D1095668

The Collected Writings of Walt Whitman

Walt Whitman

1850

WALT WHITMAN

The Correspondence

VOLUME I: 1842-1867

Edited by Edwin Haviland Miller

NEW YORK UNIVERSITY PRESS 1961

LIBRARY OF CONGRESS CATALOG CARD NUMBER: 60–15980

MANUFACTURED IN THE UNITED STATES OF AMERICA

The Collected Writings of Walt Whitman

GRATEFUL ACKNOWLEDGMENT IS MADE TO

Mr. Charles E. Feinberg,

WHOSE FINANCIAL ASSISTANCE MADE POSSIBLE
THE ILLUSTRATIONS IN THIS VOLUME AND WHO ALSO
MADE AVAILABLE TO THE PUBLISHER THE RESOURCES
OF THE FEINBERG COLLECTION.

Preface

Since his death in 1892, the letters of Walt Whitman have been appearing in print at intervals. The first to publish correspondence were the literary executors: Dr. Richard Maurice Bucke, who published books on mysticism and who supervised an insane asylum in London, Ontario; Thomas B. Harned, a Philadelphia attorney; and the most ardent disciple of all, Horace Traubel, who as a young man went to Camden to attend to the needs of an aging and dying poet, and who finally became his Boswell. The three men included some correspondence in their first joint effort, *In Re Walt Whitman* (1893). This was followed a few years later by *The Wound Dresser*, consisting of the moving letters written during the Civil War to his mother, Louisa Van Velsor Whitman, and *Calamus*, containing the correspondence with the Washington motorman Peter Doyle. In 1902, in the ten beautifully printed volumes of the Camden Edition, the executors devoted two volumes to correspondence, reprinting *The Wound Dresser* and *Calamus*, and adding other letters to his mother, as well as those to James R. Osgood, the Boston publisher of the 1881 edition of *Leaves of Grass*. Since the editors ignored not only the material in *In Re Walt Whitman* but also the numerous letters printed by William Sloane Kennedy and Thomas Donaldson in separate volumes in 1896, this first collection was not complete.

For the next two decades most large collections of letters were prepared by friends of the poet. Traubel, in 1906, began to print correspondence to and from Whitman in *With Walt Whitman in Camden*, the fourth volume of which appeared posthumously in 1953, and other volumes of which are presently being edited by his daughter and Charles E. Feinberg. In his volumes Traubel included preliminary drafts of letters which as yet have not been found in their original form. Harned shocked those who believe that the loves of famous people should be concealed from the prying eyes of posterity when he published drafts of six letters to Mrs. Gilchrist in *The Letters of Anne Gilchrist and Walt Whitman* (1918). The two admirers from Bolton, England, Dr. John Johnston and J. W. Wallace, printed almost all the letters and post cards they received during the last few years of Whitman's life.

These editors made no immodest claims to scholarship. Theirs were labors of love which occasionally reflect the lapses inherent in ardent affection. It is easy to cite their mistakes: the absence of a consistent editorial procedure, the occasionally careless transcription, the omission of a postscript or a sentence, the unindicated deletion of remarks which they considered unworthy of the man they venerated. It is simple, in short, to disparage their works, but also tasteless and shortsighted. For they preserved and publicized the writings of a great poet when most professors tilted their noses at American literature and preferred the genteel authors of other cultures to native roughs who disturbed academic aplomb.

In addition to Whitman's friends, early biographers like Bliss Perry and H. C. Binns included a few letters in their books. Other correspondence came out at intervals in magazines, in *Putnam's Monthly* in 1908 and in an obscure publication called *The Modern School* in 1918.

During his long career as a Whitman specialist Emory Holloway has printed many letters, in magazines such as *The American Mercury* and in his numerous studies. His selected letters in the Nonesuch Edition constitute the most extensive modern collection of Whitman correspondence. In this work Professor Holloway printed many previously unpublished letters which were at that time in the collections of Mrs. Frank Sprague and the late W. T. H. Howe. Clara Barrus, in *Whitman and Burroughs —Comrades* (1931), excerpted from the correspondence of these two lifelong friends, and Professor Charles I. Glicksberg, in *Walt Whitman and the Civil War* (1933), edited letters to members of the Whitman family, to soldier friends of Civil War days, and to Mrs. Abby H. Price. Later in the 1930's Professor Rollo G. Silver printed many letters from private and public collections in *American Literature* and *Colophon.*

In *Faint Clews & Indirections* (1949), Professors Clarence Gohdes and Silver edited the unprinted correspondence in the Trent Collection at Duke University. In addition, there were three fairly extensive specialized reprints of letters, two of which appeared in *Studies in Bibliography* in recent years, and one of which, the Rudolf Schmidt correspondence in the Royal Library of Copenhagen, was issued in *Orbis Litterarum* in 1949.

For almost seventy years, then, Whitman's letters have been printed sporadically in books and journals, some of which are not easy to come by. Moreover, the inadequate editorial procedures of many early compilers presented faulty texts to readers. This type of unsystematic publication constitutes a grave injustice to the poet, as well as a serious inconvenience to readers and scholars. It is no longer tolerable, when large quantities of Whitman material are available in major collections, both public and private, that the letters should be printed without clarifying annotations.

By assembling photostats and transcriptions of all known letters written by Whitman, I have had advantages not enjoyed by my predecessors. I have been able to correct erroneous dates or to suggest plausible dates in difficult cases, to identify recipients, and to illuminate obscurities by reference to other Whitman letters or to correspondence addressed to him. More important, because of the generosity of institutions and individuals, I am able to increase the number of printed letters by roughly sixty per cent.

In this volume I am indebted to the following institutions for permission to print Whitman correspondence in their collections: Clifton Waller Barrett Collection, University of Virginia; Berg Collection, New York Public Library; Estelle Doheny Collection of the Edward Laurence Doheny Memorial Library, St. John's Seminary; Ralph Waldo Emerson Memorial Association; T. E. Hanley Collection, University of Texas; Harvard University; Haverford College; Historical Society of Pennsylvania; Henry E. Huntington Library; Huntington (New York) Historical Society; Library of Congress; Oscar Lion Collection, New York Public Library; Long Island Historical Society; Missouri Historical Society; Pierpont Morgan Library; National Archives, General Services Administration; New Hampshire Historical Society; New Jersey Historical Society; New-York Historical Society; New York Public Library; Ohio Wesleyan University; University of Rochester; Rutgers University; Stanford University; Trent Collection, Duke University; Walt Whitman House, Camden; Yale University. Without exception, the librarians in charge of the various collections have assisted me in every possible way.

The following individuals have graciously allowed me to print letters: Clifton Waller Barrett; William D. Bayley; Charles E. Feinberg; Colonel Richard Gimbel; T. E. Hanley; Oscar Lion; Clifford Odets; Mrs. Joseph R. Perkins, Jr.; Mrs. Francis Frederic Phillips; Professor Rollo G. Silver; Robert H. Taylor; the late Dr. Max Thorek. I can only express publicly what I have written privately, that these women and men have invariably had a sense of public responsibility in making the manuscripts in their collections accessible. In addition, they good-naturedly put up with my importunities and infringement upon their time.

I shall always be grateful to my colleague and friend, Professor Rollo G. Silver, who some years ago argued persuasively against my reluctance to undertake a check list and finally an edition of Whitman's letters. My task has been eased by the knowledge that I have been able to rely upon him for encouragement and guidance.

I find it difficult to say anything that is not painfully trite about my obligation to Charles E. Feinberg. Over the years, with diligence and with love, he has assembled the finest collection of Whitmaniana ever brought together. More remarkably, he has encouraged the use of his material and has enthusiastically embraced the publication of the thousand letters in his possession. Like the original executors, Mr. Feinberg has considered himself a custodian, not simply a proud possessor.

It is a pleasure rather than a perfunctory duty to acknowledge my indebtedness to Dr. John Gordan and his staff in the Berg Collection at the New York Public Library; to Miss Anne Freudenberg at the University of Virginia; to Dr. Donald Gallup and his assistants at Yale University; to Professor Miriam Heffernan, executive director of the Walt Whitman Foundation of Brooklyn College; to Dr. David C. Mearns and his staff in the Manuscript Division of the Library of Congress; to Mrs. Neda M. Westlake at the University of Pennsylvania; and to Mrs. Eleanor Ray, curator of the Walt Whitman House at Camden. The librarians at Harvard University, the Boston Athenaeum, the Boston Public Library, and Simmons College have been invariably helpful. Miss Gertrude Traubel has graciously permitted quotations from the four indispensable volumes edited by her father, Horace Traubel, *With Walt Whitman in Camden.*

Professor Gay Wilson Allen has always been co-operative and most kind, and his book *The Solitary Singer*, the best of the biographical studies, has lightened my toil. Professor Holloway has contributed much valuable information. Professor Edward Grier has generously informed me of letters which he has discovered in the course of his own work. My typist, Miss Dorothy E. Buck, has been the very model of a model typist.

I am indebted to the American Philosophical Society for two grants in the early stages of the project. The research council of New York University has purchased many photostats. A fellowship from the American Council of Learned Societies permitted me freedom from classroom responsibilities in order to complete this volume.

About my unacknowledged collaborator, my wife, I need not (indeed dare not!) elaborate.

E. H. M.

Belmont, Massachusetts
December 1, 1960

CONTENTS

Introduction

WALT WHITMAN AS A LETTER WRITER

With some of the Dutch stubbornness inherited from his mother, Walt Whitman has refused to fit into the categories which contemporaries and posterity have created for him. During his lifetime his detractors seized upon his own phrase, "barbaric yawp," to stigmatize him, and his undraping of anatomical and biological facts appeared worse than vulgar to well-clothed Victorian sensibilities, both of the American and English variety. His idolaters, on the other hand, deified him: he was "the good gray poet," "the carpenter," a new half-pagan, half-Christian Messiah who uttered eternal verities in order to save man from the mechanistic and materialistic gyrations of the nineteenth-century world. He was a kind of Nietzschean overman with softer contours or a Shavian superman without disturbing and unsettling witticisms.

The twentieth century, with similar intensity but different emphasis, has continued the attempt to catalogue this enigmatic figure. Those who succumb to one current critical fashion virtually read Whitman (as well as Milton) out of the history of poetry. Those who make awareness of evil a corollary of literary greatness insist upon the inadequacy of Whitman's vision, his uneasy sublimation of the terror inherent in the life process. Avant-garde groups howl his praise, only to justify their eccentricities and to convert his vision into a tired anti-bourgeois dogma. Some biographers clutch a fragment of his personality and exaggerate it to monstrous proportions, as if Whitman, a kind of father figure, had personally betrayed them; in retaliation they set out to reduce him to size, but it is not Whitman that is reduced. Still others dote on his every word and venerate every relic as though Whitman were both a kindly preacher and a family heirloom.

And so we have a poet that is not a poet, a seer whose vision appears infantile to some observers but sublime to others, and a man who, in the judgment of one group, is dishonest, exhibitionistic, and arrogant, but who, in the opinion of others, is charitable, candid in his admission of his own contradictions, and encouragingly receptive to thwarted dreams of self-realization. Both the haters and the lovers are right, but at the same time they are wrong. Whitman was a "rough" and "the good gray poet." He was the spokesman of a mystical democratic community, but few poets have sung so musically and passionately of death. He chanted the new-old song of comradeship, or adhesiveness, but it was the chant of as lonely an individual as Huck Finn or Abraham Lincoln.

The poet, the seer, and the man, then, remain mystifying despite the impassioned outcries of defenders and opponents and despite the thousands of pages expended by biographers in quest of illumination. That people are rarely neutral where Whitman is concerned is one of the most pregnant indications of his greatness. Men neither hate nor love mediocrity. That no biography is completely satisfactory is no reflection upon its author, for the mysteries of a personality as complex as Whitman's are not reducible to simple formulas and explanations. Only those who in their own insecurity must have the security afforded by a neat categorization should find his elusiveness frustrating. For if Whitman cannot be adequately explained, the extreme reactions of partisans and the contradictory interpretations demonstrate that his magnetic but puzzling personality has been *felt*.

It would be absurd (and dishonest) to claim that the publication of Whitman's letters will suddenly unveil the truth which has escaped critics, biographers, and fanatics. Perhaps an editor (like Dr. Johnson's lexicographer, "a harmless drudge") may be forgiven if he makes an unacademic assertion: the printing of the letters, with copious annotations from the riches of material now available, will bring this baffling figure closer to readers by focusing attention on the poet of immensities engaged in the intimacies of daily experience. It is as though we have turned from gazing upon a finished canvas, complete and perfect (or nearly so) in its artistry, to examine the workshop, the tools, and the mundane (often dull) events which not even the artist can evade.

In a conversation with Horace Traubel in 1888, the poet observed that the correspondence between Carlyle and Emerson, which had just been published, "would be impossible to me, though I see it is all right in itself and for them. It is a matter of taste—of temperament. I don't believe I ever wrote a purely literary letter—ever got discussing books or literary men or writers or artists of any sort in letters: the very idea of it makes me sick. I like letters to be personal—very personal—and then stop."[1] If a reader expects to find in Whitman's correspondence discussions of poetics or to read early unfinished verses, he will be disappointed. If he seeks literary flourishes, colorful turns of speech, and notable metaphors, he must seek elsewhere. One finds few quotable phrases but many colloquialisms and grammatical lapses. If the reader anticipates a certain

1. Traubel, I, 137. 2. See 67. 3. See 63. 4. Traubel, II, 51.

amount of self-consciousness and stiffness, as though posterity were more important than the recipients of his letters, he shortly discovers that Whitman did not sacrifice his correspondents for future reputation.

In discussing letter writing at various times during his career, Whitman made his own views clear. To soldiers in the 1860's he emphasized simplicity and unhackneyed naturalness. "I never think about literary perfection in letters either," he commented to Lewis K. Brown, a Maryland soldier, "it is the *man* & the *feeling*."[2] To Hugo Fritsch he wrote: "You express your thoughts perfectly—do you not know how much more agreeable to me is the conversation or writing that does not take hard paved tracks, the usual & stereotyped, but has little peculiarities & even kinks of its own, making its genuineness—its vitality?"[3] In conversations with Traubel late in the 1880's he amplified his remarks and in effect summarized his own practice. On one occasion he said: "My main motive would be to say things: not to say them prettily—not to stun the reader with surprises—with fancy turns of speech—with unusual, unaccustomed words—but to say them—to shoot my gun without a flourish and reach the mark if I can."[4] Traubel also preserved another one of Whitman's comments on the Carlyle-Emerson letters: "If I was myself a critic, was admitted as a critic to the reviews, I would cry out against the whole business as too deliberate, too much prepared, too top-loftical—too infernally top-loftical. God never made men this way: this is the way men are made when they are made over by men—creations of strain, creations for effect."[5]

Inherent in all these remarks is a romantic fondness for personal idiosyncrasies which purportedly reveal "the *man*"—a noble ideal, perhaps, but a nebulous abstraction. At the same time Whitman was unwittingly admitting and advocating a formula no less self-conscious and deliberate than the "top-loftical" correspondence which made him sick.

Though it is true that Whitman rarely wrote "a purely literary letter" —an important letter to William D. O'Connor[6] is only one in over two thousand—he was not so impulsive or spontaneous in his correspondence as he implied. Often he carefully wrote out a letter and then recopied it. When he said to a friend, "O Hugo . . . my pen glides along writing these thoughts,"[7] he was misleading, since the quotation is from a draft letter. Or when he explained to the parents of a soldier who had recently died, "I have thus written rapidly whatever came up about Erastus, & must now close,"[8] he was claiming more spontaneity than was actually the case, because both the original and the draft of this letter are extant.

Many of the best letters in this collection exist in two states or are known only through the copies which Whitman preserved. It is true that he

5. Traubel, II, 195. 6. See 149. 7. See 84. 8. See 64.

penned less stilted letters than some artists who have been intoxicated with posterity. It is equally true, however, that Whitman was probably the greatest collector of his own letters; if he had not carefully, despite his seeming carelessness, kept his manuscripts, this edition would be about half its present size. As thousands of extant manuscripts testify, few writers have shown more concern for future renown.

Likewise, his professed (and genuine) abhorrence of "creations of strain, creations for effect," is not the simple matter he made it appear. For here was a man who at the beginning of a great career declaimed: "Walt Whitman, an American, one of the roughs, a kosmos." In 1867 the same man prepared a letter which O'Connor was to send to William Michael Rossetti for guidance in the preparation of an introduction to the English selections from *Leaves of Grass*: "That personally the author of Leaves of Grass is in no sense or sort whatever the 'rough,' the 'eccentric,' 'vagabond' or queer person, that the commentators, (always bound for the intensest possible sensational statement,) persist in making him."[9] Yet the myth of the rough was of Whitman's own creation, in his poetry, in his dress, and, if some commentators are to be trusted, in his decorum. Manliness, plain but unconventional attire, blunt speech, freedom from ordinary proprieties and formalities—these were parts of the pose. Many soldier boys did not learn until years after the Civil War that Whitman was a distinguished poet. His letters to them were deliberately "unpoetic," since he wished in their eyes and hearts to be a comrade, not a poet. He, in short, endeavored to separate the inseparable—Whitman the man and Whitman the poet. "My darling boy," he said to Lewis Brown, "when you write to me, you must write without ceremony, I like to hear every little thing about yourself & your affairs—you need never care how you write to me, Lewy, if you will only."[10] "Without ceremony" was his own favorite epithet to characterize his relations with wounded and sick soldiers, as well as for his letters. But the absence of ceremony as well as ceremony itself is a cultivated attitude, a conscious gesture.

One searches in vain in his letters for comments on nineteenth-century intellectual movements. He was not uninterested in such matters and read more extensively in philosophy and similar subjects than he ever admitted in print or in correspondence. One has only to peruse the markings in the books of his library to know that Whitman understated, or consciously misrepresented, his intellectual interests. Perhaps he wanted to appear more original than he actually was. Certainly he affected the role of the "loafer"—"I lean and loafe at my ease. . . . observing a spear of

9. See 256. This part of the letter was not among WW's papers and was therefore not printed by Traubel (III, 298–299); preserved by O'Connor, it is now in the Berg

summer grass"—which he emphatically was not. To his family and to semiliterate young friends like Peter Doyle and Harry Stafford, however, books and intellectual currents were of little importance. The intrusion of such topics into his letters would have created a barrier to friendship and communication. Not without calculation Whitman preserved the bond of affection, but at the same time these friendships were based upon concealment of important aspects of his personality. Like many artists Whitman could not resolve two conflicting tendencies: he craved fame as a poet, a successor to Homer in the words of his adulators, but he also craved acceptance as a simple human being.

Hence it is not surprising that in his letters he recorded his day-by-day observations on the topical and the immediate: the vicissitudes of war, the plight of a sick soldier, a recent train accident or murder, a political campaign, his health, his family. He assumed that his correspondents were interested in his living quarters and bad ventilation; his desk in the Attorney General's office and the view across the Potomac River; his food, including the oysters he ate in enormous quantity; the weather; the dusty Washington streets; or a play which he had recently seen. One is always aware of Whitman the man in a particular environment—reacting to the caprices of the weather, climbing to an attic room in a boardinghouse, preparing his breakfast, walking along the Washington streets or riding the ferries in New York and Philadelphia, discussing a report in the morning newspaper, or noting dizziness from the heat of the sun or suffering from a cold and later from the crippling effects of his paralysis.

Even when Whitman wrote to Tennyson or to critics like Rossetti and Edward Dowden, he avoided for the most part literary discussions, and virtually dictated the replies he received by his emphasis on his day-to-day activities. To his intellectual inferiors he was explicit: "Tell me of course all about the boys, what you do, say, any thing, every thing."[11] In another letter to the same correspondent, he asked about recent operatic performances in New York, but immediately cautioned: "Only dont run away with that theme, & occupy too much of your letter with it—but tell me mainly about all my dear friends, and every little personal item, & what you all do, & say &c."[12]

The letters, then, reveal Whitman in various nonpoetic roles. To the mother he was the dutiful son, concerned about her illnesses and the weakening effects of her age, admonishing her not to work too hard and not to be excessively frugal—loving, tactfully suggesting and guiding, never overtly directing her—and he informed her of his health (a con-

Collection.

10. See 67. 11. See 63. 12. See 84.

stantly recurring subject) and of other matters important to a parent. These letters are simple, unforced, and chatty. Whitman the son was speaking; the poet never shattered the relationship. He undoubtedly felt what his brother George stated after his death: "I remember mother comparing Hiawatha to Walt's [poetry], and one seemed to us pretty much the same muddle as the other."[13] So successfully and naturally did Whitman fit this role that if one were to read aloud the letters written by the mother and the son, and could not see her awkward handwriting and lack of punctuation, one would be fascinated with the similarities. To the soldiers whom he nursed and then watched depart from the hospitals, he was simultaneously a father (or a brother) and a comrade. Hence at times he offered the advice expected of an older person; at the same time he almost entreated the boys to write and to return to Washington. In these letters his prose was plain and colloquial, as befits communications addressed to young men who had little schooling and less command of language. But the drafts of these letters, interlined and filled with stricken passages, frequently reveal uncertainty and caution. Whitman was not always sure that his theory of comradeship, or adhesiveness, was understood.

In the case of Mrs. Anne Gilchrist, an English authoress, whose approach to Whitman was too passionate for a well-bred Victorian lady, and whose overtures were not without connubial intimations, he tactfully and delicately redirected her ardor into the safer channels of friendship. On the other hand, without restraint or fear he poured out his affection for Peter Doyle, the young Washington conductor and comrade. To William D. O'Connor he wrote chiefly of his plans for publication or of his newspaper battles for recognition in a hostile press. After one attempt, which O'Connor evidently had no taste for, Whitman did not describe his "orgies" in New York taverns. He kept "the good gray poet" before O'Connor's eyes. To Emerson and Tennyson he wrote as an equal; his intellectual peers, however, did not engage his heart.

Many years after Whitman's death, John Burroughs, who had corresponded with him for almost thirty years, complained of the poet's "brief and matter-of-fact letters," and alleged that "he let himself go only in his poems."[14] Burroughs' judgment of the letters he had received was correct, but his statement does not apply to Whitman's letters as a whole. For the best letters in this collection are hardly "matter-of-fact"; rather they are lovely prose creations. One almost hears Whitman speaking. To read aloud the letter to Erastus Haskell's parents (64) is to succumb to the tender voice of a man moved deeply by the reckless loss of youth in war. Sympathy without sentimentality and dignity pervade this letter. "Dear

13. *In Re*, 35–36. 14. Barrus, 157.

friends," it begins, "I thought it would be soothing to you to have a few lines about the last days of your son." He went on to describe Erastus' illness and his demeanor ("He never complained"). Nor did he omit the vivid detail: "While he lay sick here he had his fife laying on the little stand by his table." Toward the conclusion Whitman quietly reached a crescendo:

> Poor dear son, though you were not my son, I felt to love you as a son, what short time I saw you sick & dying here—it is as well as it is, perhaps better—for who knows whether he is not better off, that patient & sweet young soul, to go, than we are to stay? So farewell, dear boy—it was my opportunity to be with you in your last rapid days of death—no chance as I have said to do any thing particular, for nothing could be done—only you did not lay here & die among strangers without having one at hand who loved you dearly, & to whom you gave your dying kiss—

This moving document, like his greatest poems, embodies his major themes: love and death.

A great deal of the correspondence concerns publication matters, since Whitman was until late in his career his own publisher, promoter, and salesman. To follow the 1860 and 1881 editions through the presses reveals another aspect of Whitman: the practical printer minutely concerned with type faces, typography, and bindings. Even the appearance of his books was chiefly his own doing. As a publicity expert he was shrewd in obtaining newspaper space, and his releases and reviews of his own books can scarcely be termed inhibited or modest. Because he did not have a commercial publisher, he received and filled orders for his own works. This is perhaps a less glamorous side of his activities, but his business transactions are part of the total picture.

Surely it is long past time to accept Whitman in his bewildering, contradictory totality. Neither his strengths nor his weaknesses, as poet or as man, need at this date to be isolated and magnified.

WALT WHITMAN, 1842–1867

Walt Whitman (1819–1892) was the second child of Walter Whitman (1789–1855) and Louisa Van Velsor (1795–1873). His father was a carpenter, but not a very successful one. Since he died shortly after the appearance of the first edition of *Leaves of Grass* (1855), before most of the letters in this collection were written, he is rarely mentioned in these pages. Walt, furthermore, was more attached to his mother than to his father, as he revealed in "There Was a Child Went Forth":

> The mother at home quietly placing the dishes on the suppertable,
> The mother with mild words . . . . clean her cap and gown . . . .
> a wholesome odor falling off her person and clothes as she walks by:
> The father, strong, selfsufficient, manly, mean, angered, unjust,
> The blow, the quick loud word, the tight bargain, the crafty lure . . .

Mrs. Whitman, of sturdy Dutch descent, was a tireless worker who performed household drudgery into her seventies, a frugal woman who held on to her pennies, and a determined mother of a brood that included one genius, one feeble-minded son, an alcoholic, a psychotic, and a hopeless neurotic. With her Walt corresponded frequently; her replies, almost without punctuation but with a surprisingly apt vocabulary, are now in the Trent Collection at Duke University. She depended upon Walt for guidance in the family crises, which, as we see in this volume, were without end. Theirs was a close relationship, even though his poetry remained beyond her comprehension. John Burroughs described her in 1868 as "a spry, vivacious, handsome old lady, worthy of her illustrious son."[15]

That she was not wrinkled with care when Burroughs met her five years before her death is amazing. Hers had been a difficult lot. Jesse (1818–1870), the first-born, was a pathetic failure. He contracted syphilis, and on December 5, 1864, was confined to an asylum, where he died. Andrew Jackson (1827–1863), an alcoholic, was married to Nancy, also an alcoholic, as well as a streetwalker. She bore a child after Andrew's death. "So Nance has had another child," Walt wrote to his mother, "poor little one, there don't seem to be much show for it, poor little young one, these times."[16] Edward (1835–1892), the youngest of the children, was feeble-minded. He lived with his mother until her death, and then became Walt's charge.

And then there was Hannah Louisa (1823–1908), who, after being introduced by Walt to Charles L. Heyde, an artist of some reputation in his day, went off to Vermont to live with him in connubial torment. The Whitman boys blamed Heyde. Thomas Jefferson ("Jeff") wrote to Walt on April 3, 1863: "Oh I wish to God he had been in Hell before we ever saw him."[17] Walt, though less subject to outbursts than his excitable brother, was so abusive in his references to Heyde in his letters that the literary executors deleted some of his comments. The Whitman family, understandably, failed to acknowledge the other side of the coin. Hannah was neurotic, perhaps psychotic: she felt herself persecuted and masochistically bore her punishments, real and imaginary. Many of her letters, whining, self-condemning, hysterical, are preserved in the Trent Collection. Heyde's

15. Barrus, 57. 16. See 115. 17. Feinberg Collection.

letters, in the same collection, reveal not only his jealousy of Walt's success but also his deliberate efforts to wound the Whitman family. Though Heyde repeatedly threatened to send Hannah back to the family, and though the Whitmans often considered fetching her, she willingly remained with her husband.

Mary Elizabeth (1821–1899), the older of the two sisters, married Ansel Van Nostrand in 1840 and lived uneventfully (and normally) on Long Island. Though Walt wrote to her throughout his life, the relationship was not close; Hannah was his favorite sister. George Washington (1829–1901) and Thomas Jefferson (1833–1890) were, in addition to the poet, the mainstays of the family. Jeff took care of his mother while Walt was in Washington and George was serving in the Union army. When Jeff moved to St. Louis to be an engineer at the water works, George provided for Mrs. Whitman. Later she moved with him to Camden, where she died. George and his wife Louisa provided quarters for Walt after his mother's death and during the years that paralysis incapacitated him. He was fond of Louisa, who was probably more understanding than her practical husband, who was to become the most prosperous of the Whitmans. Walt was also genuinely attached to Jeff's wife Martha, who died of consumption and cancer the same year as his mother (1873), and to her two daughters, Mannahatta (1860–1886) and Jessie Louisa (1863–1957).

Such was the extraordinary family that produced and surrounded America's great poet. Because of his fame the Whitmans have a significant place, and a kind of reflected immortality, in the drama of Walt's life presented in these pages.

The earliest extant letters of Whitman, written when he was twenty-three, deal with his attempts to publish his short stories, which are as conventional and dull as his poetry is unorthodox and startling. Although the editor of the *Boston Miscellany* was, understandably, unimpressed, Whitman published "The Angel of Tears" elsewhere. Before he attempted fiction, he had drifted aimlessly from job to job: he had learned the printing trade, had briefly taught school, and had edited the *Long Islander* in Huntington, New York.

In the 1840's Walt was the editor of *The Aurora*, *The Tatler*, *The Statesman*, and the Brooklyn *Daily Eagle*. He left the *Eagle*—or was asked to leave—in January, 1848, and in the following month journeyed with Jeff to New Orleans to work for the *Crescent*. This was his first opportunity to discover for himself the vastness of the United States. Though Walt added only two brief notes, perfunctory ones at that, we at least have Jeff's four lengthy letters, reprinted here for the first time. They record the impressions of the two young men in exotic, malaria-infested New Orleans.

In May Walt resigned his position, or, more probably, was requested to resign, and was back in Brooklyn on June 15. Thus ended the first adventure in Walt's life, an adventure which in the hands of imaginative biographers has become more exciting than it was in actuality.

The next seven years were obviously important ones. A man whose published work up to that time was little different from that of the hacks of the era was preparing a volume that was to alter American literature. Unfortunately, only four letters survive. During this period Whitman supported himself by editing the Brooklyn *Freeman* in 1848–1849, by operating a printing establishment, and by constructing houses. From 1855, the *annus mirabilis*, when Emerson greeted him "at the beginning of a great career," only one communication, addressed to Senator Seward, is extant. Since his intimates were laborers and the bohemians at Pfaff's restaurant, whom he saw frequently, he probably had little occasion to write letters. In the following year Whitman printed the second edition of *Leaves of Grass*, and was visited by Alcott and Thoreau. Fame was coming slowly—as well as notoriety. He was editor of the Brooklyn *Times* from 1857 to 1859; this was the last journalistic post he was to hold.

In 1860 when two young Boston publishers, Thayer & Eldridge, requested Whitman's permission to print the third edition of *Leaves of Grass*, he went to Boston to supervise publication. At this time he began to correspond with Mrs. Abby H. Price (1814–1878), who had been active in various social-reform movements. During the 1860's Mrs. Price and her family, especially her daughter Helen, were his intimates. In a letter to Ellen O'Connor he declared with emphasis, "*They are all friends*, to prize and love deeply."[18] But, more important, in 1860 the family began to save Walt's letters, or perhaps, because he was now more certain of himself and his stature as a poet, he saw to it that his letters were not destroyed. For he was the collector in his family. If Hannah, Mary, and George had been equally conscientious, hundreds of additional letters would have been preserved for these volumes.

After the Fort Sumter incident George immediately volunteered. Though Walt followed his brother's military career with pride, and later celebrated it in a number of newspaper articles, he stayed in Brooklyn and wrote occasionally for newspapers. Jeff, who was employed at the Brooklyn Water Works, feared conscription. Andrew apparently tried to enlist, but was rejected. Jesse and Ed, of course, were unaffected by the national turmoil.

During this period Walt was intimate with a group he called the Fred

18. See 95.
19. A fuller discussion appears in the notes to 40 and 62.

Gray Association. Not much is known about this circle. Gray, the son of a noted New York physician, took a medical degree after the war. Nathaniel Bloom became a successful merchant. Hugo Fritsch was the son of the Austrian consul. The others are only names: Charles Chauncey, Charles Kingsley, Ben Knower, Charles Russell, Perkins, and Raymond.[19] From Whitman's and their letters we can deduce that they were young men, that they drank and caroused together at Pfaff's and elsewhere, and that they were more literate than the soldier-correspondents or Peter Doyle, because Whitman made a few literary allusions and adjusted his style to that of a bantering intellectual or bohemian. Some of them, certainly Gray and Russell, went off to war, and Whitman went to Washington. When he was separated from them, he wished to be in New York, but when he was with them, he wanted to return to the Washington hospitals. The association became a wartime casualty.

When George was reported wounded in December, 1862, Whitman went off to visit him at Fredericksburg, Virginia. On his way he stopped in Washington and encountered Charles W. Eldridge, who was now a clerk in the office of the army paymaster, and William D. O'Connor, who was employed in the Treasury Department. After he had seen for himself that George had not been severely wounded, he returned to Washington, which was to be his home until 1873. Eldridge obtained a desk for Walt in the office of Major Lyman Hapgood, the army paymaster.

For a time Whitman lived with William and Ellen O'Connor, who, with Eldridge and later Burroughs, were to be his close associates during the early Washington years. O'Connor (1832–1889) was the author of *Harrington*, an abolition novel published by Thayer & Eldridge in 1860. He had been an assistant editor of the *Saturday Evening Post* before he went to Washington. O'Connor was an intelligent man who deserved something better than the various governmental clerical posts he was to hold until his death. The humdrum of clerkship, however, was relieved by the presence of Whitman, whom he was to love and venerate—and defend with a single-minded fanaticism and an outpouring of vituperation and eulogy that have seldom been equaled. He was the first, and in many ways the most important, of the adulators who divided people arbitrarily into two categories: those who were for and those who were against Walt Whitman. The poet praised O'Connor in the preface to a posthumous collection of his tales: "He was a born sample here in the 19th century of the flower and symbol of olden time first-class knighthood. Thrice blessed be his memory!"[20]

20. *CW*, VII, 46.

Shortly after his arrival in Washington, Whitman began to visit the military hospitals. His white beard and haversack soon became a familiar sight. "I shall never forget the first time you came in after David & I got there," a soldier wrote to him years later. "We Loved you from the first time we spoke to you."[21] Whitman wrote letters for the injured and the illiterate. He soothed the dying with words and embraces. "When I first made your acquaintance," one of the injured said afterward, "somehow or other you seemed like a father, why it was so I am unable to say, yet such was the case, & I hav'nt the least doubt but such has been the case with thousands of other fellow soldiers."[22] "May god bless you forever," another soldier wrote, "I cant find words to tell you the love thier is in me for you. I hope you & I may live to meet again on this earth, if not I hope we shall meet in the world were thier is no more parting."[23] In 1871 an ex-soldier informed Whitman: "I have not forgot you nor your friendly kindness twards me in Arm[or]y Square Hospital. I have thought of you so many times and wondered where you was and how you was getting along. . . . Please send me some of your Poems, your choise ones, for I always enjoyed them so much when you read them to me in old ward A. I never shall forget what pains you took to help pass away our weary hours. our Heavenly Father will reward you for it."[24]

After reading the words of the soldiers themselves, O'Connor's eulogy in *The Good Gray Poet* does not appear, except for the messianic trappings, unearned: "There, in those long wards, . . . walked Walt Whitman, in the spirit of Christ, soothing, healing, consoling, restoring, night and day, for years; never failing, never tiring, constant, vigilant, faithful; performing, without fee or reward, his self-imposed duty; giving to the task all his time and means, and doing everything that it is possible for one unaided human being to do."[25] But O'Connor in his fervid praise simplified.

Whitman gave affection and love and in return received them. He eased the suffering of soldiers, as he sat by day and often by night beside their beds. But he was honest enough to admit, "It is a great privilege to me, more to me than to them I think."[26] For, he wrote to Jeff shortly after his arrival in Washington, "I never before had my feelings so thoroughly and (so far) permanently absorbed, to the very roots, as by these huge swarms of dear, wounded, sick, dying boys."[27] In the "Calamus" poems of 1860, he had sung—theoretically—of camaraderie and the love of one man for another, but "I never knew what American young men were till I have been in the hospitals."[28] Or, as he expressed it to Emerson, "I find there the

21. Benton H. Wilson to WW, July 18, 1869 (Feinberg).
22. C. L. Scott to WW, August 31, 1863 (Berg).
23. William H Millis to WW, January 12, 1865 (Berg).
24. Thomas M Woodworth to WW, February 5, 1871 (Feinberg).

best expression of American character I have ever seen or conceived."[29] In the hospitals, then, he experienced comradeship as he could never have experienced it under normal circumstances. He was father and mother to these helpless and lonely war orphans, and brother as well. "The work grows upon me, & fascinates me,"[30] he wrote to his mother in June, 1863. To Nathaniel Bloom he admitted: "It is delicious to be the object of so much love & reliance, & to do them such good, soothe & pacify torments of wounds &c."[31] And again to his mother, in September of the same year: "I believe no men ever loved each other as I & some of these poor wounded, sick & dying men love each other."[32] To another correspondent, he said: "I have never been happier than in some of these hospital ministering hours."[33]

There was also a price, as there usually is, for such ardent emotional involvement. Soldiers whom he had tended, giving solace during nights of crisis, sweating through their fevers, often recovered and left Washington to return to their regiments or to their homes. Seldom did they return, and though many wrote to Whitman, most of them were ill at ease in correspondence; besides, words were an inadequate substitute for physical presence. "I cannot bear the thought of being separated from you," Whitman wrote to Elijah Fox. "I know I am a great fool about such things, but I tell you the truth, dear son."[34] Whitman, in Robert Frost's words, "learned of finalities / Besides the grave."

In addition, there was the dangerous physical reality of continuous exposure in unhygienic hospitals to malaria, infection, and maggots, as well as the psychic strain of witnessing agonizing suffering and torturous dying. Though he remained "singularly cool" when he was in the hospitals, he confessed to his mother: "But often, hours afterward, perhaps when I am home, or out walking alone, I feel sick & actually tremble, when I recal the thing & have it in my mind and again before me."[35] By the middle of 1864 he was no longer enjoying his customary robust health: "I had spells of deathly faintness, and bad trouble in my head too, & sore throat, (quite a little budget, ain't they?)" He admitted in the same letter that "it is most too much for a fellow, & I sometimes wish I was out of it."[36] A doctor informed him that he had "absorbed too much of the virus"[37] in his system. Perhaps so. But many of his symptoms appear to be psychic reactions to an environment that artificially stimulated passionate attachments and painful separations, and that, through the daily spectacle of amputations and of death itself, aroused deep-seated anxieties and fears.

25. Bucke, 125. 26. See 108. 27. See 37.1. 28. See 78. 29. See 32. 30. See 53. 31. See 74. 32. See 76. 33. See 82. 34. See 98. 35. See 83. 36. See 133. 37. See 134.

Shortly after he complained of his "budget" of symptoms, he returned to Brooklyn. Gradually he recovered his health, and prepared *Drum-Taps* for publication. At this time he commenced what was to become a lifelong correspondence with John Burroughs (1837–1921), the naturalist, who had come to Washington in 1863 to work in the Treasury Department. Like O'Connor and many others, Burroughs was magnetically drawn to Whitman, to "his great summery, motherly soul": "I loved him as I never loved any man. We were companionable without talking. I owe more to him than to any other man in the world."[38] The correspondence between the two men, however, is, as Burroughs acknowledged, curiously "matter-of-fact."

In January, 1865, after seven months in Brooklyn, Whitman again returned to Washington when O'Connor secured a position for him in the Indian Bureau of the Interior Department. He resumed his visits to the hospitals, and did what he could to effect the release of George, who had been taken prisoner in the preceding October. After his brother's release the excitement in Walt's life subsided briefly, until the ministerial soul of James Harlan, Secretary of the Interior, quivered at the discovery that one of his employees wrote with (Biblical) frankness about sex. Whitman was fired on June 30 and, through the efforts of his friends, employed in the Attorney General's office on the following day. Because of the incident his poetry received wide publicity, and O'Connor, with assistance from the poet, composed fiery defenses, and elevated Whitman to martyrdom in *The Good Gray Poet* (1866). "The fight of a book for the world" had begun in earnest.

In 1866 and 1867 English writers began to discuss Whitman's poetry sympathetically. Moncure D. Conway (1832–1907), an American liberal clergyman who spent most of his life in London, lauded Whitman in *The Fortnightly Review* and became his foreign representative. Though the poet's admirers had misgivings about the accuracy of some of the incidents related in the article, the clergyman was a vigorous spokesman and an able emissary.[39] He was soon joined by the distinguished critic, William Michael Rossetti (1829–1919), brother of the poet, who wrote a review of *Leaves of Grass*, and began preparation of selections designed to introduce Whitman to an English audience. Soon Whitman was receiving acclaim from English critics, professors, and poets whose counterparts in America, with exceptions like Emerson and Alcott, were actively hostile or

38. Clara Barrus, *The Life and Letters of John Burroughs* (1925), I, 107, 113.

39. Of his first meeting with WW, Conway had reported: "He had so magnetised me, so charged me, as it were, with some[thing] indefinable, that for the time the only

ignored *Leaves of Grass* with majestically genteel silence. By the end of 1867, however, the tide had turned: Walt Whitman had begun to conquer the world.

THE PLAN OF THIS EDITION

This edition of Whitman's correspondence will include all known (and available) letters, post cards, and notes, without abridgment and in chronological sequence. Those who prefer to read at one time letters addressed to a particular correspondent may easily do so by referring to "A List of Whitman's Correspondents," which immediately follows this Introduction.

All the letters in this volume were written by Whitman with the following exceptions: there are four letters (3–6) from Thomas Jefferson Whitman to his family, and four letters of Ralph Waldo Emerson, two (10, 30) to Whitman, one (28) to Salmon P. Chase, and one (29) to William Henry Seward. The significance of these letters, I believe, justified their inclusion.

Wherever possible—and I have been most fortunate in this respect—I have prepared transcriptions from original manuscripts or photostats. Over ninety per cent of the letters reproduced are based upon the originals. When I have had to use printed versions of letters, I reprint either the earliest or the most complete version. Occasionally I have had to create a hypothetical text based upon excerpts from two or more books or auction catalogs; I have indicated these reconstructions in the notes. When the text is not reproduced directly from an original the word transcript appears immediately before the text.

The format of the letters printed in these volumes is, I trust, simple and clear. All letters are numbered, and cross references to letters in footnotes are to letters by number, not by page or volume. Letters received late have been placed in correct chronological sequence and given the number of the preceding letter plus a decimal—for example, 164.1. The heading contains the name of the recipient, but the date is given in the heading only if Whitman has not supplied a full and correct date at the beginning of the letter. In that case a full discussion of the date appears in a note, unless it is readily verifiable by reference to a perpetual calendar.

wise course of life seemed to be to put on a blue shirt and a blouse, and loafe about Manahatta and Paumanok." See *The Fortnightly Review*, VI (1866), 545.

A subheading before the text includes endorsements by Whitman, as well as significant endorsements by recipients. Addresses and postmarks are also cited when envelopes are extant or the address side of a post card is available. (I have not, understandably, been permitted to remove mounted post cards.) The present locations of manuscripts and printed appearances of letters are included in a list at the conclusion of the volume.

Since a handwritten letter cannot be reproduced literally except through a facsimile process, I have made certain concessions to typography and readability. Headings, salutations, and signatures are standardized. Slashes indicate the original lineal appearance of the heading. Postscripts, which Whitman sometimes wrote above the heading or on the side of a page, are uniformly placed at the conclusion of the letter, with no indication of the original placement.

I have not attempted a so-called diplomatic text, which would be a literal transcription of what Whitman wrote. Fully aware of the objections that can be, and no doubt will be, raised, I have evolved what I hope is a consistent compromise text. I have taken no extreme liberties with Whitman's correspondence, but in my judgment nothing except pedantry would be served by perpetuating in print Whitman's understandable carelessness in personal communications. Therefore, I have made modifications designed to make the letters more readable, but not to destroy their informality. I have eliminated confusing double punctuation and have silently inserted commas (and occasionally parentheses) around parenthetical expressions or last-minute interpolations. Spelling errors, on the other hand, I have not corrected, except in a few instances where he inadvertently dropped a letter (*I* for *If*), nor have I resorted to the ugly *sic* technique. (In the notes I have retained the spelling of his correspondents, although I have inserted end punctuation out of sympathy for the reader.) I have also retained Whitman's ever-present ampersand and *&c.*, as well as his dashes, since they differentiate his letters from his formal prose. I do not attempt, as some editors have done, to indicate the length of dashes. Initials and abbreviations are expanded in square brackets whenever necessary for clarity: H. S. becomes H[arry] S[tafford] and W. is rendered W[ashington]. Omitted words and conjectural readings are also in square brackets. I have not used any sort of device to designate Whitman's own interpolations, since this would have necessitated a complicated editorial apparatus that would have distracted attention from the letters. Significant material which he deleted I have placed in the notes; substitution of synonyms and minor phrasal changes I have ignored. As any one who has read Whitman's letters knows, his paragraphing is often bewildering. I have simply used my own judgment; I had no alternative. Finally, I should note that, for consistency, I have not hesitated to apply the principles outlined here to the letters which I have had to reproduce from printed sources.

Annotations are always a problem (or a nightmare) for an editor. If they are too brief, some will allege that he has not done his homework. If they explain the obvious, the informed reader is offended. If they are too voluminous, the editor is pedantic and long-winded—or worse. Since a happy compromise is an impossibility—and a subjective evaluation at that—I bow before the inevitable. I have had one guiding principle: whatever is well known or is discussed in detail in readily available works is briefly summarized; but when the letters illuminate events in Whitman's life either not thoroughly developed elsewhere or previously unknown, the notes are copious.

In the notes I have made generous use of the extensive correspondence addressed to Whitman, in the Trent Collection, the Berg Collection, and above all, the Feinberg Collection. Thus I have been able to explain many obscure points in the letters, and, by what I trust are judicious excerpts, I have been able to give the reader some of the flavor of the correspondence. If letters to Whitman have appeared in print, I cite both the present location and the published source. In most cases I have been able to examine the manuscripts and to present correct and consistent texts.

I explain topical references so far as I am able, but I have not attempted to write a miniature history of the Civil War. I have relied heavily upon contemporary newspapers because Whitman frequently was commenting upon or paraphrasing what he had read in the morning paper. The activities and crises of the Whitmans, which are especially significant in this volume because of the large number of letters to the family, are usually rendered in the words of the participants, which are far more graphic than a dull editorial summary.

I have endeavored to identify the people with whom Whitman corresponded, as well as those whom he mentioned in passing. His most important correspondents are discussed in the preceding biographical summary. Persons of importance either in their own right or because of their relationship to Whitman receive a brief biographical note. Later references to individuals previously identified are followed by a note directing the reader to the letter in which the name first appeared. Because Whitman knew scores of obscure men whose immortality rests upon his allusions to them, I have thumbed the pages of the city directories of Brooklyn, New York, and Washington. Usually I can give only the full name, occupation, and address—and the correct spelling. I have examined the poet's diaries, his manuscripts pertaining to the Civil War, and his correspondence, in order to bring together every scrap of information about the soldiers he encountered in Washington hospitals. Occasionally the vast amount of available material helped not at all in clarifying a name.

At the end of each volume of these letters appear three appendixes: a list of manuscript sources, by letter and by collection; a check list of lost letters; and a calendar of the correspondence directed to Whitman.

A LIST OF WHITMAN'S CORRESPONDENTS

This alphabetical list includes all the recipients of extant letters written between 1842 and 1867. The name is followed by the letter number.

Atlantic Monthly, The, 17
Avery, Jr., Llewellyn, 220
Babbitt, Mary A., 73
Baker, Frederick, 20, 191(?)
Bergen, Tunis G., 7
Binckley, John M., 245
Bloom, Nathaniel, 40, 68, 74
Brown, Lewis K., 60, 66, 67, 94, 141
Burroughs, John, 184, 189, 248
Church, F. P. & W. C., 242, 243, 246, 251, 253, 254, 261
Clapp, Jr., Henry, 21.2
Conway, Moncure D., 239, 255, 256
Cook, Captain William, 156
Curtis, Margaret S., 82, 93
Davis, William S., 81
Eckler, Peter, 162
Eldridge, Charles W., 96, 138, 140, 145
Emerson, Ralph Waldo, 26, 32
Ford, Gordon Lester, 244
Fox, Elijah Douglass, 98
Fritsch, Hugo, 62, 63, 84
Gray, John F. S., 40
Gregg, Miss, 75
Hale, John Parker, 9.1
Hale, Jr., Nathan, 1, 2
Harper's Magazine, 14
Haskell, Mr. & Mrs. S. B., 59, 64, 77
Irwin, Mrs., 161
Kerr, Andrew, 169, 187, 190
Kirkwood, James P., 119
Knox, John Jay, 215, 265.1
Lane, Moses, 47, 110
Lowell, James Russell, 16, 24
Muchmore, W. M., 9
New York *Sunday Courier*, 15
Northrup, Daniel L., 49
O'Connor, Ellen M., 95, 143, 146, 158, 166, 168, 222, 249
O'Connor, William D., 137, 139, 142, 144, 149, 150, 158, 159, 172, 188, 192, 235, 236, 247, 250, 256, 258, 263–265
Pratt, Alfred, 164.2, 191.1, 240, 253.1
Pratt, N. M. & John B., 164.1
Price, Abby H., 18, 86, 154, 185, 186, 194, 207, 225, 228, 241
Redpath, James, 61(?), 87, 91
Rossetti, William Michael, 257, 259
Routledge & Sons, 262
Russell, Dr. Le Baron, 99, 108
Sawyer, Thomas P., 43, 44, 52, 71, 97
Seward, William Henry, 11
Sholes, Hiram, 238
Simpson, Abraham, 237
Smith, Bethuel, 79
Stanbery, Henry, 193
Stevenson, Hannah E., 85
Stilwell, Julia Elizabeth, 90
Stuart, Carlos D., 8
Sutherland, Byron, 165, 167

*

Additional Letters Not by Whitman

ABBREVIATIONS

AL	*American Literature*
Allen	Gay Wilson Allen, *The Solitary Singer* (1955)
Allen, *Handbook*	Gay Wilson Allen, *Walt Whitman Handbook* (1946)
Barrett	Clifton Waller Barrett Collection, University of Virginia
Barrus	Clara Barrus, *Whitman and Burroughs—Comrades* (1931)
Berg	Henry W. and Albert A. Berg Collection, New York Public Library
Bucke	Richard Maurice Bucke, *Walt Whitman* (1883)
Canby	Henry Seidel Canby, *Walt Whitman: An American* (1943)
CT	Complete Text
CW	*The Complete Writings of Walt Whitman* (1902), 10 vols.
DAB	*Dictionary of American Biography*
DNB	*Dictionary of National Biography*
Doheny	Estelle Doheny Collection of the Edward Laurence Doheny Memorial Library, St. John's Seminary
Donaldson	Thomas Donaldson, *Walt Whitman the Man* (1896)
Feinberg	Charles E. Feinberg Collection
Furness	Clifton Joseph Furness, *Walt Whitman's Workshop* (1928)
Gilchrist	Herbert Harlakenden Gilchrist, *Anne Gilchrist: Her Life and Writings* (1887)
Glicksberg	Charles I. Glicksberg, *Walt Whitman and the Civil War* (1933)
Gohdes and Silver	Clarence Gohdes and Rollo G. Silver, eds., *Faint Clews & Indirections* (1949)
Hanley	T. E. Hanley Collection, University of Texas
Harned	Thomas B. Harned, ed., *The Letters of Anne Gilchrist and Walt Whitman* (1918)
Holloway	Emory Holloway, *Whitman—An Interpretation in Narrative* (1926)

Huntington	Henry E. Huntington Library
In Re	*In Re Walt Whitman* (1893), ed. by Horace L. Traubel, Richard Maurice Bucke, and Thomas B. Harned
Kennedy	William Sloane Kennedy, *Reminiscences of Walt Whitman* (1896)
LC	The Library of Congress
LC #	*Walt Whitman—A Catalog Based Upon the Collections of the Library of Congress* (1955)
Lion	Oscar Lion Collection, New York Public Library
Morgan	Pierpont Morgan Library
NEQ	*New England Quarterly*
Nonesuch	Emory Holloway, ed., *Walt Whitman—Complete Poetry & Selected Prose and Letters* (1938)
NYPL	New York Public Library
Pennsylvania	University of Pennsylvania
Perry	Bliss Perry, *Walt Whitman* (1906)
PT	Partial Text
SB	*Studies in Bibliography*
Traubel	Horace Traubel, ed., *With Walt Whitman in Camden* (1906–1953), 4 vols.
Trent	Trent Collection, Duke University
UPP	*The Uncollected Poetry and Prose of Walt Whitman* (1921), 2 vols., ed. by Emory Halloway
WW	Walt Whitman
WWR	*Walt Whitman Review*

The Correspondence of Walt Whitman

VOLUME I: 1842-1867

1842

1. *To Nathan Hale, Jr., Editor,* Boston Miscellany

6.1. [*1842*]

ENDORSED: (by WW): "Walter Whitman | Ans. July 9, '42." ADDRESS: Editor "Boston Miscellany | Present?"

The undersigned takes the liberty of offering you the accompanying MS for your "Miscellany."[1] The price is $8.

The undersigned would be glad to furnish you with an article for each number, if it would be agreeable to you.

Please forward an answer to the address given herewith, stating whether you accept or decline.

Walter Whitman

June 1st | W.W. | 12 Curtis St | N. Y.

2. *To Nathan Hale, Jr., Editor,* Boston Miscellany

6.14. [*1842*]

ENDORSED: "Ans. June 23,[2] '42." ADDRESS: N. Hale Jr— | Boston Mass.

I took the liberty, two or three weeks since, of forwarding you a MS tale "The Angel of Tears," intended for the "Boston Miscellany."

Be so kind, if you accept it, to forward a note, informing me thereof, to

1842

1. WW sent "The Angel of Tears" to the *Boston Miscellany of Literature and Fashion,* which was edited by Nathan Hale, Jr., older brother of Edward Everett Hale, who was to write one of the early sympathetic reviews of *Leaves of Grass* (see Perry, 101). After Hale rejected the manuscript, it appeared in *Democratic Review,* XI (September, 1842), 282–284, and was reprinted in *UPP,* I, 83–86.

"The Angel of Tears" is a melodramatic tale of a man who slew his brother and now "lay in chains awaiting the terrible day when the doom he himself had inflicted should be meted to his own person." Alza, the angel of tears, apparently recognizes signs of penitence in the slumbering murderer, and the last words of the tale are spoken by a chorus: "Beautiful, to the Eye of the Centre, is the sight which ushers repentance!"

WW had been fired as editor of the *Aurora* in April, 1842, but almost immediately he became editor of the *Evening Tattler.*

2. Apparently Hale rejected the manuscript in his letter of this date, but returned the manuscript on July 9; this conjecture plausibly explains why WW's first letter was answered on July 9 and his second on June 23.

this place (your agency in New York), and if you decline, please return the MS.

My stories, I believe, have been pretty popular, and extracted liberally. Several of them in the Democratic Review have received public favor, instance "Death in the School-Room," &c &c.[3]

Walter Whitman

Tuesday June 14th

3. *Democratic Review* was the foremost literary journal of the day, and included among its contributors Hawthorne, Bryant, Whittier, and Poe. Here WW had published "Death in the School-Room," IX (August, 1841), 177–181; "Wild Frank's Return," IX (November, 1841), 476–482; "Bervance; or Father and Son," IX (December, 1841), 560–568; "The Tomb-Blossoms," X (January, 1842), 62–68; "The Last of the Sacred Army," X (March, 1842), 259–264; "The Child-Ghost; A Story of the Last Loyalist," X (May, 1842), 451–459. He later published in this magazine "Revenge and Requital: A Tale of a Murderer Escaped," XVII (August, 1845), 105–111.

1848

3. *Thomas Jefferson Whitman to the Family*

[2. 18(?)–28. 1848][1]

. . .[2] Our captain though[t] he would run the risk and save the time (it takes some time longer to go through the canal) so he got a flat-boat and took out some of the freight, and we started to go over the falls. Father can judge how fast we went, when I tell him it is a fall of twenty feet, within a space of three miles. And what is most dangerous, the bottom is covered with very large rock which leave a very small channel for the boat. When you get about the middle there is a large rock in this channel, and one on each side of it, the one on the right side is a little distance from the one in the middle, just room enough for a boat to pass through. So you have to take a very sudden turn, or the boat is smashed all to peices. It happened we got off with a little bump on each rock, we should not have got that (for we had the best pilots that could be found) but one wheel would not work. The fun of the whole thing was, the *fright* we all had, some of the passengers went to bed, others walked the cabin floor, looking as gloomy as if they were going to be hung. Altho I was frightened a good deal, it was not so much as some of the *men* were. If the boat had sunk we were within a few feet of the shore, but I dont think we could have got there, the current was so swift.

Mother, you have no idea of the splendor and comfort of these western river steam-boats. The cabin is on the deck, and state rooms on each side of it, their are two beds in each room. The greatest of all these splendors is the eating (you know I always did love eating) department. Every thing you would find in the Astor house in New York, You find on these boats.

I will give you a little description of the way we live on board. For

1848

1. Because of a difference in political opinion with the owner of the Brooklyn *Daily Eagle*, Isaac Van Anden, WW resigned, or was asked to resign. On February 9, 1848, he met J. E. McClure, who was establishing a newspaper in New Orleans, the *Daily Crescent*. WW and Jeff left Brooklyn on February 11, and arrived in New Orleans on February 25. Except for the brief notes appended to 5 and 6, none of WW's correspondence is extant.

2. For WW's accounts of his travels to New Orleans, see UPP, I, 181–190, and II, 77–78; see also Allen, 91–100. WW described the passage of the "St. Cloud" over this falls "just below Louisville" in the New Orleans *Daily Crescent* of March 10 (UPP, I, 189). The first page of the letter is missing.

breakfast we have: coffee, tea, ham and eggs, beef steak, sausages, hot cakes, with plenty of good bread, sugar &c &c. For dinner: roast beef, d[itt]o mutton, d[itt]o veal, boiled ham, roast turkey, d[itt]o goose, with pie and puddings, and for supper every thing that is good to eat.[3]

Saturday noon. Last night we had a very hard storm, it rained hard and blew harder. We expect to get as far as Cairo[4] to night on the Mississippi river. Nothing has occurred since yesterday of importance.

Sunday night. We have arrived at last, at New Orleans, we came in on Friday night about ten o'clock.[5] Saturday Walter found a board in Poydrass st cor St Charles.

You must dirrect your letters thus, Walter Whitman, New Orleans, La. Saturday it was a drizzely rainy day. I hope they dont have many of them.

Monday. Yesterday was quite warm. I saw a good many peach trees in blossom to day. Walter will get the first number of his out on Sunday next.

Dear Mother, I must bid you good bye for a little while. I will write to you again pretty soon.

Dear Father, I will write to you also pretty soon, until then good bye one and all

Jefferson Whitman

New Orleans

Dear Mother, write often.

4. *Thomas Jefferson Whitman to the Family*

New Orleans, March 14, 1848.

Dear Father,

Since I wrote to Mother nothing of importance has transpired. This will be the eighth or ninth letter we have sent you, and we have not received a single one from you. Mr Wilson[6] in the Eagle office sent Walter one in which he said that he called there and that you were all well. Do

3. WW also commented on the food, in an article in the *Daily Crescent:* "The quantity is enormous, and the quality first rate" (*UPP*, I, 188).

4. WW was not impressed with Cairo: "It is doubtful whether Cairo will ever be any 'great shakes,' except in the way of ague" (*UPP*, I, 189).

5. February 25; see *UPP*, II, 77. In the following line Poydras is misspelled. The Whitman boys moved from this boarding house almost immediately; see 4.

6. Probably Peter W. Wilson, printer.

7. Probably Henry Brown; see 6. The 1848 Brooklyn Directory lists three Henry Browns: a merchant, a bookkeeper, and a well digger.

8. William J. Devoe, a carpenter.

9. In a memorandum dated March 18, WW wrote: "I get through at evening much earlier than I had anticipated, which I like, of course, very well. . . . It seems somewhat

write to us, Father, even half a sheet would be better than nothing. I go to the post office every day so we shall get it as soon as it gets here. I have written one to Mr Brown[7] and William Devoe[8] and (as Walter said in his last letter) I shall write one to you at the begining and middle of every month.

Walter and myself are very well. I am now at work in the "Crescent" office at *five* dollars per week, and my work is done by three o'clock every afternoon. I dont know how long I shall stay there, but it shall be as long as I can make it.

Walter gets home much sooner than he thought he should; he is hardly ever later than eleven o'clock, and one night he was home at half past nine o'clock, he gets a few books most every day but none of them worth much.[9]

Father, you wanted me to ask how much carpenter's wages were here. I am told they are from forty to fifty dollars a month and found, which I think is a pretty good sum, but every thing is so much here that you hardly know whether you get a good bargain or not.

To My Dear Mother

I do want to hear from you very, very much, do write to Walter or me and tell us how you have been getting along since we came away and give a description of sister Mary's visit (I wrote her a letter soon after we got here). I will give you a little bit of city news.

New Orleans is a very level place and you do not dig down above two feet before you come to the water. It is also [a] very dirty place. Mother, I never wanted your cleanliness so much before as I did at our first boarding house, you could not only see the dirt, but you could taste it, and you had to too if you ate anything at all. And the rooms too, were covered with dirt an inch thick. But now we are through with all that. We are now liveing at the Tremont house, next door to the Theatre and directly opposite the office.[10]

Their has been two or three procession (and one thing or other) days since we have been here, and some rather funny ones too.

Mr. Tombs,[11] (the man that has or will give you the letter from Walter

strange that I have not heard from home. It is now over a month, and no letter yet" (*UPP*, II, 77).

10. The *Daily Crescent* had offices at 93 St. Charles Street, and the St. Charles Theatre was at Charles Street near Poydras Street. According to a receipt in the Feinberg Collection, the Whitmans boarded with P. Irwin. On May 1 WW paid Irwin $70 "For 8 weeks & 2 days Board for Self & Brother from the 4th of March to date at $9 p[er] week"; see also *The Papers of the Bibliographical Society of America*, LII (1958), 78. Of this boarding house WW wrote: "After changing my boarding house, Jef. and I were, take it altogether, pretty comfortable.—We had good beds, and though the noise was incessant, day and night, we slept well" (*UPP*, II, 77).

11. The 1848 Brooklyn Directory listed Andrew W. Tombs, a printer.

and the bundle of papers) is a brother of the foreman of the Eagle office.

He has not heard from his Father and Mother for a year and a half yet they have written to him three or four times. (*Doubtful.* W.W.)[12] He has had the yellow fever three times within the passed summer. Last Sunday we took a walk in the old Cathilic cemmetery, and a very beautiful place it is to. Flowers of every description were on some of the tombs, large white roses and red ones too were all along the walk from one end to the other. At night too the streets are filled with women with baskets full of flowers.

On Sunday morning we took a walk down to the old French church[13] and an old looking thing it is too. Every one would go up and dip their fingers in the holy water and then go home and *whip* their *slaves.* One old black took a bottle full home to wash the sins out of her family.

I will write to you, Mother, again, you must write to me as often as you possibly can.

To George and Andrew

Dear Brothers, I should like to see you very much but as I can not you must write to me too. On Saturday the 4th of March we had a grand fireman's procession and I think it was larger than the one (the firemen part) in New York. The engines were very large and are drawn by horses (six or eaight). Right opposite here they are fixing it up for a balloon ascension on next Sunday. I suppose I shall see all the fun. I am going to night to see Mr Collins[14] and I expect some fun. You must write to me as soon as you can.

To Sister Hannah

Dear Sister. Your part of the letter comes on the part where their is no lines, so I think it will be pretty crooked, but you must not mind that.

I beleive I promised to send you something but every thing is so much that I cannot get it.

New Orleans would be just the place for you, you could have flowers all the year round which I know you are a great lover of. Bye the Bye, Walter wants to know (and you must tell him in your letter) whether the trees and flowers he sat out are living yet. Dear Sister, you must also write to me (but please pay the postage). Among the others I must not forget my dear brother.

Eddy, you must go to school and try to write and read so I can send letters to you and you can read them.

12. WW's insertion. He probably read over Jeff's letters and helped to correct the erratic spelling.

13. St. Louis Cathedral in Jackson Square. WW described the Easter services in the *Daily Crescent* of April 22 (*UPP*, I, 221–222); see also *CW*, VI, 211.

14. Probably Jeff meant Dr. Colyer's troupe of "Model Artists," described by WW in the New Orleans *Picayune* (*CW*, VI, 209–210).

15. According to A. Oakley Hall, in *The Manhattaner in New Orleans* (1851),

I must bid you all good bye but I will write again soon.
good bye, Father, good bye, Mother, good bye all.
Jefferson Whitman

5. *Thomas Jefferson Whitman and WW to the Family*

New Orleans March 27 1848

Dear Mother

To day we received the first letter from you, and glad enough we were to get it too. The passage that gave me, and Walter too, the most pleasure was the one that said you were well, and that all the rest were well also. You say the weather is very cold there, here it is just the other way, that is it is pretty warm. I have now begun to wear the summer clothes sister Hannah made me which I find very comfortble.

It would have made you laugh to see me come home from the post office this morning with your letter. Eddy never was so glad when New Year's came, as I was to get your letter.

You must write to us oftener than you have, at least twice a month, which we are going to do.

You need not be alarmed about the yellow fever[15] as that gentleman will (the folks think) not visit this place this summer. The reason they give for that is this. It does not come but once in three or four years, and last season it was very hard and killed a great many persons (I mean it does not come but once in three or four years in such a shape). Besides it is a great hum-bug, most every one in our office has had (some of them have had it twice) and got well. It is caused mostly (I think all of it) by the habits of the peo-ple, they never meet a friend but you have to go drink and such loose habits.[16]

You know that Walter is averse to such habits, so you need not be afraid of our taking it.

Yesterday we were to have a balloon ascension, but just as it was ready to go up the balloon bursted so it did not go up, this is the third time she (it was a lady that was to go up in it) has tried it and each time failed.

We are very nicely situated in our new place;—just "around the cor-ner" is a very fine public park, which we take a walk in every night.

65–73, "agitated" discussions of yellow fever began with the coming of warm weather. Bennet Dowler, M.D., in *Tableaux of New Orleans* (1852?), 27, reports that 1,800 people died of the fever in the city in 1840.

16. Dowler describes the morals of New Orleans in 1852: "Probably no city of equal size in christendom receives into its bosom every year a greater proportion of vicious people than New Orleans" (p. 22).

I believe I told you in my last letter that I was also at work at the "Crescent" office at five dollars a week, and I have the exchange papers for which I get twenty five cents per hundred, in a few weeks I expect to get two dollars a week for them.

If you do not get the paper (the "Crescent") regular you must send Andrew or George down to the Eagle office for it, I always see that two copys go every morning. My work is good and light. I have such a part of the mail (and I can do it most over night) and then I have nothing to do for the rest of the day (I generally get through with it about two o'clock) but stay in the office.

We have (I think) got along very well for such a long journey, not a single accident occurred on the way.

Dear Father, I hope you are getting along good with your work &c. Mother says it is cold so you can't work, here it is warm enough. In building houses here they do not do as they do in New York. Here they dig a hole in the ground some two feet deep and about the same width, and in length as far as the wall is to go, (they can not dig cellars here like in the north, you don't dig in the ground more than two feet before it is filled with water.) This trench they cover the bottom with boards[17] (the ground is mostly made of quick-sand) and then build the wall on it. They cannot mak[e] good brick here, so they have to come from a distance. Carpenter's wages are very high here, some forty to fifty dollars a month and found.[18]

I will write a letter to you pretty soon, but in this one I must not forget George and Andrew.

Dear brothers, I should like to see you very much indeed but I suppose I cannot, you must make Mother or Hannah write to us as often as they can. There is nothing, I beleive, there is not any thing here you would like to hear from or of.

Dear Sister,[19] I shall never forgive you if you do not write to me. I suppose you would like to hear about the ladies in N. O. They are something like the "critters" in N. Y. except they were one or two more "flonces" and live more in the open air &c&c&c&c&c&c.

To Eddy, you must go to school and learn to read and write and then you must send letters to me, besides you must be a good boy &c.

And now, Dear Mother, I must bid you good bye for a little while but will write to you again shortly.

17. Probably this sentence should read: "They cover the bottom of this trench with boards."

18. Jeff wrote "and found," but probably meant to write "I found."

19. Hannah.

20. According to a tax bill in the Feinberg Collection, WW paid taxes in February,

We are both very well and the warm air argrees with Walter very much.

I have had a little attack of the disentery but I am very very well now, in fact I have not been sick much at all.

Dear Mother, good bye,

your son Jefferson Whitman

My best respects to the rest of the family.

Tuesday morning, 28th March.

Dearest Mother;

In one of my late letters, I told Hannah that if you did not receive money, by a letter from me, to pay the interest on the 1st of May, she must go down to the bank and draw $31½, and pay it at the insurance office, and get a receipt for it.[20] However, I may send money in a letter before that time—or part of it. O, mother, how glad I was to hear that you are quite well, again. Do try to keep so; you must not work—and they must all be kind to you. If you only keep well till I get home again, I think I shall be satisfied. I began to feel very uneasy, not hearing from you so long. My prospects[21] in the money line are bright. O how I long for the day when we can have our quiet little farm, and be together again—and have Mary and her children come to pay us long visits. I wrote to Mary yesterday.

W.W.

6. *Thomas Jefferson Whitman and WW to the Family*
4.23. [1848]

New Orleans Sunday April 23th

Dear Parents,

Since I wrote to you (the night after we got your only letter) we have heard nothing from you, | It is very strange you do not write oftener to us, for we have written to you ever so many times, now we have been from home nearly three months, and we have received only one letter from you, I beg of you to write to us often.

I received a letter from Mr Brown,[22] day before yesterday, but it was a very old one, he says they are all very well, that they like Billy quite well,

1848, on "1 lot & house in Prince St. No. 23 on Saml. Fleet's map." Perhaps WW referred to the insurance on this property.

21. The rest of this paragraph, except for the last sentence, appears in *UPP*, I, xlvi, *n*.

22. See 4.

that he sprained his back gardening at his new house, that they are building up around Prince St very fast and that I can write a letter good when I am a mind to (I do not agree with him there at all.) It is one of the greatest news-letters that I ever saw.

Walter is very well indeed, he thinks this place agrees with him very much and he says he feels better than ever he did in New York.[23] And I to[o] feel pretty well but not so much so as I intend to be, I have still a kind of summer complaint, which does not feel very good but it is very far from being really sick.

I hope you are all getting along smoothly and good, Henry[24] said Mother felt better than she had for years before, I hope she will continue to feel so, (I think I mentioned in my last letter that Walter had a letter from Henry, from Brooklyn).

Walter is trying to save up all the money he can get, and allready he has quite a sum, as soon as he gets a thousand dollars he is comeing north, And I too am saveing all I can get, I give Walter five dollars (my wages) every week, and I have sold about five dollars worth of old papers, that you know is all clear gain, all the trouble it is, is to count them out and put them up in hundreds.

Yesterday evening and this morning is the finest weather we have had since we have been here. Just warm and just cool enough to make it very pleasant. We took a very long walk last night, way out Camp street beyound the limits of the city.[25] There are no hills like on old Long Island, the whole state is as level as a race course. In some of the streets they have a kind of canal or drain to let the water run off, and even then in some places there is not enough "down-hill" to make it run off good. Just a little farther up town there is a canal (of a larger kind than those in the middle of the street) where sloops &c can come up from the lake (about 7 miles westward of the city). Along by this canal (the new canal they call it) there is a road called shell road[26] where we take frequent (and very pleasant) walks, the road is nearly as hard as a brick, and on a pleasant afternoon is covered with carriages of every discription. It seems to be the fashion to drive your horse as fast as he can go.

The price of a good apple here (such a one as you could get in New York for a cent and at some places two for a cent) is the small price of ten cents.

23. In a memorandum written in June, WW observed: "My health was most capital; I frequently thought indeed that I felt better than ever before in my life" (*UPP*, II, 77).

24. Probably Henry Brown; see 4.

25. About the same time, in the April 26 issue of the *Daily Crescent*, appeared WW's "A Walk about Town" (*UPP*, I, 223–224).

Sometimes I get thinking about you all and feel quite lonesome, but not one fifth as much as I did when we first arrived here, at first I could not make myself believe that we were so far away from home, but it is something of a distance.

By this morning's mail Walter received a letter from Mr Wilson[27] of the Eagle, but there was nothing in it but what we have heard before, about the election &c. He said that "Pat" delivered the paper to you very regular and also that you were all well (which I liked best of all he said in his long letter of five pages). We get the Eagle and Brooklyn Star quite often, and also the New York Tribune, Mirror, Globe, Dispatch, Sunday Times, Atlas, &c, &c. The Sun and Herald seem to think the "Crescent" not worthey their exchange as we have not received theirs yet, altho we have sent to them ever since the paper began. Walter wrote them a letter a few days ago and I guess we shall get them before long.

You will remember that I said that we were to have a balloon ascension opposite our boarding house, the thing was tried four or five times, but as just enough persons got inside the thing would manage to burst. A few Sundays ago it was said it would go up again, they had got it all ready when it blew all to peices. The persons that had paid to see it thought it was nothing but a suck in (which I think was the case). As soon as it touched the ground they all laid hold of it, and draging it over the fence tore it all to peices, they did not leave a peice a foot square. So ended all that.

Monday April 24th

By this mornings mail I received a letter from my friend "Bill" (at Mr Smiths[28] store in Fulton st) it is a very short one however, he says nothing about you so we have not heard from you since you wrote. He said he went out on an excursion and fell overboard but his brothers got him out after a fashion.

Walter also got a sermon by Mr Johnston[29] of Brooklyn. I believe that is all we received. I am certain of one thing, that is we never got any letter from you.

To day has been a very fine clear day, the ladys were out in great numbers. The city has been very lively to day.

Mother, Just think what you would think of us if we had writtin you

26. Shell Road parallels the New Canal, which connects the First District with Lake Pontchartrain.
27. See 4.
28. Four Smiths had stores on Fulton Street at this time.
29. Jeff probably referred to E. S. or G. T. Johnston, evidently brothers who were printers in Brooklyn. The Directory did not list a clergyman of this name.

only one letter since we came away, I am afraid you would think pretty hard of us. Father and Hannah need a little "blowing up" too, but I will generously let them off if they will promise to write often in future.

I have almost wrote the whole sheet out so I must stop. I shall write to you again pretty soon, untill then good bye

your son

Jefferson Whitman

New Orleans

My love to Mary if you see her before I write again.

If you do not write to us pretty soon we will do something but I don't know what.

Dear mother, I shall write to you myself in a few days. O how I long to see you. Hannah must get $31½ from the Bank to pay the interest. If she just asks for Mr. Hegeman,[30] and tells him she is my sister, he will show her every accommodation.

Walter.

1849

7. *To Tunis G. Bergen*

Brooklyn, Jan. 15, '49

T. G. Bergen,[1] Esq:

Dear Sir: It would be a great obligation to me, if you would present the enclosed bill and start it on its passage, so that I could get my pay as quickly as possible. For, like most printers, I am horribly in need of cash.

Do, my dear sir, oblige me, in this matter, if possible.

Yours truly

Walter Whitman

30. Probably Thomas Hegeman, a bookkeeper in the Atlantic Bank.

1849

1. In one of his "Paragraph Sketches of Brooklynites," in the Brooklyn *Daily Advertizer*, June 1, 1850, WW characterized Bergen (1806–1881) as "the Nestor of the Board of Supervisors," and noted that he had been "a very Cerberus in his watch over the Treasury." He also lauded Bergen's "stout, healthy Dutch constitution" and his services in the New York legislature. Bergen was the author of *The Bergen Family: or The Descendants of Hans Hansen Bergen* (1876) and other genealogies. At this time WW was editor of the Brooklyn *Daily Freeman*, a newspaper which he founded and printed until September 11, 1849, and he also published the *Salesman*, a weekly advertising journal; see *UPP*, I, lii–liii, and Emory Holloway and Vernolian Schwarz, eds., *I Sit and Look Out* (1932), 7.

1850–1857

8. *To Carlos D. Stuart* *10.10. [1850?]*

Mr. Stuart,[1]

I take the liberty of writing, to ask whether you have any sort of "opening" in your new enterprise, for services that I could render? I am out of regular employment, and fond of the press—and, if you would be disposed to "try it on," I should like to have an interview with you, for the purpose of seeing whether we could agree to something. My ideas of salary are *very* moderate.

Would you like a Story, of some length for your paper? Please answer through P. O.

Yours, &c

Walter Whitman

106 Myrtle av. Brooklyn | Oct. 10.

9. *To W. M. Muchmore*

ADDRESS: From Walter Whitman | W. M. Muchmore, | Member Board of Supervisors | for King's county.

Tuesday afternoon, | October 21st, 1851

Mr. Muchmore,[1]

Dear Sir, If convenient, will you remind Mr. Tunis G. Bergen,[2] of my bill for advertising, ($50,) which was presented two weeks ago, and referred to Com. on Accounts—so that, if found all ship-shape, it may be

1850

1. On September 27, 1850, the following announcement appeared in *The Long Islander*: "New Penny Paper—We are glad to notice that Carlos D. Stuart late editor of the *New York Sun* is to establish a new daily in New York." Through his marriage to Catherine Oakley, who lived in West Hills, Stuart may have been known to the Whitmans. He was the author of *Ianthe and Other Poems*. For this information I am indebted to the late Mrs. Martha K. Hall, formerly librarian of the Huntington (N.Y.) Historical Society.

passed for payment this afternoon—as that would oblige me, if there is no objection.

Yours truly

Walter Whitman | Printer

Hand this note to Mr. Bergen, if you choose.

9.1 *To John Parker Hale*[1] *8.14.* [*1852*]

ENDORSED: "Walter Whitman | Aug 14, 1852."

Brooklyn, Saturday morning August 14

A word from a stranger, a young man, and a true Democrat I hope.

You must not only not decline the nomination of the Democracy at Pittsburgh, but you must accept it gracefully and cordially. It is well to know when to be firm against others' wishes; but it is better to know when to yield in a manly and amiable spirit.

Out of the Pittsburgh movement and "platform" it may be that a real live Democratic party is destined to come forth, which, from small beginnings, ridicule, and odium, (just like Jeffersonian democracy fifty years ago,) will gradually win the hearts of the people, and crowd those who stand before it into the sea. Then we should see an American Democracy with thews and sinews worthy this sublime age.

It is from the young men of our land—the ardent, and generous hearts—that these things are to come. Do you, then, yield to the decision at Pittsburgh, shape your acceptance to that idea of the future which supposes that we are at [present?] planting a renewed and vital party, fit to triumph over the effete and lethargic organizations now so powerful and so unworthy. Look to the young men—appeal specially to them. Enter into this condition of affairs, with spirit, too. Take two or three occasions within the coming month to make personal addresses directly to the people, giving condensed embodiments of the principal ideas which distinguish our liberal faith from the drag-parties and their platforms. Boldly promulge these, with that temper of rounded and good-natured moderation which is

1851

1. William M. Muchmore was a dealer in coal and wood in Brooklyn.
2. See 7.

1852

1. This important early letter was recently discovered among the Hale Papers by Richard Sewall, a graduate student at Harvard University.

John Parker Hale (1806–1873), a senator from New Hampshire, accepted the nomination of the Free-Soilers in 1852 and polled 150,000 votes. Hale, who vigorously opposed slavery, later became a Republican and served as minister to Spain from 1865 to 1869.

peculiar to you; but abate not one jot of your fullest radicalism. After these two or three speeches, which should be well-considered and not too long, possess your soul in patience, and take as little personal action in the election as may be. Depend upon it, there is no way so good as the face-to-face of candidates and people—in the old heroic Roman fashion. I would suggest that one of these addresses be delivered in New York, and one in Cincinnati—with a third either in Baltimore or Washington.

You are at Washington, and have for years moved among the great men. I have never been at Washington, and know none of the great men. But I know the people. I know well, (for I am practically in New York,) the real heart of this mighty city—the tens of thousands of young men, the mechanics, the writers, &c &c. In all these, under and behind the bosh of the regular politicians, there burns, almost with fierceness, the divine fire which more or less, during all ages, has only waited a chance to leap forth and confound the calculations of tyrants, hunkers, and all their tribe. At this moment, New York is the most radical city in America. It would be the most anti-slavery city, if that cause hadn't been made ridiculous by the freaks of the local leaders here.

O, my dear sir, I only wish you could know the sentiments of respect and personal good will toward yourself, with which, upon seeing a telegraphic item in one of this morning's papers, that you would probably decline, I forthwith sat down, and have written my thoughts and advice. I shall make no apology; for if sentiments and opinions out of the great mass of the common people are of no use to the legislators, then our government is a sad blunder indeed.

How little you at Washington—you Senatorial and Executive dignitaries—know of us, after all. How little you realize that the souls of the people ever leap and swell to any thing like a great liberal thought or principle, uttered by any well-known personage—and how deeply they love the man that promulges such principles with candor and power. It is wonderful in your keen search and rivalry for popular favor, that hardly any one discovers this direct and palpable road there.

Walter Whitman

Cumberland st. near Atlantic
Brooklyn N. Y.

1855

1. The story of this, the most famous letter in American literature, has been related many times. WW was so pleased with the letter that he not only showed it to his friends but also allowed Charles A. Dana to print it in the New York *Tribune*. WW reproduced it in the second edition of *Leaves of Grass* (1856), and quoted on the spine of that volume the sentence, "I greet you at the beginning of a great career." His unauthorized use of the letter annoyed Emerson and provoked a furor which has been periodically rekindled ever since.

10. *Ralph Waldo Emerson to WW*

ADDRESS: Walter Whitman, Esq. | Care of Fowlers & Wells, | 308 Broadway, | New York. POSTMARK: [*indecipherable*].

Concord | Massachusetts | 21 July | 1855

Dear Sir,[1]

I am not blind to the worth of the wonderful gift of "Leaves of Grass." I find it the most extraordinary piece of wit & wisdom that America has yet contributed. I am very happy in reading it, as great power makes us happy. It meets the demand I am always making of what seemed the sterile & stingy Nature, as if too much handiwork or too much lymph in the temperament were making our western wits fat & mean.

I give you joy of your free & brave thought. I have great joy in it. I find incomparable things said incomparably well, as they must be. I find the courage of *treatment*, which so delights us, & which large perception only can inspire.

I greet you at the beginning of a great career, which yet must have had a long foreground somewhere, for such a start. I rubbed my eyes a little to see if this sunbeam were no illusion; but the solid sense of the book is a sober certainty. It has the best merits, namely, of fortifying & encouraging.

I did not know until I, last night, saw the book advertised in a newspaper, that I could trust the name as real & available for a Post-office. I wish to see my benefactor, & have felt much like striking my tasks, & visiting New York to pay you my respects.

R. W. Emerson.

Mr Walter Whitman.

11. *To William Henry Seward*[2]

Brooklyn, N. Y. Dec. 7, '55.

Could you do me the favor to put my address, as enclosed, on the list of those to whom it is convenient for you to send public documents, your speeches, and any government, congressional or other publications of general interest, especially statistics, census facts &c? I should be deeply obliged for a copy of the last census returns,[3] Reports of the Smithsonian

2. Seward (1801–1872) was elected United States Senator from New York in 1848, and later was Lincoln's Secretary of State.

3. Seward probably sent a copy of *Statistical View of the United States . . . A Compendium of the Seventh Census* (1854), compiled by J. D. B. De Bow. A Senate resolution on July 12, 1854, had ordered printed "for the use of the Senate" 50,000 copies of this *Compendium*. WW apparently utilized De Bow's population statistics and projections in "The Eighteenth Presidency!"

Institute, and the like. I am a writer, for the press and otherwise. I too have at heart Freedom, and the amelioration of the people.

Walt Whitman

Brooklyn N. Y.

12. *To Sarah Tyndale* [*6*].*20. 1857*

Brooklyn, Saturday Afternoon, | June[1] 20, 1857.

Dear Friend,

Do not suppose, because I have delayed writing to you, that I have forgotten you. No, that will never be. I often recall your visits to me, and your goodness. I think profoundly of my friends—though I cannot write to them by the post office. I write to them more to my satisfaction, through my poems.

Tell Hector I thank him heartily for his invitation and letter—O it is not from any mind to slight him that I have not answered it, or accepted the friendly call. I am so non-polite—so habitually wanting in my responses and ceremonies. That is *me*—much that is bad, harsh, an undutiful person, a thriftless debtor, is me.[2]

I spent an evening with Mr. Arnold[3] and Mrs. Price[4] lately. Mrs. Price and Helen had been out all day with the sewing machine, at Mr. Beecher's —either Henry Ward's, or his father's.[5] They had done a great day's work —as much, one of the Beecher ladies said, as a sempstress could have got through with in six months. Mrs. P. and Helen had engagements for a fort-

1857

1. That WW erred in writing "July" is clear from Mrs. Tyndale's correspondence of June 24 and July 1 in the Feinberg Collection. Mrs. Tyndale was an abolitionist from Philadelphia who met WW in the company of Bronson Alcott and Henry Thoreau; see Allen, 202–204, and Odell Shepard, ed., *The Journals of Bronson Alcott* (1938), 286–290. Alcott (289) described Mrs. Tyndale as "a solid walrus of a woman spread full many a rood abroad, kindly taking the slaves' and Magdalens' parts and advocate for general justice and equality in all relations." Her son Hector was an importer of china in Philadelphia; WW described a meeting with him on February 25, 1857 (*CW*, IX, 154–155).

2. In her reply on June 24, Mrs. Tyndale commented on this passage: "I think your judgment of yourself is rather severe, I have not changed my opinion. . . . if [Emerson] or any one else expected *common* etiquette from you, after having read Leaves of Grass they were sadly mistaken in your character. Where etiquette, or what is *called* refined and exquisite taste *predominate*, I never expect to find much originality of character" (Feinberg).

3. John Arnold lived with his daughter's family in the same house as the Price family. Helen Price described him as "a Swedenborgian," with whom WW frequently argued without "the slightest irritation between them"; see Bucke, 26–27.

4. The Prices were friends of Mrs. Whitman. The husband, Edmund, operated a pickle factory in Brooklyn; see Allen, 199–200. His wife Abby, as one might expect, was closer to WW, who corresponded with her frequently in the 1860's. WW always interested himself in the Price children, Helen, Emma, and Arthur. Helen's reminiscences were included in Bucke's biography, and she printed for the first time some of WW's letters to her mother, in *Putnam's Monthly*, V (1908), 163–169.

5. Henry Ward Beecher (1813–1887), Congregational clergyman and brother of

night ahead, to go out among families and take the sewing machine. What a revolution this little piece of furniture is producing. Isn't it quite an *encouragement.*

I got into quite a talk with Mr. Arnold about Mrs. Hatch.[6] He says the pervading thought of her speeches is that *first* exists the spirituality of any thing, and *that* gives existence to things, the earth, plants, animals, men, women. But that Andrew Jackson Davis[7] puts *matter* as the subject of his homilies, and the primary source of all results—I suppose the soul among the rest. Both are quite determined in their theories. Perhaps when they know much more, both of them will be much less determined.

A minister, Rev. Mr. Porter,[8] was introduced to me this morning, a Dutch Reformed minister, and editor of the "Christian Intelligencer," N. Y. Would you believe it, he had been reading "Leaves of Grass," and wanted *more*? He said he hoped I retained the true Reformed faith which I must have inherited from my mother's Dutch ancestry. I not only assured him of my retaining faith in that sect, but that I had perfect faith in all sects, and was not inclined to reject one single one—but believed each to be about as far advanced as it could be, considering what had preceded it—and moreover that every one was the needed representative of *its* truth—or of something needed as much as truth. I had quite a good hour with Mr. Porter—we grew friends—and I am to go dine with the head man of the head congregation of Dutch Presbyterians in Brooklyn, Eastern District!

I have seen Mrs. Walton[9] once or twice since you left Brooklyn. I dined

Harriet Beecher Stowe, accepted the pastorate of the Plymouth Church, Brooklyn, in 1847. WW described him briefly in the Brooklyn *Daily Advertizer* of May 25, 1850, reprinted in UPP, I, 234–235; see also *I Sit and Look Out*, 84–85, and Traubel, I, 137–138. His father, Lyman Beecher (1775–1863), was also a clergyman, who upon his retirement lived with his son in Brooklyn.

6. Cora L. V. Hatch, a medium, was born in 1840 in Cuba, N. Y. At age ten, as she sat with slate and pencil in her hand, "she lost external consciousness, and on awaking she found her slate covered with writing." At fourteen she was a public speaker, and at sixteen married Dr. B. F. Hatch, who published and wrote an introduction to her *Discourses on Religion, Morals, Philosophy, and Metaphysics* (1858). In 1871, now Mrs. Tappan, she published a collection of poems entitled *Hisperia;* the section "Laus Natura" is dedicated to "Walt Whitman, the Poet of Nature." See also Emma Hardinge, *Modern American Spiritualism* (1870), 149.

7. Davis (1826–1910) was a famous spiritualist and, though self-educated and boastful that at thirty-one he had read only one book, was himself the author of approximately thirty works. He professed to believe that the spirit of Swedenborg had personally guided his steps after he became twenty-one.

8. Elbert Stothoff Porter was pastor of the Williamsburgh Church, Brooklyn, from 1848 to 1883, and editor of the *Christian Intelligencer*, a journal published by the Dutch Reformed Church, from 1852 to 1868. See Edward Tanjore Corwin, *A Manual of the Reformed Church in America* (1879), 407; *Americana*, XXX (1936), 478–479; and Mott, *A History of American Magazines, 1850–1865* (1938), 73–74.

9. Of Mrs. Walton, Mrs. Tyndale wrote in her reply: "Her life is not exactly in accordence with her highest views of humanity, hence the unhappyness, but she will ultimately be the better woman for the experience" (Feinberg). I have been unable to identify her.

there. I feel great sympathy with her, on some accounts. Certainly, she is not happy.

Fowler & Wells[10] are bad persons for me. They retard my book very much. It is worse than ever. I wish now to bring out a third edition—I have now *a hundred* poems ready (the last edition had thirty-two)—and shall endeavor to make an arrangement with some publisher here to take the plates from F. & W. and make the additions needed, and so bring out the third edition. F. & W. are very willing to give up the plates—they want the thing off their hands. In the forthcoming Vol. I shall have, as I said, a hundred poems, and no other matter but poems—(no letters to or from Emerson—no notices, or any thing of that sort.) I know well enough, that *that* must be the *true* Leaves of Grass—I think it (the new Vol.) has an aspect of completeness, and makes its case clearer. The old poems are all retained. The difference is in the new character given to the mass, by the additions.

Dear friend, I do not feel like fixing a day on which I will come and make my promised visit. How it is I know not, but I hang back more and more from making visits, even to those I have much happiness in being with.

Mother is well—all are well. Mother often speaks about you. We shall all of us remember you always with more affection than you perhaps suppose. Before I come to Philadelphia, I shall send you or Hector a line.

Wishing Peace & Friendship

Walt Whitman

13. *To an Unidentified Correspondent*[11]

TRANSCRIPT.

Brooklyn | July 28, 1857

O You should see me, how I look after sea-sailing. I am swarthy and red as a Moor—I go around without any coat or vest—looking so

10. The celebrated phrenologists, Orson S. and Lorenzo Fowler, formed the publishing firm of Fowler & Wells with S. R. Wells in 1844. Fowler & Wells announced the publication of *Leaves of Grass* in the New York *Tribune* of July 6, 1855, and acted as distributors of this edition. WW reviewed his book in *The American Phrenological Journal*, XXII (1855), 90. Fowler & Wells printed and advertised the second edition the following year, but on June 7, 1856, Wells wrote to WW "to insist on the omission of certain objectionable passages in Leaves of Grass, or, decline publishing it." Wells went on to assert that it would be better for WW "to have the work published by clean hands," and recommended the Partons, who "are *rich* & *enterprizing*" (Feinberg). For WW's associations with Fowler & Wells, see Edward Hungerford, "Walt Whitman and His Chart of Bumps," *AL*, II (1930–31), 350–384. Whether WW asked James Parton to publish his poetry is not known, but during the winter of 1857 he borrowed $200 from Parton; see Allen, 207–210, and letter 351.

Mrs. Tyndale concurred in WW's opinion of Fowler & Wells—"I can tell you more of their malpractice about it [*Leaves of Grass*], when you come"—and offered $50 toward the purchase of the plates. Evidently WW accepted her offer in the missing letter of

strong, ugly, and nonchalant, with my white beard—People stare, I notice, more wonderingly than ever. . . . I have thought, for some time past, of beginning the use of myself as a public Speaker, teacher, or lecturer.[12] (This, after I get out the next issue of my "Leaves")—Whether it will come to any thing, remains to be seen. . . . My immediate acquaintances, even those attached strongly to me, secretly entertain the idea that I am a great fool not to "*make something*" out of my "talents" and out of the general good will with which I am regarded. Can it be that some such notion is lately infusing itself into me also?

June 29, for on July 1 Mrs. Tyndale said that a friend of hers in the city would send a check. She also said "entrenous" that Mr. Walton might be willing to assist in getting out the third edition, and "Mr [George B.?] Arnold or Mr [Benjamin] Urner (I believe they have a press) could do it" (Feinberg). Because the correspondence between WW and Mrs. Tyndale is incomplete, the details of the plans for a third edition are not determinable. See, however, Fredson Bowers' discussion of the projected one hundred poems in *Whitman Manuscripts—Leaves of Grass (1860)* (1955), xxvii–xli.

11. Though Henkels listed this as a letter, it might have been a jotting for inclusion in one of WW's notebooks. Since only conjecture is possible until it is located, it seemed of sufficient interest to justify inclusion in the correspondence.

12. Between 1856 and 1858, as he was to do again during the Civil War Years (see 53), WW contemplated a career as a lecturer. In the Trent Collection there is a circular, dated 1858, announcing his plans: he intended to travel extensively in this country and in "Kanada" and to charge "One Dime" as well as to sell printed copies of his lectures; see Allen, 219–220.

1860

14. *To the Editors*, Harper's Magazine *1.7.1860*

ENDORSED (by WW): "Private note from Walt Whitman | *To Editors and Proprietors Harper's* | *Magazine*, accompanying 'A Chant of National Feuillage.' "

The theory of "*A Chant of National Feuillage*"[1] is to bring in, (devoting a line, or two or three lines, to each,) a comprehensive collection of touches, localés, incidents, idiomatic scenes, from every section, South, West, North, East, Kanada, Texas, Maine, Virginia, the Mississippi Valley, &c. &c. &c.—all intensely fused to the urgency of compact America, "America always"—all in a vein of graphic, short, clear, hasting along—as having a huge bouquet to collect, and quickly taking and binding in every characteristic subject that offers itself—making a compact, the-whole-surrounding, *National Poem*, after its sort, after my own style.

Is there any other poem of the sort extant—or indeed hitherto attempted?

You may start at the style. Yes, it is a new style, of course, but that is necessitated by new theories, new themes—or say the new treatment of themes, forced upon us for American purposes. Every really new person, (poet or other,) *makes* his style—sometimes a little way removed from the previous models—sometimes very far removed.

Furthermore, I have surely attained headway enough with the American public, especially with the literary classes, to make it worth your while to give them a sight of me with all my neologism.

The price is $40. Cash down on acceptance.

1860

1. Number four of the "Chants Democratic," printed in the 1860 edition of *Leaves of Grass*, 159–166. Apparently the poem was rejected by *Harper's*.

2. There are no extant copies of the New York *Sunday Courier* for 1860. "Thoughts" appeared in the third edition of *Leaves of Grass*, 408–411.

3. Lowell was editor of the *Atlantic Monthly* from 1857 to 1861. No admirer of WW, he evidently printed WW's poem at Emerson's suggestion; see Allen, 238. For other correspondence with the *Atlantic Monthly*, see 17 and 24. Portia Baker analyzes WW's relations with this magazine in *AL*, VI (1934–35), 283–301.

4. Edward Howard House (1836–1901) was music and drama critic of the Boston *Courier* from 1854 to 1858, and was appointed to the same post on the New York *Trib-*

I reserve the use of the piece in any collection of my poems I may publish in future.

Should my name be printed in the programme of contributors at any time it must not be lower down than third in the list.

If the piece is declined, please keep the MS. for me to be called for. Will send, or call, last of next week.

Walt Whitman

Jan. 7th, '60.

15. *To the Editor, the New York* Sunday Courier

1.16. 1860

ENDORSED: "Private note from Walt Whitman | To Editor Sunday Courier."

The price of the "Thoughts"[2] is $10.

I reserve the right of using it in any future edition of my poems.

I suggest, if accepted, it be placed at the top of the 2d, 3d, or 4th column, first page.

If declined, please keep the MS. till I call. I will call Wednesday morning.

Walt Whitman

Jan. 16, '60

16. *To James Russell Lowell*

Jan. 20, '60.

Dear Sir,[3]

Mr. House[4] inform'd me that you accepted, and would publish, my "Bardic Symbols."[5] If so, would you, as soon as convenient, have it put in type, and send me the proof?

About the two lines:

une in 1858. WW evidently knew House as early as 1857, for, in his "Autograph Notebook—1857" (Feinberg), he pasted a calling card signed by House. During the Civil War, House was a war correspondent for the *Tribune*. See also 235.

5. "Bardic Symbols," later entitled "As I Ebb'd with the Ocean of Life," appeared in the April issue, 445–447, and, without a title, in the third edition of *Leaves of Grass*, 195–199. The two lines were omitted in the magazine. On March 27, Henry Clapp, Jr. (see 235), wrote to WW: "The papers all over the land have noticed your poem in the Atlantic and have generally pitched into it strong: which I take to be good for you and your new publishers [Thayer & Eldridge], who if they move rapidly and concentrate their forces will make a Napolenic thing of it" (Feinberg; Traubel, I, 237).

(See from my dead lips the ooze exuding at last!
See the prismatic colors glistening and rolling!)

I have in view, from them, an effect in the piece which I clearly feel, but cannot as clearly define. Though I should prefer them in, still, as I told Mr. House, I agree that you may omit them, if you decidedly wish to.

Yours &c

Walt Whitman

Portland av. near Myrtle | Brooklyn, N. Y.

17. *To the Editor*, Atlantic Monthly

Friday morning, March 2, '60.

Your "Atlantic" has, either in type or MS. an article of mine, sent on by E. H. House, and accepted by Mr. Lowell—price $40. In lieu of that sum when the piece is printed, could you enclose me $30 immediately on receiving this, and send by mail—considering this a receipt in full?

Walt Whitman

Portland av. next to Myrtle, | Brooklyn N. Y.

You will first inquire of Mr. L. about the article, lest I am entertaining some misunderstanding about it.[6]

6. See 16. Ticknor and Fields, publishers of the *Atlantic Monthly*, sent WW a check for $30 on March 6 (Traubel, IV, 77).

7. W. W. Thayer and Charles W. Eldridge approached publication of *Leaves of Grass* with more zeal than business acumen. They wrote on February 10: "We want to be the publishers of Walt. Whitman's poems—Leaves of Grass.—When the book was first issued we were clerks in the establishment we now own. We read the book with profit and pleasure. It is a true poem and writ by a *true* man" (Feinberg; Allen, 236). On February 27 they offered "10 per cent of the retail price for your copyright," and invited WW's opinion as to size and binding. (That WW had his own way in matters of format is evident in 21.) On May 24, the firm notified WW that review copies had been sent to the "Editorial Fraternity," and, somewhat belatedly, on June 5, asked "for our consideration terms of contract for publishing L of G." The publishers reported on June 14 that "the first edition is nearly all gone, and the second is all printed and ready for binding," but noted "considerable opposition among the trade to the book. . . . Of course we intend to conquer this opposition partly born of prejudice and partly of cowardice, by creating an overwhelming demand among the mass public, which shall sweep them and their petty fears, on its resistless torrent." On July 29, the partners conjectured that the second edition would be exhausted within a month, and proposed a cheaper ($1) edition for the next printing as well as a slightly more expensive volume.

Thayer's letter of August 17 illustrates the idolatry of the publishers: "*We* too wish you could be with us in Boston, for we have *so* much to say; and our 'fanatic' wants to get under the refreshing shelter of Walt's spirit; he does not ask Walt to talk, but only for the privilege of looking into those eyes of calm, and through them to enter into that soul, so deep in its emotions, so majestic in all its thought-movements, and yet so simple and childlike. Yes, Walt Whitman, though men of the world and arch-critics do not *under-*

18. *To Abby M. Price* *3.29. [1860]*

ADDRESS: Abby M. Price, | S. W. corner Greenwich and Horatio streets, | New York | city. POSTMARK: Boston | Mar | 29 | (?).

Boston, Thursday night, | March 29.

As I know you would like to hear from me, my dear friend, I will not yet go to bed—but sit down to write to you, that I have been here in Boston, to-day is a fortnight, and that my book is well under way. About a hundred and twenty pages are set up—it will probably make from six to seven hundred pages, and of a larger size than the last edition. It is to be very finely printed, good paper, and new, rather large-sized type. Thayer & Eldridge,[7] the publishers, are a couple of young Yankees—so far very good specimens, to me, of this Eastern race of yours. They have treated me first rate—have not asked me at all what I was going to put into the book—just took me to the stereotype foundry, and given orders to follow my directions. It will be out in a month—a great relief to me to have the thing off my mind.

I am more pleased with Boston than I anticipated. It is full of life, and criss-cross streets. I am very glad I [have] come, if only to rub out of me the deficient notions I had of New England character. I am getting to like it, every way—even the Yankee twang.

Emerson called upon me immediately, treated me with the greatest courtesy—kept possession of me all day—gave me a bully dinner, &c.[8]

stand thee, yet some there be among men and women who *love* thee and hold thy spirit close by their own." But bankruptcy was facing the firm. On October 11, and again four days later, the publishers refused to advance money to WW. Thayer on December 1 advised WW not to cash a check he had recently sent, and on December 5 wrote: "We go by the boards tomorrow or next day." The Boston law firm of Jewell and Field billed WW for $20.24 on February 6, 1861. On April 19, 1861, Thayer, despite his desperate plight, wished that "I could bless you substantially with a hundred 'spot.' " (These letters are in the Feinberg Collection.)

In the same letter Thayer informed WW that the plates of *Leaves of Grass* were now in the possession of Horace Wentworth, a Boston publisher, whom Thayer characterized as "my bitter and relentless enemy" and "an illiterate man." In 1866 Wentworth offered to sell to WW the plates of the 1860 edition. When WW did not reply to his letter of November 16 (Yale), Wentworth became more threatening on November 27: "I shall unqualifiedly protest against the printing or publication of any work, bearing the title or containing in any way the same matter as the 'Leaves of Grass.' The plates and engraving are in the market at a nominal price, tho' I intend to republish if they are not soon disposed of—Also the stereotype plates of the pamphlet notices which we should be pleased to sell with the plates" (Feinberg). But on December 17 (Yale), he abandoned threats and asked for an offer.

8. It was on this occasion that, according to WW's recollections written twenty years later (*CW*, v. 26–27), Emerson attempted to persuade him not to publish the "Enfans d'Adam" poems. The date of the meeting was probably March 17, since on that day Emerson obtained reading privileges for "W. Whitman" at the Boston Athenaeum library; see Allen, 237–238.

I go on the Common—walk considerable in Washington street—and occupy about three hours a day at work in the printing office. All I have to do, is to read proofs. I wish you lived here—I should visit you regularly every day—probably twice a day. I create an immense sensation in Washington street. Every body here is so like everybody else—and I am Walt Whitman!—Yankee curiosity and cuteness, for once, is thoroughly stumped, confounded, petrified, made desperate.

Let me see—have I any thing else to say to you? Indeed, what does it all amount to—this saying business? Of course I had better tear up this note—only I want to let you see how I cannot have forgotten you—sitting up here after half past 12, to write this precious document. I send my love to Helen and Emmy.

Walt.

19. *To Thomas Jefferson Whitman* *4.1.* [*1860*]

Boston, Sunday night, | April 1st.

Dear Brother,

I have just finished a letter to mother, and while my hand is in, I will write you a line. I enclose in my letter to Mother, a note from Hyde[9]—nothing at all in it, except that Han is well, and comfortably situated—I have not heard a word from home since I left—write me a few words, Jeff, if mother does not,[10] and let me know how you all are, and whether you have took the house or given it up.[11] I suppose of course if every thing was not going on pretty much as usual, some of you would have written to tell me.

I am having a tolerable fair time here in Boston—not quite enough to occupy me—only two or three hours work a day, reading proof. Still, I am so satisfied at the certainty of having "Leaves of Grass," in a far more complete and favorable form than before, printed and really *published*, that I

9. Charles Heyde, WW's brother-in-law and Hannah's husband. That there was "nothing at all" in Heyde's letter probably came as a surprise to the Whitmans, since ordinarily he bewailed his lot and disparaged his wife and her erratic behavior. (Heyde was still in a genial mood when he wrote again on May 18 to WW; see Gohdes and Silver, 215–216.) Hannah lived in fear of her husband's letters, for he evidently threatened, or so Hannah imagined, to write candidly to her family. On July 21, 1861, for example, Hannah wrote to her mother: "Charlie has taken the greatest aversion to me, no matter what I do it is wrong. I know I should hide his faults. I do feel sensitive about it, no one knows how much so, but I must tell some little things for Charlie said he should write such a letter home that he thought some of you would come after me" (LC).

10. WW had not received his mother's letter of March 30 (Trent), in which she reported that Andrew was recovering from an illness, "made worse," according to Jeff on April 3 (Feinberg), "by an ignorent Dr. and those around him." Mrs. Whitman observed that "poor nance . . . looks as she was almost done over," and that "Jess has got to work in the navy yard again." She also requested "5 dollars the first of next month

don't mind small things. The book will be a very handsome specimen of typography, paper, binding, &c.—and will be, it seems to me, like relieving me of a great weight—or removing a great obstacle that has been in my way for the last three years. The young men that are publishing it treat me in a way I could not wish to have better. They are go-ahead fellows, and don't seem to have the least doubt they are bound to make a good spec. out of my book. It is quite curious, all this should spring up so suddenly, aint it.[12]

I am very well, and hold my own about as usual. I am stopping at a lodging house, have a very nice room, gas, water, good American folks keep it—I pay $2—eat at restaurant. I get up in the morning, give myself a good wash all over, and currying—then take a walk, often in the Common —then nothing but a cup of coffee generally for my breakfast—then to the stereotype foundry. About 12 I take a walk, and at 2, a good dinner. Not much else, in the way of eating, except that meal.

If I have any thing to communicate, dear brother, I shall write again.

Walt.

Care of Thayer & Eldridge | 116 Washington st | Boston | Mass.

20. *To Frederick Baker* — *4.24. [1860?]*

ENDORSED (by WW): "Verbatim copy of answer | to Mr. Baker's note."

Boston, April 24.

Mr. Baker,[13] In compliance with your request, I execute and return the new and explanatory deed forthwith, depending upon you that it is all right, as I know nothing at all about such things.

I paid Mr. Adams, the Commissioner, *one dollar*, which you may send me, if you please.

Yours &c

Walt Whitman

to help toward the rent."

11. In his reply on April 3, Jeff wrote: "Mother has taken the house and rented the lower part to a Mr 'John Brown' @ $14 per month" (Feinberg). The Browns lived for five years with the Whitmans on Portland Avenue, Brooklyn. He was a tailor. Relations between the two families were sometimes strained; see 112. On June 3, 1865 (Trent), Mrs. Whitman informed her son that she was glad to move away from the Browns.

12. Of the forthcoming *Leaves of Grass*, Jeff wrote on April 3: "I quite long for it to make its appearence. What jolly times we will have reading the notices of it won't we, you must expect the 'Yam Yam Yam' writer to give you a dig as often as possible" (Feinberg).

13. On April 23, Frederick Baker, attorney at law, 15 Nassau Street, New York City, wrote to WW: "The Deed executed to Lazarus Wineburgh in 1854 does not express the consideration money. Wineburgh has recently effected a sale of the property conveyed by that Deed; but objection is made to the title on the ground of such omission" (Feinberg). I have not identified Adams.

21. *To Thomas Jefferson Whitman* 5.10. [1860]

Boston, | Thursday morning, May 10.

Dear Brother,

I have nothing particular to write about, yet I know you will be glad to hear from me anyhow. The book is finished in all that makes the reading part, and is all through the press complete—It is electrotyped—that is, by a chemical process, a solution of copper, silver, zinc, &c. is precipitated in a "bath," so as to cover the face of the plates of type all over, and make it very much harder and more enduring. Plates finished by that process wear well for hundreds of thousands of copies, and are probably a neater impression. But perhaps you know about it yourself.

Thayer & Eldridge have put through 1000 copies, for the first pop. They have very accurate ideas of the whole matter. They expect it to be a valuable investment, increasing by months and years—not going off in a rocket way, (like "Uncle Tom's Cabin.")[14] The typographical appearance of the book has been just as I directed it, in every respect. The printers and foremen thought I was crazy, and there were all sorts of supercilious squints (about the typography I ordered, I mean)—but since it has run through the press, they have simmered down. Yesterday the foreman of the press-room (Rand's,[15] an old establishment where all the best work is done,) pronounced it, in plain terms, the freshest and handsomest piece of typography that had ever passed through his mill—I like it, I think, first rate—though I think I could improve much upon it now. It is quite "odd," of course. As to Thayer & Eldridge they think every thing I do is the right thing. We are just now in "suspenders" on account of the engraving. I have about decided, though, to have 1000 copies printed from it, as it is—and then let Schoff,[16] the engraver, finish it afterwards—I do not know for certain whether it is a good portrait or not—The probability is that the book will be bound and ready, May 19.

I make Thayer & Eldridge crack on the elegant workmanship of the

14. Published as a serial in 1851–1852, and as a book in 1852.

15. Rand and Avery, printers. This firm also printed the 1881 edition. It is still in business as Rand Avery–Gordon Taylor, Inc.

16. Stephen Alonzo Schoff (1818–1904) was famous for his engraved portraits of William Penn, Emerson, and others.

17. "Ned Buntline" was the pseudonym of Edward Z. C. Judson (1823–1886), the first of the dime novelists and the originator of the "Buffalo Bill" stories. *The New York Ledger*, under the editorship of Robert Bonner, was a popular weekly which featured serials, sentimental poems, and moral essays. In 1860 its circulation was 400,000; see Mott, *A History of American Magazines*, II, 356–363.

18. On April 16, Jeff had written of impending changes at the Brooklyn Water Works: "We Water Works men are all trembling in our boots, the prospects being that we are all going to be kicked out, neck and heels, from the chief down to the Axeman.

book, its material, &c. but I won't allow them to puff the poetry—though I had quite a hard struggle—as they had prepared several tremendous puff advertisements—altogether ahead of Ned Buntline and the "Ledger"[17]—I persuaded them to give me the copy to make some little corrections—which I did effectually by going straight to my lodgings, and putting the whole stuff in the fire—Oh, I forgot to tell you, they have printed a very neat little brochure, (pamphlet,) of 64 pages, called "Leaves of Grass Imprints," containing a very readable collection of criticisms on the former issues—This is given away gratis, as an advertisement and circular. Altogether, Jeff, I am very, very much satisfied and relieved that the thing, in the permanent form it now is, looks as well and reads as well (to my own notion) as I anticipated—because a good deal, after all, was an experiment—and now I am satisfied.

And how goes it with you, my dear? I watched the N. Y. papers to see if Spinola's[18] bill passed—but it didn't, of course, or I should of heard of it in many ways. So you must be on the works still—If I get a chance I will take a look at the Boston Works before I leave. The water is almost exactly like the Brooklyn water in taste. I got Mother's letter[19]—tell Mother I may not write next Monday, as I am in hopes to be home, I can't tell exactly what day, but through the week. Oh the awful expense I have been under here, Jeff, living the way I have, hiring a room, and eating at restaurants—7 cents for a cup of coffee, and 19 cts for a beefsteak—*and me so fond of coffee and beefsteak*. Tell mother I think it would have been worth while for her to have moved on here, and boarded me—

I have had a very fair time, though, here in Boston—Very, very many folks I meet I like much—I have never seen finer—they are fine in almost every respect—very friendly, very generous, very good feeling, and of course intelligent people—The great *cramper* of the Bostonian is, though, to be kept on the rack by the old idea of *respectability*, how the rest do, and what they will say. There are plenty of splendid specimens of men come from the other New England states to settle here, especially from Maine,

It seems that Mr F. Spinola started a bill at Albany some time last winter trying to oust the new commissioners. . . . It has passed one house, and I guess the chances are abt even for its passing the other" (Feinberg). The New York legislature had adjourned on April 17, and the New York *Tribune* on the following day was "reverently thankful": "We do not believe it possible that another body so reckless not merely of right but of decency—not merely corrupt but shameless—will be assembled in our halls of legislation within the next ten years."

Francis B. Spinola (1821–1891) was an alderman in Brooklyn from 1846 to 1853, a member of the New York legislature from 1855 to 1861, a brigadier general during the Civil War, and a United States Congressman from 1887 to 1891.

19. On May 3, Mrs. Whitman related family gossip and told of a recent visit from Hector Tyndale (see 12), who "behaved very friendly indeed" (Trent).

New Hampshire, Vermont, &c, that if they would *let themselves be*, and only make *that* better and finer, would beat the world. For there is no denying that these Yanks are the first-class race. But, without exception, they all somehow allow themselves to be squeezed into the stereotype mould, and wear straight collars and hats, and say "my respects"—like the rest. Of course *I* cannot walk through Washington street, (the Broadway here,) without creating an immense sensation.

I sent a couple of papers to Han this morning. Oh how much I would like to see her once more[20]—and I *must*, this summer—After I recruit a while home, I shall very likely take a tour, partly business and partly for edification, through all the N[ew] E[ngland] states—then I shall see Han—I shall write to her before I leave here—and do you write also, Jeff—don't fail—Should you write to me, in response to this, you must write so that I would get the letter not later than Wednesday morning next—as I feel the fit growing upon me stronger and stronger to move—And the fare is only $3 now from here to New York, cabin passage, in the boat—Besides I could go dead head if I was to apply—Jeff, I feel as if things had taken a turn with me, at last—Give my love to Mat, and all my dear brothers, especially Georgie.

Walt.

21.1 *To Thayer & Eldridge* [*5.(?).1860*][21]

DRAFT LETTER.

Arrived home all right, 24th, at dusk, over the "shore line"—I like that route better than the old one—no dust that day, and fine view of the water, half the time.

The package came safe to ho[me] on Friday, containing my 20 pur-

20. Hannah wrote to her mother on June 1: "I have been *very much* disappointed because Walt did not come to see us. I had felt so glad, so pleased, had spoke of it so often. I watched the cars every night . . . I will not tell you how bad I felt. you at home would think me silly and childish" (LC).

21. Apparently this draft letter was sent to Thayer & Eldridge shortly after WW's return to Brooklyn. It would appear, then, that, despite his reference in 21 to his imminent departure, WW remained in Boston until May 24, and then took the new Shore Line Railroad to New York.

22. Clapp (see 235) was editor of the New-York *Saturday Press* as well as an old friend.

23. In the next issue of the *Saturday Press*, on June 16, Clapp printed, in the columns suggested by WW, two contributions of Henry P. Leland, which had appeared earlier in the Philadelphia *City Item*: a poem entitled "Enfans de Soixante-Seize" and a swashbuckling tribute to "Walt Whitman." Leland (1828–1868) was the author of *Grey-Bay Mare, and Other Humorous American Sketches* (1856) and co-author with his brother Charles of *Ye Book of Copperheads* (1863). WW spoke many years later to Charles of Henry's support "in the darkest years of his life"; see Elizabeth Robins Pennell, *Charles Godfrey Leland* (1906). II, 111, and note 194.

ch[ased] L. of G. and 20 to give away at discretion. I shall send you a tally of the latter as I [*incomplete*].

21.2 *To Henry Clapp, Jr.*[22] *6.12.* [*1860*]

Brooklyn, | Tuesday afternoon, June 12.

Dear friend,

Fearful that, by insufficient examination you may not do justice to the articles from Mr. Leland,[23] but give them the go-by, I write to make a *special request* that, if convenient, you print them in next S[aturday] P[ress]—the poem leading first col. first page, the prose following immediately after. Those articles, (I feel it thoroughly,) have certain little grains of salt that I wish to see put in a way of "leavening" the lump of ———[24] you know what.

Walt.

Did you see what Mrs. Heenan[25] says about me in last "Sunday Mercury"—first page?

22. *To Thayer & Eldridge* [*8.(?). 1860*]

INCOMPLETE DRAFT LETTER.

[WW referred to Henry Clapp, editor of the *Saturday Press*, who "wrote more than once to me while I was in Boston, to become the solicitor and medium of pecuniary aid from you to him, to support his paper. Such solicitations I declined to act upon. He then wrote directly to you—and you advanced him $200. I think the money has been well enough invested—The paper has many original . . ."][26]

24. Probably in reply to the hostile review by Juliette H. Beach's husband which appeared in the *Saturday Press* on June 2; see Allen, 260–261.

25. The *Sunday Mercury* printed an extravagant eulogy of WW on June 3 which was written by the actress and poet Adah Isaacs Menken, who at the time was married to the prize fighter John Heenan; see Allen, 262, and Allen Lesser, *Enchanting Rebel* (1947), 61–65.

26. The entire text of this fragment, written on the verso of a poem entitled "The ball-room was swept and the floor white," is not presently available. The date is apparently August, since on August 17 Thayer & Eldridge thanked WW for his advice about the *Saturday Press*, and informed him that the firm had made an offer to Clapp (see 235) to assume financial control on September 1. Thayer & Eldridge believed that it could make the journal "pay": "Beside[s] we are deeply interested in sustaining any journal that dares in these days of literary flunkeyism to be independent, and make the literature of a country what it should be" (Feinberg). Clapp had suggested to WW on March 27 that he might get Thayer & Eldridge to "*advance me say one hundred dollars on advertising account*" (Feinberg; Traubel, I, 237). On May 14, Clapp was "in a state of despair . . . all for the want of a paltry two or three hundred dollars" which he needed to bring out the next issue (Feinberg; Traubel, II, 376).

1861

23. *To George Washington Whitman*

[B]rooklyn, | [Friday][1] July 12th, 1861.

Dear Brother,

Your letter come to-day. Every thing with us is pretty much the same. Mother is pretty much the same. Some days she [is] better, and some not so well. She has taken a good many sulphur vapor baths. She takes one every other day. She goes down in the cars to the baths, in Willoughby street near the City Hall.[2] Sometimes Mat goes with her, [and once in] a while she goes [alo]ne. They are rather agreeable to take—they make one sweat extremely. Mother goes about the same, around the house. She has better use of her arms and wrists than she did there one time—but an hour or two, now and then, generally in the morning, she has bad pains. Her appetite is pretty good. The weather here lately has been awful—three days the heat was as bad as I ever knew it—so I think that had something to do with mother's feeling weak. To-day it is much cooler.

Jeff and Martha and Cis[3] and Eddy are all well. Jess is the same as usual—he works every day in the yard. He does not seem to mind the heat. He is employed in the store-house, where they are continually busy preparing stores, provisions, to send off in the different vessels. He assists in that.

We are all very glad the 13th is coming home—mother especially. There have been so many accounts of shameful negligence, or worse, in the commissariat of your reg't. that there must be *something* in it—notwithstanding you speak very lightly of the complaints in your letters. The

1861

1. Part of the upper left-hand corner of this letter is missing, and the ink at places is badly blurred. It is one of the few letters extant from WW to his brother while the latter was in the army, although, as the Check List of Lost Letters indicates, WW wrote frequently.

2. Henry R. Piercy's sulphur baths; see also 46.

3. WW probably intended to write "Sis," his usual nickname for Jeff's daughter Mannahatta.

4. George had enlisted for three months in the Thirteenth Regiment on April 19, 1861, six days after the firing on Fort Sumter. In the letter WW referred to, George, writing to his mother from Camp Brooklyn, near Washington, had said: "Well Mother the three Months is going fast and I shall soon be with you again. I see some very foolish articles in the papers about us sutch as not haveing any thing to eat for 36 hours and

Eagle, of course, makes the worst of it, every day, to stop men from enlisting.[4]

All of us here think the rebellion as good as broke—no matter if the war does continue for months yet.

Walt.

24. *To James Russell Lowell*

ADDRESS: J. R. Lowell | Atlantic Magazine.

Brooklyn | Tuesday morning October 1st | 1861

Mr. Lowell,

Dear Sir: The price of "1861," if you print it, is $20. You are at liberty to make any verbal alterations. The envelope is of course to return it in, if you cannot use it.[5]

Yours truly

W. Whitman

being almost naked but you must not believe any thing of the kind as we are as well off as we could expect" (Trent).

5. On October 8, Lowell wrote to James T. Fields: "I enclose . . . three [poems] from Walt Whitman. '1861' he says is $20. the others $8. each"; see M. A. De Wolfe Howe, ed., *New Letters of James Russell Lowell* (1932), 102. On October 10, the editors of *Atlantic Monthly* declined "the three poems with which you have favored us, but which we could not possibly use before their interest,—which is of the present,—would have passed" (Feinberg; Traubel, II, 213). When Traubel in 1888 asked WW for the titles of these poems, he replied: "I don't just remember: I do remember that the idea that their interest was of the present struck me as being a bit odd: I always have written with something more than a simply contemporary perspective" (II, 213). "1861" appeared in *Drum-Taps* (1865), 17.

1862

25. *To Louisa Van Velsor Whitman*

Washington, Monday forenoon, | December 29, 1862.

Dear, dear Mother,

Friday the 19th inst. I succeeded in reaching the camp of the 51st New York, and found George alive and well—In order to make sure that you would get the good news, I sent back by messenger to Washington (I dare say you did not get it for some time) a telegraphic dispatch, as well as a letter—and the same to Hannah at Burlington. I have staid in camp with George ever since, till yesterday, when I came back to Washington[1]—about the 24th George got Jeff's letter of the 20th. Mother, how much you must have suffered, all that week, till George's letter came—and all the rest must too. As to me, I know I put in about three days of the greatest suffering I ever experienced in my life. I wrote to Jeff[2] how I had my pocket picked in a jam and hurry, changing cars, at Philadelphia, so that I landed here without a dime. The next two days I spent hunting through the hospitals, walking all day and night, unable to ride, trying to get information, trying to get access to big people, &c—I could not get the least clue to anything—Odell[3] would not see me at all—But Thursday afternoon, I lit on a way to get down on the government boat that runs to Aquia creek, and so by railroad to the neighborhood of Falmouth, opposite Fredericksburgh—

1862

1. The Whitman family evidently became alarmed about George during the second battle of Bull Run when they noticed in the New York *Herald* of December 16 that "First Lieutenant G. W. Whitmore" was listed among the wounded; see Allen, 281. Moses Lane (see 31) on the same day asked Captain James J. Dana to obtain a pass for WW so that he might visit George at Falmouth; on the following day Dana wrote to the Provost Marshal, Colonel W. E. Doster. (Both letters are in the Feinberg Collection.) After he lost his money in Philadelphia, WW managed to go on to Washington, where he tried to locate George in the military hospitals. He encountered two men whom he had met in Boston in 1860: William D. O'Connor lent him money, and Eldridge obtained a pass for him to Fredericksburg. Meanwhile, not having heard from WW, Jeff wrote anxiously on December 19: "We are all much worried at not hearing anything from you. . . . The Times of day before yesterday gave his name among the wounded thus 'Lieut Whitman Co. E 51st N. Y. V. cheek' [the *Times* said "face"] and we are trying to comfort ourselves with hope that it may not be a serious hurt" (Feinberg). Meanwhile, George had written to his mother on December 16 from a camp near Falmouth, Va.: "We have

So by degrees I worked my way to Ferrero's[4] brigade, which I found Friday afternoon without much trouble after I got in camp. When I found dear brother George, and found that he was alive and well, O you may imagine how trifling all my little cares and difficulties seemed—they vanished into nothing. And now that I have lived for eight or nine days amid such scenes as the camps furnish, and had a practical part in it all, and realize the way that hundreds of thousands of good men are now living, and have had to live for a year or more, not only without any of the comforts, but with death and sickness and hard marching and hard fighting, (and no success at that,) for their continual experience—really nothing we call trouble seems worth talking about. One of the first things that met my eyes in camp, was a heap of feet, arms, legs, &c. under a tree in front a hospital, the Lacy house.

George is very well in health, has a good appetite—I think he is at times more wearied out and homesick than he shows, but stands it upon the whole very well. Every one of the soldiers, to a man, wants to get home.

I suppose Jeff got quite a long letter I wrote from camp, about a week ago. I told you that George had been promoted to Captain[5]—his commission arrived while I was there. When you write, address

Capt. George W. Whitman
Co. K. 51st New York Vol.
Ferrero's brigade
near Falmouth Va.

Jeff must write oftener, and put in a few lines from mother, even if it is only two lines—then in the next letter a few lines from Mat, and so on. You have no idea how letters from home cheer one up in camp, and dissipate home sickness.

had another battle and I have come out safe and sound, although I had the side of my jaw slightly scraped with a peice of shell which burst at my feet" (Trent).

"Walter Whitman, a citizen," obtained a pass on December 27 from General Edwin Vose Summers "to Washington [by] Rail R. government steamer" (Feinberg; Traubel, II, 157), and, upon his arrival on the following day, took rooms where the O'Connors were living; see 27. Mrs. O'Connor described this meeting (her first) in "Personal Recollections of Walt Whitman," *Atlantic Monthly*, XCIX (1907), 825–834.

2. This letter is evidently lost.

3. Moses Fowler Odell (1818–1866) was a member of the House of Representatives (1861–1865) from New York.

4. Edward Ferrero (1831–1899) was appointed on October 14, 1861, colonel, Fifty-first New York Volunteers, and commanded George's regiment during the following winter. After the second battle of Bull Run, he was appointed brigadier general.

5. In an undated letter, but unquestionably written shortly after his promotion in December, George informed his mother: "Remember your galliant Son is a Capting, and expects you to keep up the dignity of the family, and darn the expense" (Trent).

While I was there George still lived in Capt. Francis's[6] tent—there were five of us altogether, to eat, sleep, write, &c. in a space twelve feet square, but we got along very well—the weather all along was very fine—and would have got along to perfection, but Capt. Francis is not a man I could like much—I had very little to say to him. George is about building a place, half-hut and half-tent, for himself—(he is probably about it this very day)—and then he will be better off, I think. Every Captain has a tent, in which he lives, transacts company business, &c. has a cook, (or man of all work,) and in the same tent mess and sleep his Lieutenants, and perhaps the 1st sergeant. They have a kind of fire-place, and the cook's fire is outside, on the open ground. George had very good times while Francis was away—the cook, a young disabled soldier, Tom,[7] is an excellent fellow, and a first-rate cook, and the 2d Lieutenant, Pooley,[8] is a tip-top young Pennsylvanian. Tom thinks all the world of George—when he heard he was wounded, on the day of the battle, he left every thing, got across the river, and went hunting for George through the field, through thick and thin. I wrote to Jeff that George was wounded by a shell, a gash in the cheek—you could stick a splint through into the mouth, but it has healed up without difficulty already. Every thing is uncertain about the army, whether it moves or stays where it is. There are no furloughs granted at present. I will stay here for the present, at any rate long enough to see if I can get any employment at any thing, and shall write what luck I have. Of course I am unsettled at present. Dear mother, my love,

Walt.

If Jeff or any one writes, address me, | care of Major Hapgood,[9] paymaster, U. S. Army, | corner 15th and F streets, 5th floor, | Washington D. C. I send my love to dear sister Mat, and little sis—and to Andrew and all my brothers. O Mat, how lucky it was you did not come—together, we could never have got down to see George.

6. George referred frequently to Henry W. Francis in his letters to his mother in 1862. His first impression, at New Bern, N. C., April 12, was favorable: "Our first Leiut. Francis is a first rate fellow so I have tip top times." Later George informed his mother that Francis had asked his wife, who was staying in Burlington, Vt., to call on Hannah. On August 3, Hannah informed her mother that "Mrs. Francis called, I liked her much." During the battle at Antietam, George commanded his company, "as the Captain was not well although he was on the field." George noted on September 30, from near Antietam, that Francis had left on a twenty-day furlough, and on November 10, he wrote: "Captain Francis has not come back yet, and I am getting almost tired of haveing the whole trouble and responsibility of the Company and some one else getting the pay for it." After his return, George related on December 8, Francis was too unwell to resume command of the company. (These letters are in the Trent Collection).

26. *To Ralph Waldo Emerson*

ENDORSED (by WW): "R. W. Emerson. | W Whitman | 1863."

Washington, D. C. | Monday afternoon, Dec. 29, '62.

Dear friend,

Breaking up a few weeks since, and for good, my New York stagnation—wandering since through camp and battle scenes—I fetch up here in harsh and superb plight—wretchedly poor, excellent well, (my only torment, family matters)—realizing at last that it is necessary for me to fall for the time in the wise old way, to push my fortune, to be brazen, and get employment, and have an income—determined to do it, (at any rate until I get out of horrible sloughs) I write you, asking you as follows:

I design to apply personally direct at headquarters, for some place. I would apply on literary grounds, not political.

I wish you would write for me something like the enclosed form of letter, that I can present, opening my interview with the great man. I wish you to write two copies—put the one in an envelope directed to Mr. Seward, Secretary of State—and the other in an envelope directed to Mr. Chase, Secretary of the Treasury—and enclose both envelopes in the one I send herewith so that I can use either one or the other. I wish you also to send me a note of introduction to Charles Sumner.[10]

It is pretty certain that, armed in that way, I shall conquer my object. Answer me by next mail, for I am waiting here like ship waiting for the welcome breath of the wind.

Indeed yours, &c

Walt Whitman

7. Tom may be Thomas McCowell, mentioned in 127. George noted, on February 1, 1863 (Trent), that Tom had received a letter from WW.

8. Samuel M. Pooley visited Mrs. Whitman on March 6, 1863 (see her letter to WW of March 7 in Trent). He was taken prisoner in 1864 along with George; see 153 and 156.

9. Lyman S. Hapgood was paymaster of the Army volunteers. Eldridge (see 86), at this time a clerk in his office, obtained employment for WW there as a copyist.

10. William Henry Seward (1801–1872), Secretary of State (1861–1869); Salmon Portland Chase (1808–1873), Secretary of the Treasury (1861–1864); Charles Sumner (1811–1874), chairman of the Committee on Foreign Affairs, United States Senate (1861–1871). Emerson wrote to Seward and Chase on January 10, and to WW on January 12, 1863.

1863

27. *To Martha Whitman* 1.2-4.1863

Washington, | Friday morning, Jan 2, 1863.

Dear sister,

You have heard of my fortunes and misfortunes of course, (through my letters to mother and Jeff,) since I left home, that Tuesday afternoon. But I thought I would write a few lines to you, as it is a comfort to write home, even if I have nothing particular to say. Well, dear sister, I hope you are well and hearty, and that little sis keeps as well as she always had, when I left home, so far. Dear little plague, how I would like to have her with me, for one day. I can fancy I see her, and hear her talk. Jeff must have got a note from me about a letter I have written to the *Eagle*[1]—you may be sure you will get letters enough from me, for I have little else to do at present. Since I laid my eyes on dear brother George, and saw him alive and well—and since I have spent a week in camp, down there opposite Fredericksburgh, and seen what well men and sick men, and mangled men endure—it seems to me I can be satisfied and happy henceforward if I can get one meal a day, and know that mother and all are in good health, and especially if I can only be with you again, and have some little steady paying occupation in N. Y. or Brooklyn.

I am writing this in the office of Major Hapgood, way up in the top of a big high house, corner of 15th and F. street—there is a splendid view, away down south, of the Potomac river, and across to the Georgetown side, and the grounds and houses of Washington spread out beneath my high point of view. The weather is perfect—I have had that in my favor ever since leaving home—yesterday and to-day it is bright, and plenty warm enough. The poor soldiers are continually coming in from the hospitals, &c. to get their pay—some of them waiting for it, to go home. They climb up here, quite exhausted, and then find it is no good, for there is no money to pay them—there are two or three paymasters desks in this room, and the scenes

1863

1. "Our Brooklyn Boys in the War" appeared in the Brooklyn *Daily Eagle* on January 5. It was a factual report of the activities of Brooklyn soldiers, particularly of

of disappointment are quite affecting. Here they wait in Washington, perhaps week after [week], wretched and heart sick—this is the greatest place of delays and puttings off, and no finding the clue to any thing—this building is the paymaster general's quarters, and the crowds on the walk and corner, of poor sick, pale, tattered soldiers, are awful—many of them day after day, disappointed and tired out. Well, Mat, I will suspend my letter for the present, and go out through the city—I have a couple of poor fellows in the Hospital to visit also.

Walt.

Saturday evening, Jan 3d.

I write this in the place where I have my lodging room, 394 L street, 4th door above 14th street. A friend of mine, William D. O'Connor,[2] has two apartments, on the 3d floor, very ordinarily furnished, for which he pays the *extra*ordinary price of $25 a month. I have a werry little bedroom on the 2d floor—Mr. & Mrs. O'Connor and their little girl have all gone out "down town" for an hour or two, to make some Saturday evening purchases, and I am left in possession of the premises—so I sit by the fire, and scribble more of my letter. I have not heard any thing from dear brother George since I left the camp last Sunday morning, 28th Dec. I wrote to him on Tuesday last—I wish to get to him the two blue woolen shirts Jeff sent, as they would come very acceptable to him—and will try to do it yet. I think of sending them by mail, if the postage is not more than $1.

Yesterday I went out to the Campbell Hospital to see a couple of Brooklyn boys, of the 51st. They knew I was in Washington, and sent me a note, to come and see them. O my dear sister, how your heart would ache to go through the rows of wounded young men, as I did—and stopt to speak a comforting word to them. There were about 100 in one long room, just a long shed neatly whitewashed inside. One young man was very much prostrated, and groaning with pain. I stopt and tried to comfort him. He was very sick. I found he had not had any medical attention since he was brought there—among so many he had been overlooked. So I sent for the doctor, and he made an examination of him—the doctor behaved very well—seemed to be anxious to do right—said that the young man would recover—he had been brought pretty low with diarroeha, and now had bronchitis, but not so serious as to be dangerous. I talked to him some time—he seemed to have entirely give up, and lost heart—he had not a cent of money—not a friend or acquaintance—I wrote a letter from him to his sister—his

Sims (see 51) and George.

2. See the Introduction.

name is John A. Holmes,[3] Campbello, Plymouth county, Mass. I gave him a little change I had—he said he would like to buy a drink of milk, when the woman came through with milk. Trifling as this was, he was overcome and began to cry. Then there were many, many others. I mention the one, as a specimen. My Brooklyn boys were John Lowery, shot at Fredericksburgh, and lost his left forearm, and Amos H. Vliet[4]—Jeff knows the latter—he has his feet frozen, and is doing well. The 100 are in a ward, (6.)—and there are, I should think, eight or ten or twelve such wards in the Campbell Hospital—indeed a real village. Then there are some 38 more Hospitals here in Washington, some of them much larger.

Sunday forenoon, Jan 4, '63.

Mat, I hope and trust dear mother and all are well, and every thing goes on good home. The envelope I send, Jeff or any of you can keep for direction, or use it when wanted to write to me. As near as I can tell, the army at Falmouth remains the same.

Dear sister, good bye.

Walt.

I send my love to Andrew and Jesse and Eddy and all—What distressing news this is of the loss of the Monitor[5]—

28. *Ralph Waldo Emerson to Salmon P. Chase*

ENDORSED: "R. W. Emerson Esq. | Recd Jany 23d | 64."

Concord Massachusetts | 10 January, 1863

Dear Sir,[6]

Mr Walt Whitman, of New York, writes me that he is seeking employment in the public service in Washington, & perhaps some application on his part has already been made to yourself.

3. WW related the harrowing story of Holmes's illness in the New York *Times*, February 26, 1863 (in CW, VII, 85–89). Though Holmes suffered from acute diarrhea, he remained with his regiment at Fredericksburg as long as he could. Finally he was evacuated (in WW's words, "dumped with a crowd of others on the boat at Aquia creek"), and was taken to Campbell Hospital, Washington, where WW met him on January 4: "As I stopped by him and spoke some commonplace remark (to which he made no reply), I saw as I looked that it was a case for ministering to the affection first, and other nourishment and medicines afterward. I sat down by him without any fuss; talked a little; soon saw that it did him good; led him to talk a little himself; got him somewhat interested" (CW, VII, 88).

4. According to WW's jottings in "New York City Veterans" (Glicksberg, 67), he discovered John Lowery (here spelled Lowerie) on December 22, 1862, "in the Hospital on the ground at Falmouth." In *Specimen Days* (CW, IV, 51), WW writes: "I saw him lying on the ground at Fredericksburg last December, all bloody, just after the arm was taken off. He was very phlegmatic about it, munching away at a cracker in the remaining hand—made no fuss." In the Brooklyn *Eagle* of March 19, 1863 (CW, VII, 95–96), WW gave a fuller account of Lowery. WW saw Amos H. Vliet in the hospital tent at Falmouth on December 22, 1862, and mentioned him briefly in the same article. According to his diary (Glicksberg, 133), WW wrote a (lost) Letter to Vliet on May 2, 1863.

Will you permit me to say that he is known to me as a man of strong original genius, combining, with marked eccentricities, great powers & valuable traits of character: a self-relying large-hearted man, much beloved by his friends; entirely patriotic & benevolent in his theory, tastes, & practice. If his writings are in certain points open to criticism, they show extraordinary power, & are more deeply American, democratic, & in the interest of political liberty, than those of any other poet.

A man of his talents & dispositions will quickly make himself useful, and, if the government has work that he can do, I think it may easily find that it has called to its side more valuable aid than it bargained for.

With entire respect,
Your obedient servant,

R. W. Emerson.

Hon Salmon P. Chase, | Secretary of the Treasury.

29. *Ralph Waldo Emerson to William H. Seward*

ADDRESS: Hon. W. H. Seward, | Secretary of State, | Washington, | D. C.

Concord | Mass^{tts} | Jan. 10 | 1863

Dear Sir,

Mr Walt Whitman, of New York, writes me, that he wishes to obtain employment in the public service in Washington, & has made, or is about making some application to yourself.

Permit me to say that he is known to me as a man of strong original genius, combining, with marked eccentricities, great powers & valuable traits of character: a self-relying, large-hearted man, much beloved by his friends; entirely patriotic & benevolent in his theory, tastes, & practice. If

5. The *Monitor* foundered at sea on December 30, 1862. The report of the disaster was received in Washington on January 3.

6. In this and the following letter Emerson fulfilled WW's request, as stated in 26. Though he was in Rochester, N. Y., at the time, Emerson, as he noted in 30, used his Concord address. Rusk, in *The Letters of Ralph Waldo Emerson*, v, 302 and 303, hypothetically reconstructs the two letters which he had not seen, and dates them "*c.* 2?" WW, who, despite his appeal to Emerson, was of two minds as far as an official position was concerned, did not immediately use the recommendations (see 36 and 40). On a wrapper of a copy of the letter to Seward (Feinberg), WW wrote, "never delivered." Trowbridge (see 102) presumably presented the letter to Chase on December 11, 1863. According to WW's account of this interview, Chase "said he considered Leaves of Grass a very bad book, & he did not know how he could possibly bring its author into the government service, especially if he put him in contact with gentlemen employed in the beaureaus" (Donaldson, 156). Chase, however, kept the letter because he wanted an Emerson autograph; see Trowbridge, *My Own Story* (1903), 388. The wrapper with this letter to Chase reads: "Clerkship | Walt Whitman | Applicant | New York: | Recommended by | R. W. Emerson | Recd. Jany 28, 1864." According to an entry in a notebook (*LC* #8), a government employee informed WW on June 30, 1862, that, on seeing *Leaves of Grass* on the table, Chase had asked: "How is it possible you can have this nasty book here?"

his writings are in certain points open to criticism, they yet show extraordinary power, & are more deeply American, democratic, & in the interest of political liberty, than those of any other poet. He is indeed a child of the people, & their champion.

A man of his talents & dispositions will quickly make himself useful, and, if the Government has work that he can do, I think it may easily find, that it has called to its side more valuable aid than it bargained for.

With great respect,
Your obedient servant,

R. W. Emerson

Hon. William H. Seward, | Secretary of State.

30. *Ralph Waldo Emerson to WW*

ENDORSED (by WW): "R W Emerson | Jan '63."
ADDRESS: Walt Whitman, Esq. | Washington.

Buffalo— | 12 Jany 1863

Dear Sir,

I am very sorry to be so late with my reply to your note, which was received by me just on leaving home to go to Canada, & thence to some of your West N.Y. cities, a journey which has left me no leisure for writing notes to diplomatists, until today.[7]

If you wish to live in that least attractive (to me) of cities, I must think you can easily do so. Perhaps better in the journalism than in the Departments.

You will see that I have dated my note from my known residence.[8] With best hope,

R. W. Emerson

Walt Whitman, Esq.

7. Emerson was at this time on one of his lyceum tours; see Ralph L. Rusk, *The Life of Ralph Waldo Emerson* (1949), 418–419, and *Letters*, v, 302 ff.

8. See 28 and 29.

9. In a letter now lost, WW must have asked his brother to raise money for his hospital work. Jeff quickly appealed to his fellow workers at the Brooklyn Water Works, and most of his letters during 1863 contained contributions. On January 13, Jeff wrote: "I wish you would take either Lane's or Probasco's money and keep an exact account of what it does and send them the particulars of just the good it does. I think it would assist them (and the rest of us) in collecting more. You can understand what an effect twould have, twould give us an oportunity to show what immense good a few shillings even will do when rightly applied, besides twould please the person sending the money hugely, twould bring his good deeds under his nose" (Feinberg).

10. Louis Probasco, a young employee in the Brooklyn Water Works, probably the son of Samuel, listed as a cooper in the Brooklyn Directory of 1861–1862.

31. *To Thomas Jefferson Whitman* 1.16.[1863]

Major Hapgood's, cor 15th & F sts | Washington,
Friday mn'g, Jan 16.

Dearest brother,

Your letter came last evening containing the $6.[9] Two days since I received one from Probasco,[10] containing $3 (not 5 as you mention.) I send a note, same mail as this, acknowledging the latter. I shall, either by letter giving specific names, hospitals, No. of the particular beds, and dates, or more likely by a letter in print in newspaper, for I am going to print a sort of hospital journal in some paper, send you and Mr. Lane[11] and Probasco, a pretty plain schedule of the manner of my outlays of the sums sent by them to the hospital soldiers through me—as it would interest you all, as you say. Meantime, dear brother, do not crowd the thing in the least—do not ask any one when it becomes unpleasant—let it be understood by our engineer friends &c. that I have mentioned the subscription affair as forwarded, to be left entirely to their sense of what they wish to do, and what they think it would be discreet for them to do. I did not wish you to send $5, for I do not think it right—it is entirely too much—nor mother $1—I think she has enough, present and future, to attend to—but since it has come, I shall use it—I distributed between 2 & $3 yesterday.

What ought to be done by our family, I feel that *I* am doing, and have done myself. I have made $27 while I have been here, and got the money, and I should think I have paid in little items and purchases and money gifts at least $10 of that to the soldiers—I wouldn't take a thousand dollars for the satisfaction it has been to me—but, Jeff, I postpone till we come together again, any attempt to make you realize this whole thing.

Of course you have received, (probably about to-day,) a long letter I have written to Mother.[12] Nothing definite appears to-day about the status or movements of the Army of the Potomac, but my guess, at a venture, is, that they either have moved down the Rappahannock toward Potomac, or

11. Moses Lane was chief engineer in the Brooklyn Water Works. Like Jeff, he collected money from his employees and friends. Lane sent WW $15.20 in his letter of January 26 (Feinberg) and later various sums which WW acknowledged in 34, 47, 51, and 77. In his letter of May 27 (Feinberg), Lane pledged $5 each month. In an unpublished manuscript in the Berg Collection, WW wrote, obviously for publication: "I have distributed quite a large sum of money, contributed for that purpose by noble persons in Brooklyn, New York, (chiefly through Moses Lane, Chief Engineer, Water Works there.)" Lane assisted WW in other ways (see 25 and 36). He was so solicitous of WW's personal welfare that on April 3 he sent through Jeff $5 "for your own especial benefit" (Feinberg).

12. This letter is not known.

are about moving. Whether it is to cross or not and whether for an attack or march, or whether as some think to Fortress Monroe, is quite unknown. You must not be alarmed at hearing of an advance, or engagement—at a distance it is more appalling than it deserves to be thought—Some think a portion goes west to Rosecrans.[13] It is so dangerous and critical for the government to make any more failures like that at Fredericksburgh, that it seems incredible to be any repetition of that most complete piece of mismanagement perhaps ever yet known in the earth's wars.[14] I have not heard from George—it is good that you got a long letter.[15] Jeff, I feel that you and dearest mother are perhaps needlessly unhappy and morbid about our dear brother—to be in the army is a mixture of danger and *security* in this war which few realize—they think exclusively of the danger.[16]

32. *To Ralph Waldo Emerson* [*1.17. 1863*]

ENDORSED: "Jan 17 '63 | to Emerson—was | it sent? | I think not."[17] DRAFT LETTER.

Your letters from Buffalo have just come to hand. They find me still hanging around here—my plans, wants, ideas, &c gradually getting into shape.

I go a great deal into the Hospitals. Washington is full of them—both in town and out around the outskirts. Some of the larger ones are towns in themselves. In small and large, all forty to fifty thousand inmates are ministered to, as I hear. Being sent for by a particular soldier, three weeks since, in the Campbell Hospital,[18] I soon fell to going there and elsewhere to like places daily. The first shudder has long passed over, and I must say I find deep things, unreckoned by current print or speech. The Hospital, I do not find it, the repulsive place of sores and fevers, nor the place of querulousness, nor the bad results of morbid years which one avoids like bad

13. William Starke Rosecrans (1819–1898), Union general, was in Tennessee in 1863 with the Army of the Cumberland.

14. A reporter of the Cincinnati *Commercial* noted: "It can hardly be in human nature for men to show more valor, or generals to manifest less judgment, than were perceptible on our side that day"; quoted by Bruce Catton, *Glory Road* (1952), 74.

15. George, however, had written to WW on January 13 from Falmouth. Though he had nothing important to say about his own activities, he was upset about Hannah: "I am sure she must be liveing in a perfect Hell . . . Walt, you or Jeff must certainly go on there and see how things are, and make arangements for bringing her home" (Trent).

16. Here WW replied to Jeff's almost hysterical letters. On January 1–2, he implored WW to urge George to quit the army and thus to spare the life of their mother, who, "if any thing should happen him . . . , could not survive it. . . . Walt, I beg

s[mells]—at least [not] so is it under the circumstances here—other hospitals may be, but not here.

I desire and intend to write a little book out of this phase of America, her masculine young manhood, its conduct under most trying of and highest of all exigency, which she, as by lifting a corner in a curtain, has vouchsafed me to see America, already brought to Hospital in her fair youth—brought and deposited here in this great, whited sepulchre of Washington itself—(this union Capital without the first bit of cohesion—this collect of proofs how low and swift a good stock can deteriorate—) Capital to which these deputies most strange arrive from every quarter, concentrating here, well-drest, rotten, meagre, nimble and impotent, full of gab, full always of their thrice-accursed *party*—arrive and skip into the seats of mightiest legislation, and take the seats of judges and high executive seats—while by quaint Providence come also sailed and wagoned hither this other freight of helpless worn and wounded youth, genuine of the soil, of darlings and true heirs to me the first unquestioned and convincing western crop, prophetic of the future, proofs undeniable to all men's ken of perfect beauty, tenderness and pluck that never race yet rivalled.

But more, a new world here I find as I would show—a world full of its separate action, play, suggestiveness—surely a medium world, advanced between our well-known practised one of body and of mind, and one there may-be somewhere on beyond, we dream of, of the soul.

Not to fly off to these clouds, however, I must abruptly say to my friends, where interested, that I find the best expression of American character I have ever seen or conceived—practically here in these ranks of sick and dying young men—nearly all I have seen, (five-sixths I think of those I have seen,) farmers' sons from the West, northwest—and from Pennsylvania, New York, and from largely among the rest your Massachusetts, &c—now after great and terrible experiences, here in their barracks they lie—in those boarded Washington hospital barracks, whitewashed outside and in, one story, high enough, airy and clean enough—one of the Wards, for sample, a long stretch, a hundred and sixty feet long, with aisle down

of you, do not neglect to see George and put this thing in its strongest light. Just think for a moment of the number of suckers that are gaining all the real benefits of the war (if that is not wicked to say) and think of George and thousands of others running all the risks while they are drawing all the pay" (Feinberg). On January 13, Jeff continued to bewail George's lot: "I wish to God that he would come home, I think that it would add 10 years to Mothers life. Write him" (Feinberg). Part of WW's letter is lost.

17. WW spent a great deal of time revising the text of this draft letter, which was part of the correspondence printed in 28–30. The earliest version of the draft, dated "Washington | Saturday morning, Jan. 17, '63," was drastically altered by the insertion of the first four paragraphs in the present text and that part of the first sentence of the following paragraph preceding "expression of American character."

18. See 27.

the middle, with cots, fifty or more on each side—and Death there up and down the aisle, tapping lightly by night or day here and there some poor young man, with relieving touch—that is one Ward, a cluster of ten or twelve make a current Washington Hospital—wherein this moment lie languishing, burning with fever or down with diarrhea, the imperial blood and rarest marrow of the North—here, at any rate, as I go for a couple of hours daily, and get to be welcome and useful, I find the masses fully justified by closest contact, never vulgar, ever calm, without greediness, no flummery, no frivolity—responding electric and without fail to affection, yet no whining—not the first unmanly whimper have I yet seen or heard.

In the Patent Office Hospital, Dr. Stone,[19] (Horatio Stone the sculptor—in his ward, some 150 men—he has been surgeon here several months—has had successive changes of soldiers in charge—some bad wounds, of course—amputations, sometimes rapidly followed by death, &c.—others from fevers, &c. &c.)—he told me last evening that he had not in memory one single case of a man's meeting the approach of death, whether sudden or slow, with fear or trembling—but always of these young men meeting their death with steady composure, and often with curious readiness—

The Army (I noticed it first in camp, and the same here among the wounded) is *very young*—and far more American than we supposed—ages range mainly from 20 to 30—a slight sprinkling of men older—and a bigger sprinkling of young lads of 17 and 18—

As I took temporary memoranda of names, items, &c of one thing and another, commissioned to get or do for the men—what they wished and what their cases required from outside, &c—these memoranda grow bulky, and suggest something to me—so I now make fuller notes, or a sort of journal, (not a mere dry journal though, I hope)—This thing I will record—it belongs to the time, and to all the States—(and perhaps it belongs to me)[20]—

19. Horatio Stone (1808–1875) was a surgeon in the Patent Office Hospital from 1862 to 1865.

20. This material, published for the first time in the New York *Weekly Graphic* in 1874 (see 569), was issued as *Memoranda During the War*. See also 91.

21. Apparently George Wood (1799–1870), who went to the Treasury Department as a clerk in 1822, and held various posts in that bureau until his death. He was the author of several satirical works, *Peter Schlemihl in America* (1858) and *The Gates Wide Open; or, Scenes in Another World* (1858); see *National Cyclopaedia of American Biography*. Undoubtedly he became acquainted with WW through the O'Connors. Mrs. O'Connor mentioned a Mr. Wood in her letter of July 5, 1864 (Feinberg). In reply to WW's letter, evidently delivered by O'Connor and dated "Thursday"—probably January 15—Wood wrote: "You sometimes find a poor soldier whom a Small Sum would relieve and I beg you will distribute these pieces of paper as you shall see best on your visit to the Hospital" (Feinberg).

22. WW described the Patent Office Hospital in the New York *Times*, Febru-

33. *To George Wood*

Washington, | Saturday morning Jan 17 '63.

Dear Mr Wood,[21]

So your generous heart moved you to send the sick and dying young men in the hospitals a handsome little contribution of money (toward $4). I thank you, dear sir, in their name, and in my own, as the organ of your charity. I have distributed part of it in Ward 6, (Dr. Leman, ward surgeon) Campbell Hospital—and shall to-day bestow the rest in the Patent Office Hosp.[22] My friend, I must meet you soon again.

Truly yours

Walt Whitman

34. *To Louisa Van Velsor Whitman*

Washington, | Friday noon, February 6, 1863.

Dearest mother,

Jeff must have got a letter[23] from me yesterday, containing George's last letter.[24] The news of your sickness, and the strange silence of Han made me feel somewhat gloomy. I wrote to George yesterday, conveying the news—and to-day I have sent him another letter, with much more comfortable news, for I was so glad to hear from Han, (her letter, enclosed in Jeff's, received this morning) that I wrote him right away, and sent Han's letter.[25]

Mother, I am quite in hopes George will get a furlough—may-be my expectations are unfounded, but I almost count on it.[26] I am so glad this morning to hear you are no worse, but changed for the better—and dear sister Mat too, and sissy, I am so glad to think they are recovering.[27] Jeff's enclosure of $10 through Mr. Lane,[28] from the young engineers, for the

ary 26, 1863 (*CW*, VII, 82–84).

23. WW's letter to Jeff is not extant. In his letter of February 6, Jeff mentioned that he had shown WW's "last letter" to Moses Lane, who thought it "was a clincher" (Feinberg). Probably Lane borrowed the letter in order to aid his solicitation of funds for WW's hospital work.

24. From his camp near Falmouth, George had written to WW on January 13 and February 1, and to his mother on January 22 (Trent).

25. These letters are not known.

26. On February 1, George vowed that if he did not receive a furlough, he would submit his resignation, "as it is hardly a fair shake for some to go home two or three times a year while others cant get away at all" (Trent). On February 6, he was still discouraged about the prospects for a leave.

27. On the day WW wrote this letter, Jeff reported that the three were recovering, and that "I think they all have had the worst colds that I know of" (Feinberg).

28. See 31.

soldiers in hospitals, the most needy cases, came safe of course—I shall acknowledge it to Mr. Lane to-morrow. Mother, I have written so much about hospitals, that I will not write any in this letter.

We have had bad weather enough here lately to most make up for the delightful weather we had for five weeks after I came from home.

Mother, I do hope you will be careful, and not get any relapse—and hope you will go on improving. Do you then think of getting new apartments, after the 1st of May? I suppose Jeff has settled about the lot[29]—it seems to me first rate as an investment—the kind of house to build is quite a consideration, (if any house,) I should build *a regular Irish shanty* myself, two rooms, and an end shed—I think that's luxury enough, since I have been down in the army.

Well, mother, I believe I will not fill out the sheet this time, as I want to go down without delay to the P. O. and send George's letter, and this one.

Good bye, dear mother,

Walt

35. *To Louisa Van Velsor Whitman*

Washington | Monday morn'g, Feb. 9th | 1863.

Dearest mother,

I write to enclose you a letter I have just received from George.[30] His corps, (Ninth Army,) and perhaps one other, are to move either to Fort Monroe, or somewhere down there—some say Suffolk. I am in hopes that when they get there, George will still have a sight for a furlough—I have written him I should think four letters since the 27th Jan—(and have sent him Han's letter to you in one)—I hope he has got most of them before this—I am afraid the $3. change I sent him is gone—He will write to you as soon as he gets settled wherever they go to—I don't know as it makes any

29. On February 6, Jeff wrote: "I think I shall be able to carry through my little 'real estate' scheme without much trouble, and I think it is a good one, at least I must try, for I am 'in' and I suppose I shall not be a true Whitman if I dont get disheartened, however I do not feel at all so just now. On the '*contrary quite the reverse*'" (Feinberg).

30. George wrote on February 6 from Falmouth (Trent). In summarizing George's letter, WW, characteristically, softened his brother's remarks about a furlough. And on February 8 George wrote to his mother: "If this movement of ours dont knock the thing in the head (and I dont know how it will be) you may expect to see me home for a short time, before many days" (Trent). On February 25, however, he notified his mother that "no furloughs would be granted, unless to save life or something of that kind" (Trent).

31 Jeff enclosed the contributions from these employees of Lane on February 10 (Feinberg). The Brooklyn Directory of 1865–1866 listed Drake as an inspector in City Hall. Martin was listed in the Directory of 1861–1862 as a surveyor, but was not cited in 1865–1866. Lane enclosed a contribution of $1 from Martin in a letter on May 2 (LC).

32. Lane wrote to E. D. Webster on February 12: "Mr. W[hitman] has been

difference in respect to danger, or fighting, from this move—One reason they have to move from the Rappahannock, up there, is that wood is all gone for miles, forage is scarce to get, and I don't know as there is any need of there staying there, for any purpose—In some haste, dearest mother, as I am off to visit for an hour or so, one of my hospitals. Your affectionate son

Walt.

36. *To Thomas Jefferson Whitman*

Office Major Hapgood, cor 15th & F. sts. | Washington,
Feb. 13th '63.

Dear brother,

Nothing new—still I thought I would write you a line this morning. The $4, namely: $2 from Theo. A. Drake and 2 [from] John D. Martin,[31] enclosed in your letter of the 10th came safe. They too will please accept the grateful thanks of several poor fellows, in hospital here.

The letter of introduction to Mr. Webster,[32] chief clerk, State Department, will be very acceptable. If convenient, I should like Mr Lane to send it on immediately. I do not so much look for an appointment from Mr. Seward as his backing me from the State of New York. I have seen Preston King[33] this morning for the second time—(it is very amusing to hunt for an office—so the thing seems to me just now—even if one don't get it)—I have seen Charles Sumner three times—he says every thing here moves as part of a great machine, and that I must consign myself to the fate of the rest—still [in] an interview I had with him yesterday he talked and acted as though he had life in him, and would exert himself to any reasonable extent for me to get something. Meantime I make about enough to pay my expenses by hacking on the press here, and copying in the paymasters offices, a couple of hours a day—one thing is favorable here, namely, pay for

for a long time connected with the New York Press and is a writer of most decided ability. His patriotism and loyalty you can rely upon under all circumstances. . . . I thought possibly you might assist him on the score of our old acquaintance" (Feinberg). In his letter on February 10, Jeff reported that Lane "tells me that he (Webster) is a '*politician*' and that he will help you without doubt provided that he thinks that it will not interfere at all with him" (Feinberg). According to the Washington Directory of 1864, Webster was not chief clerk but a clerk of the fourth class in the State Department.

33. Preston King (1806–1865) served as United States Senator from New York from 1857 to 1863. On February 11, WW called for the first time upon King, who did not "remember that Mr. Sumner had spoken to him about me. . . . King was blunt, decisive and manly . . . I think Sumner is a sort of gelding—no good." At the second interview on February 13, King gave WW "a letter to the Secretary of the Treasury [Chase]—also to Gen'l Meigs, chief of Quartermaster dep't." WW had an interview with Sumner on February 20 and asked him for "a boost" if he did not obtain a position by March 4. (This information is based upon jottings in one of WW's notebooks in the Feinberg Collection.)

whatever one does is at a high rate—I have not yet presented my letters to either Seward or Chase[34]—I thought I would get my forces all in a body, and make one concentrated dash, if possible with the personal introduction and presence of some big bug—I like fat old Preston King, very much—he is fat as a hogshead, with great hanging chops—the first thing he said to me the other day in the parlor chamber of the Senate, when I sent in for him and he came out, was, "Why, how can I do this thing, or any thing for you—how do I know but you are a secessionist—you look for all the world, like an old Southern planter—a regular Carolina or Virginia planter." I treated him with just as much hauteur as he did me with bluntness—this was the first time—it afterward proved that Charles Sumner had not prepared the way for me, as I supposed, or rather, not so strongly as I supposed, and Mr. King had even forgotten it—so I was as an entire stranger. But the same day C. S. talked further with Mr. King in the Senate, and the second interview I had with the latter, (this forenoon) he has given me a sort of general letter, endorsing me from New York—one envelope is addressed to Secretary Chase, and another to Gen. Meigs,[35] head Quartermaster's Dep't. Meantime, I am getting better and better acquainted with office-hunting wisdom, and Washington peculiarities generally.

I spent several hours in the Capitol the other day—the incredible gorgeousness of some of the rooms, (interior decorations &c)—rooms used perhaps but for merely three or four Committee meetings in the course of the whole year,) is beyond one's flightiest dreams. Costly frescoes of the style of Taylor's Saloon in Broadway,[36] only really the best and choicest of their sort, done by imported French & Italian artists, are the prevailing sorts (imagine the work you see on the fine China vases, in Tiffany's—the paintings of Cupids & goddesses &c. spread recklessly over the arched ceiling and broad panels of a big room—the whole floor underneath paved with tesselated pavement, which is a sort of cross between marble & china, with little figures drab, blue, cream color, &c).

34. Letters 28 and 29.

35. Montgomery C. Meigs (1816–1892) was appointed quartermaster general on May 14, 1861, and served in that capacity throughout the war. Catton (*Glory Road*, 96) describes Meigs as "a grave and estimable man who deserves just a little better of posterity than he seems likely ever to get."

36. John Taylor's Saloon was located at 365 Broadway. Alcott noted in his journal on December 12, 1856, that he dined there with WW, "discussing America, its men and institutions"; *The Journals*, ed. Shepard (1938), 293.

37. John Swinton (1829–1901), managing editor of the New York *Times*, frequented Pfaff's, where he probably met WW. On January 23, 1874 (WW said "1884"), Swinton wrote what the poet termed "almost like a love letter": "It was perhaps the very day of the publication of the first edition of the 'Leaves of Grass' that I saw a copy of it at a newspaper stand in Fulton street, Brooklyn. I got it, looked into it with wonder, and felt that here was something that touched on depths of my humanity. Since then you have grown before me, grown around me, and grown into me" (Feinberg; Traubel, I, 24).

These things, with heavy, elaborately wrought balustrades, columns, & steps—all of the most beautiful marbles I ever saw, some white as milk, others of all colors, green, spotted, lined, or of our old chocolate color—all these marbles used as freely as if they were common blue flags—with rich door-frames and window-casings of bronze and gold—heavy chandeliers and mantels, and clocks in every room—and indeed by far the richest and gayest, and most un-American and inappropriate ornamenting and finest interior workmanship I ever conceived possible, spread in profusion through scores, hundreds, (and almost thousands) of rooms—such are what I find, or rather would find to interest me, if I devoted time to it—But a few of the rooms are enough for me—the style is without grandeur, and without simplicity—These days, the state our country is in, and especially filled as I am from top to toe, of late with scenes and thoughts of *the hospitals*, (America seems to me now, though only in her youth, but brought *already here* feeble, bandaged and bloody *in hospital*)—*these days* I say, Jeff, all the poppy-show goddesses and all the pretty blue & gold in which the interior Capitol is got up, seem to me out of place beyond any thing I could tell—and I get away from it as quick as I can when that kind of thought comes over me. I suppose it is to be described throughout—those interiors—as all of them got up in the French style—well enough for a New York [*incomplete*]

37. *To John Swinton*

ADDRESS: John Swinton, | Care H. J. Raymond, | Editor New York Times | New York | City.
POSTMARK: Washington | Feb | 2(?) | 1863 | D. C.

Washington | Feb. 23d, 1863

John,[37] I write to call your attention to an article, (Times correspondence,) I have just written & sent about the Military Hospitals here[38]—

He praised WW in the New York *Herald* on April 1, 1876 (reprinted in Bucke, 36–37). Swinton was in 1874 a candidate of the Industrial Political Party for the mayoralty of New York. From 1875 to 1883, he was with the New York *Sun*, and for the next four years edited the weekly labor journal, *John Swinton's Paper*. When this publication folded, he returned to the *Sun*. See Robert Waters, *Career and Conversations of John Swinton* (1902), and Meyer Berger, *The History of The New York Times, 1851–1951* (1951), 250–251.

38. "The Great Army of the Sick: Military Hospitals in Washington" was printed in the *Times* of February 26; it later appeared in *The Wound Dresser* as "The Great Army of the Wounded" (CW, VII, 81–90). Swinton in his reply to WW on February 25 said: "I have crowded out a great many things to get [the article] in. . . . I am glad to see you are engaged in such good work at Washington. It must be even more refreshing [than] to sit by Pfaff's privy and eat sweetbreads and drink coffee, and listen to the intolerable wit of the crackbrains" (Feinberg; Traubel, I, 416).

as they are so generally and sadly interesting to the public. You will easily recognize the article—I enclose you my address—write me a line about it, at your leisure—(to-morrow or next day.)

Is William[39] in New York—or where?

The article is to be paid for.

Walt.

37.1 *To Thomas Jefferson Whitman* [*3.6. 1863*][40]

. . . town, I see." I asked him if he meant George, and he said yes—he saw his name, Capt. George W. Whitman, U. S. A. in the newspaper list of hotel arrivals, at the Avenue House, two days before. I was quite dumbfoundered—went right away to the Avenue House, and searching the register, I found it was Capt. George J. Whitman, 3d Wisconsin Vol. So you see there are two Capt. George Whitmans in the Army. I was a great mind to ask to see the Wisconsin Whitman—but I didn't.

I go to the Hospitals about the same as ever—the last week or so, I have been most every night to the Capitol, which has been all lit up—I should never get tired of wandering through the Senate wing at night—it is the most costly, splendid and rich-painted place in its interminable mazes (I wander around and lose myself in them) of corridors and halls, that I ever dreamed of, or thought possible to construct—The great Halls of the H[ouse] of R[epresentatives] and the Senate, are wonderful and brilliant at night—they show best then, (in some respects.) They are probably the most beautiful rooms, ornamented and gilded style, in the world.

About what is called the Conscript Bill (an improper name) I hope and pray from the bottom of my heart that, if they (the Government) are indeed going on with the war, they will carry out that bill, and enrol *every man* in the land—I would like to see the people embodied *en-masse*—I am very sure I shall see that my name is in its place on the lists, and my body in the ranks, if they do it that way—for *that* will be something like our nation getting itself up in shape. The Bill however was really meant as a warning to Louis Napoleon, or any other foreign meddler.

39. Swinton's brother William (1833–1892) was war correspondent of the New York *Times*. His hostility to Union generals and his unscrupulous tactics led to his suspension as a reporter on July 1, 1864. (WW did not have a high opinion of William's journalism; see 134.) He was professor of English at the University of California from 1869 to 1874. Thereafter he compiled extremely successful textbooks, and established the magazine *Story-Teller* in 1883.

40. At one time there were at Camden two additional pages which presumably belonged to this letter; unfortunately, no transcription was made. The pages reproduced here do not appear to be part of 31, which is also incomplete. On March 9, Jeff noted receipt of "a long letter from you Saturday" (March 7). But the principal argument for the date of March 6 is that on March 3 Jeff asked his brother: "What are they going to do to reinforce the army, will they have to enforce the conscript bill" (Feinberg).

With my office-hunting, no special result yet. I cannot give up my Hospitals yet. I never before had my feelings so thoroughly and (so far) permanently absorbed, to the very roots, as by these huge swarms of dear, wounded, sick, dying boys—I get very much attached to some of them, and many of them have come to depend on seeing me, and having me sit by them a few minutes, as if for their lives.

Jeff, I am very fat and hearty—I have found friends here—I met a lady in the street day before yesterday that was so much like Mat I could hardly keep from speaking to her. I guess she wondered what I stood and looked, and looked, at her so long for. She drest like Mat too, and was . . .

38. *To Louisa Van Velsor Whitman*

Washington, Sunday | March 8th 1863.

Dearest Mother,

Jeff must have got quite a long letter, (three sheets,) I wrote Thursday or Friday last[41]—nothing particular. This is the fifth letter I have sent with shinplasters in—(Since George's $3 got lost I am more on the alert and mention them)—

The poor Frenchman d'Almeida[42] I told you about in my last, got out of the Old Capitol prison this morning—has been in a week—it was a most ridiculous thing putting him in—he was as square a man as I am—while he was in, the chief officer of the prison laughed sarcastically one day at his broken English, and d'Almeida said, "Sir you ought not to laugh—you ought much more to weep, to see a poor traveler like me in such a misfortune"—and Mr. Chief Officer immediately called the guard and sent d'Almeida to the guard-house for that *awful offence* of making such an answer. The guard-house is a nasty, lousy dungeon without light—in it was a nigger with his wrists in manacles, and four white deserters—there is among the Old Capitol prisoners a little boy of seven years old—he and his father were taken as secesh guerillas in Virginia, and the government is holding on to the child, to exchange him for some Union prisoner south, in an exchange. Mother, my heart bleeds at all sorts of such damnable things

41. This letter is apparently lost.

42. Joseph-Charles d'Almeida (1822–1880), a professor and author of *Problèmes de physique* (1862), came to the United States in 1862. In the Feinberg Collection, there are three interesting letters from d'Almeida to O'Connor. From Memphis, Tennessee, on January 28, 1863, d'Almeida explained that because of the kindness of a Miss Rebecca Harding he had been introduced to "la société rebelle." On March 2, he asked O'Connor to visit him in the Old Capitol Prison. The Washington *National Republican* of this date listed d'Almeida among refugees who were committed to Old Capitol Prison for examination. From New York, on March 27(?), d'Almeida wrote his farewell letter after he had been to Boston, where he had been entertained by James Fields, and had met Longfellow, Emerson, and Agassiz: "I carry with me a little American library in which the LEAVES of Grass are included."

of one kind or another I meet with every day—it is not the fault of the President—he would not harm any human being—nor of Seward or Stanton[43]—but the heartless mean-souled brutes that get in positions subordinate but where they can show themselves, and their damned airs and pomposity—they think nothing of treating a man like the worst slave-owner is supposed to treat his niggers—

Meanwhile the great officers of the government have every minute occupied with pressing business, and these wretches have full swing. It seems impossible that there could be in the Free States such tyrants, as many you see hereabout—This d'Almeida is a very modest man, a real French gentleman, poor, and quite distinguished as a traveler and man of science—and is a Professor in the Academy of France. He takes or appears to take his misfortunes very goodnaturedly—yet it must have cut pretty deep on some accounts, he suffered every humiliation.

Well, dearest mother, how does it go at home? I hope you are none of you going to move—I hope it is arranged that you shall stay—there would be something dissatisfactory wherever you should go. I was real glad to hear Jeff had abandoned the idea of building, this spring—to attempt it without money is winding onesself round and round in the devil's own net.[44]

I saw Frederick Ellison here yesterday—he is a young man that used to be in Hughes's store there above Cumberland street[45]—he is in the 9th N. Y. Militia—has just come from Brooklyn, where he has been on a furlough—

I would be glad to hear about Han—I must write to her very soon. I have not heard from George since. Yesterday I spent the day at Emory Hospital—a very needy place—I gave out a great many things, and about $4 in money—it was a good day. I was covered with mud, getting there. (I dont mean good *weather*, it rained hard)—

Walt

Jeff, I shall write a few lines soon to Mr. Rae—also to the firm that contributed the $10.[46] I have not yet rec'd the engravings.

43. Edwin McMasters Stanton (1814–1869) was Secretary of War from 1862 to 1868.

44. On March 3, Jeff wrote that he had decided to "wait for cheaper times" when he discovered that what he "supposed would cost at 11 or $1200 could not be done for less than 20 or $2100" (Feinberg).

45. In the Brooklyn Directory of 1859–1860, Ellison was listed as clerk. The name did not appear in the Directories of 1861–1862 and 1865–1866. Oscar F. Hughes had a store at 373 Myrtle Avenue. In 1861–1862, the Directory cited "house furnishings," and in 1865–1866, "glass ware."

46. On February 12, Jeff sent to his brother $10 from Hill & Newman and

39. *To Thomas Jefferson Whitman*

Washington | Wednesday, March 18, 1863.

I suppose George must be about leaving you to-day,[47] to return to his regiment—and I can realize how gloomy you will all be for two or three days, especially Mother. Dear mother, you must keep up your spirits, and not get downhearted. I hope you are all well—I think about you all every day—is Mary home?[48]—you must write me all about every thing—I suppose the bundle of George's shirts, drawers, &c came safe by Adams express. I sent it last Saturday, and it ought to have been delivered Monday in Brooklyn. I did not pay the freight. Last Monday 16th I wrote to Mother, and sent her some shinplasters. Saturday previous I sent a note home, enclosing the express receipt.[49]

Jeff, I wrote a letter to the *Eagle*,[50] and sent it yesterday—if it appears, it will probably be to-day or to-morrow (or next day.) I wish you would look out for it, and buy me 20 of the papers, (the afternoon it appears,) and send them, the same as you did the other letter, direct care of Major Hapgood, the same—put the engravings (20 of the large head) in the same package—the postage will be at the rate of ½ cent per oz. You leave one end partially unsealed. Send them as *soon* as convenient, after the letter appears, but no such dreadful hurry.

I suppose you have been in quite a state of pleasure and excitement home, with the visit of dear brother George. I was much pleased to hear by mother's letter that he was so sought for, and treated with so much attention—He deserves it all—you must tell me all the particulars of his visit.

The Hospitals still engross a large part of my time and feelings—only I don't remain so long and make such exhausting-like visits, the last week —as I have had a bad humming feeling and deafness, stupor-like at times, in my head, which unfits me for continued exertion. It comes from a bad cold, gathering I think in my head. If it were not that some of the soldiers really depend on me to come, and the doctors tell me it is really necessary, I should suspend my visits for two or three days, at least. Poor boys, you

$5 "from our friend Mr. E. Rae": "I know Rae is a liberal hearted man and through his friends he could do a great deal and I am confident that he could be more earnestly interested in the matter if you write him directly" (Feinberg). This was probably E. H. Rae, a law copyist with an office at 16 Wall Street, New York.

47. According to Jeff's letter of March 9, George arrived in Brooklyn on March 7 on a ten-day furlough: "He is well and looking first rate" (Feinberg).

48. Mary Van Nostrand, WW's sister.

49. Neither letter is extant.

50. "The Great Washington Hospital" appeared in the *Eagle* on March 19, and was entitled "Life Among Fifty Thousand Soldiers" in *CW*, VII, 91–100.

have no idea how they cling to one, and how strong the tie that forms between us. Things here are just the same with me, neither better nor worse —(I feel so engrossed with my soldiers, I do not devote that attention to my office-hunting, which is needed for success.)

Jeff, you must give my best respects to Mr. and Mrs. Lane, they have enabled me to do a world of good, and I can never forget them. I see you had a great Union meeting in the Academy of Music[51]—it is impossible to tell what the government designs to do the coming season, but I suppose they will push on the war. The south is failing fast in many respects—D'Almeida,[52] the Frenchman I wrote about, told me that he was besieged every where down south to sell (for confederate money) any and every thing he had, his clothes, his boots, his haversack, &c &c. Then their niggers will gradually melt, *certain.* So the fates fight for us, even if our generals do not. Jeff, to see what I see so much of, puts one entirely out of conceit of war—still for all that I am not sure but I go in for fighting on—the choice is hard on either part, but to *cave* in the worst—good bye, dearest brother.

Walt.

40. *To Nathaniel Bloom and John F. S. Gray 3. 19 - 20. 1863*

Washington, March 19, 1863.

Dear Nat,[53] and Fred Gray:[54]

Since I left New York, I was down in the Army of the Potomac in front with my brother a good part of the winter, commencing time of the battle of Fredericksburgh[55]—have seen *war-life*, the real article—folded myself in a blanket, lying down in the mud with composure—relished salt

51. The New York *Herald* of March 17 described the meeting on the preceding day in glowing prose: "One of the largest and most truly enthusiastic meetings ever held in the new Brooklyn Academy of Music . . . The heart of every loyal man could not but throb with joy at seeing such a mass of beauty and intelligence coming forward with united voice to sustain the Government of the land."

52. See 38.

53. Nathaniel Bloom operated a fancy-goods store on Broadway for many years. What appears to be an early description of him was printed by Bucke in *Notes and Fragments* (CW, IX, 142; Trent): "Bloom—Broad-shouldered, six-footer, with a hare-lip. Clever fellow, and by no means bad looking. . . . Direct, plain-spoken, natural-hearted, gentle-tempered, but awful when roused—cartman, with a horse, cart &c, of his own—drives for a store in Maiden lane." WW referred to him in one of his notebooks (*LC* #109). Later in life Bloom was listed as an importer; his name does not appear in the Directories after 1900.

54. John Frederick Schiller Gray was a captain in the Twentieth New York Infantry and later held the same rank in the Assistant Adjutant General's Volunteers. He became a major on January 4, 1865, and resigned on December 6 of the same year; see Francis B. Heitman, *Historical Register and Dictionary of the United States Army* (1903). In 1862 he fought in the battle at Antietam and at Pfaff's gave WW "a fearful account of the battlefield at ½ past 9 the night following the engagement"; see WW's notations in Frederick W. Hedge's *Prose Writers of Germany*, reprinted in Nonesuch,

pork & hard tack—have been on the battle-field among the wounded, the faint and the bleeding, to give them nourishment—have gone over with a flag of truce the next day to help direct the burial of the dead—have struck up a tremendous friendship with a young Mississippi captain (about 19)[56] that we took prisoner badly wounded at Fredericksburgh—(he has followed me here, is in Emory hospital here, minus a leg—he wears his confederate uniform, proud as the devil—I met him first at Falmouth, in the Lacy house,[57] middle of December last, his leg just cut off, and cheered him up—poor boy, he has suffered a great deal, and still suffers—has eyes bright as a hawk, but face pale—our affection is quite an affair, quite romantic—sometimes when I lean over to say I am going, he puts his arm round my neck, draws my face down, &c. quite a scene for the New Bowery.)

I spent the Christmas holidays on the Rappahannock—during January came up hither, took a lodging room here—did the 37th Congress, especially the night sessions the last three weeks, explored the Capitol then, meandering the gorgeous painted interminable senate corridors, getting lost in them, (a new sensation, rich & strong, that endless painted interior at night)—got very much interested in some particular cases in Hospitals here—go now steadily to more or less of said Hospitals by day or night—find always the sick and dying soldiers forthwith begin to cling to me in a way that makes a fellow feel funny enough. These Hospitals, so different from all others—these thousands, and tens and twenties of thousands of American young men, badly wounded, all sorts of wounds, operated on, pallid with diarrhea, languishing, dying with fever, pneumonia, &c. open a new world somehow to me, giving closer insights, new things, exploring deeper mines than any yet, showing our humanity, (I sometimes put my-

1099. In 1864, according to one of WW's notebooks (*LC* #103), Gray was stationed at New Orleans. He graduated from the College of Physicians and Surgeons in New York in 1871, and briefly practiced medicine with his father in New York. WW referred to him during this period in a notebook (*LC* #109). Later he practiced in Paris, Nice, and Geneva. He died of Bright's disease at St. Clair Springs, Michigan, on April 18, 1891; obituaries appeared in the New York *Herald* and *Tribune* on August 19.

55. With justice, William E. Barton, in *Abraham Lincoln and Walt Whitman* (1928), 48–49, attacks WW's gross overstatement, which was undoubtedly intended to impress his New York friends.

56. WW referred with more restraint to this rebel officer in "Hospital Visits," which appeared in the New York *Times*, December 11, 1864, and later in *The Wound Dresser:* "One, a Mississippian—a captain—hit badly in the leg, I talked with some time; he asked me for papers, which I gave him. (I saw him three months afterward in Washington, with leg amputated, doing well)" (*CW*, VII, 102–103).

57. WW scribbled "Sight at the Lacy House" in his diary on December 22, 1862, when he was in the field with George: "At the foot of tree, immediately in front, a heap of feet, legs, arms, and human fragments, cut, bloody, black and blue, swelled and sickening—in the garden near, a row of graves; some distance back, a little while afterwards, I saw a long row of them" (Glicksberg, 69–70), a description substantially repeated in "Hospital Visits" (*CW*, VII, 102).

self in fancy in the cot, with typhoid, or under the knife,) tried by terrible, fearfulest tests, probed deepest, the living soul's, the body's tragedies, bursting the petty bonds of art. To these, what are your dramas and poems, even the oldest and the tearfulest? Not old Greek mighty ones, where man contends with fate, (and always yields)—not Virgil showing Dante on and on among the agonized & damned, approach what here I see and take a part in. For here I see, not at intervals, but quite always, how certain, man, our American man—how he holds himself cool and unquestioned master above all pains and bloody mutilations. It is immense, the best thing of all, nourishes me of all men. This then, what frightened us all so long! Why it is put to flight with ignominy, a mere stuffed scarecrow of the fields. O death where is thy sting? O grave where is thy victory? &c. In the Patent Office, as I stood there one night, just off the cot-side of a dying soldier, in a large Ward that had received the worst cases of 2d Bull Run, Antietam and Fredericksburgh, the surgeon, Dr. Stone, (Horatio Stone, the sculptor,)[58] told me, of all who had died in that crowded ward the past six months, he had still to find the *first man* or *boy* who had met the approach of death with a single tremor, or unmanly fear. But let me change the subject—I have given you screed enough about death and Hospitals—and too much, since I got started. Only I have some curious yarns I promise you, my darlings and gossips, by word of mouth, whene'er we meet.

Washington and its points I find bear a second and a third perusal, and doubtless indeed many. My first impressions, architectural, &c. were not favorable;[59] but upon the whole, the city, the spaces, buildings, &c make no unfit emblem of our country, so far, so broadly planned, every thing in plenty, money & materials staggering with plenty, but the fruit of the plans, the knit, the combination yet wanting—Determined to express ourselves greatly in a capital but no fit capital yet here—(time, associations, wanting, I suppose)—many a hiatus yet—many a thing to be taken down and done over again yet—perhaps an entire change of base—may-be a succession of changes. Congress does not seize very hard upon me—I studied it and its members with curiosity, and long—much gab, great fear of public opinion, plenty of low business talent, but no masterful man in Congress, (probably best so.) I think well of the President. He has a face like a hoosier Michael Angelo, so awful ugly it becomes beautiful, with its strange mouth, its deep cut, criss-cross lines, and its doughnut complexion. My notion is, too, that underneath his outside smutched

58. See 32. WW retold this incident in "Democracy," *The Galaxy*, IV (1867), 922.

59. See 36. WW became eloquent about the beauty of Washington in the article he published in the New York *Times* on October 4.

60. See 28, 29, and 36.

mannerism, and stories from third-class county bar-rooms, (it is his humor,) Mr. Lincoln keeps a fountain of first-class practical telling wisdom. I do not dwell on the supposed failures of his government; he has shown, I sometimes think, an almost supernatural tact in keeping the ship afloat at all, with head steady, not only not going down, and now certain not to, but with proud and resolute spirit, and flag flying in sight of the world, menacing and high as ever. I say never yet captain, never ruler, had such a perplexing, dangerous task as his, the past two years. I more and more rely upon his idiomatic western genius, careless of court dress or court decorums.

I am living here without much definite aim, (except going to the hospitals)—yet I have quite a good time—I make some money by scribbling for the papers, and as copyist. I have had, (and have,) thoughts of trying to get a clerkship or something, but I only try in a listless sort of way, and of course do not succeed. I have strong letters of introduction from Mr. Emerson to Mr. Seward and Mr. Chase, but I have not presented them.[60] I have seen Mr. Sumner several times anent of my office-hunting—he promised fair once—but he does not seem to be finally fascinated. I hire a bright little 3d story front room, with service, &c. for $7 a month, dine in the same house, (394 L st. a private house)—and remain yet much of the old vagabond that so gracefully becomes me. I miss you all, my darlings & gossips, Fred Gray, and Bloom and Russell and every body. I wish you would all come here in a body—that would be divine. (We would drink ale, which is here of the best.) My health, strength, personal beauty, &c. are, I am happy to inform you, without diminution, but on the contrary quite the reverse. I weigh full 220 pounds avoirdupois, yet still retain my usual perfect shape—a regular model. My beard, neck, &c. are woolier, fleecier, whiteyer than ever. I wear army boots, with magnificent black morocco tops, the trousers put in, wherein shod and legged confront I Virginia's deepest mud with supercilious eyes. The scenery around Washington is really fine, the Potomac a lordly river, the hills, woods, &c all attractive. I poke about quite a good deal. Much of the weather here is from heaven—of late, though, a stretch decidedly from the other point. To-night (for it is night, about 10) I sit alone writing this epistle, (which will doubtless devour you all with envy and admiration,) in the room adjoining my own particular. A gentleman and his wife,[61] who occupy the two other apartments on this floor, have gone to see Heron[62] in Medea—have put their little child to bed, and left me in charge. The little one is

61. William and Ellen O'Connor.

62. Matilda Agnes Heron (1830–1877) was a famous interpreter of Camille and of Legouvé's Medea; see Odell, *Annals of the New York Stage*, VI, 534–536.

sleeping soundly there in the back room, and I, (plagued with a cold in the head,) sit here in the front, by a good fire, writing as aforesaid to my gossips & darlings. The evening is lonesome & still. I am entirely alone. "O solitude where are the charms," &c &c.

Now you write to me good long letters, my own boys. You, Bloom, give me your address particular, dear friend. Tell me Charles Russell's address, particular—also write me about Charles Chauncey.[63] Tell me about every body. For, dearest gossips, as the hart panteth, &c. so my soul after any and all sorts of items about you all. My darling, dearest boys, if I could be with you this hour, long enough to take only just three mild hot rums, before the cool weather closes.

Friday Morning, 20th—I finish my letter in the office of Major Hapgood, a paymaster, and a friend of mine. This is a large building, filled with paymasters' offices, some thirty or forty or more. This room is up on the fifth floor, (a most noble and broad view from my window.) Curious scenes around here—a continual stream of soldiers, officers, cripples, &c &c. some climbing wearily up the stairs. They seek their pay—and every hour, almost every minute, has its incident, its hitch, its romance, farce or tragedy. There are two paymasters in this room. A sentry at the street door, another half way up the stairs, another at the chief clerk's door, all with muskets & bayonets—sometimes a great swarm, hundreds, around the side walk in front, waiting. (Every body is waiting for something here.) I take a pause, look up a couple of minutes from my pen and paper—see spread, off there, the Potomac, very fine, nothing petty about it—the Washington monument,[64] not half finished—the public grounds around it filled with ten thousand beeves, on the hoof—to the left the Smithsonian with its brown turrets—to the right, far across, Arlington Heights, the forts, eight or ten of them—then the long bridge, and down a ways, but

63. A Charles W. Chauncey was listed as an importer in the New York Directories of the period. In his reply on May 1, Gray wrote: "Charles Chauncey, of whose illness you have heard, is said to be much better. . . . Charley Russell was in town some weeks ago, he told me not to fail to send his warmest love to you. He is on Genl. Meade's staff as Medical Inspector General of the 5th Corps d'Armée—a first rate position and one that he has earned by his industry and talents" (Hanley).

64. Construction of the Washington Monument began in 1848, was abandoned from 1855 to 1877, and finally completed in 1884.

65. Dr. John F. Gray (1804–1882), a celebrated homeopath.

66. In *Old Friends, Being Literary Recollections of Other Days* (1909), 66, 88, William Winter mentions Edward F. Mullen, an artist and a Pfaffian. On August 16, 1881, in *Specimen Days* (CW, v, 21), WW recorded a visit to Pfaff's Restaurant, during which the proprietor and he recalled "ante-bellum times" and the deaths of old habitués like "Mullin."

67. Benjamin Knower was listed as a clerk (1862–1863) and later as a New York merchant. In an 1863 diary, WW noted the receipt of a letter from Knower on May 6 (Glicksberg, 135); he was also mentioned in two other diaries (LC #104 and #108).

68. This letter was sent to Charles S. Kingsley, who replied on March 21: "I received your letter and I delivered the enclosed one to Gray (not knowing where to

quite plain, the shipping of Alexandria—opposite me, and in stone throw, is the Treasury building—and below the bustle and life of Pennsylvania avenue. I shall hasten with my letter, and then go forth and take a stroll down "the avenue" as they call it here.

Now, you boys, don't you think I have done the handsome thing by writing this astounding, magnificent letter—certainly the longest I ever wrote in my life. Fred, I wish you to present my best respects to your father.[65] Bloom and all, one of these days we will meet, and make up for lost time, my dearest boys.

Walt.

Address me, care Major Hapgood, paymaster, U. S. Army, cor 15th & F sts. Washington. How is Mullen?[66] give him my respects—How is Ben Knower?[67] how the twinkling and temperate Towle? remember me to them.[68]

41. *To Louisa Van Velsor Whitman*

Washington March 31, 1863.

Dearest mother,

I have not heard from George, except a note he wrote me a couple of days after he got back from his furlough—I think it likely the regiment has gone with its corps to the west, to the Kentucky or Tennessee region[69]—Burnside at last accounts was in Cincinnati—Well it will be a change for George, if he is out there—I sent a long letter to Han last Saturday, enclosed George's note to me. Mother, when you or Jeff writes again, tell me if my papers & MSS are all right—I should be very sorry indeed if they got scattered, or used up or any thing—*especially* the copy of Leaves of

find Bloom)" (Berg). On May 5, one of Burroughs' friends wrote to him: "He lent me some letters from some of his young friends in New York. They call him 'Walt,' and by reading you would judge him to be a young fellow, and indeed, he is young, with his perfect health and youthful tastes" (Barrus, 4).

On May 1, Gray excused his neglect in replying because of his military duties and "bothering my brain with the detestable clerical duties incidental to my position": "I have just come from my Mother, who, together with my Father, desires to be kindly remembered to you. . . . I lead a very different life from what I did last summer—no more beer houses and disreputable 'cakes and ale.' Sometimes when I think of my poor little Clothilde and you I feel as if I were not as happy now as then. However, a man must work and woman must weep, I suppose! . . . I detest writing letters to a dear friend like you—it's such a devilish slow and insufficient way of communicating your thoughts. . . . the other day I took a walk in the central park with Perk; the park was so heavenly that it actually made me as sentimental and lachrymose as a school boy. I'm damned if I wouldn't have given up all my hopes in the future to have had you and my little girl with me then. Don't fail to write me, will you, old Boy! Be Christlike and forgive!" (Professor Holloway supplied me with a typescript of this letter.)

69. There are no extant letters from George until April 2 (Trent), when, as WW predicted, he wrote to his mother from Paris, Ky.

Grass covered in blue paper, and the little MS book "Drum Taps," & the MS tied up in the square, spotted (stone-paper) loose covers—I want them all carefully kept.

Mother, it is quite a snow storm here this morning—the ground is an inch and a half deep with snow—and it is snowing & drizzling—but I feel very independent in my stout army-boots, I go any where. I *have* felt quite well of my deafness and cold in my head for four days or so, but it is back again bad as ever this morning.

Dear mother, I wrote the above, in my room—I have now come down to Major Hapgood's office. I do not find any thing from home, and no particular news in the paper this morning—no news about the Ninth Army Corps, or where they are. I find a good letter from one of my New York boys, (Fifth Avenue)—a young fellow named Hugo Fritsch,[70] son of the Austrian Consul General—he writes me a long first-rate letter this morning—he too speaks about the opera, (like Jeff) he goes there a good deal—says that Medori,[71] the soprano, as Norma, made the greatest success ever seen—says that the whole company there now, the singers, are very fine—all this I write for Jeff & Mat—I hope they will go once in a while when it is convenient—

It is a most disagreeable day here, mother, walking poshy and a rain and drizzle—

There is nothing new with me—no particular sight for an office, that I can count on. But I can make enough with the papers, for the present necessities—I hear that the paymaster, Major Yard,[72] that pays the 51st, has gone on West. I suppose to Cincinnati, or wherever the brigade has gone—of course to pay up—he pays up to 1st of March—All the Army is going to be paid up to 1st March every where.

70. Three drafts of letters to Fritsch appear below—62, 63, and 84. According to his diary, WW sent a letter on April 23 to "Futch," possibly Fritsch (Glicksberg, 132). In diary entries in 1867 and 1870, WW noted Fritsch's address at the American Papier Maché Company (*LC* #108, #109). His name did not appear in the New York Directories of the period, unless he (not his father) was the vice-consul listed in 1873–1874.

71. Giuseppini Medori was introduced to New York by Max Maretzek in the 1862–1863 season. She made a sensational debut as Norma on March 23, 1863; see Odell, *Annals of the New York Stage*, VII, 514–515. Jeff described his visits to the opera on March 21 and April 3 (Feinberg).

72. Major Thomas W. Yard, paymaster, entered the army June 1, 1861, and resigned March 18, 1865.

73. Jeff wrote to WW on March 21: "We are having glorious spring weather and sissy [Mannahatta] wants to know if I wont write and tell Uncle Walt to come home and take her out on Fort Green" (Feinberg).

74. See 31.

75. Raphael Semmes (1809–1877), Confederate naval officer, commanded the "Alabama" and sank the U.S.S. "Hatteras" off Galveston on January 11. WW printed an account of this engagement in the New York *Daily Graphic* in 1874; see *AL*, XV (1943), 58–59.

Mother, I hope you are well and hearty as usual—I am so glad you are none of you going to move—I would like to have the pleasure of Miss Mannahatta Whitman's company, the first fine forenoon, if it were possible—I think we might have first rate times, for one day at any rate—I hope she will not forget her Uncle Walt[73]—I received a note from Probasco,[74] requesting me not to put his name in my next letter—I appreciate his motive, and wish to please him always—but in this matter I shall do what I think appropriate—Mother, I see some very interesting persons here —a young master's mate, who was on the Hatteras, when surprised & broadsided by the Alabama, Capt. Semmes[75]—he gave me a very good acc't of it all—then Capt. Mullin,[76] U. S. Army (engineer), who has been six years out in the Rocky Mt's, making a gov't road, 650 miles from Ft. Benton to Walla Walla—very, very interesting to know such men intimately, and talk freely with them—Dearest mother, I shall have great yarns to spin, when I come home—I am not a bit home sick, yet I should [like] to see you & Mat, very very much—One thinks of the *vimmen* when he is away.

Walt

Shall send the shirts in a day or two.

42. *To Louisa Van Velsor Whitman*

Washington, Wednesday | forenoon, April 15, '63.

Dearest Mother,

Jeff's letter of the 11th, acknowledging the books, also the one about five days previous, containing the $10 from Van Anden, came safe.[77] Jeff's letters are always first rate and welcome—the good long one with so much about home, and containing Han's & George's, was especially so. It

76. Captain John Mullan (1830–1909), an army engineer, was associated with General Isaac I. Stevens in his surveys for a railroad route to the West. Mullan's explorations were described in *Reports of Explorations and Surveys. . . . for a Railroad from the Mississippi River to the Pacific Ocean, 1853–5* (1860), XII, 123–125, 168–172, 176–182. When WW met Mullan, he was about to publish *Report on the Construction of a Military Road from Walla-Walla to Fort Benton* (1863). In a notebook entry for April, 1863 (*LC* #76), WW referred to both reports. A transcontinental railroad had long fascinated WW; he had written an editorial on the subject in 1858 while he was editor of the Brooklyn *Daily Times* (see Allen, 213), and, of course, celebrated the completed feat in "Passage to India."

77. In his letter of April 6(?), Jeff included $10 from Isaac Van Anden (1812–1875), the founder of the Brooklyn *Eagle*. WW was editor of this newspaper in 1846–1847, but left after a political disagreement with the proprietor; see Allen, 90–91. On April 2, Jeff had requested "a copy of the Pacific R. R. Exploration &c Reports. . . . I find them of great use in giving me ideas about my business and they are too cursed costly to buy" (Feinberg). By April 11, he had received two books: "I am extremely obliged . . . and shall, Oliver Twist like, ask for more" (Feinberg).

is a great pleasure, though sometimes a melancholy one, to hear from Han, under her own hand. I have writ to George—I wrote last Friday—I directed the letter to "*Lexington* or elsewhere, *Kentucky*"—as I saw in a letter in a Cincinnati paper that Gen. Ferrero[78] was appointed provost marshal at Lexington—the 51st is down there somewhere, and I guess it is about as well off there as anywhere—there is much said about their closing up the regimental companies—that is, where there are ten companies of 40 men each, closing them up to five companies, of 80 men each. It is said the government purposes something of this kind—it will throw a good many captains & lieutenants out—I suppose you know that LeGendre[79] is now Col. of the 51st—it's a pity if we havn't Americans enough to put over our old war regiments—(I think less and less of foreigners, in this war—what I see, especially in the hospitals, convinces me that there is no other stock, for emergencies, but native American—no other name by which we can be saved.)

Mother, I feel quite bad about Andrew[80]—I am so in hopes to hear that he has recovered—I think about him every day—he must not get fretting and disheartened—that is really the worst feature of any sickness—diseases of the throat and bronchia are the result always of bad state of the stomach, blood, &c. (they never come from the throat itself)—the throat and bronchia are lined like the stomach and other interior organs with a fine lining like silk or crape, and when all this gets ulcerated or inflamed or what not, (it is Dr. Sammis's *mucous membrane*, you know,) it is bad, and most distressing—medicine is really of no great account, except just to pacify a person—this lining I speak of is full of little blood vessels, and the way to make a *real cure* is by gentle and steady means to recuperate the whole system—this will tell upon the blood, upon the blood vessels, and so finally & effectually upon all this coating I speak of that lines the throat &c. But as it is a long time before this vital lining membrane (*very important*) is injured, so it is a long time before it can be made all healthy & right again—but Andrew is young & strong enough and good constitution for basis—& of course by regular diet, care, (& *nary*

78. See 25.

79. Charles W. LeGendre (1830–1899). WW was unkind to this soldier who was born in France and educated at the University of Paris. LeGendre helped to recruit the Fifty-first New York Volunteer Infantry. He was severely wounded at New Bern, N. C., on March 14, 1862, as George observed in his letter of March 16–18 to his mother (Trent). LeGendre was appointed lieutenant colonel on September 20, 1862, and later succeeded Edward Ferrero (see 25) and Robert B. Potter (see 51) as commanding officer of the Fifty-first Regiment. During the second battle of the Wilderness, May 6, 1864, he lost his left eye and the bridge of his nose, and was honorably discharged on October 4 of the same year. See WW's account of LeGendre's hospitalization in 126.

80. On February 12, Jeff informed WW that "Andrew had been discharged from the [navy] yard. Tis too bad but I presume it is on account of his not being there much of the time" (Feinberg). This was but the first of the disasters that befell Andrew in 1863. On April 3, Jeff noted that Andrew's health was poor, and that the doctor had

whiskey under any circumstances) I am sure he would not only get over that trouble, but be as well & strong as he ever was in his life. Mother, you tell him I sent him my love, and Nancy the same, and the dear little boys the same. The next time you or Mat goes down there you take this & show him.

Mat, I am quite glad to hear that you are not hurried & fretted with work from New York this spring—I am sure I should think sis & housekeeping &c would be enough to attend to. I was real amused with sis's remarks, and all that was in the letter about her. You must none of you notice her smartness, nor criticisms, before her, nor encourage her to spread herself nor be critical, as it is not good to encourage a child to be too sharp—and I hope sissy is going to be a splendid specimen of good animal health—for the few years to come I should think more of that than any thing—that is the foundation of all, (righteousness included)—as to her mental vivacity & growth, they are plenty enough of themselves, and will get along quite fast enough of themselves, plenty fast enough—don't stimulate them at all—dear little creature, how I should like to see her this minute—Jeff must not make his lessons to her in music any ways strong or frequent on any account—two lessons a week, of ten minutes each, is enough—But then I dare say Jeff will think of all these things, just the same as I am saying.[81]

Jeff writes he wonders if I am as well and hearty, and I suppose he means as much of a beauty as ever—whether I look the same[82]—well, not only as much, but more so—I believe I weigh about 200 and as to my face, (so scarlet,) and my beard and neck, they are terrible to behold—I fancy the reason I am able to do some good in the hospitals, among the poor languishing & wounded boys, is that I am so large and well—indeed like a great wild buffalo, with much hair—many of the soldiers are from the west, and far north—and they take to a man that has not the bleached shiny & shaved cut of the cities and the east. I spent three to four hours yesterday in Armory Hospital—One of my particular boys there was dying,[83] pneumonia—he wanted me to stop with him awhile—he could not

advised him to stop drinking and "to work out-doors" (Feinberg).

81. On April 11, Jeff, like a typical father, boasted of Mannahatta's verbal ability: "Yesterday one of the Hearkness children was in our rooms and they were talking about rolling their hoops, one told sis—4½ yrs old—that she had rolled her hoop down the 'teet'; sis says 'I rolled mine down *the street*, thats the way to say it'" (Feinberg). On April 6(?), Jeff wrote: "Every day I give her a little exercise in singing, two or three notes only. I think she could be made a fine musician and am going to try it" (Feinberg).

82. On April 6(?), Jeff said: "Walt, how I should like to see you, do you look the same as ever or has the immense number of unfortunate and heart-working cases given you an sober and melancholy look" (Feinberg). WW always endeavored to allay Jeff's fears.

83. Possibly "M. de F.," of Connecticut, mentioned in *Specimen Days* (CW, IV, 44). WW spent most of his time in Armory Square Hospital because, he wrote on June 30, "it contains by far the worst cases."

articulate—but the look of his eyes, and the holding on of his hand, was deeply affecting. His case is a relapse—eight days ago, he had recovered, was up, was perhaps a little careless—at any rate took cold, was taken down again and has sunk rapidly. He has no friends or relatives here—Yesterday he labored & panted so for breath, it was terrible—he is a young man from New England, from the country—I expect to see his cot vacated this afternoon or evening, as I shall go down then. Mother, if you or Mat was here a couple of days, you would cry your eyes out. I find I have to restrain myself and keep my composure—I succeed pretty well. Good bye, dearest mother.

Walt.

Jeff, Capt. Mullen[84] remains here yet for some time. He is bringing out his Report. I shall try to send you a copy. Give my best respects to Dr. Ruggles.[85]

Mother, my last letter home was a week ago to-day—We are having a dark rainy day here—it is now ½ past 3—I have been in my room all day, so far—shall have dinner in ½ an hour, and then down to Armory.

43. *To Thomas P. Sawyer* [*4.21.1863*]

ENDORSED (in unknown hand): "21 April 1863."
DRAFT LETTER.

Tom,[86] I thought I would write you a few words, and take chances of its getting to you—though there is great excitement now about the Army of the Potomac,[87] no passes allowed, mails held over, &c. &c.—still I thought I would write, and take chances.

84. See 41.

85. Edward Ruggles (1817?–1867) was a Brooklyn physician and friend of the Whitman family. Jeff referred to him frequently in his letters. Toward the end of his life, Ruggles virtually abandoned his practice in order to paint cabinet pictures called "Ruggles Gems." See *The Round Table*, v (1867), 173. See also 226.

86. This, apparently the first extant letter WW addressed to a soldier, is a revealing—and in many respects a pathetic—document. For WW was destined to write many others like it, and with the same results. Always WW was both an anxious father-figure and an ardent comrade desirous of establishing permanent ties with soldiers whom he had known and nursed in Washington hospitals. Like some of the others, Sawyer was evidently perplexed, possibly frightened, by WW's extravagant protestations of enduring friendship.

The reply to WW's letter, dated April 26, though it is signed "Thos. B. Sawyer," is not in Sawyer's holograph, as WW noted in 52. The author of the letter addressed WW as "Dear Brother," and continued: "I fully reciprocate your friendship as expressed in your letter and it will afford me great pleasure to meet you after the war will have terminated or sooner if circumstances will permit" (Berg). However, on April 12, Sawyer himself had written to Brown: "I want you to give my love to Walter Whitman and tell him I am very sorry that I could not live up to my Prommice because I came away so soon that it sliped my mind and I am very sorry for it, tell him that I shall write to him my self in a few days, give him my love and best wishes for ever" (Berg). Though WW wrote several times during 1863, Sawyer did not reply until January 21, 1864:

There is nothing very special here about Washington—they seem to be shoving troops off from here now all the time, in small or large bodies—the convalescents are doing guard duty &c in the Hospitals—even the old regiments doing patrol, & provost, are sent off. So I suppose something is up. Tom, I was at Armory last evening, saw Lewy Brown,[88] sat with him a good while, he was very cheerful, told me how he laid out to do, when he got well enough to go from hospital, (which he expects soon), says he intends to go home to Maryland, go to school, and learn to write better, and learn a little bookkeeping, &c.—so that he can be fit for some light employment. Lew is so good, so affectionate—when I came away, he reached up his face, I put my arm around him, and we gave each other a long kiss, half a minute long. We talked about you while I was there. I saw Hiram[89] but did not speak to him. He lay pale and pretty sick, sound asleep. I could not help stopping before I came away, and looking at him—it was pitiful to see him, so pale, sound asleep—Poor Hiram—he is a good boy—he gets no better. Johnny Mahay[90] does not get any better, in Ward E. He is going to have an operation performed on him by Dr. Bliss.[91] Tom, I do not know who you was most intimate with in the Hospital, or I would write you about them.

As to me, there is nothing new with me, or my affairs. I manage to pay my way here in Washington, what I make writing letters for the New York papers, &c. When I stopped here, last January, on my return from Falmouth, I thought I would stop only a few days, before returning to New York, and see if I could not get some berth, clerkship or something—but I have not pushed strong enough—have not got anything—and I don't know as I could be satisfied with the life of a clerk in the departments

"Dear Brother, I hardly know what to say to you in this letter for it is my first one to you. . . . I hope you will forgive me and in the future I will do better and I hope we may meet again in this world" (Berg).

87. The Army of the Potomac was preparing for the assault at Chancellorsville.

88. See 60.

89. Hiram Sholes lay next to Brown in Armory Square Hospital, according to Sholes's letter to WW on May 24, 1867 (Feinberg); see also 238. Glicksberg (155) records: "Hiram Scholis—bed 3—Ward E.—26th N. York—wants some pickles—a bottle of pickles."

90. John Mahay, Hundred and First New York, was wounded in the bladder at second Bull Run, August 29, 1862. On February 4, in *Specimen Days* (CW, IV, 46), WW notes that Mahay, despite his pain, "was of good heart" and "was delighted with a stick of horehound candy I gave him." He is referred to as in poor health in 60 and 67. Evidently he died later in the year. In describing his death (CW, IV, 98–99), WW writes: "Poor Mahay, a mere boy in age, but old in misfortune." See also Glicksberg, 149.

91. D. Willard Bliss (1825–1889) was a surgeon with the Third Michigan Infantry, and afterward in charge of Armory Square Hospital. See John Homer Bliss, *Genealogy of the Bliss Family in America* (1881), 545. He practiced medicine in Washington after the war; see 238. When a pension for WW was proposed in the House of Representatives in 1887, Dr. Bliss was quoted: "I am of opinion that no one person who assisted in the hospitals during the war accomplished so much good to the soldiers and for the Government as Mr. Whitman" (Donaldson, 169).

anyhow. So I have hung along here ever since. I guess I enjoy a kind of vagabond life any how. I go around some, nights, when the spirit moves me, sometimes to the gay places, just to see the sights. Tom, I wish you was here. Somehow I don't find the comrade that suits me to a dot—and I won't have any other, not for good.

Well, Tom, the war news is not lovely, is it? We feel disappointed here about Charleston[92]—I felt as blue about it as anybody. I was so in hopes they would take the conceit out of that gassy city. It seems to me always as if Charleston has done the biggest business of blowing & mischief, on a small capital of industry or manliness, of any city the world ever knew. But for all our bad success at Charleston, and even if we fail for a while elsewhere, I believe this Union will conquer in the end, as sure as there's a God in heaven. This country can't be broken up by Jeff Davis, & all his damned crew. Tom, I sometimes feel as if I didn't want to live—life would have no charm for me, if this country should fail after all, and be reduced to take a third rate position, to be domineered over by England & France & the haughty nations of Europe &c and we unable to help ourselves. But I have no thought that will ever be, this country I hope would spend her last drop of blood, and last dollar, rather than submit to such humiliation.

O I hope Hooker[93] will have good success in his plans, whatever they may be. We have been foiled so often in our plans, it seems as though it was too much. And our noble Army of the Potomac, so brave, so capable, so full of good men, I really believe they are this day the best in the world. God grant Hooker may have success, and his brave boys may at last achieve the victory they deserve. O how much I think about them though. I suppose that does no good. Tom, you tell the boys of your company there is an old pirate up in Washington, with the white wool growing all down his neck—an old comrade who thinks about you & them every day, for all he don't know them, and will probably never see them, but thinks about them as comrades & younger brothers of his, just the same.[94]

These lines may never reach you, as it is talked here that the Army of the Potomac is in for a real fighting march, at last, may be something desperate, it may continue some time when it once begins. Tom, I thought I would write you a few words, hoping they might reach you. Dear com-

92. Admiral Samuel F. du Pont was severely defeated at Charleston, on April 7, in the worst naval loss of the Civil War.

93. Joseph Hooker (1814–1879) replaced Burnside as commanding general of the Army of the Potomac on January 26, 1863. He was defeated at Chancellorsville on May 2–4, and was succeeded by Meade on June 28, a few days before the battle of Gettysburg.

94. At this point WW deleted the following sentence: "My old mother, in Brooklyn,

rade, you must not forget me, for I never shall you. My love you have in life or death forever. I don't know how you feel about it, but it is the wish of my heart to have your friendship, and also that if you should come safe out of this war, we should come together again in some place where we could make our living, and be true comrades and never be separated while life lasts—and take Lew Brown too, and never separate from him. Or if things are not so to be—if you get these lines, my dear, darling comrade, and any thing should go wrong, so that we do not meet again, here on earth, it seems to me, (the way I feel now,) that my soul could never be entirely happy, even in the world to come, without you, dear comrade.[95] And if it is God's will, I hope we shall yet meet, as I say, if you feel as I do about it—and if [it] is destined that we shall not, you have my love none the less, whatever should keep you from me, no matter how many years. God bless you, Tom, and preserve you through the perils of the fight.

Good bye, my darling comrade, my dear darling brother, for so I will call you, and wish you to call me the same.

44. *To Thomas P. Sawyer* [*4.26. 1863*]

ENDORSED (in unknown hand): "26 April '63."
DRAFT LETTER.

Dear comrade,

I have not heard from you for some time, Lewy Brown has received two letters from you, & Walter[96] in Ward E has received one three weeks ago. I wrote you a letter about a week ago, which I hope you have received. I was sorry you did not come up to my room to get the shirt & other things you promised to accept from me and take when you went away. I got them all ready, a good strong blue shirt, a pair of drawers & socks, and it would have been a satisfaction to me if you had accepted them. I should have often thought now Tom may be wearing around his body something from *me*, & that it might contribute to your comfort, down there in camp on picket, or sleeping in your tent.

Lewy Brown and Hiram are about the same. I saw Lewy & sat with

New York, when she sees the troops marching away, or returning, always begins to cry."

95. The following sentence, corrected several times, was omitted: "What I have written is pretty strong talk, I suppose, but I mean exactly what I say."

96. To Brown, on April 12, Sawyer wrote that he had "received a short letter from Walter yesterday" (Berg). I have not identified Walter; perhaps he was an orderly in Armory Square Hospital. For Brown, see 60.

him last evening. I go to see him almost every evening. He sets up a little in the chair, during the middle of the day—his foot is doing pretty well. There is quite a time at Armory about Dr. Bliss[97]—some say he is under arrest for defrauding the government. There is a new surgeon in charge—I have not seen him. In Ward K there is a new surgeon, Dr. Rose.[98] There is quite a change, with men & doctors, going and coming.

Well, Tom, how did you stand the gay old rain storm of Thursday & Friday last?[99] It rained here enough to wet hell itself, and swamp the fires. But yesterday & to-day here have been fine. The talk here previously was all about Hooker's advance—we expected a big fight, on the jump—but of course the storm has laid an injunction on that for some days.

Yet I suppose Hooker must move soon, & that there will be fighting and lots of marches and skirmishes, &c before the summer is through. O my dear comrade & brother, I hope it will prove your good luck to come safe through all the engagements & marches of this war, & that we shall meet again, not to part. I hope this letter will find you in good health & spirits.

Tom, I will not write a long yarn at present. I guess I have not made out much of a letter, anyhow at present, but I will let it go, whatever it is, hoping it may please you, coming from old wooly-neck, who loves you. You must let that make up for all deficiencies now and to come. Not a day passes, nor a night but I think of you. Now, my dearest comrade, I will bid you *so long*, & hope God will put it in your heart to bear toward me a little at least of the feeling I have about you. If it is only a quarter as much I shall be satisfied.

Your faithful friend & brother,

Walt

Tom, it is now about 9 o'clock, a fine moonlight night. I am going to close this up, and then scud out for a walk to the post office. Good by again, & God bless you, dear brother.

97. WW noted—in 52—that Bliss was later confined to Old Capitol Prison. The only reference I have found to Bliss's imprisonment appears in court testimony quoted by Lafayette C. Baker, *History of the United States Secret Service* (1867), 624.

98. Perhaps George S. Rose, assistant surgeon, though he was reported to have entered military service on September 24, 1863. WW deleted the following comment: "He is a sharp little fellow."

99. WW excised the next sentence: "I thought about you many times."

1. Jeff wrote to WW on April 25: "Mother had a little attack of her rheumatism yesterday and to-day and I am somewhat afraid that she will have more of it. She has been wonderful foolish in cleaning house as she calls it and has overworked herself. I dont think that she ought to do so, and so I tell her but she always answeres that it's got to be done and that there is no one but her to do it, &c" (Feinberg).

45. *To Louisa Van Velsor Whitman*

Washington, April 28th | 1863.

Dearest mother,

A letter from Jeff came this morning[1]—mother, I was sorry to hear you had a return of your rheumatism—I do hope you will favor yourself more, it depends so much on that—& rheumatism is so obstinate, when it gets hold of one.

Mother, you rec'd a letter from me, sent last Wednesday, 22d.[2] of course, with a small quantity of shinplasters. Next time you or Jeff writes, I wish you would tell me whether the letters come pretty regularly, *the next morning after I write them*—this now ought to reach you Wednesday forenoon, April 29th. Mother, did a Mr. Howell call on you?—he was here last week to see about his boy, died a long while ago in hospital in Yorktown. He works in the Navy Yard—knows Andrew. You will see about him, (the boy,) in a letter I sent yesterday to the Eagle—it ought to appear to-day or to-morrow.[3]

Jeff, I wish you would take 10 cts I send in this letter & get me ten copies of the Eagle with it in—put in 5 more of my pictures, (the big ones in last edition "Leaves"), & a couple of the photographs carte visites (the smaller ones,) & send me to the same direction as before. Jeff, I wish you would do up the parcel same as before, it came very well. I will send an Eagle to Han and George. The stamps & 10 cts. are for Jeff, for the papers, & postage.

I have written to Han, & sent her George's last two letters from Kentucky, one I got last week from Mount Sterling. I write to George, & send him papers. Sam Beatty[4] is here in Washington again, I saw him, & he said he would write to George. Mother, I have not got any new clothes yet, but shall very soon I hope. People are more rough and free & easy drest than your way. Then it is dusty or muddy most of the time here.

Mother dear, I hope you have comfortable times—at least as com-

2. This letter is not known.

3. Apparently this letter did not appear in the Brooklyn *Eagle*, as WW acknowledged in 51. He probably submitted it to the Brooklyn *Daily Union*, in which appeared a letter, dated September 21 and printed on September 22, describing "Benjamin D. Howell, Company D, 87th New York, Aged 18." The son of Henry D. Howell, who was employed, like Andrew, in the Navy Yard, died at Yorktown in June, 1862. Howell went to Washington in the following spring "to see if he could get any certainty about the boy"; see *UPP*, II, 28–29, and Glicksberg, 133 and *n*.

4. Samuel A. Beatty lived at 40 Prince Street, Brooklyn. According to the Directories of 1850–1851 and 1856–1857 he was a shoemaker; later he was listed as a "gas-fitter" or "gas regulator." His name did not appear in the Directory of 1865–1866.

fortable as the law allows—I am so glad you are not going to have the trouble of moving this 1st of May. How are the Browns?[5] Tell Will I should like to see him first rate—if he was here, attached to the suite of some big officer, or something of that kind, he would have a good time & do well. I see lots of young fellows not half as capable & trustworthy as he, coming & going, in Washington, in such positions. The big generals & head men, all through the armies, & provosts &c like to have a squad of such smart nimble young men around them. Give my respects to Mr. & Mrs. Brown.

Tell Jeff I am going to write to Mr. Lane, either to-day or to-morrow.[6] Jeff asks me if I go to hospitals as much as ever. If my letters home don't show it, you don't get 'em. I feel sorry sometimes after I have sent them, I have said so much about hospitals, & so mournful. O mother, the young man in Armory Square, Dennis Barrett,[7] in the 169th N. Y., I mentioned before, is probably going to get up after all—he is like one saved from the grave. Saturday last I saw him & talked with him & gave him something to eat, & he was much better—it is the most unexpected recovery I have yet seen.

Mother, I see Jeff says in the letter you don't hear from me very often —I will write oftener especially to Jeff. Dear brother, I hope you are getting along good & in good spirits. You must not mind the failure of the sewer bills, &c. &c.[8] It don't seem to me it makes so much difference about worldly successes (beyond just enough to eat & drink, and shelter, in the moderatest limits) any more, since the last four months of my life especially, & that merely to *live*, & have one fair meal a day, is *enough*—but then you have a family, & that makes a difference.

Matty, I send you my best love, dear sister—how I wish I could be with you one or two good days. Mat, do you remember the good time we had that awful stormy night we went to the opera, New York, & had the front seat, & heard the handsome-mouthed Guerrabella?[9] And then the good oyster supper at Fulton Market—("pewter them ales"—) O, Mat, I hope & trust we shall have such times again.

5. See 19. The son, William A. Brown, was listed in the Directory of 1865–1866 as a bookkeeper.

6. According to Lane's letter of April 30 (LC), WW wrote to him on the twenty-ninth. Lane promised to "make an effort among my friends here to keep you supplied with funds all summer."

7. Barrett (or Barret), Hundred and Sixty-ninth New York Volunteers. On April 18 WW wrote to him; see Glicksberg, 132. (The editors of the *Complete Works* assume, doubtfully, that Barrett is referred to in 42. It seems more likely that WW spoke for the first time of Barrett in the apparently lost letter of April 22; see Glicksberg, 132.)

8. On April 25, Jeff complained that "We dont hear from you as often as we used to," and described the defeat of a bill in the state legislature which would have empowered the Brooklyn Sewer Commission to construct a sewer. Since Jeff was to have

Tell Andrew he must remember what I wrote about the throat, &c. I am sure he will get all right before long, & recover his voice. Give him my love—& tell Mannahatta her Uncle Walt is living now among the sick soldiers. Jeff, look out for the Eagles, & send the portraits. Dearest mother, I must bid you & all for the present good bye.

Walt.

46. *To Louisa Van Velsor Whitman*

Washington | Tuesday May 5th '63.

Dearest Mother,

Your letter came safe, and was very welcome, & always will be—Mother, I am sorry about your rheumatism—If it still continues, I think it would be well for me to write a line to Mrs. Piercy,[10] & get Jeff to stop with it, so that you could take the baths again, as I am sure they are very beneficial—Dear mother, you write me, or Jeff must in the next letter, how you are getting along, whether it is any better, or worse—I want to know.

Mother, about George's fund in the bank, I hope by all means you can scratch along so as to leave $250 there—I am so anxious that our family should have a little ranch, even if it is the meanest kind, off somewhere that you can call your own, & that would do for Ed, &c.—it might be a real dependence, & comfort—and may-be for George as much as any one. I mean to come home one of these days, and get the acre or ½ acre somewhere out in some by-place on Long Island, & build it, you see if I dont. About Hannah,[11] dear mother, I hardly know what advice to give you—from what I know at present, I cant tell what course to pursue. I want Han to come home, from the bottom of my heart. Then there are other thoughts & considerations that come up. Dear mother, I cannot advise, but shall acquiesce in any thing that is settled upon, & try to help.

The condition of things here in the Hospitals is getting pretty bad—the wounded from the battles around Fredericksburgh are coming up in

been in charge of the project, he had "had quite a disappointment in a small way" (Feinberg).

9. Genevra Guerrabella, who was a New York girl named Genevieve Ward, made her operatic debut in Paris in 1859. Her acting was unusually effective (for the operatic stage) in such roles as Violetta, Leonora, and Elvira. She evidently appeared for the first time in New York on November 10, 1862.

10. Henry R. Piercy operated sulphur baths at 5 Willoughby Avenue, Brooklyn.

11. Jeff wrote of Hannah on May 2: "We have not heard from Han since the letter that I sent you. I suppose she is about the same. Mother speaks of sending for her &c and then says she hardly knows what to do. Tis rather a puzzling question I confess. I hope however that she will come home herself before long. It certainly is a great relief not to be cursed with letters from Heyde every few days" (Feinberg).

large numbers.[12] It is very sad to see them. I have written to Mr. Lane, asking him to get his friends to forward me what they think proper—but somehow I feel delicate about sending such requests, after all.[13]

I have almost made up my mind to do what I can personally, & not seek assistance from others.

Dear Mother, I have not received any letter from George. I write to him & send papers to Winchester. Mother, while I have been writing this, a very large number of southern prisoners, I should think 1000 at least, has past up Pennsylvania avenue, under a strong guard. I went out in the street, close to them, to look at them. Poor fellows, many of them mere lads—it brought the tears, they seemed our own flesh & blood too, some wounded, *all* miserable in clothing, all in dirt & tatters—many of them fine young men. Mother, I cannot tell you how I feel to see these prisoners marched [*incomplete*]

47. *To Moses Lane* [*5.11. 1863*]

ENDORSED (by WW): "letter to | Moses Lane | May 11th 1863." DRAFT LETTER.

Dear friend,[14]

Your letters of the 6th & 7 have arrived, with timely contributions from D. L. Northrup, John H. Rhodes, Thos. Cotrel, Nicholas Wyckoff, & Thomas Sullivan,[15] for my poor men here in hospital. With these, as with other funds, I aid all I can soldiers from all the states. Most heartily do I thank you, dear friend, for your kind exertions—& those gentlemen above named—it is a work of God's charity, never cases more deserving of aid, never more heart-rending cases, than these now coming up in one long bloody string from Chancellorsville and Fredericksburgh battles, six or seven hundred every day without intermission. We have already over 3000 arrived here in hospital from Hooker's late battles. I work somewhere among them every day or in the evening. It is not so exhausting as one might think—the endurance & spirit are supplied. My health, thank God, was never better—I feel strong & elastic—an obstinate cold & deafness

12. In his diary WW noted on May 4: "Tonight the wounded begin to arrive from Hooker's command"; on May 6: "Very bad for Hooker"; and on May 7: "Last night we heard of Hooker recrossing the Rappahannock—news very distressing" (Glicksberg, 134–135). The New York *Tribune* printed lengthy lists of the wounded on May 9 and 11.

13. This letter to Lane is not known. WW wrote again on May 11. Lane had sent dollar contributions from six individuals on May 2 (LC).

14. See 31.

15. Daniel L. Northrup was a member of the Brooklyn Water Commission; Rhodes, a water purveyor in Brooklyn; Cotrel, a bookkeeper or accountant; Wyckoff, the president of the First National Bank of Brooklyn. Sullivan I have been unable to identify.

some weeks, seems to be broken up at last. Yesterday I spent nearly all day at Armory Square Hospital. This forenoon I take an intermission, & go again at dusk.

You there north must not be so disheartened about Hooker's return to this side of the Rappahannock and supposed failure.[16] The blow struck at Lee & the rebel sway in Virginia, & generally at Richmond & Jeff Davis, by this short but tremendous little campaign, of 2d, 3d, 4th & 5th inst's, is in my judgment the heaviest and most staggering they have yet got from us, & has not only hit them nearer where they live than all Maclellan ever did, but all that has been levelled at Richmond during the war. I mean this deliberately. We have I know paid for it with thousands of dear noble lives, America's choicest blood, yet the late battles are not without something decisive to show for them. Hooker will resume operations forthwith—may be has resumed them. Do not be discouraged. I am not even here—here amid all this huge mess of traitors, loafers, hospitals, axe-grinders, & incompetencies & officials that goes by the name of Washington. I myself yet believe in Hooker & the A[rmy] of P[otomac]—yet say he is a good man.

Jeff writes me about your boy Horace Tarr,[17] 20th Connecticut. I will endeavor to make immediate inquiry about him—there are some of the 20th Conn. here in hospital—will write you forthwith, if I get any information.

I have written to Nicholas Wyckoff,[18] to your care, a hospital &c. letter.

Love & thanks to you, dear friend, & to those who are aiding my boys.

48. *To Louisa Van Velsor Whitman*

Washington, Wednesday forenoon, | May 13th 1863.

Dearest Mother,

I am late with my letter this week—my poor, poor boys occupy my time very much—I go every day, & sometimes nights—I believe I mentioned a young man in Ward F, Armory Square, with a bad wound in the leg, very agonizing, had to have it propt up, & an attendant all the while

16. On May 8, the New York *Times* reported that Hooker was rumored to have retired to the northern side of the Rappahannock River. It would seem as though WW were anticipating Jeff's letter of May 9: "Of course we all feel pretty well down-hearted at the news but then we try to look on it in the most favorable light. God only knows what will be the next. I had certainly made up my mind that we should meet with partial success certainly, but it seems otherwise" (Feinberg).

17. Jeff wrote on May 9 (Feinberg) that Lane was concerned about the whereabouts of his nephew Horace G. Tarr, a lanquet-major. On July 8, Jeff informed his brother that "Lane is again very anxious about his boy" (Feinberg).

18. But see 49.

dripping water on night & day—I was in hopes at one time he would get through with it, but a few days ago he took a sudden bad turn, & died about 3 o'clock the same afternoon—it was horrible—he was of good family (handsome, intelligent man, about 26, married) his name was John Elliott[19] of Cumberland Valley, Bedford Co., Penn., belonged to 2d Pennsylvania Cavalry. I felt very bad about it—I have wrote to his father—have not rec'd any answer yet—no friend nor any of his folks was here & have not been here nor sent, probably didnt know of it at all. The surgeons put off amputating the leg, he was so exhausted, but at last it was imperatively necessary to amputate—mother, I am shocked to tell you, that he never came alive off the amputating table—he died under the operation—it was what I had dreaded & anticipated—poor young man, he suffered much, very *very* much, for many days & bore it so patiently—so it was a release to him—Mother, such things are awful—not a soul here he knew or cared about, except me—yet the surgeons & nurses were good to him—I think all was done for him that could be—there was no help but to take off the leg—he was under chloroform—they tried their best to bring him to—three long hours were spent, a strong smelling bottle held under his nostrils, with other means, three hours. Mother, how contemptible all the usual little worldly prides & vanities & striving after appearances, seems in the midst of such scenes as these—such tragedies of soul & body. To see such things & not be able to help them is awful—I feel almost ashamed of being so well & whole.

Dear mother, I have not heard from George himself—but I got a letter from Fred McReady,[20] a young Brooklyn man in 51st—he is intimate with George, said he was well & hearty—I got the letter about five days ago—I wrote to George four days since, directed to Winchester, Kentucky. I got a letter from a friend[21] in Nashville, Tenn., yesterday, he told me the 9th Army Corps was ordered to move to Murfreesboro, Tenn. I don't know whether this is so or not. I send papers to George almost every day. So far, I think it was fortunate the 51st was moved west, & I hope it will prove to continue so. Mother, it is all a lottery, this war, no one knows what will come up next.

Mother, I rec'd Jeff's letter of May 9th, it was welcome, as all Jeff's

19. WW's notations in his diary add interesting details to this account: "Did he shoot himself. Operated on chloroform—Leg taken off. Dies under operation" (Glicksberg, 149).

20. While WW was with George after the battle of Fredericksburg in 1862, he noted in his diary that, among others, Fred B. McReady, then an orderly sergeant in George's regiment, "used me well" (Glicksberg, 70). McReady sent WW a lengthy account of the activities of the Fifty-first Regiment from February 9 to April 29 (Berg). In the Brooklyn *Daily Union* of September 22, WW noted: "Fred. McReady I know to be as good a man as the war has received out of Brooklyn City" (*UPP*, II, 29).

letters are, & all others from home. Jeff says you do not hear from me at home but seldom—Mother, I write once a week to *you* regular—but I will write soon to Jeff a good long letter—I have wanted to for some time, but have been much occupied. Dear brother, I wish you to say to Probasco & all the other young men on the Works, I send them my love & best thanks —never any thing came more acceptable than the little fund they forwarded me, the last week, through Mr. Lane[22]—Our wounded, from Hooker's battles, are worse wounded & more of them, than any battle of the war & indeed any I may say of modern times (we have lost from 15,000 to 20,000)—besides, the weather has been very hot here, very bad for new wounds. Yet as Jeff writes so downhearted I must tell him the rebellion has lost worse & more than we have—the more I find out about it, the more I think they, the confederates, have rec'd an irreparable harm & loss in Virginia. I should not be surprised to see them (either voluntarily or by force) leaving Virginia, before many weeks. I don't see how on earth they can stay there—I think Hooker is already reaching after them again—I myself do not give up Hooker yet—

Dear mother, I should like to hear from Han, poor Han—I send my best love to Sister Mat & all. Good bye, dearest mother.

Walt.

49. *To Nicholas Wyckoff or Daniel L. Northrup*[23]

[*5.14. 1863*]

ENDORSED (by WW): "sent May 14 | letter to | Nicholas Wyckoff | or Northrup." DRAFT LETTER.

I adapt myself to each case, & to [*indecipherable*][24]—some need to be humored, some are rather out of their head—some merely want me to sit down [near] them, & hold them by the hand—one will want a letter written to mother or father, (yesterd[ay] I wrote over a dozen letters)—some like to have me feed them (wounded perhaps in shoulder or wrist) perhaps a few bits of my peaches—some want a cooling drink, (I have some very nice syrups from raspberries &c.)—others want writing paper,

21. Probably John Barker; see 53 and 79. However, another soldier, Will W. Wallace, wrote on July 1 from Nashville, Tenn.: "I wrote to you some time since and have received no reply" (Berg).

22. See 46.

23. See 47. Since the two men had sent contributions to WW through Lane, he probably wrote to both men. The paragraph reproduced is the type of thing WW composed while he sat in the hospital and later inserted into a letter to a friend or donor.

24. The manuscript is water-stained and mutilated in the upper right-hand corner.

envelopes, a stamp, &c.—I could fill a sheet with one day's items—I often go, just at dark, sometimes stay nearly all night—I like to go just before supper, carrying a pot or jar of something good & go around with a spoon distributing a little here and there. Yet after all this succoring of the stomach (which is of course most welcome & indispensable) I should say that I believe my profoundest help to these sick & dying men is probably the soothing invigoration I steadily bear in mind, to infuse in them through affection, cheering love, & the like, between them & me. It has saved more than one life. There is a strange influence here. I have formed attachments here in hospital, that I shall keep to my dying day, & they will the same, without doubt.

50. *To Louisa Van Velsor Whitman*

Washington, Tuesday | forenoon, May 19th | 1863.

Dearest mother,

I received a letter from Heyde this morning, one of the usual sort, about as interesting as a dose of salts. Says Han has not been able to stand erect for the past five months—the doctor told her lately that she might possibly recover in one year if she was careful—then says he thinks, & he don't think, & has taken a little place, & Han has a girl to wait on her, &c. &c. All amounts to nothing more than we knew before, & only serves to make one feel almost heart-sick about Han, & the awful snarl in which we are all fixed about it all, & what to do. I wrote to Han yesterday, (before I received this letter of Heyde's), I wrote a short letter of my own, & sent her George's letter to you, (I cut out what was said about the money, as I did not wish Heyde to see it.)[25]

I also sent George a letter yesterday—have not got any letter myself from Georgy, but have sent him quite a good many & papers—Mother, what a tramp the 51st has had—they only need now to go to California, & they will finish the job complete—

O mother, how welcome the shirts were—I was putting off, & putting off, to get some new ones, I could not find any one to do them as I wear them, & it would have cost such a price—& so my old ones had got to be, when they come back from the wash I had to laugh, they were a lot of rags, held together with starch—I have a very nice old black aunty for a washwoman, but she bears down pretty hard I guess when she irons them, & they showed something like the poor old city of Fredericksburgh

25. The material up to this point was omitted in earlier printings of this letter. Perhaps WW's executors considered the reference to Heyde unusually offensive. Note also the omissions in 69 and 70.

26. According to Jeff's letter of May 27, Andrew planned to go to New Bern,

does, since Burnside bombarded it—Well, mother, when the bundle came, I was so glad—& the coats too, worn as they are, they come in very handy —& the cake, dear mother, I am almost like the boy that put it under his pillow—& woke up in the night & eat some—I carried a good chunk to a young man wounded, I think a good deal of, & it did him so much good —it is dry, but all the better, as he eat it with tea & it relished—I eat a piece with him & drinked some tea, out of his cup, as I sat by the side of his cot—Mother, I have neglected I think what I ought to have told you two or three weeks ago, that is that I had to discard my old clothes, somewhat because they were too thick & more still because they were worse gone in than any I ever yet wore I think in my life, especially the trowsers—wearing my big boots had caused the inside of the legs just above the knee to wear two beautiful round holes right through cloth & partly through the lining, producing a novel effect, which was not necessary, as I produce a sufficient sensation without—then they were desperately faded—I have a nice plain suit, of a dark wine color, looks very well, & feels good, single breasted sack coat with breast pockets &c. & vest & pants same as what I always wear, (pants pretty full,) so upon the whole all looks unusually good for me, my hat is very good yet, boots ditto, have a new necktie, nice shirts, you can imagine I cut quite a swell—I have not trimmed my beard since I left home, but it is not grown much longer, only perhaps a little bushier—I keep about as stout as ever, & the past five or six days I have felt wonderful well, indeed never did I feel better—about ten or twelve days ago, we had a short spell of very warm weather here, but for about six days now it has been delightful, just warm enough.

I generally go to the hospitals from 12 to 4—& then again from 6 to 9—some days I only go either in the middle of the day, or evening, not both—& then when I feel somewhat opprest, I skip over a day, or make perhaps a light call only, as I have received several cautions from the doctors, who tell me that one must beware of continuing too steady & long in the air & influences of the hospitals—I find the caution a wise one.

Mother, you or Jeff must write me what Andrew does about going to North Carolina[26]—I should think it might have a beneficial effect upon his throat.

I wrote Jeff quite a long letter Sunday[27]—Jeff must write to me whenever he can, I like dearly to have them, & whenever you feel like it you too, dear mother—tell sis her uncle Walt will come back one of these days

N. C., with a friend: "Andrew is going to take charge of the building of some fortifications I believe . . . I think he would get well easy enough if he took better care of himself and did not drink so much" (Feinberg).

27. This letter is not extant.

from the sick soldiers & take her out on Fort Greene again—Mother, I received a letter yesterday from John Elliott's[28] father, in Bedford co[unty,] Pennsylvania, (the young man I told you about, who died under the operation)—it was very sad, it was the first he knew about it—I don't know whether I told you of Dennis Barnett,[29] pneumonia, three weeks since, had got well enough to be sent home—

Dearest mother, I hope you will take things as easy as possible & try to keep a good heart—Matty, my dear sister, I have to inform you that I was treated to a splendid dish of ice cream Sunday night, I wished you was with me to have another—I send you my love, dear sister. Mother, I hope by all means it will be possible to keep the money whole, to get some ranch next spring, if not before, I mean to come home & build it.[30] Good bye for the present, dear mother.

Walt

51. *To Louisa Van Velsor Whitman*

Washington, Tuesday forenoon, | May 26th 1863.

Dear Mother,

I got a long letter from George, dated near Lancaster, Kentucky, May 15th[31]—he seems to be well & in good spirits, says he gets some letters from me & papers too—At the time he wrote, the 51st was doing provost duty at Lancaster, but would not probably remain so very long—seem to be moving toward southeast Kentucky—had a good camp, & good times generally. LeGendre[32] is colonel—Gen. Ferrero[33] has left the service—Col. Potter[34] (now Brig. Gen.) is in Cincinnati—Capt. Sims[35] &c are all well—George describes Kentucky as a very fine country—says the people are about half & half, secesh & union. This is the longest letter I have yet rec'd from George. Did he write you one about the same time? Mother, I have

28. See 48.

29. WW wrote "Barnett," but spelled it "Barrett" in 45 and "Barret" in his hospital notes (Glicksberg, 132).

30. WW was again referring to the money George sent home to his mother; see 46.

31. This letter to WW and one to his mother on the following day are apparently lost. There is a letter from George to Jeff, dated May 15, in the Missouri Historical Society. On May 29, from "Heusonville" [Hustonville], Ky. (Trent; Gohdes and Silver, 156–158), George described the recent movements of his regiment.

32. See 42.

33. WW's or George's information about Ferrero (see 25) was incorrect; he did not leave the service at this time.

34. Robert Brown Potter (1829–1887) was a lawyer who enlisted as a private at the beginning of the war. He rose rapidly and became a lieutenant colonel on November 1, 1861, in George's regiment. On March 16–18, 1862, George described Potter's bravery in the battle at New Bern, N. C.: "I went up to him and asked him if he was struck, he said only with a spent ball that did not hurt him mutch, and he got up and went into the thickest of it again and did not give up untill the fighting was over which was an hour after I spoke to him, when he found a ball had struck him just above the hip

not rec'd any word from home in over a week—the last letter I had from Mr. Lane was about 12 days ago, sending me $10 for the soldiers, (5 from Mr. Kirkwood[36] & 5 from Conklin Brush.)[37]

Mother dear, I should like to hear from Martha, I wish Jeff would write me about it[38]—has Andrew gone? & how is your wrist & arm, mother—We have had some very hot weather here—I don't know what I should have done without the thin grey coat you sent—you don't know how good it does, & looks too—I wore it three days, & carried a fan & an umbrella, (quite a Japanee)—most every body here carries an umbrella, on acc't of the sun—yesterday & to-day however have been quite cool, east wind—Mother, the shirts were a real godsend, they do first rate, I like the fancy Marseilles collar & wristbands—

Mother, how are you getting along—I suppose just the same as ever—I suppose Jess & Ed are just the same as ever—when you write, you tell me all about every thing, & the Browns,[39] & the neighborhood generally. Mother, is George's trunk home & of no use, there? I wish I had it here, as I must have a trunk—but do not wish you to send it, until I send you word—I suppose my letter never appeared in the Eagle,[40] well I shall send them no more, as I think likely they hate to put in any thing which may celebrate me a little, even though it is just the thing they want for their paper & readers. They altered the other letter on that account, very meanly. I shall probably have letters in the N. Y. Times & perhaps other papers in about a week[41]—Mother, I have been pretty active in hospitals for the past two weeks, somewhere every day or night—I have written you so much about cases &c I will not write you any more, on that subject this time—O the sad, sad things I see, the noble young men with legs & arms taken off—the deaths—the sick weakness, sicker than death, that some endure, after amputations—(there is a great difference, some make little of it, others lie after it for days, just flickering alive, & O so deathly

and passed through his side" (Trent). WW described Potter's courage in the New York *Times*, October 29, 1864 (*UPP*, II, 38–39).

35. WW stayed in the tent of Samuel H. Sims (or Simms) when he visited George at Fredericksburg (Glicksberg, 69–70), and commended him in the Brooklyn *Daily Union* of September 22, 1863 (*UPP*, II, 29). According to the *New York State Muster Rolls*, Sims had recruited George for the Fifty-first Regiment. He was killed in the Petersburg mine explosion in 1864; see *CW*, IV, 134, and letter 143.

36. James P. Kirkwood was a New York engineer; he probably heard of WW's hospital work through Moses Lane. See WW's letter to him, 119.

37. Conklin Brush was president of the Mechanics' Bank, Brooklyn, according to the Directories of 1861–1862 and 1865–1866.

38. Martha was pregnant. Jeff wrote on May 27: "Mattie is well yet but how long she will continue so is a question, she is getting along first rate, she has a young girl to help her do the house work and is in the best of spirits" (Feinberg).

39. See 19.

40. See 45.

41. I have not been able to identify these "letters."

weak & sick)—I go this afternoon to Campbell Hospital, out a couple of miles.

Mother, I should like to have Jeff send me 20 of the large sized portraits & as many of the standing figure, do them up flat. I think every day about Martha. Mother, have you heard any further about Han? Good bye for the present, dearest mother.

Walt

52. *To Thomas P. Sawyer*

DRAFT LETTER.

Washington, May 27, 1863.

Dear brother,

I sit down to rattle off in haste a few lines to you. I do not know what is the reason I have been favored with nary a word from you, to let me know whether you are alive & well—that is, if you are so, which I pray to God you are. My thoughts are with you often enough, & I make reckoning when we shall one day be together again—yet how useless it is to make calculations for the future. Still a fellow will.

Tom, I wrote you one letter April 21st, & then another April 26th. The first one must have gone all right, as a letter was received by me April 28th,[42] (very pretty written)—but I have not heard whether you got my second letter. I enclosed in it an envelope with my address on, in hopes you would write to me.

Well, dear brother, the great battle between Hooker & Lee came off, & what a battle it was—without any decisive results again, though at the cost of so many brave men's lives & limbs—it seems too dreadful, that such bloody contests, without settling any thing, should go on. The hospitals here are filled with the wounded, I think the worst cases & the plentiest of any fighting yet. Was you in the fight? I have made inquiries of two of the 11th Mass. here in hospital, but they could not tell me about you for certain.

Lewy Brown[43] seems to be getting along pretty well. I hope he will be up & around before long—he is a good boy, & has my love, & when he is discharged, I should feel it a comfort to share with Lewy whatever I might have—& indeed if I ever have the means, he shall never want.

Dr. Bliss[44] was removed from Armory & put for a few days in the Old Capitol prison—there is now some talk however of his going back to Armory.

42. See 43. 43. See 60. 44. See 44.
45. WW changed "celestial" to "gay."

There is no particular change in my affairs here—I just about manage to pay my way, with newspaper correspondence &c. Tom, I believe I shall have to lay pipe for some office, clerkship, or something—

We had awful hot weather here three or four days ago—O how the grease run off of me—I invested in an umbrella & fan—it must have been gay[45] down there about Falmouth—didn't you want some *ice cream* about last Sunday?

My dearest comrade, I cannot, though I attempt it, put in a letter the feelings of my heart—I suppose my letters sound strange & unusual to you as it is, but as I am only expressing the truth in them, I do not trouble myself on that account. As I intimated before, I do not expect you to return for me the same degree of love I have for you.

53. *To Louisa Van Velsor Whitman*

Washington, Tuesday morning | June 9th 1863.

Dearest mother,

Jeff's letter came yesterday & was very welcome, as I wanted to hear about you all—I wrote to George yesterday & sent Jeff's letter enclosed. It looks from some accounts as though the 9th Army corps might be going down into East Tennessee, (Cumberland Gap or perhaps bound for Knoxville.) It is an important region, & has many southern unionists—the staunchest union man I have ever met is a young southerner in the 2d Tennessee (union reg't)—he was ten months in southern prisons, came up from Richmond paroled about ten weeks ago, & has been in hospital here sick until lately—he suffered every thing but death, he is the one they hung up by the heels, head downwards, & indeed worse than death, but stuck to his convictions like a hero—John Barker,[46] a real manly fellow, I saw much of him & heard much of that country that can be relied on. He is now gone home to his reg't.

Mother, I am feeling very well these days—my head that was stopt up so & hard of hearing seems to be all right. I only hope you have had similar good fortune with your rheumatism, & that it will continue so—I wish I could come in for a couple of days & see you—if I should succeed in getting a transportation ticket that would take me to New York & back, I should be tempted to come home for two or three days, as I want some MSS & books, & the trunk, &c. But I will see—Mother, your letter week before last was very good—whenever you feel like it, you write me, dear mother, & tell me every thing about the neighborhood, & all the items of our

46. Barker's career is detailed in 78. After Barker left the hospital, he wrote to WW from Camp Summerset, Ky., on June 5 and 19 (Hanley).

family. And sister Mat, how is she getting along—I believe I will have to write a letter especially to her & Sis, one of these times.

It is awful dry weather here, no rain of any consequence for five or six weeks—we have strawberries good & plenty, 15 cents a quart, with the hulls on—I go down to market sometimes of a morning & buy two or three quarts, for the folks I take my meals with—Mother, do you know I have not paid, as you may say, a cent of board since I have been in Washington, that is for meals—four or five times I have made a rush to leave the folks & find a moderate priced boarding house, but every time they have made such a time about it, that I have kept on—it is Mr. & Mrs. O'Connor, (he is the author of "Harrington")[47]—he has a $1600 office in the Treasury, & she is a first rate woman, a Massachusetts girl—they keep house in a moderate way—they have one little girl, (lost a fine boy about a year ago)—they have two rooms in the same house where I hire my room, & I take breakfast (½ past 8) & dinner (½ past 4) with them, as they will have it so—that's the way it has gone on now over five months, & as I say they won't listen to my leaving—but I shall do so, I think—I can never forget their kindness & real friendship & it appears as though they would continue just the same, if it were for all our lives. But I have insisted on going to market, (it is pleasant in the cool of the morning,) and getting the things, at my own expense, two or three times a week lately—I pay for the room I occupy now $7 a month—the landlord is a mixture of booby, miser & hog, his name is Gwin[48]—the landlady is a good woman, Washington raised—they are quite rich—he is Irish of the worst kind—has had a good office for ten years until Lincoln came in—They have bought another house, smaller, to live in, & are going to move (were to have moved 1st of June)—they had an auction of the house we live in yesterday, but nobody came to buy, so it was ridiculous—we had a red flag out, & a nigger walked up & down ringing a big bell, which is the fashion here for auctions.

Well, mother, the war still goes on, & every thing as much in a fog as ever—& the battles as bloody, & the wounded & sick getting worse & plentier all the time. I see a letter in the Tribune from Lexington, Ky., June 5th, headed "the 9th Army Corps departing for Vicksburgh"[49]—but I cannot exactly make it out, on reading the letter carefully—I don't see any thing in

47. Of the O'Connors, Jeff wrote on June 13: "I am real glad, my dear Walt, that you are among such good people. I hope it will be in the power of some of our family to return their kindness some day. I'm sure twould be done with a heartfelt gratitude. Tis pleasant, too, to think, that there are still people of that kind left" (Feinberg).

48. Carey Gwynne. Mrs. O'Connor, in a letter on November 10 (Feinberg), related with malice Gwynne's failure to rent an unfurnished house for $100 a month, but, like WW, spoke sympathetically of his wife. Gwynne was listed in the 1866 Directory as a clerk in the Treasury Department.

49. A dispatch with this heading appeared in the New York *Times* on June 8.

50. In his letter of June 13, Jeff had reservations about WW's lecture plans: "I

the letter about the 9th corps moving for Vicksburgh—at any rate I think the 2d division is more likely to be needed in Kentucky (or as I said, in Eastern Tennessee) as the secesh are expected to make trouble there—But one can hardly tell—the only thing is to resign onesself to events as they occur—it is a sad & dreary time, for so many thousands of parents & relatives, not knowing what will occur next—Mother, I told you I think last week that I had wrote to Han, & enclosed George's last letter to me—I wrote a week ago last Sunday—I wonder if she got the letter—About the pictures, I should like Jeff to send them, as soon as convenient—might send 20 of the big head, 10 or 12 of the standing figure, & 3 of the carte visite.

I am writing this in Major Hapgood's office—it is bright & pleasant, only the dust here in Washington is a great nuisance. Mother, your shirts do first rate. I am wearing them—the one I have on today suits me better than any I have ever yet had. I have not worn the thin coat the last week or so, as it has not been very hot lately.

Mother, I think something of commencing a series of lectures & readings &c.[50] through different cities of the north, to supply myself with funds for my Hospital & Soldiers visits—as I do not like to be beholden to the medium of others—I need a pretty large supply of money &c. to do the good I would like to—& the work grows upon me, & fascinates me—it is the most affecting thing you ever see, the lots of poor sick & wounded young men that depend so much, in one ward or another, upon my petting or soothing or feeding, sitting by them & feeding them their dinner or supper, some are quite helpless—some wounded in both arms—or giving some trifle (for a novelty or a change, it isn't for the value of it,) or stopping a little while with them—nobody will do but me—So, mother, I feel as though I would like to inaugurate a plan by which I could raise means on my own hook, & perhaps quite plenty too. Best love to you, dearest mother, & to sister Mat & Jeff.

Walt

fear that you would not meet with that success that you deserve. Mr Lane and I talked about the matter and both came to the conclusion that it would be much better if you could be appointed dispensing agent, or something of that kind, for some of the numerous aid societies" (Feinberg). Probably about this time, WW wrote in his "Hospital Note Book" (Huntington): "*Lectures*—pieces must not be dry opinions & prosy doctrines, &c—must be animated life-blood, descriptions, full of movement—with questions—apostrophes—declamatory passages, &c (a little ad captandum is allowable)."

Except for the concluding sentences, this paragraph appeared in *November Boughs* (*CW*, VI, 232), erroneously dated May 26, 1863.

54. *To Louisa Van Velsor Whitman*

Washington | Monday morning June 22 '63

Dear mother,

Jeff's letter came informing me of the birth of the little girl,[51] & that Matty was feeling pretty well, so far. I hope it will continue—Dear sister, I should much like to come home & see you & the little one, I am sure from Jeff's description it is a noble babe, & as to its being a girl it is all the better. (I am not sure but the Whitman breed gives better women than men.)

Well, mother, we are generally anticipating a lively time here or in the neighborhood,[52] as it is probable Lee is feeling about to strike a blow on Washington, or perhaps right into it—& as Lee is no fool, it is perhaps possible he may give us a good shake—he is not very far off—yesterday was a fight to the southwest of here all day, we heard the cannons nearly all day—the wounded are arriving in small squads every day, mostly cavalry, a great many Ohio men—they send off to-day from the Washington hospitals a great many to New York, Philadelphia, &c. all who are able, to make room, which looks ominous—indeed it is pretty certain that there is to be some severe fighting, may be a great battle again, the pending week—I am getting so callous that it hardly arouses me at all—I fancy I should take it very quietly if I found myself in the midst of a desperate conflict here in Washington.

Mother, I have nothing particular to write about—I see & hear nothing but new & old cases of my poor suffering boys in Hospitals, & I dare say you have had enough of such things—I have not missed a day at Hospital I think for more than three weeks—I get more & more wound round—poor young men—there are some cases that would literally sink & give up, if I did not pass a portion of the time with them—I have quite made up my mind about the lecturing &c project—I have no doubt it will succeed well enough, the way I shall put it in operation—you know, mother, it is to raise funds to enable me to continue my Hospital ministrations, on a more free handed scale—As to the Sanitary Commissions & the like, I am sick of them all, & would not accept any of their berths—you ought to see the way the men as they lie helpless in bed turn away their faces from the sight of

51. Jessie Louisa Whitman was born June 17 (Glicksberg, 136). Evidently the baby was not so named immediately, since WW referred to her in later letters as "black head" and "California."

52. Rumors were widespread that Lee was about to attack Washington, for the War Department on June 23, according to the New York *Times*, issued a report, "for the purpose of contradicting all erroneous reports, and giving quiet to the public mind," that "*No enemy is on or near the old Bull Run battle-field.*"

53. WW described the career of Hicks (1748–1830), the famous American

these Agents, Chaplains &c. (*hirelings* as Elias Hicks[53] would call them—they seem to me always a set of foxes & wolves)—they get well paid, & are always incompetent & disagreeable—As I told you before the only good fellows I have met are the Christian Commissioners—they go everywhere & receive no pay[54]—

Dear, dear mother, I want much to see you & dear Matty too, I send you both [my] best love, & Jeff too—the pictures came—I have not heard from George nor Han. I write a day earlier than usual.

Walt

We here think Vicksburgh is ours[55]—the probability is that it has capitulated—& there has been no general assault—can't tell yet whether the 51st went there—we are having very fine weather here to-day—rained last night.

55. *To Louisa Van Velsor Whitman*

Washington June 30 1863

Dearest Mother,

Your letter with Han's I have sent to George, though whether it will find him or not I cannot tell, as I think the 51st must be away down at Vicksburgh—I have not had a word from George yet—Mother, I have had quite an attack of sore throat & distress in my head for some days past, up to last night, but to-day I feel nearly all right again. I have been about the city same as usual, nearly—to the Hospitals, &c, I mean—I am told that I hover too much over the beds of the hospitals, with fever & putrid wounds, &c. One soldier, brought here about fifteen days ago, very low with typhoid fever, Livingston Brooks,[56] Co B 17th Penn Cavalry, I have particularly stuck to, as I found him in what appeared to be a dying condition, from negligence, & a horrible journey of about forty miles, bad roads & fast driving—& then after he got here, as he is a simple country boy, very shy & silent, & made no complaint, they neglected him—I found him something like I found John Holmes[57] last winter—I called the doctor's attention to him, shook up the nurses, had him bathed in spirits, gave him lumps of ice, & ice to his head, he had a fearful bursting pain in his head, & his body was like fire—he was very quiet, a very sensible boy, old fashioned—he did

Quaker, in *November Boughs* (CW, VI, 241–280).

54. Here WW replied to Jeff's letter of June 13, quoted in note 50 above.

55. The city surrendered formally on July 4.

56. Eventually Brooks recovered and, after a furlough, returned to his regiment. He wrote to WW on November 21, from Culpepper, Va. (Berg); WW's reply of December 19 is lost (Glicksberg, 140). WW noted the case in his diary (Glicksberg, 149–150).

57. See 27.

not want to die, & I had to lie to him without stint, for he thought I knew everything, & I always put in of course that what I told him was exactly the truth, & that if he got really dangerous I would tell him & not conceal it.

The rule is to remove bad fever patients out from the main wards to a tent by themselves, & the doctor told me he would have to be removed. I broke it gently to him, but the poor boy got it immediately in his head that he was marked with death, & was to be removed on that account—it had a great effect upon him, & although I told the truth this time it did not have as good a result as my former fibs—I persuaded the doctor to let him remain—for three days he lay just about an even chance, go or stay, with a little leaning toward the first—But, mother, to make a long story short, he is now out of any immediate danger—he has been perfectly rational throughout—begins to taste a little food, (for a week he eat nothing, I had to compel him to take a quarter of an orange, now & then)—& I will say, whether any one calls it pride or not, that if he *does* get up & around again, it's me that saved his life. Mother, as I have said in former letters, you can have no idea how these sick & dying youngsters cling to a fellow, & how fascinating it is, with all its hospital surroundings of sadness & scenes of repulsion & death.

In this same hospital, Armory Square, where this cavalry boy is, I have about fifteen or twenty particular cases I see much too, some of them as much as him—there are two from East Brooklyn, George Monk,[58] Co A 78th N Y, & Stephen Redgate,[59] (his mother is a widow in E[ast] B[rooklyn], I have written her,) both are pretty badly wounded—both are youngsters under 19—O mother, there seems to me as I go through these rows of cots, as if it was too bad to accept these *children*, to subject them to such premature experiences—I devote myself much to Armory Square Hospital because it contains by far the worst cases, most repulsive wounds, has the most suffering & most need of consolation—I go every day without fail, & often at night—sometimes stay very late—no one interferes with me, guards, doctors, nurses, nor any one—I am let to take my own course.

Well, mother, I suppose you folks think we are in a somewhat dubious position here in Washington, with Lee in strong force almost between us

58. In July, 1863, WW recorded the case of George W. Monk in his hospital notes: "Brooklyn boy—father Wm D. Monk, Brooklyn E[ast] D[istrict]—gun shot wound in head—feet benumbed—fine manly quiet boy" (Glicksberg, 149). The father was listed as a roof maker in the Directory of 1861–1862, as a ropemaker in 1865.

59. A drummer in the Seventy-eighth Regiment; see *A Record of the Commissioned Officers, Non-Commissioned Officers and Privates . . . in the State of New York* (1864), III, 229.

60. The New York *Times* reported that Lee was in Pennsylvania, at or near Chambersburg.

61. Perhaps in part WW was directing these words to Jeff, who was no admirer

& you northerners[60]—Well it does look ticklish, if the rebs cut the connection, then there will be fun—The reb cavalry come quite near us, dash in & steal wagon trains, &c—It would be funny if they should come some night to the President's country house, (soldier's home,) where he goes out to sleep every night—it is in the same direction as their saucy raid last Sunday—Mr. Lincoln passes here (14th st) every evening on his way out—I noticed him last evening about ½ past 6, he was in his barouche, two horses, guarded by about thirty cavalry. The barouche comes first under a slow trot, driven by one man in the box, no servant or footman beside—the cavalry all follow closely after with a lieutenant at their head—I had a good view of the President last evening—he looks more careworn even than usual—his face with deep cut lines, seams, & his *complexion gray*, through very dark skin, a curious looking man, very sad—I said to a lady who was looking with me, "Who can see that man without losing all wish to be sharp upon him personally? Who can say he has not a good soul?" The lady assented, although she is almost vindictive on the course of the administration, (thinks it wants nerve &c., the usual complaint).[61] The equipage is rather shabby, horses indeed almost what my friends the Broadway drivers would call *old plugs*. The President dresses in plain black clothes, cylinder hat—he was alone yesterday—As he came up, he first drove over to the house of the Sec[retary] of War, on K st about 300 feet from here, sat in his carriage while Stanton came out & had a 15 minutes interview with him (I can see from my window)—& then wheeled around, & slowly trotted around the corner & up Fourteenth st., the cavalry after him—I really think it would be safer for him just now to stop at the White House, but I expect he is too proud to abandon the former custom—Then about an hour after, we had a large cavalry regiment pass, with blankets, arms, &c, on the war march over the same track—the reg't was very full, over a thousand, indeed thirteen or fourteen hundred—it was an old reg't, veterans, *old fighters*, young as they were—they were preceded by a fine mounted band of sixteen, (about ten bugles, the rest cymbals & drums)—I tell you, mother, it made every thing ring—made my heart leap, they played with a will—then *the accompaniment*—the sabres rattled on a thousand men's sides—they had pistols, their heels spurred—handsome

of Lincoln. On May 27, apparently in answer to a lost letter, Jeff wrote: "I cannot agree with you, Walt, in relation to the President. I think that he is not a man for the times, not big enough. He dont seem to have even force enough to stop bickerings between his own Cabinet and Generals nor force enough to do as he thinks best. . . . No, A. L. is not the man and I hardly know if we have one that is equal to the thing." Jeff returned to the subject on June 13: "Well, Walt, you and I cannot agree in regard to 'Uncle Abe.' . . . He lends himself to the speculators, in all the ways that it can be done. He says 'yes' to the last man or 'No' as that man wants him to. Everything he does reminds me of an old woman" (Feinberg).

American young men, (I make no acc't of any other)—rude uniforms, well worn, but good cattle, prancing—all good riders, full of the devil, nobody shaved, all very sunburnt. The regimental officers (splendidly mounted, but just as roughly drest as the men) came immediately after the band, then company after company, with each its officers at its head—the tramping of so many horses (there is a good hard turnpike)—then a long train of men with led horses, mounted negroes, & a long long string of baggage wagons, each with four horses—& then a strong rear guard—I tell you it had the look of *real war*—noble looking fellows—a man looks & feels so proud on a good horse, & armed—They are off toward the region of Lee's (supposed) rendezvous, toward the Susquehannah, for the great anticipated battle—Alas, how many of these healthy handsome rollicking young men will lie cold in death, before the apples ripe in the orchards[62]—

Mother, it is curious & stirring here, in some respects—smaller or larger bodies of troops are moving continually—many just well men are turned out of the hospitals—I am where I see a good deal of them—There are getting to be *many black troops*—there is one very good reg't here black as tar—they go armed, have the regular uniform—they submit to no nonsense—others are constantly forming—it is getting to be a common sight—they press them. [*Incomplete*]

56. *To Louisa Van Velsor Whitman* [*7.7. 1863*][63]

Tuesday afternoon.

Mother, it seems to be certain that Meade[64] has gained the day, & that the battles there in Pennsylvania have been about as terrible as any in the war—O what a sight must have been presented by the field of action—I think the killed & wounded there on both sides were as many as eighteen or twenty thousand—in one place, four or five acres, there were a thousand dead, at daybreak on Saturday morning—Mother, one's heart grows sick of war, after all, when you see what it really is—every once in a while I feel so horrified & disgusted—it seems to me like a great slaughter-house & the men mutually butchering each other—then I feel how impossible it ap-

62. Compare the lines in "Come Up from the Fields Father," which appeared in *Drum-Taps*, 39:

Lo, 'tis autumn; . . .
Where apples ripe in the orchards hang, and grapes on the trellis'd vines . . .

63. Since this letter (previously printed with 76) obviously refers to the engagements at Gettysburg, it has been placed in correct sequence. Note also the first sentence in 57.

64. George Gordon Meade (1815–1872) unexpectedly replaced Hooker as commander of the Army of the Potomac on June 28, two days before the engagement at Gettysburg. On July 7, Jeff was writing to his brother: "We are awfully pleased and excited at the war news. Feel as if the man had been appointed that was thinking less of political affairs than of licking the rebs. . . . Bully for Meade! He has not only licked

pears, again, to retire from this contest, until we have carried our points —(it is cruel to be so tossed from pillar to post in one's judgment).

Washington is a pleasant place in some respects—it has the finest trees, & plenty of them every where, on the streets, & grounds. The Capitol grounds, though small, have the finest cultivated trees I ever see—there is a great variety, & not one but is in perfect condition—After I finish this letter I am going out there for an hour's recreation—The great sights of Washington are the public buildings, the wide streets, the public grounds, the trees, the Smithsonian Institute & grounds—I go to the latter occasionally—the Institute is an old fogy concern, but the grounds are fine[65]— Sometimes I go up to Georgetown, about two & a half miles up the Potomac, an old town—just opposite it in the river is an island, where the niggers have their first Washington reg't encamped—they make a good show, are often seen in the streets of Washington in squads—since they have begun to carry arms, the secesh here & in Georgetown (about ⅗ths) are not insulting to them as formerly.

One of the things here always on the go, is long trains of army wagons —sometimes they will stream along all day, it almost seems as if there was nothing else but army wagons & ambulances—they have great camps here in every direction, of army wagons, teamsters, ambulance camps, &c. Some of them are permanent, & have small hospitals—I go to them, (as no one else goes, ladies would not venture)—I sometimes have the luck to give some of the drivers a great deal of comfort & help. Indeed, mother, there are camps here of every thing—I went once or twice to the Contraband Camp,[66] to the Hospital, &c. but I could not bring myself to go again— when I meet black men or boys among my own hospitals, I use them kindly, give them something, &c.—I believe I told you that I do the same to the wounded rebels, too—but as there is a limit to one's sinews & endurance & sympathies, &c. I have got in the way after going lightly as it were all through the wards of a hospital, & trying to give a word of cheer, if nothing else, to every one, then confining my special attentions to the few where the investment seems to tell best, & who want it most—Mother, I have real pride in telling you that I have the consciousness of saving quite a little

the rebs but the peace party headed by McClellan. Hope that he will not let them off but will poke it into them" (Feinberg). Unfortunately, like his predecessors, Meade failed to press his advantage and destroy the "old fox." WW evaluated Meade's strengths and weaknesses in 119.

65. WW visited the Smithsonian Institute for the first time on April 17, with one of his soldier friends, Calving P. Riegel: "The Building is good, solid, &c.—the grounds around are fine—I must go walk there oftener" (Glicksberg, 132). In a notebook, "The Congress of the United States" (1863), WW noted: "Smithsonian Institute—at night, under unfavorable circumstances—all dark—pokerish to walk through there in the dark" (Feinberg).

66. On February 27, the New York *Herald* published a grim account of squalor in the Contraband Camp.

number of lives by saving them from giving up & being a good deal with them—the men say it is so, & the doctors say it is so—& I will candidly confess I can see it is true, though I say it of myself—I know you will like to hear it, mother, so I tell you—

I am finishing this in Major Hapgood's office, about 1 o'clock—it is pretty warm, but has not cleared off yet—the trees look so well from where I am, & the Potomac—it is a noble river—I see it several miles, & Arlington heights—Mother, I see some of the 47th Brooklyn every day or two—the reg't is on the Heights—back of Arlington House, a fine camp ground—O, Matty, I have just thought of you—dear sister, how are you getting along? Jeff, I will write you truly—Good bye for the present, dearest mother, & all—

Walt

57. *To Louisa Van Velsor Whitman*

ENDORSED (by WW): "for Mother."

Washington, | July 10 1863.

Dear mother,

I suppose you rec'd a letter from me last Wednesday as I sent you one Tuesday, (7th)—dear mother, I was glad enough to hear from George, by that letter from Snyder's Bluffs, June 28th—I had felt a little fear on acc't of some of those storming parties Grant sent against Vicksburgh the middle of June & up to the 20th—but this letter dispels all anxiety—I have written to George many times, but it seems he has not got them—Mother, I shall write immediately to him again—I think he will get the letter I sent last Sunday, as I directed it to Vicksburgh—I told him all the news from home. Mother, I shall write to Han & inclose George's letter—I am real glad to hear from Mat & the little one, all so favorable—We are having pleasant weather here still—I go to Campbell Hospital this afternoon—I still keep going, mother—the wounded are doing rather badly I am sorry to say, there are frequent deaths. The weather, I suppose, which has been peculiarly bad for wounds, so wet & warm, (though not disagreeable outdoors)—

Mother, you must write as often as you can, & Jeff too—you must not get worried about the ups & downs of the war—I don't know any course but to resign onesself to events—if one can only bring one's mind to it—

67. Jeff wrote a vivid account of the mob on July 19: "We have passed through a wonderful week for our New York. A week that I think will eventually be productive of great good to our country, but had at a fearful cost. From my own personal observations I think that the newspapers would give one the most perverted kind of an idea of the

Good bye once more for the present, dearest mother, Mat & the dear little ones.

Walt

Mother, do you ever hear from Mary—

58. *To Louisa Van Velsor Whitman*

Washington | Wednesday forenoon July 15 | 1863

Dear mother,

So the mob has risen at last in New York[67]—I have been expecting it, but as the day for the draft had arrived & every thing was so quiet, I supposed all might go on smoothly—but it seems the passions of the people were only sleeping, & have burst forth with terrible fury, & they have destroyed life & property, the enrolment buildings &c as we hear—the accounts we get are a good deal in a muddle, but it seems bad enough—the feeling here is savage & hot as fire against New York, (the mob—"*copperhead mob*" the papers here call it,) & I hear nothing in all directions but threats of ordering up the gunboats, cannonading the city, shooting down the mob, hanging them in a body, &c &c—meantime I remain silent, partly amused, partly scornful, or occasionally put a dry remark, which only adds fuel to the flame—I do not feel it in my heart to abuse the poor people, or call for rope or bullets for them, but that is all the talk here, even in the hospitals—

The acc'ts from N Y this morning are that the gov't has ordered the draft to be suspended there—I hope it is true, for I find that the deeper they go in with the draft, the more trouble it is likely to make—I have changed my opinions & feelings on the subject—we are in the midst of strange & terrible times—one is pulled a dozen different ways in his mind, & hardly knows what to think or do—Mother, I have not much fear that the troubles in New York will affect any of our family, still I feel somewhat uneasy—about Jeff, if any one, as he is more around—I have had it much on my mind what could be done, if it should so happen that Jeff should be drafted—of course he could not go, without its being the downfall almost of our whole family, as you may say, Mat & his young ones, & a sad blow to you too, mother, & to all—I didn't see any other way than to try to raise the $300, mostly by borrowing if possible of Mr Lane—mother, I have no doubt I shall make a few hundred dollars by the lectures I shall certainly

riot. The big type, the general 'skeery' look of the articles, was something that did not make its appearance on the public face" (Feinberg). See also Lawrence Lader, "New York's Bloodiest Week," in *American Heritage*, x (June, 1959).

commence soon, (for my hospital missionary purposes & my own, for that purpose) & I could lend that am't to Jeff to pay it back—May be the draft will not come off after all—I should say it was very doubtful if they can carry it out in N Y & Brooklyn—& besides it is only one chance out of several, to be drawn if it does—I dont wonder dear brother Jeff feels the effect it would have on domestic affairs. I think it is right to feel so, full as strongly as a man can. I do hope all will go well, & without such an additional trouble falling upon us, but as it can be met with money, I hope Jeff & Mat & all of you, dear mother, will not worry any more about it—I wrote to Jeff a few lines last Sunday, I suppose he got[68]—Mother, I don't know whether you have had a kind of gloomy week the past week, but somehow I feel as if you all had, but I hope it has passed over—How is dear sister Mat, & how is Miss Mannahatta & little black head—I sometimes feel as if I *must* come home & see you all, I want to very much—

My hospital life still continues the same—I was in Armory all day yesterday & day & night before—they have the men wounded in the railroad accident at Laurel station (bet[ween] here & Baltimore) about 30 soldiers, some of them horribly injured at 3 o'clock a m last Saturday by collision—poor, poor, poor men—I go again this afternoon & night—I see so much of butcher sights, so much sickness & suffering I must get away a while I believe for self preservation—I have felt quite well though the past week—we have had rain continually—Mother, I have not heard from George since, have you? I shall write Han to-day & send George's letter—if you or Jeff has not written this week I hope Jeff will write on receiving this. Good bye for present, dearest mother, & Jeff & Mat.

Walt

Mother, the army is to be paid off two months more, right away. Of course George will get two months more pay. Dear mother, I hope you will keep untouched & put in bank every cent you can. I want us to have a ranch somewhere by or before next spring.

68. This letter is evidently lost.

69. WW noted in his diary: "Rank musician—typhoid fever—I visited him from the time he was brought in the hospitals—he told me he had been sick off & on for several months" (Glicksberg, 148–149). See also 64 and 78. On the verso of the letter is a pass, dated August 1, issued to Samuel B. Haskell for the purpose of visiting his son. The New-York Historical Society has a letter written by J. M. Jansen—like Erastus, a musician in the Hundred and Forty-first Regiment, New York Volunteers—on April 5, 1863, in which he informed Mr. Haskell that his son would surely receive "his discharge after a spel, so take things cool and dont borrow any trouble about him." Erastus added a note to Jansen's letter: "I am not doing any duty any where now, I havent been on duty since the 20th day of December."

70. Lewis K. Brown (1843–1926) was wounded in the left leg near Rappahannock Station on August 19, 1862, and lay where he fell for four days. Eventually he was transferred to Armory Square Hospital, where WW met him, probably in February, 1863.

59. *To Mr. and Mrs. S. B. Haskell*

Washington | July 27 1863

Mr and Mrs Haskell

Your son Erastus Haskell,[69] of Co K 141st New York, is now lying sick with typhoid fever here in hospital.

I have been with him quite a good deal, from day to day, was with him yesterday & indeed almost every day, & feel much interested in the young man. He has been very sick, & seems to be so now, as I should judge, but the doctor says he will recover. I had a talk with the doctor yesterday, & he says so still. But Erastus seems to me very sick, & I thought I would write to you. He had some one write to you about two weeks ago, but has received no answer.

Erastus does not talk much, so I do not understand much about his affairs. I am merely a friend. The address of Erastus is

Ward E, Armory Square Hospital | Washington D C

should you wish to write to him direct.

Walt Whitman

care Major Hapgood, paymaster | U S A cor 15th & F st | Washington | D C

Upon second thought I enclose you an envelope to send your letter to Erastus—put a stamp on it, & write soon. I suppose you know he has been sick a great deal since he has been in the service.

60. *To Lewis K. Brown*[70]

Washington August 1 1863

Both your letters have been received, Lewy[71]—the second one came this morning, & was welcome, as any thing from you will always be, & the sight of your face welcomer than all, my darling—I see you write in good

In a diary in the Feinberg Collection, WW described Brown on February 19 as "a most affectionate fellow, very fond of having me come and sit by him." Because the wound did not heal, the leg was amputated on January 5, 1864. WW was present and described the operation in a diary (*LC* #103). Brown was mustered out in August, 1864, and was employed in the Provost General's office in September; see 144. The following September he became a clerk in the Treasury Department, and was appointed Chief of the Paymaster's Division in 1880, a post which he held until his retirement in 1915. (For this material I have drawn upon a memorandum prepared by Brown's family, now in the Library of Congress.)

Brown replied to this letter from Elkton, Md., on August 10 (Berg). After advising WW to give himself a furlough, he chatted about his reception among Maryland copperheads, the crops, and his father's farmhouse.

71. Brown had written from Judiciary Square Hospital on July 6 and 18 (Berg).

spirits, & appear to have first-rate times—Lew, you must not go around too much, nor eat & drink too promiscuous, but be careful & moderate, & not let the kindness of friends carry you away, lest you break down again, dear son—I was at the hospital yesterday four or five hours, was in ward K—Taber[72] has been down sick, so he had to lay abed, but he is better now, & goes around as usual—Curly[73] is the same as usual—most of the others are the same—there have been quite a good many deaths—the young man who lay in bed 2 with a very bad leg is dead—I saw Johnny Mahay[74] in ward E—poor fellow, he is very poorly, he is very thin, & his face is like wax—Lew, I must tell you what a curious thing happened in the chaplain's[75] house night before last—there has been a man in ward I, named Lane, with two fingers amputated, very bad with gangrene, so they removed him to a tent by himself—last Thursday his wife came to see him, she seemed a nice woman but very poor, she stopt at the chaplain's—about 3 o'clock in the morning she got up & went to the sink, & there she gave birth to a child, which fell down the sink into the sewer runs beneath, fortunately the water was not turned on—the chaplain got up, carried Mrs Lane out, & then roused up a lot of men from the hospital, with spades &c. dug a trench outside, & got into the sink, & took out the poor little child, it lay there on its back, in about two inches of water—well, strange as it may seem, the child was alive, (it fell about five feet through the sink)—& is now living & likely to live, is quite bright, has a head of thick black hair—the chaplain took me in yesterday, showed me the child, & Mrs Jackson, his wife, told me the whole story, with a good deal I havn't told you—& then she treated me to a good plate of ice cream—so I staid there nearly an hour & had quite a pleasant visit. Mrs Lane lay in an adjoining room.

Lew, as to me & my affairs there is nothing very new or important—I have not succeeded in getting any employment here yet, except that I write a little (newspaper correspondence &c), barely enough to pay my expenses—but it is my own fault, for I have not tried hard enough for any thing—the last three weeks I have not felt very well—for two or three days I was down sick, for the first time in my life, (as I have never before been sick)—I feel pretty fair to-day—I go around most every day the same as usual. I have some idea of giving myself a furlough of three or four weeks, & going home to Brooklyn, N Y, but I should return again to Washington, probably. Lew, it is pretty hot weather here, & the sun affects me—(I had a

72. On July 18, 1864, Brown wrote to WW: "I suppose you herd that J. A. Tabor was killed. . . . in the wilderness the second days battle. I seen some men out of his company & they say that he fell dead when he was shot" (Berg).

73. "Curly," a soldier from Ohio, is again referred to in 238.

74. See 43.

75. Eliphalet W. Jackson, a chaplain in Armory Square Hospital, was ardently patriotic. On March 7, the Washington *National Republican* noted that at a hospital party

sort of sun stroke about five years ago)—You speak of being here in Washington again about the last of August—O Lewy, how glad I should be to see you, to have you with me—I have thought if it could be so that you, & one other person & myself could be where we could work & live together, & have each other's society, we three, I should like it so much—but it is probably a dream—

Well, Lew, they had the great battle of Gettysburgh, but it does not seem to have settled any thing, except to have killed & wounded a great many thousand men—It seems as though the two armies were falling back again to near their old positions on the Rappahannock—it is hard to tell what will be the next move—yet, Lewy, I think we shall conquer yet—I don't believe it is destined that this glorious Union is to be broken up by all the secesh south, or copheads north either—

Well, my darling, I have scribbled you off something to show you where I am & that I have rec'd your welcome letters—but my letter is not of much interest, for I don't feel very bright to-day—Dear son, you must write me whenever you can—take opportunity when you have nothing to do, & write me a good long letter—your letters & your love for me are very precious to me, for I appreciate it all, Lew, & give you the like in return. It is now about 3 o'clock, & I will go out & mail this letter, & then go & get my dinner—So good bye, Lewy—good bye, my dear son & comrade, & I hope it will prove God's will that you get quite well & sound yet, & have many good years yet—

Walt

Address my letters care Major Hapgood, paymaster U S A, cor. 15th & F st Washington D C—

61. *To James Redpath(?)* [*8.6. 1863*]

DRAFT LETTER.

Dear friend,[76]

I am going to write you to ask any friends you may be in communication with for aid for my soldiers. I remain here in Washington still occupied among the hospitals—I have now been engaged in this over

Jackson proposed a lengthy resolution which began: "Resolved, That the rebellion now waged against our Government is the most wicked and atrocious of any since the days of Satan, Absalom, or Judas."

76. When WW gave this letter to Traubel on August 12, 1888, he observed: "I don't know for sure who it was written to—probably one of those Boston women—the Curtis people, it may be" (Traubel, II, 127). It seems probable, however, that this draft letter was addressed to James Redpath, who gave the original to Dr. Le Baron Russell

seven months. As time passes on it seems as if sad cases of old & lingering wounded accumulate, regularly recruited with new ones every week—I have been most of this day in Armory Square Hospital, Seventh st. I seldom miss a day or evening. Out of the six or seven hundred in this Hosp[ital] I try to give a word or a trifle to every one without exception, making regular rounds among them all. I give all kinds of sustenance, blackberries, peaches, lemons & sugar, wines, all kinds of preserves, pickles, brandy, milk, shirts & all articles of underclothing, tobacco, tea, handkerchiefs, &c &c &c. I always give paper, envelopes, stamps, &c. I want a supply for this purpose. To many I give (when I have it) small sums of money—half of the soldiers in hospital have not a cent. There are many returned prisoners, sick, lost all—& every day squads of men from [the] front, cavalry or infantry—brought in wounded or sick, generally without a cent of money. Then I select the most needy cases & devote my time & services much to them. I find it tells best—some are mere lads, 17, 18, 19 or 20. Some are silent, sick, heavy hearted, (things, attentions, &c. are very rude in the army & hospitals, nothing but the mere hard routine, no time for tenderness or extras)—So I go round—Some of my boys die, some get well—

O what a sweet unwonted love (those good American boys, of good stock, decent, clean, well raised boys, so near to me)—what an attachment grows up between us, started from hospital cots, where pale young faces lie & wounded or sick bodies. My brave young American soldiers—now for so many months I have gone around among them, where they lie. I have long discarded all stiff conventions (they & I are too near to each other, there is no time to lose, & death & anguish dissipate ceremony here between my lads & me)—I pet them, some of them it does so much good, they are so faint & lonesome—at parting at night sometimes I kiss them right & left—The doctors tell me I supply the patients with a medicine which all their drugs & bottles & powders are helpless to yield.

I wish you would ask any body you know who is likely to contribute—It is a good holy cause, surely nothing nobler—I desire you if possible could

(see 99), who in turn gave it to Mrs. Charles P. Curtis (see 82). An envelope in the Feinberg Collection is endorsed: "letter to Jas. Redpath | Aug 6th '63."

Redpath (1833–1891) was the author of *The Life of John Brown* (1860), a correspondent for the New York *Tribune* during the war, the originator of the "Lyceum" lectures, and editor of the *North American Review* in 1886. He met WW in Boston in 1860 (*LC* #90), and remained an enthusiastic admirer; see Traubel, III, 459–461. He concluded his first letter to WW on June 25, 1860: "I love you, Walt! A conquering Brigade will ere long march to the music of your barbaric yawp" (Feinberg; Traubel, III, 460). See also Charles F. Horner, *The Life of James Redpath* (1926).

In February, 1863, WW had evidently written to Redpath for assistance with his work in the hospitals. Redpath reported on March 10 (Donaldson, 143) that he had called WW's appeal to the attention of Emerson, who replied on February 23: "I shall make some trial whether I can find any direct friends and abettors for him and his beneficiaries, the soldiers" (Donaldson, 144). Redpath, however, noted on May 5 that "Emerson tried

raise for me, forthwith, for application to these wounded & sick here, (they are from Massachusetts & all the New England states, there is not a day but I am with some Yankee boys, & doing some trifle for them)—a sum—if possible $50—if not, then less—$30—or indeed any am't—

I am at present curiously almost alone here, as visitor & consolator to Hospitals—the work of the different Reliefs & Commissions is nearly all off in the field—& as to private visitors, *there are few or none*—I wish you or some of your friends could just make a round with me, for an hour or so, at some of my hospitals or camps—I go among all our own dear soldiers, hospital camps & army, our teamsters' hospitals, among sick & dying, the rebels, the contrabands, &c &c. What I reach is necessarily but a drop in the bucket but it is done in good faith, & with now some experience & I hope with good heart.

62. *To Hugo Fritsch* [*Before 8.7. 1863*]

DRAFT LETTER.

My honest thanks to you, Hugo,[77] for your letter posting me up not only about yourself but about my dear boys, Fred, Nat Bloom[78]—always so welcome to me to hear personally or in any way any & every item about them. Dear friend, the same evening I rec'd your letter, I saw in the New York papers (which get here about 5 every evening) the announcement of Charles Chauncey's death.[79] When I went up to my room that night towards 11 I took a seat by the open window in the splendid soft moonlit night, and, there alone by myself, (as is my custom sometimes under such circumstances), I devoted to the dead boy the silent cheerful tribute of an hour or so of floating thought about him, & whatever rose up from the thought of him, & his looks, his handsome face, his hilarious fresh ways, his sunny smile, his voice, his blonde hair, his talk, his caprices—the way he & I first met—how we spoke together impromptu, no introduction—

to have something done about you, but failed" (Donaldson, 144), and explained: "There is a prejudice agst you here among the 'fine' ladies & gentlemen of the transcendental School. It is believed that you are not ashamed of your reproductive organs, and, somehow, it wd seem to be the result of their logic—that eunuchs only are fit for nurses. If you are ready to qualify yourself for their sympathy & support, that you may not unnecessarily suffer therefrom, is the sincere wish of your friend" (Historical Society of Pennsylvania; omitted in Donaldson's transcription of the letter). See also WW's letters to Redpath, 87 and 91.

77. See 41. Until the date of Chauncey's death is established, this letter cannot be dated precisely. In the absence of this information I have placed it next to the dated letter to Fritsch.

78. For "Fred" Gray and Nathaniel Bloom, see 40.

79. See 40. Since at this point WW noted in the draft: "reserve for Fred Gray," he probably intended to include the material in another letter.

then our easy falling into intimacy—he with his affectionate heart thought so well of me, & I loved him then, & love him now—I thought over our meetings together, our drinks & groups so friendly, our suppers with Fred & Charley Russell[80] &c. off by ourselves at some table, at Pfaff's[81] off the other end—O how charming those early times, adjusting our friendship, I to the three others, although it needed little adjustment—for I believe we all loved each other more than we supposed—Chauncey was frequently the life & soul of these gatherings—was full of sparkle, & so good, really witty—then for an exception he would have a mood come upon him & right after the outset of our party, he would grow still & cloudy & up & unaccountably depart—but these were seldom—then I got to having occasionally quite a long walk with him, only us two, & then he would talk well & freely about himself, his experiences, feelings, quite confidential, &c. All these I resumed, sitting by myself.

Hugo, that's the way I sat there Wednesday night till after midnight (the pleasant Virginia breeze coming up the Potomac) and certainly without what they call mourning thought of the boy.

Dear Hugo, you speak of your all remembering me and wish to see me, it would be happiness for me to be with you all, at one of your friendly meetings, especially at Fred's room,[82] so pleasant, with its effect I remember of pictures, fine color, &c. to have the delight of my dear boys' company & their gayety & electricity, their precious friendship, the talk & laughter, the drinks, me surrounded by you all, (so I will for a moment fancy myself,) tumbled upon by you all, with all sorts of kindness, smothered with you all in your hasty thoughtless, magnificent way, overwhelmed with questions, Walt this, Walt that, & Walt every thing. Ah, if one could float off to New York this afternoon. It is Sunday afternoon now, & perhaps you are at this moment gathered at Fred's or at your house, & having a good time.

I suppose you were at Charles Chauncey's funeral—tell me about it, & all particulars about his death. When you write, tell.[83]

80. See 40.

81. Charles Pfaff had opened—about 1854—a restaurant on Broadway near Bleecker Street which shortly became a famed meeting place for literary and theatrical people. In "Pfaff's privy," as the wits described it, in the late 1850's, Henry Clapp (see 235) was king and Ada Clare (see 247) was queen of the bohemians. Here WW met writers like Howells, Stoddard, and Aldrich, editors like Garrison (see 247) and John Swinton (see 37), and eccentrics like Count Adam Gurowski (see 177). "My own greatest pleasure at Pfaff's was to look on—to see, talk little, absorb," WW observed to Traubel in 1888 (I, 417). Here too his nonliterary friends like Fritsch also assembled for their "orgies."

For accounts of the Pfaffian days, see William Winter, *Old Friends, Being Recollections of Other Days* (1909), 63–106; W. L. Alden, "Some Phases of Literary New York in the Sixties," *Putnam's Monthly*, III (1907–8), 554–558; and Albert Parry, *Garrets and Pretenders: A History of Bohemianism in America* (1933), 3–48.

63. *To Hugo Fritsch* [*8.7.1863*]

ENDORSED (by WW): "To Hugo | Aug 7 '63."
DRAFT LETTER.

Dear Hugo,[84]

I rec'd a letter from Bloom yesterday—but, before responding to it (which I will do soon) I must write to you, my friend. Your good letter of June 27th was duly rec'd—I have read it many times—indeed, Hugo, you know not how much comfort you give, by writing me your letters—posting me up.

Well, Hugo, I am still as much as ever, indeed more, in the great military hospitals here. Every day or night I spend four, five, or six hours, among my sick, wounded, prostrate boys. It is fascinating, sad, & with varied fortune of course. Some of my boys get well, some die. After I finish this letter (and then dining at a restaurant), I shall give the latter part of the afternoon & some hours of the night to Armory Square Hospital, a large establishment & one I find most calling on my sympathies & ministrations. I am welcomed by the surgeons as by the soldiers—very grateful to me. You must remember that these government hospitals are not filled as with human débris like the old established city hospitals, New York, &c., but mostly [with] these good-born American young men, appealing to me most profoundly, good stock, often mere boys, full of sweetness & heroism—often they seem very near to me, even as my own children or younger brothers. I make no bones of petting them just as if they were—have long given up formalities & reserves in my treatment of them.

Let me see, Hugo. I will not write any thing about the topics of the horrible riots of last week,[85] nor Gen. Meade, nor Vicksburgh, nor Charleston—I leave them to the newspapers. Nor will I write you this time so much about hospitals as I did last. Tell Fred his letter was received—I appreciate it, received real pleasure from it—'twas a true friend's letter, charac-

82. Gray's father, Dr. John F. Gray, lived at 1 East Twenty-sixth Street.

83. Traubel (III, 386) notes his difficulties in deciphering this draft letter—"it was so criss-crossed and interlined." WW could not remember the date: "I think it was in '63—about the same time as the other." When Traubel finished reading this letter aloud, "Walt's eyes were full of tears. He wiped the tears away with the sleeve of his coat. Put on a make-believe chuckle" (III, 388).

84. On December 23, 1888, Traubel records that "W. gave me one of what he calls his 'soger boy letters'. . . . he even had me read it to him. I don't like to read these letters aloud. They move me too much. I notice that he too is stirred strangely over them hearing them again" (III, 367). The New York friends mentioned in this letter are discussed briefly in the notes to 40. The envelope with this draft was stationery from the United States Christian Commission.

85. If WW referred to the New York riots of July 15, the date of this letter may be incorrect. There was, however, a draft drawing in Washington on August 3 and 4.

teristic, full of vivacity, off hand, & below all a thorough base of genuine remembrance & good will—was not wanting in the *sentimental* either—(so I take back all about the *apostate*, do you understand, Freddy, my dear?)—& only write this for you till I reply to that said letter a good long (especial) missive to yourself.

I[86] meant to [tell] Nat Bloom that if he expects to provoke me into a dignified not mentioning him, nor writing any thing about him, by his studious course of heart-breaking neglect, (which has already reduced me to a skeleton of but little over 200 lbs & a countenance of raging hectic, indicating an early grave), I was determined not to do any thing of the sort, but shall speak of him every time, & send him my love, just as if he were adorned with faithful troth instead of (as I understand) beautiful whiskers—Does he think that beautiful whiskers can fend off the pangs of remorse? In conclusion I have to say, Nathaniel, you just keep on if you think there's no hell.

Hugo, I suppose you were at Charles Chauncey's[87] funeral—tell me all you hear about the particulars of his death—Tell me of course all about the boys, what you do, say, any thing, every thing[88]—

Hugo, write oftener—you express your thoughts perfectly—do you not know how much more agreeable to me is the conversation or writing that does not take hard paved tracks, the usual & stereotyped, but has little peculiarities & even kinks of its own, making its genuineness—its vitality? Dear friend, your letters are precious to me—none I have received from any one are more so.

Ah, I see in your letter, Hugo, you speak of my being reformed—no, I am not so frightfully reformed either, only the hot weather here does not admit of drinking heavy drinks, & there is no good lager here—then besides I have no society—I expect to prove to you & all yet that I am no backslider—But here I go nowhere for mere amusement, only occasionally a walk.

And Charles Russell—how I should like to see him—how like to have one of our old times again—Ah Fred, and you, dear Hugo, & you repentant one with the dark-shining whiskers[89]—must there not be an hour, an eve-

86. As Traubel read this letter, WW said that he did not think that this paragraph had been sent: "It was too damned nonsensical for a letter otherwise so dead serious" (III, 368). It is lined through in the manuscript.

87. See 62.

88. WW deleted the following: "did you go out to Bloom's for 4th of July? I heard about your bold(?) & aquatic excursion to Bloo[m's]."

89. Nat Bloom.

90. In a notebook, WW described Kingsley as "a young man, upper class, at Pfaff's &c—fond of training for boat-racing &c.—June, July, 1862" (*LC* #8). He was listed in the Directory of 1865–1866 as the proprietor of a furniture store; his name did not appear thereafter.

91. I have not identified Perkins, who was mentioned again in 74 and 84.

ning in the future, when we four returning concentrating New York-ward or elsewhere, shall meet, allowing no interloper, & have our drinks & things, & resume the chain & consolidate & achieve a night better & mellower than ever—we four?

Hugo, I wish you to give my love to all the boys—I received a letter from Ben Knower, very good—I shall answer it soon—Give my love to Ben—If Charles Kingsley[90] is in town same to him—ditto Mullen—ditto Perk,[91] (I hope to hear that sweet, sweet fiddler one of these days, that strain again.)

I wish to have Fred Gray say something from me, giving my love to his mother & father—I bear them both in mind—I count on having good interviews with them when I see New York.

64. *To Mr. and Mrs. S. B. Haskell*

ADDRESS: S B Haskell | Breseport | Chenning Co. New York. POSTMARK: Washington D. C. | Aug | 10 | 1863.

Washington August 10 1863

Mr and Mrs Haskell,[92]

Dear friends, I thought it would be soothing to you to have a few lines about the last days of your son Erastus Haskell of Company K, 141st New York Volunteers. I write in haste, & nothing of importance—only I thought any thing about Erastus would be welcome. From the time he came to Armory Square Hospital till he died, there was hardly a day but I was with him a portion of the time—if not during the day, then at night. I had no opportunity to do much, or any thing for him, as nothing was needed, only to wait the progress of his malady. I am only a friend, visiting the wounded & sick soldiers, (not connected with any society—or State.) From the first I felt that Erastus was in danger, or at least was much worse than they in the hospital supposed. As he made no complaint, they perhaps [thought him][93] not very bad—I told the [doctor of the ward] to

92. See 59. After WW handed the draft of this letter to Traubel, on May 7, 1888, the latter wrote: "I read the letter. I must have shown I was much moved. W. said gently: 'I see that you understand it. Well, I understand it, too. I know what you feel in reading it because I know what I felt in writing it. When such emotions are honest they are easily passed along.' I asked W.: 'Do you go back to those days?' 'I do not need to. I have never left them. They are here, now, while we are talking together—real, terrible, beautiful days!'" (I, 115).

With the draft letter, written on the stationery of the United States Christian Commission, there is an envelope which contains the following: "sent about Aug 15 or 16 '63 | letter to | S B Haskell | Breseport | Chenning Co N Y."

93. Where the letter was folded, it is now difficult to transcribe. I have checked doubtful readings with the draft.

look him over again—he was a much [sicker boy?] than he supposed, but he took it lightly, said, I know more about these fever cases than you do—the young man looks very sick, but I shall certainly bring him out of it all right. I have no doubt the doctor meant well & did his best—at any rate, about a week or so before Erastus died he got really alarmed & after that he & all the doctors tried to help him, but without avail—Maybe it would not have made any difference any how—I think Erastus was broken down, poor boy, before he came to the hospital here—I believe he came here about July 11th—Somehow I took to him, he was a quiet young man, behaved always correct & decent, said little—I used to sit on the side of his bed—I said once, You don't talk any, Erastus, you leave me to do all the talking—he only answered quietly, I was never much of a talker. The doctor wished every one to cheer him up very lively—I was always pleasant & cheerful with him, but did not feel to be very lively—Only once I tried to tell him some amusing narratives, but after a few moments I stopt, I saw that the effect was not good, & after that I never tried it again—I used to sit by the side of his bed, pretty silent, as that seemed most agreeable to him, & I felt it so too—he was generally opprest for breath, & with the heat, & I would fan him—occasionally he would want a drink—some days he dozed a good deal—sometimes when I would come in, he woke up, & I would lean down & kiss him, he would reach out his hand & pat my hair & beard a little, very friendly, as I sat on the bed & leaned over him.

Much of the time his breathing was hard, his throat worked—they tried to keep him up by giving him stimulants, milk-punch, wine &c—these perhaps affected him, for often his mind wandered somewhat—I would say, Erastus, don't you remember me, dear son?—can't you call me by name?—once he looked at me quite a while when I asked him, & he mentioned over in[audibly?] a name or two (one sounded like [Mr. Setchell]) & then, as his eyes closed, he said quite slow, as if to himself, I don't remember, I dont remember, I dont remember—it was quite pitiful—one thing was he could not talk very comfortably at any time, his throat & chest seemed stopped—I have no doubt at all he had some complaint besides the typhoid—In my limited talks with him, he told me about his brothers & sisters by name, & his parents, wished me to write to his parents & send them & all his love—I think he told me about his brothers living in different places, one in New York City, if I recollect right—From what he told me, he must have been poorly enough for several months before he came to Armory Sq[uare] Hosp[ital]—the first week in July I think he told me he was at the regimental hospital at a place called Baltimore Corners not many

94. WW probably drew upon this account of Haskell in his "Notebook of September–October, 1863": "He used to have his fife lying by him on a little stand by his cot, once told me that when he got well he would play me a tune" (Feinberg).

miles from White House, on the peninsula—previous to that, for quite a long time, although he kept around, he was not at all well—couldn't do much—was in the band as a fifer I believe—While he lay sick here he had his fife laying on the little stand by his side—he once told me that if he got well he would play me a tune on it[94]—but, he says, I am not much of a player yet.

I was very anxious he should be saved, & so were they all—he was well used by the attendants—poor boy, I can see him as I write—he was tanned & had a fine head of hair, & looked good in the face when he first came, & was in pretty good flesh too—(had his hair cut close about ten or twelve days before he died)—He never complained—but it looked pitiful to see him lying there, with such a look out of his eyes. He had large clear eyes, they seemed to talk better than words—I assure you I was attracted to him much—Many nights I sat in the hospital by his bedside till far in the night—The lights would be put out—yet I would sit there silently, hours, late, perhaps fanning him—he always liked to have me sit there, but never cared to talk—I shall never forget those nights, it was a curious & solemn scene, the sick & wounded lying around in their cots, just visible in the darkness, & this dear young man close at hand lying on what proved to be his death bed—I do not know his past life, but what I do know, & what I saw of him, he was a noble boy—I felt he was one I should get very much attached to. I think you have reason to be proud of such a son, & all his relatives have cause to treasure his memory.

I write to you this letter, because I would do something at least in his memory—his fate was a hard one, to die so—He is one of the thousands of our unknown American young men in the ranks about whom there is no record or fame, no fuss made about their dying so unknown, but I find in them the real precious & royal ones of this land, giving themselves up, aye even their young & precious lives, in their country's cause—Poor dear son, though you were not my son, I felt to love you as a son, what short time I saw you sick & dying here—it is as well as it is, perhaps better—for who knows whether he is not better off, that patient & sweet young soul, to go, than we are to stay? So farewell, dear boy—it was my opportunity to be with you in your last rapid days of death—no chance as I have said to do any thing particular, for nothing [could be done—only you did not lay] here & die among strangers without having one at hand who loved you dearly, & to whom you gave your dying kiss—

Mr and Mrs Haskell, I have thus written rapidly whatever came up about Erastus,[95] & must now close. Though we are strangers & shall prob-

95. Since WW composed a rough copy of this letter and then copied it before sending it, the artlessness of the letter was in part contrived.

ably never see each other, I send you & all Erastus' brothers & sisters my love—

Walt Whitman

I live when home, in Brooklyn, N Y. (in Portland avenue, 4th door north of Myrtle, my mother's residence.) My address here is care of Major Hapgood, paymaster U S A, cor 15th & F st, Washington D C.

65. *To Louisa Van Velsor Whitman*

Washington, August 11 1863

Dear mother

I sent Jeff a letter on Sunday, I suppose he got at the office—I feel so anxious to hear from George, one cannot help feeling uneasy, although these days sometimes it cannot help being long intervals without one's hearing from friends in the army—O I do hope we shall hear soon, & that it is all right with him—it seems as if the 9th corps had returned to Vicksburgh, & some acc'ts say that part of the corps had started to come up the river again—toward Kentucky I suppose—I have sent George two letters within a week past,[96] hoping they might have the luck to get to him, but hardly expect it either—

Mother, I feel very sorry to hear Andrew is so troubled in his throat yet, I know it must make you feel very unhappy—Jeff wrote me a good deal about it, & seems to feel very bad about Andrew's being unwell—but I hope it will go over, & that a little time will make him recover—I think about it every day[97]—

Mother, it has been the hottest weather here that I ever experienced, & still continues so—yesterday & last night was the hottest—still I slept sound, have good ventilation through my room, little as it is, (I still hire the same room in L street)—I was quite wet with sweat this morning when I woke up, a thing I never remember to have happened to me before, for I was not disturbed in my sleep & did not wake up once all night—Mother, I believe I did not tell you that on the 1st of June (or a while before) the O'Connor's, the friends I took my meals with so long, moved to other apartments, far more room & pleasanter—not far off though, I am there every

96. George's lengthy letter to his mother on July 23 from Milldale, Miss. (Trent), in which he described the regiment's recent activities, evidently had not reached the family when WW wrote. WW's letters to George and Jeff are not known.

97. On August 4, Jeff discussed Andrew's illness at length: "Andrew is not getting any better I fear. I think that he will hardly get well again, Walt. The doctors all say that he must go out from the seashore if he wants to get well. . . . He is badly off. He can hardly speak, nor eat anything, but worse than all I guess that his home comforts are not much. I dont think Nancy has the faculty of fixing things to eat for a sick man.

day almost, a little—so for nearly two months & a half I have been in the habit of getting my own breakfast in my room & my dinner at a restaurant —I have a little spirit lamp, & always have a capital cup of tea, & some bread, & perhaps some preserved fruit—for dinner I get a good plate of meat & plenty of potatoes, good & plenty, for 25 or 30 cents—I hardly ever take any thing more than these two meals, both of them are pretty hearty —eat dinner about 3—my appetite is plenty good enough, & I am about as fleshy as I was in Brooklyn—Mother, I feel better the last ten days, & at present, than I did the preceding six or eight weeks—there was nothing particular the matter with me, but I suppose a different climate & being so continually in the hospitals—but as I say I feel better, more strength & better in my head &c.—About the wound in my hand & the inflammation, &c.[98] it has thoroughly healed, & I have not worn any thing on my hand, nor had any dressing for the last five days—Mother, I hope you get along with the heat, for I see it is as bad or worse in New York & Brooklyn—I am afraid you suffer from it, it must be distressing to you—dear mother, do let things go, & just sit still & fan yourself—I think about you these hot days—I fancy I see you down there in the basement—I suppose you have your coffee for breakfast—I have not had three cups of coffee in six months, tea altogether—(I must come home & have some coffee for breakfast with you)—

Mother, I wrote to you about Erastus Haskell,[99] co K 141st N Y—his father, poor old man, come on here to see him, & found him dead three days, he had the body embalmed & took home—they are poor folks but very respectable—I was at the hospital yesterday as usual—I never miss a day—I go by my feelings—if I should feel that it would be better for me to lay by a while, I should do so, but not while I feel so well as I do the past week, for all the hot weather, & while the chance lasts I would improve it, for by & by the night cometh when no man can work, (ain't I getting pious?)

I got a letter from Probasco[1] yesterday, he sent $4 for my sick & wounded—I wish Jeff to tell him that it came right, & give him the men's thanks & my love—

Mother, have you heard any thing from Han? And about Mary's Fanny[2]—I hope you will write me soon & tell me everything—tell me exactly as things are, but I know you will—I want to hear family affairs be-

Andrew still goes to the Navy Yard and thereby gets his pay, but I hardly think he does anything. Sometimes he is much better than others but as a general thing he is mighty badly off" (Feinberg).

98. Evidently WW mentioned this inflammation in letters no longer extant.

99. The letter referred to is evidently lost. For Haskell, see 59, 64, and 78.

1. See 31.

2. Fanny Van Nostrand, mother-in-law of Mary, WW's sister. See also 69, 70, and 80.

fore any thing else—I am so glad to hear Mat is good & hearty—you must write me about Hat & little black head too—Mother, how is Eddy getting along—and Jess, is he about the same—I suppose Will Brown is home all right, tell him I spoke about him, & the Browns too[3]—dearest mother, I send you my love, & to Jeff too—must write when you can—

Walt

66. *To Lewis K. Brown*

Washington | August 11 1863

Dear Lewy,

I thought I would write you a few lines to-day—I suppose you rec'd a letter from me eight or nine days ago[4]—I hope this will find you in good health & spirits—I wrote to you not to go about too much, & eat & drink too freely, & I must repeat the caution—a fellow can keep himself in good condition by a little care & prudence—

Well, Lewy, the presentation to Dr Bliss[5] came off last Saturday evening—it was in ward F—the beds were all cleared out, the sick put in other wards—the room cleaned, hung with greens &c., looked very nice—the instruments were there on exhibition the afternoon. I took a view of them, they were in four cases, & looked very fine—in the evening they were presented—speeches were made by one & another—there was a band of music &c—I stopt about 20 minutes, but got tired, & went off among the boys that were confined to their beds—the room was crowded, & every thing passed off right I heard—

Lewy, we have had the hottest weather here I ever experienced—it has been now about ten days, & no let up yet—Yesterday & last night was the hottest, no rain for some time & the air prickly & burning—Still I am enjoying very good health, thank God—better this last week than I have had for two or three months—I have some thought of going on to New York for a short time, as I have not been home now in eight months, but if I do, I shall pretty surely return here before long—Lewy, the draft has been put through here in Washington the past week—they drafted lots of secessionists & quite a good many darks—(I wonder if it wouldn't be a good plan to draft all of both them kinds)—I don't hear any particular war news—the Army of the Potomac is down around Warrenton—there are conscripts arriving there to fill up the reg'ts, more or less every day—it will be a great & sudden change of life to many, especially such weather as this.

3. See 19.
4. See 60. WW had not received the letter Brown wrote on August 10; see the following letter.
5. The Washington *National Republican* of August 10 carried a two-column ac-

I believe I told you in my last letter about the strange way the baby was born in the Chaplain's—well the baby is alive & growing like a pig, & the father Mr Lane is getting well, Mrs Lane ditto—Dr Bliss is just going off on a furlough—the Chaplain & wife have left on a furlough—Taber[6] & the rest in ward K are all right—there have been quite a good many deaths in hospital the past week or so, the heat is bad for the poor wounded men—

Well, Lewy, I must now wind up—I send you my love, my darling son & comrade, & request you to write me soon as convenient, how you are getting along & all about things—I will write again before very long, till then good bye & God bless you, dear son—

Walt Whitman

address | care Major Hapgood paymaster U S A cor 15th & F st Washington D C—

67. *To Lewis K. Brown*

Washington | August 15 1863

Lewy, your letter of August 10 came safe, & was glad to hear all about you, & the way you are spending the time—Lew, you must be having first rate times out there—well you need something to make up what you have suffered—You speak of being used well out there—Lewy, I feel as if I could love any one that uses you well, & does you a kindness—but what kind of heart must that man have that would treat otherwise, or say any thing insulting, to a crippled young soldier, hurt in fighting for this union & flag? (Well I should say damned little man or heart in the business)—

Should you meet any such, you must not mind them, dear comrade, & not allow your feelings to be hurt by such loafers—(I agree with you that a rebel in the southern army is much more respectable than a northern copperhead.) Dear son, when I read about your agreeable visit of a week, & how much you enjoyed yourself, I felt as much gratified as though I had enjoyed it myself—& I was truly thankful to hear that your leg is still doing well, & on the gain—you must not mind its being slowly, dear son, if it only goes forward instead of backward, & you must try to be very careful of your eating & drinking &c., not indulge in any excesses, & not eat too much flummery, but generally plain food, for that is always best, & it helps along so much.

count of the presentation of five cases of surgical instruments to Bliss. Chaplain Jackson (see 60) declared with fervor: "We all love you, sir, for the kindness and urbanity with which you have always treated us."

6. See 60.

Lewy, I believe I wrote you an acc't of the presentation to Dr Bliss—he is now off north for three weeks—Dr Butler[7] (ward D) is in charge—some of the doctors & wardmasters have been drafted—poor Johnny Mahay[8] is not in very good spirits—he was to have an operation performed before Bliss went, but he went off & did not do it—Johnny is pretty low some days—Things in ward K are pretty much the same—they had some improvem'ts in the Hospital, new sinks, much better, & the grounds in front & between the wards nicely laid out in flowers & grass plots &c.—but, Lew, it has been awful hot in the wards the past two weeks, the roofs burnt like fire—

There is no particular war news—they are having batches of conscripts now every day in the Army—Meade is down on the upper Rappahannock & fords, & around Warrenton—Lee stretches down toward Gordonsville, they say his head quarters is there—folks are all looking toward Charleston—if we could only succeed there, I don't know what secesh would do—the ground seems to be slipping more & more from under their feet—Lew, the *Union* & the *American Flag* must conquer, it is destiny—it may be long, or it may be short, but that will be the result—but O what precious lives have been lost by tens of thousands in the struggle already—

Lew, you speak in your letter how you would like to see me—well, my darling, I wonder if there is not somebody who would be gratified to see you, & always will be wherever he is—Dear comrade, I was highly pleased at your telling me in your letter about your folks' place, the house & land & all the items—you say I must excuse you for writing so much foolishness—nothing of the kind—My darling boy, when you write to me, you must write without ceremony, I like to hear every little thing about yourself & your affairs—you need never care how you write to me, Lewy, if you will only—I never think about literary perfection in letters either, it is the *man* & the *feeling*—Lewy, I am feeling pretty well, but the sun affects me a little, aching & fulness in the head—a good many have been sun-struck here the last two weeks—I keep shady through the middle of the day lately—Well, my dear boy, I have scribbled away any thing, for I wanted to write you to-day & now I must switch off—good by, my darling comrade, for the present, & I pray God to bless you now & always.

Walt.

Write when you feel like it, Lewy, don't hurry—address still care Major Hapgood, paymaster U S A, cor 15th & F st Washington D C.

7. Not identified. 8. See 43. 9. See 40.
10. George wrote to his mother from Covington, Ky., on August 16 (Trent).
11. The rest of this paragraph was omitted in earlier printings of the letter. Note

68. *To Nathaniel Bloom*

INCOMPLETE DRAFT LETTER.

Washington | August 15 1863

Dear Nat,[9]

Your letter came safe & was received with cordial & forgiving welcome, (there is more joy over one sinner that repenteth at the last, than, &c &c) —But I don't know what right I have to lecture you—

69. *To Louisa Van Velsor Whitman*

Washington | August 18 1863

Dear Mother,

I was mighty glad to get George's letter, I can tell you—you have not heard since, I suppose—they must be now back again in Kentucky, or that way, as I see a letter from Cairo, (up the Mississippi river,) that boats had stopt there with the 9th Corps on, from Vicksburgh, going up toward Cincinnati—I think the letter was dated Aug 10. I have no doubt they are back again up that way somewhere.[10] I wrote to George, four or five days ago, I directed it Ohio, Mississippi or elsewhere—

Mother, I was very glad indeed to get your letter—I am so sorry Andrew does not get any better, it is very distressing—about losing the voice, he must not be so much alarmed, as that continues sometimes years, & the health otherwise good[11]—Mother, you must have had a very unhappy day Heyde's first letter came, writing all such stuff as I guess no man living but he can tack together—I know how you must have felt, with your other annoyances, & every thing, mother. I do hope you will try not to let things cast you down, for they pass over somehow, & it hurts one so in old age to be taken down even for a day—Heyde is bound to make as much unhappiness as he can—(he is worse than bed bugs.)

Mother, I wrote to Han about five days ago, told her we had heard from George, & all the news—I must write to Mary too, without fail—I should like to hear from them all, & from Fanny—There has been a young man here in hospital, from Farmingdale, he was wounded, his name is Hendrickson, he has gone home on a furlough, he knows the Van Nostrands very well, I told him to go & see Aunt Fanny.[12] I was glad you gave Emma Price my direction here, I should like to hear from Mrs Price[13] & her

also the excisions in 50 and 70.

12. See 80. 13. See 12.

girls first rate, I think a great deal about them, &, mother, I wish you to tell any of them so, they always used me first rate, & always stuck up for me—if I knew their street & number I should write—

It has been awful hot here, now for twenty one days—ain't that a spell of weather?—the first two weeks I got along better than I would have thought, but the last week I have felt it more, have felt it in my head a little—I no more stir without my umbrella, in the day time, than I would without my boots. I am afraid of the sun affecting my head, & move pretty cautious—Mother, I think every day, I wonder if this hot weather is affecting mother much, I suppose it must a good deal, but I hope it cannot last much longer—mother, I had a letter in the N Y Times of last Sunday[14] —did you see it?

I wonder if George can't get a furlough & come home for a while, that furlough he had was only a flea bite—if he could it would be no more than right, for no man in the country has done his duty more faithful, & without complaining of any thing or asking for any thing, than George—I suppose they will fill up the 51st with conscripts, as that seems the order of the day —a good many are arriving here, from the north, & passing through to join Meade's army—we are expecting to hear of more rows in New York, about the draft—it commences there right away I see—this time it will be no such doings as a month or five weeks ago, the gov't here is forwarding a large force of regulars to New York to be ready for any thing that may happen—there will be no blank cartridges this time—Well, I thought when I first heard of the riot in N Y[15] I had some feeling for them, but soon as I found what it really was, I felt it was the devil's own work all through—I guess the strong arm will be exhibited this time, up to the shoulder.

Mother, I want to see you & all very much—As I wish to be here at the opening of Congress, & during the winter, I have an idea I will try to come home for a month, but I don't know when—I want to see the young ones & Mat & Jeff & every body—Well, mother, I should like to know all the domestic affairs home, don't you have the usual things, eating &c. Why, Mother, I should think you would eat nearly all your meals with Mat—I know you must when they have any thing good, (& I know Mat will have good things if she has got a cent left)—Mother, don't you miss *Walt*—loafing around, & carting himself off to New York, toward the latter part of every afternoon?—how do you & the Browns get along?—that hell-hole

14. "Washington in the Hot Season," New York *Times*, August 16; later included in *Specimen Days* (*CW*, IV, 70–74). WW wrote the draft letter to Sawyer (71) on the verso of this manuscript.

15. See 58.

16. George wrote to his mother from Covington, Ky., on August 16: "I have been perfectly healthy all through the Vicksburg campaign although there has been considerable sickness in our regt. especially during the last two weeks of our stay at Milldale"

over the way, what a nuisance it must be nights—here it is very quiet nights, & I generally have a very good sleep—mother, I suppose you sleep in the back room yet—I suppose the new houses next door are occupied—how I should like to take a walk on old Fort Greene, tell Mannahatta her uncle Walt will be home yet, from the sick soldiers, & have a good walk all around, if she behaves good to her grandmother & don't cut up—Mother, I am scribbling this hastily in Major Hapgood's office, it is not so hot today, quite endurable. I send you my love, dear mother, & to all, & wish Jeff & you to write as often as you can—

Walt

70. *To Louisa Van Velsor Whitman*

Washington | August 25 1863

Dear Mother,

The letter from George & your lines, & a few from Jeff came yesterday, & I was glad indeed to be certain that George had got back to Kentucky safe & well[16]—while so many fall that we know or, what is about as bad, get sick or hurt in the fight, & lay in hospital, it seems almost a miracle that George should have gone through so much, south & north & east and west, & been in so many hard-fought battles, & thousands of miles of weary & exhausting marches, & yet have stood it so, & be yet alive & in good health & spirits—O mother, what would we [have] done if it had been otherwise—if he had met the fate of so many we know—if he had been killed or badly hurt in some of those battles—I get thinking about it sometimes, & it works upon me so I have to stop & turn my mind on something else—

Mother, I feel bad enough about Andrew, & I know it must be so with you too—one don't know what do do—if we had money he would be welcome to it, if it would do any good—if George's money comes from Kentucky this last time & you think some of it would do Andrew any real good I advise you to take some & give him—I think it would be proper & George would approve of it[17]—I believe there is not much but trouble in this world, & if one hasn't any for himself he has it made up by having it brought close to him through others, & that is sometimes worse than to have it touch one'sself—Mother, you must not let Andrew's case & the poor condition of his household comforts &c. work upon you, for I fear you will,

(Trent).

17. In a letter written between August 16–25, WW's mother spoke of using some of the $175 George promised to send her to aid Andrew: "If he could see Andrew i know he would say mother give him some and let him go on in the country if it will doo him good. I went down there the other day but O walt how poverty stricken every thing looked, it made me feel bad all night and so dirty every thing" (Trent).

but, mother, it's no use to worry about such things—I have seen now so much horrors that befal men, (so bad & such suffering & mutilations, &c that the poor men can defy their fate to do any thing more or any harder misfortune or worse agony) that I sometimes think I have grown callous—but, no, I don't think it is that, but nothing of ordinary misfortune seems as it used to, & death itself has lost all its terrors—I have seen so many cases in which it was so welcome & such a relief—

Mother, you must just resign yourself to things that occur—but I hardly think it is necessary to give you any charge about it, for I think you have done so for many years, & stood it all with good courage—

We have a second attack of the hot weather—Sunday was the most burning day I ever yet saw—it is very dry & dusty here, but to-day we are having a middling good breeze—I feel pretty well, & whenever the weather for a day or so is passably cool I feel really first rate, so I anticipate the cooler season with pleasure—

Mother, I believe I wrote to you I had a letter in N Y Times, Sunday 16th[18]—I shall try to write others & more frequently—the three Eagles came safe, I was glad to get them—I sent them & another paper to George—Mother, you none of you ever mention whether you get my letters, but I suppose they come safe—it is not impossible I may miss some week, but I have not missed a single one for months past—I wish I could send you something worth while & I wish I could send something for Andrew—Mother, write me exactly how it is with him[19]—I see you still have letters from Heyde, I hope they dont never come just as you are setting down to the table, for they would take away your appetite I know—Mother, I have some idea Han is getting some better, it is only my idea somehow—I hope it is so from the bottom of my heart—did you hear from Mary's Fanny[20] since?

And how are Mat's girls—so, Mannahatta, you tear Uncle George's letters, do you?[21]—you mustn't do so, little girl, nor Uncle Walt's either, but when you get to be a big girl, you must have them all nice, & read them, for grandmother will perhaps leave them to you in her will, if you behave like a lady—Matty, my dear sister, how are you getting along? I really want to see you, bad—& the baby too—well may be we shall all come together & have some good times yet—Jeff, I hope by next week this time we shall be in possession of Charleston—some papers say Burnside

18. See 69.

19. The next sentence was deleted by the executors. See omissions of references to Heyde in 50 and 69.

20. Fanny Van Nostrand. See 65 and 80.

21. Mrs. Whitman was not amused in her terse postscript: "Miss hattie has torn

is moving for Knoxville, but it is doubtful—I think the 9th Corps might take a rest awhile anyhow—good bye, mother—

Walt

71. *To Thomas P. Sawyer* [*8.(?). 1863*]

ENDORSED (by WW?): "July '63." DRAFT LETTER.

Dear brother,[22]

You did not write any answer to my last two letters, now quite a while ago, still I will write again. I still remain here in Washington, finding just about work enough to pay my expenses. Occasionaly go to Armory Hospital. I see Lewy Brown always, he has returned from his furlough, he told me a few days ago he had written to you, & had sent you my best respects—I told him he must never send my respects to you but always my love. Lewy's leg has not healed, gives him trouble yet. He goes around with crutches, but not very far. He is the same good young man as ever, & always will be.

Well, Tom, it looks as though secesh was nearly played out—if they lose Charleston, as I believe they will soon, seems to be they may as well give it up—Some think that Lee will make another dash up this way, but I should think Gettysburgh might last him a while yet.

Dear brother, how I should like to see you—& would like to know how things have gone with you for three months past. I cant understand why you have ceased to correspond with me. Any how I hope we shall meet again, & have some good times. So, dearest comrade, good bye for present & God bless you.

72. *To Louisa Van Velsor Whitman*

Washington | September 1 1863

Dear Mother,

I have been thinking to-day & all yesterday about the draft in Brooklyn, & whether Jeff would be drafted—you must some of you write me just as soon as you get this[23]—I want to know, I feel anxious enough I can tell you—& besides it seems a good while since I have rec'd any

this letter as usual" (Trent).

22. See 43 for details of WW's correspondence with Sawyer. On the verso of this letter is a draft of the article mentioned in note to 69.

23. Jeff was not drafted; see 77.

letters from home—Of course it is impossible for Jeff to go, in case it should turn out he was drafted—the way our family is all situated now, it would be madness—If the Common Council raise the money to exempt men with families dependent on them, I think Jeff ought to have no scruples in taking advantage of it, as I think he is in duty bound—but we will see what course to take, when we know the result &c. Write about it right away.

The Eagles came, this is the second time—I am always glad to get them—Jeff, wait till you get four or five, & then send them with a two cent stamp—I have not had any letter from George[24]—Mother, have you heard any thing? did the money come? Dear mother, how are you nowadays—I do hope you feel well & in good spirits—I think about you every day of my life out here—sometimes I see women in the hospitals, mothers come to see their sons, & occasionally one that makes me think of my dear mother—one did very much, a lady about 60, from Pennsylvania, come to see her son, a Captain, very badly wounded, & his wound gangrened, & they after a while removed him to a tent by himself—another son of hers, a young man, came with her to see his brother—she was pretty full-sized lady, with spectacles, she dressed in black, looked real Velsory. I got very well acquainted with her, she had a real Long-Island old fashioned way—but I had to avoid the poor Captain as it was that time that my hand was cut in the artery, & I was liable to gangrene myself—but she and the two sons have gone home now, but I doubt whether the wounded one is alive as he was very low—

Mother, I want to hear about Andrew too, whether he went to Rockland lake[25]—You have no idea how many soldiers there are who have lost their voices, & have to speak in whispers—there are a great many, I meet some almost every day—As far as that alone is concerned Andrew must not be discouraged, as the general health may be good as common irrespective of that—I do hope Andrew will get along better than he thinks for—it is bad enough for a poor man to be out of health even partially, but he must try to look on the bright side—

Mother, have you heard any thing from Han since, or from Mary's

24. There are no extant letters from George to the family between August 16 and September 7, when he again wrote from Kentucky.

25. See notes to 77.

26. Apparently WW replied to Mrs. Price's letter before September 15, but the letter is lost.

27. The letter appeared on October 4; see 83.

28. As WW informed Mrs. Curtis in 93, Caleb Babbitt suffered a sun stroke in July and was admitted to Armory Square Hospital. According to the "Hospital Note Book" (Huntington), Babbitt had been in Mobile earlier. About August 1, he left Washington on furlough. On August 18, Mary A. Babbitt informed WW of Caleb's arrival in Barre, Mass.; because of his exhaustion he was unable to write. Mary acknowledged WW's letter on September 6, and wrote that Caleb was "not quite as well as when I wrote you

folks? I got a letter from Mrs Price[26] last week, if you see Emma tell her I was pleased to get it, & shall answer it very soon—Mother, I have sent another letter to the N Y Times,[27] it may appear, if not to-day, within a few days—I am feeling excellent well these days, it is so moderate & pleasant weather now, I was getting real exhausted with the heat. I thought of you too, how it must have exhausted you those hot days—I still occupy the same little 3d story room, 394 L st, & get my breakfast in my room in the morning myself, & dinner at a restaurant about 3 o'clock—I get along very well & very economical (which is a forced put, but just as well). But I must get another room or a boarding house soon, as the folks are all going to move this month—My good & *real* friends the O'Connors live in the same block, I am in there every day—

Dear Mother, tell Mat & Miss Mannahatta I send them my love—I want to see them both—O how I want to see Jeff & you, mother, I sometimes feel as if I should just get in the cars & come home—& the baby too, you must always write about her—dear mother, good bye for present—

Walt

73. *To Mary A. Babbitt*

INCOMPLETE DRAFT LETTER.

Washington | September 3, 1863

Mary A. Babbitt,[28]

I write you regarding your brother Caleb—I rec'd your letter of August 18th & I have written to Caleb three letters since. But I have not heard a word about him, only your letter of August 18th—

74. *To Nathaniel Bloom*

Washington | September 5 1863

Dear Nat[29]

I wish you were here if only to enjoy the bright & beautiful weather we are having here now for about two weeks—then it is sufficiently cool, &

before. . . . he wishes me to tell you to keep writing . . . for your letters do him more good than a great deal of medicine." On September 18, at the expiration of his forty-day furlough, Caleb was strong enough to write: "Walt—In your letters you wish me to imagine you talking with me when I read them, well I do, and it does very well to think about, but it is nothing compared with the original." On October 1, Babbitt was depressed —"dark clouds seem to be lying in my pathway and I can not remove them nor hide them from my mind"—until he mentioned his beloved, Nellie F. Clark, who "has saved me." On October 26, S. H. Childs wrote for Caleb from the Massachusetts General Hospital, Boston: "He Is unable to set up & suffers considerable pain In his head" (Berg). See also 93, 102, and 106. (This letter is in two pieces, on the verso of which appears the draft letter to Bethuel Smith, 75.)

29. For accounts of WW's New York friends, see 40 and 41.

the air buoyant & inspiriting—dear friend, how long it is since we have seen each other, since those pleasant meetings & those hot spiced rums & suppers & our dear friends Gray & Chauncey, & Russell, & Fritschy too, (who for a while at first used to sit so silent,) & Perkins & our friend Raymond—how long it seems—how much I enjoyed it all. What a difference it is with me here—I tell you, Nat, my evenings are frequently spent in scenes that make a terrible difference—for I am still a hospital visitor, there has not passed a day for months (or at least not more than two) that I have not been among the sick & wounded, either in hospitals or down in camp—occasionally here I spend the evenings in hospital—the experience is a profound one, beyond all else, & touches me personally, egotistically, in unprecedented ways—I mean the way often the amputated, sick, sometimes dying soldiers cling & cleave to me as it were as a man overboard to a plank, & the perfect content they have if I will remain with them, sit on the side of the cot awhile, some youngsters often, & caress them &c.—It is delicious to be the object of so much love & reliance, & to do them such good, soothe & pacify torments of wounds &c—You will doubtless see in what I have said the reason I continue so long in this kind of life—as I am entirely on my own hook too.

Life goes however quite well with me here—I work a few hours a day at copying &c, occasionally write a newspaper letter, & make enough money to pay my expenses—I have a little room, & live a sort of German or Parisian student life—always get my breakfast in my room, (have a little spirit lamp) & rub on free & happy enough, untrammeled by business, for I make what little employment I have suit my moods—walk quite a good deal, & in this weather the rich & splendid environs of Washington are an unfailing fountain to me—go down the river, or off into Virginia once in a while—All around us here are forts, by the score—great ambulance & teamsters' camps &c—these I go to—some have little hospitals, I visit, &c &c—

Dear Nat, your good & friendly letter came safe, & was indeed welcome—I had not thought you had forgotten me, but I wondered why you did not write—What comfort you must take out there in the country, by the river—I have read your letter many times, as I do from all my dear friends & boys there in New York—Perkins lately wrote me a first-rate letter, & I will reply to it soon—I wish to see you all very much—I wish you to give my love to Fritschy, & Fred Gray—I desire both to write to me—Nat, you also, my dear comrade, & tell me all about the boys & every-

30. See 63.
31. I have not been able to identify this nurse. She is referred to in 94 and 95.

thing, all the little items are so good—should Charles Russell visit New York, I wish you to say to him I send him my love—I wish you the same to Perk, & to Kingsley[30] & Ben Knower—So good bye, my comrade, till we meet, & God bless you, dear friend—

Walt

address me care Major Hapgood, Paymaster U S A, cor 15th & F Washington D C—

75. *To Miss Gregg*

ENDORSED (by WW): "Note to Miss Gregg." DRAFT LETTER.

Sept 7, '63

Dear friend,[31]

You spoke the other day, partly in fun, about the men being so undemonstrative. I thought I would write you a line, as I hear you leave the hospital tomorrow for a few weeks. Your labor of love & disinterestedness here in Hospital is appreciated. I have invariably heard the Ward A patients speak of you with gratitude, sometimes with enthusiasm. They have their own ways (not outside eclat, but in manly American hearts, however rude, however undemonstrative to you). I thought it would be sweet to your tender & womanly heart, to know what I have so often heard from the soldiers about you, as I sat by their sick cots. I too have learnt to love you, seeing your tender heart, & your goodness to those wounded & dying young men—for they have grown to seem to me as my sons or dear young brothers.

As I am poor I cannot make you a present, but I write you this note, dear girl, knowing you will receive it in the same candor & good faith it is written.

76. *To Louisa Van Velsor Whitman*

Washington | September 8 1863

Dearest mother,

I wrote to Jeff Sunday last that his letters sent Sept 3d containing your letter & $5 from Mr Lane had miscarried—this morning when I came down to Major Hapgood's office I found it on my table, so it is all right—singular where it has been all this while as I see the post mark on it is Brooklyn Sept 3 as Jeff said[32]—Mother, what to do about Andrew I hardly

32. Jeff wrote to WW twice on September 3 (Feinberg). The earlier letter contained the contribution from Moses Lane; the second, written in the evening after a visit to Dr. Ruggles with Andrew, arrived in Washington first.

know—as it is I feel about as much pity for you as I do for my poor brother Andrew, for I know you will worry yourself about him all the time—I was in hopes it was only the trouble about the voice &c but I see I was mistaken, & it is probably worse—I know you & Jeff & Mat will do all you can—& will have patience with all (it is not only the sick who are poorly off, but their friends—but it is best to have the greatest forbearance, & do & give &c whatever one can—but you know that, & practice it too, dear mother)[33]—

Mother, if I had the means, O how cheerfully I would give them, whether they availed any thing for Andrew or not—yet I have long made up my mind that money does not amount to so much, at least not so very much, in serious cases of sickness—it is judgment, both in the person himself, & in those he has to do with—& good heart is every thing—(Mother, you remember Theodore Gould,[34] how he has stuck it out, though sickness & death has had hold of him as you may say for fifteen years)—but any how I hope we will all do what we can for Andrew—Mother, I think I must try to come home for a month—I have not given up my project of lecturing, I spoke about before,[35] but shall put it in practice yet, I feel clear it will succeed enough. (I wish I had some of the money already, it would be satisfaction to me to contribute something to Andrew's necessities, for he must have bread)—I will write to you of course before I come—

Mother, I hope you will live better—Jeff tells me you & Jess & Ed live on poor stuff, you are so economical[36]—Mother, you mustn't do so, as long as you have a cent—I hope you will at least four or five times a week have a steak of beef or mutton, or something substantial for dinner—I have one

33. Andrew's condition was rapidly deteriorating. Toward the end of August he went off to the country with one of his cronies, after he had gone on his first spree in three months. "He went home to get his things," Mrs. Whitman wrote to her son on September 3, "and nancy had not put them up. she told him to put them up himself and his having drank some he was very angry and he went away without taking any thing." Later in the same letter, the mother admitted that Andrew looked "very bad indeed," and reported that "he says he wouldent care about living only for his children. i think nance might do better at any rate. she might keep things a little cleaner" (Trent).

Jeff, devoting almost an entire letter to Andrew's illness, reported Dr. Ruggles' diagnosis: "That he could think of no medicine that would be likely to do him any good, That . . . what would cure him would be to take heart, go in the country again, and to resolve to get well." Jeff had proposed to his mother that she permit Andrew to occupy a room in her house while Martha nursed and fed him. Mrs. Whitman refused because she feared Andrew's entire family would move in. "I tell her to send the whole family back again, but she saing that 'she cant let him have it and that is the end of it.' . . . Perhaps it would not do any good, but I *think* it would save his life" (Feinberg). Since the family was feuding, Mrs. Whitman, on September 3(?), suggested to WW, "Write on a piece of paper [apart?] from the letter if you say any thing you dont want all to read" (Trent). Though he was tactful, Jeff was not pleased that WW remained in Washington and thus escaped direct participation in the family crisis: "What do you think about coming to Brooklyn. I think you better, for awhile any way. I wish you would

good meal of that kind every day, or at least five or six days out of the seven—but for breakfast I never have any thing but a cup of tea & some bread or crackers, (first rate tea though with milk & good white sugar)—well I find it is hearty enough—more than half the time I never eat any thing after dinner, & when I do it is only a cracker & cup of tea—Mother, I hope you will not stint yourselves—as to using George's money for your & Jess's & Ed's needful living expenses, I know George would be mad & hurt in his feelings, if he thought you was afraid to—Mother, now have a comfortable time as much as you can, & get a steak occasionally, won't you?

I suppose Mat got her letter last Saturday, I sent it Friday—O I was so pleased that Jeff was not drawn,[37] & I know how Mat must have felt too, & you too—I have no idea the government will try to draft again, whatever happens—they have carried their point, but have not made much out of it—O how the conscripts & substitutes are deserting down in front, & on their way there—you don't hear any thing about it, but it is incredible—they don't allow it to get in the papers—Mother, I was so glad to get your letter, you must write again—can't you write to-morrow, so I can get it Friday or Saturday?—you know though you wrote more than a week ago I did not get it till this morning—I wish Jeff to write too, as often as he can—mother, I was gratified to hear you went up among the soldiers[38]—they are rude in appearance, but they know what is decent, and it pleases them much to have folks, even old women, take an interest & come among them—mother, you must go again, & take [Hat]—Well, dear mother, I must close—I am first rate in health, so much better than a month & two mo's ago—my hand has entirely healed—I go to hospital every day, or night—I believe no men ever loved each other as I & some

write to Andrew" (Feinberg).

34. Not identified. 35. See 53 and 54.

36. Jesse was not in good health, according to the mother's letter of September 3: "Jesse aint very well. he has such sick spells. he rocks the cradle for martha day in and day out" (Trent). In his letter of the same day, Jeff agreed that Jesse was "a mere shadow of what he ought to be," but attributed the condition to his mother's frugality: "I have not the least doubt in my own mind that it all comes of his not having anything to eat that he can eat. Somehow or another, Mother seems to think that she ought to live without spending any money. Even to-day she has 25 or $30 in the house and I will bet that all they have for dinner will be a quart of tomats and a few cucumbers, and then Mother wonders why Jess vomits up his meals" (Feinberg). See also notes to 86.

37. Jeff was not drafted, as he reported in the earlier letter on September 3: "I was not one of the elected, I feel thankful. In our ward the screws were put rather tight, out of a little over 3000 names they drew 1056, nearly one in three. . . . If this is the last of it I feel thankful but I believe Uncle Abe left off some on account of [Governor Horatio] Seymour, if so I suppose there will be another spurt. However we wont worry till the time comes" (Feinberg). The letter to Martha is apparently lost.

38. Mrs. Whitman had noted that "there is part of two regments encamped on fort green. the indiana and 94th california . . . sis and i went up there this afternoon. poor fellows, they looked like hard times. i spoke to some of them" (Trent).

of these poor wounded, sick & dying men love each other—good bye, dearest mother, for present—

Walt

77. *To S. B. Haskell*

Washington | Sept 9 1863

Dear Sir,[39]

Your friendly letter acknowledging mine & telling me more of the previous life of Erastus was duly rec'd. Dear boy, death has not blotted out my love for him, the remembrance will be not sad only but sweet. You will either see me or hear of me in Brooklyn at my mother's, Louisa Whitman, Portland avenue, 4th door north of Myrtle, about two miles from Fulton ferry (Myrtle av cars)—

Walt Whitman

I send love to Erastus' mother & brothers & sisters—

78. *To Louisa Van Velsor Whitman*

ENDORSED (by WW): "letter ab't Jack Barker."

Washington | September 15 1863

Dear Mother

Your letters were very acceptable—one came just as I was putting my last in the post office—I guess they all come right—I have written to Han & George, & sent George papers—Mother, have you heard any thing whether the 51st went on with Burnside, or did they remain as a reserve in Kentucky[40]—Burnside has managed splendidly so far, his taking Knoxville & all together, it is a first class success—I have known Tennessee union men here in hospital, & I understand it therefore—the region where Knoxville is, is mainly union but the southerners could not exist without it, as it is in their midst—so they determined to pound & kill & crush out the unionists—all the savage & monstrous things printed in the papers about their treatment are true, at least that kind of thing is—as bad as the Irish in the mob treated the poor niggers in New York[41]—we north[erners] dont understand some things about southerners, it is very

39. See 59 and 64.

40. From a camp near Nicholasville, Ky., George reported to his mother on September 7 that, as he wrote, orders for his regiment to move to join Burnside's forces were countermanded. On September 22, from Camp Nelson, near Hickman's Bridge, Ky., George informed Jeff that "as our regt. was pretty well used up . . . we were left here to do guard duty" (Trent). Like WW, George was pleased with Burnside's victory: "Jeff, that was rather a slick thing 'old Burny' did up there wasent it, he fooled the rebs that time nicely."

41. Lader has recently explained the racial tensions in New York City preceding

strange—the contrast—if I should pick out the most genuine union men & real patriots I have ever met in all my experience, I should pick out two or three Tennesse & Virginia unionists I have met in the hospitals, wounded or sick—one young man I guess I have mentioned to you in my letters, John Barker,[42] 2d Tennessee Vol. (union)—was a long while a prisoner in secesh prisons in Georgia, & in Richmond—three times the devils hung him up by the heels to make him promise to give up his unionism, once he was cut down for dead—he is a young married man with one child—his little property destroyed, his wife & child turned out—he hunted & tormented, & any moment he could have had any thing if he would join the confederacy—but he was firm as a rock—he would not even take an oath to not fight for either side—they held him about 8 months—then he was very sick, scurvy, & they exchanged him & he came up from Richmond here to hospital, here I got acquainted with him—he is a large, slow, good natured man (somehow made me often think of father), shrewd, very little to say—wouldn't talk to any body but me—his whole thought was to get back & fight, he was not fit to go, but he has gone back to Tennessee—he spent two days with his wife & young one there & then to his regiment—he writes to me frequently, & I to him—he is not fit to soldier, for the rebels have destroyed his health & strength (though he is only 23 or 4), but nothing will keep him from his regiment, & fighting—he is uneducated, but as sensible a young man as I ever met, & understands the whole question—well, mother, Jack Barker is the most genuine Union man I have ever yet met—I asked him once very gravely why he didn't take the southern oath & get his liberty—if he didn't think it was foolish to be so stiff &c—I never saw such a look as he gave me, he thought I was in earnest—the old devil himself couldn't have had put a worse look in his eyes—

Mother, I have no doubt there are quite a good many just such men—he is now down there with his regiment, (one of his brothers was killed)—when he fails in strength, he gets the Colonel to detach him to do teamster's duty for a few days, on a march till he recruits his strength—but he always carries his gun with him—in a battle he is always in the ranks—then he is so sensible, such decent manly ways, nothing shallow or mean, (he must have been a giant in health, but now he is weaker, has

the draft riots: "The mob's savagery to the Negro sprang from complex motivations—economic, social, and religious. Most of its members were Irish. Comprising over half the city's foreign-born population of 400,000, out of a total of about 814,000, the Irish were the main source of cheap labor, virtually its peon class. Desperately poor and lacking real roots in the community, they had the most to lose from the draft. Further, they were bitterly afraid that even cheaper Negro labor would flood the North if slavery ceased to exist" *American Heritage*, x (June, 1959), 48.

42. See 53.

a cough too)—Mother, can you wonder at my getting so attached to such men, with such love, especially when they show it to me—some of them on their dying beds, & in the very hour of death or just the same when they recover, or partially recover—I never knew what American young men were till I have been in the hospitals—

Well, mother, I have got writing on—there is nothing new with me, just the same old thing—as I suppose it is with you there—Mother, how is Andrew, I wish to hear all about him—I do hope he is better, & that it will not prove any thing so bad—I will write to him soon myself, but in the mean time you must tell him to not put so much faith in medicine, drugs I mean, as in the true curative things, namely diet & careful habits, breathing good air, &c—you know I wrote in a former letter[43] what is the cause & foundation of the diseases of the throat, & what must be the remedy that goes to the bottom of the thing—sudden attacks &c are to be treated with applications & medicines, but diseases of a seated character are not to be cured by them, only perhaps a little relieved, (& often aggravated, made firmer)—

Dearest mother, I hope you yourself are well, & getting along good—About the letter in the Times,[44] I see ever since I sent it they have been very crowded with news that must be printed—I think they will give it yet. I hear there is a new paper in Brooklyn,[45] or to be one—I wish Jeff would send me some of the first numbers without fail, & a stray Eagle in same parcel to make up the 4 ounces—I was glad to hear Mat was going to write me a good long letter—every letter from home is so good, when one is away—(I often see the men crying in the hospital when they get a letter)—Jeff too I want him to write whenever he can, & not forget the new paper—we are having pleasant weather here, it is such a relief from that awful heat—(I can't think of another such seige without feeling sick at the thought)—Mother, I believe I told you I had written to Mrs. Price—do you see Emma? Are the soldiers still on Fort Greene?[46]

Well, mother, I have writ quite a letter—it is between 2 & 3 o'clock—

43. See 42. 44. See 83.
45. The first issue of the Brooklyn *Standard-Union* appeared on September 14.
46. See 76.
47. Perhaps the Boyle referred to in 378.
48. According to his diary (Glicksberg, 136), WW sent a letter to Smith on September 16.
49. Bethuel Smith, Company F, Second U. S. Cavalry, was wounded in 1863. He wrote to WW on September 17, from the U. S. General Hospital at Carlisle, Pa., "I left the armory hospital in somewhat of A hurry." He expected, he explained on September 28, to rejoin his regiment shortly, and was stationed near Washington when he wrote on October 13. He wrote on December 16, from Culpepper, Va., that he was doing provost duty, and on February 28, 1864, he was in a camp near Mitchell Station, Va., where "the duty is verry hard." He was wounded again on June 11, so his parents reported to WW (August 29), was transported to Washington, and went home on fur-

I am in Major Hapgood's all alone—from my window I see all the Potomac, & all around Washington—Major & all gone down in the Army to pay troops & I keep house—I am invited to dinner to-day at 4 o'clock at a Mr Boyle's[47]—I am going—(hope we shall have something good)—dear Mother, I send you my love, & same to Jeff & Mat & all, not forgetting Mannahatta (who I hope is a help & comfort to her grandmother)—well I must scratch off in a hurry, for it is nearly a hour later than I thought—good bye for present, dear mother—

Walt

79. *To Bethuel Smith* [*9.16(?).*[48] *1863*]

DRAFT LETTER.

Dear Comrade,[49]

I thought I would write you a few lines & see if they would reach you—I was very much disappointed when I went to Armory that evening to find my dear comrade was gone so sudden & unexpected.[50]

Thuey, did you take the envelope you had with my address?—if you did why have you not written to me, comrade?

What kind of accommodations have you at Carlisle, Thu, & how is the foot? I want to hear all about it—If you get this you must write to me, Thu, you need not mind ceremony—there is no need of *ceremony* between dear friends for that I hope we are, my loving boy, for all the difference in our ages.

There is nothing new with me here—I am very well in health & spirits, & only need some employment, clerkship or something, at fair wages to make things go agreeable with me—no, there is one thing more I need & that is Thuey, for I believe I am quite a fool, I miss you so.[51]

Well, Thu, it seems as though they were moving again in front—Pleasonton[52] has been advancing & fighting—he had all the cavalry mov-

lough on July 1. He returned on August 14 to Finley Hospital, where, on August 30, he wrote to WW: "I would like to see you verry much, I have drempt of you often & thought of you oftener still." He expected to leave the next day for Carlisle Barracks to be mustered out, and on October 22 he wrote to WW from Queensbury, N. Y. When his parents communicated with WW on January 26, 1865, Bethuel was well enough to perform tasks on the farm. (These letters are in the Feinberg Collection.) Smith was one of the soldiers to whom WW wrote ten years later; see 647.

50. At this point WW deleted: "Thuey, I think about you often & miss you more than you have any idea of—I hope you will . . ."

51. Compare the similar phrasing in 98.

52. Alfred Pleasonton (1824–1897) commanded the Union cavalry in 1863. After Gettysburg, he participated in battles at Culpepper Courthouse and Brandy Station.

ing, had quite a fight last Sunday, driving Stuart[53]—a good many wounded were brought here very late Monday night 12 o'clock—some 70 to Armory Hospital—all cavalry. In Ward A things go on the same—I dont go as often there as I did—Pyne & I went on quite a spree Monday, went to the mystic Varieties & elsewhere, (saw the ghost as they call it)[54]—had an oyster supper, ale, &c. quite a time—

Well I will not write any more this time—so good bye for present, Thuey, & I pray God bless you, my dear loving comrade, & I hope he will bring us together again—good by, dear boy, from your true friend—

Thuey, I enclose an envelope but will write my address here too for future—

Thuey, you went away without getting paid, aint you broke? I can send you a little, a few 10ct bills, my darling—You write to me, Thu, just how it is—you need not be afraid, my darling comrade—it is little, but it may be some use—Thuey, you write to me just as you would to your own older brother—

80. *To Louisa Van Velsor Whitman*

Washington | Sept 29 1863

Dear Mother,

Well here I sit this forenoon in a corner by the window in Major Hapgood's office—all the Potomac & Maryland & Virginia hills in sight—writing my Tuesday letter to you, dearest mother—Major has gone home to Boston on sick leave, & only the clerk & me occupy the office & he not much of the time—at the present moment there are two wounded officers come in to get their pay, one has crutches—the other is drest in the light blue uniform of the invalid corps—way up here in the 5th floor it is pretty hard scratching for cripples & very weak men to journey up here—often they come up here very weary & faint, & then find out they can't get their money, some red tape hitch, & the poor soldiers look so disappointed—it always makes me feel bad—

Mother, we are having perfect weather here nowadays, both night & day—the nights are wonderful, for the last three nights as I have walked

53. James Ewell Brown Stuart (1833–1864), the Confederate cavalry leader.

54. Washington theaters were featuring "ghosts" in September. The "Original Ghost" appeared at the Varieties on September 7. The Washington Theatre and Canterbury Hall also advertised ghosts on the same date, and Ford's New Theatre announced the imminent appearance of a specter.

55. In the Brooklyn *Daily Union* of September 22 appeared WW's communication "From Washington," which is adequately described by its subheadings: "Waiting and Speculating," "The Weather—The President," "Signs of Next Session," "The Wounded in the Hospitals," "The Army Young and American," "Benjamin D. Howell, Company D, 87th New York, Aged 18," and "Fifty-first New York Volunteers." It is reprinted in

home from the hospital pretty late, it has seemed to me like a dream, the moon & sky ahead of any thing I ever see before—Mother, do you hear any thing from George, I wrote to him yesterday & sent him your last letter & Jeff's enclosed—I shall send him some papers to-day—I send papers quite often—(why hasn't Jeff sent me the Union[55] with my letter in—I want much to see it, & whether they have misprinted it.)

Mother, I dont think the 51st has been in any of the fighting we know of down there yet—what is to come of course nobody can tell—As to Burnside I suppose you know he is among his *friends*, & I think this quite important, for such the main body of East Tennesseans are, & are far truer Americans any how than the Copperheads of the North—the Tennesseans will fight for us too—Mother, you have no idea how the soldiers, sick &c. (I mean the American ones to a man) all feel about the copperheads, they never speak of them without a curse & I hear them say with an air that shows they mean it, they would shoot them sooner than they would a rebel—Mother, the troops from Meade's army are passing through here night & day, going west & so down to reinforce Rosecrans I suppose—the papers are not permitted to mention it, but it is so—two Army Corps I should think have mostly passed—they go through night & day—I hear the whistle of the locomotive screaming away any time at night when I wake up, & the rumbling of the trains—

Mother dear, you must write to me soon, & so must Jeff—I thought Mat was going to send me a great long letter, I am always looking for it, I hope it will be full of every thing about family matters & doings, & how every body really is—I go to Major's box three or four times a day—I want to hear also about Andrew, & indeed about every one of you & every thing, nothing is too trifling, nothing uninteresting.

O mother, who do you think I got a letter from, two or three days ago—Aunt Fanny, Ansel's mother—She sent it by a young man, a wounded soldier who has been home to Farmingdale on furlough, & lately returned—she writes a first rate letter, Quaker all over[56]—I shall answer it—She says Mary & Ansel & all are well—I have rec'd another letter from Mrs Price, she has not good health, I am sorry for her from my heart, she is a good noble woman, no better kind—Mother, I am in the hospitals

UPP, II, 26–29.

56. Fanny Van Nostrand, Mary's mother-in-law, wrote to WW from Farmingdale, Long Island, on September 25: "I have raiced my pen unexpectedly to address thee with a few lines thinking thee will be pleased to hear from us as thee was so kind to let us know thee had not foregotton us in our old age, we wos very pleased with them few lines thee favord us with . . . I have roat more than I expected to with asking thee to over look and excuse all blunders and mistaks, thee must consider that it is from and old woman and vary laim" (LC). WW's letter is apparently lost. Mrs. Van Nostrand's letter was evidently delivered by the soldier Hendrickson mentioned in 69.

as usual—I stand it better the last three weeks than ever before—I go among the worst fevers & wounds with impunity—I go among the small pox, &c just the same—I feel to go without apprehension, & so I go—nobody else goes, & as the darkey said there at Charleston when the boat run on a flat & the reb sharpshooters were peppering them, *somebody must jump in de water* (& shove the boat off)—

Walt

81. *To William S. Davis*[57] [*10.1.1863*]

ENDORSED: "Sent Oct 1 1863 | to W S Davis | Worcester | Massachusetts." DRAFT LETTER.

The noble gift of your brother Joseph P Davis of [$20?] for the aid of the wounded, sick, dying soldiers here came safe to hand—it is being sacredly distributed to them—part of it has been so already—I may another time give you special cases—I go every day or night in the hospitals a few hours—

As to physical comforts, I attempt to have something—generally a lot of—something harmless & not too expensive to go round to each man, even if it is nothing but a good home-made biscuit to each man, or a couple of spoonfuls of blackberry preserve, I take a ward or two of an evening & two more next evening &c—as an addition to his supper—sometimes one thing, sometimes another, (judgment of course has to be carefully used)—then, after such general round, I fall back upon the main thing, after all, the special cases, alas, too common—those that need special attention, some little delicacy, some trifle—very often, far above all else, soothing kindness wanted—personal magnetism—poor boys, their sick hearts & wearied & exhausted bodies hunger for the sustenance of love or their deprest spirits must be cheered up—I find often young men, some hardly more than children in age yet—so good, so sweet, so brave, so decorous, I could not feel them nearer to me if my own sons or young brothers—Some cases even I could not tell any one, how near to me, from their yearning ways

57. Davis, a lawyer in Worcester, Mass., acting upon instructions from his brother Joseph, who was in Peru, sent Jeff $50 for WW's hospital work. On September 24, Jeff advised WW to acknowledge the gift and to describe his hospital work: "I consider it an opportunity for you to make this $50 the father of 100's without in the least seeming like one asking for it" (Feinberg). Joseph returned from Peru in 1865, and went with Jeff later to St. Louis; see 234. The brothers were descendants of a distinguished Massachusetts family. See John Davis Estabrook, *Three Generations of Northboro Davises, 1781–1894* (1908), 35–36; and E. A. Davis, *Eager–Davis Genealogy* (1859).

58. According to WW's notations, the material in this paragraph up to this point was to have been incorporated into the preceding paragraph. Since there are no indications in the manuscript as to where he intended to place it, I have transcribed literally.

59. When Traubel read this letter aloud on May 23, 1888, WW commented: "Some-

& their sufferings—it is comfort & delight to me to minister to them, to sit by them—some so wind themselves around one's heart, & will be kissed at parting at night just like children—though veterans of two years of battles & camp life—

I always carry a haversack with some articles most wanted—physical comforts are a sort of basis—I distribute nice large biscuit, sweet-crackers, sometimes cut up a lot of peaches with sugar, give preserves of all kinds, jellies, &c. tea, oysters, butter, condensed milk, plugs of tobacco, (I am the only one that doles out this last, & the men have grown to look to me) —wine, brandy, sugar, pickles, letter-stamps, envelopes & note-paper, the morning papers, common handkerchiefs & napkins, undershirts, socks, dressing gowns, & fifty other things[58]—I have lots of special little requests. Frequently I give small sums of money—shall do so with your brother's contribution—the wounded are very frequently brought & lay here a long while without a cent. I have been here & in front 9 months doing this thing, & have learned much—two-thirds of the soldiers are from 15 to 25 or 6 years of age—lads of 15 or 16 more frequent than you have any idea—seven-eighths of the Army are Americans, our own stock—the foreign element in the army is much overrated, & is of not much account anyhow—As to these hospitals, (there are dozens of them in [&] around Washington) [there] are no hospitals you must understand like the diseased half-foreign collections under that name common at all times in cities—in these here, the noblest, cleanest stock I think of the world, & the most precious.[59]

82. *To Margaret S. Curtis* — *10.4.* [*1863*]

ENDORSED (by WW): "Oct 5, '63. | Margarete S Curtis | care Charles P Curtis | Boston | Mass."
DRAFT LETTER.

Washington, | Armory Sq Hospital, Sunday evening Oct 4

Dear Madam,[60]

Your letter reached me this forenoon with the $30 for my dear boys, for very dear they have become to me, wounded & sick here in the

times I am myself almost afraid of myself—afraid to read such a letter over again: it carries me too painfully back into old days—into the fearful scenes of the war. I don't think the war seemed so horrible to me at the time, when I was busy in the midst of its barbarism, as it does now, in retrospect" (I, 198).

60. Margaret S. Curtis, wife of a Boston counsellor, and her sister, Hannah E. Stevenson (see 85), sent sums of money to WW. Mr. and Mrs. Curtis had sent $30 on October 1; see Donaldson, 147. According to the Boston Directory of 1888, Mrs. Curtis died on March 13 of that year. After WW gave this letter to Traubel on July 27, 1888, he observed: "My main motive would be to say things: not to say them prettily—not to stun the reader with surprises—with fancy turns of speech—with unusual, unaccustomed words—but to say them—to shoot my gun without a flourish and reach the mark if I can. The days in the hospitals were too serious for that" (II, 51).

government hospitals—As it happens I find myself rapidly making acknowledgment of your welcome letter & contribution from the midst of those it was sent to aid—& best by a sample of actual hospital life on the spot, & of my own goings around the last two or three hours—As I write I sit in a large pretty well-fill'd ward by the cot of a lad[61] of 18 belonging to Company M, 2d N Y cavalry, wounded three weeks ago to-day at Culpepper—hit by fragment of a shell in the leg below the knee—a large part of the calf of the leg is torn away, (it killed his horse)—still no bones broken, but a pretty large ugly wound—I have been writing to his mother at Comac, Suffolk co. N Y—She must have a letter just as if from him, about every three days—it pleases the boy very much—has four sisters—them also I have to write to occasionally—Although so young he has been in many fights & tells me shrewdly about them, but only when I ask him—He is a cheerful good-natured child—has to lie in bed constantly, his leg in a box—I bring him things—he says little or nothing in the way of thanks—is a country boy—always smiles & brightens much when I appear—looks straight in my face & never at what I may have in my hand for him—I mention him for a specimen as he is within reach of my hand & I can see that his eyes have been steadily fixed on me from his cot ever since I began to write this letter.

There are some 25 or 30 wards, barracks, tents, &c in this hospital—This is ward C, has beds for 60 patients, they are mostly full—most of the other principal wards about the same—so you see a U S general hospital here is quite an establishment—this has a regular police, armed sentries at the gates & in the passages &c.—& a great staff of surgeons, cadets, women & men nurses &c &c. I come here pretty regularly because this hospital receives I think the worst cases & is one of the least visited—there is not much hospital visiting here now—it has become an old story—the principal here, Dr Bliss, is a very fine operating surgeon[62]—sometimes he performs several amputations or other operations of importance in a day—amputations, blood, death are nothing here—you will see a group absorbed [in] playing cards up at the other end of the room.

I visit the sick every day or evening—sometimes I stay far in the night, on special occasions. I believe I have not missed more than two days in past six months. It is quite an art to visit the hospitals to advantage. The amount of sickness, and the number of poor, wounded, dying young men are appalling. One often feels lost, despondent, his labors not even a drop in the bucket—the wretched little he can do in proportion.

61. James S. Stilwell; see 90 and 95. Stilwell was mentioned in the "Notebook: September–October, 1863" (Feinberg) and "Hospital Notes" (Huntington). He wrote to WW on September 2(?) and 27, 1864 (Berg).

I believe I mentioned in my letter to Dr Russell[63] that I try to distribute something, even if but the merest trifle, all round, without missing any, when I visit a ward, going round rather rapidly—& then devoting myself, more at leisure, to the cases that need special attention. One who is experienced may find in almost any ward at any time one or two patients or more, who are at that time trembling in the balance, the crisis of the wound, recovery uncertain, yet death also uncertain. I will confess to you, madam, that I think I have an instinct & faculty for these cases. Poor young men, how many have I seen, & known—how pitiful it is to see them—one must be calm & cheerful, & not let on how their case really is, must stop much with them, find out their idiosyncrasies—do any thing for them—nourish them, judiciously give the right things to drink—bring in the affections, soothe them, brace them up, kiss them, discard all ceremony, & fight for them, as it were, with all weapons. I need not tell your womanly soul that such work blesses him that works as much as the object of it. I have never been happier than in some of these hospital ministering hours.

It is now between 8 & 9, evening—the atmosphere is rather solemn here to-night—there are some very sick men here—the scene is a curious one—the ward is perhaps 120 or 30 feet long—the cots each have their white musquito curtains—all is quite still—an occasional sigh or groan—up in the middle of the ward the lady nurse sits at a little table with a shaded lamp, reading—the walls, roof, &c are all whitewashed—the light up & down the ward from a few gas-burners about half turned down—It is Sunday evening—to-day I have been in the hospital, one part or another, since 3 o'clock—to a few of the men, pretty sick, or just convalescing & with delicate stomachs or perhaps badly wounded arms, I have fed their suppers—partly peaches pealed, & cut up, with powdered sugar, very cool & refreshing—they like to have me sit by them & peal them, cut them in a glass, & sprinkle on the sugar—(all these little items may-be may interest you).

I have given three of the men, this afternoon, small sums of money—I provide myself with a lot of bright new 10ct & 5ct bills, & when I give little sums of change I give the bright new bills. Every little thing even must be taken advantage of—to give bright fresh 10ct bills, instead of any other, helps break the dullness of hospital life—

62. Originally WW wrote: "the principal surgeon, Dr Bliss, is a capital surgeon, & a pretty good head manager of hospital."

63. See 99. The letter WW referred to, probably written in September, is not extant.

83. *To Louisa Van Velsor Whitman*

Washington | October 6 1863

Dearest mother

Your letter & George's came safe—dear brother George, one dont more than get a letter from him before you want to hear again, especially as things are looking pretty stormy down that way—but, mother, I rather lean to the opinion that the 51st is still in Kentucky at or near where George last wrote,[64] but of course that is only my guess—I send George papers often & occasionally letters—mother, I sent him enclosed your letter before the last, though you said in it not to tell him how much money he had home, as you wanted to surprise him, but I sent it—Mother, I think Rosecrans & Burnside will be too much for the rebels down there yet—I myself make a great acc't of Burnside being in the midst of *friends*, & *such* friends too—they will *fight* & fight up to the handle & kill somebody—(it seems as if it was coming to that pass where we will either have to destroy or be destroyed)—

Mother, I wish you would write soon after you get this, or Jeff or Mat must, & tell me about Andrew, if there is any thing different with him—I think about him every day & night. I believe I must come home even if it is only for a week—I want to see you all very much—Mother, I know you must have a good deal to harrass & trouble you, I dont mean about Andrew personally, for I know you would feel to give your life to save his, & do any thing to nourish him, but about the children & Nancy—but, mother, you must not let any thing chafe you, & you must not be squeamish about saying firmly at times not to have little Georgy[65] too much to trouble you (poor little fellow, I have no doubt he will be a pleasanter child when he grows older) & while you are pleasant with Nancy, you must be sufficiently plain with her—only, mother, I know you will & Jeff & Mat will too be *invariably* good to Andrew, & not mind his being irritable at times, it is his disease, & then his temper is naturally fretful, but it is such a misfortune to have such sickness, & always do any thing for him that you can in reason—Mat, my dear sister, I know you will, for I know your nature is to come out a first class girl in times of trouble & sickness, & do any thing—

Mother, you dont know how pleased I was to read what you wrote

64. Apparently George's last letter was written on September 22 from Camp Nelson, near Hickman's Bridge, Ky. (Trent).

65. Mrs. Whitman had complained of Andrew's son on September 3(?): "georgie is so cross, he aint a nice child at all" (Trent).

66. About October 5, Mrs. Whitman described Jeff's new baby as "fat and prettyer than hatty," and earlier in the same letter complained that Mannahatta was "very obstropdous" (Trent).

about little sis,[66] I want to see her so bad I dont know what to do, I know she must be just the best young one on Long Island—but I hope I will not be understood as meaning any slight or disrespect to Miss Hat, nor to put her nose out of joint, because Uncle Walt I hope has heart & gizzard big enough for both his little neices, & as many more as the Lord may send—

Mother, I am writing this in Major Hapgood's office as usual—I am all alone to-day—Major is still absent, unwell, & the clerk is away somewhere—O how pleasant it is here, the weather I mean, & other things too for that matter—I still occupy my little room 394 L st., get my own breakfast there, had good tea this morning, & some nice biscuit, (yesterday morning & day before had peaches cut up)—My friends the O'Connors that I wrote about re-commenced cooking the 1st of this month, (they have been as usual in summer taking their meals at a family hotel near by.) Saturday they sent for me to breakfast & Sunday I eat dinner with them, very good dinner, roast beef, lima beans, good potatoes &c. They are truly friends to me—I still get my dinner at a restaurant usually. I have a very good plain dinner, which is the only meal of any acc't I make during the day, but it is just as well, for I would be in danger of getting fat on the least encouragement, & I have no ambition that way.

Mother, it is lucky I like Washington in many respects, & that things are upon the whole pleasant personally, for every day of my life I see enough to make one's heart ache with sympathy & anguish here in the hospitals, & I do not know as I could stand it, if it was not counterbalanced outside—it is curious—when I am present at the most appaling things, deaths, operations, sickening wounds (perhaps full of maggots), I do not fail, although my sympathies are very much excited, but keep singularly cool—but often, hours afterward, perhaps when I am home, or out walking alone, I feel sick & actually tremble, when I recal the thing & have it in my mind again before me—

Mother, did you see my letter in the N Y Times of Sunday Oct 4?[67] That was the long delayed letter—Mother, I am very sorry Jeff did not send me the Union with my letter in[68]—I wish very much he would do so yet, & always when I have a letter in a paper I would like to have one sent—if you take the *Union*, send me some once in a while—Mother, was

67. "Letter from Washington," dated October 1, 1863, appeared in the New York *Times* on October 4; reprinted in *UPP*, II, 29–36. This letter is typical of WW's newspaper correspondence—chatty, discursive, and informal. WW described the Capitol and various Washington sights; only one section, "Army Wagons and Ambulances," was topical. Burroughs termed the article "one of the finest pieces of writing I have ever seen" (Barrus, 13).

68. See 80.

it Will Brown sent me those? tell him if so I was much obliged, & if he or Mr & Mrs Brown[69] take any interest in hearing my scribblings, mother, you let 'em read the letters of course—O I must not close without telling you the highly important intelligence that I have cut my hair & beard—since the event, Rosecrans, Charleston, &c &c have among my acquaintances been hardly mentioned, being insignificant themes in comparison—Jeff, my dearest brother, I have been going to write you a good gossipy letter for two or three weeks past, will try [to] do it yet, so it will reach you for Sunday reading—so good bye, brother Jeff, & good by for present, Mother dear, & all, & tell Andrew he must not be discouraged yet—

Walt

84. *To Hugo Fritsch* [*10.8. 1863*]

ENDORSED (by WW): "To Hugo | Oct 8 '63."
DRAFT LETTER.

Dear Hugo.[70]

I don't know why I have delayed so long as a month to write to you, for your affectionate & lively letter of September 5th gave me as much pleasure as I ever received from correspondence—I read it even yet & have taken the liberty to show it to one or two persons I knew would be interested. Dear comrade, you must be assured that my heart is much with you in New York, & with my other dear friends, your associates—&, my dear, I wish you to excuse me to Fred Gray, & to Perk, & Ben Knower, for not yet writing to them, also to Charley Kingsley, should you see him—I am contemplating a tremendous letter to my dear comrade Fredericks, which will make up for deficiencies—my own comrade Fred, how I should like to see him & have a good heart's time with him, & a mild orgie, just for a basis, you know, for talk & interchange of reminiscences & the play of the quiet lambent electricity of real friendship—O Hugo, as my pen glides along writing these thoughts, I feel as if I could not delay coming right off to New York & seeing you all, you & Fred & Bloom, & every body—I want to see you, to be within hand's reach of you, & hear your voices, even if only for one evening, for only three hours—I want to hear Perk's fiddle—I want to hear Perk himself, (& I will humbly submit to drink to the Church of England)—I want to be with Bloom, (that wretched young man who I hear continually adorns himself outwardly,

69. See 19.

70. For accounts of these New York friends, see 40 and 63. After Traubel read this letter on January 20, 1889, WW observed: "I was always between two loves at that time: I wanted to be in New York, I had to be in Washington: I was never in the one place but

but I hear nothing of the interior &c)[71] & I want to see Charley Russell, & if [when?] he is in N. Y. you see him I wish you to say that I sent him my love, particular, & that he & Fred & Charles Chauncey remain a group of itself in the portrait-gallery of my heart & mind yet & forever—for so it happened for our dear times, when we first got acquainted, (we recked not of them as they passed,) were so good, so hearty, those friendship-times, our talk, our knitting together, it may be a whim, but I think nothing could be better or quieter & more happy of the kind—& is there any better kind in life's experiences?

Dear comrade, I still live here as a hospital missionary after my own style, & on my own hook—I go every day or night without fail to some of the great government hospitals—O the sad scenes I witness—scenes of death, anguish, the fevers, amputations, friendlessness, of hungering & thirsting young hearts, for some loving presence—such noble young men as some of these wounded are—such endurance, such native decorum, such candor—I will confess to you, dear Hugo, that in some respects I find myself in my element amid these scenes—shall I not say to you that I find I supply often to some of these dear suffering boys in my presence & magnetism that which nor doctors nor medicines nor skill nor any routine assistance can give?

Dear Hugo, you must write to me often as you can, & not delay it, your letters are very dear to me. Did you see my newspaper letter in N Y Times of Sunday Oct 4? About my dear comrade Bloom, is he still out in Pleasant Valley? Does he meet you often? Do you & the fellows meet at Gray's or any where? O Hugo, I wish I could hear with you the current opera—I saw Devereux[72] in the N Y papers of Monday announced for that night, & I knew in all probability you would be there—tell me how it goes, and about the principal singers—only dont run away with that theme, & occupy too much of your letter with it—but tell me mainly about all my dear friends, & every little personal item, & what you all do, & say &c.

I am excellent well. I have cut my beard short, & hair ditto: (all my acquaintances are in anger & despair & go about wringing their hands). My face is all tanned & red. If the weather is moist or has been lately, or looks as if it thought of going to be, I perambulate this land in big army boots outside & up to my knees. Then around my majestic brow, around my well-brimmed felt hat—a black & gold cord with acorns. Altogether the effect is satisfactory. The guards as I enter or pass places often salute

I was restless for the other: my heart was distracted" (III, 581).

71. Evidently WW enjoyed this witticism; see 63.

72. Maretzek opened his operatic season on October 5 with a performance of Donizetti's *Roberto Devereux*.

me. All of which I tell, as you will of course take pride in your friend's special & expanding glory.

Fritschy, I am writing this in Major Hapgood's office, fifth story, by a window that overlooks all down the city, & over & down the beautiful Potomac, & far across the hills & shores for many a mile. We have had superb weather lately, yes for a month—it has just rained, so the dust is provided for, (that is the only thing I dread in Washington, the dust, I dont mind the mud). It is now between one & two o'clock Thursday afternoon. I am much alone in this pleasant far-up room, as Major is absent sick, & the clerk lays off a good deal. From three to five hours a day or night I go regularly among the sick, wounded, dying young men. I am enabled to give them things, food &c. There are very few visitors, amateurs, now. It has become an old story. The suffering ones cling to me, poor children, very close. I think of coming to New York quite soon to stay perhaps three weeks, then sure return here.

85. *To Hannah E. Stevenson*

ENDORSED (by WW): "sent Oct 8 '63 | Hannah E Stevenson | 80 Temple st | Boston | Mass." DRAFT LETTER.

Washington October 8 | 1863

Dear friend[73]

Your letter was received, enclosing one from Mary Wigglesworth with $30 from herself & her sisters Jane & Anne—As I happened stopping at one of the hospitals last night Miss Lowe just from Boston came to me & handed the letters—My friend, you must convey the blessings of the poor young men around me here, many amid deepest afflictions not of body only but of soul, to your friends Mary, Jane, & Anne Wigglesworth.[74] Their & all contributions shall be sacredly used among them. I find more & more how a little money rightly directed, the exact thing at the exact moment, goes a great ways, to make gifts comfort & truly nourish these American soldiers, so full of manly independence, is required the spirit of love & boundless brotherly tenderness, hand in hand with greatest tact. I

73. Hannah E. Stevenson heard of WW's hospital work from Dr. Russell, and wrote to WW on October 6 (Hanley; Donaldson, 150). She had been, Dr. Russell wrote to WW, "an ardent worker in one of the Georgetown Hospitals" (Hanley; Donaldson, 148). She was also associated with William Lloyd Garrison and Wendell Phillips in the abolitionist movement, and was a patron of the Home for Aged Colored Women in Boston. She died in 1887; see the Boston *Evening Transcript*, June 11, 1887. On presenting this letter to Traubel, Whitman exclaimed: "That was a great woman" (I, 26).

74. Like Miss Stevenson, Anne and Mary Wigglesworth were patrons of various

do not find any lack in the storehouses, nor eager willingness of the North to unlock them for the soldiers—but sadly everywhere a lack of fittest hands to apply, & of just the right thing in just the right measure, & of all being vivified by the spirit I have mentioned—

Say to the sisters Mary & Jane & Anne Wigglesworth, & to your own sister, Margaret,[75] that as I feel it a privilege myself to be doing a part among these things, I know well enough the like privilege must be sweet to them, to their compassionate & sisterly souls, & need indeed few thanks, & only ask its being put to best use, what they feel to give among sick & wounded. I have received L B Russell's[76] letter & contribution by same hand, & shall try to write to him to-morrow—

Walt Whitman

Address | care Major Hapgood | paymaster U S A cor 15th & F st | Washington D C.

86. *To Abby H. Price* *10. 11 - 15. 1863*

Washington October 11 1863

Dear friend,

Your letters were both received, & were indeed welcome. Don't mind my not answering them promptly, for you know what a wretch I am about such things. But you must write just as often as you conveniently can. Tell me all about your folks, especially the girls, & about Mr Arnold[77]—of course you won't forget Arthur,[78] & always when you write to him send him my love. Tell me about Mrs Urner[79] & the dear little rogues. Tell Mrs Black[80] she ought to be here hospital matron—only it is a harder pull than folks anticipate. You wrote about Emma, her thinking she might & ought to come as nurse for the soldiers—dear girl, I know it would be a blessed thing for the men to have her loving spirit & hand, & whoever of the poor fellows had them would indeed feel it so. But, my darling, it is a dreadful thing—you dont know these wounds, sicknesses &c—the sad condition in which many of the men are brought here, & remain for days, sometimes the wounds full of crawling corruption &c—

benevolent organizations in Boston. Mary died in 1882 and Anne in 1891; see the Boston *Evening Transcript*, August 29, 1882, and January 6, 1891. I have been unable to trace Jane's career, nor have I identified Miss Lowe.

75. Margaret S. Curtis; see 82.

76. See note 73 and letter 99.

77. John Arnold; see 12.

78. Mrs. Price's son was a naval officer.

79. Probably the wife of Benjamin Urner, publisher, 160 Fulton Street, New York; see notes to 12.

80. Probably one of Mrs. Whitman's neighbors.

Down in the field hospitals in front they have no proper care & attention, & after a battle go for many days unattended to—

Abby, I think often about you, & the pleasant days, the visits I used to pay you & how good it was always to be made so welcome. O I wish I could come in this afternoon, & have a good tea with you, & have three or four hours of mutual comfort & talk, & be all of us together again. Is Helen home, & well? And what is she doing now? And you, my dear friend, how sorry I am to hear that your health is not rugged—but, dear Abby, you must not dwell on anticipations of the worst. (But I know that is not your nature, or did not use to be.) O I hope this will find you feeling quite well, & in good spirits—I feel so well myself—I will have to come & see you I think—I am so fat, out considerable in the open air, & all red & tanned worse than ever. You see therefore that my life amid these sad & unhealthy hospitals has not yet told upon me, for I am this fall running over with health, so I feel [as] if I ought to go on that account [working] among all the sick & deficient [who are deprived of] it—& O how gladly I would [bestow upon you a] liberal share, dear Abby, [if such a][81] thing were possible.

I am continually moving around among the hospitals. One I go to oftenest the last three months is Armory Square, as it is large, generally full of the worst wounds & sicknesses, & is one of the least visited—to this, or some one, I never miss a day or evening. I am enabled to give the men something—add perhaps some trifle to their supper all round. Then there are always special cases, needing something special. Above all the poor boys welcome magnetic friendship, personality (some are so fervent, so hungering for this)—poor fellows, how young they are, lying there with their pale faces, & that mute look in the eyes. O how one gets to love them, often, particular cases, so suffering, so good, so manly & affectionate—Abby, you would all smile to see me among them—many of them like children, ceremony is mostly discarded—they suffer & get exhausted & so weary—lots of them have grown to expect as I leave at night that we should kiss each other, sometimes quite a number, I have to go round—poor boys, there is little petting in a soldier's life in the field, but, Abby, I know what is in their hearts, always waiting, though they may be unconscious of it themselves—

I have a place where I buy very nice home-made biscuits, sweet crackers &c—Among others, one of my ways is to get a good lot of these & for supper go through a couple of wards & give a portion to each man—

81. The letter has been repaired in the lower left-hand corner; the insertions, however, appear to be in WW's hand.

82. See 83.

83. The publisher of the third edition of *Leaves of Grass* (see 18) and the man who obtained a position for WW in Major Hapgood's office (see 25).

next evening two wards more, & so on—then each marked case needs something to itself—I spend my evenings altogether at the hospitals—my day, often. I give little gifts of money in small sums, which I am enabled to do. All sorts of things indeed, food, clothing, letter-stamps (I write lots of letters), now & then a good pair of crutches &c &c. Then I read to the boys—the whole ward that can walk gathers around me & listens—

All this I tell you, my dear, because I know it will interest you. I like Washington very well (did you see my last letter in N Y Times of Oct 4, Sunday?)[82] I have three or four hours work every day copying & in writing letters for the press, &c., make enough to pay my way—live in an unexpensive manner any how—I like the mission I am on here, & as it is deeply holding me I shall continue—

October 15

Well, Abby, I guess I will send you letter enough—I ought to have finished & sent off the letter last Sunday, when it was written—I have been pretty busy—we are having new arrivals of wounded & sick now all the time—some very bad cases—Abby, should you come across any one who feels to help, contribute to the men through me, write me. (I may then send word some purchases I should find acceptable for the men)—but this only if it happens to come in that you know or meet any one, perfectly convenient—

Abby, I have found some good friends here, a few, but true as steel—W D O'Connor & wife, above all. He is a clerk in Treasury—she is a Yankee girl—then C W Eldridge[83] in paymaster's department. He is a Boston boy too—their friendship has been unswerving.

In the hospitals among these American young men, I could not describe to you what mutual attachments & how passing deep & tender these boys—some have died, but the love for them lives as long as I draw breath—those soldiers know how to love too when once they have the right person & the right love offered them. It is wonderful. You see I am running off into the clouds—but this is my element—

Abby, I am writing this note this afternoon in Major Hapgood's office—he is away sick—I am here a good deal of the time alone—it is a dark rainy afternoon—we don't know what is going on down in front, whether Meade is getting the worst of it, or not[84]—(but the result of the big elections cheers us)[85]—I believe fully in Lincoln—few know the rocks & quick-

84. Meade was unable to prevent a massive rebel movement across the Rapidan River.

85. The New York *Times* on October 15 headed its account of the New York election "Copperheads Crushed," and printed an editorial entitled "The Great Union Victory."

sands he has to steer through. I enclose you a note Mrs O'Connor handed me to send to you, written I suppose upon impulse—she is a noble Massachusetts woman, is not very rugged in health—I am there very much—her husband & I are great friends too—Well I will close—the rain is pouring, the sky leaden—it is between 2 & 3—I am going to get some dinner & then to hospital—good by, dear friends, & I send my love to all—

Walt Whitman

Address | Care Major Hapgood paymaster U S A | cor 15th & F st Washington D C.

87. *To James Redpath* [*10.12. 1863*]

ENDORSED (by WW): "to J Redpath | Oct 12 | '63."
DRAFT LETTER.

Your note of Oct 8,[86] enclosing Dr Russell's of 4th to you,[87] is just rec'd. Yours with $5, some weeks ago, came safely. The generosity of Dr. Russell, Mrs. Curtis, and the other friends, I will briefly say, tells daily & nightly & shall tell to the best of my power, upon my dear boys here, in hospital. I do not miss one day or night. (I guess we, I & the wounded &c, were made for each other.) I have written to Dr Russell, to Mrs Curtis & to Miss Stevenson.[88]

Do you want to print a little 30 or 50ct book about the scenes, war, camp, hospitals &c (especially the &c.)[89]

I shall probably remain here, in this thing. I am very happy. I never was so beloved. I am running over with health, fat, red & sunburnt in face &c. I tell thee I am just the one to go [to] our sick boys. Good by, my friend.

86. Redpath (see 61) wrote to "Nurse Walt" on October 8: "I didn't answer your letter by words, as you asked for cash; & to get cash, being minus the article myself, required time." He evidently had sent $9 in an earlier letter, including a contribution of $1 from Emerson. Redpath concluded: "By the Bye—how about your Hospital Sketches? Are they ready yet for press?" (Historical Society of Pennsylvania). Redpath replied to WW's letter on October 14: "I will do all I can here in one direction to keep you supplied with funds" (Donaldson, 151).

87. Russell's letter to Redpath appears in Donaldson, 148–149.

88. See 82 and 85.

89. See 91. After this sentence WW deleted the following: "Do you want to print my new little volume of poetry 'Ban . . ."

90. While WW remained in Washington, tension was increasing among the Whitmans in Brooklyn. Jeff was incensed by his mother's frugality. On September 24, he commented to WW: "I certainly think Mother is following a mistaken notion of economy. I think the only decent meals that any of them have had for three months is what they have eaten with Mat and I"; and again on October 8: "There is no doubt, Walt, in my mind but that mother is doing injury both to herself and Jess by her economy, they do

88. *To Louisa Van Velsor Whitman*

Washington Oct 13 | 1863

Dearest mother,

[Nothing] particular new with me. I am well & hearty—think a good deal about home. Mother, I so much want to see you, even if only for a couple of weeks—for I feel I must return here & continue my hospital operations. They are so much needed, although one can do only such a little in comparison, amid these thousands. Then I desire much to see Andrew.[90] I wonder if I could cheer him up any—does he get any good from that treatment with the baths, &c. Mother, I suppose you have your hands full with Nancy's poor little children, & one worry & another (when one gets old little things bother a great deal). Mother, I go down every day looking for a letter from you or Jeff—I had two from Jeff latter part of the week.[91] I want to see Jeff much. I wonder why he didn't send me the Union with my letter in.[92] I am disappointed at not getting it. I sent Han [a] N Y Times with my last letter, & one to George too. Have you heard any thing from George or Han?

There is a new lot of wounded now again.[93] They have been arriving, sick & wounded, for three days—First long strings of ambulances with the sick. But yesterday many with bad & bloody wounds, poor fellows. I thought I was cooler & more used to it, but the sight of some of them brought tears into my eyes—Mother, I had the good luck yesterday to do quite a great deal of good—I had provided a lot of nourishing things for the men, but for another quarter—but I had them where I could use them immediately for these new wounded as they came in faint & hungry, & fagged out with a long rough journey, all dirty & torn, & many pale as ashes, & all bloody—I distributed all my stores, gave partly to the nurses I knew that were just taking charge of them—& as many as I could I fed

not have enough *good* things to eat . . . I have spoken of it till I have tired and it dont accomplish anything" (Feinberg). See also notes to 76.

Meanwhile, Andrew refused the advice of Dr. Ruggles and of Jeff, and accepted the expensive ministrations of a quack who, Jeff said on October 15, "told Andrew yesterday that he must not come there again till he brought him $45 more. Only think of it. The infernal son of a bitch. I would like to hang him for a thousand years, ten times a second." Dr. Ruggles, according to Jeff's letter of October 8, "thinks that it is more than wicked to take his [Andrew's] money and make believe to cure him, for in his opinion that is almost impossible . . . his lungs are much diseased." Repeatedly, and with some hostility, Jeff urged WW to return home. Writing on October 15, he pleaded: "Dear Walt, do come home if only for a short time. And unless you come quite soon you certainly will never see Andrew alive" (Feinberg). Though there was little excuse for delay, WW remained in Washington until November 2.

91. WW, presumably, inked out the next line of the letter.

92. See 80.

93. This paragraph was later printed in *November Boughs* (CW, VI, 225–226) with alterations that reduced the original effectiveness of the material.

myself—Then besides I found a lot of oyster soup handy, & I procured it all at once—Mother, it is the most pitiful sight I think when first the men are brought in—I have to bustle round, to keep from crying—they are such rugged young men—all these just arrived are cavalry men—Our troops got the worst of it, but fought like devils. Our men engaged were Kilpatrick's[94] cavalry. They were in the rear as part of Meade's retreat—& the reb cavalry cut in between & cut them off & [attacked] them & shelled them terribly. But Kilpatrick brought them out mostly—this was last Sunday.

Mother, I will try to come home before long, if only for six or eight days. I wish to see you, & Andrew—I wish to see the young ones & Mat. You must write. I am about moving,[95] I have been hunting for a room to-day—I shall write next how I succeed. Good by for present, dear mother.

Walt

89. *To Louisa Van Velsor Whitman*

Washington | October 20, 1863

Dearest mother,

I got your last letter Sunday morning, though it was dated Thursday night. Mother, I suppose you got a letter from me Saturday last, as I sent one the day before, as I was concerned about Andrew—If I thought it would be any benefit to Andrew I should certainly leave everything else & come back to Brooklyn—mother, do you recollect what I wrote last summer about throat diseases,[96] when Andrew was first pretty bad—well that's the whole groundwork of the business, any true physician would

94. Hugh Judson Kilpatrick (1836–1881), distinguished himself as a commander of cavalry. He was with Meade at Gettysburg and in the campaigns in Virginia from August to November, 1863. In his "Hospital Book 12" (Feinberg), WW, after " 'chinning' with some soldier in hospital," elaborated on Kilpatrick's conduct. His cavalry cut off and outnumbered, the general ordered his two bands to play: "They joined, & played Yankee Doodle, it went through the men like lightning, every man seemed a giant. They charged & cut their way out with the loss of 20 men." See also *November Boughs* (CW, VI, 171).

95. See 89.

96. See 42. WW was obviously trying to allay Jeff's fears, as related in note 90.

97. On September 22, George informed Jeff that Captain Sims (see 51) was in Brooklyn to recruit for the regiment. Evidently McReady (see 48) had also gone to Brooklyn for the same purpose, since George referred to both in a letter to Mrs. Whitman on October 16 (Trent). According to a notation on the verso of 97, WW saw McReady while he was in New York in November. The Fifty-first Regiment was still on guard duty at Camp Nelson, Ky.

98. See 80.

99. WW, evidently, inked through the next three lines of this letter.

1. WW misunderstood his mother's letter (now lost), and Jeff explained the situation on October 22: "It is not like you think in regard to cutting down my wages. I was working for the two boards of Commissioners, one at $40 and the other at $50 per month,

confirm it—there is no great charm about such things—as to any costly & mysterious baths, there are no better baths than warm water, or vapor, (& perhaps sulphur vapor,) there is nothing costly or difficult about them—one can have a very good sweating bath, at a pinch, by having a pan of warm water under a chair & heating a couple of bricks or stones or any thing to put in one after another, & sitting on the chair with a couple of blankets around him to enclose the vapor—it is a very wholesome sweat too, & not to be sneezed at if one wishes to do what is salutary, & thinks of the sense of a thing, & not what others do—Andrew mustn't be discouraged, those diseases are painful & tedious, but he can recover & will yet—

Dear mother, I sent your last letter to George with a short one I wrote myself, I sent it yesterday—I sent a letter last Wednesday 14th to him also, hoping that if one don't reach him another will—hasn't Jeff seen Capt Sims or Lieut McReady[97] yet, & don't they hear whether the 51st is near Nicholasville, Kentucky, yet? I send George papers now & then—Mother, one of your letters contains part of my letter to the Union,[98] (I wish I could have got the whole of it.) It seems to be mostly as I intended it, barring a few slight misprints—was my last name signed at the bottom of it? tell me when you write next[99]—Dear mother, I am real sorry & mad too that the water works people have cut Jeff's wages down to $50[1]—this is a pretty time to cut a man's wages down—the mean old punkin heads—mother, I can't understand it at all—tell me more the particulars—Jeff, I often wish you was on here, you would be better appreciated, there is big salaries paid here sometimes to civil engineers—Jeff, I know a fellow, E C Stedman,[2] has been here till lately, is now in Wall street, he is poor but he is in with the big bankers (Hallett & Co) who are in with Fremont[3] in *his* line of Pacific railroad—I can get his (Stedman's) ad-

and I have got all the work for one board finished (the one at $40) . . . It is not the meanness or anything of that kind of anybody and they would pay me more if they could and will probably in a short time" (Feinberg).

2. Edmund Clarence Stedman (1833–1908) was a man of diverse talents. He edited for a year the *Mountain County Herald* at Winsted, Conn., wrote "Honest Abe of the West," presumably Lincoln's first campaign song, and served as correspondent of the New York *World* from 1860 to 1862. In 1862 and 1863 he was in the Attorney General's office until he entered the firm of Samuel Hallett and Company in September, 1863. The next year he opened his own brokerage office. He published many volumes of poems and was an indefatigable compiler of anthologies, among which were *Poets of America* (2 vols., 1885) and *A Library of American Literature from the Earliest Settlement to the Present Time* (11 vols., 1889–1890).

3. After Congress had endowed a Pacific Railroad, John Charles Frémont (1813–1890) was ready to take charge, with the assistance of Hallett. They planned to build a railroad from Kansas City to the West. Stedman was engaged by Hallett to edit *The American Circular*, which propagandized for the new railroad. Frémont was one of the New York *Tribune's* candidates to succeed Lincoln in 1864. See Allan Nevins, *Frémont: Pathmarker of the West* (1939), 570; and Laura Stedman and George M. Gould, *Life and Letters of Edmund Clarence Stedman* (1910), I, 322–323.

dress, & should you wish it any time I will give you a letter to him—I shouldn't wonder if the big men, with Fremont at head, were going to push their route, works, road, &c &c. in earnest, & if a fellow could get a good managing place in it, why it might be worth while—I think after Jeff has been with the Brooklyn W[ater] W[orks] from the beginning, & so faithful & so really valuable, to put down to $50, the mean low-lived old shoats. I have felt as indignant about it, the meanness of the thing, & mighty inconvenient too, $40 a month makes a big difference—Mother, I hope Jeff won't get & keep himself in a perpetual fever, with all these things & others & botherations, both family & business ones—if he does, he will just wear himself down before his time comes—I do hope, Jeff, you will take things equably all round, & not brood or think too deeply—So I go giving you all good advice—

O Mother, I must tell you how I get along in my new quarters, I have moved to a new room, 456 Sixth street, not far from Pennsylvania avenue, (the big street here,) & not far from the Capitol—it is in 3d story, an addition back, seems to be going to prove a very good winter room, as it is right under the roof & looks south, has low windows, is plenty big enough, I have gas—I think the lady will prove a good woman, she is old & feeble, (there is a little girl of 4 or 5, I hear her sometimes calling *grandma*, *grandma* just exactly like Hat, it made me think of you & Hat right away)—one thing is I am quite by myself, there is no passage up there except to my room, & right off against my side of the house is a great old yard with grass & some trees back, & the sun shines in all day &c. & it smells sweet & good air, good big bed, I sleep first rate—there is a young wench of 12 or 13, Lucy, (the niggers here are the best & most amusing creatures you ever see)—she comes & goes, gets water &c., she is pretty much the only one I see—then I believe the front door is not locked at all at night—(in the other place the old thief the landlord had two front doors, with four locks & bolts on one, & three on the other—& a big bull-dog in the back yard—we were well fortified I tell you—sometimes I

4. WW probably referred to the house his mother purchased on April 10, 1856, from John H. and George Wheeler, at the corner of Graham Street and Willoughby Avenue. See Allen, 600.

5. On October 15, Jeff wrote: "Mother, Mat and Sis are all suffering from bad colds, Mother particularly I think is failing rapidly" (Feinberg).

6. The postscript was omitted in earlier printings.

7. James S. Stilwell, Second New York Cavalry, was confined in Ward C of Armory Square Hospital with a gunshot wound in his left leg; see "Notebook: September–October, 1863" (Feinberg) and "Hospital Notes" (Huntington). He recovered slowly from his injury. About the end of May in the following year he was sent to Mower Hospital, Chestnut Hill, Pa., where he remained until he was granted a furlough in August, 1864. He later returned to Mower Hospital, and wrote to WW on September 27 that his

had an awful time at night getting in)—I pay $10 a month, this includes gas, but not fuel—Jeff, you can come on & see me easy now—Mother, to give you an idea of prices here, while I was looking for rooms, I went in to see a couple of furnished rooms about like our two in Wheelers houses[4] (2d story), nothing extra about them, either in location or any thing, & the rent was $60 a month—yet quite curious vacant houses here are not so very dear, very much the same as in Brooklyn—dear mother, Jeff wrote in his letter[5] latter part of last week you was real unwell with a very bad cold, (& that you didn't have enough good meals)—mother, I hope this will find you well & good spirits—I think about you every day & night—Jeff thinks you show your age more, & failing like—O my dear mother, you must not think of failing yet—I hope we shall have some comfortable years yet. Mother, don't you allow things, troubles, to take hold of you—write a few lines whenever you can, tell me exactly *how* things are—Mother, I am first rate & well, only a little of that deafness again—good bye for present.

Walt

Mother, I am of course every day in hospitals—they are pretty full now, some very bad wounds—Mother, it is the opinion here this morning that Lee has vamosed back into lower Virginia again but there's no telling—he's a cunning old fox—he may make a dash at us here before we know it[6]—

90. *To Julia Elizabeth Stilwell*

DRAFT LETTER. Washington October 21 1863

Dear friend,[7]

Jimmy is getting along favorably as usual but of course somewhat slowly. I was with him night before last, & am going again this afternoon. It requires a good deal of patience in him to lay so steadily confined in

wound was "most healed up," and that he expected either to be discharged or to be transferred to New York. (The Berg Collection contains three letters from James to WW—July 5, September 2(?), and September 27, 1864.)

When Traubel received this draft letter from WW, he noted that "it was addressed to Julia Elizabeth Stilwell, South Norwalk, Connecticut" (I, 434). After Traubel had read the letter, WW said "fervently": "I thank God for having permitted me to write that letter." As WW indicated in 82, he corresponded frequently with members of the Stilwell family. Mrs. Stilwell on October 20 wrote: "I hope God will bless you in your basket and in your Store, in your Soul and in your body. . . . be a father and a Mother to him"; and on December 28: "You have been More than a brother to James and to his Sisters and to us his parents More than a Son" (Berg).

bed, but he still has the good luck to continue remarkably free from any acute suffering. Night before last he had some pain & swelling in the foot & leg below the wound, but nothing of serious account. They bandaged it pretty tightly, & that seemed to relieve it. Jim wished me to write to *you* this time, & I promised him night before last to do so. I wrote at that time from the hospital to your parents at Comac, & sent the letter yesterday. Jim is dissatisfied unless I write pretty often, whether there is any thing to write about or not—My friend, I rec'd your note about your folks getting your dear brother's body from down in Virginia.[8] Dear friend, the rebels have lately advanced upon us, as you doubtless know, & held Culpepper & thereabout for many days past—but the rumor now is that they are falling back, & that Meade will probably take possession of his old ground[9] —but at present I doubt if any thing could be done—the authorities here do not grant passes yet, they are stricter than ever—

Dear friends all, I would say to you as I have written to Jimmy's parents, that I shall try to keep watch of the boy, as I shall probably continue in Washington for some time yet—& if any thing should occur I will write to you—as it may be some reliance to you & make you feel less uneasy, to feel that Jim can have nothing occur in his case without your being informed—though as far as now appears, he will go on favorably, & his wound is likely to heal so that he can sit up, & then gradually move about, & so in due time be able to travel—

So, my friend, farewell for present, & I pray that God may be with you, & though we are strangers I send my love to you & all Jimmy's sisters & brothers in law—for in times of trouble & death folks draw near in spirit regardless of being separated by distance, or of being personally strangers—

Walt Whitman

care Major Hapgood, paymaster U S A | cor 15th & F st | Washington | D C.

8. John Stilwell was evidently killed at Culpepper about the time that James was wounded, for Julia Stilwell wrote to WW about both brothers on October 13 (Berg). WW was mistaken about the body, however, since, according to Margaret Stilwell's letter of October 25 (Berg), members of the family had been refused a pass to Culpepper.

9. The New York *Herald* reported this rumor on the following day.

10. WW probably chose Redpath (see 61 and 87) as the publisher of his proposed book because earlier in the year he had printed Louisa May Alcott's *Hospital Sketches*, which relates the experiences of Tribulation Periwinckle in a military hospital in Georgetown. (Miss Periwinckle, actually the authoress, had expected to go to Armory Square Hospital, but at the last minute was sent to "Hurly-burly House.") In his reply on October 28, Redpath said that there was "a lion in the way—$. I could easily publish a small Book, but the one you propose. . . . implies an expenditure that may be be-

91. *To James Redpath* [*10.21. 1863*]

ENDORSED: "letter to Redpath about | Memoranda of a Year | (publisher's announcement) | sent Oct 21 '63." DRAFT LETTER.

Dear friend,[10]

My idea is a book of the time, worthy the time—something considerably beyond mere hospital sketches—a book for sale perhaps in a larger American market—the premises or skeleton memoranda of incidents, persons, places, sights, the past year (mostly jotted down either on the spot or in the spirit of seeing or hearing what is narrated)—(I left New York early last December, & have been around in the front[11] or here ever since)—full of interest I surely think—in some respects somewhat a combination in handling of the Old French Memoires, & my own personality (things seen through my eyes, & what my vision brings)—a book full enough of mosaic, but all fused to one comprehensive thing—one of the drifts is to push forward the very big & needed truth, that our national military system needs shifting, revolutionizing & made to tally with democracy, the people[12]—The officers should almost invariably rise from the ranks—there is an absolute want of democratic spirit in the present system & officers—it is the feudal spirit exclusively—nearly the entire capacity, keenness & courage of our army are in the ranks—(what has been done has been unavoidable so far, but the time has arrived to discuss the change)—

I have much to say of the hospitals, the immense national hospitals—in them too most radical changes of premises are demanded—(the air, the spirit of a thing is every thing, the details follow & adjust themselves). I have many hospital incidents, [that] will take with the general reader—I ventilate my general democracy with details very largely & with reference to the future—bringing in persons, the President, Seward, Congress, the Capitol, Washington City, many of the actors of the drama—have

yond my means" (Traubel, IV, 418). WW's proposal was not to be realized until the publication of *Specimen Days*. Accompanying this draft is WW's sketch of the title page. (An editor fully sympathizes with Traubel's remark [IV, 416] when he received this letter from WW: "It made me sweat to look at it." It is a maze of interlineations.)

11. Once again WW overstated his involvement in the war.

12. In his "Notebook: September–October, 1863," WW made this entry on September 23: "Talk with Ben in Ward A about tyrannous and unnecessary exposure of the soldiers—how many officers there are who dare not go into engagements nor even out on picket with their men, for fear of their lives from their own men—the 8th N Y Cav Col Davis, (killed afterward) who . . . made the poor sick men (sick with diarrhea) dismount & mount 13 times to make them do it in military style—I have seen not a single officer that seemed to know American men" (Feinberg).

something to say of the great trunk America, the West &c &c—do not hesitate to diffuse *myself*—the book is very rapid—is a book that can be read by the five or ten minutes at (being full of small parts, pieces, paragraphs with their dates, incidents &c)—I should think two or three thousand sale ought to be certainly depended on here in hospitals in Washington, among departments &c—

My idea is a book of handy size & form, 16 mo or smallish 12 mo, *first rate paper* (this last indispensable), ordinary binding, strongly stitched, to cost including copyright not more than 35 or 40cts or thereabouts to make, to retail for a dollar. It should be got out *immediately*. I think an edition, elegantly bound, might be pushed off for books for presents &c for the holidays, if advertised for that purpose. It would be very appropriate. I think it a book that would please women. I should expect it to be popular with the trade.

Of course I propose the affair to you publisherially as something to invest in, to make out of (for both of us)—I take it it would be a very handsome speculation. Only it is to be done while the thing is warm, namely *at once*. I have been & am in the midst of these things, I feel myself full of them, & I know the people generally now are too (far more than they know,) & would readily absorb & understand my mem[oranda]. Wherefore let us make & publish the book, & out with it so as to have it for sale by middle or 20th of November.

92. *To Louisa Van Velsor Whitman*

Washington | Oct 27 1863

Dearest mother,

Yours & George's letter came, & a letter from Jeff too, all good.[13] I had received a letter a day or so before from George too—I am very glad he is at Camp Nelson, Kentucky, & I hope & pray the reg't will be kept there—for God knows they have tramped enough for the last two years, & fought battles & been through enough. I have sent George papers to Camp Nelson, & will write to-morrow. I send him the Unions, & late New York papers. Mother, you or Jeff write & tell me how Andrew is, I hope he will prove to be better, such complaints are sometimes very alarming for awhile, & then take such a turn for the better. Common means, & steadily pursuing them, about diet, especially, are so much more reliable than any course of medicine whatever. Mother, I have written to Han. I

13. Mrs. Whitman sent George's letter of October 16, on which she wrote a note (Trent), and Jeff wrote on October 22 (Feinberg).

14. See note 1 above.

15. This paragraph, rearranged, appeared in *November Boughs* (CW, VI, 226–227).

sent her George's letter to me, & wrote her a short letter myself. I sent it four or five days ago.

Mother, I am real pleased to hear Jeff's explanation[14] how it is that his wages was cut down, & that it was not as I fancied, from the meanness of the old coons in the Board—I felt so indignant about it, as I took it into my head, (though I don't know why), that it was done out of meanness, & was a sort of insult—I was quite glad Jeff wrote a few lines about it—& glad they appreciate Jeff too—

Mother,[15] if any of my soldier boys should ever call upon you, (as they are often anxious to have my address in Brooklyn,) you just use them as you know how to without ceremony, & if you happen to have pot luck & feel to ask them to take a bite, dont be afraid to do so—there is one very good boy, Thos Neat,[16] 2d N Y Cavalry, wounded in leg—he is now home on furlough, his folks live I think in Jamaica, he is a noble boy, he may call upon you, (I gave him here $1 toward buying his crutches &c.)—I like him very much—Then possibly a Mr. Haskell,[17] or some of his folks, from western New York, may call—he had a son died here, a very fine boy. I was with him a good deal, & the old man & his wife have written me, & asked me my address in Brooklyn, he said he had children in N Y city, & was occasionally down there—Mother, when I come home I will show you some of the letters I get from mothers, sisters, fathers &c. They will make you cry—There is nothing new with my hospital doings—I was there yesterday afternoon & evening, & shall be there again to-day—

Mother, I would like to hear how you are yourself—has your cold left you, & do you feel better?—do you feel quite well again? I suppose you have your good stove all fired-up these days—we have had some real cool weather here—I must rake up a little cheap second hand stove for my room, for it was in the bargain that I should get that myself—Mother, I like my place quite well, better on nearly every account than my old room, but I see it will only do for a winter room—they keep it clean, & the house smells clean, & the room too—my old room they just left every thing lay where it was, & you can fancy what a litter & dirt there was—still it was a splendid room for air, for summer, as good as there is in Washington—I got a letter from Mrs Price this morning—does Emmy ever come to see you?

Matty, my dear sister, & Miss Mannahatta, & the little one (whose name I dont know, & perhaps han't got any name yet,) I hope you are all well & having good times. I often, often think about you all. Mat, do you

16. Neat was cited in the "Notebook: September–October, 1863" (Feinberg) as a patient in Ward H, Armory Square Hospital. According to an 1864 Notebook (*LC* #103), he was attached to the headquarters of Kilpatrick's cavalry.

17. See 59 and 64.

go any to the opera now?—they say the new singers are so good—when I come home we'll all try to go[18]—

Mother, I am very well—have some cold in my head & my ears stopt up yet, making me sometimes quite hard of hearing—I am writing this in Major Hapgood's office—last Sunday I took dinner at my friends the O'Connors, had two roast chickens, stewed tomatoes, potatoes, &c. I took dinner there previous Sunday also.

Well, dear Mother, how the time passes away[19]—to think it will soon be a year I have been away—it has passed away very swiftly somehow to me—O what things I have witnessed during that time—I shall never forget them—& the war is not settled yet, & one does not see any thing at all certain about the settlement yet, but I have finally got for good I think into the feeling that our triumph is assured, whether it be sooner or whether it be later, or whatever roundabout way we are led there, & I find I dont change that conviction from any reverses we meet, or any delays or government blunders—there are blunders enough, heaven knows, but I am thankful things have gone on as well for us as they have—thankful the ship rides safe & sound at all—then I have finally made up my mind that Mr Lincoln has done as good as a human man could do—I still think him a pretty big President—I realize here in Washington that it has been a big thing to have just kept the United States from being thrown down & having its throat cut—& now I have no doubt it will throw down secession & cut its throat—& I have not had any doubt since Gettysburgh—Well, dear, dear Mother, I will draw to a close, Andrew & Jeff & all, I send you my love—good bye, dear Mother, & dear Matty & all hands—

Walt

93. *To Margaret S. Curtis* [*10.28. 1863*]

ENDORSED: "to Margaret S Curtis | care Charles P Curtis | Boston | Mass | Oct. 28 '63 (about Caleb H | Babbitt." DRAFT LETTER.

Dear Madam.

Since I last wrote you[20] I have continued my hospital visitations daily or nightly without intermission & shall continue them this fall &

18. WW kept his word when he returned to Brooklyn in November; see 95.

19. In the printed version of this paragraph (*CW*, VI, 227), WW made significant alterations. He, to put it mildly, exaggerated his wartime activities: "To think it is over a year since I left home suddenly—and have mostly been down in front since." WW also attempted to create the impression that he had never wavered about the outcome of the conflict, when he altered "I have finally got for good I think into the feeling" to "I do not lose the solid feeling, in myself." The latter part of this paragraph, following the remarks about "government blunders," was drastically abridged, and again minimized WW's day-by-day doubts about the war and Lincoln's leadership: "One realizes here in

winter. Your contributions, & those of your friends, sent me for the soldiers wounded & sick, have been used among them in manifold ways, little sums of money given, (the wounded very generally come up here without a cent & in lamentable plight,) & in purchases of various kinds, often impromptu, as I see things wanted on the moment, for instance [when a] train is standing tediously waiting, &c. as they often are here. But what I write this note for particularly is to see if your sister, Hannah Stevenson,[21] or yourself, might find it eligible to see a young man whom I love very much, who has fallen into deepest affliction, & is now in your city. He is a young Massachusetts soldier from Barre. He was sun-struck here in Washington last July, was taken to hospital here, I was with him a good deal for many weeks—he then went home to Barre—became worse—has now been sent from his home to your city—is at times (as I infer) so troubled with such distress—I received a letter from Boston this morning from a stranger about him,[22] telling me (he appears too ill to write himself) that he is in Mason General Hospital, Boston. His name is Caleb H. Babbitt[23] of Co E 34th Mass Vol. He must have been brought there lately. My dear friend, if you should be able to go, or if not able yourself give this to your sister or some friend who will go—it may be that my dear boy & comrade is not so very bad, but I fear he is. Tell him you come from me like, & if he is in a situation to talk, his loving heart will open to you at once. He is a manly, affectionate boy. I beg whoever goes would write a few lines to me how the young man is. I send my thanks & love to yourself, your sister, husband, & the sisters Wigglesworth.[24] Or else give this to Dr. Russell.[25] The letter from the stranger above referred to is dated also Pemberton square hospital.

94. *To Lewis K. Brown* *11. 8 - 9. 1863*

ADDRESS: Lewis K Brown | Ward K Armory Square Hospital | Washington | D C. POSTMARK: N(?) | Nov | 9 | 1863.

Brooklyn, November 8, 1863

Dear son & comrade,[26] | & all my dear comrades in the hospital,

I sit down this pleasant Sunday forenoon intending to write you

Washington the great labors, even the negative ones, of Lincoln; that it is a big thing to have just kept the United States from being thrown down and having its throat cut. I have not waver'd or had any doubt of the issue, since Gettysburg."

20. October 4; see 82. 21. See 85.

22. WW probably referred to the letter written by S. H. Childs for Babbitt on October 26 (Berg); see 73.

23. See 73. 24. See 85. 25. See 99.

26. See 60. When WW presented this letter to Traubel on November 15, 1888, he said: "You'll find two versions—that is, the vague notes, then the inked letter—the letter

all a good stout letter, to try to amuse you as I am not able at present to visit you, like I did—yet what I shall write about I hardly know until I get started—but, my dear comrades, I wish to help you pass away the time, for a few minutes any how—I am now home at my mother's in Brooklyn, N Y—I am in good health as ever & eat my rations without missing one time—Lew, I wish you was here with me, & I wish my dear comrade Elijah Fox[27] in Ward G was here with me—but perhaps he is on his way to Wisconsin—Lewy, I came through from Washington to New York by day train, 2d Nov., had a very pleasant trip, every thing went lovely, & I got home in the evening between 8 and 9—Next morning I went up to the polls bright & early—I suppose it is not necessary to tell you how I voted—we have gained a great victory in this city—it went union this time, though it went democratic strong only a year ago, & for many years past—& all through the state the election was a very big thing for the union—I tell you the copperheads got flaxed out handsomely[28]—indeed these late elections are about as great a victory for us as if we had flaxed General Lee himself, & all his men—& as for personal good will I feel as if I could have more for Lee or any of his fighting men, than I have for the northern copperheads—

Lewy, I was very glad to get your letter of the 5th—I want you to tell Oscar Cunningham[29] in your ward that I sent him my love & he must try to keep up good courage while he is confined there with his wound. Lewy, I want you to give my love to Charley Cate[30] & all the boys in Ward K, & to Benton[31] if he is [there still]—I wish you would go in Ward C and see James S Stilwell,[32] & also Thomas Carson[33] in same ward, & Chambers[34] that lays next to him, & tell them I sent them my

that went was passed around: they don't essentially differ, if at all: I got the sent letter back from Lew Brown" (III, 100). On the following day he remarked to Traubel: " 'Did you read the huge hospital letter? Did it remind you of anything? My relations with the boys there in Washington had fatherly, motherly, brotherly intimations—touched life on many sides: sympathetically, spiritually, dynamically: took me away from surfaces to roots. I don't seem to be able to review that experience, that period, without extreme emotional stirrings—almost depressions . . . I don't seem to be able to stand it in the present condition of my body' " (III, 110–111).

27. See 98.

28. On November 5, the New York *Times* observed that the elections in Brooklyn two days earlier "resulted in the choice of a majority of the Union candidates for county and state offices." On the same day the New York *Herald* proclaimed: "The agony is over . . . The copperheads . . . have been routed, horse, foot and artillery."

29. See 121.

30. According to Alonzo S. Bush's letter on December 22 (Yale), Cate was ward master in Armory Square Hospital.

31. Benton Wilson; see 230. 32. See 90.

33. Thomas J. Carson, Fourth Ohio Volunteers, had a compound fracture of the knee, according to the "Hospital Notebook" (Huntington).

34. Not identified.

35. Wintersteen, of the Sixth Ohio Cavalry, was wounded in the left shoulder, and, according to the "Notebook: September–October, 1863" (Feinberg), "came in frozen"

love. Give Carson this letter to read if he wishes it. Tell James Stilwell I have writ from here to his folks at Comac, L. I., & it may be I shall go down there next week on the L I railroad; & let him have this letter to read if he wishes it—Tell Manvill Winterstein[35] that lays next to him in Ward C that I send him my love, & I hope his wound is healing good. Lew, I wish you to go in Ward B and tell a young cavalry man, his first name is Edwin,[36] he is wounded in the right arm, that I sent him my love, & on the opposite side a young man named Charley[37] wounded in left hand, & Jennings,[38] & also a young man I love that lays now up by the door just above Jennings, that I sent them all my love. So, Lew, you see I am giving you a good round job, with so many messages—but I want you to do them all, dear son, & leave my letter with each of the boys that wish it, to read for themselves—tell Miss Gregg[39] in Ward A that I send my love to Pleasant Borley,[40] if he is still there, & if so I hope it will be God's will that he will live & get strong to go home yet—I send my love to little Billy,[41] the Ohio boy in Ward A, & to Miss Gregg herself—& if Mrs Doolittle is in Ward B, please ask her to tell the boys in the ward I sent them my love, & to her too, & give her this letter some evening to read to the boys, & one of these days I will come back & read to them myself—& the same to Mrs Southwick in Ward H, if she wishes to read it to the boys for my sake.

Lew, I wish you would go in Ward G & find a very dear friend of mine in bed 11, Elijah D Fox, if he is still there. Tell him I sent him my best love, & that I make reckoning of meeting him again, & that he must not forget me, though that I know he never will—I want to hear how he is, & whether he has got his papers through yet—Lewy, I wish you would go

from a "cav[alry] fight." In his hospital notes, WW termed him "a noble sized young fellow" (Glicksberg, 150), and referred to him briefly in *Specimen Days* (*CW*, IV, 134). In 1875 WW wrote to Wintersteen, who, on March 1, replied: "I can not place you as I did not learn your name but havent forgot the kindness I recived while in the Arm[or]y Square Hospital" (Berg). On March 10 of the same year, Wintersteen acknowledged receipt of WW's picture, and on August 5 described his not-so-prosperous circumstances. WW's letters to Wintersteen are evidently not extant.

36. Probably Edwin H. Miller, Ninth New York Cavalry; see Glicksberg, 157.

37. "Charley" may be Charles H. Harris, who wrote to WW from West Brattleboro, Vt., on May 30, 1864 (Berg).

38. In the "Notebook: September–October, 1863" (Feinberg), a J. E. Jennings is referred to.

39. See 75.

40. Borley, Company A, First U. S. Cavalry, was admitted to the hospital on August 2, with a wound in the left leg, which gangrened. According to the "Notebook: September–October, 1863" (Feinberg), his "principal disease," however, was consumption. WW recorded a "dying scene night of October 22": "—speaks of the doctor, the lady nurse so kind, so tender, 'the doctor thinks he cant do any thing for you'—'I can die'—a pause—'I dont think the doctor cares much any how.' "

41. On December 22 (Yale), Alonzo S. Bush referred to "Billy Clements."

to him first & let him have this letter to read if he is there—Lewy, I would like you to give my love to a young man named Burns in Ward I, & to all the boys in Ward I—& indeed in every ward, from A to K inclusive, & all through the hospital, as I find I cannot particularize without being tedious—so I send my love sincerely to each & all, for every sick & wounded soldier is dear to me as a son or brother, & furthermore every man that wears the union uniform & sticks to it like a man, is to me a dear comrade, & I will do what I can for him though it may not be much—& I will add that my mother & all my folks feel just the same about it, & would show it by their works too when they can—

Well, dear comrades, what shall I tell you to pass away the time? I am going around quite a great deal, more than I really desire to. Two or three nights ago I went to the N Y Academy of Music, to the Italian opera.[42] I suppose you know that is a performance, a play, all in music & singing, in the Italian language, very sweet & beautiful. There is a large company of singers & a large band, altogether two or three hundred. It is in a splendid great house, four or five tiers high, & a broad parquette on the main floor. The opera here now has some of the greatest singers in the world—the principal lady singer (her name is Medori) has a voice that would make you hold your breath with wonder & delight, it is like a miracle—no mocking bird nor the clearest flute can begin with it—besides it is [a] very rich & strong voice—& besides she is a tall & handsome lady, & her actions are so graceful as she moves about the stage, playing her part. Boys, I must tell you just one scene in the opera I saw—things have worked so in the piece that this lady is compelled, although she tries very hard to avoid it, to give a cup of poisoned wine to her lover—the king her husband forces her to do it—she pleads hard, but her husband threatens to take both their lives (all this is in singing & music, very fine)—so the lover is brought in as a prisoner, & the king pretends to pardon him & make up, & asks the young man to drink a cup of wine, & orders the lady to pour it out. The lover drinks it, then the king gives her & him a look, & smiles & walks off the stage. And now came as good a piece of performance as I ever saw in my life. The lady as soon as she saw that her husband was really gone, she sprang to her lover, clutched him by the arm, & poured out the greatest singing you ever heard—it poured like a raging river more than any thing else I could compare it to—she tells him he is

42. Medori (see 41) appeared in Donizetti's *Lucrezia Borgia* at the New York Academy of Music on November 4.

43. In view of Jeff's frequent references to his mother's frugality (see notes to 76 and 88), this remark seems somewhat ironic.

44. From George's letters to his mother, it is possible to pinpoint Andrew's military service. On June 9, 1862, George wrote: "So Bunkum [Andrew] has gone Sogering too

poisoned—he tries to inquire &c and hardly knows what to make of it—she breaks in, trying to pacify him, & explain &c—all this goes on very rapid indeed, & the band accompanying—she quickly draws out from her bosom a little vial, to neutralize the poison, then the young man in his desperation abuses her & tells her perhaps it is to poison him still more as she has already poisoned him once—this puts her in such agony, she begs & pleads with him to take the antidote at once before it is too late—her voice is so wild & high it goes through one like a knife, yet it is delicious—she holds the little vial to his mouth with one hand & with the other springs open a secret door in the wall, for him to escape from the palace—he swallows the antidote, & as she pushes him through the door, the husband returns with some armed guards, but she slams the door to, & stands back up against the door, & her arms spread wide open across it, one fist clenched, & her eyes glaring like a wild cat, so they dare not touch her—& that ends the scene. Comrades, recollect all this is in singing & music, & lots of it too, on a big scale, in the band, every instrument you can think of, & the best players in the world, & sometimes the whole band & the whole men's chorus & women's chorus all putting on the steam together—& all in a vast house, light as day, & with a crowded audience of ladies & men. Such singing & strong rich music always give me the greatest pleasure—& so the opera is the only amusement I have gone to, for my own satisfaction, for last ten years.

But, my dear comrades, I will now tell you something about my own folks—home here there is quite a lot of us—my father is not living—my dear mother is very well indeed for her age, which is 67—she is cheerful & hearty, & still does all her light housework & cooking—She never tires of hearing about the soldiers, & I sometimes think she is the greatest patriot I ever met, one of the old stock—I believe she would cheerfully give her life for the Union, if it would avail any thing—and the last mouthful in the house to any union soldier that needed it[43]—then I have a very excellent sister-in-law—she has two fine young ones—so I am very happy in the women & family arrangements. Lewy, the brother I mentioned as sick, lives near here, he is very poorly indeed, & I fear will never be much better[44]—he too was a soldier, has for several months had throat disease—he is married & has a family—I believe I have told you of still another brother in the army, down in the 9th Army Corps, has been in the service

has he, well they will have good times in Baltimore." On July 21, he noted: "I shall try and go down to see Bunkum at Suffolk." George's last reference to Andrew's military career appears in the letter of September 30, 1862, from Antietam, Md.: "Bunkum I guess is around somewhere looking for a good chance to go sogering" (Trent). Undoubtedly Andrew was released from service because of his health.

over two years, he is very rugged & healthy—has been in many battles, but only once wounded, at first Fredericksburgh.

Monday forenoon November 9.

Dear comrades, as I did not finish my letter yesterday afternoon, as I had many friends come to see me, I will finish it now—the news this morning is that Meade is shoving Lee back upon Richmond, & that we have already given the rebs some hard knocks, there on the old Rappahannock fighting ground. O I do hope the Army of the Potomac will at last gain a first-class victory, for they have had to retreat often enough, & yet I believe a better Army never trod the earth than they are & have been for over a year.

Well, dear comrades, it looks so different here in all this mighty city, every thing going with a big rush & so gay, as if there was neither war nor hospitals in the land. New York & Brooklyn appear nothing but prosperity & plenty. Every where carts & trucks & carriages & vehicles on the go, loaded with goods, express-wagons, omnibuses, cars, &c—thousands of ships along the wharves, & the piers piled high, where they are loading or unloading the cargoes—all the stores crammed with every thing you can think of, & the markets with all sorts of provisions—tens & hundreds of thousands of people every where, (the population is 1,500,000), almost every body well-drest, & appearing to have enough—then the splendid river & harbor here, full of ships, steamers, sloops, &c—then the great street, Broadway, for four miles, one continual jam of people, & the great magnificent stores all along on each side, & the show windows filled with beautiful & costly goods—I never saw the crowd thicker, nor such goings on & such prosperity—& as I passed through Baltimore & Philadelphia it seemed to be just the same.

I am quite fond of crossing on the Fulton ferry, or South ferry, between Brooklyn & New York, on the big handsome boats. They run continually day & night. I know most of the pilots, & I go up on deck & stay as long as I choose. The scene is very curious, & full of variety. The shipping along the wharves looks like a forest of bare trees. Then there are all classes of sailing vessels & steamers, some of the grandest & most beautiful steamships in the world, going or coming from Europe, or on the California route, all these on the move. As I sit up there in the pilot house, I can see every thing, & the distant scenery, & away down toward the

45. See 43.
46. On the envelope of this letter there is the following note: "This letter has been Read by Isaac Linensparger in Ward D. I think it is a very good letter & I am very much

sea, & Fort Lafayette &c. The ferry boat has to pick its way through the crowd. Often they hit each other, then there is a time—

My loving comrades, I am scribbling all this in my room in my mother's house. It is Monday forenoon—I have now been home about a week in the midst of relations, & many friends, many young men, some I have known from childhood, many I love very much. I am out quite a good deal, as we are glad to be with each other—they have entertainments &c. But truly, my dear comrades, I never sit down, not a single time, to the bountiful dinners & suppers to which I am taken in this land of wealth & plenty without feeling it would be such a comfort to all, if you too, my dear & loving boys, could have each your share of the good things to eat & drink, & of the pleasure & amusement. My friends among the young men make supper parties, after which there is drinking &c., every thing prodigal & first rate, one, Saturday night, & another last night—it is much pleasure, yet often in the midst of the profusion, the palatable dishes to eat, & the laughing & talking, & liquors &c, my thoughts silently turn to Washington, to all who lie there sick & wounded, with bread & molasses for supper—

Lewy, dear son, I think I shall remain here ten or twelve days longer, & then I will try to be with you once again. If you feel like it I would like to have you write me soon, tell me about the boys, especially James Stilwell, Pleasant Borley, Cunningham, & from the cavalry boy Edwin in ward B—tell me whether Elijah Fox in ward G has gone home—Lew, when you write to Tom Sawyer[45] you know what to say from me—he is one I love in my heart, & always shall till death, & afterwards too—I wish you to tell a young man in ward D, 2d bed below the middle door, (his first name is Isaac,[46] he is wounded in left leg, & it has had erysipelas), that I sent him my love, & I wish him to have this letter to read if he desires it, & I will see him again before long.

So, Lew, I have given you a lot of messages but you can take your time to do them, only I wish each of the boys I have mentioned to have my letter that wishes it, & read it at leisure for themselves, & then pass to another. If Miss Hill in ward F or the lady nurse in ward E cares about reading it to the boys in those wards for my sake, you give it them some evening, as I know the boys would like to hear from me, as I do from them.

Well, Lewy, I must bid you good bye for present, dear son, & also to

pleased & delited with it. I love to read such letters. I am yours truly." Linensparger wrote to WW on May 7, 1864 (Berg), after he returned home to Bloom, Ohio.

all the rest of my dear comrades, & I pray God to bless you, my darling boys, & I send you all my love, & I hope it will be so ordered to let things go as easy as possible with all my dear boys wounded or sick, & I hope it will be God's will that we shall all meet again, my dear loving comrades, not only here but hereafter.

Walt Whitman

Portland avenue near Myrtle Brooklyn New York

95. *To Ellen M. O'Connor*

Brooklyn November 15 1863

Dear Nelly

I have received your letter, also Charles Eldridge's & Mrs Cooper's. Nelly, I hope this will find you better of your cold, & that you & all the rest are well & [in] good spirits. Tell Mrs Cooper I heartily accept her invitation to visit at Philadelphia, & if I can work it so I will come gladly.[47] I think about you all, & frequently. I have told my mother & sister about you all. I send my love to William. I feel that I have never had a better friend, & that no truer nor warmer heart beats. Tell Charles Eldridge too I send him my love. I regret his not likely meeting me in New York to go around together. But, Charley, we will have it yet, dear comrade. I received the letters you sent under envelope. For all & sundry, & the year's most valuable kindness, from you three, what can I say, more than that I am sure I appreciate it.

Nelly, I had a pleasant trip that Monday from the start, & all through —clear & cool & no dust—I got home about 8 in evening—was up bright & early to the polls next morning &c. How well the election went in this state, you know.[48] Here Brooklyn gave a stunning union vote, the biggest ever dreamed of here—Mayor, assemblymen, judges, all elected.

47. According to WW's notation on Mrs. O'Connor's letter of November 10 (Feinberg), Mrs. Cooper included "a note." On November 21 (Feinberg), Mrs. O'Connor informed WW that Eldridge was going to stay at Mrs. Cooper's home in Philadelphia for several days. This is undoubtedly the Hattie B. Cooper (listed in the Directory as C. H. B. Cooper, "gentlewoman") who in an undated letter sent a "Christmas Greeting" to WW—"from one who has the *heart*—but not the *head*—of a poet, and consequently feels a sincere admiration and reverence for those Gifted Mortals, who possess both" (Feinberg). Another (probably) Mrs. Cooper was referred to by Fred Vaughan, a New York driver, on March 27, 1860: "Mrs. Cooper says if you will make love to her you had better do so personally the next time you call, as she cannot put much faith in a profession made in a letter to an outside party" (Feinberg).

48. See note 28.

49. Edward and Jesse were mentally retarded.

50. Max Maretzek (1821–1897), opera impressario, was the most successful producer of Italian opera in New York City from 1849 to 1879.

Nelly, I am writing this from my room at my mother's house. It is Sunday afternoon, dripping & rainy, the air thick & warm, & the sky lowering. My poor brother Andrew is very ill. It is not likely he can live. His voice is quite gone. Still he moves about & is here all the time during the day. My sister Martha is untiring, feeding & nursing him. Of her children, little Hattie is well—the new baby is immense, & I take to her in proportion. I want her to be called California. She is fully worthy the name. She is large, calm, not pretty but something ahead of that, full of latent fire in the eyes (which are grey) & a complete success every way. Mother is very well & active & cheerful—she still does her own light housework, & keeps up handsomely under her surroundings of domestic pressure—one case of sickness & its accompanying irritability—two of grown helplessness[49]—& the two little children, very much with her, & one of them unsurpassed in volatility & restlessness—Nelly, I have thought before that the real & best bravery is to be discovered somewhere else than in the bravery of war, & beyond the heroisms of men. My brother Jeff is well—he is a noble young man & one to love.

I find my New York boys the same gay-hearted, joyous fellows, full of friendship & determined to have pleasure. We have been together quite a good deal. They have given me little supper parties, men only, with drinking &c. Of course we have great times. I have been several times to the Opera & to French theatre. The opera here, Maretzek's troupe,[50] is very fine. Medori, soprano, is pretty near perfection—Mazzoleni, tenor, ditto—Biachi, base, ditto. Miss Kellogg is also good. The pieces were Lucrezia, Sonnambula, &c.[51]

Nelly, I have seen Charles Howells.[52] He is well—apparently indeed better than he was in Washington (in health I mean). I have been at the place, 15 Charles street. In the parlor is hung up a large blue placard "Headquarters of the Pantarchy" in white letters. I did not stop to dinner, although I was prest hard. I saw a man named Newbold.[53] Charles Howells

51. Clara Louise Kellogg (1842–1916) sang in *La Sonnambula* on November 13. Giuseppini Medori sang Lucrezia Borgia on November 2; see WW's account of this opera in 94. In Peri's *Judith* on November 11 appeared Medori, Mazzoleni, and Biachi. See Odell, *Annals of the New York Stage*, VIII, 580–581.

52. On November 10, Mrs. O'Connor melodramatically implored WW to see Mr. Howells, "and with all the skill and talent of which you are master do what you can to disenchant him with those people. . . . If he could but know the real truth in regard to 'the great head' and leader of the reform it would surely open his eyes. He evidently thinks Mr. A[ndrews] a 'great light' & a saint of a man, sincere and true" (Feinberg). Joseph Charles Howells, according to entries in New York Directories, must have been versatile (and perhaps eccentric): in 1864–1865 he was an "inventor," in 1865–1866 an inspector in the Custom House, in 1866–1867 simply an "inspector," and in 1867–1868 a seller of hairpins.

53. Perhaps John A. Newbould, who, according to the Directory of 1863–1864, managed a hardware store in New York and lived in Brooklyn.

is cheerful. We had quite a walk. He told me he was doing well in a business point of view, had made more while in New York than his salary would have been in Idaho. I did not see Mr nor Mrs Andrews.[54] I did not make any demonstration upon Charles, except what was probably significant enough during the course of his flourishing & somewhat elaborated statement of the Pantarchian scheme which I listened to in dead silence, broken only by one or two running questions of a very brief & dry character. Charles was full of friendship & our interview was one in which he imprest me more agreeably than ever before. Surely he is a good man. The impression I received (maybe casual) is that he is partially absorbed there, his own yearning & eager nature supplying the fuel of the flame, but that he is really shrewd at bottom, & may prove more able to pick his way through the humbugs of the world than we were thinking.

Nelly, I have seen Mrs Price, but not to have much true & friendly talk, as there were many present. She is much *less* well than I expected —has a hacking cough. She preserves the same quiet cheerful way—& her daughters—dear girls—*they are all friends*, to prize & love deeply.

Nelly, if you go down to Armory Square—or if Mrs Howells should, (& if you feel well, & like going, I much wish you would very soon) please find if Pleasant Borley[55] is living, he is in bed 40 in Ward A—tell him I am coming back soon, (or tell Miss Gregg,[56] for him)—Also see James S Stilwell[57] in Ward C, & Thomas Carson[58] in same ward—also Lewis K Brown[59] in Ward K, (I have sent him a long letter)—also Oscar Cunningham[60] in Ward K—also tell Mrs Doolittle[61] in Ward B, I want to see the boys there. I shall probably stay five or six days longer. I count on our all being together again. My head & hearing &c. are better yesterday & to-day than for two weeks—sometimes have been rather disagreeable. Well, Nelly, I will now bid you good bye for present, my truly dear friend, & good bye to the rest, & God bless you all.[62]

Walt Whitman

54. Stephen Pearl Andrews (1812–1886), an abolitionist and philosopher, was absorbed in utopian schemes to establish a universal language, to reconcile all great thought, to discover a science of the universe ("Universology"), and to institute a new social order which he called Pantarchy. Trowbridge related WW's adverse opinion of Andrews' schemes in *The Independent*, LV (1903), 497–501; note also R. A. Coleman, "Trowbridge and Whitman," *PMLA*, LXIII (1948), 266, and E. C. Stedman's description of the "Pantarchial scheme" in *Life and Letters* (1910), I, 174–175. Mrs. O'Connor voiced her distaste for Andrews in "Personal Recollections of Walt Whitman," *Atlantic Monthly*, XCIX (1907), 829.

55. See 94. 56. See 75. 57. See 90. 58. See 94. 59. See 60.
60. See 121. 61. Mentioned in 94.

96. *To Charles W. Eldridge*

Brooklyn | Nov 17, 1863

Dear friend[63]

I suppose Nelly has received a letter from me posting you up of my doings, &c. Any letters that come to me, up to Saturday next, please send on here. After that, do not send any, as I shall return Monday or Tuesday next. The weather here the last three days is very unpleasant, sloppy & thick. I was at the opera last night, Trovatore[64]—very, very good singing & acting—

I feel to devote myself more to the work of my life, which is making poems. I must bring out Drum Taps. I *must* be continually bringing out poems—now is the hey day. I shall range along the high plateau of my life & capacity for a few years now, & then swiftly descend. The life here in the cities, & the objects, &c of most, seem to me very flippant & shallow somehow since I returned this time—

My New York boys are good, too good—if I staid here a month longer I should be killed with kindness—The great recompense of my journey here is to see my mother so well, & so bravely sailing on amid many troubles & discouragements like a noble old ship—My brother Andrew is bound for another world—he is here the greater part of the time—

Charley, I think sometimes to be a woman is greater than to be a man—is more eligible to greatness, not the ostensible article, but the real one. Dear comrade, I send you my love, & to William & Nelly, & remember me to Major [Hapgood][65]—

Walt

97. *To Thomas P. Sawyer* [*11.20(?). 1863*]

ENDORSED (by WW): "Nov. 63." DRAFT LETTER.

Dear brother,

I am here in Brooklyn, New York, spending a few weeks home at my mother's. I left Washington Nov 2d, & shall return there next week. I

62. The affection of the O'Connors for WW was evident in Ellen's reply on November 21: "Dear Walt, we long for you, William sighs for you, & I feel as if a large part of myself were out of the city—I shall give you a good big kiss when you come, so depend upon it" (Feinberg).

63. See 86.

64. *Il Trovatore* was performed at the Academy of Music on November 16, with a cast that included Medori, Mazzoleni, and Fernando Bellini.

65. Mrs. O'Connor wrote on November 21 that Eldridge "got your letter, & was delighted with it, he said it was worthy to be set in a gold frame—to which Wm. & I assented most heartily" (Feinberg).

wrote to you six or seven weeks ago, the last time.[66] I am well & fat, eat my rations regular, & weigh about 200—so you see I am not very delicate. Here in Brooklyn & New York where I was raised, I have so many friends, I believe, now I am here they will kill me with kindness, I go around too much, & I think it would be policy for me to put back to Washington. I have a brother here, very sick, I do not think he can recover, he has been in the army—I have another brother in the 9th Army Corps, has been out 26 months. But the greatest patriot in the family is my old mother. She always wants to hear about the soldiers, & would give her last dime[67] to any soldier that needed it.

Every thing looks on the rush here in these great cities, more people, more business, more prosperity, & more of every thing to eat & wear, than ever. Tom, I was home in time to vote. The elections went bully. How are you copperheads? I think these last elections will be a settler for all traitors north, & they are the worst.

I shall be back in Washington next Tuesday. My room is 456 Sixth street. But my letters are still addrest care of Major Hapgood, paymaster U S A, Washington D C.

Well, comrade, I must close. I do not know why you do not write to me. Do you wish to shake me off? That I cannot believe, for I have the same love for you that I exprest in my letters last spring, & I am confident you have the same for me. Anyhow I go on my own gait, & wherever I am in this world, while I have a meal, or a dollar, or if I should have some shanty of my own, no living man will ever be more welcome there than Tom Sawyer. So good by, dear comrade, & God bless you, & if fortune should keep you from me here, in this world, it must not hereafter.

98. *To Elijah Douglass Fox*

ENDORSED (by WW): "to Elijah Fox | Portage | Kalamazoo Co | Mich | sent Nov 22 '63." DRAFT LETTER.

Brooklyn | Saturday night Nov 21, '63

Dear son & comrade,[68]

I wrote a few lines about five days ago[69] & sent on to Armory

66. This letter is not extant. For Sawyer, see 43.
67. Originally WW wrote: "& would take the clothes off her back to give . . ."
68. According to the "Notebook: September–October, 1863" (Feinberg), Fox, of the Third Wisconsin, entered Armory Square Hospital on September 26.
69. Apparently not extant.
70. On November 10, Fox wrote from Washington: "Dear Father | You will allow me to call you Father wont you. I do not know that I told you that both of my parents were dead but it is true and now, Walt, you will be a second Father to me won't you. for my

Square, but as I have not heard from it I suppose you have gone on to Michigan. I got your letter of Nov 10th,[70] & it gave me much comfort. Douglass, I shall return to Washington about the 24th, so when you write direct to care of Major Hapgood, paymaster U S A, Washington D. C.—Dearest comrade, I only write this, lest the one I wrote five days ago may not reach you from the hospital. I am still here at my mother's, & feel as if [I] have had enough of going around New York—enough of amusements, suppers, drinking, & what is called *pleasure*—Dearest son, it would be more pleasure if we could be together just in quiet, in some plain way of living, with some good employment & reasonable income, where I could have you often with me, than all the dissipations & amusements of this great city—O I hope things may work so that we can yet have each other's society—for I cannot bear the thought of being separated from you—I know I am a great fool about such things, but I tell you the truth, dear son. I do not think one night has passed in New York or Brooklyn when I have been at the theatre or opera or afterward to some supper party or carouse made by the young fellows for me, but what amid the play or the singing, I would perhaps suddenly think of you—& the same at the gayest supper party, of men, where all was fun & noise & laughing & drinking, of a dozen young men, & I among them, I would see your face before me in my thought as I have seen it so often there in Ward G, & my amusement or drink would be all turned to nothing, & I would realize how happy it would be if I could leave all the fun & noise & the crowd & be with you—I don't wish to disparage my dear friends & acquaintances here, there are so many of them & all so good, many so educated, traveled, &c., some so handsome & witty, some rich &c., some among the literary class—many young men—all good—many of them educated & polished, & brilliant in conversation, &c[71]—& I thought I valued their society & friendship—& I do, for it is worth valuing—But, Douglass, I will tell you the truth, you are so much closer to me than any of them that there is no comparison—there has never passed so much between them & me as we have—besides there is something that takes down all artificial accomplishments, & that is a manly & loving soul—My dearest comrade, I am sitting here writing to you very late at night—I have been reading—it is indeed after 12, & my mother & all the rest have gone to bed two hours ago, & I am here alone

love for you is hardly less than my love for my natural parent. I have never before met with a man that I could love as I do you. Still there is nothing strange about it for 'to know you is to love you,' and how any person could know you and not love you is a wonder to me" (Lion).

71. Originally this passage read: "you must not be offended if I say much more of what the world calls educated & polished, & brilliant in conversation, &c, than you, my dear son."

writing to you, & I enjoy it too, although it is not much, yet I know it will please you, dear boy—If you get this, you must write & tell me where & how you are. I hope you are quite well, & with your dear wife, for I know you have long wished to be with her, & I wish you to give her my best respects & love too.

Douglass, I havn't written any news, for there is nothing particular I have to write. Well, it is now past midnight, pretty well on to 1 o'clock, & my sheet is most written out—so, my dear darling boy, I must bid you good night, or rather good morning & I hope it may be God's will we shall yet be with each other—but I must indeed bid you good night, my dear loving comrade, & the blessing of God on you by night & day, my darling boy.[72]

99. *To Dr. Le Baron Russell*[73] [*12.3. 1863*]

TRANSCRIPT.

. . . I have told you how young & how American they mostly are—so on my own account I shall continue as a Missionary among them as surely as I live—& shall continue for years . . . I reject none of course—not rebel wounded nor blacks nor any when I find them suffering and dying.

72. When Traubel observed, "That letter to Elijah Fox . . . is better than the gospel according to John for love," WW replied: "What [it says] to me is the most important something in the world—something I tried to make clear in another way in Calamus—yes, something, something" (Traubel, II, 380). On December 9, when Fox replied to WW's letter of November 24 (now lost), he was in Wyoming, Ill.: "I expect to go into business here with Brother but do not know certain." Fox realized that, like most of the soldiers whom WW tended, he too was about to disappoint his friend: "Since coming here I have often thought of what you told me when I said to you I am certain I will come back to Washington. you said to me then that a great many of the boys had said the same but none had returned. I am sorry it is so but after I had thought it over I concluded it would be better for me to go into some business that would be a periminent thing" (LC). On hearing of WW's illness, Fox wrote, on July 14, 1864: "Oh! I should like to have been with you so I could have nursed you back to health & strength . . . I shall never be able to recompense you for your kind care and the trouble I made you while I was sick in the hospital . . . I am sure no Father could have cared for their own child, better than you did me" (Berg).

73. Russell (1814–1889) was a Boston abolitionist and friend of Carlyle and Emerson. He was instrumental in having the former's works printed in the United States. See the Boston *Evening Transcript*, August 20, 1889; and William T. Davis, *Plymouth Memories of an Octogenarian* (1906), 342. Russell, after reading WW's letter to Redpath on August 6, sent money on September 21 (Hanley; Donaldson, 145–146). On October 4 (Hanley; Donaldson, 147–148), he enclosed $50 and noted that he had sent WW's letter (not extant) to Hannah Stevenson (see 85) and to her sister Mrs. Charles P. Curtis (see 82). Russell sent a contribution of $20 on November 8 (Hanley; Donaldson, 151).

74. This note to George was written on the verso of Jeff's letter of December 3: "I have just telegraphed to you that Andrew was dead. Poor boy, he died much easier than one would have supposed. I do hope to God you will come on. I have been with him, Mary, Mother, Mat and I, almost all the time since you left. Mary and I watched last

100. *To George Washington Whitman*

Washington | Dec 6 '63

Dear brother,[74]

I sent you a letter four days ago that Andrew was gone at last, poor fellow. I have written to Han. I did not go on to Andrew's funeral, (I suppose it was yesterday)—but I am very very sorry now that I did not stay while I was home—I am well—Write when you can—

Walt

101. *To Louisa Van Velsor Whitman*

Washington | Dec 15 1863

Dearest mother

The last word I got from home was your letter written the night before Andrew was buried, Friday night, nearly a fortnight ago—I have not heard any thing since from you or Jeff[75]—Mother, Major Hapgood has moved from his office cor 15th st. & I am not with him any more—he has moved his office to his private room—I am writing this in my room 456 Sixth st—but my letters still come to Major's care, they are to be addrest same as ever, as I can easily go & get them out of his box—(only

night. He has been dying ever since Wednesday morning—fully 24 hours—Poor Nancy, she takes it woful hard. Mary has acted like the best of Women. It is very affecting to see Nancy and the children. Mattie did everything that she possibly could. She watched with us till near 3 o'clock this morning. Andrew was very desirous of having us all around him when he died. The poor boy seemed to think that that would take nearly all the horror of it away" (Feinberg; Allen, 306).

75. On December 4 (Trent), Mrs. Whitman had described the death scene. Nancy went to bed on Wednesday night and "in the morning she brought such a smell that Jeffy got sick." Meantime Jesse had been so affected by the crisis that he had threatened Mannahatta and Martha, an incident which led the explosive Jeff to exclaim: "I love Mat as I love my life—dearer by far—and to have this infernal pup—a perfect hell-drag to his Mother—treat [Martha] so—threaten to brain her—call her all the vile things that he could think of—is a little more than I will stand. He says he dont know any better—he lies—he does know better. I wish to God he was ready to put along side of Andrew. There would be but few tears shed on my part I can tell you. . . . To think that the wretch should go off and live with an irish whore, get in the condition he is by her act and then come and be a source of shortening his mother's life by years" (Feinberg). Jeff finally proposed that Jesse be hospitalized.

On December 15(?) (Trent), Mrs. Whitman minimized Jesse's behavior, and gave WW details of the funeral, including Nancy's "adue" to friends that "we had taken [Andrew] away from her," when the body was brought to the Whitman house. Evidently WW had agreed with Jeff that something must be done about Jesse, for on December 28 Jeff wrote: "You wrote Mother abt getting Jess in the Asylum—It does not seem to meet with her wishes—when I wrote you my idea was that by each of us paying—say a $ a week—you and I and George—that we could keep him in some one of the hospitals around New York—I think it would be best yet. . . . I feel as if it was our duty to relieve Mother of him" (Feinberg). (Jesse was admitted to the Brooklyn State Hospital on December 5, 1864; see Allen, 318.)

nothing need be sent me any time to the old office, as I am not there nor Major either—any thing like a telegraphic dispatch or express box or the like should be addrest 456 Sixth st, 3d story back room)—

Dear mother, I hope you are well & in good spirits—I wish you would try to write to me every thing about home & the particulars of Andrew's funeral, & how you all are getting along—I have not rec'd the Eagle with the little piece in[76]—I was in hopes Jeff would have sent it—I wish he would yet—or some of you would—I want to see it—I think it must have been put in by a young man named Howard,[77] he is now editor of the Eagle, & is very friendly to me—

Mother, I am quite well—I have been out this morning early, went down through the market, it is quite a curiosity—I bought some butter, tea, &c—I have had my breakfast here in my room, good tea, bread & butter &c—

Mother, I think about you all more than ever—& poor Andrew, I often think about him—Mother, write to me how Nancy & the little boys are getting along—I got thinking last night about little California—O how I wished I had her for an hour to take care of—dear little girl, I dont think I ever saw a young one I took to so much—but I mustn't slight Hattie—I like her too—Mother, I am still going among the hospitals, there is plenty of need, just the same as ever—I go every day or evening—I have not heard from George—I have no doubt the 51st is still at Crab Orchard[78]—

Mother, I hope you will try to write—I send you my love, & to Jeff & Mat & all—so good bye, dear Mother—

Walt

76. In her letter of December 4, Mrs. Whitman wrote that "there was a very good little peice in the eagle last night about you" (Trent), and promised that Jeff would send it. In a note appended to a letter from George, dated December 9, Mrs. Whitman said that she thought that the article had been written by Dr. Ruggles. The "Personal" in the *Eagle* on December 3 read in part: "Who is there in Brooklyn who doesn't know Walt Whitman? Rough and ready, kind and considerate, generous and good, he was ever a friend in need. . . . Surely such as he will find their reward here and hereafter."

77. Joseph Howard, Jr. (1833–1908), was war correspondent for the New York *Times* until he was appointed city editor of the Brooklyn *Daily Eagle*. See Louis M. Starr, *Bohemian Brigade: Civil War Newsmen in Action* (1954), 315.

78. WW evidently had not received the letter written by George to his mother on December 9 (Trent), in which he told her that the regiment had moved from Camp Orchard to Camp Pittman, near London, Ky.

79. Trowbridge (1827–1916), novelist, poet, and author of juvenile stories, read *Leaves of Grass* in 1855, and in the following year described WW to his sister as "a sort of Emerson run wild." He met the poet for the first time when WW was in Boston to supervise the Thayer & Eldridge edition of *Leaves of Grass*, and again in Washington in 1863, when Trowbridge stayed with Secretary Chase in order to gather material for his biography, *The Ferry Boy and the Financier* (1863); he described their meetings in *My Own Story* (1903), 360–401. On December 11, Trowbridge had presented to Chase Emerson's letter recommending WW; see 28. Though Trowbridge was not an idolator of

102. *To John Townsend Trowbridge*

TRANSCRIPT.

Washington | Dec 27 1863

Dear friend,[79]

I have left word at the office Armory Square hospital about Caleb Babbitt's descriptive list.[80] Poor boy, I should like much to see him & soothe him—I hope he will yet keep up his spirits. About the package of books, direct them to me, (if you should find convenient to send them) to Washington, 456 Sixth St north, 3d story back room—Should you see Mr. Shillaber[81] tell him I see Frank McDonald every day or so—I saw him last evening, saw his wound and examined it—he still lies constantly in bed—The wound is not in a very favorable way, yet nothing really serious —Mr. S must write and send papers to him &c, often as convenient—I am well & in hospitals every day—So, dear friend, good bye for present—

Walt Whitman.

Address care Major Hapgood, paymaster U. S. A., Washington D. C.

WW, he wrote to O'Connor in 1867: "Every year confirms my earliest impression, that no book has approached the power and greatness of this book, since the Lear and Hamlet of Shakespeare"; R. A. Coleman, "Trowbridge and O'Connor," *AL*, XXIII (1951–2), 327. For WW's high opinion of Trowbridge, see Traubel, III, 506. See also Coleman, "Trowbridge and Whitman," *PMLA*, LXIII (1948), 262–273.

80. At WW's request, Trowbridge visited Babbitt (see 73) in Mason Hospital, and wrote on December 21 that his discharge was delayed because of Dr. Bliss's failure to send a descriptive list. "What [Babbitt] needs is sympathizing friends around him. He is very lonesome lying here on his back, with no Walt Whitman to cheer him up" (Feinberg). Trowbridge's letter of December 30 informed WW that the descriptive list had arrived, and that the package contained two copies of *The Drummer Boy, a Story of the War in Verse* (1862) by "Cousin John," one of which "I wish you would leave at Mr. Chase's" (Traubel, IV, 290).

81. Benjamin Penhallow Shillaber (1814–1890) was a celebrated humorist and newspaperman. While he was with the Boston *Post*, he invented the American version of Mrs. Mallaprop, and *The Life and Sayings of Mrs. Partington* (1854) was a best-seller. Trowbridge was associated with Shillaber in the short-lived comic journal *Carpet Bag*, in which appeared the first writings of Artemus Ward and Mark Twain. Shillaber wrote to WW about Babbitt on December 14 (Feinberg; Traubel, II, 96–97). See Trowbridge, *My Own Story* (1903), 179–182; and Cyril Clemens, "Benjamin Shillaber and His 'Carpet Bag,'" *NEQ*, XIV (1941), 519–537.

1864

103. *To Louisa Van Velsor Whitman*

Washington | Friday afternoon Jan 29 1864

Dear Mother

Your letter of Tuesday night came this forenoon—the one of Sunday night I rec'd yesterday—Mother, you don't say in either of them whether George has re-enlisted or not—or is that not yet decided positively one way or the other?[1]

O Mother, how I should like to be home, (I dont want more than two or three days)—I want to see George, (I have his photograph on the wall, right over my table all the time)—& I want to see California—you must always write in your letters how she is—I shall write to Han this afternoon or to-morrow morning, & tell her probably George will come out & see her, & that if he does you will send her word beforehand—

Jeff, my dear brother, if there should be the change made in the works & things all overturned, you mustn't mind—I dare say you will pitch into something better—I believe a real overturn in the dead old beaten track of a man's life, especially a young man's, is always likely to turn out best, though it worries one at first dreadfully—

Mat, I want to see you most sincerely—they havn't put in anything in the last two or three letters about you, but I suppose you are well, my dear sister—

Mother, the young man that I took care of, Lewis Brown,[2] is pretty well, but very restless—he is doing well now, but there is a long road before him yet—it is torture for him to be tied so to his cot, this weather—he is a very noble young man, & has suffered very much—he is a Maryland boy, & (like the southerners when they *are* union,) I think he is as strong & resolute a union boy as there is in the United States—he went out in Maryland reg't but transferred to a N Y battery—But I find so many noble men in the ranks, I have ceased to wonder at it—I think the soldiers from the New England States & the Western states are splendid, & the country

1864

1. George came home on a thirty-day furlough in January, and re-enlisted.

2. Brown's leg had been amputated on January 5. WW was present at the operation, which he described in his diary (Glicksberg, 93). See also 60.

3. A member of the House of Representatives; see 25.

4. Martin Kalbfleisch (1804–1873) was an important Brooklyn politician, an alder-

parts of N Y & Pennsylvania too—I think less of the great cities than I used to—I know there are black sheep enough, even in the ranks, but the general rule is the soldiers are noble, very—

Mother, I wonder if George thinks as I do about the best way to enjoy a visit home, after all—When I come home again, I shall not go off gallivanting with my companions half as much, nor a quarter as much as I used to, but shall spend the time quietly home with you, while I do stay—it is a great humbug spreeing around, & a few choice friends for a man, the real right kind, in a quiet way, are enough—

Mother, I hope you take things easy, dont you? Mother, you know I was always advising you to let things go, & sit down & take what comfort you can while you do live—

It is very warm here, this afternoon it is warm enough for July—the sun burns where it shines on your face—it is pretty dusty in the principal streets—Congress is in session, I see Odell,[3] Kalbfleisch,[4] &c. often—I have got acquainted with Mr Garfield,[5] an M C from Ohio, & like him very much indeed—(he has been a soldier west, was a Major General & I believe a good brave one)—I don't go much to the debates this session yet—Congress will probably keep in session till well into the summer—as to what course things will take, political or military, there's no telling—I think though the secesh military power is getting more & more shaky—how they can make any headway against our new, large & fresh armies next season passes my wit to see—

Mother, I was talking with an (pretty high) officer, here, who is behind the scenes—I was mentioning that I had a great desire to be present at a first class battle—he told me if I would only stay around here three or four weeks longer, my wish would probably be gratified—I asked him what he meant, what he alluded to specifically—but he would not say any thing further—so I remain as much in the dark as before—only there seemed to be some meaning in his remark, & it was made to me only as there was no one else in hearing at the moment—(he is quite an admirer of my poetry)—

The re-enlistment of the veterans is the greatest thing yet, it pleases every body but the rebels—& surprises every body too—

Mother, I am well & fat, (I must weigh about 206)—So Washington must agree with me—I work three or four hours a day copying—Dear mother, I send you & Hattie my love, as you say she is a dear little girl—

man from 1855 to 1861, and mayor in 1862–1864 and again in 1867–1871. He served one term in Congress from 1863 to 1865.

5. James Garfield (1831–1881) entered the House of Representatives in 1863 and served until 1880, when he was elected President. WW eulogized him in "The Sobbing of the Bells"; see also Allen, 495.

Mother, try to write every week, even if only a few lines—love to George & Jeff & Mat—

Walt

104. *To Louisa Van Velsor Whitman*

Washington | Feb 2 1864

Dearest Mother,

I am writing this by the side of the young man you asked about, Lewis Brown,[6] in Armory Square hospital—He is now getting along very well indeed—The amputation is healing up good, & he does not suffer any thing like as much as he did. I see him every day. We have had real hot weather here, & for the last three days wet & rainy—it is more like June than February—

Mother, I wrote to Han, last Saturday—she must have got it yesterday—I have not heard any thing from home since a week ago, (your last letter)—I suppose you got a letter from me Saturday last—I am well as usual—there has been several hundred sick soldiers brought in here yesterday—

I have been around among them to-day all day—it is enough to make one heart-sick, the old times over again—they are many of them mere wrecks, though young men—(sickness is worse in some respects than wounds)—one boy[7] about 16, from Portland, Maine, only came from home a month ago, a recruit, he is here now, very sick & downhearted, poor child, he is a real country boy, I think has consumption—he was only a week with his reg't—I sat with him a long time—I saw [it] did him great good—I have been feeding some their dinners—it makes me feel quite proud, I find so frequently I can do with the men what no one else at all can, getting them to eat, (some that will not touch their food otherwise, nor for any body else)—it is sometimes quite affecting I can tell you—I found such a case to-day, a soldier with throat disease, very bad—I fed him quite a dinner—the men, his comrades around, just stared in wonder, & one of them told me afterwards that he (the sick man) had not eat so much at a meal, in three months—Mother, I shall have my hands pretty full now for a while—write all about things home—

Walt

Lewis Brown says I must give you his love—he says he knows he would like you if he should see you—

6. See 103.

7. William Rackliffe (or Racliffe) died December 15, 1866, and was buried in the National Cemetery (*LC* #108). See also 208.

8. WW's "Hospital Book 12" (Feinberg) contains two entries from Culpepper dated February 7 and 9. Both are descriptive accounts, the first of the movement of troops and

105. *To Louisa Van Velsor Whitman* 2.5. [*1864*]

Washington | Friday afternoon Feb 5

Dearest Mother

I am going down in front, in the midst of the Army, to-morrow morning, to be gone for about a week[8]—so I thought I would write you a few lines now, to let you know—

Mother, I suppose you got my letter written last Tuesday—I have not got any from home now for a number of days—I am well & hearty—the young man Lewis Brown is able to be up a little on crutches—there are quite a number of sick young men, I have taken in hand, from the late arrivals, that I am sorry to leave—sick & downhearted & lonesome, they think so much of a friend, & I get so attached to them too—but I want to go down in camp once more very much—& I think I shall be back in a week—I shall spend most of my time among the sick & wounded in the Camp hospitals—if I had means I should stop with them, poor boys, or go down among them periodically, dispensing what I had, as long as the war lasts, down among the worst of it—(although what are collected here in hospital, seem to me about as severe and needy cases as any after all)—

Mother, I want to hear about you all,[9] & about George & how he is spending his time home—Mother, I do hope you are well & in good spirits & Jeff & Mat & all, & dear little California & Hattie—I send them all my love—Mother, I may write to you from down in front—so good bye, dear mother, for present—

Walt

I hope I shall find several letters waiting for me when I get back here—

106. *To John Townsend Trowbridge*

TRANSCRIPT.

Culpepper Va. | Feb 8 1864

Dear friend[10]

I ought to have written to you before, acknowledging the good package of books, duly received by express, & actively used since, changing them around in places where most needed among the soldiers—(I found a small hospital of U. S. teamsters, entirely without reading, I go there con-

the second of the scenery near the town. See also note to 107.

9. No letters from the family are extant in January and February, except for Jeff's brief note on January 8 (Feinberg).

10. See 102.

siderable, & have given them largely of your reading contribution)—I am down here pretty well toward the extreme front of the Army, eight or ten miles south of headquarters, (Brandy Station)—We had some fighting here, below here on picket lines, day before yesterday—We feared they, the rebs, were advancing upon us in our depleted condition, especially feared their making a flank movement up on our right. We were all ready to skedaddle from here last night, & expected it—horses harnessed in all directions, & traps packed up, (we have held & lost Culpepper three or four times already)—but I was very sleepy & laid down & went to sleep, never slept fresher or sweeter—but orders came during the night to stay for the present, there was no danger—during the night I heard tremendous yells, I got up & went out, & found it was some of the men returning from the extreme front—As day before yesterday a strong force, three corps, were moved down there—These were portions of them now returning—it was a curious sight to see the shadowy columns coming in two or three o'clock at night—I talked with the men—how good, how cheerful, how full of manliness & good nature our American young men are—I staid last night at the house of a real secesh woman, Mrs. Ashby—her husband (dead) a near relation of the famous reb Gen Ashby[11]—she gave me a good supper & bed—There was quite a squad of our officers there—she & her sister paid me the compliment of talking friendlily & nearly altogether exclusively with me—she was dressed in very faded clothes but her manners were fine, seems to be a travelled educated woman—quite melancholy—said she had remained through fearful troubles & changes here on acct of her children—she is a handsome middle-aged woman—poor lady, how I pitied her, compelled to live as one may say on chance & charity, with her high spirit—

Dear friend, I am moving around here among the field hospitals—(O how the poor young men suffer)—& to see more of camp life & war scenes, & the state of the army this winter—Dear friend, I have much to tell you, but must abruptly close—

Walt Whitman

Write to me same address Washington, D. C.—has Caleb Babbitt gone home from Mason Hospital—I left the book at Mr. Chase's[12]—
J. T. Trowbridge, | Somerville, Massachusetts.

11. Turner Ashby (1828–1862), Confederate cavalry officer, was killed on June 6, 1862, while he fought a rear-guard action for Stonewall Jackson's troops. This sentence does not appear in the Stanford transcription.

12. Trowbridge replied, on February 12 (Feinberg; Traubel, II, 524), that Babbitt had left the hospital in late December, and that he had heard from another soldier-patient that Babbitt had regained "his strength, though not his voice." Trowbridge also reported that he had written "a few days ago" to Chase on WW's behalf, and that Chase had received the book—evidently the copy of *Drummer Boy* referred to in 102.

13. Henry Loud Cranford entered the army as a first lieutenant in the Eighty-fourth

107. *To Louisa Van Velsor Whitman*

Culpepper Virginia | Friday night Feb 12th | 64.

Dearest Mother,

I am still stopping down in this region. I am a good deal of the time down within half a mile of our picket lines, so that you see I can indeed call myself in the front. I stopped yesterday with an artillery camp, in the 1st Corps, at the invitation of Capt Cranford,[13] who said that he knew me in Brooklyn. It is close to the lines—I asked him if he did not think it dangerous—he said no, he could have a large force of infantry to help him there, in very short metre, if there was any sudden emergency—The troops here are scattered all around, much more apart than they seemed to me to be opposite Fredericksburgh last winter—they mostly have good huts & fireplaces, &c—I have been to a great many of the camps, & I must say I am astonished how good the houses are almost every where—I have not seen one regiment nor any part of one, in the poor uncomfortable little shelter tents that I saw so common last winter, after Fredericksburgh—but all the men have built huts of logs & mud—a good many of them would be comfortable enough to live in under any circumstances[14]—

I have been in the Division hospitals around here—there are not many men sick here, & no wounded—they now send them on to Washington—I shall return there in a few days, as I am very clear that the real need of one's services is there after all—there the worst cases concentrate, & probably will, while the war lasts—

I suppose you know that what we call hospital here in the field, is nothing but a collection of tents, on the bare ground for a floor, rather hard accommodations for a sick man—they heat them here by digging a long trough in the ground under them, covering it over with old railroad iron & earth, & then building a fire at one end & letting it draw through & go out at the other, as both ends are open—this heats the ground through the middle of the hospital quite hot—I find some poor creatures crawling about pretty weak with diarrhea—there is a great deal of that—they keep them till they get very bad indeed, & then send them to Washington—the journey aggravates the complaint, & they come into Washington in a terrible condition—O mother, how often & how many I have seen come into

New York Infantry on May 23, 1861, and was appointed captain on February 19, 1863.

14. At Culpepper WW noted in his "Hospital Book 12" about February 9: "Around through the landscape for miles, in pleasant situations, are . . . little villages of tents, log & mud huts, &c. There are scores of these little improvised [villages]. I see them in all directions. Some of the camps are quite large. I amuse myself by examining one of them, a mile or so off, through a strong glass. Some of the men are cooking, others washing, cleaning their clothes, others playing ball, smoking lazily, or lounging about. I watch the varied performance long. It is better than any play" (Feinberg).

Washington, from this awful complaint, after such an experience as I have described—with the look of Death on their poor young faces—they keep them so long in the field hospitals with poor accommodations, the disease gets too deeply seated—

To-day I have been out among some of the camps of the 2d division of the 1st Corps—I have been wandering around all day, & have had a very good time, over woods, hills, & gullys, indeed a real soldier's march—the weather is good & the traveling quite tolerable—I have been in the camps of some Massachusetts, Pennsylvania, & New York regiments—I have friends in them, & went out to see them, & see soldiering generally, as I never cease to crave more & more knowledge of actual soldiers' life, & to be among them as much as possible—This evening I have also been in a large wagoners' camp—they had good fires, & were very cheerful—I went to see a friend there too, but did not find him in—it is curious how many I find that I know & that know me—Mother, I have no difficulty at all in making myself at home among the soldiers, teamsters, or any—I most always find they like to have me very much, it seems to do them good, no doubt they soon feel that my heart & sympathies are truly with them, & it is both a novelty & pleases them & touches their feelings, & so doubtless does them good—& I am sure it does that to me—

There is more fun around here than you would think for—I told you about the theatre the 14th Brooklyn has got up,[15] they have songs & burlesques &c, some of the performers real good—As I write this I have heard in one direction or another two or three good bands playing—& hear one tooting away some gay tunes now, though it is quite late at night—Mother, I dont know whether I mentioned in my last letter that I took dinner with Col Fowler[16] one day early part of the week—his wife is stopping here—I was down at the 14th as I came along this evening too—one of the officers told me about a presentation to George of a sword &c, he said he see it in the papers[17]—the 14th invited me to come & be their guest while I staid here, but I have not been able to accept—Col Fowler uses me tip top—he is provost marshal of this region, makes a good officer—Mother, I could get no pen & ink tonight—Well, dear Mother, I send you my love & to George & Jeff & Mat & little girls & all—

Walt

15. This letter is not known.

16. Edward Brush Fowler (1827–1896) became the commanding officer of the Fourteenth New York Regiment on December 9, 1862. He was badly wounded and mustered out on June 6, 1864. His statue is in Washington Park, not far from the Brooklyn home of the Whitmans.

17. An article in the Brooklyn *Daily Eagle* on February 12 noted that on the preceding evening, at the Uris' Dancing Academy, George had received a sword "in recognition of his services in the field . . . The guest of the evening was the observed of all

direct to care Major Hapgood, as before, & write soon—Mother, I suppose you got a letter I wrote from down here last Monday—

108. *To Dr. Le Baron Russell* [2.(?). *1864*]

ENDORSED (by WW): "February, 1864 | Down in the Army at | Culpepper & Brandy Station | describe | army field hospitals, &c." DRAFT LETTER.

The hospitals here in & around Washington are still pretty full, and contain in some respects the most needy cases of all the suffering—(though there are plenty such every where.) For the past few weeks I have been on a tour down to the front, through the division hospitals, especially those around Culpepper & Brandy Station, mostly of the 1st, 2d, & 3d corps, to see how the sick were situated there. A year ago I spent December & part of January[18] (after 1st Fredericksburgh) among the wounded in front from Aquia Creek to Falmouth, and saw perhaps the saddest scenes of the war then. But there is nothing like it now. I have made up my mind that the camp hospitals are pretty well cleaned out, the worst cases are here in Washington, & so I have returned here for good.[19] In the field hospitals I find diarrhea, getting more & more prevalent, & chronic. It is the great disease of the army. The doctors, as always, give too much medicine, & hold on to the poor young men in camp too long, then when the thing is deeply rooted, send them up here. How many such wrecks of young men have I seen, from boat & railroad, from front, come crawling pale & faint along here, many to linger a while, & die, during the past year, sent up in this way after being kept too long.

I suppose you will be interested in knowing that our troops in the field in Virginia are this Winter remarkably well in health, however, as a general thing & in the cheeriest temper. They have better houses than ever before, no shelter tents now, but huts of logs & mud, with fireplaces. In the tour I allude to, I was much in contact with the rank in file, lived among them in their camps, among the common soldiers & teamsters, &c. I never go among the Army in this way, but what, after making all allowances, I feel that our general stock of young men shows all other races, meagre & pale & puny in comparison. The more I see of them in the Army, the higher

observers . . . It was a very fine affair and worthy of the occasion which brought it forth."

18. Once again (see 92) WW overstated the duration of his stay at the front; he wrote to his mother from Washington on December 29, 1862 (see 25).

19. The rest of this paragraph appeared in slightly altered form in the New York *Times*, December 11, 1864, and in "Hospital Visits," in *The Wound Dresser* (CW, VII, 114).

& broader my estimate of them. (I mean the Americans, I dont make account of any other—Americans both West & East, & from all the agricultural regions of the great states). And then to be among them also as I have been for past fifteen months, among them, seeing them in hospitals, thousands, so young & manly, with such fearful suffering, wounds, amputations, & weary sickness. O how one gets to love them—indeed it brings people very, very close, such circumstances.

As to the temper of the Army in Virginia, I should say it was never so resolute, so full of the right spirit for endurance & work as it is to-day. The filled-up regiments, gathering around the nucleus of the old veterans, make better regiments than any. I was with several such, & found them excellent. These re-enlisted regiments, returning from their furloughs, thus filled up, are streaming down to front fast already. The opinion of Meade is full of respect for him—he is thought an earnest, alert, concientious, cautious commander.

I write these, doctor, thinking they may interest you, coming from late direct contact with the army on the ground.

So, doctor, I still remain here in Washington, occupying my time nearly altogether among the wounded & sick, as when I last wrote you.[20] I act as an independent visitor & helper among the men, fixing as before on the cases that most need. I never miss a single day or night, week day or Sunday, visiting some poor, young soul in bodily & mental tribulation. It is a great privilege to me, more to me than to them I think.

109. *To Louisa Van Velsor Whitman*

Washington | March 2 1864

Dear mother

You or Jeff must try to write as soon as you receive this & let me know how little Sis is, tell me if she got entirely over the croup & how she is—also about George's trunks,[21] I do hope he recovered them, it was such a misfortune—I want to hear the end of it, I am in hopes I shall hear that he has got them—I have not seen in the papers whether the 51st has left New York yet—Mother, I want to hear all about home & all the occurrences, especially the two things I have just mentioned, & how you are, dearest mother, you must write me exactly how you are for somehow I was

20. See 99.

21. On March 6, George wrote to his mother: "I found my trunk up at Fort Schuyler all right the morning I left home" (Trent). When he wrote, George was in Nashville, Tenn., on his way to Knoxville, Ky.

22. See 45.

23. WW wrote about his lecture plans in 53. Evidently spurred by the enthusiasm of John Burroughs, he had agreed to lecture in Washington on January 20 or 25. "If we

thinking from your letters lately whether you was as well as usual or not —write how my dear sister Mat is too, & whether you are still going to stay there in Portland av. the coming year—Well, dear mother, I am just the same here, nothing new, I am well & hearty, & constantly moving around among the wounded & sick—there are a great many of the latter coming up—the hospitals here are quite full—lately they have [been] picking out in the hospitals all that had pretty well recovered, & sending them back to their regiments, they seem to be determined to strengthen the army this spring, to the utmost—they are sending down many to their reg'ts that are not fit to go, in my opinion—then there are squads & companies & reg'ts too passing through here in one steady stream going down to front, returning from furlough home—but then there are quite a number leaving the army on furlough, re-enlisting, & going north for a while—they pass through here quite largely—

Mother, Lewis Brown is getting quite well, he will soon be able to have a wooden leg put on, he is very restless & active, & wants to go around all the time—

Sam Beatty[22] is here in Washington—We have had quite a snow storm, but is clear & sunny to-day here, but sloshy, I am wearing my army boots—any thing but the dust—Dear mother, I want to see you & Sis, & Mat & all very much—if I can get a chance I think I shall come home for a while—I want to try to bring out a book of poems, a new one to be called "Drum Taps" & I want to come to New York for that purpose too—

Mother, I havn't given up the project of lecturing[23] either—but whatever I do, I shall for the main thing devote myself for years to come to these wounded & sick, what little I can—Well good bye, dear mother, for present—write soon—

Walt

110. *To Moses Lane(?)* [*3.13(?). 1864*]

DRAFT LETTER.

Dear friend,[24]

I rec'd this morning your additional contribution of $5 for the wounded & sick. The same am't from you was also duly & thankfully re-

succeed here," Burroughs wrote to a friend, "he proposes going North to New York, Brooklyn, Boston, etc."; see Barrus, 18. The plans, however, did not materialize.

24. This appears to be a rough copy of a letter to Moses Lane (see 31), who, according to his letter on May 27, 1863 (Feinberg), had promised to send WW $5 each month for his hospital work. March 13 is a plausible date, since Jeff had enclosed $5 from Lane on March 11 (Feinberg).

ceived last month. It is some time since I have written you.[25] I have lately been down to front a second time through the field hospitals—they are breaking them up & sending the bad cases up here. I suppose preparatory to some movement of course. Among the sick diarrhea & rheumatism are prevalent. Many of the cases of the latter suffer fearfully. I am writing this in hospital as I am watching here to-night over a bad case.

(Describe scene.)[26]

With me here things are about the same. I have first-rate health & strength. My hospital ministrations are very fascinating with all of their sadness. The wounded & sick get incredibly near to one. Poor young men, they respond so affectionately to kindness & magnetism.[27]

I suppose you hear of Grant's plan to improve enormously the communication between here & the southwest by rail &c. so that he can transport the army by immense trains hither & yon at short notice. They say he has staked all on taking Richmond within three months. God prosper him.

Our Virginia Army is in prime condition. This I know from personal observation. All its defeats & slaughters have only hardened it, & made it an army of fighters. I believe Grant realizes in his secret heart that it is the clear superior in fibre & soul of his Western Army, but of course he would not say so.

Dear friend, the sick are coming in here now from front pretty freely. I have need of means additional—The new sick & wounded generally come in without a cent. I give aid of all kinds, sometimes little sums of money. You have been generous & regular in your aid, & I cannot call on you for any thing more than you are doing, but I would like you to cast around among your friends, show them this note, & tell them the case—see if you could raise among them some 20 or $25 the ensuing week, if possible, for it is for a sacred object.

111. *To Louisa Van Velsor Whitman*

Washington | March 15 1864

Dearest mother,

I got a letter from Jeff last Sunday—he says you have a very bad cold indeed—dear mother, I feel much concerned about it—I do hope it has passed over before this—Jeff wrote me about the house, I hope it will be so you can both remain in the same house,[28] it would be much more satisfaction [*line cut out*] very sick of brain fever, I was with—the poor boy is

25. Although WW ran vertical lines through the salutation and the first three sentences, I have retained them, since they permit reasonable conjectures as to the date and recipient.

26. This is, of course, a direction to WW. Here he undoubtedly intended to include material similar to that in 49.

27. WW deleted the following at this point: "It is wonderful to go round among

dead,[29] he was only 19, & a noble boy, so good, though out of his senses some eight days, though still having a kind of idea of things, no relative or friend was with him, it was very sad, I was with him considerable, only just sitting by him soothing him, he was wandering all the time, his talk was so affecting it kept the tears in my eyes much of the time, the last 24 hours he sunk very rapidly—he had been sick some months ago, & was put in the 6th invalid corps—they ought to have sent him home instead—the next morning after his death his brother came, a very fine man, postmaster at Lyme Ridge, Pa.—he was much affected, & well he might be.

Mother, I think it is worse than ever here in the hospitals, we are getting the dregs as it were of the sickness & awful hardships of the past three years—there is the most horrible cases of diarrhea you ever conceived of, & by the hundreds & thousands, I suppose from such diet as they have in the army—

Well, dear mother, I will not write any more on the sick—& yet I know you wish to hear about them—every one is so unfeeling, it has got to be an old story—there is no good nursing—O I wish you were—or rather women of such qualities as you & Mat—were here, in plenty, to be stationed as matrons among the poor sick & wounded men—just to be present would be enough—O what good it would do them—

Mother, I feel so sick when I see what kind of people there are among them, with charge over them, so cold & ceremonious, afraid to touch them —Well, Mother, I fear I have written you a flighty kind of a letter—I write in haste—

Walt

The papers came right, mother—[*line cut out*] love to Jeff, Mat & all—

112. *To Louisa Van Velsor Whitman*

Washington | March 22 1864

Dearest Mother,

I feel quite bad to hear that you are not well, have a pain in your side, & a very bad cold—dear Mother, I hope it is better—I wish you would write to me, or Jeff would, right away, as I shall not feel easy until I hear—I rec'd George's letter, Jeff wrote with it, about your feeling pretty sick, & the pain—Mother, I also rec'd your letter a few days before—you say the Brown's acted very mean & I should think they did indeed, but as it is go-

them, & twice blessed. One wonders too where all the enormous proceeds . . ."

28. On March 11 (Feinberg), Jeff had reported that his mother had "the worst cold that I ever knew of," and that they were having troubles with the Browns (see 19) about the rent.

29. Thomas B. Low died on March 7. His brother was George L. Low. See "Hospital Book 12" (Feinberg).

ing to remain the same about the house, I should let it all pass[30]—I am very glad Mat & Jeff are going to remain, I should not have felt satisfied if they & you had been separated—I have written a letter to Han, with others enclosed, a good long letter, (took two postage stamps)—I have written to George too, directed it to Knoxville.[31]

Mother, every thing is the same with me, I am feeling very well indeed, the old trouble of my head stopt & my ears affected, has not troubled me any since I came back here from Brooklyn—I am writing this in Major Hapgood's old office, cor 15th & F st., where I have my old table & window—it is dusty & chilly to-day, any thing but agreeable—Gen Grant is expected every moment now in the Army of the Potomac, to take active command—I have just this moment heard from the front—there is nothing yet of a movement, but each side is continually on the alert, expecting something to happen—O mother, to think that we are to have here soon what I have seen so many times, the awful loads & trains & boat loads of poor bloody & pale & wounded young men again—for that is what we certainly will, & before very long—I see all the little signs, getting ready in the hospitals &c.—it is dreadful, when one thinks about it—I sometimes think over the sights I have myself seen, the arrival of the wounded after a battle, & the scenes on the field too, & I can hardly believe my own recollection—what an awful thing war is—Mother, it seems not men but a lot of devils & butchers butchering each other—

Dear Mother, I think twenty times a day about your sickness—O I hope it is not so bad as Jeff wrote, he said you was worse than you had ever been before—& he would write me again—well he must, even if only a few lines —what have you heard from Mary & her family, anything?

Well, dear Mother, I hope this will find you quite well of the pain, & of your cold—write about the little girls & Mat & all—

Walt

113. *To Louisa Van Velsor Whitman* [*3.29. 1864*]

Washington | Tuesday afternoon M[arch 29]

Dearest mother

I have written [to] George again to Knox[ville]—things seem to be quiet down there so far—We think here that our forces are going to be

30. About his mother Jeff wrote on March 19: "She has a very steady and severe pain, she thinks a gathering or enlargement, in the right side of her chest. For a day or two she was almost helpless. . . . I am really fearful that she has permanently hurt herself" (Trent). As this quotation indicates, Jeff rarely, if ever, understated; he always foresaw disaster, particularly in any situation in which his mother was involved. Again he complained that her parsimony kept her from hiring household help. The difficulties with the Browns had been settled, and both families were to remain on Portland Avenue

made strongest here in Virginia this spring, & every thing bent to take Richmond—Grant is here, he is now down at headquarters in the field, Brandy Station—we expect fighting before long, there are many indications—I believe I told you they had sent up all the sick from front[32]—about four nights ago we [had a] terrible rainy afternoon [& night]—Well in the middle [of the w]orst of the rain at [night? th]ere arrived a train [of sick?] & wounded, over 600 [soldiers], down at the depot—[It w]as one of the same [old] sights, I could not keep the tears out of my eyes—many of the poor young men had to be moved on stretchers, with blankets over them, which soon soaked as wet as water in the rain—Most were sick cases, but some badly wounded—I came up to the nearest hospital & helped—Mother, it was a dreadful night (last Friday night)—pretty dark, the wind gusty, & the rain fell in torrents—One poor boy (this is a sample of one case out of the 600) he seemed to me quite young, he was quite small, (I looked at his body afterwards)—he groaned some as the stretcher-bearers were carrying him along—& again as they carried him through the hospital gate, they set down the stretcher & examined him, & the poor boy was dead—they took him into the ward, & the doctor came immediately, but it was all of no use—the worst of it is too that he is entirely unknown—there was nothing on his clothes, or any one with him, to identify him—& he is altogether unknown—Mother, it is enough to rack one's heart, such things—very likely his folks will never know in the world what has become of him—poor poor child, for he appeared as though he could be but 18—

I feel lately as though I must have some intermission, I feel well & hearty enough, & was never better, but my feelings are kept in a painful condition a great part of the time—things get worse & worse, as to the amount & sufferings of the sick, & as I have said before, those who have to do with them are getting more & more callous & indifferent—Mother, when I see the common soldiers, what they go through, & how every body seems to try to pick upon them, & what humbug there is over them every how, even the dying soldier's money stolen from his body by some scoundrel attendant, or from some sick ones, even from under his head, which is a common thing—& then the agony I see every day, I get almost frightened at the world—Mother, I will try to write more cheerfully next time—but I see so much—well, good bye for present, dear Mother—

Walt

for another year.

31. According to George's letter of April 3 to his mother (Trent), WW wrote on March 19.

32. The upper right-hand corner of the first page of this letter is missing; hence, in earlier printings, editors summarized the next few lines and omitted the postscript, which appears at the top of the first page.

Mother, I got your letter telling [me you were] better—have you got quite we[ll?—I] wish you would write very so[on again] too—I feel uneasy about [you]—I send my love to Jeff & Mat & all—

114. *To Louisa Van Velsor Whitman*

Washington | Thursday afternoon | March 31st '64

Dearest mother,

I have just this moment received your letter dated last Monday evening—dear mother, I have not seen any thing in any paper where the 51st is, nor heard any thing, but I do not feel any ways uneasy about them, I presume they are at Knoxville, Tennessee[33]—Mother, they are now paying off many of the regiments in this army—but about George I suppose there will be delays in sending money &c—dear mother, I wish I had some money to send you, but I am living very close by the wind—Mother, I will try somehow to send you something worth while, & I do hope you will not worry & feel unhappy about money matters—I know things are very high—Mother, I suppose you got my letter written Tuesday last, 29th March, did you not?

I have been going to write to Jeff for more than a month—I laid out to write a good long letter, but something has prevented me, one thing & another—but I will try to write to-morrow sure—

Mother, I have been in the midst of suffering & death for two months worse than ever—the only comfort is that I have been the cause of some beams of sunshine upon their suffering & gloomy souls & bodies too—many of the dying I have been with too—

Well, mother, you must not worry about the grocery bill &c, though I suppose you will say that is easier said than followed—(As to me I believe I worry about worldly things less than ever, if that is possible)—Tell Jeff & Mat I send them my love—Gen Grant has just come in town from front—the country here is all mud again—I am going to a spiritualist

33. In his letter of April 3 from Annapolis, Md., to his mother, George traced the itinerary of the Fifty-first Regiment: "When I last wrote you [March 6] from Nashville Tenn. we were just about leaving that place for the front. Well we went to Knoxville by way of Chattanooga, stopped at Knoxville a day or two, and then were ordered to a place called Mossy Creek, about 40 miles beyond Knoxville. The next day after we arrived at the Creek we were ordered to bout face and travel over the same ground again back to this place. We arrived here yesterday having been nearly two weeks on the journey, our Regt. came nearly all the way by Rail Road" (Trent).

34. The celebrated medium, Charles H. Foster. WW referred to the seance again in 115. Foster's career is described by George C. Bartlett, *The Salem Seer* (1891), and by Arthur Conan Doyle, *A History of Spiritualism*, II, 30–34. Note also WW's interest in Mrs. Hatch in 12.

34.1. One of Andrew's sons.

medium[34] this evening, I expect it will be a humbug of course, I will tell you next letter—dear mother, keep a good heart—

Walt

How is Californy?—tell Hat her uncle Walt will come home one of these days, & take her to New York to walk in Broadway—poor little Jim,[34.1] I should like to see him—there is a rich young friend of mine wants me to go to Idaho with him to make money[35]—

115. *To Louisa Van Velsor Whitman*

Washington | Tuesday afternoon April 5th | '64

Dearest Mother,

I got a letter from Jeff yesterday—he says you often work too hard, exposing yourself, I suppose scrubbing &c. and the worst of it is I am afraid it is true—Mother, I would take things easy, & let up on the scrubbing & such things, they may be needed perhaps, but they ain't half as much needed as that you should be as well as possible, & free from rheumatism & cold[36]—Jeff says that sis has had the chicken pox—has she got all over it—I want to hear—So Nance[37] has had another child, poor little one, there don't seem to be much show for it, poor little young one, these times.

We are having awful rainy weather here—it is raining to-day, steady & spiteful enough—the soldiers in camp are having the benefit of it, & the sick, many of them—there is a great deal of rheumatism & also throat diseases, & they are affected by the weather—I have writ to George again, directed to Knoxville—Mother, I got a letter this morning from Lewis Brown,[38] the young man that had his leg amputated two months or so ago—(the one that I slept in the hospital by several nights for fear of hemorrhage from the amputation)—he is home at Elkton, Maryland, on furlough, he wants me to come out there, but I believe I shall not go, he is doing very well—there are many very bad now in hospitals—so many of the soldiers

35. Possibly Captain John Mullan; see 41. Apparently Mrs. Whitman's letter to which this is an answer is not extant.

36. Jeff's letter to WW is apparently lost, but he obviously repeated the complaint voiced in earlier letters (see note 30) that Mrs. Whitman refused to engage domestic help. George, in his letter of April 14, reinforced the injunctions of his brothers: "I am quite sure, Mother, that you are not half carefull enough of yourself, and if you would only hire someone to come and work for you two or three days every week, and let them do all the scrubing and cleaning, I am sure you would not be trobled so much with colds and lameness. You needent say you cant afford it, Mammy, for I will guarentee to send you money enough to keep the Institution running (without your working the way you always have) and, Mammy, dont you be backward in useing it" (Trent).

37. Andrew's wife. 38. See 103.

are getting broke down after two years, or two & a half, exposure, & bad diet, pork, hard biscuit, bad water or none at all, &c &c—so we have them brought up here. O it is terrible, & getting worse, worse, worse—I thought it was bad to see the wounded, but to see these I sometimes think is more pitiful still—

Well, mother, I went to see the great spirit medium Foster, there were some little things some might call curious perhaps, but it is a shallow thing & a humbug—a gentleman who was with me was somewhat impressed, but I could not see any thing in it worth calling supernatural—I wouldnt turn on my heel to go again & see such things, or twice as much—we had table rappings & lots of nonsense—I will give you particulars when I come home one of these days—

Jeff, I believe there is a fate on your long letter, I thought I would write it to-day, but as it happens I will hardly get this in the mail I fear in time for to-day—O how I want to see you all, & sis & Hat—Well I have scratched out a great letter, just as fast as I could write—

Wednesday forenoon—Mother, I didn't get the letter in the mail yesterday—I have just had my breakfast, some good tea & good toast & butter —I write this in my room, 456 Sixth st.—the storm seems to be over—dear Mother, I hope you are well & in good spirits—Write to me often as you can & Jeff too—any news from Han?

Walt

115.1 *To George Washington Whitman*

ADDRESS: Capt George W Whitman | vet 51st New York Vol | Annapolis | Maryland. POSTMARK: Brooklyn, N.Y. | Apr | 26 | 186(?).

Washington | Saturday mn'g April 9 '64

Dear brother

I got a letter from Mother this morning, & she sends one to you for me to direct—I will just enclose both—you *must* write to Mother oftener—before she got this last letter it was too long, & seemed ten times longer than

39. George wrote to his mother on April 3; apparently his last letter had been written on March 6 (Trent).

40. This letter is not known.

41. In December, 1863, Jeff had made surveys at Springfield, Mass., and, in February and March, he had been in Connecticut "making surveys for an 'Iron Co.'" (Feinberg).

42. See 103. 43. See 25.

44. WW adapted the material in this letter for inclusion in *November Boughs* (CW, VI, 229–230). The sentence "this is a pretty time to talk of recognizing such villains" was attributed there to "a Pennsylvania officer in hospital." After this paragraph,

it was[39]—if she don't hear from you in a long while she just gets sick about it—she is getting pretty old, & shows it at last—still I think she is pretty well—

Nothing new with me—I wrote you three days ago,[40] to Annapolis, I suppose you got it—Jeff is away a good deal of the time, surveying &c[41] —We are having another rain-storm set in here this morning—Congress is splurging away, doing some good things too—I see Kalbfleisch[42] & Odell[43] here frequently—have you writ to Han? Well, brother, good bye for present—

Walt

116. *To Louisa Van Velsor Whitman*

Washington | April 10th 1864.

Dearest Mother,

I rec'd your letter & sent the one you sent for George immediately —he must have got it the next day—I had got one from him before yours arrived—I mean to go to Annapolis & see him—

Mother, we expect a commencement of the fighting below very soon, there is every indication of it—we have had about as severe rain storms here lately as I ever see—it is middling pleasant now—there are exciting times in Congress[44]—the Copperheads are getting furious, & want to recognize the Southern Confederacy—this is a pretty time to talk of recognizing such villains after what they have done, and after what has transpired the last three years—After first Fredericksburgh I felt discouraged myself, & doubted whether our rulers could carry on the war—but that has past away, the war *must* be carried on—& I would willingly go myself in the ranks if I thought it would profit more than at present, & I don't know sometimes but I shall as it is—

Mother, you dont know what a feeling a man gets after being in the active sights & influences of the camp, the Army, the wounded &c.—he gets to have a deep feeling he never experienced before[45]—the flag, the tune of Yankee Doodle, & similar things, produce an effect on a fellow never such before—I have seen some bring tears on the men's cheeks, & others turn

WW added in the published version: "Then there is certainly a strange, deep, fervid feeling form'd or arous'd in the land, hard to describe or name; it is not a majority feeling, but it will make itself felt."

45. In the printed version in *November Boughs*, WW once more (see notes to 92) encouraged readers to infer that his services during the war were not confined to hospital visits: "M[other], you don't know what a nature a fellow gets, not only after being a soldier a while, but after living in the sights and influences of the camps, the wounded, &c.—a nature he never experienced before" (*CW*, VI, 229).

pale, under such circumstances[46]—I have a little flag (it belonged to one of our cavalry reg'ts) presented to me by one of the wounded—it was taken by the secesh in a cavalry fight, & rescued by our men in a bloody little skirmish, it cost three men's lives, just to get one little flag, four by three—our men rescued it, & tore it from the breast of a dead rebel—all that just for the name of getting their little banner back again—this man that got it was very badly wounded, & they let him keep it—I was with him a good deal, he wanted to give me something he said, he didn't expect to live, so he gave me the little banner as a keepsake—I mention this, Mother, to show you a specimen of the feeling—there isn't a reg't, cavalry or infantry, that wouldn't do the same, on occasion—

Tuesday morning April 12th

Mother, I will finish my letter this morning—it is a beautiful day to-day—I was up in Congress very late last night,[47] the house had a very excited night session about expelling the men that want to recognize the Southern Confederacy—You ought to hear the soldiers talk—they are excited to madness—we shall probably have hot times here not in the Army alone—the soldiers are true as the north star—I send you a couple of envelopes, & one to George—Write how you are, dear Mother, & all the rest—I want to see you all—Jeff, my dear brother, I wish you was here, & Mat too—Write how sis is—I am well as usual, indeed first rate every way —I want to come on in a month, & try to print my "Drum Taps"[48]—I think it may be a success pecuniarily too—Dearest Mother, I hope this will find you entirely well, & dear sister Mat & all.

Walt

117. *To Louisa Van Velsor Whitman*

Washington | Tuesday noon April 19 '64

Dearest Mother,

I havn't heard any news from home now in more than a week, I hope you are well, dear Mother, & all the rest too—there is nothing new or different with me—I can only write you the same old story about going to the hospitals &c &c.—I have not heard any thing since from George—have you heard any thing further?[49] I have writ to him, to Annapolis—We

46. WW was probably thinking of an incident which a soldier of Kilpatrick's cavalry had related to him, and which he recorded in "Hospital Book 12" (Feinberg) about this time. See 88 and *CW*, VI, 171.

47. The expulsion of Alexander Long; see 117. This paragraph up to "true as the north star" appeared in *November Boughs* (*CW*, VI, 230).

48. On April 14, George informed his mother that WW in a recent letter wrote of "publishing a small book this Spring" (Trent).

49. George replied to 115.1 from Annapolis, Md., on April 16 (Trent).

50. After Alexander Long (1816–1866), Democratic Representative from Ohio,

are having it pretty warm here to-day, after a long spell of rain storms, but the last two or three days very fine—Mother, I suppose you got my letter of last Tuesday, 12th—

I went down to the Capitol the nights of the debate on the expulsion of Mr Long[50] last week—they had night sessions, very late—I like to go to the House of Representatives at night, it is the most magnificent hall, so rich & large, & lighter at night than it is days, & still not a light visible, it comes through the glass roof—but the speaking & ability of the members is nearly always on a low scale, it is very curious & melancholy to see such a rate of talent there, such tremendous times as these—I should say about the same range of genius as our old friend Dr Swalm,[51] just about—you may think I am joking, but I am not, Mother—I am speaking in perfect earnest—the Capitol grows upon one in time, especially as they have got the great figure on top of it now, & you can see it very well, it is a great bronze figure, the Genius of Liberty[52] I suppose—it looks wonderful toward sundown, I love to go down & look at it, the sun when it is nearly down shines on the head-piece & it dazzles & glistens like a big star, it looks quite curious—

Well, Mother, we have commenced on another summer, & what it will bring forth who can tell?—the campaign of this summer is expected here to be more active & severe than any yet—As I told you in a former letter Grant is determined to bend every thing to take Richmond & break up the banditti of scoundrels that have stuck themselves up there as a "government"—he is in earnest about it, his whole soul & all his thoughts night & day are upon it—he is probably the most in earnest of any man in command or in the government either—that's something, ain't it, Mother—& they are bending every thing to fight for their last chance—calling in their forces from southwest &c—Dear Mother, give my love to dear brother Jeff & Mat & all—I write this in my room, 6th st—

Walt

118. *To Louisa Van Velsor Whitman*

Washington | April 26 1864

Dearest Mother

Burnside's army passed through here yesterday—I saw George & walked with him in the regiment for some distance & had quite a talk—he is

assailed the North's moral position in the Civil War, in April, Schuyler Colfax, Speaker of the House of Representatives, moved for the expulsion of Long, but later approved a resolution of censure: "That the said Alexander Long be, and he hereby is, declared to be an unworthy member of this House." On April 15, the New York *Herald* observed sardonically: "One beneficial effect of this discussion has been to secure a full attendance of members." Long was defeated for re-election in the fall.

51. Samuel J. Swalm, physician, lived at 129 Buffield Street, Brooklyn.

52. The "Statue of Freedom" was formally unveiled on December 2, 1863; see Glenn Brown, *History of the United States Capitol* (1900–1903), II, 138, 177.

very well, he is very much tanned & looks hardy, I told him all the latest news from home—George stands it very well, & looks & behaves the same good & noble fellow he always was & always will be—it was on 14th st.—I watched three hours before the 51st came along—I joined him just before they came to where the President & Gen Burnside were standing with others on a balcony, & the interest of seeing me &c. made George forget to notice the President & salute him—he was a little annoyed at forgetting it—I called his attention to it, but we had passed a little too far on, & George wouldn't turn round even ever so little—however there was a great many (more than half the army) passed without noticing Mr Lincoln & the others, for there was a great crowd all through the streets, especially here, & the place where the President stood was not conspicuous from the rest—The 9th Corps made a very fine show indeed—there were I should think five very full regiments of new black troops under Gen Ferrero,[53] they looked & marched very well—It looked funny to see the President standing with his hat off to them just the same as the rest as they passed by—then there [were] Michigan regiments, one of them was a reg't of sharpshooters, partly composed of indians—then there was a pretty strong force of artillery—& a middling force of cavalry, many New York, Pennsylvania, Massachusetts, R[hode] I[sland], &c reg'ts—all except the blacks were veterans, seen plenty of fighting—Mother, it is very different to see a real army of fighting men, from one of those shows in Brooklyn, or New York, or on fort Greene—

Mother, it was a curious sight to see these ranks after ranks of our own dearest blood of men, mostly young, march by, worn & sunburnt & sweaty, with well worn clothes & their bundles & knapsacks, tin cups & some with frying pans, strapt over their backs, all dirty & sweaty—nothing real neat about them except their muskets, but they were all as clean & bright as silver—they were four or five hours passing along, marching with wide ranks pretty quickly too—it is a great sight to see such a big Army, 25 or 30,000, on the march—they are all so gay too, poor fellows—nothing dampens their spirits—they all got soaked with rain the night before—I saw Fred McReady & Capt Sims, & Col LeGendre[54] &c—I dont know exactly where Burnside's army is going—among other rumors it is said they [are] to go [with] the Army of the Potomac to act as a reserve force, &c—another is that they are to make a flank march, to go round & get Lee on the side &c—We know nothing—I havn't been out this morning & dont know what

53. See 25.
54. On April 16, when George wrote to WW, LeGendre (see 42) and Sims (see 51) were still in New York recruiting for the regiment. In the same letter, George reported that McReady (see 48) was now a second lieutenant (Trent).
55. Possibly Albert G. Knapp, who wrote to WW on April 2, 1876 (Berg), and recalled their meetings at the Judiciary Square Hospital in 1863 and at Armory Square

news, only that there is without doubt to be a terrible campaign here in Virginia this summer, & that all who know deepest about it, are very serious about it—Mother, it is serious times—I do not feel to fret or whimper, but in my heart & soul about our country, the army, the forthcoming campaign with all its vicissitudes & the wounded & slain—I dare say, Mother, I feel the reality more than some because I [am] in the midst of its saddest results so much—Others may say what they like, I believe in Grant & in Lincoln too—I think Grant deserves to be trusted, he is working continually—no one knows his plans, we will only know them when he puts them in operation—Our Army is very large here in Virginia this spring & they are still pouring in from east & west—you dont see about it in the papers, but we have very large army here—

Mother, I am first rate in health, thank God, I never was better—dear mother, have you got all over that distress & sickness in your head? You must write particular about it—Dear brother Jeff, how are you, & how is Matty?—& how the dear little girls—Jeff, I believe the devil is in it about my writing you, I have laid out so many weeks to write you a good long letter, & something has shoved it off each time—never mind, mother's letters keep you posted—you must write & don't forget to tell me all about sis, is she as good & interesting as she was six months ago? Mother, have you heard any thing from Han? Mother, I have just had my breakfast, I had it in my room, some hard biscuits warmed on stove, & a first rate bowl of strong tea, with good milk & sugar—I have given a Michigan soldier[55] his breakfast with me, he relished it too, he has just gone—Mother, I have just heard again that Burnside's troops are to be a reserve to protect Washington, so there may be something in it—

Walt

It is very fine weather here yesterday & to-day—the hospitals are very full, they are putting up hundreds of hospital tents—

119. *To James P. Kirkwood*[56] [*4.27(?). 1864*]

ENDORSED (by WW): "for J P Kirkwood | 44 Union Square | New York City." DRAFT LETTER.

I forget whether I wrote to you acknowledging the receipt of the $10 sent for the wounded & sick, 1st Feb.[57] It came safe—also the $5 you

Hospital in 1864. Knapp remained in Washington until the summer of 1865.

56. Kirkwood, an engineer, sent sums of money to WW for his hospital work; see 51 and 120. I have dated the draft on the basis of the reference in the next letter: "I wrote to Mr Kirkwood yesterday."

57. Jeff had enclosed $5 from Kirkwood on January 8 (Feinberg).

sent some ten days since. My dear sir, your contributions are very, very welcome—they go to the direct sustenance, cheer, & comfort of special cases of wounded & sick.[58] I have now been over a year among the wounded. I find that personal application, tact, & insight, with entire sympathy, are the only means effectual in hospitals—every case wants some peculiar adaptation—to some, some little article purchased—many the tender hand & word, oft repeated, never slacking up, till danger is past. Some, while prostrated, are out of money, & too proud to speak of it, to these a little gift of two or three [cents?]—to some a little tobacco is a great treasure. Any thing like beggars or deceivers, are very rare—indeed I dont meet one a fortnight. The soldiers are nearly altogether young American men of decent breeding, farmers' sons ordinarily educated, but well behaved & their young hearts full of manliness & candor. Their condition makes deepest attachments[59] under their sufferings & wounds often brought right to the bitterness of death. Some, indeed, one feels to love deeply, & they return it with interest.

I have lately been down front, on a short tour through the Army, part of the time being in camp among the men, (I know a great many soldiers in the ranks) & part visiting the division hospitals. The hospitals in the field are at present thin—the main cases are here. The condition of the Army the past winter has been surpassingly good—(go on with acc't)[60]—the talk here is that Grant is going to make things hop in this region presently—The idea is that the means of railway transportation between here & the southwest are to be increased to the extremest practical degree, so that he can swing large bodies to & fro, with unprecedented dispatch, & have the use of the Army, in either quarter, at a few days notice. We hear he (Grant) thinks it indispensable that we should smash Lee & the Richmond junta this summer, though more for our prestige than for any practical need of Richmond as a locality. I can assure you from personal knowledge that the Army of the Potomac is in splendid condition, physically & in soul—it has now the fibre of the most veteran troops, one of the historic armies. It is very youthful. I think well of Meade. He is very cautious & conscientious, yet very alert—(would be perfect if he fused those qualities with the lightning of audacity & venturing all when it was worth it, but he has not that dangerous but necessary crowning merit, Napoleon's.)

I make no calculations on the course & result of the ensuing summer campaign, except that I believe it will be vehement. Meantime we are liable at any moment to have an incipient caving in of the South, parts of it

58. The text up to this point was lined through, and perhaps was not included in the actual letter.

59. WW originally wrote: "One gets so attached to them."

60. It is impossible to know what WW meant by this parenthetical remark. Con-

like North Carolina, but the shrewd ones here still reckon on a desperate fight of the Richmond junta, ferocious, carrying things with as high hand as ever the ensuing year.

I see the President often. I think better of him than many do. He has conscience & homely shrewdness—conceals an enormous tenacity under his mild, gawky western manner. The difficulties of his situation have been unprecedented in the history of statesmanship. That he has conserved the government so far is a miracle itself. The difficulties have not been the south alone. The north has been & is yet honeycombed with semi-secesh sympathisers ever ready to undermine—& I am half disposed to predict that after the war closes, we shall see bevics of star-straps, two or three of our own Major Generals, shot for treachery, & fully deserve their fate.

I write this in hospital, having leisure here. I am sitting by the side of a soldier of the 6th Maine—he had his leg amputated lately.

The sick are coming in pretty freely here, poor wrecks & phantoms—a sign of action, as they are breaking up the field hospitals. One's heart bleeds for them. Every day I am among them as usual. I desire you, if you have any friends able to send me aid, & that feel to do so, that you would show them this letter, as I would like more means. It shall be sacredly [*incomplete*]

120. *To Louisa Van Velsor Whitman*

Washington | April 28 1864

Dearest mother

I thought I would write you just a line, though I have nothing of importance—only the talk of the street here seems more & more to assert that Burnside's army is to remain near here to protect Washington & act as a reserve, so that Grant can move the Army of the Potomac upon Richmond, without being compelled to turn & be anxious about the Capital—also that Burnside can attend to Lee if the latter should send any force up west of here, (what they call the valley of the Shenandoah)—or invade Pennsylvania again—I thought you would like to hear this—it looks plausible, but there are lots of rumors of all kinds—I cannot hear where Burnside's army is as they dont allow the papers to print army movements—but I fancy they are very near Washington, the other side of Arlington heights, this moment[61]—

Mother, I wrote yesterday to Han, & sent one of George's last letters

ceivably the letter itself was to be rearranged drastically.

61. George wrote WW on the following day from Bristoe Station, Va.: "We arrived here last night about dark, and are going to fall in, in a few minutes, to move on towards Warrenton, I believe" (Trent).

from Annapolis—Mother, I suppose you got my letter of Tuesday 26th—I have not heard any thing from you in quite a little while—I am still well—the weather is fine, quite hot yesterday—Mother, I am now going down to see a poor soldier who is very low with a long diarrhea—he cannot recover—when I was with him last night, he asked me before I went away to ask God's blessing on him, he says, I am no scholar & you are—poor dying man, I told him I hoped from the bottom of my heart God would bless him, & bring him up yet—I soothed him as well as I could, it was affecting, I can tell you—Jeff, I wrote to Mr Kirkwood[62] yesterday to 44 Pierrepont st., he sent me some money last Monday—is Probasco[63] still in the store in N Y?—dear sister Mat, I quite want to see you & California, not forgetting my little Hattie too—

Walt

2 o'clock, 28th April

Dearest mother,

Just as I am going to mail this, I receive authentic information. Burnside's army is now about 16 or 18 miles south of here, at a place called Fairfax court house—They had last night no orders to move at present, & I rather think they will remain there, or near there—What I have written before, as a rumor, about their being to be held as a reserve, to act wherever occasion may need them, is now quite decided on—You may hear a rumor in New York that they have been shipped in transports from Alexandria—there is no truth in it at all—Grant's Army of the Potomac is probably to do the heavy work—his army is strong & full of fight. Mother, I think it is to-day the noblest army of soldiers that ever marched—nobody can know the men so well as I do, I sometimes think—

Mother, I am writing this in Willard's hotel,[64] on my way down to hospital after I leave this at post office—I shall come out to dinner at 4 o'clock & then go back to hospital again in evening—

Good bye, dear Mother, & all—

Walt

121. *To Louisa Van Velsor Whitman*

Washington | May 3 1864

Dearest Mother

I rec'd your letter dated last Friday afternoon, with one from Mr Heyde—it seems by that Han is better, but as you say it would be much

62. The draft (119), however, was addressed "44 Union Square."
63. See 31.
64. Willard's Hotel was located on Pennsylvania Avenue between Fourteenth and

more satisfactory if Han would write to us herself—Mother, I believe I told you I sent a letter to Han last week, enclosing one of George's from Annapolis—I was glad to get Heyde's letter though, as it was—Mother, I am sorry you still have returns of your cold, does it affect your head like it did?—dear Mother, I do hope you will not expose yourself, nor work too much, but take things easier—

I have nothing different to write about the war, or movements here—what I wrote last Thursday about Burnside's corps being probably used as a reserve, is still talked of here, & seems to be probable—a large force is necessary to guard the railroad between here & Culpepper, & also to keep for any emergency that might happen, & I shouldn't wonder if the 9th would be used for such purpose, at least for the present—I think the 51st must be down not very far from Fairfax Court House yet, but I havn't heard certain—

Mother, I have seen a person up from front this morning—there is no movement yet & no fighting started—the men are in their camps yet—Gen Grant is at Culpepper—You need not pay the slightest attention to such things as you mention in the Eagle,[65] about the 9th corps—the writer of it, & very many of the writers on war matters in those papers dont know one bit more on what they are writing about than Ed does—

Mother, you say in your letter you got my letter the previous afternoon—why, Mother, you ought to got it Wednesday forenoon, or afternoon at furthest—this letter now will get in New York Wednesday morning, by day light—you ought to get it before noon—the postmaster in Brooklyn must have a pretty set of carriers, to take twice as long to take a letter from New York to you as it does to go from Washington to N Y—Mother, I suppose you got a letter from me Friday also—as I wrote a second letter on Thursday last, telling you the 9th Corps was camped then about sixteen miles from here—

About George's pictures, perhaps you better wait till I hear from him, before sending them—

I remain well as usual—the poor fellow I mentioned in one of my letters last week, with diarrhea, that wanted me to ask God's blessing on him, was still living yesterday afternoon, but just living, he is only partially conscious, is all wasted away to nothing, & lies most of the time in half stupor, as they give him brandy copiously—yesterday I was there by him a few minutes, he is very much averse to taking brandy, & there was some trouble in getting him to take it, he is almost totally deaf the last five or six days—

Fifteenth Streets.

65. See 36.

there is no chance for him at all—Quite a particular friend of mine, Oscar Cunningham,[66] an Ohio boy, had his leg amputated yesterday close up by the thigh, it was a pretty tough operation—he was badly wounded just a year ago to-day at Chancellorsville, & has suffered a great deal, lately got erysipelas in his leg & foot—I forget whether I have mentioned him before or not—he was a very large noble looking young man when I first see him—the doctor thinks he will live & get up, but I consider [it] by no means so certain—he is very much prostrated—

Well, dear Mother, you must write, & Jeff too—I do want to see you all very much—how does Mat get along, & how little sis & all? I send my love to you & Jeff & all—we are having a very pleasant coolish day here—I am going down to post office to leave this, & then up to my old friends O'Connors, to dinner, & then down to hospital—Well good by, dear Mother, for present—

Walt

Tuesday afternoon 3 o'clock—Mother, just as I was going to seal my letter, Major Hapgood has come in from the P O & brings me a few lines from George, which I enclose—you will see they were written four days ago[67]—

122. *To Louisa Van Velsor Whitman*

Washington | May 6, 1864

Dearest mother

I write you a few lines, as I know you feel anxious these times—I suppose the New York papers must have it in this morning that the Army of the Potomac has made a move, & has crossed the Rapidan river[68]—at any rate that is the case—as near as I can learn about Burnside's army, that lies in the rear of the Army of the Potomac, (from Warrenton, Virginia, & so to Rappahannock river & up toward Manassas)—it still appears to be kept as a reserve, & for emergencies &c. I have not heard any thing from the 51st.

66. The rapid decline of Oscar Cunningham is traced in 122, 124, 130, 132, and 133. In his diary, on April 12, before the amputation, WW wrote, "The chances are against him, poor fellow" (Glicksberg, 150). In a manuscript written as he sat in Armory Square Hospital, about the time of this letter, WW observed: "Right opposite is a young Ohio boy, Oscar Cunningham, badly wounded in right leg—his history is a sad one—he has been here nearly a year—he & I have been quite intimate all that time—when he was brought here I thought he ought to have been taken to a sculptor to model for an emblematical figure of the west, he was such a handsome young giant over 6 feet high, with a great head of brown yellow shining hair thick & longish & a manly noble manner & talk—he has suffered very much since—the doctors have been trying to save his leg but it will probably have to be taken off yet. He wants it done, but I think he is too weak at present" (LC). The Berg Collection possesses a cheerful letter from Cunningham's sister Helen, dated May 15; another from a friend in Lincoln Hospital, May 17; and a letter from Helen to WW on June 11, in which she requested details of her brother's

Mother, of course you got my letter of Tuesday, 3d, with the letter from George dated Bristoe station—I have writ to George since, and addressed the letter Warrenton, Va., or elsewhere, thinking he might get it—

Mother, the idea is entertained quite largely here that the rebel army will retreat to Richmond, as it is well known that Grant is very strong, (most folks say too strong for Lee)—I suppose you know we menace them almost as much from up Fortress Monroe as we do from the Rapidan—Butler & W F Smith[69] are down there with at least fifty or sixty thousand men, & will move up simultaneously with Grant—the occasion is serious, & anxious, but somehow I am full of hope—& feel that we shall take Richmond—(I hope to go there yet before the hot weather is past)—dear mother, I hope you are well & little California—love to Jeff & Mat & all—

Walt

Mother, you ought to get this letter Saturday forenoon, as it will be in N Y by sunrise Saturday 7th—

Mother,[70] the poor soldier with diarrhea is still living, but O what a looking object, death would be a boon to him, he cannot last many hours—Cunningham, the Ohio boy with leg amputated at thigh, has picked up beyond expectation, now looks altogether like getting well—the hospitals are very full—I am very well indeed—pretty warm here to-day—

2 o'clock p m Friday 6th[71]

Mother, just as I put this letter in the mail there is an extra out here that Grant has advanced his army or a portion of it to the region of the Chancellorsville battle of just a year ago, & has either flanked Lee, as they call it, (got in on his army between him & Richmond)—or else that Lee has hurried back, or is hurrying back to Richmond—

Whether there is any thing in this story or not, I cannot tell—the city is full of rumors & this may be one of them—the government is not in receipt of any information to-day—Grant has taken the reins entirely in his own hands—he is really dictator at present—we shall hear something important within two or three days—Grant is very secretive indeed—he

death.

67. The letter of April 29 from Bristoe Station; see notes to 120.

68. Grant was engaged in the Battle of the Wilderness and was about to achieve a major victory. On May 9, the New York *Times* reported: "GLORIOUS NEWS | Defeat and Retreat | of Lee Army. | Two Days Battle in Virginia."

69. Benjamin Franklin Butler (1818–1893), controversial Massachusetts politician and controversial administrator of New Orleans until his removal on December 16, 1862, was in command of the Army of the James in 1863 and 1864. William Farrar Smith (1824–1903) was one of Butler's general officers. He attacked Petersburg in the following month, but his delays led to his loss of command on July 19, 1864.

70. This paragraph was printed in *November Boughs* (CW, VI, 230), with minor changes; "pretty warm" in the last line, for example, became "Hot here to-day."

71. This part of the letter, which is in the Estelle Doheny Collection, has never been reprinted.

bothers himself very little about sending news even to the President or Stanton—time only can develope his plans—I still think *he is going to take Richmond & soon*, (but I may be mistaken as I have been in past)—Well, dearest mother, keep up good courage, good bye for present—I wish you would write soon—

Walt

123. *To Louisa Van Velsor Whitman* 5.9. [1864]

Washington | Monday 2 o'clock—May 9th

Dearest Mother

There is nothing from the army more than you know, in the N Y papers—the fighting has been hard enough, but the papers make lots of additional items, & a good deal that they just entirely make up—there are from 600 to 1000 wounded coming up here—(not 6 to 8000 as the papers have it)[72]—I cannot hear what part the 9th corps took in the fight, of Friday & afterwards, nor whether they really took any at all—(they, the papers, are determined to make up just any thing)—

Mother, I rec'd your letter & Han's—& was glad indeed to get both—Mother, you must not be under such apprehension, as I think it is not warranted[73]—

So far as we get news here, we are gaining the day, so far, *decidedly*—if the news we hear is true that Lee has been repulsed & driven back by Grant, & that we are masters of the field, & pursuing them—then I think Lee will retreat, south—& Richmond will be abandoned by the rebs—but of course time only can develope what will happen—

Mother, I will write again Wednesday, or before if I hear any thing to write—love to Jeff & Mat & all—

Walt

124. *To Louisa Van Velsor Whitman*

Washington | May 10 '64 (½ past 2 | p m)

Dearest Mother,

There is nothing perhaps more than you see in the N Y papers—the fighting down in the field on the 6th I think ended in our favor, though

72. These figures were cited in the New York *Times* of this date, in the official release from the office of the Secretary of War.

73. Mrs. Whitman's letter is not extant, but Hannah wrote, on May 10, an hysterical letter about George's safety: "Mother, will you *be sure* and send me word the minute you hear that he is safe. I am like you, I cannot see a bit of peace till I hear. I feel this time as if he would be safe, and, Mother, if he only is, I will try to never complain again of anything as long as I live" (LC). Of the Whitmans, only WW apparently remained

with pretty severe losses to some of our divisions—the fighting is about 70 miles from here & 50 from Richmond—on the 7th & 8th followed up by the rebel army hauling off, they say retreating, & Meade pursuing—it is quite mixed yet, but I guess we have the best of it—if we really have, Richmond is a goner, for they cannot do any better than they have done—how much the 9th corps was in the fight, & where, I cannot tell yet, but from the wounded I have seen I dont think that corps was deeply in—I have seen 300 wounded, they came in last night, I asked for men of 9th corps, but could not find any at all—these 300 men were not badly wounded, mostly in arms, hands, trunk of body, &c.—they could all walk, though some had an awful time of it—they had to fight their way, with the worst in the middle, out of the region of Fredericksburgh, & so on where they could get across the Rappahannock & get where they found transportation to Washington—the gov't has decided (or rather Gen Meade has) to occupy Fredericksburgh,[74] for depot & hospitals—(I think that a first rate decision)—so the wounded men will receive quick attention & surgery, instead of being racked through the long journey up here—still may come in here—Mother, my impression is that we have no great reason for alarm or sadness about George so far—of course I *know* nothing—Well good by, dearest mother,

Walt—

Mother, I wrote you yesterday too—tell dear brother Jeff to write me—love to Mat—the poor diarrhea man[75] died, & it was a boon—Oscar Cunningham, 82d Ohio, has had a relapse, I fear it is going bad with him—lung diseases are quite plenty—night before last I staid in hospital all night tending a poor fellow—it has been awful hot here—milder to-day—

125. *To Louisa Van Velsor Whitman* 5.12. [*1864*]

May 12th | ½ past 5 P M

Dearest Mother

George is all right, unhurt, up to Tuesday morning, 10th inst—the 51st was in a bad battle last Friday, lost 20 killed, between 40 & 50 wounded—I have just seen some of the 51st wounded, just arrived, one of them Fred Saunders, Corp[oral], Co K, George's company—he said when

impassive. George had not helped matters when he noted in his letter of April 29: "I hear that Grant has issued an order, that no letters will be allowed to be sent from this army for the next Sixty days" (Trent).

74. So reported in the New York *Times* of this date. The *Times* printed a detailed account of the fighting around Fredericksburg on May 13.

75. See 120.

he left the 51st was in rear on guard duty—he left Tuesday mn'g last—the papers have it that Burnside's Corps was in a fight Tuesday, but I think it most probable the 51st was not in it—

Fred McReady is wounded, badly, but not seriously—Sims is safe—you see LeGendre is wounded—he was shot through the bridge of nose[76]—

Mother, you ought to get this Friday forenoon, 13th—I will write again soon—wrote once before to-day[77]—

Walt

126. *To Louisa Van Velsor Whitman*

Washington | May 13 1864 | 2 o'clock p m

Dearest Mother

I wrote you a hurried letter late yesterday afternoon, but left it myself at the P O in time for the mail—you ought to have got it this forenoon, or afternoon at furthest—I sent you two letters yesterday—I hope the carrier brings you your letters the same day—I wrote to the Brooklyn postmaster about it—

I have heard from George up to Tuesday morning last, 10th, till which time he was safe—the battle of Friday 6th was very severe—George's co. K lost one acting Lt Sturgis killed, 2 men killed, 4 wounded—as I wrote yesterday I have seen here Corp Fred Sanders of Co K who was wounded in side, nothing serious, in Friday's fight, & came up here—I also talked with Sgt Brown,[78] co F, 51st—rather badly wounded in right shoulder—Sanders said when he left Tuesday morning, he heard (or saw them there, I forget which) the 51st & its whole division were on guard duty toward the rear—the 9th Corps however has had hard fighting since, but whether the division, or brigade the 51st is in, was in the fights of Tuesday, 10th (a pretty severe one,) or Wednesday I cannot yet tell, & it is useless to make calculations—& the only way is to wait & hope for the best—as I wrote yesterday there were some 20 of 51st reg't killed & 50 wounded in Friday's battle, 6th inst—

I have seen Col LeGendre, he is here in Washington, not far from where I am—485 12th st is his address—poor man, I felt sorry indeed for him, he is badly wounded & disfigured, he is shot through the bridge

76. In his "Hospital Book 12" (Feinberg), WW recorded substantially the same information given here and in 126. Corporal Saunders (or Sanders) was confined in Finley Hospital. WW methodically cited the names and locations of the wounded soldiers from the Fifty-first Regiment who had been transferred to hospitals in or near Washington. For McReady, see 48; Sims, 51; and LeGendre, 42.

77. This letter is not known.

78. In the "Hospital Book 12" (Feinberg), Sgt. James C. Brown was listed as a patient in Finley Hospital.

of the nose, & left eye probably lost—I spent a little time with him this forenoon—he is suffering very much—spoke of George very kindly, said "your brother is well"—his orderly told me he saw him (George) Sunday night last well—Fred McReady is wounded in hip, I believe bone fractured, bad enough, but not deeply serious—I cannot hear of his arrival here, if he comes I shall find him immediately & take care of him myself—he is probably yet at Fredericksburgh, but will come up I think[79]—

Yesterday & to-day the badly wounded are coming in—the long lists of *previous arrivals*, (I suppose they are all reprinted at great length in N Y papers)[80] are of men ¾ths of them quite slightly wounded, & the rest hurt pretty bad—I was thinking, mother, if one could *see* the men who arrived in the first squads, of two or three hundred at a time, one wouldn't be alarmed at those terrible long lists—Still there is a sufficient sprinkling of deeply distressing cases—I find my hands full all the time, with new & old cases—poor suffering young men, I think of them, & do try, Mother, to do what I can for them, (& not think of the vexatious skedaddlers & merely scratched ones, of whom there are too many lately come here)—

Dearest Mother, I hope you & all are well—you must keep a good heart —still the fighting is very mixed, but it *seems steadily turning into real successes* for Grant—the news to-day here is very good—you will see it in N Y papers—I steadily believe Grant is going to succeed, & that we shall have Richmond—but O what a price to pay for it—We have had a good rain here & it is pleasanter & cooler—I shall write very soon again—

Walt.

127. *To Louisa Van Velsor Whitman*

Washington | May 18 1864

Dearest Mother,

I will only write you a hasty note this time, as I am pretty tired, & my head feels disagreeable, from being in too much—I was up yesterday to Carver hospital & again saw the man of the 51st, Thos McCowell,[81] who told me of George, up to latter part of Thursday, 12th inst. I questioned him, & his story was very clear, so I felt perfectly satisfied—he is

79. George essentially corroborated WW's report in his letter to his mother of May 16: "We had a pretty hard battle on the 6th. . . . Our Regt. suffered severely loseing 70 in killed and wounded. I lost nearly half of my Co. but we won the fight . . . We came here [Spotsylvania] on the 8th and there has been fighting going on every day since we came here. . . . We had a severe fight here on the 12th and the loss was heavy on both sides, our Regt lost 20 killed and wounded" (Trent).

80. The New York *Times* printed a lengthy casualty list on May 12.

81. This may be the "Tom" referred to in 25.

wounded in hand, will be transferred soon to New York & may call on you—he is a young Irishman, & seems to be a very good fellow indeed—

I have written to George, day before yesterday. Did you send my last letter to Han?—if not send it yet—Mother, I see such awful things—I expect one of these days, if I live, I shall have awful thoughts & dreams—but it is such a great thing to be able to do some real good, assuage these horrible pains & wounds, & save life even—that's the only thing that keeps a fellow up—

Well, dear mother, I make such reckoning of yet coming on & seeing you—how I want to see Jeff too—O it is too bad I have not written to him so long—& Mat too & little California & all—I am going out now a little while—I remain first rate & well as ever—

Walt

128. *To John Townsend Trowbridge*

TRANSCRIPT.

Washington | May 20 1864

Dear friend[82]

Your welcome gift of money for wounded here, ($5) came safe to-day & is most acceptable—Most of wounded brought up here now are without a cent—Many of the cases appeal very strongly—(I sometimes think only one going among the men as I do, with personal feeling & my own way of investigation understands how deep & what sort the appeal is)—the hospitals are very full—Armory Square has more inmates than many a well known New England village—I go as usual to one or another hospital & to Alexandria, day & night—

Dear friend, I shall always be glad to hear from you—Should you find any you know who are able & who feel to aid the wounded, through me, it would come *very acceptable now*—sure to reach addressed

Walt Whitman

Care Major Hapgood | Paymaster U S Army | Washington D C

J T Trowbridge | Somerville | Massachusetts

82. See 102.

83. From Spotsylvania, Va., on May 20, George described to his mother a skirmish of his regiment which cost "22 killed and wounded." "About One O'clock yesterday morning," he continued, "we were relieved in the rifle pitts and withdrawn to the rear, where we are now, resting ourselves and having good times. Mother, I suppose you know how we are getting along, better than we do ourselves, for I expect the newspaper correspondents keep you pretty well posted as to our movements, and here there are so many rumors flying around, that a fellow only knows, what he sees himself" (Trent).

129. *To Thomas Jefferson Whitman*

Washington | Monday forenoon May 23 '64

Dear brother Jeff

I received your letter yesterday—I too had got a few lines from George dated on the field, 16th—he said he had also just written to mother —I cannot make out there has been any fighting since in which the 9th Corps has been engaged—I do hope Mother will not get despondent & so unhappy—I suppose it is idle to say I think George's chances are very good for coming out of this campaign safe, yet at present it seems to me so—but it is indeed idle to say so, for no one can tell what a day may bring forth[83]—

Sometimes I think that should it come, when it *must* be, to fall in battle, one's anguish over a son or brother killed, would be tempered with much to take the edge off—I can honestly say it has no terrors for me, if I had to be hit in battle, as far as I myself am concerned—it would be a noble & manly death, & in the best cause—then one finds, as I have the past year, that our feelings & imaginations make a thousand times too much of the whole matter—Of the many I have seen die, or known of, the past year, I have not seen or heard of *one* who met death with any terror—Yesterday afternoon I spent a good part of the afternoon with a young man of 17, named Charles Cutter,[84] of Lawrence City, Mass, 1st Mass heavy artillery, battery M—he was brought in to one of the hospitals mortally wounded in abdomen—Well I thought to myself as I sat looking at him, it ought to be a relief to his folks after all, if they could see how little he suffered—he lay very placid, in a half lethargy, with his eyes closed, it was very warm, & I sat a long while fanning him & wiping the sweat, at length he opened his eyes quite wide & clear, & looked inquiringly around. I said, What is it, my dear, do you want any thing?—he said quietly with a good natured smile, O nothing, I was only looking around to see who was with me—his mind was somewhat wandering, yet he lay so peaceful, in his dying condition—he seemed to be a real New England country boy, so good natured, with a pleasant homely way, & quite a fine looking boy—without any doubt he died in course of night—

84. Cutter's unexpectedly delayed death is reported in 130–132. When WW printed his abridged version of this letter in *November Boughs* (CW, VI, 230–232), he evidently forgot that Cutter had lingered for two weeks: "His mind was somewhat wandering, yet he lay in an evident peacefulness that sanity and health might have envied. I had to leave for other engagements. He died, I heard afterward, without any special agitation, in the course of the night." In addition, he altered phraseology: "What is it, my dear" became "What is it, my boy?"; "it was very warm" was rendered "it was extremely hot."

There dont seem to be any war news of importance very late—We have been fearfully disappointed with Sigel[85] not making his junction from the lower part of the valley, & perhaps harrassing Lee's left, or left rear, which (the junction or equivalent to it) was an indispensable part of Grant's plan, we think—this is one great reason why things have lagged so with the Army—some here are furious with Sigel, you will see he has been superseded—his losses in his repulse are not so important, though annoying enough, but it was of the greatest consequence that he should have hastened through the gaps ten or twelve days ago at all hazards & come in from the west, keeping near enough to our right to have assistance if he needed it—Jeff, I suppose you know that there has been quite a large army lying idle, mostly of artillery reg'ts manning the numerous forts around here, they have been the fattest & heartiest reg'ts any where to be seen, & full in numbers, some of them numbering 2000 men—well, they have all, every one, been shoved down to the front—lately we have had the militia reg'ts pouring in here mostly from Ohio, they look first rate, I saw two or three come in yesterday, splendid American young men, from farms mostly—we are to have them for a hundred days & probably they will not refuse to stay another hundred—Jeff, tell mother I shall write Wednesday certain (or if I hear any thing I will write to-morrow)—I still think we shall get Richmond—

Walt—

Jeff, of course you must take this up to mother soon as you go home—Jeff, I have changed my quarters—I moved Saturday last—I am now at 502 Pennsylvania av, near 3d st.—I still go a little almost daily to Major Hapgood's, cor 15th & F st., 5th floor, am apt to be there about 12 or 1. —I am well, go the same among wounded day & night—see Fred McReady, & others of 51st—George's letter to me of 16th I sent to Han—should like to see Mr Worthen[86] if he comes here—give my best remembrance to Mr Lane[87]—

I have writ to George several times in hopes one at least may reach him —Matty, my dear sister, how are [you] getting along—O how I should like to see you this very day—

I may very likely go down for a few days to Bell Plain & Fredericksburgh, but one is wanted here permanently more than any other place—

85. Franz Sigel (1824–1902), a German-born Union general, was in command of the department of West Virginia when he was seriously defeated at New Market in the Shenandoah Valley on May 15. He was relieved of his command.

86. William E. Worthen was an engineer, evidently employed in the Croton Aque-

130. *To Louisa Van Velsor Whitman*

Washington | May 25 1864

Dearest Mother

I have not heard any thing of George or the reg't or Corps more than I have already written—I got Jeff's letter on Sunday, & wrote to him next day, which you have seen, mother, of course—I have written to Han & sent her George's letter to me dated 16th—I have heard that the 9th Corps has been moved to the extreme left of the Army—I should think by acc'ts this morning that the Army must be nearly half way from Fredericksburgh to Richmond[88]—the advance can't be more than 30 to 35 miles from there—

I see Fred McReady about every other day, I have to go down to Alexandria, about 6 miles from here—he is doing quite well, but very tired of the confinement—I still go around daily & nightly among wounded —Mother, it is just the same old story, poor suffering young men, great swarms of them come up here, now, every day, all battered & bloody—there have 4000 arrived here this morning, & 1500 yesterday—they appear to be bringing them all up here from Fredericksburgh—the journey from the field till they get aboard the boats at Bell Plain is horrible—I believe I wrote several times about Oscar Cunningham, 82d Ohio, amputation of right leg, wounded over a year ago, a friend of mine here, he is rapidly sinking, said to me yesterday, O if he could only die—the young lad Cutter, of 1st Massachusetts heavy artillery, I was with Sunday afternoon, (I wrote about in Jeff's letter,) still holds out, poor boy, there is no chance for him at all—

But, Mother, I shall make you gloomy enough if I go on with these kind of particulars—Only I know you like to hear about the poor young men, after I have once begun to mention them—Mother, I have changed my quarters—am at 502 Pennsylvania av. near 3d street, only a little way from the Capitol—where I was, the house was sold & the old lady I hired the room from had to move out & give the owner possession—I like my new quarters pretty well—I have a room to myself, 3d story hall bedroom, I have my meals in the house.

Mother, it must be sad enough about Nance, & the young ones—is the little baby still hearty, I believe you wrote a few weeks after it was born

duct Department, New York. See 130.

87. See 31.

88. A dispatch in the New York *Times*, signed "Swinton," simply noted that Grant's army was "on the march toward Richmond."

that it was quite a fine child[89]—I see you had a draft in the 3d Congressional district, I was glad enough to see Jeff's name was not drawn—We have had it awful hot here, but there was a sharp storm of thunder & lightning last night, & to-day it is fine—Mother, do any of the soldiers I see here, from Brooklyn or New York, ever call upon you?—they sometimes say they will, here—tell Jeff I got a letter yesterday from W E Worthen, in which he sent me some money for the men, I have acknowledged it to Mr W by letter[90]—Well, dear mother, I must close, O how I want to see you all—I will surely have to come home as soon as this Richmond campaign is decided—then I want to print my next book—love to Mat—write to a fellow often as you can—

Walt

131. *To Louisa Van Velsor Whitman*

Washington | May 30 1864

Dearest Mother

I have no news at all to write this time—I have not heard any thing of the 51st since I last wrote you, & about the general war news only what you see in the papers—Grant is gradually getting nearer & nearer to Richmond—Many [here] anticipate that should Grant go into Richmond, Lee will make a side movement & march up west, into the north, either to attempt to strike Washington, or to go again into Pennsylvania—I only say if that should happen, I for one shall not be dissatisfied so very much—

Well, mother, how are you getting along home—how do you feel in health these days, dear mother—I hope you are well & in good heart yet—I remain pretty well, my head begins to trouble me a little with a sort of fulness, as it often does in the hot weather—Singular to relate the 1st Mass artillery boy, Charles Cutter, is still living, & may get well—I saw him this morning—I am still around among wounded same, but will not make you feel blue by filling my letter with sad particulars—

I am writing this in Willard's hotel, hurrying to catch this afternoon's mail—Mother, do you get your letters now next morning, as you ought? I got a letter from the Post Master of Brooklyn about it—he said if the letters were neglected again to send him word—I have not heard from home now in some days—I am going to put up a lot of my old things in a box & send

89. See 115.

90. Worthen sent $20 to WW on May 23: "I hope I shall be able to send more from time to time" (Feinberg). WW's reply is not known. See also note 86 above.

91. Grant was moving toward Richmond. The headline in the New York *Times* of this date read: "Encouraging Success at Every Point."

them home by express, I will write when I send them—Have you heard any thing from Mary or Han lately—I should like to hear—

Tell Jeff he must write, & you must too, Mother—I have been in one of the worst hospitals all the forenoon, it contains about 1600—I have given the men pipes & tobacco, (I am the only one that gives them tobacco)—O how much good it does some of them—the chaplains & most of the doctors are down upon it—but I give them & let them smoke—to others I have given oranges, fed them, &c—well, dear mother, good bye—love to Matty & sis—

Walt

Fred McReady is coming home very soon on furlough—have any of the soldiers called on you?

132. *To Louisa Van Velsor Whitman*

Washington | June 3 1864

Dearest mother

Your letter came yesterday—I have not heard the least thing from the 51st since—no doubt they are down there with the Army near Richmond—I have not written to George lately—I think the news from the Army is very good—Mother, you know of course that it is now very near Richmond indeed, from five to ten miles[91]—

Mother, if this campaign was not in progress I should not stop here, as it is now beginning to tell a little upon me,[92] so many bad wounds, many putrified, & all kinds of dreadful ones, I have been rather too much with —but as it is I shall certainly remain here while the thing remains undecided—it is impossible for me to abstain from going to see & minister to certain cases, & that draws me into others, & so on—I have just left Oscar Cunningham,[93] the Ohio boy—he is in a dying condition—there is no hope for him—it would draw tears from the hardest heart to look at him—he is all wasted away to a skeleton, & looks like some one fifty years old—you remember I told you a year ago, when he was first brought in, I thought him the noblest specimen of a young western man I had seen, a real giant in size, & always with a smile on his face—O what a change, he has long been very irritable, to every one but me, & his frame is all wasted away—the

92. WW began to complain of his health on May 18, when he noted that his "head feels disagreeable"; on May 30, he wrote that "my head begins to trouble me a little with a sort of fulness, as it often does in the hot weather." The attacks increased in severity, as succeeding letters indicated.

93. See 121.

young Massachusetts 1st artillery boy, Cutter, I wrote about is dead—he is the one that was brought in a week ago last Sunday, badly wounded in breast—the deaths in the principal hospital I visit, Armory Square, average one an hour—I saw Capt Baldwin[94] of the 14th this morning, he has lost his left arm—is going home soon—

Mr Kalbfleisch[95] & Anson Herrick,[96] (M C from New York) came in one of the wards where I was sitting writing a letter this morning, in the midst of the wounded—Kalbfleisch was so much affected by the sight that he burst into tears—O I must tell you I gave the boys in Carver hospital a great treat of ice cream a couple of days ago, went round myself through about 15 large wards, (I bought some ten gallons, very nice)—you would have cried & been amused too, many of the men had to be fed, several of them I saw cannot probably live, yet they quite enjoyed it, I gave everybody some—quite a number western country boys had never tasted ice cream before—they relish such things, oranges, lemons, &c—Mother, I feel a little blue this morning, as two young men I knew very well have just died, one died last night, & the other about half an hour before I went to the hospital, I did not anticipate the death of either of them, each was a very, very sad case, so young—well, mother, I see I have written you another gloomy sort of letter—I do not feel as first rate as usual—

Walt—

You don't know how I want to come home & see you all, you, dear Mother, & Jeff & Mat & all—I believe I am homesick, something new for me—then I have seen all the horrors of soldier's life & not been kept up by its excitement—it is awful to see so much, & not be able to relieve it—

133. *To Louisa Van Velsor Whitman*

Washington | June 7 1864

Dearest mother,

I cannot write you any thing about the 51st, as I have not heard a word—I felt much disturbed yesterday afternoon, as Major Hapgood came up from the Paymaster General's office, & said that news had arrived that Burnside was killed, & that the 9th Corps had had a terrible slaughter—he said it was believed at the Paymaster general's office—Well I went out to see what reliance there was on it—the rumor soon spread over town, & was believed by many—but as near as I can make it out, it proves to be

94. William M. Baldwin entered the army at age twenty-nine, became a captain on October 1, 1862, was wounded at Laurel Hill, Va., on May 10, 1864, and was mustered out on June 6 of the same year. See *The History of the Fighting Fourteenth* (1926?), 260.

one of those unaccountable stories that get started these times—Saturday night we heard that Grant was routed completely &c &c—so that's the way the stories fly—I suppose you have the same big lies there in Brooklyn—Well the truth is sad enough, without adding any thing to it—but Grant is not destroyed yet, but I think is going into Richmond yet, but the cost is terrible—

Mother, I have not felt well at all the last week—I had spells of deathly faintness, and bad trouble in my head too, & sore throat, (quite a little budget, ain't they?)—My head was the worst, though I don't know, the faint weak spells were not very pleasant—but I feel so much better this forenoon I believe it has passed over—There is a very horrible collection in Armory Building, (in Armory Square hosp.) about 200 of the worst cases you ever see, & I had been probably too much with them—it is enough to melt the heart of a stone—over one third of them are amputation cases—

Well, mother, poor Oscar Cunningham is gone at last—he is the 82d Ohio boy, (wounded May 3d '63)—I have written so much of him I suppose you feel as if you almost knew him—I was with him Saturday forenoon & also evening—he was more composed than usual, could not articulate very well—he died about 2 o'clock Sunday morning—very easy they told me, I was not there—It was a blessed relief, his life has been misery for months—the cause of death at last was the system absorbing the pus, the bad matter, instead of discharging it from wound—I believe I told you in last letter I was quite blue from the deaths of several of the poor young men I knew well, especially two I had strong hopes of their getting up—things are going pretty badly with the wounded—They are crowded here in Washington in immense numbers, & all those that come up from the Wilderness, & that region, arrived here so neglected, & in such plight, it was awful—(those that were at Fredericksburgh & also from Belle Plaine)—The papers are full of puffs, &c. but the truth is, the largest proportion of worst cases got little or no attention—we receive them here with their wounds full of worms—some all swelled & inflamed, many of the amputations have to be done over again—one new feature is that many of the poor afflicted young men are crazy, every ward has some in it that are wandering—they have suffered too much, & it is perhaps a privilege that they are out of their senses—Mother, it is most too much for a fellow, & I sometimes wish I was out of it—but I suppose it is because I have not felt first rate myself—

I am going to write to George to-day, as I see there is a daily mail to

95. See 103.

96. Herrick (1812–1868) established the New York *Atlas* in 1836, and served one term in the House of Representatives (1863–1865). He was defeated for re-election in 1864.

White House—O I must tell you that we get the wounded from our present field near Richmond much better than we did from the Wilderness & Fredericksburgh—We get them now from White House, they are put on boats there, & come all the way here, about 160 or 70 miles—White House is only twelve or fifteen miles from the field, & is our present depot & base of supplies—It is very pleasant here to-day, a little cooler than it has been—a good rain shower last evening—the western reg'ts continue to pour in here, the 100 days men, may go down to front, to guard posts, trains, &c—

Well, Mother, how do things go on with you all—it seems to me if I could only be home two or three days, & have some good teas with you & Mat, & set in the old basement a while, & have a good time & talk with Jeff, & see the little girls, &c—I should be willing to keep on afterward among these sad scenes for the rest of the summer—but I shall remain here until this Richmond campaign is settled, any how, unless I get sick, & I don't anticipate that—Mother dear, I hope you are well & in fair spirits—you must try to—have you heard from sister Han?

Walt

You know I am living at 502 Pennsylvania av. (near 3d st)—it is not a very good place, I don't like it so well as I did cooking my own grub—& the air is not good—Jeff, you must write—

134. *To Louisa Van Velsor Whitman*

Washington | June 10 1864

Dearest mother

I got your letter dated last Wednesday—I do not always depend on Swinton's[97] accounts—I think he is apt to make things full as bad as they are, if not worse—

Mother, I was so glad to get a letter from Jeff this morning enclosing one from George dated June 1st—it was so good to see his handwriting once more—I have not heard any thing of the reg't—there are all sorts of rumors here, among others that Burnside does not give satisfaction to Grant & Meade, & that it is expected some one else will be placed in command of 9th Corps—Another rumor, more likely, is that our base of the army is to be changed to Harrison's Landing on James river instead of White House on Pamunky—

Mother, I have not felt well again the last two days as I was Tuesday,

97. William Swinton was a correspondent of the New York *Times;* see 37. At this time he was at Grant's headquarters; signed dispatches appeared in the *Times* on May 24 (see note 88 above) and 30. On July 5, Mrs. O'Connor reported that Swinton

but I feel a good deal better this morning, I go around, but most of the time feel very little like it—the doctor tells me I have continued too long in the hospitals, especially in a bad place, armory building, where the worst wounds were, & have absorbed too much of the virus in my system—but I know it is nothing but what a little relief & sustenance of right sort, will set right—

I am writing this in Major Hapgood's office—he is very busy paying off some men whose time is out, they are going home to New York—I wrote to George yesterday—we are having very pleasant weather here just now—Mother, you didn't mention whether Mary had come, so I suppose she has not, I should like to see her & Ansel too[98]—

The wounded still come here in large numbers—day & night trains of ambulances—tell Jeff the $10 from Mr Lane for the soldiers came safe—I shall write to Jeff right away—I send my love to Mat & all—Mother, you must try to keep good heart—

Walt.

135. *To Louisa Van Velsor Whitman*

Washington | June 14 1864

Dearest mother

I am not feeling very well these days—the doctors have told me not to come inside the hospitals for the present—I send there by a friend every day, I send things & aid to some cases I know, & hear from there also, but I do not go myself at present—it is probable that the hospital poison has affected my system, & I find it worse than I calculated—I have spells of faintness & very bad feeling in my head, fullness & pain—& besides sore throat—my boarding place, 502 Pennsylvania av, is a miserable place, very bad air—But I shall feel better soon, I know—the doctors say it will pass over—they have long told me I was going in too strong—some days I think it has all gone & I feel well again, but in a few hours I have a spell again—

Mother, I have not heard any thing of the 51st—I sent George's letter to Han—I have written to George since—I shall write again to him in a day or two—if Mary comes home tell her I sent her my love—if I dont feel better before the end of this week or beginning of next, I may come home for a week or fortnight for a change—the rumor is very strong here that Grant is over the James river on south side—but it is not in the papers—we are having quite cool weather here—Mother, I want to see you &

was in Washington: "He looked sick, & says he is. He has had chills & fever, caught on the James River" (Feinberg). Swinton's name was deleted in earlier printings.

98. Ansel Van Nostrand, Mary's husband.

Jeff so much—I have been working a little at copying, but have stopt it lately—

Walt

136. *To Louisa Van Velsor Whitman*

Washington | June 17 1864

Dearest Mother

I got your letter this morning—this place & the hospitals seem to have got the better of me—I do not feel so badly this forenoon—but I have bad nights & bad days too, some of the spells are pretty bad—still I am up some & around every day—the doctors have told me for a fortnight I must leave, that I need an entire change of air, &c—

I think I shall come home for a short time, & pretty soon—(I will try it two or three days yet, though, & if I find my illness goes over, I will stay here yet awhile—all I think about is to be here if any thing should happen to George)—

We dont hear any thing more of the Army than you do there in the papers—

Walt

Mother, if I should come I will write a day or so before—

137. *To William D. O'Connor*

ENDORSED: "Answ'd." ADDRESS: Wm D O'Connor | Washington | D C. POSTMARK: Brooklyn N Y | Jun | 2(?).

Brooklyn | June 25 1864

Dear friend

I write just a line to let you know I got home all safe—I do not feel very well yet, but expect to, or begin to, pretty soon—I send my love to you & Nelly & to Charles Eldridge[99]—

Walt Whitman

99. WW left Washington on June 22. On July 5, Ellen O'Connor wrote: "It will be two weeks to-morrow since you left us, and I have missed you terribly every minute of the time. I think I never in my life felt so wholly blue and unhappy about any one's going away as I did, and have since, about your going. I began to be really superstitious I felt so badly. I did not think that you were going to die, but I could not possibly overcome the feeling that our dear and pleasant circle was broken, and it seemed to me that we four [the O'Connors, Eldridge, and WW] should not be together any more as we have been. . . . Ah! Walt, I don't believe other people need you as much as we do. I am *sure* they don't need you as much as *I* do" (Feinberg).

1. On June 18, George wrote to his mother of additional engagements of his regi-

138. *To Charles W. Eldridge*

ADDRESS: Charles W Eldridge | care Major Hapgood | Paymaster U S Army | Washington | D C. POSTMARK: Brooklyn | Jun | (?).

Brooklyn | Tuesday afternoon June 28 | '64

Dear comrade

I have been improving for the last two days, & think I shall be up & around soon, as well as ever—I have had the services of a good physician, who has allowed me to get well quite naturally—he decided that the only thing needing serious watching was the throat, & had prepared if the disease there went beyond a certain point to call in a skilful New York doctor, for consultation, but fortunately we were saved the trouble—I felt a good deal like myself the most of yesterday, & the same to-day—so I don't think I am hurrahing before I am out of the woods.

We have a letter from my brother George, down to 18th inst. he was all safe.[1] My mother & folks are all well—

I rece'd the letter enveloped to me 25th—I sent a line to Wm O'Connor, 25th, which I suppose he rec'd—has Nelly gone yet? I shall write to her next time—remember me to Ashton[2] with friendship—also to Arnold Johnson[3] with sincere thanks & tell him I am getting well—& give my best respects & thanks to Major Hapgood.

Walt Whitman

139. *To William D. O'Connor*

ENDORSED: "Answ'd." ADDRESS: Wm D O'Connor | Washington | D C. POSTMARK: [*indecipherable*].

Brooklyn | Tuesday even'g July 5 1864

My dear friend

I have had the misfortune to fall back a little since I wrote to you—I have had three or four pretty bad days & nights—but I am feeling decidedly brighter this afternoon, & have no doubt I shall be myself again before long. The trouble has been as before, bad spells of weakness with

ment, and was confident that "it will not be long before the long covetted City of Petersburg will be in our possession. I notice by the papers that our Corps is very little spoken of, but for all that they have done some splendid fighting, although we seem to be rather outsiders here in the Army of the Potomac" (Trent).

2. J. Hubley Ashton, the assistant Attorney General, actively interested himself in WW's affairs, and obtained a position for the poet in his office after the Harlan fracas; see 164.

3. A friend of the O'Connors and private secretary to Senator Sumner; see Barrus, 10. He was listed in the 1866 Directory as a clerk in the Treasury Department.

heavy aching head—I think the throat is no worse, but it is not well yet—

William, I rec'd your letter to-day, also one from Charles Eldridge, with one in envelope—as to the future, & as to our meeting again, I have no doubt we shall meet again & have good times[4]—if Nelly has not gone when this reaches you, I wish her to consider it just the same as if written to her—I do not write much, nor do any thing hardly, but keep as quiet as possible—my physician thinks that time, with the change of locality, & my own latent recuperative power, will make me well, but says my system is probably saturated with the virus of the hospitals &c which eludes ordinary treatment—&c &c &c—

I have nothing new or interesting to write you. I intend to move heaven & earth to publish my "Drum-Taps" as soon as I am able to go around.

So Eldridge is down at Petersburgh[5]—if I were there at Washington & well I should want no better fun than accompanying them—When you see Count[6] tell him I sent him my love—also Ashton—I will write should there be any change in my condition—

Good bye for present, my dear friend, & God bless you[7]—

Walt

140. *To Charles W. Eldridge*

Brooklyn | July 9 1864

My dear friend

I rec'd the letters this afternoon, two in the envelope with a note from you. I wrote to William some five days ago—has he not rec'd it? I had grown worse, quite a good deal, & I was about making up my mind that I would have to stand a good seige—but yesterday the current changed, & I felt better all day, & in the afternoon went out riding with my brother, the

4. In his letter of July 2, O'Connor was deeply moved by WW's departure from Washington: "Many thoughts of you have come to me since you went away, and sometimes it has been lonely and a little like death. Particularly at evening when you used to come in . . . I wonder what the future for us is to be. Shall we triumph over obscurities and obstacles and emerge to start the Pathfinder, or whatever the name of it is to be? . . . Or shall we never meet, never work together, never start any Pathfinder, never do anything but fade out into death, frustrated, lost in oblivion? . . . I hardly believe you will come back here. But I hope you will" (Feinberg; Traubel, IV, 366–368).

5. According to Mrs. O'Connor's letter of July 5 (Feinberg), Eldridge had gone to pay the staff officers of the Fifth Corps.

6. Count Adam Gurowski; see 177.

7. On July 5, Mrs. O'Connor asked WW what she should do with "Mrs. Beach's notes." Mrs. Juliette H. Beach was one of those enigmatic women associated with WW about whom imaginative biographers have spun ingenious theories. Mrs. Beach was to have reviewed the 1860 edition of *Leaves of Grass* for the *Saturday Press*, but when her husband's unfavorable review was published instead, the journal had to take public note of matrimonial discord in order to correct the error (Allen, 260–262). Mrs. O'Connor contributed her bit to the theory that Mrs. Beach and WW had a love affair when she asserted that "Out of the Rolling Ocean, the Crowd," published in *Drum-Taps*, was

first time I have been out of the house since I got home—& to-day I remain feeling better.

The doctor to-day tells me my throat is markedly better—In my letter to William I told him I had rec'd his—I have also rec'd one from Nelly—it was very welcome, & I shall try to answer it soon—When you write tell me the impressions you got in the army, & the probabilities as far as you can make them out—As to me, I still believe in Grant, & that we shall get Richmond—we have heard from my brother to July 2[8]—tell me about Ashton[9]—in a day or two as I get strength I shall probably go down the island—

Walt

141. *To Lewis K. Brown*

Brooklyn | July 11 1864

Dear comrade

I have rec'd your letter of the 6th[10] as it has been sent on to me by Major Hapgood. My dear comrade, I have been very sick, and have been brought on home nearly three weeks ago, after being sick some ten days in Washington—The doctors say my sickness is from having too deeply imbibed poison into my system from the hospitals—I had spells of deathly faintness, & the disease also attacked my head & throat pretty seriously—

The doctors forbid me going any more into the hospitals—I did not think much of it, till I got pretty weak, & then they directed me to leave & go north for change of air as soon as I had strength—But I am making too long a story of it—I thought only to write you a line—My dear comrade, I am now over the worst of it & have been getting better the last three days—my brother took me out in a carriage for a short ride yesterday which is the

composed for "a certain lady" who had angered her husband because of her correspondence with the poet (*UPP*, I, lviii, *n.*). "Mrs. Beach's notes" may be the letters to WW, which later Burroughs vainly asked Mrs. Beach to print; see Clara Barrus, *The Life and Letters of John Burroughs* (1925), I, 120 *n.* If these were love letters, WW hardly treated Mrs. Beach's heart-stirrings discreetly. See also Allen, 340–342.

8. On July 2, George wrote from "near Petersburg instead of from Richmond." WW here echoed George's optimism: "We all believe in Grant, and as far as I can hear the opinion is universal in the army, that before the campaign is over Petersburg and Richmond will be in our posession" (Trent).

9. On July 5, Mrs. O'Connor wrote: "Poor Ashton is sick in bed with rheumatism, a fearful attack of it" (Feinberg).

10. Brown (see 60) had written from the Judiciary Square Hospital in an attempt to locate WW (Berg). Brown, usually inarticulate, was deeply moved in his reply to WW on July 18: "I was also very sory to hear of your illness & to think that it was brought on by your unselfish kindness to the Soldiers. There is a many a soldier now that never thinks of you but with emotions of the greatest gratitude & I know that the soldiers that you have bin so kind to have a great big warm place in their heart for you. I never think of you but it makes my heart glad to think that I have bin permited to know one so good" (Berg).

first I have been out of the house since I have been home—the doctor tells me to-day I shall soon be around which will be very acceptable—This is the first sickness I have ever had & I find upon trial such things as faintness, headache & trembling & tossing all night, & all day too, are not proper companions for a good union man like myself—

Lewy, I dont know any news to send you—the acc'ts here to-night are that the railroad & telegraph between Baltimore & Washington are cut, & also between Philadelphia by the rebel invasion[11]—

My dear boy, you say you would like to see me—well I would give any thing to see your face again too—I think of you often—tell Jo Harris & Bartlett[12] I have not forgotten them—

And now good bye, Lewy, & accept my heartfelt & true love, my dearest comrade—& I will try to write again before a great while & tell you how I am getting along, & which way I expect to move, &c. And I hope you will do the same to me—

So good bye again, Lew, & God bless you, dear son, now & through life—

Walt Whitman

Portland av near Myrtle | Brooklyn | New York

142. *To William D. O'Connor*

ENDORSED: "Answ'd." ADDRESS: William D O'Connor | Treasury Dep't *Light house bureau* | Washington | D C. POSTMARK: Brooklyn N.Y. | Jul | 25 | 1864.

Brooklyn | Sunday afternoon July 24 1864

My dear friend

Since I last wrote to you my illness has been gradually alleviated, until now I go about pretty much the same as usual—I keep pretty old-fashioned hours, rise early, dine at 1, & go to bed before 10—My head feels clear & comfortable, & my strength has returned almost, but not quite up

11. In his letter of July 18, Brown gave a colorful firsthand account of the attempted invasion of Washington. He had hobbled to the front on his crutches and had remained there until witnesses near him were killed. John Burroughs was also a participant in this skirmish; see his letter to WW on August 2 (Feinberg; Barrus, 19).

12. Brown, on July 18, reported that he had not seen Adrian Bartlett and Joseph Harris since they returned from a spree to Baltimore on July 4. According to his letter of September 5 (Berg), the three young men were living in a Washington boardinghouse; Harris was not in good health, and Bartlett worked in the Treasury Department. Harris enclosed a letter with Brown's on September 5 (Berg). Brown and Bartlett were still clerks in the Treasury on May 30, 1867; see 238.

13. On July 18 (Feinberg), Mrs. O'Connor had informed WW that she would be in

to what it was. I rec'd Nelly's letter, I could not get over to New York that afternoon—Nelly, my dear friend, you must excuse me—I wished much to see you, too[13]—I hope you are having a good time & feeling well physically & in good spirits—& the little one, little Jenny, this line is for you, my dear. I hope you too are well—William, I rec'd the volume of Navy Reports, transactions of iron clads, fights, &c. for '62 & '3[14]—it will probably give me material for some pieces, thumb-nail sketches, for my "*Drum Taps*" —I take it you had that in view in sending it to me—

I am trying to make arrangements to publish my volume—I shall probably try to bring [it] out myself, stereotype it, & print an edition of 500—I could sell that number by my own exertions in Brooklyn & New York in three weeks.

I rec'd Charles Eldridge's last letter—so he is to go down to front again —how I wish I was in Washington to go with him & Major—I should try it as I am, & be glad of the chance—O I almost forgot the big raid—it is already a thing of the past, I find by my own thoughts & memory, but I suppose it would not do to write a letter to Washington so soon & not mention it—

We have heard from my brother George up to the 18th inst.[15]—he was living & well up to that time—At home here all well as usual—Mother's age I think begins to just show—in a few weeks, she will commence her 70th year—still she does most of her light housework—My sister & her children are well—(Nelly, I write these particulars for you)—

Well, William, about the war I have to inform you that I remain hopeful & confident yet[16]—I still think Grant will go into Richmond—My brother describes the spirit of the troops as confident & sanguine under all their trials—I wish you to enclose this in your next letter to Nelly—I wish you to give my remembrance & love to the Howells,[17] to Miss Howard[18] & to Arnold Johnson[19]—Write soon & tell me all the news—tell me how is Ashton—Good bye & God bless you, my dear friend—

Walt

New York on July 20, and wanted to see him.

14. *Report of the Secretary of the Navy in Relation to Armored Vessels* (1864). Of this volume O'Connor wrote on August 13: "I thought it might yield hints for poems. At all events, it gives one a good idea of what the Monitors are and can do. They are . . . an upheld finger of warning to all despotocracy" (Feinberg; Traubel, III, 338).

15. George's letter is not known; probably it was sent to Hannah.

16. On August 13, O'Connor, who never emulated WW's calm faith in the outcome of the war, wrote: "Alas, Walt! There is no hope of Richmond. The campaign has proved a failure. . . . It is sad to think of the eighty thousand men, veterans, lost so fruitlessly" (Feinberg; Traubel, III, 339).

17. See 95. 18. See 149. 19. See 138.

143. *To Ellen M. O'Connor*

ENDORSED: "Ans'd." ADDRESS: Ellen M O'Connor | Little Compton | Rhode Island. POSTMARK: Brooklyn N.Y. | Sep | 11 | 18(?).

Brooklyn | September 11 1864

My dear friend[20]

Well I am still home & no event of importance to write you about. My illness has passed over, & I go around the same as formerly, only a lingering suspicion of weakness now & then—I go out fishing & have been out riding frequently—

There is a hospital[21] here, containing a couple of hundred soldiers, it is only a quarter of a mile from our house, & I go there a good deal—am going this afternoon to spend the afternoon & evening—Strange as it may seem days & days elapse without their having any visitors—So you see I am still in business—Some of the cases are very interesting—

My mother is very well, & the rest the same—We have heard from my brother up to the beginning of this month, he is well[22]—We felt pretty gloomy some little time since, as two young men of the 51st N Y, friends of my brother George & of our family (officers of 51st), were killed in battle within ten days of each other & their bodies brought on for burial here[23]—Mother was at the funeral of each of them, & I also—the regiment is on the Weldon road & in a position of danger—

I have seen Mrs Price, she speaks of you & hopes to know you, she is only tolerably well—I have not seen Charles Howells[24] for some time—I shall write to William to-day—I rec'd a letter from Charles Eldridge yesterday, he was to pass through New York yesterday on his way to Boston for two or three weeks—"Drum Taps" is not yet begun to be printed—Nelly, I was much obliged for the photograph—it reminds me of you & is good—how is dear little Jennie?—& you, my dear dear friend, how are you

20. Mrs. O'Connor was hurt when WW did not reply to her letters of July 5, 18, 24, and August 18. In her last letter, she said: "You will not think me foolish if I tell you that it hurt me a little, will you? You know what a foolish, absurd person I am, where I love any one as I do you, and knowing this, and now I having confessed, you will pardon" (Feinberg).

21. Brooklyn City Hospital, which WW visited in August and September; see his notebook (*LC* #102).

22. Throughout August George's regiment was engaged in especially heavy fighting near Petersburg, in which he repeatedly distinguished himself. Major John G. Wright (see 163) reported on August 8 that, when he had to relinquish command of the regiment, George "discharged the duties of the responsible position to my entire satisfaction, and it affords me great pleasure to speak of the gallant manner in which he has Sustained himself during the entire campaign" (Trent).

in health & spirits, & have you had a good time—O how I should like to see you all again—

Walt

I think it quite probable I shall be in Washington again this winter—(but not certain)—Give Dr & Mrs Channing[25] my friendly remembrance—Who have you met & what seen or heard that I would like to hear of, for you must tell me—

144. *To William D. O'Connor*

ENDORSED: "Answ'd." ADDRESS: William D O'Connor | Light house Board Treasury | Department | Washington | D C. POSTMARK: Brooklyn N.Y. | Sep | 11 | 1864.

Brooklyn | September 11 1864

Dear friend

I have nothing of consequence to write, but I thought I would send you a few lines anyhow. I have just written Nelly a letter, & send to Little Compton—We are full of politics here, the dispute runs high & hot everywhere—I think the Republicans are going to make a stout fight after all, as there is confusion in the opposition camp—the result of course I do not pretend to foretell—

My health is quite re-established, yet not exactly the same unconscious state of health as formerly—The book is still unprinted—Our family are all well as usual—I go two or three times a week among the soldiers in hospital here—

I go out quite regularly, sometimes out on the bay, or to Coney Island—& occasionally a tour through New York life, as of old—last night I was with some of my friends of Fred Gray association,[26] till late wandering the east side of the City—first in the lager bier saloons & then elsewhere—

23. Captain Samuel H. Sims (see 51) was killed on July 30 at Petersburg, according to George's letter of August 9–10 (Trent). I have not identified the other officer.

24. See 95.

25. William F. Channing (1820–1901), son of William Ellery Channing, and Ellen O'Connor's brother-in-law, was by training a doctor, but devoted most of his life to scientific experiments. With Moses G. Farmer, he perfected the first fire-alarm system. He was the author of *Notes on the Medical Applications of Electricity* (1849). Ellen O'Connor visited him frequently in Providence, R. I., and WW stayed at his home in October, 1868; see 317–322.

26. See 40. Since Gray had written on May 7, 1864, to WW that "we are suddenly ordered away to the South-west. I will write when we get settled" (Berg), he was probably not present.

one crowded, low, most degraded place we went, a poor blear-eyed girl bringing beer. I saw her with a McClellan medal on her breast—I called her & asked her if the other girls there were for McClellan[27] too—she said yes every one of them, & that they wouldn't tolerate a girl in the place who was not, & *the fellows* were too—(there must have been twenty girls, sad sad ruins)—it was one of those places where the air is full of the scent of low thievery, druggies, foul play, & prostitution gangrened—

I don't know what move I shall make, but something soon, as it is not satisfactory any more in New York & Brooklyn—I should think nine tenths, of all classes, are copperheads here, I never heard before such things as I hear now whenever I go out—then it seems tame & indeed unreal here, life as carried on & as I come in contact with it & receive its influences—

How is Ashton? & is he there again?[28] I got a letter from Charley Eldridge yesterday—I suppose he is now in Boston—My dear friend, I often often think of you, & count on our being together again, may be quite soon—meantime good bye & God bless you & I send you my best best love—

Walt

We are having a sloppy rainy dark Sunday here to-day—Lewis Brown (that was in ward K Armory Square) is a clerk in the Provost Marshall's office, cor 18th & I sts[29]—I got a letter from him the other day—perhaps you may see him some time—I am going off for a couple of weeks soon, to Burlington, Vt.[30]—O how the rain is pouring down as I write—at the other window sits my mother reading the Sunday Herald—quiet & pleasant & soothing—only us two home to-day—not a word spoken in a long time—

145. *To Charles W. Eldridge*

ADDRESS: Charles W Eldridge | care J F Eldridge & Co | 31 School street | Boston | Massachusetts.
POSTMARK: New York | Oct | 8.

Portland av near Myrtle | Brooklyn Oct 8 '64

Dear friend,

Your letters from Washington have all reached me, with the others enclosed. The last from you was dated Sept 27. You did not mention Wil-

27. George Brinton McClellan (1826–1885), deposed Union general, was nominated as Democratic candidate for President in 1864.

28. On August 13, O'Connor had reported that Ashton was "at Schooley's Mountain, New York, vacationizing" (Traubel, III, 339).

29. Brown informed WW of his appointment on September 5 (Berg).

30. There is no indication in Hannah's letter to WW on October 17 (Trent) of a visit to her in September.

31. The family had not received George's letter of October 2 from Petersburg: "Here

liam in it—I should always like to hear about him & from him. Is Nelly in Boston? If so say I sent my best love, not forgetting little Jennie. The last letter I received from Nelly was from Little Compton Aug 18—I have written subsequently & directed there, which I suppose she received—I have not heard from her since—

I am pretty well, perhaps not so unconsciously hearty as before my sickness—We are deprest in spirits home here about my brother George, (2d div 9th Corps)—if not killed, he is a prisoner—he was in the engagement of Sept 30 on the extreme left.[31]

My book is not yet being printed. I still wish to stereotype it myself. I could easily still put it in the hands of a proper publisher then, & make better terms with him.

If you write to William I wish you to enclose him this letter—I wish him to receive again my faithful friendship—while breath & sense remain I cannot forget what he has been to me—I love him dearly—

The weather here is fine of late—to-day a little blowy—The political meetings in New York & Brooklyn are immense—I go to them as to shows, fireworks, cannon, clusters of gaslights, countless torches, banners & mottos, 15, 20, 50,000 people—Per contra I occasionally go riding off in the country, in quiet lanes, or a sail on the water, & many times to the sea shore at Coney Island—

All the signs are that Grant is going to strike forthwith, perhaps risk all—One feels solemn who sees what depends. The military success, though first-class of war, is the least that depends—

Good bye, dearest comrade, write me whenever you can—if I make any move I shall let you know—

Walt

146. *To Ellen M. O'Connor*

ENDORSED: "Ans'd." ADDRESS: Mrs Ellen M O'Connor | 400 L st corner of 14th | Washington | D C. POSTMARK: Brooklyn N.Y. | Dec | 4 | 1864.

Brooklyn | December 4 1864

My dear friend

Your letter of November 30 came safe, & was truly welcome—if

I am perfectly well and unhurt, but a prisoner. I was captured day before yesterday . . . I am in tip top health and Spirits, and am as tough as a mule and shall get along first rate. Mother, please dont worry and all will be right in time if you will not worry" (Trent). According to his letter of October 23, he was taken prisoner near the Weldon Railroad. William E. Babcock, a lieutenant in the Fifty-first Regiment, informed WW on October 18 (Berg) that George's effects were to be sent to his mother. On December 12 (Berg), Babcock promised to send George's "large Trunk," and, in a memorandum dated December 26, WW noted receipt of the trunk (Yale; Allen, 318).

you have seen Mrs Howells[32] she has told you that I intend returning to Washington this winter—I do not know how soon, but I shall come, almost certainly—Then Charles Eldridge is to be transferred to Boston—I am indeed sorry, on my own account, & yours & Williams, for he will be missed by us all, I believe more than he thinks for[33]—

We are all well as usual. Mother remains well, & in pretty good spirits, better than I would have expected—My brother George still remains a prisoner—as near as we can judge he is at Columbia, S C—we have had no word from him[34]—

About my book nothing particular to tell—I shall print it myself—also my new edition of Leaves of Grass—Most likely shall do it in the way we have talked of, namely by subscription—I feel that it is best for me to print my books myself, (notwithstanding some very good objections to that course, but the reasons in favor are far stronger)[35]—

Dear Nelly, you & William have neither of you any idea how I daily & nightly bear you in mind & in love too—I did not know myself that you both had taken such deep root in my heart—few attachments wear & last through life, but ours *must*—

Good bye, dear Nelly, & good bye, dear William, & God bless you both—

Walt

147. *To an Editor* [*12.26(?). 1864*]

DRAFT LETTER.

Sir: whether it agrees with your own opinion or not I hope you will open your columns to this communication of mine, seeking to stir up the government to a general exchange of prisoners. I hope also you may feel to say a word about it editorially—if you could call attention to it.

As I have sent similar communications this afternoon to one or two other papers, I would particularly solicit that you find room for it in tomorrow's issue.[36]

32. See 95.

33. Although Eldridge did not depart until January, Ellen O'Connor feared further changes in the little Washington group of WW admirers. On November 30, she wrote to WW: "Every evening we talk of you, & wish you were here, & almost every evening we read from Leaves of Grass, read & admire. I don't believe, dear Walt, that you have in all the world, two heartier lovers & appreciators than William & Charley" (Feinberg).

34. The last extant letter from George in 1864 is that of October 23, mentioned in note 31 above.

35. On August 13, William O'Connor admitted "many misgivings about your plan of getting out the book yourself. I want it to have a large sale, as I think it well might,

Walt Whitman
in 1855

Washington
April 29th 1863.

Dear wife,

I am now to inform you that I have been now sick for two weeks — have been for the past week in Armory Square Hospital — have a pretty bad cold, the doctor does not call my disease by any particular name — I have considerable cough — but I think I shall be up all right before a great while so you must not be uneasy — I have pretty good care taken of me here, & shall do well

—I send you an envelope for you to put a letter in, as I wish you to write to me.

I send you my love. I have this letter written by a friend who sometimes calls in to see me, & the other boys.

Good bye for the present. & God bless you & all.

David Ferguson.

The above letter is written by Walt Whitman, a visitor to the hospitals

Louisa Whitman
1871

Washington, Wednesday forenoon,
May 13th 1863.

Dearest mother, I am late with my letter this week—my poor, poor boys occupy my time very much—I go every day, & sometimes nights—I believe I mentioned a young man in Ward F. Armory Square with a bad wound in the leg, very agonizing, had to have it propt up, & an attendant all the while dripping water on, night & day—I was in hopes at one time he would get through with it, but ~~he~~ a few days ago he took a sudden bad turn, & died about 3 o'clock the same afternoon—it was horrible—he was of good family, (handsome intelligent man, about 26, married) his name was John Elliott of Cumberland Valley Bedford Co. Penn. belonged to 2d Pennsylvania Cavalry. I felt very bad about it—I have wrote to his father—have not rec'd any answer yet—no friend nor any of his folks was here & have not been here nor sent, probably don't know of it at all—the surgeons put off amputating the leg, he was so exhausted, but at last it was imperatively necessary to amputate—mother, I am

shocked to tell you, that he never
came alive off the amputating table—
he died under the operation—it
was what I had dreaded & anticipated—poor young man, he suffered
much, very <u>very</u> much, for many days
& bore it so patiently—so it was
a release to him—Mother,
such things are awful—not a soul
here he knew or cared about, except
me—yet the surgeons & nurses
were good to him—I think all was
done for him that could be—
there was no help but to take
off the leg—he was under chloroform—they tried their best
to bring him to—three long hours
were spent, a strong smelling bottle
held under his nostrils, with
other means, three hours. Mother
how contemptible all the usual
little worldly prides & vanities
& striving after appearances, seems
in the midst of such scenes as
these—such tragedies of soul
& body. To see such things & not
be able to help them is awful—I feel
almost ashamed of being so well & whole.

Dear mother I have not heard from George himself — but I got a letter from Fred McReady & a young Brooklyn man in 51st — he is intimate with George, said he was well & hearty — I got the letter about five days ago — I wrote to George four days since, directed to Winchester, Kentucky. I got a letter from a friend in Nashville, Tenn. yesterday, he told me the 9th Army Corps was ordered to move to Murfreesboro, Tenn. I dont know whether this is so or not. I send papers to George almost every day. So far, I think it was fortunate the 51st was moved west, & I hope it will prove to continue so. Mother, it is all a lottery, this war, no one knows what will come up next. Mother I rec'd Jeff's letter of May 9th it was welcome as all Jeff's letters are, & all others from home. Jeff says you do not hear from me at home but seldom — mother I write once

a week to you, regular—but I will write soon to Jeff a good long letter—I have wanted to for some time, but have been much occupied. Dear brother, I wish you to say to Probasco & all the other young men on the Works, I send them my love & best thanks—never any thing came more acceptable than the little fund they forwarded me, through Mr. Lane the last week.—Our wounded, from Hooker's battles, are worse wounded & more of them, than any battle of the war & indeed (we have lost from 15,000 to 20,000) any I may say of modern times—besides the weather has been very hot here, very bad for new wounds. Yet as Jeff writes so downhearted I must tell him the rebellion has lost worse & more than we have—the more I find out about it the more I think they the confederates have recd an irreparable harm & loss in Virginia,—I should not be surprised to see them (either voluntarily or by force) leaving Virginia, before many weeks. I don't see how on earth they can stay there—I think Hooker is already reaching after them again—I myself do not give up Hooker yet—
Dear mother, I should like to hear from Han, poor Han—I send my best love to Sister Mat & all.
Good bye dearest mother. Walt.

Walt Whitman
taken from life 1863
war time Washington
D C
to Horace L Traubel
from his friend W W
June 1888-

Washington
June 10. 1865.

Mr. & Mrs. Pratt:

As I am visiting your son Alfred occasionally to cheer him up in his sickness in hospital, I thought you might like a few words, though from a stranger, yet a friend to your boy. I was there last night, and sat a while by the bed, as usual, & he showed me the letter he had just received from home. He wrote to you yesterday. He has had diarrhea pretty bad, but is now improved & goes about the hospital—but as the weather is pretty hot & powerful in the midst of the day, I advised him not to go out doors much at present. What he wants most is rest, and a chance to get his strength again. I expect he will

improve by degrees, & I hope it will not be very long before he will be sent home — though I don't know, as I am only a friend, occasionally visiting the hospitals. Alfred has good accommodations where he is, & a good doctor, & nursing — so you must not worry about him.
I shall stop & see him a little every day, as he likes to have me, & I like him too. Poor young men, there are hundreds & thousands of them here, wounded or sick, in the great Army hospitals — many of them suffering with amputations & wounds — others with sickness, & so faint & weak this weather — it is enough to make one's heart bleed —
— As to Alfred, he is comparatively well off, there are so many with bad wounds &c. — the deaths are quite frequent. He will soon be restored according to present appearances.

We are having very hot weather here, & it is dry & dusty—The City is alive with soldiers from both the Army of the Potomac & the Western Armies, brought here by Sherman. There have been some great Reviews here, as you have seen in the papers—& thousands of soldiers are going home every day.

You must write to Alfred often, as it cheers up a boy sick & away from home. Write all about domestic & farm incidents, and as cheerful as may be. Direct to him, in Ward C. Armory Square Hospital, Washington, D.C. Should any thing occur, I will write you again, but I feel confident he will continue doing well. For the present farewell.

Walt Whitman

Washington

D C

148. *To an Editor*

Dec 29 1864

Private note to Editor:[37]

Sir, I send you a communication which I hope you will publish for sake of the soldiers dying & suffering in Southern prisons—Would it be convenient also to say a few words editorially? I have taken the liberty to send you a few lines myself—if they are not acceptable, substitute something else—

Walt Whitman

122 Portland av near Myrtle Brooklyn

and I am afraid that this sort of private publication will keep it from being known or accessible to any considerable number of people" (Feinberg; Traubell, III, 338–339). See also 236.

36. This is the draft of a letter written to the editor of the Brooklyn *Daily Eagle* or the New York *Times* to accompany a communication entitled "The Prisoners," which was to appear on December 27 (reprinted by Glicksberg, 178–180). WW assailed the Secretary of War and General Butler for their attitudes toward the exchange of prisoners.

37. WW evidently sent "The Prisoners" to other newspapers in addition to the Brooklyn *Daily Eagle* and the New York *Times*. Later in life he sometimes sent a communication to as many as twelve newspapers.

1865

149. *To William D. O'Connor*

ADDRESS: Wm D O'Connor | Light House Board | Treasury Department | Washington | D C.
POSTMARK: New York | Jan | 6.

Brooklyn January 6 1865

Dear friend

Your welcome letter of December 30 came safe. I have written & sent my application to Mr Otto,[1] & also a few lines to Mr Ashton, with a copy of it.[2] I am most desirous to get the appointment, as enclosing, with the rest of the points, my attentions to the soldiers & to my poems, as you intimate.

It may be Drum-Taps may come out this winter, yet, (in the way I have mentioned in times past.) It is in a state to put right through, a perfect copy being ready for the printers—I feel at last, & for the first time without any demur, that I am satisfied with it—content to have it go to the world verbatim & punctuation. It is in my opinion superior to Leaves of Grass—certainly more perfect as a work of art, being adjusted in all its proportions, & its passion having the indispensable merit that though to the ordinary reader let loose with wildest abandon, the true artist can see it is yet under control. But I am perhaps mainly satisfied with Drum-Taps because it delivers my ambition of the task that has haunted me, namely, to express in a poem (& in the way I like, which is not at all by directly stating it) the pending action of this *Time* & *Land we swim in*, with all

1865

1. William Tod Otto (1816–1905) was appointed assistant Secretary of the Interior in January, 1863, and took an active interest in Indian affairs. He resigned from this post in 1871, but held various other governmental posts for many years. See also note 11 below.

2. On December 30, O'Connor informed WW that Ashton had spoken to Otto "in your behalf. . . . We shall fetch it this time. I have every confidence that you will get a good and an easy berth, a regular income, &c, leaving you time to attend to the soldiers, to your poems, &c" (Feinberg; Traubel, II, 401).

3. Of the 1867 edition Allen observes: "What makes it important is Whitman's great exertion to rework the book by deletion, emendation, and rearrangement of the poems" (*Handbook*, 173). He omitted from the "Calamus" poems "Long I thought that knowledge alone would suffice me" (#8), "Hours continuing long, sore and heavy-hearted" (#9), and "Who is now reading this?" (#16).

4. George's last known letter was the one of October 23. Though the family did not hear from George for some time, it did everything possible to send provisions to him and

their large conflicting fluctuations of despair & hope, the shiftings, masses, & the whirl & deafening din, (yet over all, as by invisible hand, a definite purport & idea)—with the unprecedented anguish of wounded & suffering, the beautiful young men, in wholesale death & agony, everything sometimes as if in blood color, & dripping blood. The book is therefore unprecedently sad, (as these days are, are they not?)—but it also has the blast of the trumpet, & the drum pounds & whirrs in it, & then an undertone of sweetest comradeship & human love, threading its steady thread inside the chaos, & heard at every lull & interstice thereof—truly also it has clear notes of faith & triumph.

Drum Taps has none of the perturbations of Leaves of Grass. I am satisfied with Leaves of Grass (by far the most of it) as expressing what was intended, namely, to express by sharp-cut self assertion, *One's-Self* & also, or may be still more, to map out, to throw together for American use, a gigantic embryo or skeleton of Personality, fit for the West, for native models—but there are a few things I shall carefully eliminate in the next issue, & a few more I shall considerably change.[3]

I see I have said I consider Drum-Taps superior to Leaves of Grass. I probably mean as a piece of wit, & from the more simple & winning nature of the subject, & also because I have in it only succeeded to my satisfaction in removing all superfluity from it, verbal superfluity I mean. I delight to make a poem where I feel clear that not a word but is indispensable part thereof & of my meaning.

Still Leaves of Grass is dear to me, always dearest to me, as my first born, as daughter of my life's first hopes, doubts, & the putting in form of those days' efforts & aspirations—true, I see now, with some things in it I should not put in if I were to write now, but yet I shall certainly let them stand, even if but for proofs of phases passed away—

Mother & all home are well as usual. Not a word for over three months from my brother George[4]—the probabilities are most gloomy. I see the Howells[5] now & then. I am well, but need to leave here—need a change. If you see Miss Howard tell her Jesse Mullery[6] has been to see me—came

to arrange for a prisoner exchange. On January 4, Dana F. Wright wrote to WW to explain that a gentleman who had a relative in an Ohio prison camp was anxious to arrange for an exchange: "Your brother's name was given & the party promised to act upon it immediately" (Berg).

5. See 95.

6. According to WW's "Hospital Book 12" (Feinberg), Sergeant Jesse Mullery, Company K, Fifteenth New Jersey, was in Ward A, Armory Square Hospital, on May 14, 1864. The twenty-year-old boy had been "shot through shoulder, ball in lung—(ball still in probably near lung)—lost right finger." On June 23, 1864, he went home to Vernon, N. J., on furlough, and then served as assistant cook in the army hospital in Newark. On December 26, Mullery proposed a visit to Brooklyn. He was still at the Newark hospital on January 23, 1865. According to his letters of May 3 and June 11, 1865, he later was able to return to active duty. (In the Berg Collection there are four letters from Mullery and one from his father to WW.)

yesterday & has just left this forenoon. He talked of nothing but her. His life is saved, & he will have tolerably good strength & health, at least for present. His address is Ward 7, Centre st Hospital, Newark New Jersey. I was up at Mrs Price's the other night. She is better this winter. Mrs Paulina Wright Davis[7] is stopping with her this winter. I have sent a paper with sketch of Hospital Visits, to Dr Wm F Channing.[8] I cannot forgive myself for not acknowledging his assistance for the Hospitals, by letter at the time. I send you another paper also, as you might like it. I take it by a line in your letter that Charles Eldridge has not gone to Boston.[9] I have been reading the strange articles from the Richmond press.[10] A thousand Satans baffled, with terror, hatred, malignant squirming, appear in every paragraph. Little California is playing around me as I finish, & has been for half an hour. Love to dear Nelly & Jeannie & all.

Walt Whitman

150. *To William D. O'Connor*

ADDRESS: William D. O'Connor | Light House Bureau, | U S Treasury Department, | Washington, | D. C. POSTMARK: New York | Jan | 20.

Brooklyn January 20 1865

My dear friend

I suppose you must have heard from Ashton that I received Mr. Otto's letter,[11] & that I returned for answer that I would report myself to him on or about Tuesday 24th instant. During the week previous to 16th I was quite sick, but this week I am about as well as usual.

I intend to leave here on Monday 23d—shall take the 8 o'clock morning train, which will probably arrive in Washington about 7 in the evening.

In several letters Mullery referred to the kindnesses of a Miss Howard while he was in the hospital, and another soldier, Charles H. Harris, on May 30, 1864 (Berg), asked to be remembered to Miss Howard and her sister. On February 20, 1866, Mullery wrote that one of the Howard sisters had died the preceding fall, and recalled "the Same Sad Smile on her countenance" (LC). Probably these were the Misses Sallie and Carrie Howard listed in the 1866 Directory, or the Miss Garaphelia Howard mentioned in 576.

7. Pauline Wright Davis (1813–1876) was a well-known abolitionist and suffragette. She was the wife of Thomas Davis (1805–1895), a manufacturer of jewelry in Providence, R. I., and a Congressman from 1853 to 1855. WW stayed at their home in October, 1868.

8. See 143.

9. Eldridge had spent Thanksgiving and Christmas with the O'Connors, according to William's letter on December 30.

10. The New York *Times* of this date quoted the following from the Richmond *Sentinel*: "Our authorities *must do more.* They must take care, whatever befalls us, to save us from the Yankees. *If adverse gales and devouring billows should constrain our storm-lost ship into some port, let it be no Yankee port. If an unpropitious Providence should condemn us to a master, let it not be a Yankee master.* Of all the people on earth,

William, if you could hear of a room, I wish you would engage it for me—if Gwinne[12] has one, it would do—take the first good room you find, if any, irrespective of price—it would do for a week or so, any how—would like convenience for a fire, as I am susceptible to chill this winter.

We got word yesterday by means of an exchanged prisoner, from my brother George, but only up to November 27—at that time he was at Danville, Virginia, in confinement with 350 other officers. We hear that he is full of fortitude & even good nature, but like all the rest, starved, miserable & naked, to the last degree.

We are all well, home here. Last night another snow-storm, but fine & sunshiny this morning—So far this winter, snow, rain, mud, melt, fog, with spells of sharp cold. I have received a letter from Charles Eldridge, from an island off in the sea, far beyond Boston. I suppose you got my letter of some ten days since. Nelly, I send you my love, & hope you are well & [in] good spirits. Farewell.

Walt Whitman

151. *To Thomas Jefferson Whitman*

Washington | January 30 1865.

My dear brother,

Your letter has only just reached me though I see the Brooklyn post office stamp is January 27th—I was gratified with Babcock's and Smith's letters, though I am very sorry they neither of them mentioned the date of Lt Caldwell's letter from Danville.[13] If it should be much later than George's, which was November 27th, it would be a relief to know it—but I presume it was one of the same batch. Jeff, I have this morning written to Capt Mason,[14] telling him where George is, & asking him, as

we should have most reason to loathe and to dread them. *Any terms with any other would be preferable to subjugation to them.*"

11. Otto (see 149) wrote to WW on January 12 to advise him that upon "passing a satisfactory examination you will be appointed to a First Class Clerkship" (Lion; Traubel, III, 470); and, on January 24, informed WW of his appointment as clerk at the salary of "$1200 per annum" (Lion; Traubel, III, 471).

12. Carey Gwynne; see 53.

13. Babcock, a lieutenant in George's regiment (see 145), on January 21, informed WW that the prisoners were "pretty hard up for grub" and wanted things like "Salt Pork and hard tack" sent to them. Since Babcock was in the field near Petersburg, he hoped that WW "would look out for all hands" (Feinberg). Aaron Smith, probably of the Fifty-first Regiment, wrote to WW on May 14 and July 13, 1864 (Berg), while he was a patient at Carver Hospital, Washington. On January 21, 1865 (Feinberg), from Petersburg, he asked WW to send supplies to the Danville Military Prison. Lieutenant William Caldwell had been captured at the same time as George. He was a captain when WW mentioned him again in 163. According to jottings in a notebook, dated May 23–24 (Barrett), Caldwell was born in Scotland and was 27; he had been "in the same fights as George."

14. See 152.

that would be ten times more likely to get through, if he will have (or direct some proper person) to put up a box of things to eat, & given him George's address to send it through the lines, & said that I or you would pay the bill of course, & be most deeply obliged to him & that I would have enclosed the money in the letter I sent him, but thought it safer to wait & see whether it reached him.[15] I have written to George since I have been here in Washington. Also a few lines to Han. We have had very cold mean weather here ever since I arrived till to-day—it is now moderated & very pleasant overhead.

I am quite comfortable, have a comfortable room enough, with a wood stove, & a pile of wood in the room, a first rate & good big bed, & a very friendly old secesh landlady whose husband & son are off in the Southern army—she is different from any I have found yet here, is very obliging, starts my fire for me at 5 o'clock every afternoon, & lights the gas, even, & then turns it down to be ready for me when I come home. I get my meals where I can—they are poor & expensive—You speak of the Indian office—it is a Bureau in the Department of the interior, which has charge of quite a large mass of business relating to the numerous Indian tribes in West & Northwest, large numbers of whom are under annuities, supplies, &c for the government. All I have hitherto employed myself about has been making copies of reports & Bids, &c for the office to send up to the Congressional Committee on Indian Affairs. It is easy enough—I take things very easy—the rule is to come at 9 and go at 4—but I don't come at 9, and only stay till 4 when I want, as at present to finish a letter for the mail—I am treated with great courtesy, as an evidence of which I have to inform you that since I began this letter, I have been sent for by the cashier to receive my *PAY* for the arduous & invaluable services I have already rendered to the government—I feel quite well, perhaps not as completely so as I used to was, but I think I shall get so this spring—as I did indeed feel yesterday better than I have since I was taken sick last summer.

I spent yesterday afternoon in Armory Square Hospital,[16] & had a real good time, & the boys had too. Jeff, you need not be afraid about my overdoing the matter. I shall go regularly enough, but shall be on my guard against trouble. I am also going to some of the camps about here,

15. Jeff wrote to WW on January 31: "I have almost come to the conclusion that it is hardly possible that the things that we send to George can reach him (yet I propose to keep sending, hoping that a proportion may do so)" (Feinberg).

16. This visit is described in *Specimen Days* (CW, IV, 101–102).

17. Jeff informed WW on January 26 (Feinberg) that he had used "hoop iron" to strap the box he sent to George.

18. See 31 and 42, respectively.

19. Probably Julius W. Mason, a lieutenant colonel in the Fifth Cavalry. On February 10, 1863, Jeff mentioned a J. W. Mason, who "used to be in my party on the Water

there is a great chance among them to do good, & they are interesting places every way, for one who goes among the men. I have thought every day of Mother—dear Mother, I hope she gets along well this bitter weather—(about the hoop iron, I think it was the right thing to do[17]—the least they can do is to take it off)—My dear brother, you must by all means *come* & see me—Martha, my dear sister, I send you & the dear little torments my best, best love—Jeff, give my respects to Mr. Lane & Dr Ruggles[18]—

Walt

152. *To Louisa Van Velsor Whitman*

Washington | February 1 1865

Dear Mother,

I sent Jeff a letter three or four days ago, which I suppose he received. There is nothing very new with me—I see in the U. S. Senate yesterday they passed a resolution that it was the sense of the Senate that there ought to be an exchange of prisoners. I feel as if there was a fair chance of the box you sent getting to George—I wrote to Jeff how I was so much surer that a box from City Point, would go through, that I had sent a letter to Julius Mason[19] asking him to have a box made up there, & sent, giving him the address, & I or Jeff would pay the bill—if he writes to me that he has done so, I asked him to write if he got mine, I will send him the money myself—

Well, mother, how are you getting along—we had a cold week, but the past three days has been much moderated—I am satisfied in the main with my room. I have such a good bed—& my stove does very well—it is a little bit out of the way in location—My work as clerk in the Indian office is quite easy—I am through by 4—I find plenty who know me—I received a week's pay on Monday, came very acceptable—My appetite is not very good, but I feel very well upon the whole—I wish you would ask Wm Fosdick[20] in the corner house for the *Times*, & also sketch of 51st I lent him, & put them away—I am very glad I have employment (& *pay*)—I must try to keep it—I send you an envelope, so that you can write me a letter soon

Works" (Feinberg). When George considered staying in the army after the war, Jeff conferred with Mason; see his letter of May 14, 1865 (Feinberg). Mason remained in the army until his death in 1882. WW wrote to "Captain" Mason on January 30; on February 7 (Feinberg), Jeff noted that Mason had complied with WW's request. WW wrote again on February 13, and Mason replied from City Point on February 16 that a box had been sent to George on February 10, and that WW's letter would be forwarded by "1st Flag of Truce" (Yale).

20. Not listed in the 1865–1866 Directory.

as convenient. I send $1 for Nancy, the other for you—I may not write again till about the 12th, or perhaps 10th—

Tell Hattie & sis Uncle Walt sent them his love. I see Gen. Butler[21] says the fault of not exchanging the prisoners is not his but Grants.

Walt.

My room is 468 M street, 2d door west of 12th—from 10 till 4, I am in the Indian Bureau, north-east corner Patent Office, basement.[22]

153. *To John Swinton*

Washington, Feb 3, 1865

My dear friend,[23]

From the deep distress of my mother whose health is getting affected,[24] & of my sister—& thinking it worth the trial myself, I write this hastily to ask you to do, or rather if you have an objection to do, as follows:

Write a brief letter, not filling more than one page, letter paper, to Lt. Gen. Grant. Date it from the office of the *Times*, which will add to its effect, & recal you to Gen. Grant. It is to request him to give directions, that one of the special exchanges (of which they are now making quite a number) shall be made, in favor of my brother George, and also another officer same regiment. State in short terms that Capt. Whitman has been in active military service of U. S. since April, 1861, nearly four years, has borne his part bravely in battles in nearly every part of the war in the United States, east & west, including Vicksburgh & Jackson, Miss.—has an aged widowed mother in deepest distress. Ask Gen. G. to order a special exchange of

Capt George W. Whitman, 51st New York Vol.
& Lieut Samuel Pooley,[25] 51st New York Vol.

both of whom are now, or were lately, in C. S. Military Prison, in Dan-

21. In a speech at Lowell, Mass., on January 29, Butler blamed Grant for the collapse of the prisoner exchange. In an editorial on the following day, the New York *Times* termed Butler's address "exceedingly able, defiant and mischievous."

22. When Traubel read this letter on December 13, 1888, WW was unusually moved: "O God! that whole damned war business is about nine hundred and ninety parts diarrhoea to one part glory: the people who like the wars should be compelled to fight the wars . . . I say, God damn the wars—all wars" (III, 293).

23. Jeff suggested on January 31 that WW write to John Swinton: "Now, Walt, if you will remember among the first men that blowed for Grant and wrote him up, so to speak, was our friend John Swinton. . . . Now I am positive that a letter could be got from Swinton to Grant signed as Editor of the Times asking that a special exchange might be made in George's case" (Feinberg). Swinton replied to WW on February 5 and included a letter to Grant in which he closely paraphrased WW's letter; see Traubel, II,

ville, Va. (both the above officers have been promoted from the ranks for conduct on the field)—

Walt Whitman

My address is simply to Washington D. C. as I go to post office for my letters.

154. *To Abby H. Price*

Washington | February 4 1865

My dear friend,

As you see by the date of this, I am again back in Washington. I spend a portion of my time around among the Hospitals as formerly—I find quite a good many bad old lingering wounds, & also a good many down with sickness of one sort or another—& the latter are receiving accessions every day—especially as they appear to be breaking up the Corps Hospitals in front, down in Grant's army—a good many of the men have been sent up here—day before yesterday I saw a string of over a hundred ambulances, bringing up the men from the depot, to distribute them around to the different Hospitals.

My health is pretty good, & I remain in good spirits considering.

I have a little employment here, of three or four hours every day. It is regular, & sufficiently remunerative—Sundays I spend most of the day in the Hospitals—during the week a few hours from time to time, & occasionally in the evening.

Abby, I write in haste to catch this evening's mail, so will not make out much of a letter. I was not able to get over and make you a parting visit, as I wished.

I send my love to Emily and Helen and all—

Walt Whitman

Direct to me simply to Washington, D. C. as I go to post office for my letters.

426–427. In a lost letter, WW informed his family that he had written to Swinton, and, on February 7, Jeff replied that "we are all very joyful," and that Dr. Ruggles had visited Swinton "to urge him to write to Gen Grant" (Feinberg). According to Williamson's *Catalogue of A Collector of Books, Letters, and Manuscripts Written by Walt Whitman* (1903), with WW's letter there is another from Lieutenant Colonel E. S. Parker, Grant's military secretary, dated February 13, 1865, informing Swinton that the cases of the two officers "had been ordered to be made a subject of special exchange." Swinton endorsed the envelope: "W. W. 1865 Asking me to help his captured brother. Successful."

24. WW overstated, for on the same day Jeff, who took nothing calmly, wrote from Brooklyn: "Mother is quite well—I think to-day [she] seems in better spirits than usual" (Feinberg).

25. See 25.

155. *To John Townsend Trowbridge*[26]

TRANSCRIPT.

Washington, Monday February 6, 1865.

My dear Friend:

As you see by the date of this, I am back again in Washington, moving around regularly, but not to excess, among the hospitals. . . . My health is pretty good, but since I was prostrated last July, I have not had that unconscious and perfect health I formerly had. The physician says my system has been penetrated by the malaria—it is tenacious, peculiar and somewhat baffling—but tells it will go over in due time. It is my first appearance in the character of a man not entirely well.

The talk here is about the late Peace Conference[27]—the general statement accepted is that it has been a failure and a bubble—even the war is to go on worse than ever—but I find a few shrewd persons whose theory is that it is not at all sure of its being a failure—they say that the President and Mr. Seward are willing to avoid at present the tempest of rage which would beat about their heads, if it were known among the Radicals that Peace, Amnesty, *every thing*, were given up to the Rebels on the single price of re-assuming their place in the Union—so the said shrewd ones say the thing is an open question yet. For *my* part I see no light or knowledge in any direction on the matter of the conference, or what it amounted to, or where it left off. I say nothing, and have no decided opinion about it—not even a guess (but rather leaning to the generally accepted statement above).

My dear friend, I haven't your last letter at hand to see whether there is anything that needs special answer—I hope to hear from you often. For the present Farewell.

Walt Whitman

Direct to me simply Washington, D. C., as I call for my letters daily at the post office. Should you have an opportunity to see Dr. Le Baron Russell,[28] 3 Mt. Vernon St., tell him I wished you to thank him for many favors and contributions to the men in times past, and that I am now back

26. See 102. Glicksberg (98 *n.*) based his text on a transcription prepared by Professor Will S. Monroe.

27. Seward left on February 1 to meet southern representatives at Fortress Monroe, Va., and on the following day summoned Lincoln. The actual meeting took place on February 3, and Lincoln and Seward returned to Washington the next day. The New York *Times* of February 6 contained a full account of the negotiations.

28. See 99.

29. The Boston *Saturday Evening Gazette;* see 102. I have not found the para-

in Washington. If perfectly eligible, it might help me in the cause of the men, if you were to prepare a paragraph for Mr. Shillaber's paper,[29] if he were willing to publish it, stating that I am now as a volunteer nurse among the Hospitals at Washington & in the field as formerly. Write soon as convenient.

W. W.

156. *To Captain William Cook*

Washington Feb. 27, 1865.

Captain:

Could you give me a little further information about my brother Capt. George W. Whitman, 51st New York, who gave you the slip you sent from Annapolis Feb. 19, with his & mother's address, Feb. 14th? Why did not he, & the other officers, 51st N. Y., come up with the main body, for exchange? Were the other officers 51st there at Danville, time you left? Please tell me all you know, or think probable, on this subject of why they did not come? Have they been sent further south, to avoid exchanging them, or are they still at Danville? *Was* my brother *really well* & hearty? Was Lieut. Sam'l Pooley, 51st N. Y., there, & how was he? Do you know whether my brother got letters & boxes we sent him? Was he in the attempt to escape, Dec. 10, last? My dear sir, if you could take a leisure half hour & write me, *soon as possible*, what you know on these, or any points relating to my brother, it would deeply oblige me—address[30]—

Walt Whitman

Washington D C

157. *To John Townsend Trowbridge*

TRANSCRIPT.

Washington Friday, March 3, '65.

My dear Trowbridge,

Your letter has reached me—my best thanks for your contribution to the wounded & sick, & shall be applied in most needy cases. You speak

graph, although it evidently appeared; see 157.

30. Cook replied, on the back of WW's letter (Feinberg; Traubel, III, 202–203), that he assumed George was now in Annapolis, since all the Danville prisoners had arrived there on February 23 and 24. George had written to his mother from the Officers' Hospital, Annapolis, Md., on February 24. He had left the Danville prison on February 19, stopped at Richmond for three days, and arrived in Annapolis the day before. "If ever a poor devil was glad to get in a Christian Country it was me" (Trent). By oversight on his mother's part, George's letter was not sent to WW immediately.

of seeing Dr. Russell[31]—has he not rec'd a N. Y. Times of two months since containing a sketch of my Visits to Hospitals[32]—I thought one had been sent him. If he has not had one I should like to send one to him. The paragraph in the Gazette by Mr Shillaber[33] is very kind. I do not wish you to send me any of the papers. Nothing new or special with me—I believe I told you I was working a few hours a day, a sufficiently remunerative desk in Indian office—I spend a couple of hours day or evening in the hospitals. Farewell.

Walt Whitman.

Washington, D. C.

158. *To William D. and Ellen M. O'Connor*

ENDORSED: "Answ'd." ADDRESS: Wm. D. O'Connor | Washington | D C. POSTMARK: Brooklyn (?) | Mar | 27 | (?).

ENGINEER'S OFFICE, NASSAU WATER DEPT.
355 *Fulton Street,* | *Brooklyn, N. Y.,* March 26 *1865*

My dear William & Nelly O'Connor,

I write a few lines to tell you how I find the folks at home—Both my mother & brother George looked much better than I expected—Mother is quite well, considering—she goes about her household affairs pretty much the same as ever, & is cheerful.

My brother would be in what I would almost call fair condition, if it were not that his legs are affected—it seems to me it is rheumatism, following the fever he had[34]—but I don't know—He goes to bed quite sleepy & falls to sleep—but then soon wakes, & frequently little or no more sleep that night—he most always leaves the bed, & comes downstairs, & passes the night on the sofa. He goes out most every day though—some days has to lay by—He is going to report to Annapolis promptly when his

31. See 99.

32. "Our Wounded and Sick Soldiers—Visits among the Hospitals," New York *Times*, December 11, 1864; reprinted as "Hospital Visits" in *The Wound Dresser* and *CW*, VII, 101–127. On December 30, O'Connor had informed WW that he had read this letter "with a swelling heart and wet eyes. It was very great and touching to me. I think I could mount the tribune for you on that and speak [a] speech which jets fire and drops tears. Only it filled me with infinite regrets that there is not a book from you, embodying these rich and sad experiences. It would be sure of immortality. No history of our times would ever be written without it" (Feinberg; Traubel, II, 402).

33. See 155.

34. About March 5, Mrs. Whitman described George's illness in prison camp: "he

furlough is up—I told him I had no doubt I could get it extended, but he does not wish it—He says little, but is in first rate spirits.

I am feeling finely—& never enjoyed a visit home more than I am doing this.

I find myself perplexed about printing my book. All the printers tell me I could not pick a more inopportune time—that in ten days prices of paper, composition &c will all be very much lower &c. I shall decide to-morrow.

My brother Jeff wishes me to give you his sincerest thanks for your good will &c in the matter of the engineer's situation[35]—Mother says he has talked much about it, & feels your kindness in it thoroughly.

Martha & the little girls are well. My sister at Burlington Vt. is not well, & mother will probably pay a long visit there this summer.

Walt.

159. *To William D. O'Connor*

ADDRESS: Wm. D. O'Connor, | Light House Board, | Treasury Department, | Washington, | D. C.
POSTMARK: New York | Apr | 7.

Brooklyn, April 7, 1865.

Dear friend,

I am stopping longer than first intended, as I have decided to print the book, and am now under way with it. Probably I will not be back till 16th or 17th.

I have been to Christiern's,[36] the great importer of foreign & special London books—he said he had no Hugo's Shakspeare & had heard of none—English I mean—if any, Scribner would know about it—I have been to Scribner's to-day—He thinks he has seen one announced in English literary announcements—but thinks it is not yet printed—has not had or seen any such book.

The grand culminations of past week impress me profoundly of course.

was very sick at one time. i think it was in january with the lung fever. he was six weeks in the hospital so bad that the doctor thought he would die . . . he was dilerious and lay in a stupor till the night the fever turned. he says he felt a thrill run through him and thought he was dying. he was in the dark. he cald to one of the nurses to bring a light and to raise him up and give him a piece of paper and pencil and he wrote to me that was his last night and what was due him from the goverment" (Trent; Gohdes and Silver, 190).

35. O'Connor recommended Jeff for a position as a "draughtsman," but Jeff, in a letter to O'Connor on March 17 (Berg), declined because of lack of experience.

36. WW misspelled the name of Frederick W. Christern, 763 Broadway.

I feel more than ever how America has been entirely re-stated by them—and they will shape the destinies of the future of the whole of mankind.

My dear mother is well. My brother George has been unwell, again, & has sulkily permitted me to get an extension of his leave of absence, 30 days longer.

Please go to the Post Office & get all letters & send me. Please inquire for last week's advertised letters, & the present weeks also. I will not trouble to send any after next Wednesday night. My book will be small & not thick at all—but will be well printed.[37] (The Commissioner has granted me the two weeks longer).

Walt.

160. *To a Soldier* [*4(?).(?). 1865*]

TRANSCRIPT

My Dear Comrade:[38]

. . . I believe I have told you all that occurs to me, only I must let you know that your notion I may have forgotten you is not regular by a long shot. I do not forget any one so easily, where the friendship has been formed as it was under such circumstances as yours & mine in the hospital. You must write to me whenever you feel like it—tell me all about things & people down there in Kentucky—God bless you, my loving soldier boy, & for the present, Farewell.

Walt Whitman

161. *To Mrs. Irwin* [*5.1. 1865*]

TRANSCRIPT.

Dear madam:

No doubt you and Frank's friends have heard the sad fact of his death in hospital here, through his uncle, or the lady from Baltimore, who took his things. (I have not seen them, only heard of them visiting Frank.) I will write you a few lines—as a casual friend that sat by his death-bed. Your son, Corporal Frank H. Irwin, was wounded near Fort Fisher, Virginia, March 25th, 1865—the wound was in the left knee, pretty bad. He

37. The financial details of printing *Drum-Taps* are related in the notes to 162.

38. Excerpts from five of WW's letters to an unidentified ex-soldier were printed by Florence Hardiman Miller in the *Overland Monthly*. Because of the fragmentary nature of her quotations, I have not been able to date most of the letters or to offer any conjectures about the identity of the recipient. Evidently he came from Kentucky and later

was sent up to Washington, was receiv'd in ward C, Armory-square hospital, March 28th—the wound became worse, and on the 4th of April the leg was amputated a little above the knee—the operation was perform'd by Dr. Bliss, one of the best surgeons in the army—he did the whole operation himself—there was a good deal of bad matter gather'd—the bullet was found in the knee. For a couple of weeks afterwards he was doing pretty well. I visited and sat by him frequently, as he was fond of having me. The last ten or twelve days of April I saw that his case was critical. He previously had some fever, with cold spells. The last week in April he was much of the time flighty—but always mild and gentle. He died first of May. The actual cause of death was pyaemia, (the absorption of the matter in the system instead of its discharge). Frank, as far as I saw, had everything requisite in surgical treatment, nursing, &c. He had watches much of the time. He was so good and well-behaved and affectionate I myself liked him very much. I was in the habit of coming in afternoons and sitting by him, and soothing him, and he liked to have me—liked to put his arm out and lay his hand on my knee—would keep it so a long while. Toward the last he was more restless and flighty at night—often fancied himself with his regiment—by his talk sometimes seem'd as if his feelings were hurt by being blamed by his officers for something he was entirely innocent of—said, "I never in my life was thought capable of such a thing, and never was." At other times he would fancy himself talking as it seem'd to children or such like, his relatives I suppose, and giving them good advice; would talk to them a long while. All the time he was out of his head not one single bad word or idea escaped him. It was remark'd that many a man's conversation in his senses was not half as good as Frank's delirium. He seem'd quite willing to die—he had become very weak and had suffer'd a good deal, and was perfectly resign'd, poor boy. I do not know his past life, but I feel as if it must have been good. At any rate what I saw of him here, under the most trying circumstances, with a painful wound, and among strangers, I can say that he behaved so brave, so composed, and so sweet and affectionate, it could not be surpass'd. And now like many other noble and good men, after serving his country as a soldier, he has yielded up his young life at the very outset in her service. Such things are gloomy—yet there is a text, "God doeth all things well"—the meaning of which, after due time, appears to the soul.

moved to California. Her transcripts are not reliable, as evidenced by a comparison of the facsimile (63) with the transcription (61). Miss Miller, who generally is more exuberant than factual, seems to imply that the correspondence continued into the early 1870's. Until the originals are found, this admittedly feeble attempt at reconstruction will have to suffice; see 170, 171, 179, and 203.

I thought perhaps a few words, though from a stranger, about your son, from one who was with him at the last, might be worth while—for I loved the young man, though I but saw him immediately to lose him. I am merely a friend visiting the hospitals occasionally to cheer the wounded and sick.

W. W.

162. *To Peter Eckler*

Washington | May 2 1865.

Mr. Eckler:[39]

Dear Sir: I enclose $20 in further liquidation. I wish you would send me a copy of each of the printed sheets, by mail—as I suppose Alvord has printed them.

Before I left New York I paid Bradstreet[40] $20 in advance for binding the first 100.

I rec'd the copyright & receipt. I thank you for your kindness in getting the copyright.

Walt Whitman

163. *To Louisa Van Velsor Whitman*

Indian Bureau, basement of Patent Office.
—house 468 M st 2d door west of 12th
Washington, Thursday, May 25, '65

Dear Mother,

I received your letter of the 22d—I feel uneasy about you all the time, & hope I shall get a letter to-day, & find you have recovered.

Well, the Review is over, & it was very grand—it was too much & too impressive, to be described—but you will see a good deal about it in the papers. If you can imagine a great wide avenue like Flatbush avenue, quite flat, & stretching as far as you can see, with a great white building half as big as fort Greene on a hill at the commencement of the avenue,

39. From the receipts and letters in the Feinberg Collection, F. DeWolfe Miller has recently clarified the printing history in his edition of *Drum-Taps* (xxxiv–xlv). On April 1, WW signed a contract with Eckler to stereotype 500 copies for $254.00: "The workmanship is to be first class in every respect & to be completed, & the printed sheets delivered within one month from this date" (xxxv). The contract called for "one hundred & twenty pages," but since the book contained only 72 pages, Eckler submitted on April 12 a bill for $192.85, of which $138.00 had been paid. According to WW's notations on the statement, he paid $20.00 on April 26 and again on May 2. He either included the unpaid balance in his letter of May 2, or sent another (missing) letter in answer to Eckler's request of May 1 that the balance be paid. On May 4, Eckler issued a receipt for

& then through this avenue marching solid ranks of soldiers, 20 or 25 abreast, just marching steady all day long for two days, without intermission, one regiment after another, real war-worn *soldiers*, that have been marching & fighting for years—sometimes for an hour nothing but cavalry, just solid ranks, on good horses, with sabres glistening, & carbines hanging by their saddles, & their clothes showing hard service, but they mostly all good-looking hardy young men—then great masses of guns, batteries of cannon, four or six abreast, each drawn by six horses, with the gunners seated on the ammunition wagons—& these perhaps a long while in passing, nothing but batteries—(it seemed as if all the cannon in the world were here)—then great battalions of blacks, with axes & shovels & pick axes, (real southern darkies, black as tar)—then again hour after hour the old infantry regiments, the men all sunburnt—nearly every one with some old tatter all in shreds, (that *had been* a costly & beautiful *flag*)—the great drum corps of sixty or eighty drummers massed at the heads of the brigades, playing away—now and then a fine brass band—but oftener nothing but the drums & whistling fifes—but they sounded very lively—(perhaps a band of sixty drums & fifteen or twenty fifes playing "Lannigan's ball")—the different corps banners, the generals with their staffs &c—the Western Army, led by Gen. Sherman,[41] (old Bill, the soldiers all call him)—well, dear mother, that is a brief sketch, give you some idea of the great panorama of the Armies that have been passing through here the last two days.

I saw the President several times, stood close by him, & took a good look at him—& like his expression much—he is very plain & substantial—it seemed wonderful that just that plain middling-sized ordinary man, dressed in black, without the least badge or ornament, should be the master of all these myriads of soldiers, the best that ever trod the earth, with forty or fifty Major-Generals, around him or riding by, with their broad yellow-satin belts around their waists—and of all the artillery & cavalry—to say nothing of all the Forts & Ships, &c, &c.

I saw Gen. Grant too several times—He is the noblest Roman of them all—none of the pictures do justice to him—about sundown I saw him again riding on a large fine horse, with his hat off in answer to the

$34.85, and included a receipt from Coridon A. Alvord, printer, for the stereotype plates, which he had placed in his vault. On April 26, Eckler had informed WW that the book was "now to press" and would "be ready for the Binders next Monday morning" (Feinberg; Miller, xliii). See Rollo G. Silver's reservations, in *WWR*, v (1959), 36. See also 168.

40. This receipt, dated April 21 and signed by Abraham Simpson, is in the Feinberg Collection; see also Miller, xxxvi. J. M. Bradstreet & Son, printers, had their establishment at 8 Spruce Street, New York.

41. William Tecumseh Sherman (1820–1891).

hurrahs—he rode by where I stood, & I saw him well, as he rode by on a slow canter, with nothing but a single orderly after him—He looks like a good man—(& I believe there is much in looks)—I saw Gen. Meade, Gen. Thomas,[42] Secretary Stanton, & lots of other celebrated government officers & generals—but the *rank & file* was the greatest sight of all.

The 51st was in the line Tuesday with the 9th Corps. I saw George, but did not get a chance to speak to him. He is well. George is now *Major* George W. Whitman[43]—has been commissioned & mustered in. (Col. Wright[44] & Col. Shephard[45] have done it, I think.) The 51st is over to the Old Convalescent camp, between here and Alexandria, doing provost duty. It (the old camp) is now called Augur General Hospital. If you should write direct,

Major G. W. Whitman | 51st New York V. V. | on provost duty at | Augur Gen'l Hospital | near Alexandria | Va.

It is thought that the 51st will not be mustered out for the present—It is thought the Government will retain the re-enlisted veteran regiments, such as the 51st—If that is so, George will remain as he is for the summer, or most of it—The reason I havn't seen him is, I knew they had left provost duty in the Prince st. prison, but didn't know where they had gone till Tuesday—I saw Capt. Caldwell[46] Tuesday, also Col. Wright Tuesday night—they said they all have pleasant quarters over there.

Dear brother Jeff, I was very sorry you wasn't able to come on to see the Review—we had perfect weather & every thing just as it should be—the streets now are full of soldiers scattered around loose, as the armies are in camp near here, getting ready to be mustered out. I am quite well & visit the Hospitals the same. Mother, you didn't write whether you

42. George Henry Thomas (1816–1870) served under Sherman and Grant, and in 1864 and 1865 commanded the Army of the Cumberland.

43. George's official appointment as major, dated May 13, is in the Missouri Historical Society.

44. John Gibson Wright rose from captain to colonel in the Fifty-first Regiment; he was appointed to the latter position May 18, 1865. He was taken prisoner with George in 1864. See also 143.

45. Elliott F. Shepard, of the Fifty-first Regiment, informed George of his promotion on April 16, 1862 (Traubel, II, 201), and wrote to WW about George's imprisonment on February 16, 1865 (Feinberg). George had returned to his regiment, probably about the first of the month, and, when he wrote to his mother on May 8 (Trent), he was in charge of the Prince Street Military Prison in Alexandria. According to Jeff's letter of May 14 (Feinberg), George wanted an appointment in the regular army as captain.

46. See 151.

47. Probably this is *The Odyssey of Homer*, translated by Theodore Alois Buckley (1863), now in the Feinberg Collection. On the flyleaf WW wrote: "Possess'd by me from 1868 to 1888 and read by me during those times—Sometimes in Washington & sometimes in Camden—Small or larger readings—Often in Camp or Army Hospitals—WW." Obviously either the reference to the hospitals or the date "1868" is in error. In "Whitman Studies Homer" (1872) he termed the Buckley translation "best of all" (Feinberg).

48. On June 30, James Harlan (1820–1899), a United States Senator and a member of Lincoln's cabinet, relieved WW of his position in the Indian Office (Lion; Traubel, III, 471). He was immediately consigned to the *Dunciad* by WW and his admirers.

got the package of 5 Drum-Taps—I keep thinking about you every few minutes all day—I wish I was home a couple of days—Jeff, you will take this acc't of the Review, same as if it was written to you.

Walt

164. *To John Swinton(?)*

Washington | June 9, 1865.

My dear friend,

The *Homer*[47] has come & is now lying before me. I thank you deeply. I am very well, this summer, & go to the Hospitals daily & nightly—as I find a greater proportion of sad cases than ever—& for some reason or other there are few or no visitors. I enjoy my visits with a sad but profound joy & satisfaction—especially at night, when the light is nearly turned off, & I am soothing some suffering one.

I send you, same mail with this, two copies of the little book Drum-Taps. Farewell.

Walt Whitman[48]

164.1 *To N. M. and John B. Pratt*

Washington | June 10, 1865.

Mr. & Mrs. Pratt:

As I am visiting your son Alfred[49] occasionally, to cheer him up in his sickness in hospital, I thought you might like a few words, though from a stranger, yet a friend to your boy. I was there last night, and sat a while by the bed, as usual, & he showed me the letter he had just re-

Count Gurowski erupted in his *Diary;* see notes to 177. O'Connor strained syntax in vilifying Harlan in *The Good Gray Poet.* In our century H. L. Mencken remarked savagely: "Let us repair, once a year, to our accustomed houses of worship and there give thanks to God that one day in 1865 brought together the greatest poet America has ever produced and the damndest ass"; see *Prejudices, First Series* (1929), 249–250. Ashton intervened with Harlan, and, according to WW's version of this interview (Traubel, III, 472–474), Harlan acknowledged that WW "was a both competent and faithful clerk," but that he objected to "outrageous" material he found in a copy of *Leaves of Grass* which was "in or on" the poet's desk. On July 21, O'Connor prepared, with WW's assistance, a lengthy letter defending the poet's character and expounding the theory of his poetry which he intended to have Ashton sign and forward to Harlan. The document, now in the Berg Collection, was reprinted by F. DeWolfe Miller, *Tennessee Studies in Literature,* III (1958), 92–95. Harlan remained silent until 1894, when he explained in a personal letter that upon assuming office in 1865 he was determined "to weed out the needless and worthless material" in the department, and that WW was dismissed on the recommendation of William P. Dole, Commissioner of Indian Affairs, "on the ground that his services were not needed." See Johnson Brigham, *James Harlan* (1913), 122–123. Ashton wrote to Eldridge about the affair on June 13, 1902; see Barrus, 27–30. The fullest account of the incident appears in Barrus, 25–35.

WW was employed in the Attorney General's office on July 1.

49. All that is known about Alfred Pratt is contained in this letter and in the continuation of the correspondence; see 164.2, 191.1, 240, and 253.1. The letter from Pratt's father is in the Feinberg Collection.

ceived from home. He wrote to you yesterday. He has had diarrhea pretty bad, but is now improved & goes about the hospital—but as the weather is pretty hot & powerful in the midst of the day, I advised him not to go outdoors much at present. What he wants most is rest, and a chance to get his strength again. I expect he will improve by degrees, & I hope it will not be very long before he will be sent home—though I don't know, as I am only a friend, occasionally visiting the hospitals. Alfred has good accommodations where he is, & a good doctor, & nursing—so you must not worry about him. I shall stop & see him a little every day, as he likes to have me, & I like him too. Poor young men, there are hundreds & thousands of them here, wounded or sick, in the great army hospitals—many of them suffering with amputations & wounds—others with sickness, & so faint & weak, this weather—it is enough to make one's heart bleed—

As to Alfred, he is comparatively well off, there are so many with bad wounds &c.—the deaths are quite frequent. He will soon be restored, according to present appearances.

We are having very hot weather here, & it is dry & dusty—The City is alive with soldiers from both the Army of the Potomac & the Western Armies, brought here by Sherman. There have been some great Reviews here, as you have seen in the papers—& thousands of soldiers are going home every day.

You must write to Alfred often, as it cheers up a boy sick & away from home. Write all about domestic & farm incidents, and as cheerful as may be. Direct to him, in Ward C, Armory Square Hospital, Washington, D. C. Should any thing occur, I will write you again, but I feel confident he will continue doing well. For the present farewell.

Walt Whitman

Washington | D C

164.2 *To Alfred Pratt*

ATTORNEY GENERAL'S OFFICE,

Washington, Aug. 26, *1865*.

Dear Al,[50]

Your letter came all right—& I was glad to hear from you, boy, & to know that you had got home to your own folks at last—& now I hope you will get well & strong again, dear son—& I hope it may be God's will that you will not only get so, but keep so. Armory Square hospital is

50. On August 7 (Feinberg), Pratt informed WW from Williamson, in Wayne County, N. Y., that he had arrived home late in July and was about to receive his discharge.

51. Pratt told WW that he had given "to no. 6 thare in the ward 70cts to give to

broken up, & all the sick & wounded have been taken away, or forwarded home. I have not seen No. 6. in Ward C. that you speak of, but shall no doubt meet him soon, & that little matter is all right any how.[51] Al, you was quite low, one time there in the Hospital—& the worst of it was you was down-hearted & homesick, & said nothing to any body—only when I came around, & we soon had quite a love toward each other, & no doubt that did you good—only I now regret that I did not do more for you, & come to see you oftener.

I am working now in the Attorney General's office. This is the place where the big southerners now come up to get pardoned—all the rich men & big officers of the reb army have to get special pardons, before they can buy or sell, or do any thing that will stand law—Sometimes there is a steady stream of them coming in here—old & young, men & women—some of the men are odd looking characters—I talk with them often, & find it very interesting to listen to their descriptions of things that have happened down south, & to how things are there now, &c. There are between 4 & 5000 pardons issued from this Office, but only about 200 have been signed by the President—The rest he is letting wait, till he gets good & ready—What I hear & see about Andrew Johnson, I think he is a *good man*—sometimes some of the letters he gets are sent over to this office to be answered—& occasionally that job falls to me—One of them was a letter a few days ago from a widow woman in Westfield, N Y. Her husband was in Texas when the war broke out, joined *our* army—& was killed by the rebels—they also confiscated his property in Texas, leaving his family helpless—this lady wrote to the President for aid, &c—I wrote the President's answer—telling her that she should have her husband's pension, which would be pretty good, as he was a captain—& that the rebs in Texas could not hold any such property, but that she could bring a suit & get it back, &c.—then put in a few words to cheer her up, &c.—

Aug 29.

Dear son, I did not finish my letter because I have not been able to get the little picture of Lincoln & Washington[52]—but I succeeded in getting one this morning—I send it as a little present to my dear boy, & I hope it will please him, for there is something about it that is both pleasing & solemn to me, though but a small picture—We are having a cloudy drizzly day here & heavy mist—There is nothing very new or special—

you" (Feinberg). Probably in reference to this matter, Pratt wrote on the side of WW's letter: "the Draft I will send Monday. I went to the bank Saturday but was closed."

52. In a postscript to his letter, Pratt had asked WW "to sennd me that potograph of Abe and Washington like yours if you can find them."

There was a big match played here yesterday between two base ball clubs, one from Philadelphia & the other a Washington club—& to-day another is to come off between a New York & the Philadelphia club I believe—thousands go to see them play[53]—

I keep well, & every body says I am getting fat & hearty—I live at the same place in M street, 468—only I have moved into the front room—it is pleasanter—I have my meals brought up to me—my landlady gives me very good grub, $32.50 a month—Well I must draw to a close, as the sheet is most full—When you write, to let me know how you are, & if you have rec'd this, direct to me, *Attorney General's office*, Washington D. C.

Now, Ally, I must bid you good by, & I send you my love, my darling boy, & also to your parents, for your sake—you must try to be a good young man & behave right & manly, for that is far more than worldly prosperity—Farewell, dear son,

Walt Whitman

165. *To Byron Sutherland*

ATTORNEY GENERAL'S OFFICE

Washington, Aug 26, *1865*.

Dear friend,

Your letter from Dewittville came safe, about nine days ago—& I have been expecting to hear from you since. Byron, I am still here, and as far as appears at present am likely to remain employed here, through the fall—but may ask for leave of absence for two or three weeks before long. There is a great stream of Southerners comes in here day after day, to get *pardoned*[54]—All the rich, and all high officers of the rebel army cannot do any thing, cannot buy or sell, &c. until they have special pardons —(that is hitting them where they *live*)—so they all send or come up here in squads, old & young, men & women—

They come to this office to get them—sometimes the rooms are filled

53. The Philadelphia Athletics defeated the Washington Nationals 87 to 12 on August 28. On the following day the Nationals played the New York Atlantics.

54. WW described the same scene in a memorandum dated August 22, printed in *November Boughs* (CW, VI, 217–218). WW corresponded with this soldier on occasions between 1865 and 1870. On September 20, 1868, he wrote to Sutherland: "I retain just the same friendship I formed for you the short time we were together, (but intimate,) in 1865" (Berg); see 303.

55. In his jottings for "Sept. 8, 9 &c.," WW noted that Johnson was signing the pardons "very freely of late. The President, indeed, as at present appears, has fix'd his mind on a very generous and forgiving course toward the return'd secessionists" (CW, VI, 219).

56. Sutherland replied on September 5 from Corry, a lumber and oil center in Pennsylvania. He was working on a farm and "managing to save $30 per month," had

with a curious gathering—I talk with them frequently, listen to their stories, descriptions, opinions &c. &c—As you know, almost every thing of that sort (& especially all odd characters) are interesting to me—Some 4 or 5000 pardons have been passed through here—but the President hasn't signed more than 200—The rest are all blank yet—Andy Johnson seems disposed to be in no hurry about it—What I learn & know about him (the President), I think he is a *good man.*[55]

Byron, there is nothing new or special with me. I have changed my back room to the front room, & have my meals sent up by the landlady—She gives me very good grub, & I like it, both room & board, ($32.50 a month)—The last ten or twelve days here have been very pleasant & sufficiently cool—after the melting hot summer—I am writing this in the office, by my big window, looking out on a splendid view across & down the Potomac for several miles, & over into Virginia, along Arlington heights—The trees, grass, river, & sky are splendid.

Well, my dear comrade, how are you, & how does it go? You must write & let me hear about you—& I shall want to know also if you get this. I wish it was so we could see each other, & be together once in a while. Well, Byron, I must close. I send you my love, & God bless you, dearest comrade—Write soon, dear son, & give me all particulars.[56]

Direct | Walt Whitman | Attorney Generals Office | Washington, D. C.

166. *To Ellen M. O'Connor*

ENDORSED: "Ans'd." ADDRESS: Mrs. E. M. O'Connor, | 326 H st. near Vermont av. | Washington, | D. C. POSTMARKS: New York | Oct | 12; Carrier | Oct | 13 | 1865(?) | (?)AM.

Brooklyn, | October 12, 1865.

My dear Nelly,[57]

I sit down home here in the front basement alone to write you a few lines. Mother is still at Burlington,[58] & I am waiting to hear from her,

"considerable leisure time" for "light reading," and expected during the winter to "learn a trade or go to School" (Feinberg). See also 167.

57. WW must have arrived in Brooklyn early in October for "a month's furlough" (see 167), and evidently returned to Washington on November 7 (see 169). He went to Brooklyn in order to supervise the binding of the *Sequel to Drum-Taps*, which was printed in Washington; see Allen, 353.

58. Mrs. Whitman arrived in Burlington, Vt., on September 5. She wrote to WW on that date, as well as on September 11, 21, and 27 (Trent). She "found hanna quite as well and better than i expected." Mrs. Whitman returned on October 16 (see 167). On July 16, Jeff had described a long letter which Heyde had written to his mother : "He says he shall leave Han, and go out west—I wish he was in Hell—Mother of course is considerably exercised about it—and thinks she will go on there and bring Han home" (Feinberg).

what she decides, about coming home—I shall probably go for her very shortly. I find it makes a mighty difference in my visit—(What is home without—&c)—

My dear little California is sick—infantile remittent fever—for the past week has just been lying quiet & pale, eats literally nothing—it is pitiful, & throws a gloom over every thing—doctor comes every day, & sometimes twice a day—when I ask him about the chances, he is rather non-committal—saying the disease in such a case as hers is expected to run fourteen days, before a turn for either better or worse—the fourteen days are up next Sunday—meanwhile she grows weaker & weaker—

I am middling well—My brother George has resumed carpentering[59] —he is well, & looks fine—I see him every day—the rest of the folks all well. I send my love to Charles Eldridge—same to Ashton—when you write tell me the latest from the baby & Mrs. Ashton. Send William the enclosed piece[60]—it is one of those I spoke of—When you write direct to me, *Portland av. near Myrtle.*

Walt.

167. *To Byron Sutherland*

TRANSCRIPT.

Brooklyn, October 15, 1865.

Dear Friend:[61]

I write you a few lines to let you know that I have come home on a month's furlough—there is nothing very new or special with me. I am still employed in the Attorney Gen'l's office, & shall return there before the middle of next month. I often think about you, & wish it was so we could have each others society frequently—Byron, I don't know certain whether I have written to you since I rec'd your last letter or not—but it came safe, & was glad to hear from you—write soon, my dear comrade, & direct

59. After toying with several offers, including an appointment in the New York Custom House, George decided to return to housebuilding. "I am quite sure," Jeff wrote to WW on September 29, "that if he can keep devoted to his present undertaking he will make a handsome fortune in 8 or ten years—he certainly has the prospect of it" (Feinberg). George had been mustered out in July. Nothing came of his plans to remain a commissioned officer in the regular army.

60. A review of WW in the London *Leader* for June 30, 1860. O'Connor was so impressed that he planned to incorporate "a great deal of it" into his manuscript, *The Good Gray Poet* (13–14), which he was revising when he wrote on October 19: "But oh, Walt, the literary shortcomings of it oppress me. It is not the thing that should be said of your book—not the thing that it is in even me to say" (Feinberg; Traubel,

your letter to me, Portland Av. near Myrtle, Brooklyn, New York. Soon as I get back to Washington, I will send you word.

Here in this place & New York, I go around quite a good deal—it is a great excitement to go around the busiest parts of New York, Broadway, & the wharves, & great ferries—The oceans of people, the trucks & omnibuses, go all jammed together, & such bustle & noise—I like it much for a few hours now and then—but don't want to be continually in it—I have made an addition to the little book "Drum Taps,"[62] & will send you one of the perfect copies soon—we had a fine long pouring rain here all last night—I am writing this home at my mother's, in the front basement sitting by the stove, as the weather is cool—Mother is absent at Burlington, Vt, but returns to-morrow—the others have gone to church, etc—so I am entirely alone to-day—so I thought I couldn't do better than write to you. Dear comrade, I hope you are well & doing well—write soon, boy—from your loving friend and comrade—

Walt Whitman.

168. *To Ellen M. O'Connor*

ENDORSED: "Ans'd." ADDRESS: Mrs. E. M. O'Connor | 326 H st. near Vermont av. | Washington | D. C. POSTMARK: New York | Oct | 20.

Brooklyn | October 20 | 1865

Dear friend,

Your letter came right—& was glad to hear from you, Nelly, & Charles Eldridge & dear little Jeannie—(I will not add William because I did not hear any thing about him.)[63]

Nelly, the skies are brighter here than when I wrote you last. Little sis is so much better, that she has been twice brought down here to the front basement, & has in every respect improved much since last Saturday—Then my mother arrived home last Tuesday—and now it looks something like *home* in reality—I am quite well—

Drum Taps will be bound (a small edition) before you get this—& will

I, 85). At this time O'Connor had not found a publisher for his polemic.

61. See 165. 62. *Sequel to Drum-Taps;* see 166.

63. William's letter of October 19, from New Ipswich, N. H., had not reached WW. O'Connor submitted a review of *Drum-Taps* to the New York *Times* in November, but, according to William Swinton's letter to O'Connor on November 27, it arrived too late to appear in the newspaper. John Swinton, on January 11, 1866, wrote to O'Connor: "I was sorry for it [the review]; and the matter should have been treated otherwise had I been managing editor." Because of poor health, Swinton was now on the editorial staff of the *Times* and had "no control of such matters" (Feinberg).

next week be put in the hands of a New York publisher & launched on the market—at least that's my design at present[64]—

When you write tell me all about William—My mother returns bringing cheerful intelligence upon the whole—& is herself in splendid condition—havn't seen her look & apparently feel better in many years—My brother George (or did I tell you?) is working again at his trade & has grand health—Love & Farewell—

Walt.

169. *To Andrew Kerr*[65]

Brooklyn | October 29, 1865.

Andy, my dear comrade—I rec'd yours of 24th, with enclosure of letter. Two others previously.

I am sincerely sorry for Mr. Stewart.

Andy, my programme is, to vote here early Tuesday forenoon,[66] & then start immediately for Washington—So Love—& farewell—till we meet, dear boy.

Walt Whitman

(I wish you to say to Mr. Ashton, however, that if there is any pressure in the clerical duties of the Office, I will come *immediately*, if needed.)

170. *To a Soldier*[67] [*Late 1865?*]

TRANSCRIPT.

. . . Blue coats are getting quite scarce in Washington. I envy you the fresh country air, healthy influences, and, I doubt not, the fine scenery and quiet. I am in that part of the office where pardons are attended to. There is a stream of rebels passing in all the time to be pardoned. All of the Confederates who are worth more than $20,000 in property have to have a special pardon, and all who have been officers of the rank of Brigadier-General and upwards the same. There are some real characters among them, and you know I have a fancy for anything out of the ordinary.

64. Announcements of the publication of *Drum-Taps* by Bunce & Huntington appeared in the New York *Tribune* on October 28, and in *The Round Table* on November 4; see F. DeWolfe Miller, *WWR*, v (1959), 15, and also his edition of *Drum-Taps* (1959), l. The *Sequel* was printed by Gibson Brothers of Washington, who issued a receipt to WW on October 2 for 1,000 copies (Feinberg; Miller, xlviii). On September 20, Abraham Simpson wrote: "When I receive your extra sheets will then bind your 500 'Drum Taps'" (Feinberg; Miller, xlviii). Simpson on October 20 acknowledged $50

A good many women come up to Washington to look after pardons. All are dressed in deep black. Then there are bushels of applications arriving by every mail. When they are recommended by the Provisional Government or by some well known Union men they get them. There are 3,000 or 4,000 waiting for the President's signature now. He is not in any hurry to sign them.

paid on account for binding 300 copies and, on November 1, billed WW for 500 copies (Feinberg).

65. Kerr was, according to the 1866 Directory, a clerk in the Attorney General's office.

66. The elections of November 7 resulted in what the New York *Times* described as a "Great Republican Victory."

67. See 160.

1866

171. *To a Soldier*[1] [*Early 1866*]

TRANSCRIPT.

I keep stout as ever, my face red and a great beard just the same. I am writing this in the office by a bay window with a splendid view of the Potomac and Arlington Heights. I send my love to you, darling boy.

172. *To William D. O'Connor* [*1.25. 1866*][2]

ENDORSED: "Jan. 25, 1866." ADDRESS: Mr. O'Connor.

TREASURY DEPARTMENT,
OFFICE OF THE LIGHT HOUSE BOARD.

Washington *186*

May come around & take a cup of tea with you after dinner.

Walt

173. *To Louisa Van Velsor Whitman*

ATTORNEY GENERAL'S OFFICE,

Washington, March 23 *1866*

Dearest Mother,

I ordered the draft to be paid to you, of course. All you have to do is to go down & present it—they may ask you who you expected money from, & where.

I dont know, but I expect Jeff or Mat would do just as well.

Walt.

1866

1. See 160.

2. The only evidence for the date is the endorsement, which appears to be in O'Connor's hand.

3. George B. Lincoln.

4. Hannah's letter of March 24 (LC) was almost cheerful, although she was "lonesome" and looked forward to WW's promised visit in the summer.

5. On March 27(?), Mrs. Whitman added in a postscript: "i got all the letters you have sent."

6. According to Mrs. Whitman's letter of March 27(?), George was alarmed about his business prospects: "george is building his shop and he gets veary tired. he had never

Mr. Lincoln,[3] the post master, knows about the letters & money being stolen—the Post office here has conferred with him on the subject.

174. *To Louisa Van Velsor Whitman*

ATTORNEY GENERAL'S OFFICE,

Washington, March 28, *1866*

Dearest Mother,

Your letter come safe this morning, enclosing Han's[4]—I was very glad to get both—Mother, I wrote you three letters last week, the second one was in a big envelope, & the last was a small one you ought to have got Saturday—I feel quite unsettled how to send any thing[5]—the letters seem to be so liable to be stolen—but I shall certainly fix it so as you get something every week, mother, some how—Seems to me George's arrangements, & the buying of the lots, &c. are very good—also the shop—As Jeff says, he must have patience[6]—Love to Matty & the children—& good bye for present, mother dear,

Walt.

175. *To Louisa Van Velsor Whitman*

ATTORNEY GENERAL'S OFFICE,

Washington, | Monday | April 23, *1866*

Dearest Mother,

I received your letter on Saturday—I am well as usual—shall write to Han to-day—Mother, write soon as convenient after you get this, as I shall want to know if it reached you all right—I have no doubt George will do well in his business—of course there will be slack times once in a while—I have seen the "Radical"[7]—Mother, I sometimes think the old letter carrier you had, must be the thief[8]—We have fine weather, plenty of rain to keep down the dust. We had the greatest black procession here last Thursday—I didn't think there was so many darkeys, (especially

aught to have commenced to work at his trade he says. he had aught to have staid in the army" (Trent).

7. A favorable review of *Drum-Taps* appeared in *The Radical: A Monthly Magazine, Devoted to Religion*, I (April, 1866), 311–312: "The author of 'Leaves of Grass,' is as unquestionably a true poet, as the greatest of his contemporaries. He seems to us more purely permeated with the subtile essence of poetry than almost any other." Anne Gilchrist's "A Woman's Estimate of Walt Whitman" also appeared in this journal, VII (1870), 345–359.

8. See 173 and 174.

wenches,) in the world—it was the anniversary of emancipation in this District—

Mother, you must try to take the moving [cooly][9]—Well I believe that is all this time—Good bye, dearest mother—Love to sister Mat & the little girls.

Walt.

176. *To Louisa Van Velsor Whitman*

ATTORNEY GENERAL'S OFFICE,

Saturday afternoon, | *Washington*, April 28, *1866*

Dearest Mother,

I got both your letters—the last one has just come—It is too bad to be so troubled about a house—but then, Mother, there might be troubles a great deal worse than that—Mother, when you get there, & feel able, you must write me a few lines, & give me the No. of the house, & the right address, &c.

Well, mother, you must all try to get along the best you can. Try to take it easy as possible.

Walt

177. *To Thomas Jefferson Whitman*

ATTORNEY GENERAL'S OFFICE,

Washington, May 7, *1866.*

Dear brother Jeff,

By Mother's letter I have heard about the moving & the new quarters—Mother says that she is glad they are no worse, under all the

9. The Whitmans moved to 840 Pacific Street; see 185.

10. Henry Stanbery (1803–1881) was appointed Attorney General on July 23, 1866, and served until March 12, 1868, when he resigned to serve as President Johnson's chief counsel in the impeachment proceedings. When, at the conclusion of the trial, Johnson renominated Stanbery, the Senate refused to confirm him. Failing eyesight—to which WW referred in 197 and 200—forced Stanbery to retire from legal practice in 1878. Speaking to Traubel in 1888 (III, 156), WW affirmed his fondness for Stanbery.

11. Count Adam Gurowski (1805–1866), a Polish exile, published an eccentric three-volume *Diary* (1862–1866), a day-by-day account of the war written with a marked partiality toward extreme abolitionists. The Count was a colorful figure: he covered his lost eye with a "green blinder," and "he had a Roman head . . . a powerful top-knot, in and out: people always stopped to look at him" (Traubel, III, 79, 96). O'Connor, who apparently Englished Gurowski's manuscripts (see the letter from Gurowski to O'Connor in Feinberg), reported to WW, on August 13, 1864, that "he is a madman with lucid intervals"—he had attempted "to discipline the firemen with a pistol" (Feinberg; Traubel, III, 340). WW maintained to Traubel, in 1888, that "he was truly a remarkable, almost phenomenal, man," and that "he was, no doubt, very crazy, but also very sane" (Traubel, III, 79, 340). Mrs. O'Connor related in a letter on November 24,

circumstances. I enclose an envelope to mother, with a little money in it. As you see, I am still in the same place, with easy times enough, & a good place as I could expect. The Attorney General[10] is absent now in Kentucky. There is not much work. I can't tell whether I shall keep on here, or not. There is nothing at present that looks like a change—I feel quite well this spring—but a clerk's life here is not very interesting—I went down last Thursday to Mt Vernon, 16 miles down the Potomac—I think it is the pleasantest spot & farm I ever saw—went through the house & grounds &c—I was very glad I went—Yesterday we had the funeral here of a man you must have seen mentioned in the papers, old Count Gurowski. I have been very well acquainted with him since I have lived here—he was a strange old man, a great lord in his own country, Poland, owned 30,000 serfs & great estates—an exile for conspiring against the government—he knew every thing & growled & found fault with everybody—but was always very courteous to me, & spoke very highly of me in his book, his "Diary," printed last winter—his funeral was simple but very impressive—all the big radicals were there[11]—

The fight between Congress & the President is still going on—I think the President is rather afraid of going too far against Congress, for Stevens & the rest of 'em are very determined.[12]

My hospitals are dwindled down to a small force—but there are plenty of cases to occupy me a couple of visits a week—I always go Sunday, & sometimes in the middle of the week—Julius Mason[13] is here in barracks yet—Jeff, I wish I could now & then be home & see you all, even if was only a couple of hours—

Give my best respects to Mr. Lane,[14] and the Doctor[15]—I send my love to Mat & the little girls. Write & tell me all about home affairs, & how

1863, that the Count had said to her recently: "My Gott, I did not know that [WW] was such a poet, tell him so, I have been trying every where to find him to tell him myself" (Feinberg). In the last volume of the *Diary*, Gurowski placed WW's name in the first category of his threefold evaluation of persons "mentioned in this volume": "Praise," "Half and Half," and "Blame." The Count referred in his entry for April 18, 1864, to WW as among "the most original and genuine American hearts and minds" (187). In a footnote (372–373), appended September 12, 1865, Gurowski abused Harlan, who had "shown himself to be animated by a spirit of narrow-minded persecution which would honor the most fierce Spanish or Roman inquisitor." Gurowski was recently praised by Robert Penn Warren, in Malcolm Cowley, ed., *Writers at Work*, (1958), 189. See also LeRoy Fischer, *Mississippi Valley Historical Review*, XXXVI (1949–1950), 415–434, and *DAB*, Supplement I.

12. Thaddeus Stevens (1792–1868), fiery Congressman from Pennsylvania, violently opposed Johnson's moderate policy toward the South. He introduced the impeachment resolution in February, 1868.

13. See 152.

14. See 31.

15. Dr. Ruggles; see 42.

George is getting along—dear old Mother, as she gets older & older, I think about her every day & night—

Walt.

178. *To Louisa Van Velsor Whitman*

ATTORNEY GENERAL'S OFFICE,

Monday, | *Washington*, May 14, *1866*.

Dearest Mother,

I hope you are entirely over that sickness of last week—When you write you must tell me—and also how you all get along with the new quarters—I think you must be pretty badly cramped—All goes on as usual with me—I spent yesterday afternoon at the Quarter Master's hospital—it is the old dregs & leavings of the war, old wounds, brokendown sick, discharged soldiers, who have no place to go, &c.—It is a shame that the Government has provided no place for such cases, of the Volunteer Army—they are just taken in here, to prevent them dying in the street—others go to the poor house—a good many break down after discharge, & have no pensions—& what is $8 a month these days anyhow?

Mother, have [you] heard any thing lately from Han? I write to her every now & then—It is very pleasant weather here, quite cool to-day—Good by, dear mother,

Walt.

179. *To a Soldier*[16]

TRANSCRIPT.

Attorney General's Office, | May 16, 1866.

. . . As to me, I lead rather a dull life here. I wish you were nearer, that we might be together frequently. I do not associate much with the depart-

16. See 160.

17. Hugo Eicholtz was listed in the Washington Directory of 1869 and in one of WW's address books (*LC* #109). He evidently lived with his mother, a dressmaker.

18. Sergeant Hiram W. Frazee, Second New York Artillery, was wounded in "one of the last battles near Petersburg" (*CW*, VI, 236).

19. Probably Dr. Thomas C. Smith, a Washington physician.

20. Mrs. Whitman informed WW on June 7 that she had sent "a short note to the honorable mr Heyde as i received a veery lengthy epistle from him the other day. i really think the world never produced such another man or devil. i think he is nearest the last named. i wrote very short with no compliment that i was not surprised at his wishing to get rid of han, that he had expressed that wish many times before this letter" (Trent).

In a letter to WW in April, Heyde had accused Mrs. Whitman of fomenting trouble between him and his wife:

"Much of this difficulty has arisen from the miserable teachings of her mother, who

ment clerks, yet many appear to be good fellows enough. The contest between Congress and the President is quite exciting. I go up to the Capitol and listen to the speeches and arguments. Sometimes I feel as if one side had the best of it and then the other. Well, my dear comrade, I believe I have told you all the news—of Eicholtz,[17] the German sergeant with the bad compound fracture, of Frazee[18] and Dr. Smith.[19]

180. *To Louisa Van Velsor Whitman*

ATTORNEY GENERAL'S OFFICE,

Washington, June 12, *1866*.

Dearest mother,

I rec'd your letter of last Thursday—I suppose you got one from me the Saturday before, with some envelopes in, & $1—Well, mother, you have got a letter from that good for nothing pup again[20]—it is too bad to be worried so—but one is powerless to do any thing, under present circumstances—I hope George will do well, in the houses, if he & the others put them up on Portland av.—I see there are cases of cholera once in a while in New York—you must all be careful of yourselves—it is very healthy here this summer—I havn't been troubled by the heat yet—my head is much better—

Mother, I must tell you I am having some *new shirts* made—quite an event—I can't hardly believe it when I think how those old ones you fixed, & fixed again, have held out—but, poor old things, they have got played out pretty well—why I believe I have got one or two that you fixed for me when I went to Boston there six years ago, & more—I have 'em made in the same way as ever, & I think they are going to be very good—I expect to have half a dozen—so you see I *am* coming out—had quite a clearing out the other day, collected all my old tattered duds & socks, & boots &

enjoined upon her, when we were first married, not to perform these little services for me, which naturally would suggest themselves to a kind and considerate wife, and endear her to her husband: Because I might be spoild, by it.

"Mrs Whitman has been toward me, a silly old woman—for why I do not know—I never was under obligations to her for anything. If she brought a half loaf of bread to my house, she took butter or tea away in return for it, and I never had a meal at her table that I did not pay for. But Mrs Whitman never did possess a particle of honest frankness—on the contrary, in one instance, I will not here mention, a more than mean, a wicked duplicity toward myself.

"Perhaps I would not look upon 'Leaves of Grass' with so much melancholy regard, if I was not experiencing a practical version of it: Irregular—disorderly: indifferent, or defiant—the lower animal instincts—no accountability, no moral sense or principle—No true, inherent, practical sympathy for anything; myself; disappointments, or endeavours. Nothing of me, or of the future to arise for me, out of my labour, and progressions" (Trent; Gohdes and Silver, 222–223).

slippers &c &c. into a great heap—and when Sally, our black girl, brought up my breakfast, I told her she could have 'em all, if she wanted 'em—she was most tickled to death—took 'em all off home—there was nothing but what was all give out, though—

There is nothing new with me in my affairs—if things would only work so that I could get a higher grade, with more pay, it would come very acceptable—but here I remain, in the same way as at first—however I am very glad to have what I have—Tell Jeff I should like to see him very much—I think he would find it pleasant to come here for a few days, even this season—Well, dear mother, my sheet is full—love to all—

Walt.

181. *To Louisa Van Velsor Whitman*

ADDRESS: Mrs. Louisa Whitman | 840 Pacific st. bet. Washington & | Grand av's. | Brooklyn, | New York.
POSTMARK: Washington, D. C. | Jun | 26(?) | Free.

ATTORNEY GENERAL'S OFFICE,

Washington, June 26, *1866*.

Dearest mother,

Well, I suppose you have the hot weather too—it has been very hot here for the last four or five days, but I have got along very well—I think of you every day, with the work & the heat, &c.—I believe you said that it was good air around there in Pacific st., well I should think that was one great advantage over Portland av. any how. Mother, I rec'd your letter of last week—I do not go much to the hospital this hot weather—I think I feel better than usual now for a couple of weeks past—if I can only get through the summer as well as I am, I shall be satisfied—Mrs. Grayson gives me plenty of good vegetables, peas, string beans, squash & new potatoes, with fruit now & then, which is better than too much meat—Old Mrs. Mix[21] is well as usual—the house is very pleasant this weather—as cool as it can be any where—

I should like to hear from Han, but I suppose she is getting along in the same old way—As I am writing this letter at my table, the celebrated Mrs. Cobb[22] has just come in, to see about some rebel pardon, some

21. Mrs. Edward B. Grayson, 468 M North, took in boarders. Her mother, Mrs. Mary Mix, a widow, lived with her. Mrs. Grayson died on January 7, 1867; see 213. After her daughter's death, Mrs. Mix left Washington; see 216.

22. Mrs. Lucy Livingston Cobb became notorious when she brought a court action against General Lafayette C. Baker, chief of the National Detective Police, who ordered her arrested for her dealings in the pardons racket. Baker, who was no friend of Johnson, implied that she was intimate with the President. Baker defended his actions at length

profitable job for her, I suppose—she is a great piece—she is what most people would call a very pretty little woman—dresses gay, &c—but she has too brazen & silly a way, ever to be taken for a lady by any one that knows—she has got lots of pardons, & probably made a fortune—is half the time at the President's—is not a good character. This Washington is a great place—you see how funny the world is governed—& lots of queer doings that outsiders never dream of—

Well, mother, my new shirts are done, half a dozen, very satisfactory—I havn't bought any new clothes this summer except a new hat, a big brim, light drab—makes me look like a southern planter, but is very light & comfortable—Mother, I wish you could sit here by the window I have so often mentioned, & have the cool breeze blow on you, as it is now, & the trees & river & hills beyond, so pleasant—

Dear mother, you must try to take things moderate—because folks that worry & overdo are apt to get the cholera, you know—I hope brother Jeff feels all right again[23]—how I should like to see him, & all of you.

Walt.

182. *To Louisa Van Velsor Whitman*

ATTORNEY GENERAL'S OFFICE,

Washington, | Friday, | June 29, *1866.*

Dearest Mother,

I rec'd your letter this morning—I hope you have had as pleasant a change in the weather, as we have here—it rained yesterday & the night before—& to-day the weather is just right—cool enough—poor old Mrs. Mix[24] is quite sick—Hector Tyndale[25] has been to see me again—always talks about you—When in the army he had a very bad wound in the head—was a year getting over it—

I think George must mind how he exposes himself to the sun, or gets overheated—I find I have to maneuvre through the very hot days, like a general in fight—I carry an umbrella, and if the sun gets to fall on me good & strong, any of the real hot days, my head gets swimming, & I have to stop in the street, or rather get inside some store or something, & sit down—I have had just that happen to me twenty times—so now I am very

in *History of the United States Secret Service* (1867), 589–693; but see also Hugh McCulloch, *Men and Measures of Half a Century* (1887), 393–394.

23. On June 7, Mrs. Whitman reported that "Jeff looks bad, he dont complain but i think he ought to have a month of leave from all cares" (Trent).

24. See 181. 25. See 12.

slow & careful—I think George might find a suit of good blue navy flannel first-rate for the hot weather—I am wearing mine—the suit I wore last summer—I never had any thing for heat that suited me so well—

Jeff, I hope you had, (or will have,) a first rate time on your fishing excursion—I should like greatly to be with you—

Well good bye for this time, dear mother—I send you some envelopes. Love to sister Mat, & the little girls.

Walt.

183. *To Louisa Van Velsor Whitman*

ATTORNEY GENERAL'S OFFICE,

Washington, July 2, *1866*.

Dearest mother,

I got your letter of last Thursday—I wrote to Han two or three days ago—poor Mrs. Mix is very bad—she has her old complaint neuralgia—she suffers very much indeed—it makes me almost sick, some spells she has, the agony is terrible, & her screams are heartrending—fortunately her nights are comparatively easy—it is doubtful if she recovers—

We are having delightful weather—just right—I went to the Post Hospital[26] yesterday, Sunday, & who do you think was one of the first persons I found there—Jo. Velsor,[27] poor fellow, he has had jaundice pretty bad, but is now getting very near well—so he goes out & around—he expects to go to work again in a day or two—he has work in the Quartermasters Dept. driving an ambulance—

Mother, I suppose you got the letter Saturday last with the envelopes—

I hope you have as pleasant weather in Brooklyn as we have had here for a week past, & now—

It is generally expected Congress will adjourn the last of this month, & then there will be some high old times in politics & the Departments—most of us think that A[ndrew] J[ohnson] is only waiting for that, to lay around him & kick up his heels at a great rate. Well, we shall see what

26. After the war, all the hospitals except this one were converted to other purposes. Armory Square Hospital, as WW observed in 238, became a clothing depot.

27. Undoubtedly Joseph A. Velsor, who was later listed in an address book (*LC* #108), and who had a drugstore in New York after 1868.

28. Jimmy and George were presumably Andrew's children.

29. This is the first letter in a correspondence that continued until WW's death. It should be noted that the text given here is hypothetical, since it is based on excerpts from Mrs. Barrus' volumes; see "A List of Manuscript Sources."

30. Probably WW sent this issue of the *Atlantic Monthly* because of Lowell's poem "To J. B." According to an annotation in the Harvard Library copy of the magazine, J. B. is John Bartlett, the compiler of quotations. One of Burroughs' friends,

comes to pass—but I guess the Republicans are just every bit as ferocious as he is—they won't back down an inch—

Mother, the small bills I send you, you might distribute, (or get some fire crackers or something,) for Ed, & Jimmy & George[28]—not forgetting Hat & sis—

Walt.

184. *To John Burroughs*[29] [*7.2. 1866*]

TRANSCRIPT.

I went up to your house this morning and took a look at the garden —Everything growing first rate—potatoes, tomatoes, corn, cabbages, and all—I guess upon the whole the garden never looked better at this time of year. We have had opportune rains—I inquired about the cow, and received a favorable report. . . .

John, about coming, I am not able to say anything decisive in this letter. . . . Up in your Bureau all seems to go on as usual . . . John, I send you the July Atlantic.[30] . . .

I am feeling hearty and in good spirits—go around more than usual—go to such doings as base-ball matches and the music Performances in the Public grounds—Marine Band, etc. . . .

I hope your parents are well—I wish you to give them my love—tho' I don't know them, I hope to one of these days—remember me to the wife, also.

I am writing this by my window in the office—the breeze is blowing moderate, and the view down the river and off along Virginia hills opposite is most delightful—the pardon clerks are middling busy—I have plenty of leisure, as usual—I spent yesterday afternoon at the Hospital, and took tea in the evening at O'Connor's.

Piatt[31] is trying to get transferred to New York, to the Custom House—Well, good by for present, you dear friend, and God bless you and wife, and bring you both safe back—

Walt

interestingly, was Joel Benton, a poet and reviewer; see Barrus, 18. The magazine also contains an account of Ferrero's (and therefore George's) siege at Knoxville.

31. John J. Piatt met WW on New Year's Day, 1863. Piatt was a versifier and author of *Poems by Two Friends* in collaboration with W. D. Howells; see Barrus, 43. On February 12, 1866, he wrote a sympathetic account of WW and *The Good Gray Poet* for the Columbus (Ohio) *Morning Journal;* see Barrus, 10, and Kennedy, *The Fight of a Book for the World* (1926), 17. Burroughs quoted from Piatt's article in *Notes on Walt Whitman, As Poet and Person* (1867), 84–85. The Washington Directory of 1866 listed Piatt as a clerk in the Treasury Department; according to Barrus (12), he was later librarian of the House of Representatives and then consul at Cork.

185. *To Abby H. Price*

ADDRESS: Abby H. Price, | 279 East 55th st. | New York City. POSTMARK: Washington | Jul | 30 | Free.

ATTORNEY GENERAL'S OFFICE,

Washington, July 30, *1866*.

My dear friend,

I write mainly to see whether I have got the right address—to find whether this reaches you—If so please give me an answer as soon as convenient.

As you see, I am still in Washington—have a small place in the Attorney General's office—pleasant, agreeable, &c. but pretty moderate pay. My health has been good—& I have got through the hot weather all right —It is a long while since I have heard from you—& indeed it is nearly a year since I have been in New York—Direct to me Attorney Gen's. office, Washington—I expect to come north soon for a short time—Love to Helen, Emily, Arthur & all.

Walt.

Mother is living at 840 Pacific st. bet. Washington & Grand av's Brooklyn.

186. *To Abby H. Price*

ADDRESS: Mrs. Abby H. Price, | 279 East 55th street, | New York City. POSTMARK: Washington D. C. | Aug | 4.

ATTORNEY GENERAL'S OFFICE,

Washington, Aug. 1, *1866*.

Dear friend,

I have just received your letter, & respond immediately, because by what you have written, it may be that you can do me a great favor—I have obtained leave of absence, & am coming to New York, principally to bring out a new & much better edition of Leaves of Grass complete—that *unkillable* work!—Mother's apartments in Pacific st are very limited, & I had decided to get a lodging room in N. Y. or Brooklyn, so as not to incommode my folks at home—taking my meals at the restaurants, & home &c— leaving my time free for my work &c—Now *have you such a room for me*, at a fair price? I hope you have, for that would be very agreeable—Your going off for a week or two would not make any difference—as a lodging is my main object—write *immediately* & let me know, as my leave of absence will probably date from Monday next, 6th inst—

Mrs. O'Connor has gone west, with her mother, for the summer—Wm O'Connor is well—We all speak of you—The weather is almost perfect here now-a-days—I am writing this by my window in the south front of the Treasury building, looking down the beautiful grounds in front, and across & down the Potomac for miles, & across to the green hills all along Arlington Heights, very beautiful & cool—a view of great expanse, & very comforting every way—also a pleasant breeze coming in steadily from the river.

I have an agreeable situation here—labor moderate—& plenty of leisure—My principal work is to make (from rough drafts) the letters, answers, law opinions, &c that go from the Attorney General to the President, or to the Secretary of State, & the other Heads of Departments—The rule is that none but such officers as just named have a right to require information from Attorney Generals—So you see I have to do only with the big men—

There is one regular Soldiers Hospital left here, in K street—I go there once or twice every week—it is still a great privilege to go—You would be amazed, as well as distressed, to know how many old wounds are lingering along yet—youth & hope struggling against fate—but the latter, alas! almost always conquering at last—it is indeed a great privilege to soothe the lingering days & months of many of these cases.

Walt.

Mother is quite well, & comfortable—considering her age—brothers, sisters & the children, all well, at last accounts.

187. *To Andrew Kerr*

New York City | August 25, 1866.

Dear friend,[32]

The letters arrive safe—I have received three—& I am much obliged to you, Andy, for your attention. I am having good times here, rather quiet—My book is being printed—gets along rather slowly. I ride out on Long Island, & up New York, Central Park, &c. occasionally—the country is beautiful now—I take a walk on Broadway almost every afternoon—then sometimes a sail on the river or bay—so you see I am enjoying

32. See 169.

myself in my way—with three or four hours work every day reading my proofs, &c—

Andy, I suppose you are all getting along as usual—I enclose a line to Mat,[33] which please give him—I send my love to you, Frank,[34] Mat & Lewis—& for present, Farewell.

Walt

P.S. Andy, should any more letters come, you may direct them to me at 279 East 55th st. New York City[35]—I expect to return about 12th Sept.

Finally, I must not neglect to impress upon your youthful mind—also upon that of Mr. F. Stitt—the original & solemn advice, "Be *virtuous*—& you will be happy."

—from your Christian friend—*Walter.*

188. *To William D. O'Connor* *8.26. [1866]*

ADDRESS: William D. O'Connor | Light House Board —Treasury Depart- | ment. | Washington, | D. C. POSTMARK: New York | Aug | 26.

279 East 55th st. New York. | Sunday morning, Aug. 26.

Dear friend,

Your letter came safe, & was indeed welcome. I will leave out "orgies" since you dislike it so much. I have been much delayed in the printing—but I believe they have now fairly got to work, & will go on expeditiously. I found a printer, Chapin,[36] 24 Beekman st., who was getting new type of the kind I wanted, & I waited for him—He engages to have the composition & presswork done in from two to three weeks. It will be typographically about the same as Drum-Taps, only about five times as thick—Upon calling on Huntington & Son,[37] I found that Drum-Taps has sold somewhat better than I anticipated—I was treated very courteously, & they promised to advertise D. T. & push it this fall—I did not say any thing about the coming new Leaves—but may propose to

33. Matthew F. Pleasants, who later became chief clerk in the Attorney General's office.

34. Frank N. Stitt was pardon clerk in the same office.

35. WW was staying at Mrs. Price's home; see 186.

36. William E. Chapin was the printer of the 1867 edition of *Leaves of Grass.*

37. F. J. Huntington & Company, 459 Broome Street; see also 168.

38. Mrs. Whitman had written on May 31: "he has got to be very economical, very different from when he was in the army, but every body changes, some for the better and some for the worser" (Trent). She also had noted that "he appears to be very much

Messrs. H. to be the agents before I return—I shall probably return about the 12th of September—

When I arrived here, I found my mother & the rest lately moved (again) in a large old house out in Brooklyn suburbs, & in a good deal of confusion &c.—Mother was not well, & seemed generally fagged out—But since then things have come round somewhat—Mother has improved a good deal—yesterday felt quite like herself again—I spend three or four hours there every day—Jeff is very well, & George pretty well—in the latter I can see that campaigning & Danville prison have left their mark[38]—I am stopping at Mrs. Price's, am most pleasantly situated in personal comforts, &c.—Mrs. P. has asked much about you—hopes to see you yet—The weather here is really perfect—I have been to the Central Park, had a long ride & foot ramble—the place is probably looking its best just now—I go out on Broadway occasionally & take a walk, or a ride on the omnibus—I am received by the drivers with renewed rapture—it is more marked than ever.

I havn't learned any thing worth mentioning about literary persons or doings here. I doubt whether the article will be accepted in the Galaxy[39]—don't know who edits it—I send my love to John Burroughs—Also the same to Charles Eldridge—I hope to be able to write to Nelly—I wish you when you write to say I send my love to her. And now for a while, my dear friend, Farewell.

Walt.

189. *To John Burroughs* [*9.10. 1866*]

TRANSCRIPT.

The book is going to suit me pretty well—it will make a volume of 500 pages, size and style &c fully equal to 'Drum Taps'—I shall feel glad enough when it is completed—I have a constant struggle with the printers—They are good fellows and willing enough—but it seems impossible to prevent them making lots of ridiculous errors—it is my constant dread that the book will be disfigured in that way—though we have got along pretty well thus far.[40] . . .

taken with some one," and, on June 7, "i think george will get married" (Trent). George, however, did not marry until 1871.

39. *The Galaxy* was edited by W. C. and F. P. Church; see 242. When W. C. Church wrote on June 13 to O'Connor (Feinberg), requesting an article, he suggested that the magazine publish Burroughs' "Walt Whitman and His 'Drum-Taps,' " which appeared on December 1; *The Galaxy*, II (1866), 606–615.

40. According to Barrus, WW in this letter also asked Burroughs to send him a draft for $100.

190. *To Andrew Kerr*

New York, Sept. 10, 1866.

Dear Andy,[41]

I rec'd your letter last Saturday—I intended to return day after to-morrow, but shall not be able to, till the last of the week, or the early part of next week. The reason is that my book, which is a little more than half done, does not get along as fast as the printers agreed—& if I do not stay & finish it, (the supervision of it,) it will be botched & full of blunders.

I am in good health & all goes well. Andy, dear boy, I hope my delay of a few days will not put you out—Write to me, & tell me about the office, & my friends there. Don't forward any letters that come after Friday next, but put them in my drawer. Once more—I send my love to you & all.

Walt

191. *To Mr. Baker*[42] *9.25.* [*1866*]

TRANSCRIPT.

Mr. O'Connor's address is Wm. D. O'Connor, Light House Board, Treasury Dep't. Washington, D. C.

Yours respectfully,

Walt Whitman

191.1 *To Alfred Pratt*

ATTORNEY GENERAL'S OFFICE,

Washington, Sept. 27, *1866*

Dear boy, & comrade,[43]

I am not only alive, but as well & hearty as ever I was—& more [than] that, I often think about you, Alfred, & retain the same friendship that we formed when I used to sit down on your bed when you was so low in the hospital. If I hadn't got your letter of 23d, I should likely have written to you very soon, of my own accord, for I thought about you the last few weeks in particular. I have been home in Brooklyn the last two months, to see my mother, & pay a visit to New York, &c. and I only re-

41. See 187.

42. This may be—though there is no certainty—the man to whom WW wrote in 20.

43. See 164.1 and 164.2.

turned day before yesterday. I am still employed in this Department, shall probably remain here through the winter, (although nothing is certain now-days)—Washington is rather dull—no more soldiers around like there used to be—no more patrols marching around the streets—no more great racks of hospitals—I get along well enough in this city in pleasant weather, when one can go around, but it's rough in bad weather.

Al, I got the picture, dear boy, & I have it yet, & take good care of it, & take a good look at it every now & then—I think it is a good likeness. It is now a year ago since you sent it—you spoke in that letter of your parents—You must give my love to them, & if it should be practicable I should like much to make them a call—but yet it does not seem likely as things are at present. But I wonder whether we shall ever come together again, you & I, my loving soldier boy. O how much comfort it would be to me, if things were so that we could have each other's society—for I think so much of such things.

I am writing this at my table by a big window in the Office, where I can look out & see the Potomac away down to Alexandria, & across all up & down Arlington Heights, & near at hand the grounds south of the President's House—it is a splendid day to-day, bright & clear & just cool enough—& I feel in good health—& all the better on account of your letter arriving. Well I must draw to a close.

I hope, dear comrade, you are trying to be an honorable & upright young man, for that is more than the greatest worldly prosperity, or learning either.

I send you my love, & must now bid you farewell for present, dear soldier boy.

Walt Whitman

192. *To William D. O'Connor*[44] [*9(?). (?). 1866*]

TRANSCRIPT.

I assume that Poetry in America needs to be entirely recreated. On examining with anything like deep analysis what now prevails in the United States, the whole mass of current poetical works, long and short, consists either of the poetry of an elegantly weak sentimentalism, at bottom nothing but maudlin puerilities, more or less musical in verbiage, arising out of a life of depression and enervation, and producing depres-

44. Sometime during 1866, O'Connor sent to Moncure D. Conway a "Memoranda" (Yale), in which he quoted from WW's letter, and commented on the poet's life and works. Conway used this material in his article "Walt Whitman," *The Fortnightly Review*, VI (1866), 538–548. WW undoubtedly wrote to O'Connor with publication in mind.

sion and enervation as their result;—or else that class of poetry, plays, &c, of which the foundation is feudalism, with its ideas of lords and ladies, its imported standards of gentility, and the manners of European high-life-below-stairs in every line and verse. Such to me is the existing condition of poetry; such the product of the poets and poems of the time. To me, nothing can be more utterly contemptible. Instead of mighty and vital breezes, proportionate to our continent, with its powerful races of men, its tremendous historic events, its great oceans, its mountains and its illimitable prairies, I find a few little silly fans languidly moved by shrunken fingers. [My ambition is] to give something to our literature which will be our own; with neither foreign spirit, nor imagery nor form, but adapted to our case, grown out of our associations, boldly portraying the West, strengthening and intensifying the national soul, and finding the entire fountains of its birth and growth in our own country.

192.1 *To Louisa Van Velsor Whitman* *10.16. [1866?]*

ENDORSED (in unknown hand): "1867?"[45]

ATTORNEY GENERAL'S OFFICE,

Washington, Oct. 16, *186*

Dearest mother,

I have not heard any thing from you the last week, but I hope you are well & every thing goes right. I sent you a letter last Tuesday, as usual. I suppose you have got your copy of the new book—I feel satisfied with the looks of it—it might be better, & handsomer paper, &c—but I am glad it turns out as good as it is—for, in making a book, you can't be certain how it is going to look, till it is all completed. Then I feel sure it tells the meaning better than any of the former editions—My enemies, & those who are determined to find fault, will of course still do so—But I feel that the book proves itself to any fair person—& will have a fair chance now, & go ahead. But the best thing is, it is *done*—& I shant worry myself any more with fixing & revising it—

I have sent a copy to Han—& wrote her a letter—I am feeling first rate in health—I have a good place to eat—get good victuals & plenty of 'em—

45. This letter has been consistently misdated. WW referred to the recently completed printing of the fourth edition of *Leaves of Grass*, and, more important, according to the second sentence, he was writing on Tuesday, October 16, which could only be 1866.

46. The Prices became interested in the case of Erastus Otis Parker, as Helen Price wrote years later, "through his niece an intimate friend who beleived most absolutely in her Uncle's innocence" (Morgan). They asked WW to investigate the circumstances of Parker's conviction and to appeal for a pardon. WW sent this concise

After the biggest rain-storm I ever knew, we have splendid weather here just now. In the office here, every thing goes on the same as usual. I like Mr. Stanbery—Ashton, the Assistant, will probably remain here this winter—I hope Jeff won't neglect to vote—George of course will vote—Love to Mat—Well good bye, dear mother, till next time.

Walt.

193. *To Henry Stanbery*

Washington City | Oct. 26. 1866.

To | Hon. Henry Stanbery | Attorney General. | Sir:[46]

I hereby respectfully apply for the pardon of Erastus O. Parker, aged 55 years, formerly Postmaster at the village of Monument, Mass. on the Cape Cod Railroad—now in prison at Plymouth Jail, Plymouth, Mass.

The following is a statement of his case, condensed from the accompanying documents:[47]

At a term of U. S. Circuit Court, at Boston, Mass. in October, 1862, Parker was tried on an indictment of [please notice][48] *Seven Counts*; the 1st charged him with, on Oct. 22, 1860, unlawfully detaining a package sent by mail from the Falmouth Bank, containing a sum of money; the 2d charged him with opening the packet; the 3d charged him with embezzlement of $500, part of the contents of said packet; the 4th charged him with stealing & taking out said $500; the 5th charged him with advising & assisting one Joseph S. Hewins to steal & take out said valuable packet; the 6th charged him with advising & assisting one Henry C. Hewins to steal said valuable packet; & the 7th charged him with receiving & concealing a bank-note of $500, which had been stolen from the mail, & which he, Parker, knew had been stolen.

The evidence proved that on Oct. 22, 1860, the Falmouth Bank sent through the mail a package containing some $5000, (of which about $1700 was in cash, & the rest in drafts,) to Suffolk Bank, Boston—that the mail from Falmouth in due course passes through Monument, at which place the bag is usually opened to put in the Boston matter—& that the package with the $5000 never reached Suffolk Bank.

summary of the evidence to Stanbery. Though the wrapper in the National Archives reads, "Filed Oct 27th 1866 | Pardoned same day," WW had worked for months on the case. The Court Record was certified on May 31. The letter from the sheriff was dated May 30, and the one from the jailer at Plymouth, July 14. The petition from the citizens of Monument was marked, in WW's hand, "July 1866."

47. The wrapper of this certified record of the case is in WW's hand: "Record of In- | dictment, with counts, &c. | (Conviction on 7th | count.)"

48. WW's brackets.

Furthermore, that on the 12th of Jan. 1861, Joseph S. Hewins, of Monument, a mail contractor & driver of the mail (implicated with Parker, as just seen in the 6th count of the indictment,) receives from Monument post office a letter postmarked Boston, which, on opening, he, to his amazement, finds to contain a $500 note, & nothing else;—that on the 15th of Jan. said Joseph Hewins sends a younger brother Henry C. Hewins, with this $500 note to Falmouth Bank, to get it changed into small bills. The cashier, (the same man who had made up & sent the $5000 package to Suffolk Bank,) gives Henry Hewins the small bills as requested. Some time afterward a question is raised of this $500 note being identical with one in the stolen or missing package. Joseph Hewins is sent for, answers all questions frankly, cannot account for the $500, openly acknowledges that he has no idea who sent it to him, & produces the envelope it was sent in. This is the basis of suspicion against Parker.

The prosecution charges the handwriting of the direction on the envelope to Parker. Witnesses are called to prove the handwriting on him. Several witnesses testify to its being Parker's writing to the best of their belief; but the preponderance of the testimony is against it. The best experts swear positively that it is not Parker's hand.

Parker proves a remarkably good character all his previous life, by a long train of witnesses, of the best standing in the county & town. No attempt is made to prove a bad character. As to the identity of the $500 note, with one in the stolen package, the testimony makes that identity probable, but not certain.

The foregoing contains every point made against Parker.

Incredible as it would seem, the Jury, who, with the Court, had been thoroughly wearied out with several preceding long & tedious trials—though they brought in a verdict of *Not Guilty* on the 1st, 2d, 3d, 4th, 5th, & 6th counts, [see, back,][49] found him *Guilty* on the 7th count.

On this finding Parker was sentenced to Five Years imprisonment, & sent to Jail Oct. 22, 1862—& has been incarcerated there since.

Joseph S. Hewins was also tried & convicted; but was soon after *pardoned*. He immediately resumed his station as a respectable member of the community at Monument, & has been for some time, & is now, occupying his old position as mail carrier & contracter under the Post Office Department.

49. WW's brackets.

50. WW included what he labeled a "Memorial of | persons holding | Municipal & | other positions | in Monument, | (fellow citizens) | for Mr. Parker's | pardon." The petition, with twenty-one signatures, advanced five reasons for pardoning Parker, the most important of which was the first: "We think that evidence did not sufficiently show that Mr Parker was guilty of any offence against the laws."

When Parker was arrested he was station master on the Cape Cod Railroad, as well as postmaster of the village. Both are small positions in a pecuniary point of view. I may mention that ever since, & at this time, the officers of the Road have been & are, keeping his place for him; & his daughter is performing the duties of the post, to support the family.

The belief is universal in Monument & the neighborhood that old Mr. Parker is innocent.[50] It seems to be one of those curious & helpless cases that sometimes occur in judicial trials, where the accused becomes a victim in defiance of law & common sense. I am informed by the Sheriff, & the Jailer at Plymouth,[51] that the old man is one of the most truthful & benevolent persons they ever knew; they use him as an assistant & messenger, and have for years allowed him to go about the jail premises & grounds on his own parole. Both warmly join in the application for his pardon, & one of them adds his belief in Parker's innocence.[52]

I have but respectfully to add, that as the whole theory on which he was convicted was but an inference from an inference—that, as on the substantial counts of his indictment he was pronounced *not guilty*—that as the sentence, on that comparatively mild 7th count, was a cruel & heavy one—& that, waiving my claim of his innocence, (which, after a thorough examination of the Case, I devoutly believe in)[53]—I submit, that he has already served four years in prison, & is now a most proper subject for Warrant of Pardon.

Walt Whitman

364 Thirteenth st.

194. *To Abby H. Price*

ADDRESS: To | Mrs. Abby H. Price, | 279 East 55th st. bet. 1st & 2d Av's. | New York City. POSTMARK: Washington D. C. | Oct | 27 | Free.

ATTORNEY GENERAL'S OFFICE,

Washington, Oct. *27*, *1866*.

Mrs. Price, & all | My dear friends,

I sent you a telegram, ten minutes ago, telling you that I have just succeeded in getting an order from the Attorney General for Mr. Parker's

51. WW included letters from Sheriff James Bates and jailer James B. Hollingswood.

52. Although Bates was careful to disclaim personal knowledge of Parker's innocence, Hollingswood considered him "entirely innocent of the crime for which he is committed."

53. Note, however, the opinion quoted in the next note.

pardon. The pardon will probably go from here, (from the State Department,) on Monday next—the day you will receive this note—it will be directed to the Jail at Plymouth. I have had much more of a struggle than I anticipated—the pardon clerk knew the case, & was filled with Mr. Dana's[54] reports upon it. When we meet, (or perhaps by letter, before) I will give you a more detailed account of the progress of the affair here, & its fluctuations. But no matter—it has ended successfully.

I have written to Aurelia Parker, & sent the news, the same mail as this.

I am fearfully well—indeed so red & fat that people stop in the street & gaze at me.

In the office, & my work, every thing goes on as usual. We are having delicious weather, coolish & bright.

Has Arthur[55] gone, then? Well you will value him all the more, when you have him again.

Helen & Emmy, my dear friends, I send you my best love—Go over & see my mother when you can—Best remembrance to Mr. Arnold—also to Mr. Price.

Walt

195. *To Louisa Van Velsor Whitman*

ADDRESS: Mrs. Louisa Whitman | p. o. Box 218 | Brooklyn, New York. POSTMARK: Washington, D. C. | Oct | 30.

ATTORNEY GENERAL'S OFFICE,

Washington, Oct. 30, *1866*.

Dearest Mother,

I am well as usual, & having good times—There is nothing new to tell you—I hope you are well, mother dear—& Mat & the little girls & Jeff & Georgy—I begin to want to see you all again—I hear there is a long & favorable piece about me & Leaves of Grass in an English magazine called the *Fortnightly Review*[56]—one of the highest rank, too—

54. Richard Henry Dana, Jr. (1815–1882), author of *Two Years Before the Mast*, was the United States attorney for the district of Massachusetts from 1861 to 1866. On July 9, 1864, Dana informed Montgomery Blair, Postmaster General, that a pardon was being requested for Parker "on the ground of failing health." On March 19, 1866, in a letter to M. F. Pleasants, pardon clerk in WW's office (see 187), Dana explained what had transpired two years earlier: "Parker's friends tried to get President Lincoln to issue a pardon without its coming to his knowledge that Parker had admitted his guilt; and for that purpose, contrived to get the thing out of the regular track of the Pardon Bureau, with a report from me. I think they did get an order for a pardon, conditioned on Mr. Blair's assent. But, Mr. Blair sent the papers to me; and when the President learned the facts, and the deception that had been practiced upon him, he revoked the order. . . . The case is a very bad one, almost as bad in the fraudulent attempts to

Well, I am now going to leave off, & drink a cup of tea—near us there is a room where the Treasury ladies work—about noon they have tea—one of our own clerks has a sort of sweetheart in there who sends him every day a cup of splendid green tea—which as he dont drink the article—he always makes over to *me*—

Well, mother dear, good bye for this time—

Walt.

196. *To Louisa Van Velsor Whitman* [*10(?). 1866?*][57]

FRAGMENT.

. . . not sick with rheumatism or any thing—I see the carpenters in Brooklyn are demanding $4 a day—I was thinking perhaps George & Smith would just take[58] . . .

Write how George & Smith make out—George, how would it do for you to put up a couple of small houses, to be worth about $2000 a piece, in some good spot, outer part of the city—one of the two for *us*—& the other for sale—I could raise $800 cash—to leave 1200 on bond & mortgage—some such plan—you & Smith could do much of the work yourselves—I only mention it to see whether it would be practicable. Good bye, dear mother,

Walt.

197. *To Louisa Van Velsor Whitman*

ATTORNEY GENERAL'S OFFICE,

Washington, Nov. 13, *1866*.

Dearest Mother,

I have had a very bad cold the past week or so, but am feeling better to-day. I am at the office as usual every day. The promotion I spoke

get signatures and a pardon, as in the original guilt" (National Archives).

55. Arthur joined the navy, and became second assistant engineer on the steamer "Ossipee"; see WW's address book (*LC* #109).

56. See 192.

57. The date of this fragment can only be conjectural. In 1866, George was in business with Smith. According to his mother's letter of June 7 to WW, "George and smith and french the mason has bought 5 lots on portland ave opposite the arsenal, 950 a lot, going to put up brick houses" (Trent). On October 10, she wrote: "george says if you will buy smiths half of that lot he will fix the shop (the carpenters shop acrost the street) for me . . . for about 1200 twelv hundred dollars" (Trent).

58. Only the lower half of the letter is extant.

about last week hasn't come yet[59]—I guess I had better make no reckoning of it till it comes—Mother, I havn't received any letter from you the past week—I sent you day before yesterday a paper with the piece in (or most of it) from the London *Fortnightly Review*—it was meant well, but a good deal of it is most ridiculous.[60] Here in the office every thing goes on as usual. The Attorney General and Assistant are very busy getting themselves ready to argue their cases in the U. S. Supreme Court, which holds a session here every winter, & all the big cases, in which the U. S. are a party, come off on such occasions. We are having pleasant weather yet—a little dusty though. The O'Connors are all well—they have got to move, & are worrying a good deal about it.

Well, I believe that is all—so good bye for this time, mother dear. I send my love to Jeff & George & Mat & all.

Walt.

198. *To Louisa Van Velsor Whitman*

ATTORNEY GENERAL'S OFFICE,

Washington, Nov. 16, *1866*.
Friday afternoon.

Dearest Mother,

I only write again this week (I wrote last Tuesday) to inform you that the Attorney General has promoted me. I have now a real good berth, what they call a third class clerk with the pay of $1600 a year.[61] I shall have about $127 a month (they take a little off, every time they pay, on acc't of gov't tax.) Besides I have now a regular appointment, instead of being a temporary clerk, as before. I was appointed last Wednesday, my

59. See 198. The letter referred to is not known.

60. Conway's article; see 192. Burroughs called it "an eloquent article . . . but it told untruths about him. Walt said it did" (Barrus, 39). O'Connor wrote to Conway on December 5, 1866: "A great deal of it I liked very much, and I think the general effect of it was very good. In part of it, there was a tone I regretted. Pardon me. I think the time is past when this august man should be written of as a curiosity, or his poem mentioned as something monstrous. You do not do this, it is true, but there are, here and there, lines and touches in your article, which suggest such a treatment and leave me unsatisfied" (Yale). However, to Trowbridge, O'Connor labeled it "a frightful mess of misstatement and fiction" (Barrus, 40). WW, and therefore his friends, objected to two of Conway's anecdotes in particular: WW's lying on his back at Coney Island with the temperature at 100 degrees, and the description of his room in 1855. In 1888 WW observed: "I can't help feeling still a little suspicion of Conway's lack of historical veracity: he romances: he has romanced about me: William says lied: but romanced will do" (Traubel, III, 16). Rossetti repeated the Coney Island tale in *Poems by Walt Whitman* (1868), 15–16.

new grade & pay commence on Nov. 1st—I haven't got a letter from home for ten or twelve days. The Attorney General has gone to New York—he is badly afflicted with sore eyes, & has gone there to see the best oculists—

My cold, or whatever it is, is better to-day—I hope you are all well—Good bye, dear mother. *Write soon.*

Walt.

Mother, I send some envelopes—You must have paper—you know I left you a great lot, when I was home. I hope you are not sick, dear mother.

199. *To Bayard Taylor*

ATTORNEY GENERAL'S OFFICE,

Washington, Nov. 18, *1866.*

My dear Mr. Taylor,[62]

I have received your letter of the 12th. The friendly pages thereof have given me pleasure, & I wish to proffer you my friendship in response. Should I not see you at the lecture, I hope you will do me the honor to call upon me at the Attorney General's office here, in the Treasury Building, where I am employed.

Your book also came safely. I accept it, as a kind & valuable gift—& heartily thank you.

Permit me to send you, in return, a copy of the new edition of Leaves of Grass. I send it herewith by same mail.

Truly hoping to see you—for the present, Farewell.

Walt Whitman.

61. WW's copy of Stanbery's "Order Book" is in the Feinberg Collection.

62. Bayard Taylor (1825–1878), translator of *Faust*, journalist, and traveler, sent his *Picture of St. John* to WW on November 12. He commended WW's "remarkable powers of expression" and "deep and tender reverence for Man" (Feinberg; Traubel, II, 148–149). His letter of December 2 was even more unreserved in its praise: "I may say, frankly, that there are two things in [*Leaves of Grass*] which I find nowhere else in literature, though I find them in my own nature. I mean the awe and wonder and reverence and beauty of Life, as expressed in the human body, with the physical attraction and delight of mere contact which it inspires, and that tender and noble love of man for man which once certainly existed, but now almost seems to have gone out of the experience of the race" (Feinberg; Traubel, II, 153). Taylor was to deliver a lecture in Washington on December 27. Later Taylor's enthusiasm for WW was to change dramatically. In *The Echo Club* (2d ed., 1876), 154–158, 168–169, Taylor burlesqued WW's poetry. Kennedy lists him among WW's "Bitter and Relentless Foes and Vilifiers"; see *The Fight of a Book for the World* (1926), 288. See also 211.

200. *To Louisa Van Velsor Whitman*

ADDRESS: Mrs. Louisa Whitman | p. o. Box 218, | Brooklyn, New York. POSTMARK: Washington D. C. | Nov | 20.

ATTORNEY GENERAL'S OFFICE,

Washington, Nov. 20, *1866*.

Dearest mother,

I suppose you got two letters from me last week, Wednesday & Saturday—My cold still troubles me some—I have a good deal of pain in the head—I think it is neuralgia—but I guess I shall get over it—I have good meals, I do not cook for myself, at present—but get my grub at a good New England restaurant—Mother, I received your letter a week ago—there is nothing new in the office—the poor Attorney General has a cataract forming on one of his eyes, & will have to undergo a surgical operation—Mother, I told you all about my promotion & appointment to a regular berth, in Saturday's letter—

Well, mother dear, I will bid you good bye for this week—

Walt.

201. *To Louisa Van Velsor Whitman*

ATTORNEY GENERAL'S OFFICE,

Washington, Nov. 23, *1866*.

Dearest mother,

I feel middling well to-day. I go to the office just the same as usual —If I had a good home where I could have a decent time, & keep in for three or four days, I should get all right—the principal trouble with me, I think, is neuralgia—it gives me great distress in the head at times—but the spells do not last long at a time—I eat pretty nearly the same as usual—but do not sleep well—But I think I am making too much of it—I thought I would write you just a few lines, you would get Saturday.

You must tell Jeff or George to get the "Galaxy" of Dec. 1.—it is a magazine—it is for sale at most of the book-stands—30 cts—it has a

63. See 188. In his letter to Conway on December 5, O'Connor asserted fervidly that Burroughs' was "the first article . . . that reveals real critical power and insight, and a proper reverence, upon the subject of Walt Whitman's poetry" (Yale). WW's most recent biographer, Gay Wilson Allen, concurs in O'Connor's judgment: Burroughs "deserves credit for having lifted the criticism of Whitman's poems to the plane of reason and intellectual appreciation" (375).

64. See 197.

piece in about me[63]—I think it is very good—John Burroughs is a young man from Delaware county, New York—he lives here, now, is married—I am well acquainted with him, & he & his wife have been very hospitable & friendly to me.

Mr. Conway's article[64] was about as impudent as it was friendly—quite a mixture of good & bad.

I am glad you like Emily Price—she is a good girl. She seems to me one that you needn't make any fuss or change—but let domestic things go on just as they may be, when she comes to visit you.

It is pleasant this afternoon—the sun is shining out—the river & hills on the other side look beautiful.

I sent Han a book—"Lady Audley's Secret"[65]—& shall send her a letter to-day.

Dont forget, George or Jeffy, to get the Galaxy of Dec. 1.

Mother, if any of you want another copy of the new "Leaves of Grass," I can send you an order for one on the binder in New York, & you can get it.

Well, mother dear, I believe that is all—except that I am getting a new pair of trowserloons—Shall not get any other new clothes this winter—

Love to George & all.

Walt.

202. *To Louisa Van Velsor Whitman*

ADDRESS: Mrs. Louisa Whitman | P. O. Box 218, | Brooklyn, New York. POSTMARK: Washington D. C. | Nov | 27.

ATTORNEY GENERAL'S OFFICE,

Washington, Nov. 27, *1866*

Dearest Mother,

I suppose you got a letter last Saturday as well as the previous Wednesday—I am better than I was last week—not as well as I would like to be, but well enough to keep on with my work, &c. just the same as ever—I feel real well, sometimes, for a day—but then comes the trouble in the head again—

65. Mary Elizabeth Braddon (Maxwell), English novelist (1837–1915), established a phenomenal reputation after the publication of *Lady Audley's Secret*, which appeared in 1862 in *The Sixpenny Magazine* and later in the year as a three-volume novel. According to the DNB, "in various forms nearly a million copies must have gone into circulation; it has been translated into every civilized tongue, several times piratically dramatized, and twice filmed."

Did you get the "Galaxy" of Dec. 1st? I think it a very good piece. Every thing here in the office goes on as usual. I got your letter, mother. I wrote to Han last week. It is beautiful weather here to-day—I have got my new trowsers—$20!!—only think of that!—it is lucky I wear my clothes a long while—

Walt.

Mother, I would rather you would use the money to get things for yourself—shoes, stockings, underclothes[66]—

203. *To a Soldier*[67] [*11(?). 1866*]

TRANSCRIPT.

We have a new Attorney-General.[68] One of the first things he did was to promote me. Sensible man, wasn't he? May the Lord reward him. . . .

I enclose you a little picture. You shall have a better one, dear son. The picture in shirt sleeves was taken in 1854.[69] You would not know it was me now, but it was taken from real life and was first-rate then.

204. *To Louisa Van Velsor Whitman*

ATTORNEY GENERAL'S OFFICE,

Washington, Dec. 3, *1866*.
Monday afternoon.

Dearest Mother,

I thought I would write a day before the usual time, as I did not send any letter last Saturday. For the last two days I have felt a good deal better—My head is much better, & I feel more like myself every way. I sent Han a short letter last Friday, & sent the piece from the "Galaxy"[70]—I thought it would please her.

I went to the Hospital yesterday afternoon—took a lot of tobacco, &c. I wrote several letters—there are quite a good many, some with sickness, some with old wounds—two or three in the last stages of consumption, &c.

66. The postscript was omitted in earlier printings.
67. See 160. 68. Henry Stanbery; see 177.
69. The frontispiece to the first edition of *Leaves of Grass*.
70. Burroughs' article; see 201.
71. In his letter of December 1(?), Heyde excitedly described his first reading of Swinburne, and then wrote of WW's poetry: "There is enough beauty in your 'Leaves'

I go every Sunday, & sometimes Wednesday also—There are many of the patients, very young men, country boys—several from the Southern states, whose parents & homes & families are gone or broke up—& they have enlisted in the regular army—then they get down with fever or something, & are sent to Hospital—I find most of them can't read or write—there are many of these homeless Southern young men now enlisted in the regulars —they have no other resource—

We have quite a procession here to-day to "welcome Congress"—two-thirds of it consists of darkies—they look very well too—the streets are jammed with darkies—I tell you when they do turn out here they are thicker than crows in a cornfield—

The O'Connors have got to move—but can't get a house suitable—Every thing in the office same as usual—We are having beautiful bright, coolish weather—

Thursday last, Thanksgiving day, four of us went out in Maryland 15 miles, to see the Great Falls, on the Potomac. We carried a basket of grub, built a fire & made tea, &c—had a first rate, quiet time—the Falls were a fine sight—almost as impressive as Niagara—I much enjoyed the ride & every thing, & it did me good—I felt well, all day, & have felt quite well ever since. Love to you, dearest mother, & to all.

Walt.

205. *To Louisa Van Velsor Whitman*

ATTORNEY GENERAL'S OFFICE,

Washington, Dec 4, *1866*.

Dearest Mother,

I wrote you yesterday, (Monday,) which I suppose you rec'd, with the money. I have just heard from Han, & I write to-day because I knew it would be a comfort to you to know right away. Heyde has just sent me a letter—he seems to be in a very good humor—writes a lot of stuff—but *not* about domestic affairs this time—on "poetry" & "criticism" &c. &c—of no interest at all to me—then at the close of the letter he says:

"Han is much better than usual, & is constantly promising to write to her mother."[71]

to make a rare book, and not without sensuous extravagance either. But you are wonderfully, woefully mistaken in the privileage you take of being merely savagely material, and subsequently offensively vulgar" (Trent; Gohdes & Silver, 223–224). About the same time, Heyde must have written to Raymond of the New York *Times;* see 209.

Mother, I send you the part of the N. Y. Times, containing a good long piece about me. It is the N. Y. Daily Times, of Sunday, Dec 2—but perhaps George or Jeff brought it to you last Sunday.

I feel pretty well generally—with now & then a poorish spell—

I am going to hear the great actress Ristori[72] to-morrow night. One of my fellow clerks has taken a seat for me, & made me a present of it—the play is "Queen Elisabeth"—I wish you & Mat could go with me—

The piece in the *Times* is by O'Connor.[73] He grows stronger & stronger, & fiercer & fiercer in his championship of "Leaves of Grass"—no one can ever say a word against it in his presence, without a storm. Did you get the "Galaxy" of Dec 1—?

William Swinton[74] is here in Washington, temporarily. He is interested in speculating in gold. It is very fine weather here to-day. I am writing this by my big window, where I can look out on the water—the sun is shining bright as silver.

Walt.

206. *To Louisa Van Velsor Whitman*

ATTORNEY GENERAL'S OFFICE,

Washington, Dec. 10, *1866.*

Dearest Mother,

I have grown better the last four or five days, & don't have that pain in my head now.

Well, mother, it is the middle of Tuesday afternoon, & the carrier has just brought your letter, (though I see it was written Saturday.) Mother, your letter is the first news I have had of the fire—it must have been quite an exciting time—& quite a sad loss, anyhow—

I went to see Ristori, the great actress, the other night, & was very much pleased—but don't want to go again.

It has got pretty cold here the last two days—I wear my big old overcoat. Every thing goes on the same in the office—I have written again to Han—I send her some book or something to read, occasionally—I got a letter from Mrs. Price—Helen is not very well—

72. Adelaide Ristori (1822–1906), a famous Italian tragedienne, appeared at the National Theatre in *Elizabeth, Queen of England* on December 6. The Washington *National Republican* reported on December 7 that the house had been sold out, and that during the week she would also appear in *Macbeth* and *Mary, Queen of Scotland.* The Washington *National Intelligencer* printed a lengthy biography of the actress on December 3.

73. Raymond, on December 2, granted O'Connor four columns for a review of the new *Leaves of Grass;* see Allen, 376.

Mother, I will send you another *Times*, with Wm O'Connor's piece in. It seems as if things were going to brighten up about "Leaves of Grass." I rather think it is going to be republished in England.

Well, mother, you must keep a good heart—and good bye for this time—

Walt.

207. *To Abby H. Price*

ADDRESS: Abby H. Price, | 279 East 55th st. | New York City. POSTMARK: Washington | Dec | 11 | D. C.

ATTORNEY GENERAL'S OFFICE,

Washington. Dec. 10, *1866.*

My dear friend,

Yours of the 8th has just come. I am glad indeed to hear that you are free from asthma, & are feeling well.

I should be truly happy to become acquainted with Mrs. Andrews[75]—I am sure I should like her much.

For a month or so, I have not been very well—my trouble takes the form, sometimes, of neuralgia—but is a complication—(the doctor says it probably all dates from that time I got saturated with hospital malaria)—But I keep around, & go to the office just the same—& now for four of five days have felt much better—

The O'Connors are well—The consul at Rio Janeiro is James Munroe—Our Minister to Brazil, resident in Rio Janeiro, is James Watson Webb.[76]

I send my love to Helen and Emmy & all—I have rec'd a letter from mother to-day—she seems to be about the same as usual—I hope Helen or Emmy will just go over & visit her without ceremony as often as possible. Give my respects to Mr. Arnold[77]—also to Mr. Price—It would give me the greatest pleasure to see you or Helen here in Washington. I rec'd your friend's (Katy Hinds)[78] letter at the time—I have had no letter from

74. See 37.
75. Possibly the wife of Stephen Pearl Andrews; see 95.
76. James Monroe was the American consul at Rio de Janeiro from 1863 to 1869, and was later, after service in the Ohio legislature, professor of political science and modern history at Oberlin College. James Watson Webb (1802–1884) was an editor and later Minister to Brazil from 1861 to 1869.
77. See 12. 78. Mentioned again in 320.

Mr. Parker's family[79]—I am writing this by my window in the office—it is a fine view, ten miles of river, & away across to Virginia hills, ever so far—My place is an easy & pleasant one here in the Att'y Gen's. office—And now for the present, dear friend, Farewell.

Walt.

208. *To Louisa Van Velsor Whitman*

ATTORNEY GENERAL'S OFFICE,

Washington. Dec. 18, *1866.*

Dearest Mother,

I rec'd your letter Sunday morning last—It has been very cold here too, but is pleasant now. I sent you a copy of "Leaves of Grass"—which I suppose you have rec'd. Every thing here with me remains the same—I am free from the distress in my head—Mrs. Grayson[80] is very sick—she sent my old washerwoman, old Aunt Kitty, around this morning to see if I had any of "that bread my mother used to send me"—I suppose she meant the sweet Dyer bread—I gave her a piece a long while ago, & she liked it—poor woman, I think she is on her dying bed—Mother, you must write to me how Jeff is, & how he is getting along—tell Hattie I hope she will take a lesson on the piano every day, and learn to play for her Uncle Walt—so when he comes home, she can play a beautiful tune[81]—

I have been down to the Hospital a great deal lately—A friend of mine that I have known over three years, a Maine soldier named Racliffe,[82] was very low with consumption & bleeding at the lungs—He died Sunday morning—it was a great relief, for he suffered much—

Well, mother, I believe that is all this time.

Walt.

79. See 193–194.
80. WW had boarded with Mrs. Grayson; see 181.
81. Jeff liked WW's reference to his daughter. He wrote, on December 21: "Wish when you write Mother you would always say something abt Hattie's learning to read and play &c, it sets her ahead wonderfully—you know how such things please Children" (Feinberg).
82. See 104.
83. On December 21, Jeff had sent $31 collected from employees at the Water Works: "Hope you wont be disappointed in the smallness of the amount" (Feinberg). Evidently WW had also written to William E. Worthen (see 129) for funds, since Jeff noted that he had "sent letter to Worthen." See also 210 and 211.

209. *To Louisa Van Velsor Whitman*

ATTORNEY GENERAL'S OFFICE,

Washington. Dec. 24, *1866.*

Dearest mother,

I got Jeff's letter sending the money toward the soldiers' dinner—it was more than I asked for, & was very good of them all[83]—I have not had any trouble myself, worth mentioning—the dinner has been got up at my instigation—I have contributed handsomely—but they, (the Hospital steward, &c.) have done the work.

Mother, I sent Han a handsome little volume of "Florence Percy's Poems,"[84] & $5 for a Christmas present. Sent it to-day. Poor Han—I suppose every such thing does her so much good—

Don't you believe that fool Heyde lately wrote a long letter to Mr. Raymond,[85] editor of the N. Y. Times—in it he said "Walt was a good fellow *enough—but*"—& then he went on to run down Leaves of Grass, like the rest of 'em—

The way I know is, Wm. O'Connor was invited by Raymond to come & see him—& he told O'Connor he had received a number of letters about that piece in the *Times* of Dec. 2, which I sent you. He said they all praised the piece, & thanked him (Raymond) for printing it, except one he got from a fellow in Vermont who called himself Walt Whitman's relation—a brother in law, he believed—quite a good deal of stuff. Raymond seemed to think the man was either crazy or a fool, & he treated the letter with contempt.

I dont want you to write any thing about it, to Han, of course—only if she was here, we would tell her. The puppy thought I suppose that he could get his letter printed, & injure me & my book.

We are likely to have a pleasant day for Christmas—when I next write I will tell you about the dinner—I must inform you that I have had a present of a beautiful knife, a real Rogers' steel, to-day from the Attorney

84. Elizabeth Chase Allen (1832–1911), one of the favorite nineteenth-century household poets, used the pseudonym Florence Percy. *Poems*, published in 1866 by Ticknor and Fields, includes her most famous poem "Rock Me to Sleep." She married Burroughs' friend, E. M. Allen, in October, 1866; she heartily disliked WW (Barrus, 12). Hannah acknowledged receipt of the book in her letter to her mother on March 20, 1867 (Trent).

85. Henry Jarvis Raymond (1820–1869) established the New York *Daily Times* on September 18, 1851. Raymond termed *The Good Gray Poet* "the most brilliant monograph in our literature" (Barrus, 35), and invited O'Connor to review *Leaves of Grass* on December 2 (see 205). He later asked O'Connor to write for the *Times;* see 231.

General—Mother, $2 is for Nance[86]—you can give it to her in money, or any way you like—

Well, dear mother, this is Christmas eve, & I am writing it in the office by gas light, so as it will be ready to go to-morrow—I have not heard since from Mrs. Grayson. Good night, mother dear.

Walt.

210. *To George Wood*

ATTORNEY GENERAL'S OFFICE,

Washington. Dec. 29, *1866.*

My dear Mr. Wood,[87]

I write to solicit from you $2, for helping my soldier boys to some festivities these holiday & New Year times.

Yours

Walt Whitman

86. Andrew's wife. 87. See 33.

1867

211. *To Louisa Van Velsor Whitman*

ATTORNEY GENERAL'S OFFICE,

Washington. Jan. 1, *1867*

Dearest Mother,

I have just rec'd your letter—I thought of you during that storm—it was very severe here too, & awful gales of wind one or two nights—The dinner in the Hospital[1] was a complete success—there was plenty, & good too—turkey & four or five kinds of vegetables, & mince pie, &c—then I purchased a large quantity of navy plug, & smoking tobacco, & pipes, &c. and after dinner every body that wanted to, had a good smoke—& I had a lot of oranges, apples, &c. & a large sugar cake for supper—then I read some amusing pieces to them for three quarters of an hour, for a change—& sat down by those who were worst off—&c. &c. Nobody else came in that day. They have a Chaplain, but he is miserable coot, like the rest of his tribe.

I have written again to Han—I am writing this in the office, all alone—I am going down to the Hospital for a little while, & to carry some tobacco—& then I am invited to O'Connor's to dinner at 4 o'clock—we are to have cold turkey, hot vegetables, &c—They are going to stay where they are till next March. We have had quite a snow storm here—it is snowing moderately now. Some are out with their sleighs. I am glad to hear such a good account of Eddy. It makes me feel quite satisfied.

I had a visit from Bayard Taylor, a few days since.[2]

Well good bye for this time, dear mother.

Walt.

1867

1. See 209–210. 2. See 199.

212. *To Louisa Van Velsor Whitman* *1.8. [1867]*[3]

ATTORNEY GENERAL'S OFFICE,

Washington. Jan. 8, *1866*

Dearest mother,

Well, every thing is just about the same. I rec'd your letter New Years. I have rec'd a small present from Heyde[4]—he sent me a small stereoscope, that is to put pictures in, & look through it, & it magnifies them, & makes them look like the real thing—it has some beautiful views of scenes in Vermont—I forget whether I told you that I sent Han some gloves & a $5 bill, Christmas—so I suppose this is in return—He says Han rec'd the parcels.[5] Mrs. Grayson[6] is still living—she is slightly better—I go [to] the hospital now oftener than usual—there are several very low—I just go, for an hour or so, at [a] time—I had rather go than not—

Every thing is covered with snow here, looks wintry enough—cold weather, but somehow I like it—I have no fire in my room, so far, this winter—I have rec'd a letter from Mrs. Price. You must tell me how George is getting along with his business. You might ask George whether any thing could be done with $500 cash about getting a lot & moderate-sized two story house to have say 15 or $1600 on mortgage?—whether they could get some one to take the rest on mortgage, so as to save themselves[7]—

Mat, I went to the opera last [night]—went alone—I was much pleased—the piece was Ernani[8]—first amusement I have been to in a year, except once to hear Ristori[9]—Good by, mother dear.

Walt.

I sent Jeff some envelopes for you a week ago.

213. *To Louisa Van Velsor Whitman*

ATTORNEY GENERAL'S OFFICE,

Washington. | Tuesday | Jan. 15, *1867.*

Dearest Mother,

I received your letter of Wednesday evening last—I thought it

3. WW wrote "1866."

4. Heyde sent this package to Senator George Franklin Edmunds, of Vermont, who so informed WW on January 4 (Feinberg).

5. Heyde mentioned WW's gifts in a letter to Mrs. Whitman, written in January: "Walter is very kind" (Trent). In commenting on this passage, on January 17, Mrs. Whitman, who was not without a sense of humor, wrote: "i suppose you will take it as a great complement" (Trent). Hannah, with her customary guilt about her procrastination, acknowledged the gifts in a letter to her mother on March 20 (Trent).

6. See 181, 209, and 213. 7. See 196.

would be very blustering & cold there on the hill this winter, & I know you must have freezing times, especially in the west rooms—We have had a great deal of snow here, & very cold weather. I get along very well, considering.

Mother, I have to inform you that poor Mrs. Grayson has gone at last. I wrote in my last letter that I had met her son Willy in the street, Monday Jan. 7, & he told me she was somewhat better—well, it was that very night, she died, & was buried the next Wednesday—they sent me word that the funeral was to be at ½ past 2—but the man didn't tell me any thing about it till 4—so I was not at the funeral—poor woman, she is at rest, & it is a blessed thing for her—she had an easy & peaceful death, I hear—But that devil, old Grayson, it is he that was the cause of her dying—about three days before her death, he had a fight in the house, with his son-in-law—there was great excitement, & Old Grayson put them all out of the house, son-in-law, children, &c—I suppose that hastened Mrs. Grayson's death—I have not been there, but shall go & see poor old Mrs. Mix[10]—She will not last long now—Old Aunt Kitty, the washwoman, says that Mrs. Grayson spoke much about me, & wanted me to come & see her—but I never knew any thing of it—(Mother, I believe there can be a greater nuisance & devil even than Heyde.)

Well, we are having pretty serious times here, in Congress, &c—I rather think they are going to impeach Johnson & bring him to trial—it is a serious business—I cannot tell how it will turn out—only I know both sides seem determined, & neither will give an inch[11]—

There have been several died in the hospital, that I was with a good deal, since I last wrote—one of consumption—one of abscess on the liver, very bad—I was down there Sunday afternoon, carried a great big 12 pound cake, for the men's supper—there was a piece for all, & very acceptable—as the supper consisted of plain bread, a thin wash they called tea, & some miserable apple sauce—that was all—I carry a big cake often of Sunday afternoons—I have it made for me by an old mulatto woman, cook, that keeps a stand in the market—it is sort of molasses pound cake, common but good.

I have received a letter from old Uncle Otis Parker,[12] the old man

8. Verdi's *Ernani* was performed at the National Theatre, with a cast that included Carmen Poch, Mazzoleni, and Bellini.

9. See 205–206.

10. For Mrs. Grayson and Mrs. Mix, see 181. On January 17, Mrs. Whitman commented: "she must have been tortured to death, probabley a happy exchange" (Trent).

11. Attempts to impeach President Johnson continued throughout the session until its adjournment on March 3. A Senate committee which studied an impeachment resolution submitted an inconclusive report. See 223.

12. See 193.

that I got pardoned down at Cape Cod, Mass. He is very grateful.

Every thing in the office here goes on as usual. I have a little more work to do than I have had. One of the clerks, the youngest, was dismissed, (or suspended,) lately for selling some information about pardons to the *Herald*—the Attorney Gen'l was very mad about it, & gave him a sharp talking to.[13] We are having quite good sleighing here to-day.

Well good bye, dear mother—& give my love to George, & Jeff, & Matty, & all.[14]

Walt.

214. *To Louisa Van Velsor Whitman*

ADDRESS: Mrs. Louisa Whitman | p. o. box 218, | Brooklyn, New York. POSTMARK: Washington D. C. | Jan | 22.

ATTORNEY GENERAL'S OFFICE,

Washington. | Tuesday noon | Jan. 22, 1867.

Dearest mother,

I rec'd your letter of the 17th—I have been thinking about you this cold weather—& especially the storm latter part of last week, that is, since the date of your letter—I see you have had it very heavy indeed—I see a piece in the *Tribune*, about a new book, a history of the Campaigns of the Ninth Corps[15]—I send it, for George—but it may be he has already seen it in the paper.

I am glad you treated Emmy Price so kindly[16]—they were so hospitable to me—I should think it would be pretty hard to reach you up there on the hill, so you can't have many visitors. I see young Van Brunt Bergen[17] here last week, he is in Jeff's office, the Water Works. I havn't seen Julius Mason[18] for a long while—I think he must have left here. The O'Connors are all well as usual—I was there to tea Sunday evening.

We have had very rough weather here too—Sunday it snowed hard, & the wind blew in gusts, with now & then quite a gale. After dinner, I started to go to the Hospital, as I had provided a big molasses pound

13. I have discovered nothing about this incident in the newspapers of the period.

14. According to Mrs. Whitman's reply on January 17 (Trent), WW enclosed $5 in this letter, as well as paper and envelopes.

15. Augustus Woodbury, *Burnside and the Ninth Army Corps: A Narrative of Operations in North Carolina, Maryland, Virginia, Ohio, Kentucky, Mississippi, and Tennessee* (Sidney S. Rider & Bros., Publishers, Providence, R. I.)

16. Mrs. Whitman, on January 17, spoke of a visit from Emma Price: "i told her if shed wait till the teakettle boiled i would make her some tea, so she took off her hat and i fried her a fresh egg and bread and butter" (Trent).

17. This son of Tunis G. Bergen (see 7) was born in 1844, graduated from the Rensselaer Polytechnic Institute, and was employed in the Brooklyn Water Department.

cake for supper—but the snow was too hard, & the wind right in my face, & I gave it up—I postponed going till next day.

I spend quite a good deal of time, evenings & Sundays, in the office at my desk, as I can get in the Treasury Building any time, as the doorkeepers all know me—nearly all of them are broken down or one-legged soldiers—The office is warm & nice, with gas, & all the modern improvements—& I am all alone. I would like you to see our rooms—they are a suite of seven rooms, all in a row, or rather in the shape of an L, each room opening from the other—five of them are very large & high—one is the library, filled with books of law, mostly—but we have five or six hundred miscellaneous works—I have described to you before, my desk & window looking out south, down the Potomac. In the Attorney General's room, there are nearly a hundred pictures, portraits of all the different Attorney Generals, from the days of Washington.

I went round one evening last week to see Mrs. Mix. Poor old woman, yet she bears up bravely—it was real affecting—Mother, she makes me think of grandmother Whitman in her last days[19]—She & all of them are going to scatter—the house was all in confusion, every thing torn up, & things being boxed up to be taken away—Mrs. Mix is going to Brooklyn to live with her granddaughter Mrs. Haskell, (that is Mrs. Graysons daughter that married the young man, the protegé of Mr. Beecher.)[20] The poor old lady said she was going on the train from Here to New York, last Friday night—but it was so bitter cold, & snow on the track, I hardly think she went then—but I havnt heard yet—Living here for her or any of them is a perfect hell—I have heard that old Grayson is just as bad since his wife's death as ever—he gets drunk, & then tries to choke his son & daughter, & ends by getting in a fury, & trying to beat every body out of the house—but enough of the old villain.

Mother, I will write to you old Mrs. Mix's address in Brooklyn.

To-day we are having it quite bright & pleasant—I am feeling well as usual—It looks like winter at the far north as I look from my window—every thing as far as the eye can reach is white with a deep snow—Ashton,[21] the Assistant Attorney Gen'l, has just had a bad fall on the

See *The Bergen Family: or The Descendants of Hans Hansen Bergen* (1876), 151. (For this information I am indebted to Miss Edna Huntington, librarian of the Long Island Historical Society.) According to Jeff's letter of December 21, 1866 (Feinberg), Bergen contributed $2 to the fund raised for the soldiers' dinner mentioned in 209.

18. See 152.

19. Hannah Brush Whitman died on January 6, 1834.

20. Mrs. Mary Mix (see 181) evidently went to live with Samuel S. Haskell, Jr., who was associated with his father, an importer of bags. For Henry Ward Beecher, see 12.

21. See 138.

sidewalk, cut his face badly, & stunned him—will lay him up a few days —Love to Jeff & Mat & all.

Walt.

215. *To John Jay Knox*

ADDRESS: Mr. Knox, | Sec. of the Treasury's Office.

ATTORNEY GENERAL'S OFFICE,

Washington. | Jan 28 *1867*

Mr. Knox,[22]

The Copy of Opinion of Mr. Attorney Gen. Bates, in title case, will be sent up to you at 2 o'clock, according to your request.

Yours,

Walt Whitman

216. *To Louisa Van Velsor Whitman*

ATTORNEY GENERAL'S OFFICE,

Washington. | Tuesday noon, | Jan. 29, *1867*.

Dearest mother,

I wrote to Han last Saturday. I hope you manage to keep comfortable this cold winter—it must be pretty tough up there on that bleak hill—It has been very cold here, but I have not minded it—My thick overcoat that Nelson[23] made comes in first-rate this winter—it is quite good yet—I have not bought any new clothes for a long while—suppose I must get some next spring.

There is a Bill before Congress to give extra pay to the clerks—if it passes I shall have something extra, too—but I make no calculations on it, for I think it quite uncertain. The debates in Congress now are quite exciting—sometimes they hold their sessions quite late in the night, & things get to be quite stormy. William Hunter (who is in the House, from Brooklyn, to fill out James Humphrey's term)[24] called a Republican

22. Knox (1828–1892) was appointed to the Treasury Department by Chase. On October 10, 1867, he became Deputy Comptroller of the Currency, and from 1872 to 1884 he served as Comptroller. WW forwarded to Knox an opinion of Edward Bates (1793–1869), Lincoln's Attorney General. See also 265.1.

23. There were two tailors by this name in the Brooklyn Directory of 1865–1866: Andrew, 372 Myrtle Avenue, and N., 739 Atlantic Avenue.

24. John Ward Hunter (1807–1900), not William, was elected to complete the term of James Humphrey (1811–1866), who was a Congressman from 1859 to 1861, and, after two unsuccessful attempts, was elected for the second time in 1864.

25. See 214. 26. See 240. 27. See 60.

member "a liar"—so the Speaker had Mr. Hunter up before him & gave him a formal reprimand—it was last Saturday. Mrs. Mix[25] went that cold Friday night, twelve days ago—I have not heard from her. It was a bad night for a journey, & the track was blocked with snow.

I receive letters from the soldiers every now & then. Within a week I have had two invitations—one is from a young fellow named Alfred Pratt.[26] I knew him in one of the hospitals two years ago, & more. His folks are farming people out in northwestern New York, near the shores of Lake Erie—he writes half the letter, & his father & mother write the other half, inviting me to come there & pay them a visit—the parents say they "will do every thing they can to make a country visit agreeable"—the letter is very old fashioned, but very good. Then I had another invitation, from a Michigan boy. He has got married, & has a small farm, not far from Detroit.

Do you remember Lewis Brown,[27] the Maryland boy, who had such a time with his leg, & had it amputated at last in Armory Square hospital? He is quite well otherwise, & has got a place in the Treasury Dep't. I send the advertisement of the new book about the Ninth Corps—if George wants it, I think he can find it at the American News Co. 121 Nassau st. New York[28]—We have ill luck among the clerks &c in our office—I send a little slip from the Washington *Star*[29]—then another clerk, Mr. Rowland,[30] is lying very sick. It is doubtful if he recovers. Wm. O'Connor has just been in to see me—He is well & flourishing.

Walt.

Mother, no letter from you the past week—

217. *To Louisa Van Velsor Whitman*

ATTORNEY GENERAL'S OFFICE,

Washington. | Tuesday afternoon | Feb. 5, *1867*.

Dearest mother,

I received your letter of Sunday week, Jan. 26—Mother, I hope that lameness in the wrist is better by this time.[31] There is no news to

28. See 214. WW pasted on the advertisement of the book.

29. The clipping from the *Star* read: "Accidents.—On Tuesday morning, as Mr. J. Hubley Ashton, Assistant Attorney General, was leaving his residence, corner of 14th and F streets, he fell and cut his face so badly as to confine him to his room for a few days. On the following day, Mr. F. U. Stitt, the pardon clerk of the same office, received a fall, by which his left arm was badly injured."

30. John A. Rowland, a clerk in the Attorney General's office, substituted for WW when he was on leave in 1870; see 374.

31. In this letter (Trent), Mrs. Whitman described the lameness and told WW that Jeff planned to visit him in Washington the following week. See 219.

write you this time—I have heard that old Mrs. Mix got through safe to Brooklyn the next day—I looked for Jeff, but he didn't come—When you write, tell me how Jeff is—

I suppose you have had a great change in the weather in Brooklyn —we have here—for several days past, it has been thawing & melting—Here in the office, it is the same old story—it is now about 12 o'clock—the Attorney Gen'l. & Ashton have gone to the Supreme Court—they go most every day now from 11 till 2—& I have little or nothing to do a good deal of the time when they are away—

Mother, write whether Jeff got the books, for himself & Dr. Ruggles[32] —write how Hattie is—Well, the sun is shining, & as I look out this morning on the Potomac, I see the ice is broke up, & the river is all open —I hope we shall have but little more cold weather—I have not had a very agreeable winter—I have not had a satisfactory room & arrangements—I think I shall look around & get one more suitable—

Mother, do you still have the office partly in your house—there in the long room?

Sometimes I feel as though I want to come home for about a week—I think it quite likely I shall come before long—I should not be able to stay longer than a week—I will tell you though, in time—

Well, mother dear, I believe that is all this time. Give my love to George, & Jeff & Mat.

Walt.

218. *To Louisa Van Velsor Whitman*

ATTORNEY GENERAL'S OFFICE,

Washington. | Tuesday noon, | Feb. 12, *1867.*

Dearest mother,

I rec'd your letter of Wednesday last all right. I shall begin to look for Jeff, to-morrow—I do hope he will come.

I have just changed my quarters—I moved to-day back again to the same house Mrs. Grayson used to live in—it is now occupied by a Mr. & Mrs. Benedict[33]—I have not got my old-room but a room right over it —it is in the attic, it is true, but I think it will be pleasant, & cool in summer—& all the quieter for being in the attic—every thing is new & clean, new bedstead, mattress, &c—I can't tell till I try, but I think I shall like it —that is, as well as one is apt to like any quarters here in Washington—I will write you how I like it in my next—I want Jeff to come & stay there

32. See 42 and 226.
33. Newton Benedict. The 1869 Directory listed him as a clerk in the State De-

with me—it will be pleasant & comfortable—it is 472 M st. 2d door west of 12th—

Mother, it may be I write kind of sober sometimes, but I have been this winter, & am now, in as good health as usual, & very good spirits—So, brother Jeff, I don't feel a bit "pegged out"—only getting old—most 50, you know—

We have had another cold spell here, pretty nearly as cold as ever—There is great excitement in Congress—they have night sessions[34]—

I went to the hospital Sunday afternoon last—there is a friend of mine there that got shot at Cold Harbor in June 1864—& he has had the bullet in him ever since—it was in a very bad place, the lower part of the stomach, just in the waist—last Saturday he had an operation & had it extracted—it was in, the length of my little finger—it was a very critical operation indeed—but he got through with, & is going to get well, according to all appearances now—There are lots of things left by the war, yet.

I hope Jeff will not disappoint me—the prospect, as I write, is for pleasant weather—& Jeff can stop with me just as well as not—Love to George and Matty, & all.

Walt.

219. *To Louisa Van Velsor Whitman*

ATTORNEY GENERAL'S OFFICE,

Washington. | Tuesday noon, | Feb. 19, *1867*.

Dearest mother,

Well, mother, Jeff has been to see me at last—he left yesterday morning—I wish he could have staid a few days longer—He seemed to be well pleased with his visit, & I am sure it was a great comfort to me—

I rather like my new quarters—at any rate they are better than where I was previously—they are very good on some accounts, & not so good on others—but one must not expect perfection. When you write tell me how Jeff got home—We are having pleasant weather here now—the ice & snow are all gone—Mother, do you see the papers much? I can send papers to you, only they would be rather old by the time you get them.

Well, mother, I left my letter awhile, & have been out taking a walk, & now return & finish my letter—It is quite like summer—I looked for an Almanac but couldn't find any to suit me—I am going out to Georgetown, & will find one there—I will send it to-morrow—

partment and Mrs. Benedict as a clerk in the First Comptroller's office; see 229.

34. A reconstruction bill under discussion aroused bitter controversy.

The O'Connors are much pleased with Jeff—Mrs. O'Connor has taken a real liking to him[35]—

I hope this will find you relieved of your rheumatism—I send my love to Matty & George & all.[36]

Walt.

220. *To Llewellyn Avery, Jr.*

ADDRESS: Llewellyn Avery, Jr. | Washington, | D. C. POSTMARK: Washington | Feb | 20 | D. C.

ATTORNEY GENERAL'S OFFICE,

Washington. Feb. 20, *1867*.

Mr. Avery,[37] | Dear Sir:

In answer to your note of 15th, I would inform you that a small edition has just been published of "Leaves of Grass" complete, (including "Drum Taps," &c)—price $3. I think Hudson Taylor's bookstore, on Penn'a. Av, has them—If not, I can supply you with a copy, by your calling on me at this Office.

Yours, respectfully,

Walt Whitman

221. *To Louisa Van Velsor Whitman*

ATTORNEY GENERAL'S OFFICE,

Washington. | Tuesday noon | Feb. 26, *1867*.

Dearest mother,

I rec'd your letter day before yesterday—We have had some stormy weather here too, but nothing so bad as you must have had—I wrote to Hannah last Saturday—I was down to the Hospital last Sunday, & also yesterday—there is a soldier there very bad with bleeding at the lungs—it is doubtful if he recovers—he is from Harper's Ferry, W. Va.—He is not willing to have me write to his folks, nor will he write himself—his mother is feeble, & he says it would hurt her—he is an only son—he

35. According to Mrs. Whitman's letter of February 20, "Jeff . . . likes the Oconors very much, says he spent a very agreable evening there" (Trent).

36. WW enclosed $5 in this letter for his mother, who wrote on February 21: "i feel Walt sometimes as if you was too liberall with me but its all i have except sometimes 15 or 20 cents" (Trent).

37. On the verso of the envelope, presumably in Avery's hand, appear several notations: "Received February 20th, 1867. | Walt Whitman was forty years | old during the 83d Anniversary | of American Independence. . . . 'I am Walt Whitman liberal and lusty | as nature.' " I have not identified Avery.

38. John H. Surratt, who had been a secret dispatch bearer for the Confederacy

is in the 44th Reg. Infantry—He likes to have me come & sit a while with him—so I go—I do not allow him to talk much, as it is best for him to keep very quiet. He is quite a southerner, although in our army—& takes great interest in politics—his name is Andrew J. Kephart—Mother, I tell you all the particulars, as I know you will be interested tho' a perfect stranger. There are all kinds of soldiers in the hospitals, some good & some the other thing. But there are always some that appreciate deeply any kindness & friendship—& it helps them along too, more than one would think.

Mother, I suppose you got your almanacks—both are calculated for *this* region, not New York, & one is a sort of Catholic almanac—I saw it had all the Saints' days.

O'Connor, & the wife too, were both very much taken with Jeff, & speak about him often.

Surratt is here in jail—his sister Anna goes to see him most every day —poor girl.[38]

It is pleasant here this forenoon—as I look out of my window, the river looks fine—there is a slight haze in the air but the warm sun is shining—O'Connor has just been in to see me a few moments—they have invited me up there to dinner, but I believe I don't care to go to-day.[39]

I was up at the Capitol last night, to see the House in session, & walk around—there was nothing very interesting—they were debating some appropriation Bill.

Mother dear, I hope this will find you all right, & free from rheumatism—Love to George & Mat & all—

Walt.

222. *To Ellen M. O'Connor* 2.26. [*1867*]

ENDORSED: "Ans'd." ADDRESS: Ellen M. O'Connor.

Tuesday afternoon | February 26.

My dear Nelly,

I will be at the house in time to go with you & see the Capitol

and involved, with his mother Anna, in Booth's conspiracy, fled the country before the murder of Lincoln. He remained a fugitive until he was arrested in Egypt in 1866. Unlike his mother, who had been convicted by a military tribunal and ordered hanged on July 7, 1865, the son was tried in a civil court, between June 10 and August 10; WW described the trial in 240. When the jury could not agree, a new trial was ordered, but because of inadequate evidence the government quietly released Surratt on June 22, 1868. His sister Anna sought clemency for her mother in 1865, but, presumably because of a conspiracy, her plea never reached the desk of President Johnson. See David Miller DeWitt, *The Assassination of Abraham Lincoln* (1909).

39. See 222.

lighted. About the dinner, (thank you for your kind invitation,) I fear I shall not be with you to-day.

Walt.

223. *To Louisa Van Velsor Whitman*

ATTORNEY GENERAL'S OFFICE,

Washington. March 5, *1867*, | Tuesday forenoon.

Dearest mother,

I rec'd the letter you wrote last Wednesday[40]—It has been rainy weather again here, & plenty of mud—Sunday afternoon I was at the Hospital—that young man that was so low with bleeding at the lungs, Kephart,[41] was easier—he was very bad just after I wrote last week—but Sunday it seemed as though he might recover yet if he had good luck—he has written to his folks at Harper's Ferry, West Va.

I went up to the Capitol Sunday night—Congress was in full blast in both houses—they paid no more attention to its being Sunday, than if it was any other day—which I thought a very good sign—the Radicals have passed their principal measures over the President's vetos—as you will see in the papers. There is much talk about impeachment—but I think it is very doubtful if there is any impeachment[42]—

O mother, I must not forget to tell the *great news among Clerks* (far more important than Reconstruction, or impeaching Andy)—that is, we are going to have 20 percent addition to our pay, for the present year—that is, I shall get quite a handsome little sum, back pay, & about $25 additional, a month, till 1st of July next—if I stay here. We havnt got the money yet, but I suppose it is sure—

I like my boarding house very well, take it altogether—we have a tip-top table—& the folks are kind & accommodating.

The Old Congress went out yesterday, & the new one (the 40th) organized right away—the Republicans have a strong majority[43]—

It is dark & rainy this forenoon here—snow & drizzle—

Mother, you must not imagine any thing about me—I am having good times enough—"eat well & sleep well," as Dr. Ruggles[44] says—&

40. Mrs. Whitman's letter of February 27 (Trent) was filled with complaints about her health ("i feel my age more this winter then i ever did before"), about Jeff's children, and about George's business difficulties.

41. See 221.

42. In order to complete its business before the beginning of the new session on March 4, Congress held a marathon session that finally ended on Sunday morning.

43. The new Congress, according to the New York *Herald*, had 128 Republicans

have a pocket full of money—which you can call upon when you want any—as I look out of the window while I write, I see we are having a little snow for a change—So good bye for this time, mother dear—Love to George & Jeff & all,

Walt.

224. *To Louisa Van Velsor Whitman*

ADDRESS: Mrs. Louisa Whitman, | p. o. Box 218, | Brooklyn, | New York. POSTMARK: Washington | Mar | 12 | D. C.

ATTORNEY GENERAL'S OFFICE,

Washington. | Tuesday, | March 12, *1867.*

Dearest mother,

I rec'd Jeff's letter on Monday—I am sorry to hear you suffer so much with the rheumatism, & it is so bad in the wrist—Jeff thinks it is because you wash & do the rough work, & expose yourself too much—Mother, I would like if you would get some woman to come every week, or every other week, for a day, & do the washing, &c.[45]—As to the little girls, Jeff says they *will* be with you, & bother you sometimes too much—When one is old, one is easily tired and annoyed—& I have long been sorry you can't have more quiet to yourself & rest.

Every thing goes the same as usual with me—The young man that had bleeding at the lungs[46] seemed to be getting along pretty well, till Saturday & Sunday last, when he had a return of the sweating spells—they weaken him very much—I was down there Sunday—He has been very dissipated though only 24 years old—I believe I told you he is an only son.

We had a warm & clear day here yesterday—after the usual long spell of rainy & dark weather—Washington is nothing but mud—

I took tea at O'Connors last Sunday night—they are all well as usual—have got to move, the end of this month—they have found no place yet—

Ashton, the Assistant Attorney Gen'l, has gone on to Philadelphia with wife & child, to spend three or four days—I like my new boarding place very well, take it altogether—

Mother, I am writing this at my table, by the big window I have

and 35 Democrats in the House and 40 Republicans and 12 Democrats in the Senate.

44. See 42 and 226.

45. Mrs. Whitman dutifully replied on March 15: "i shall certainly do so for i find i cant do much in the way of any thing that is laborious, its hard to give up but old age will creep on us" (Trent).

46. Kephart; see 221.

mentioned several times in former letters—it is very pleasant indeed—the river looks so fine, & the banks & hills in the distance—I can sit sometimes & look out for a long time—It is mighty lucky for me I fell in with such a good situation—Mother, if it was only so where I could come home oftener, & see you & all—I have not thought any thing decided of the visit I spoke of—I will send you word in good time, if I should come—I should rather stop home, this time,[47] if I come, as I should only be for a few days, not more than a week—I can sleep in the room George did—or any how. O, I must tell you I am getting a new coat—sack-coat, dark blue—I have pants of the same—& shall have to get a new vest—when I shall come out quite spruce—I had 6 shirts made last July, & they are good yet—So much for the clothing department.

Jeff don't say whether you got my last Tuesday's letter, (March 5,) with the envelopes, &c.[48]—but I suppose of course you did—Yesterday was such a fine day, I went off about 1 o'clock & had quite a jaunt—went to Georgetown, &c. & walked so, I got very tired, when I arrived home—We don't have dinner till 5 o'clock—but I always take a good lunch in my pocket—the table is furnished with plenty, & good—Mother, I think about you a great deal—I think, what if mother is sick & bothered, & every thing—& I feel as if I should fly—I go evenings up to the office frequently—I have got me a splendid astral-lamp, to burn gas by a tube, & it works to admiration, (all at the expense of the office)—& there I can sit, & read &c. as nice as you please—then I am getting many books for the Library (our office Library) that I have long wanted to read at my leisure—& can get any book I want, in reason—so you see it is a great privilege I have here. Love to dear sister Mat, & little ones, & all.

Walt.

225. *To Abby H. Price*

ADDRESS: Abby H. Price, | 279 East 55th street, | New York City. POSTMARK: Washington | Mar | 13 | D. C.

ATTORNEY GENERAL'S OFFICE,

Washington. | Wednesday | March 13, *1867.*

Dear friends, all,

I have just rec'd the letter of the 10th—I sympathise deeply with those of you that have suffered with pains & illness—but hope, from the wording of what you write, that it is now all over.

47. WW stayed with the Prices in 1866; see 186–190.
48. Mrs. Whitman acknowledged, on March 15 (Trent), receipt of $15 and envelopes.
49. Someone, probably Helen Price, has written above this word "(Ear ache)."

Poor Emily—it must have been such agony—that kind of distress[49] is about as severe as any thing can be, for human endurance—I hope Emily will try to go over, soon, and make a good call on Mother—

Mother isn't well—she has rheumatism pretty bad—I am sorry to hear that Helen has attacks of sick head-ache—& that you too have been unwell—I do hope you are now both of you well, & may continue so.

There is nothing important or new in my affairs here—I am still in the same Office—find my work mild & agreeable, & the place one remarkably well suited to a lazy, elderly, literary gentleman—

The O'Connors are well as usual—They have to move, the end of this month. Mr. Parker[50] wrote me, some time since, & I have written an answer & sent it.

I still go to the Hospitals—always go Sunday afternoons.

We are having a dark, cloudy, rainy time here, just now—*not* for a novelty—I have good health, & good spirits. I send love to you & Helen & Emmy & all, not forgetting Mr. Arnold—Remember me to Arthur, when you write—God give you health, in body & in spirit—Farewell,

Walt Whitman

226. *To Louisa Van Velsor Whitman*

ATTORNEY GENERAL'S OFFICE,

Washington. March 19, *1867.*

Dearest mother,

I got both your letters last week, & they were a relief to my mind—I want to hear whether sis got over swallowing the penny[51]—don't forget to write about it—It has been cold & disagreeable here, and another snow storm—but the sun shone all day yesterday—it keeps pretty backward here.

I went down to the Hospital Sunday—that young man Kephart[52] was sitting up by the stove—he looked very pale & thin, but is doing far better than I anticipated.

I have written a letter to Han—I have received a letter from Mrs. Price—they have most all of them been sick this winter—I see quite a good many notices of Dr. Ruggles' death in the papers—I enclose one

50. See 193.
51. In a postscript on March 20, Mrs. Whitman added: "last evening sis swallowed a penny, Jeff was very much alarmed about it but she is bright enough now" (Trent).
52. See 221 and 223.

printed in the paper here—taken from N. Y. Post—there is quite a long one in the Round Table, of March 16.[53]

Every thing is exactly the same in the office, & with me—Ashton has returned from Philadelphia—he tells me, confidentially, that he has decided to resign, early this summer—I am sorry to hear it—

I hope George will have good luck with the houses[54]—he must take things cool—don't fail to write to me how every thing goes—

Well, I believe that is all, for this time, dear mother.

Walt.

227. *To Louisa Van Velsor Whitman*

ATTORNEY GENERAL'S OFFICE

Washington | Tuesday forenoon | March 26, *1867*.

Dearest mother,

Your letter, including Han's, arrived, & I was glad to hear that sis's penny had a safe journey—I was very glad to hear George had sold one of the houses—& also to hear from Han.[55]

Mother, all the news I have to write about my affairs, is the same old thing—we have had another long spell of stormy weather here, rain, & snow, & mud—In the office, every thing as usual—I spend a good deal of the time there, nights & Sundays—it is quiet & agreeable—It is likely Surratt's trial will come on before long—I have become acquainted with St Marie,[56] the man who discovered Surratt in Rome—it was quite curious, & I will tell you when I come home. He goes here by a false name—he is very unhappy, & is in dread of assassination, from Surratt's friends—He came to me for advice, & wanted me to intercede for him with some members of Congress, as he says the government is treating him very coldly, as if they didn't consider he had done them any favor. I declined to mix up at all in the matter, in any way. He talked a good deal, & told me a good deal about Surratt. It is quite an interesting story, & I will tell you all about it when I come home.

53. See 42. Obituaries appeared in the New York *Evening Post*, March 11, and *The Round Table*, v (1867), 173. The author of the obituary in the New York *Tribune*, on March 12, lamented the fact that Ruggles had abandoned his profession to produce "Ruggles Gems": "The public gained nothing by the change, and we regret Dr. Ruggles' death, not because we have lost an artist, but because an excellent man and a worthy citizen has gone to his rest." Jeff and Martha attended the funeral, according to Mrs. Whitman's letter of March 15 (Trent).

54. On March 15, Mrs. Whitman said that George expected to sell one of his houses, but had to borrow $200 from Jeff: "he is well but begins to look quite old" (Trent).

55. On March 20 (Trent), Hannah wrote excitedly about her mother's lameness, begged her or one of the boys to visit her in the summer, and extolled WW's kindness to her.

56. Henry Ste. Marie reported the hiding place of John H. Surratt (see 221) to

It was so stormy, the walking so dreadful, (half-melted snow,) that I didn't go to the hospital last Sunday. I have rec'd another epistle from Heyde—one of his regular damned fool's letters—I never answer them, nor make any allusion to them—it was full of complaints[57]—

To-day it is bright sunshiny weather—yesterday too—but rather cool—Congress is to adjourn this week—they have carried all their measures successfully over the President—I am writing this at my desk—the air is very clear, & I can see a great distance over the Potomac off into Virginia—the river is high & muddy to-day—I hope this will find you feeling well, & free from rheumatism. Love to George & Jeff & Mat.

Walt.

228. *To Abby H. Price*

ADDRESS: Abby H. Price, | 279 East 55th street, | New York City. POSTMARK: Washington | (?) | (?) | D. C.

ATTORNEY GENERAL'S OFFICE,

Washington. March 27, 1867.

My dear friend,

Although your letter I see has the N. Y. post office stamp, Mar. 25, I have only just rec'd it, (2 o'clock Wednesday P.M.)—I have talked with Thomas Harlan[58]—he treated me very well. My impression is, there is little or no chance of getting Congress to pass, at this time, a special resolution or law putting the ruffles on the list of exempts—There is no Committee of Ways & Means yet appointed in the H[ouse] of R[epresentatives]—True, any member could offer such a Bill, & if it had powerful influence, they *might* suspend the rules & pass it—but there are too many, both in House & Senate, who would almost certainly object—one objection would be that ruffles are matters of extra ornament &c. &c. and ought to pay a tax, if any thing does[59]—

the American consul in Montreal when the latter fled there shortly before Lincoln's murder; see DeWitt, *The Assassination of Abraham Lincoln* (1909), 187–188, 205–206.

57. Heyde complained of Hannah's sloppy attire ("her appearance would disgrace any servant in the vicinity"), her laziness, her lack of "womanly sensibility . . . and intellectual imbecility" (Trent). He wrote much more temperately about the same time to Mrs. Whitman (Trent).

58. Undoubtedly Thomas Harland, chief clerk in the Patent Office, to whom Mrs. Price referred in her letter; see the following note.

59. WW was replying to Mrs. Price's undated letter, in which she made a tempting offer: "I write now in great haste to ask your assistance in behalf of Our Ruffle Manufacture and if you succeed in doing what we ask, or in getting it done I am authorized to offer you a 1000 dollar check as soon as it is done! think of *that.* Tis only a simple act of Justice that we ask either" (Yale). Mrs. Price as a dressmaker feared the effect on her business of a projected tax on ruffles; see Allen, 381.

Still, I will try what I can do—I will see a few of the members, forthwith—I have one in my mind, I think may be the best one I can get to offer a Bill, & if he is willing, we will try it on—Had I known it when the Committee & House were cooking the Bill, I have no doubt I could have got it put in with the ¶ including shirt-bosoms, &c.—But that's poor consolation.

There is nothing new or important with me. I am well as usual, & working the same, (not much.) Love to Helen and Emmy & all.

Walt.

229. *To Louisa Van Velsor Whitman*

ATTORNEY GENERAL'S OFFICE,

Washington, April 2, *1867*.

Dearest mother,

I rec'd your letter of March 28—you must have had rather a dreary time this winter, the cold & storms, & being left so much alone[60]—but now I think the spring is upon us, & I think it will be pleasant enough there all summer—

Dear mother, I have not much to write this time—I am feeling very well—no trouble in the head, nor any thing, so far—I get along very well in my boarding house—the landlady[61] is a young woman, from New York State—but she works in the Treasury & leaves things to her servants, black women—I like her very well—& the place is probably as good a one as I could get—In the Office every thing is just the same—Ashton expects to leave next May or June.

We have had very pleasant weather here this week—only sometimes the dust is bad—I went to the Hospital Sunday & shall go again this afternoon—Kephart,[62] that had bleeding at the lungs, & pneumonia, is

60. Mrs. Whitman continued in her letters to complain of the severe winter. On March 21, she lamented: "it has been almost as much as your life was worth to get to the privy"; and on March 28: "it will be spring one of these days i hope" (Trent).

61. Mrs. Newton Benedict; see 218. 62. See 221.

63. The friendship of WW with this former soldier can be reconstructed from Wilson's letters in the Feinberg Collection. On July 18, 1869, Wilson recalled his confinement in Armory Square Hospital (see 94), "when your kind face & pleasant words cheered the soldier Boys & won their hearts. I never shall forget the first time you came in after David & I got there. We Loved you from the first time we spoke to you." In Wilson's first letter, written on November 11, 1865, he began: "I suppose you will think that I have forgotten you long before this time but I have not, your kindness to me while in the hospital will never be forgotten by me." After a lapse in the correspondence, he wrote on December 16, 1866: "I wish if aggreable to yourself to keep up a regular correspondence between us . . . I think it will be of benefit to me morally, and perhaps will not be of any detriment to you." In this letter he admitted that he had just discovered that WW was a poet. On January 27 of the following year, he informed WW that he had been reading *Leaves of Grass*, but complained: "I wrote to you a year and more ago

quite recovered—when I came away, he walked out a few blocks with me —there are one or two pretty bad cases that I go to see, yet—

Washington is filled with *darkies*—the men & children & wenches swarm in all directions—(I am not sure but the North is like the man that won the elephant in a raffle)—I was glad you wrote about the little girls—Tell Hattie and sis Uncle Walt sends his love to them, & is coming home to see them.

Walt.

230. *To Benton H. Wilson* [*4.12. 1867*]

DRAFT LETTER.

Dear boy,[63]

Your letter has come to hand. According to request, I send you immediately a few hurr[ied] lines in response. My dear loving boy, I wish things were situated so you could be with me, & we could be together for a while, where we could enjoy each others society & sweet friendship & you could talk freely. I am sure it would do you good, & it would be a great pleasure to me. But we must take things as they are. I have thought over some passages in the letter, but will not at present say much to you on the subject, in writing. One or two things I will say briefly at present—One is, that it is every way the best & most natural condition for a young man to be married, having a companion, a good & affectionate wife—& another is, that contentment with one's situation in life does not depend half so much on what that situation is, as on the mood & spirit in which one accepts the situation & makes the best of it.

But these are bits of cold wisdom. I must put something to you better than that in my letter. So I will cheer my boy [&] tell you again,

that I was married but did not receive any reply, so I did not know but you was displeased with it"; he concluded the letter: "I remain as ever your | Boy Friend | with Love | Benton H. Wilson." WW replied (lost), and sent *The Good Gray Poet*, which Wilson acknowledged on February 3. On April 7, after he informed WW that his wife had gone to the hospital for her first confinement (the child was to be named Walt Whitman), he complained: "I am poor and am proud of it but I hope to rise by honesty and industry. I am a married man but I am not happy for my disposition is not right. I have got a good Woman and I love her dearly but I seem to lack patience or something. I think I had ought to live alone, but I had not ought to feel so." On April 21, Wilson acknowledged WW's reply of April 12: "I do not want you to misunderstand my motives in writing to you of my Situation & feelings as I did in my last letter or else I shall have to be more guarded in my letters to you. I wrote so because you wanted me to write how I was situated, and give you my mind without reserve, and all that I want is your advice and Love, and I do not consider it cold lecture or dry advice. I wish you to write to me just as you feel & express yourself and advise as freely as you wish and will be satisfied." On September 15, Wilson wondered why WW had not replied. See also 360.

Benton, that I love you dearly, & always keep you in mind, though we are separated by hundreds of miles. Remember this, dearest comrade, when things are cloudy with you, for it is true—& such thoughts are often a balm & comfort to the mind.

Write to me often as you can. Don't mind because we are separated now, as things are. We will meet one day, I have no doubt. Try to keep up the same brave heart in the affairs of peace, that I know you did when you were a soldier. A young man's life is a battle any how. Noble—thrice noble is he who steadily carries throughout the march, through defeat or whatever happens, a gay, unconquered spirit.

231. *To Louisa Van Velsor Whitman*

ATTORNEY GENERAL'S OFFICE,

Washington. | Tuesday forenoon | April 16, *1867.*

Dearest mother,

I rec'd your letter last week a couple of hours after I sent mine. I have written to Hannah. Well, mother, we have had a spell of warm weather here—& last night & this morning we are having quite a rain—I can see the difference this morning already—the grass & trees are beginning to look green—they have made a large flower garden right in front of my window at the office.

Wm O'Connor is coming on to New York to stop three days—he goes on to-night—he may call on Jeff at the City Hall—but may-be not—H. J. Raymond wants him to come to New York & write for the *Times* &c—but I don't know as he will go[64]—

I went to a concert last night—Brignoli & Parepa[65]—nothing very great—

There is nothing new at the office—I went up to the Supreme Court last Friday, & heard the Attorney General Mr. Stanbery make quite a great speech—he is a good speaker—you would have liked it.

I was down at the hospital Sunday—there was one poor young man, a Maryland boy, very bad from delirium tremens—(such cases are getting quite common)—this young man saw such sights & terrible things, he took it into his head that the Almighty was in a rage, & punishing him—

64. Evidently Raymond (see 209) was considering O'Connor for a position on the New York *Times*. On May 9, O'Connor wrote that he had heard from Raymond—"a sort of hankering treatment of the subject, but no offer" (Feinberg; Traubel, III, 521).

65. Pasquale Brignoli (1824–1884), the Italian tenor, and Euphrosyne Parepa-Rosa (1836–1876), the English soprano, gave a recital at Metzerott Hall, of which the *National Republican* reported: "Their performances last evening were all that heart and cultivated taste could demand." According to Allen (*Handbook*, 195), "The Singer in the Prison"

& he just got on his knees, & *remained so for over 12 hours*, praying away for mercy—so the wardmaster told me—I sat by him some time—he told me, "*they*" went away while I was with him—he said he could hear "*them*," a good ways off—but they wouldn't come near him while I was there—he got into quite a little nap while I remained—you know if the delirium tremens patients can only get a few hours good sleep the worst is over—they are rational on most things—One of these men, in the hospital, had an idea there was a great cat gnawing at his arm, & eating it—he had this idea for days & days, & of course suffered awfully—One of the watchmen of the Treasury, (formerly a Captain in the army, in an Ohio reg't,) is there in the hospital, with delirium tremens—So you see what troubles there are in the world, of one kind & another—

We are quite busy at the office—have a good many people coming —so it is quite lively—We had a clerk here, who was a great nuisance to every body, a young sprig of a Virginian—he has cleared out, forced to resign—we are all very glad—it makes a great relief—all the rest of us get along like brothers—I like them all, & they like me.

Walt

If Mary & the girls come, you must give them my love, & tell Mary I shall send her a small package of books soon—I will send word before.

Tell Hattie she must behave like a lady & try to learn—Uncle Walt is coming home soon, to see her[66]—

232. *To Louisa Van Velsor Whitman*[67] *4.23. 1867*

ATTORNEY GENERAL'S OFFICE,

Washington, 186

Dearest mother,

William O'Connor has returned, & has brought me news from you all, & about Jeff's offer to go to St. Louis.[68] I don't know what to advise about it—but feel as if I was rather in favor of accepting the offer. Jeff must take it cool, & not get excited about it—& after he has *decided* which to do, must go ahead for good, & not doubt his decision, or fear he has done wrong, &c—I believe that's about all I wish to say on it, at present. Wm. O'Connor was much pleased with his visit, & speaks

described Parepa-Rosa's concert in Sing Sing Prison.

66. The postscript was omitted in the Camden Edition.

67. The first part of this letter has never been published.

68. Jeff's offer, as the next few letters make clear, was to cause excitement and confusion in the Whitman household. Martha bustled about in feverish haste (and waste); Mrs. Whitman did not know where she was to live, and complained about Martha and the general turmoil.

about you & all—he is a good fellow, & has been a good friend to me.

Mother, I send you the Harper's Weekly, with the picture of Abraham Lincoln & the Drummer Boy[69]—I think it is tip top—We are having warm weather here—I am feeling very well indeed—I was down at the hospital Sunday afternoon—the young man that had delirium tremens, that prayed so long, has got quite well—his prayers seemed to be answered—at any rate, he is well & gone back to duty—while several others with the same complaint, are lying there not yet recovered—One soldier, 12th Infantry, was dying while I was there—he had pneumonia—it was a very sudden & dangerous attack, only taken two or three days before—he had been in the war, & had been wounded badly—but sickness took him off at last—I sat by him about half an hour—breathing was very oppressive indeed—It was a fine afternoon, & very still in the ward—& off a block or so there is a big Catholic church, St. Aloysius Church—they were ringing a chime of bells, three or four bells playing a sort of tune, sounded loud & joyful—I sat and listened for a long while—the poor dying man kept looking at me with such a look—

ATTORNEY GENERAL'S OFFICE,
Washington. | Tuesday, | April 23, *1867.*

Dearest mother,

Since the other sheet was written & just as I was going to enclose, your letter of Saturday came. You must not be uneasy about a place—there will be some way provided—If not one way, it will be another, I hope—

So mother, keep a good heart—I guess I must try to come on to Brooklyn & set you all right—

Walt.

233. *To Thomas Jefferson Whitman*

ATTORNEY GENERAL'S OFFICE,

Washington. April 29, *1867.*

Dear brother Jeff,

I heard by William O'Connor of the St. Louis proposition—& as far as I could judge by his account—& since by your letter & Mother's—it seems to me best to accept the offer, & go, by all means—

It is a great work—a noble position—& will give you a good big field.

Jeff, I wish to hear about the family arrangements—whether Mother

69. The issue of April 27 contained this cartoon by Thomas Nast (1840–1902).
70. See 31. 71. See 81.

& Martha &c are going to stay there this summer, or not—(I hope they are.)

There is nothing special with me, to write about. In the office, all goes on as usual. I still board at 472 M st. Love to Mat & the little girls. Remember me to Mr. Lane[70] & Davis[71]—So good bye for this time, Jeffy, dear brother.

Walt.

234. *To Louisa Van Velsor Whitman*

ATTORNEY GENERAL'S OFFICE,

Washington. | Tuesday, | April 30, *1867.*

Dearest mother,

I received your letter—also one from Jeffy. I wrote to Jeffy yesterday—I suppose it is for the best that he should go to St. Louis—as it seems to be a great position—I was much pleased to hear that it was Mr. Kirkwood[72] who was the designing Engineer—& also that Davis is to go to St. Louis on the works—

Well, mother, about domestic matters—I hardly know what to say at present—Jeff did not say in his letter what was proposed, or how he & Mat thought of doing—I can tell better after I hear—But, Mother, you must not worry about it—it will be arranged some way—

There is nothing new in my affairs—I have a little more work these days than usual, but get along first rate—am satisfied with the boarding-house as well as could be expected. Love to you & all, dear mother. I write this at my desk—spring is quite advanced here—it is a damp, misty, cloudy forenoon—but pleasant—I can send you whatever money you need, dear mother, any time—or can come on for a few days—try to take things coolly.

Walt.

235. *To William D. O'Connor* *5.5. [1867]*

ADDRESS: Wm. D. O'Connor, | Light House Board, | U. S. Treasury Dep't. | Washington, | D. C.
POSTMARK: New-York | May | 8 | (?).

Brooklyn | Sunday afternoon, May 5th.

Dear William O'Connor,

When I arrived home yesterday I found my brother worse than I

72. See 51. On September 29, 1865 (Feinberg), Jeff wrote to WW that Kirkwood had gone to St. Louis to construct a water works.

had anticipated.[73] It is a case of malignant erysipelas, with great swelling, sores, & for a while complete blindness, now partially relieved. There are spells also of lethargy & flightiness—all bad enough, yet, as far as the case stands at this present writing, *he will come out safe*, I somehow feel *certain.*

Mother is well as usual—defers every thing else, & does the nursing, &c. for George. When I came, yesterday, I found her standing with a cup of warm tea, feeding slowly with a spoon, to some one wrapt in a great blanket, & seated in an arm chair, by the stove—I did not recognize my brother at first—he was so disfigured, & the features out of all proportion & discolored. Mother put down the cup, &c. & began to cry—this affected poor George—yet I preserved my composure, though much distrest, as you will understand.

The rest of the family are well. Jeff leaves to-morrow evening for St. Louis. It is cold here, with raw easterly wind. I met Henry Clapp[74] in Broadway yesterday—he has a $1500 clerkship in a public office in New York—I met Edward H. House[75]—also other of my young men friends—they are all very, very cordial & hospitable—I shall go over & make Mrs. Price a short visit this afternoon.

They all talk of you here—as of the good person, the desired one,

73. On May 2, Mrs. Whitman reported that George was not well, but was still able to go to work; she did not indicate the gravity of his illness. She was upset by all the turmoil involved in Jeff's moving. Martha, somewhat impulsively, sold all the furnishings "and spent the money as fast as it came in for clothes to go in the country" (Trent). Under the circumstances, since the family desperately needed some one who could "take things coolly," it is understandable that WW decided to hurry to Brooklyn.

74. Henry Clapp (1814–1875) was one of WW's intimates from the Pfaffian days. Restless and adventurous, Clapp roamed to Paris, returned in the 1840's to Lynn, Mass., to edit the *Essex County Washington* (later *The Pioneer*), and eventually went to New York, where he became "king of the Bohemians." As editor of the short-lived *Saturday Press* (1858–1860), he printed "A Child's Reminiscence" ("Out of the Cradle Endlessly Rocking"), and, in 1860, praised *Leaves of Grass* when others condemned it; see Allen, 242–244, 260–261. "Henry Clapp," WW said to Traubel in 1888, "stepped out from the crowd of hooters—was my friend: a much needed ally at that time (having a paper of his own) when almost the whole press of America when it mentioned me at all treated me with derision or worse. If you ever write anything about me in which it may be properly alluded to I hope you will say good things about Henry Clapp" (Traubel, I, 236). In his reply to WW on May 9, O'Connor was amused that Clapp was "becoming a respectable citizen. When once a man enters upon the downward path, &c. . . . one can see as the guilty result of Bohemianism, a place in the Common Council or Board of Aldermen!" (Feinberg; Traubel, III, 522).

Two letters from Clapp to WW, March 27, 1860, and October 3, 1867 (Feinberg), appear in Traubel, I, 236–237, 267. Clapp is also referred to in 247–248. See William Winter's sympathetic account in *Old Friends, Being Literary Recollections of Other Days* (1909), 57–63.

75. At this time House was not with the New York *Tribune* (see 16); he was engaged in theatrical management in New York and London.

76. O'Connor, much flattered by this paragraph, compared himself to "a young girl finding herself beloved or admired by some one unsuspected before." In the same letter, May 9, he went on to describe how deeply WW's mother "affected" him: "Her cheerfulness, her infinite gentleness and tenderness, were like the deep smile of the evening sky. As I saw her that night, with the children on each side, and each leaning a head upon her, I thought of the Madonna grown old" (Feinberg; Traubel, III, 522).

exhilarating, whose presence gives sun, & whose talk nourishes—(I think you must have laid yourself out that evening.)[76]

Dear Nelly, I send you my love—also to Charles Eldridge—shall probably remain here the ensuing week.

Walt

236. *To William D. O'Connor* *5.12. [1867]*

ADDRESS: Wm. D. O'Connor, | Light House Board, | Treasury Department, | Washington, | D. C.
POSTMARK: New-York | May | 13.

Sunday Afternoon | May 12.

Dear friend,

My brother does not get on quite as well as I had anticipated. Yet I still hold to the judgment in my previous letter. He has been, & is, very sick—has had improved spells, & then goes down again. To-day he is in the latter condition.

William, I received the letter, with Ramsdells note.[77] Also Allen's. (Also the first letter soon after my arrival here.)

As to Allen,[78] refusing &c. giving his views, reasons, &c. &c. it is

77. H. J. Ramsdell was a clerk in Washington; in a hospital notebook (Huntington), WW called him "chief clerk." In the 1869 Directory, he was listed as a correspondent. On May 8, Ramsdell reported the high praise that George Townsend, the journalist (1841–1914), accorded to WW—"a stupendous genius," "the song of a God." On July 17, he asked WW to do whatever he could for Judge Milton Kelly, of Idaho, against whom charges had been brought by "a very bad man," Congressman Edward D. Holbrook (1836–1870). Actually, on July 12, WW had submitted to the Attorney General a "Report | on the | *Charges* submitted by | *Hon. E. D. Holbrook,* | Del[egate] from Idaho Terr[itory], | *against* | *Hon. Milton Kelly,* | Asso[ciate] Just[ice] Supreme Court of Idaho" (National Archives). To this forty-one page summary of the evidence, all in WW's hand, there is appended a letter signed by Stanbery but written by WW, dated July 20: "The Conclusion in the preceding Report is hereby adopted by me, & ordered to stand as the decision of this Office in the Case, so far as now presented." On July 22, Ramsdell apologized for his "aggressiveness." (Ramsdell's letters are in the Feinberg Collection.) Judge Kelly wrote to WW on June(?) 21 (National Archives) and again on August 9 (Yale). On November 15, 1875, Ramsdell, among others, petitioned Benjamin H. Bristow, Secretary of the Treasury, that WW "be appointed to a position in the Treasury Department" (National Archives).

78. On May 9, O'Connor wrote: "I enclose a letter I got from that child of a burnt father, Allen . . . It is truly Pecksniffian, and seems to have been written on all-fours. You will see that it ends the matter of publishing the book, and he doesn't say a word about John Burroughs' book . . . I think, on the whole, it is probably altogether best that Carleton should have nothing to do with 'Leaves of Grass,' though I would well enough like to have him publish the 'Notes'" (Feinberg; Traubel, III, 521–522). George W. Carleton was a New York publisher, and Henry Stanley Allen was evidently associated with him, since the 1867 Directory listed them at the same business address. In 1864 O'Connor had suggested Carleton as the publisher of *Drum-Taps;* see Trowbridge's letter to WW (Feinberg; Traubel, II, 524). In 1865 O'Connor proposed to George William Curtis (1824–1892), the editor of *Harper's Weekly,* that he write to Carleton about the publication of *The Good Gray Poet;* see Traubel, I, 86. Since O'Connor was not successful in either attempt, it is surprising that he once again sought to interest Carleton in publication schemes. See also Miller, ed., *Drum-Taps,* xxv.

perhaps one of those services to a thing, (precious, rare & precious, in philosophy, & life too,) rendered by showing not only how that thing appears from the point of view of intensest vermin & filth, exclusively, but of vermin & filth diluted with shallowness to the last degree that life will bear.

If my brother does not get worse, & no crisis takes place, I think, (as at present intending) I shall leave for Washington Wednesday morning next.

Mother is well, (considering). All the rest are first rate. Jeff is in St. Louis. Nelly, I send you my true love, my darling.

Walt.

237. *To Abraham Simpson*

ENDORSED (by WW): "sent to Abm Simpson— | May 20 '67." DRAFT LETTER.

ATTORNEY GENERAL'S OFFICE,

Washington. May 20, *1867.*

Abm. Simpson.[79] | My dear Sir:

I have been absent in New York & Brooklyn & only returned three days ago. I have rec'd your note, & wish to answer it elaborately soon. At present, I can only say that if you are going into publishing & if you feel like taking hold of my productions, I should cordially open negotiations with you—But the papers are in error in giving the idea that I am writing a book on a new subject—it is only a new & far more perfected edition of *Leaves of Grass*—which work, though printed, has really never been

79. Simpson, who, while working for J. M. Bradstreet & Son, had supervised the binding of *Drum-Taps* (see 162), wrote on May 10 that he was going into business for himself: "Hearing you are writing another book, [I] would like to print and publish it for you and will give you better advantages than any other publishing house. . . . One of my reasons for securing your friendship is my appreciation for you as a man, with knowing your life has been devoted to help among those most in need of your assistance." On May 31, he informed WW that "we have established a Ptg & Publishing House." But, on July 3, he advised WW that after consultation "with several eminent literary men, . . . though we are favorably impressed, . . . we deem it injudicious to commit ourselves to its publication at the present time." (These letters are in the Feinberg Collection.)

80. After seeing WW's name in a newspaper, Sholes (mentioned in 43) wrote to him from Albany on May 24. Sholes had occupied a bed next to Lewis Brown's in Armory Square Hospital in 1862 and 1863, and recalled WW's visits: "My kind friend (for so you must permit me to call you) I have thought of you many times since I left Washington and how well can I remember you as you came into the Wards with the Haversack under your arm, giving some little necessary here, a kind word there, and when you came to Louis [Brown's] bed and mine how cordialy you grasped our hands and

published at all. I shall be happy to hear any thing from you. My address is at this office.

Walt Whitman

238. *To Hiram Sholes* [*5.30. 1867*]

DRAFT LETTER.

Dear friend Hiram,[80]

Your letter of 27th May[81] has come safe to hand, & I was truly glad to hear from you. Hiram, you must not think I have forgotten you, for I have thought of you too many times since the days we used to see each other there in the Hospital. Lewis Brown is well. I see him often. He has a place here as Clerk, at $1200 a year. He is in the 4th Auditor's Office, Treasury Department, & that is his address. Did you know Adrian Bartlett—in Ward K? He is also a clerk in 4th Auditor's. Thompson,[82] the one so low with diarrhea, went home to New Jersey, & I have never heard from him since. Taber was killed in one of the Battles of the Wilderness. Shot in the head & fell instantly. Tom Sawyer, (Lewy Brown's friend), passed safe through the war—but we have not heard from him now for two years. Dr. Bliss is practising here in Washington. Dr Bowen[83] also. Old Armory Square is now used as an Army Clothing depot. Of course all the big hospitals are long broken up—there now remain only the Post Hospital, U. S. A. on K st. & two or three small regimental hospitals in & around the city.[84]

As to me & my fortunes I am in pretty good health, thank God—& I am working in the Attorney General's office (as the heading of this letter.)

anxiously enquired into our condition. I thank you for all this and you in your lonely moments must be happy in thinking of the good you have done to the many suffering ones during the war" (Feinberg). In his reply of June 8 (Feinberg), Sholes reported that his health was excellent, but not his economic lot: he had been an attendant in an insane asylum, a watchman, and a doorkeeper, positions he was able to hold for only short periods of time.

WW's letter supplies details about soldiers mentioned earlier: Brown (see 60), Bartlett (see 141), Taber (see 60), Sawyer (see 43), Dr. Bliss (see 43), Harris (see 141), Curley (see 60), and Cate (see 94).

81. WW was in error: Sholes's letter was dated May 24.

82. Perhaps H. B. Thompson, who wrote to WW on July 22, 1869: "You will not remember the writer of this letter. . . . I wont forget Walt Whitman. I have just read that you have completed your half century. May you live to a ripe old age, loving and beloved. I was reading 'Drum Taps' last night, no man can depict Army life so vividly that had not spent his time amongst the boys" (Yale).

83. Dr. Charles H. Bowen was a Washington physician.

84. This sentence was lined through, but, contrary to my usual practice, I have transcribed it because it seemed of interest.

It is an easy kind of place—the other clerks are all young men, friendly & jovial—So I have things pleasant enough. The pay is 1000 a year.[85]

Miss Lowell[86] is still around—is interested in the African schools. Lewy Brown has just been in to see me—he says he wrote two letters & wrote to your mother—Joe Harris often asks for you & is doing well—is in the State Office—Mrs & Miss Martins are well.

Curly, at last accounts, was home in Ohio. Cate is home in New Hampshire—he has been committing matrimony—& is now supposed to be suffering the consequences—poor reckless young man—Mrs. Wright[87] is at Flushing, L. I., New York. She is in the Soldiers' orphan home.

Hiram, you ought to have put in your letter how you got along with your leg since, & how you are now in health, & how you are situated. I want to hear all about you generally—all the particulars.

Well I believe that is all this time. I send you my love, dear friend & soldier, & I hope this will find you well in health & in good spirits. So God bless you, boy, & for the present I must bid you Farewell—

239. *To Moncure D. Conway*

Washington, | Wednesday afternoon, | July 24, 1867.

Dear friend,[88]

I avail myself of an opportunity to send you, by hands of Mr. Philp,[89] just starting for London, a copy of my Poems, prepared with care for the printers, with reference to republication in England. The Introduction is written by William O'Connor. All is sent you, so that in case there comes any opening, you may have a proper copy, of latest date, prepared by me, to publish from. Of course I do not expect you, & would not permit you, to make yourself the job of running around & seeking after a publisher. Only, please take charge of the Copy—(I hereby

85. This is an error. WW's salary was $1,600 (see 198), and he later received a "20 percent addition" (see 223). Perhaps WW sensed that Sholes was about to ask for a loan (see note 80).

86. In a letter to WW, on December 22, 1863, Alonzo S. Bush, a soldier, referred to Anna Lowell, a nurse during the war in Armory Square Hospital: "Tell Miss Lowell that her Kindness to the Solders undr her charge While I was there I never Shall forget" (Yale).

87. Mrs. H. J. Wright was a nurse during the Civil War at the Mansion House Hospital in Alexandria, Va. (*LC* #104). In a reprint of an unidentified newspaper article, "The Soldiers, &c.," dated February, 1865, WW wrote: "I have known her for over two years in her labors of love" (Yale). The passage referring to her did not appear with the rest of the article in *Specimen Days* (*CW*, IV, 100–104).

88. When WW wrote this letter, a London edition of his poem was under consideration. On April 30, Conway had informed O'Connor of a conference, attended by Swinburne, William Michael Rossetti, and John Camden Hotten, the publisher, at which

clothe you with full power over it)—& should any good chance befal, it is what I would wish a London edition set up from.

Mr. O'Connor has shown me your note of April 30, last, to him. I wish to send you, as also to those other friends & well-wishers whom it seems I have in England, my true thanks & love.

Many serious & wonderful things have occurred in our dear country, since you & I last met, my friend. But of these I will not now talk. I also have had many deep experiences since.

Mr. Philp leaves Washington this evening, & I must hasten my letter. I will add that I remain well & hearty. For occupation I hold a clerkship in the Attorney General's Office here, of pay sufficient, & duties entirely agreeable & consistent with my tastes.

I may write you further, by mail, about the book, & other matters. Write me, on receipt of this. Farewell.

Walt Whitman.

240. *To Alfred Pratt*

Washington, | July 25, 1867.

Dear boy & comrade,[90]

It is a long while since I have written to you—I believe it is six months, or over—but you must not think I have forgotten you—I have thought of you often, & wished we could be together.

Al, I believe the last letter I got from you was last April.[91] I went home about that time to Brooklyn, N. Y., & remained home quite a long time—one of my brothers, (who had been a soldier & all through the war, in the 9th Corps,) was sick with erysipelas, & lay very low for a while—but has recovered. My Mother, & the rest of the folks, are all well. I have had good health since I last wrote to you. I am still working in the At-

it was decided that a complete edition of *Leaves of Grass* could not be published in England without "legal prosecution on any publisher" (Berg; Perry, 185). This statement was later denied; see Conway's letter to Burroughs (Barrus, 47). A volume of selections was eventually decided upon; see 255. Since WW was determined to guide the London edition, he sent to Conway an "Introduction" which he had composed but had attributed to O'Connor, who was thus to introduce WW to English readers. A WW manuscript in the Morgan Library, "Introduction to the London Edition," is dated August, 1867, and was later corrected to read September, 1871; it is reprinted by Furness, 150–154.

89. According to one of WW's notebooks (*LC* #109), Philp was to leave New York on July 27: "(Ought to get in London Aug 9—answer ought to get here last of Aug.)" This may be James B. Philp, listed as a lithographer and engraver in the New York Directory of 1867, or Franklin Philp, of Philp & Solomon, Washington booksellers.

90. See 164.1.

91. Only two of Pratt's letters are extant—August 7, [1865], and September 29, [1867]—both of which are in the Feinberg Collection.

torney General's Office, here—I am writing this letter at my desk in the office, seated by the same old open window, where I can look out & have a splendid view of the Potomac river, & the hills & trees & banks, for miles & miles. It looks pleasant enough—but we are having it very hot indeed, just now—last night was very oppressive—then the air is so close & stale in the city in hot weather any how—I sometimes feel as I could hardly breathe.

Alfred, I suppose you read in the papers about the trial of John H. Surratt[92] for taking part in the murder of President Lincoln. I went down to the trial, day before yesterday. Surratt is very young—I sat near him & looked at him a long time—he sits most of the time fanning himself with a big palm leaf fan, & watches the witnesses with his sharp eyes—& his brother,[93] a young farmer-looking man from Texas, sits close by him. The lawyers on both sides are very smart—sometimes the evidence goes strongly against him, & then again for him. It is very interesting to sit & hear the witnesses & the speeches of the lawyers. It has been a tedious trial, & it is hard to tell how it will end.

Al, you mentioned about your father buying a new farm, last spring. You must tell me how it goes—& also how you are getting along yourself, for I want to hear every thing, & all the particulars about you.

Tell your father & mother I would write to them, but I suppose writing to you is almost the same. I send them my love, & a full share to you, dearest comrade. My address is the same as you directed your former letters. Well, I must draw to a close. Alfred, your love for me, & the kind invitations you have sent me, & from the kind father & mother also, to come & pay you all a visit, are fully appreciated by me.[94] I hope & intend to come & see you all, one of these days. Write & let me know if you get this. Farewell, my darling boy, & God bless you, & bless the dear parents also.

Walt Whitman.

92. See 221.

93. Isaac was John Surratt's elder brother. His counsels were Joseph H. Bradley and Richard T. Merrick, and the government was represented by Edwards Pierrepont; see DeWitt, *The Assassination of Abraham Lincoln* (1909).

94. See 216.

95. Edwin L. Godkin (1831–1902) was the founder of the *Nation*, and a publisher, with a shop at the address WW cited.

241. *To Abby H. Price*

ADDRESS: Mrs. Abby H. Price, | 279 East 55th street, | New York City. POSTMARK: Washington | Jul | (?) | D. C.

ATTORNEY GENERAL'S OFFICE

Washington July 27, *1867*.

My dear friend,

Will some of you, the first time you go down town, stop at office (or shop) of E. Godkin,[95] 130 Nassau st. & see if you can get me two or three copies of a new paper, the *London Chronicle*,[96] with a piece about *Leaves of Grass* &c. I think it must be the paper for June 22—(though it may be June 29—or June 15)—but you must look & see—Godkin is the American agent.

I am well as usual—work in the same office—all goes on the same in the office & generally. Mother has moved to 1194 Atlantic street—(not *av.*)—opposite Hamilton st. You take Fulton av. cars. Ellen O'Connor is going for the summer to coast of Rhode Island—her little girl Jenny is afflicted with bad swellings &c of joints—appears to be scrofulous—William O'Connor is well—

How are you all? Write me a good long letter—tell me all the news—all about the girls, & Mr. Arnold—& the last from Arthur, & every thing—

So good bye for this time—I send you my love, dear friend, & same to the dear girls—& to all.

Walt.

If you can get the papers, direct them to me Attorney Gen's Office—

242. *To W. C. Church*

Washington, | Wednesday afternoon, | Aug. 7, 1867.

My dear Mr. Church,

In response to your letter to William O'Connor, I send herewith the piece,

96. William Michael Rossetti's article on WW appeared on July 6. As Burroughs observed to a friend, it "had a profound effect" (Barrus, 48). On April 30, Rossetti had called on Conway and had borrowed the 1867 *Leaves of Grass*, as well as the proofs of Burroughs' *Notes on Walt Whitman as Poet and Person;* see the *Rossetti Papers* (1903), 181, and Allen, 383. He probably had also seen the material which O'Connor had sent Conway on December 5, 1866 (Yale)—a copy of Burroughs' article in *The Galaxy* (see 201) and his own article in the New York *Times* on December 2, 1866.

"*A Carol of Harvest, for 1867*,"

for the Galaxy.[97] I presume it will be in time for the September number. I wish, if acceptable, you would have it set up *immediately*, proved, read carefully by copy, carefully corrected, & then a *good proof* taken & sent to me here. I would mail it back again the same day I get it, so you would receive it next day.

If practicable, I should like to have the piece commence on an odd-numbered page of the magazine—& wish it could come the second article in the Number.

The "Carol" will make about five pages more or less.

Please acknowledge the receipt of this. Direct to me, Attorney General's Office.

Walt Whitman

243. *To W. C. or F. P. Church*

Washington | Sunday afternoon, Aug. 11, '67.

Mr. Church, | Dear Sir:

I have not, as yet, received any proof of the *Carol of Harvest.*

I neglected to mention, in my former note, that I reserve the right of incorporating & printing the *Carol*, in future, in the copyrighted collection of *Leaves of Grass*. I shall not avail myself of this right, however, within six months following Sept. 1, 1867, without permission of the publishers of the *Galaxy.*[98]

Walt Whitman.

244. *To Gordon Lester Ford*

Washington, | August 23, 1867.

Mr. Ford.[99] | Dear Sir,

Your note has been received.

I have a vague impression, or memory, of some copies of the first

97. On August 1, W. C. Church, from the office of *The Galaxy*, wrote to O'Connor: "It seems to me that this glorious harvest of 1867, sown & reaped by the returned soldiers, ought to be sung in verse. . . . Walt Whitman is the man to chaunt the song. Will you not ask him to do it for The Galaxy?" (Feinberg). The editors, in a letter to WW on August 8, considered "A Carol of Harvest, for 1867" (later titled "The Return of the Heroes") "to rank with the very best of your poems" (Feinberg). It appeared in the September issue, 605–609.

William Conant Church (1836–1917), journalist and publisher, was a correspondent for several New York newspapers until he founded *The Army and Navy Journal* in 1863. With his brother Francis Pharcellus (1839–1906), he established *The Galaxy* in 1866. Financial control of *The Galaxy* passed to Sheldon & Company in 1868, and it was absorbed by the *Atlantic Monthly* in 1878. W. C. published a biography of his life-long friend

edition of Leaves of Grass being for sale at Dion Thomas's Bookstore,[1] in Nassau st. near Spruce, New York, some time since.

Andrew Rome, printer, now in Fulton st. opposite City Hall, Brooklyn, did the printing of the first edition.

Walt Whitman

245. *To John M. Binckley*

ENDORSED: "Leave of Absence, | from Sept. 9 to Oct. 12, | '67."

ATTORNEY GENERAL'S OFFICE

Washington. | Aug 31, *1867.*

Hon. Mr. Binckley,[2] | Acting Attorney General. | Sir:

The undersigned respectfully asks leave of absence from the 9th of September to the 12th of October.

Walt Whitman.

Leave granted as above

John M. Binckley
Acting Attorney General

246. *To W. C. and F. P. Church*

Washington, | September 7, 1867.

W. C. & F. P. Church. | Gentlemen:

The check for $60. arrived safely this morning. Please consider this a receipt for said sum.

I received, some ten days since, the six proof-impressions of the *Carol*—& am much obliged. (No copies of magazine.)

I forward herewith another poem for the *Galaxy*. If acceptable, please, after correcting, let me have a good proof in time.

U. S. Grant in 1897, and F. P. wrote for the New York *Sun* "Yes, Virginia, there is a Santa Claus." See E. F. Grier, "Walt Whitman, the *Galaxy*, and *Democratic Vistas*," *AL*, XXIII (1951–1952), 332–350; D. N. Church, *William Conant Church & "The Army and Navy Journal"* (1952); J. R. Pearson, Jr., "Story of a Magazine: New York's Galaxy, 1866–1878," *Bulletin of the New York Public Library*, LXI (1957), 217–237, 281–302.

98. On August 13 (Feinberg), *The Galaxy* replied that it had no objection to WW's using the poem in a book.

99. Ford practiced law in New York and lived in Brooklyn.

1. See 252.

2. Binckley, a Washington lawyer, was associated with the *National Intelligencer*, was in the Attorney General's office for several years, and in 1869 was Solicitor of Internal Revenue. Except for Binckley's signature, this letter is in WW's hand.

The right of publishing *Ethiopia Commenting*,[3] in future book, is reserved to me.

The price of the piece is $25.

I have, in composition, an article, (prose,) of some length—the subject opportune—I shall probably name it *Democracy*. It is partly provoked by, & in some respects a rejoinder to, Carlyle's *Shooting Niagara*.[4] I think it might be specially appropriate to your purposes & scope. I would propose it to you for a leading article for January '68 *Galaxy*. Please write me how the idea suits you. Or, as I am coming to Brooklyn in a few days, perhaps I may as well call personally, & get your notions about it.

Walt Whitman.

247. *To William D. O'Connor* *9.15. [1867]*

ADDRESS: William D. O'Connor, | Light House Board, | Treasury Department, | Washington, | D. C.
POSTMARK: New York | (?) | 15.

Brooklyn, | Sunday, Sept. 15.

My dear friend,

I find my mother in excellent spirits & fair health & strength, considering her age, doing her own housework as usual. We have talked

3. This poem was never published in *The Galaxy*. It probably became "Ethiopia Saluting the Colors"; see Grier, *AL*, XXIII (1951–1952), 337. WW withdrew it on November 2, 1868.

4. "Shooting Niagara: and After?" *Macmillan's Magazine*, XVI (1867), 319–336. It was published in the December issue. See also Grier, *AL*, XXIII (1951–1952), 337–338; and Allen, 389–391.

5. Though none of WW's letters to the family is extant between the periods of his two visits to Brooklyn in 1867, it is possible to reconstruct the activities of the family from correspondence addressed to him. Jeff was in St. Louis, and Martha and her children boarded with friends in New Jersey, until they returned to Brooklyn, about the time WW was writing. George, not completely recovered from his illness, was working and living with his mother. The family was considering, as WW noted, building a home. Heyde, in June, complained vituperatively of Hannah's vulgarity and meanness, and described an encounter with her which he came out of with "the back of my right hand so badly lacerated by her nails that I am compelld to bandage it" (Trent). Ed, at least, caused no one any trouble. (Jesse had been confined to an asylum in December, 1864.)

6. See WW's description of his meeting with F. P. Church in 250.

7. See 235.

8. According to Donaldson (206), WW said that he had not visited Pfaff's (see 62) between 1865 and 1881.

9. A clerk, according to the New York Directory of 1867–1868.

10. William Winter (1836–1917) was a "sub-editor" of the *Saturday Press* and drama critic of the New York *Tribune* from 1865 to 1909. He was one of the "vilifiers" of *Leaves of Grass*, and was the butt of WW's idolators. WW himself termed Winter "a dried-up cadaverous schoolmaster" (Traubel, II, 93), "miserable cuss" (I, 61), and "an arrant damned fool" (III, 431). In 1888 Winter voiced his hostility to WW before an English audience; see Kennedy, *The Fight of a Book for the World* (1926), 81–82. In *Old Friends, Being Literary Recollections of Other Days* (1909), Winter depicted the Pfaffians unsympathetically.

11. These men were WW's companions during the Pfaff's days, most of whom,

much about you & Nelly. I am not at all satisfied with the quarters we occupy, & shall make, probably in conjunction with George, some arrangements to have a house, or home for her & the youngest brother, before I leave.[5] George is very well, lives home mainly, & looks & feels as hearty as can be—which is a pleasant surprise to me. I called at the *Galaxy* office yesterday, but found the Churches out of town—shall call again to-morrow or Tuesday.[6]

I saw Henry Clapp[7]—chatted pleasantly an hour with him at Pfaff's[8] over some lager—he was very cordial & communicative—I saw George Clapp[9]—he is the same good creature, apparently not shined upon by fortune's bright sun, any more than formerly. H. C. spoke of the remnants of the old Bohemian crowd—expressed contempt for William Winter[10]—called him Turvey-drop, &c.—Stoddard, Steadman, Aldrich, Howells, Garrison,[11] &c. were mentioned—there appears to be nothing new to tell about them. Garrison is the man of all work on the *Nation*. Stoddard still has his place in the Custom House. Ada Clare[12] is an actress—has lately been playing at Memphis, Tenn—is now about playing at Albany—Clapp remains as clerk in the City Hall—Spoke of your pamphlet—says he considers it absolutely one of the most vital productions in Literature. He read it through several times. It seems to have had lasting effect upon him

like Henry Clapp himself and Winter, had moved from bohemianism to respectability; they had entered upon O'Connor's "downward path." Richard Henry Stoddard (1825–1903) was appointed custom inspector in New York through the influence of Nathaniel Hawthorne. He was from 1860 to 1870 a literary reviewer for the New York *World*. A poet as well as an anthologist, he was often characterized as the "Nestor of American literature" (*DAB*). He referred briefly to WW in *Recollections Personal and Literary* (1903), 266. For Edmund Clarence Stedman, one of the few Pfaffians with whom WW remained friendly throughout his life, see 89. Thomas Bailey Aldrich (1836–1907) was associated with Clapp's *Saturday Press* from 1858 until its final number in 1860; see Ferris Greenslet, *The Life of Thomas Bailey Aldrich* (1908), 37–49. In 1865 Aldrich left New York and returned to Boston—to gentility and Longfellow. He was editor of the *Atlantic Monthly* from 1881 to 1890. For Aldrich's opinion of WW's poetry, see Greenslet, 138–139. William Dean Howells (1837–1920), the novelist, described his first meeting with WW at Pfaff's in *Literary Friends and Acquaintances* (1900), 73–76. Wendall Phillips Garrison (1840–1907), son of the celebrated abolitionist, was literary editor of the *Nation*.

12. Ada Clare, the stage and pen name of Jane McElheney (or McElhinney) (1836–1874), made her stage debut on August 15, 1855, at Wallack's Theatre in New York; see Odell, *Annals of the Theater*, VI, 365. She was an intimate of the bohemians who gathered at Pfaff's, and wrote for the New York *Leader*. W. W. Thayer, on August 31–September 6, 1862, wrote to WW: "How's Bohemia and its Queen the charming Ada? She talks with us every week in the Leader in articles that wify and I *love* to read" (Feinberg). Her autobiographical novel, *Only a Woman's Heart* (1866), relates the sufferings of a woman in love with a young actor who becomes famous in the role of Romeo. Except for the contrived romantic conclusion and some melodramatic plotting, the book is an interesting, and occasionally penetrating, study of an Ophelia-like woman (Ada herself). She returned to the stage in 1867–1868. See Charles Warren Stoddard, "Ada Clare, Queen of Bohemia," *National Magazine*, XXII (1905), 637–645; Albert Parry, *Garrets and Pretenders: A History of Bohemianism in America* (1933), 14–37; Donaldson, 208; Holloway and Adimari, eds., *New York Dissected* (1936), 232–233; Barrus, 2–4.

both intellectually & emotionally. Says there is nothing of its special character, ever produced, that is, upon the whole, equal to it. It is peerless. Clapp speaks in a tone of seriousness & deference I never heard him use toward any other work or person[13]—

I have seen Haggerty[14]—Just at dusk I was up Broadway, waiting for a Fulton ferry stage, when he came down upon me with genuine Irish warmth & volubility—I was glad to see him, & we had a talk of some fifteen minutes there on the street—He too spoke of the pamphlet—he said when he first heard of it he went down to Huntington's[15] & bought a copy, took it home, & sat down & read it to his wife—when through he read it a second time—& then still a third time. He says he now regularly keeps the pamphlet within reach, & whenever he feels the want of something to rouse him up, & put his mental energies on the alert, he resorts to it.

I have seen Mrs. Price—she asked particularly about you—Mrs. Rhinds is unwell, & has been taken home by her sister, to recuperate—John's book[16] has been largely read—at least by those interested in L. of G. and its virtuous & accomplished author—& has had deepest appreciation & acceptance in good quarters. Show John this letter—I send him my love—William, I have not yet rec'd any letters—when any come, send them to me 1194 Atlantic st. opposite Hamilton st. My sister Mat & her children are here. Farewell.

Walt Whitman

248. *To John Burroughs*

Brooklyn, | September 21, 1867.

My dear friend,

I suppose you saw my letter to William O'Connor, a week since, with notice of my safe arrival home, & account of one thing & another

13. When O'Connor had belatedly sent Clapp a copy of his pamphlet, he had written defensively: "You *don't* believe in heroes, and I *do*! So I know beforehand that my pamphlet comes to you at a disadvantage" (Feinberg).

14. Possibly Thomas Haggerty (or Hagerty), listed in Washington Directories as a clerk in the Treasury Department.

15. *The Good Gray Poet* was published by Bunce & Huntington, 459 Broome Street, New York. The correspondence between the publishers and O'Connor is in the Feinberg Collection. The authorship of this impassioned tract has been debated since the appearance of Nathan Resnick's *Walt Whitman and the Authorship of The Good Gray Poet* (1948); see the refutations of E. H. Eby in *MLQ*, XI (1950), 445–449, and W. G. Milne in *AL*, XXV (1953–1954), 31–42.

16. Burroughs' *Notes on Walt Whitman as Poet and Person* was printed in Washington at the author's expense and was published in New York by the American News Company; see Barrus, *The Life and Letters of John Burroughs* (1925), I, 116. See also 236. It was composed with some assistance from O'Connor and WW; see Allen, 383, and Frederick P. Hier, Jr., "The End of a Literary Mystery," *American Mercury*, I (1924),

up to that date. I have called at the American News Company store. They have not sold many of the Notes—not more than a hundred. It seems to be well-known, however, & often talked about. I have procured & given Henry Clapp[17] a copy, at his particular request.

I have seen F. P. Church, who treated me with great courtesy—he was anxious about the article on *Democracy*—wishes to have it for the December number—said he would publish the little piece *Ethiopia Commenting*[18]—but thought it best to keep it back till after the Democracy article had appeared.

I have not done anything further to the latter-named piece—but shall try to have it ready in time for the December number. I think it likely I shall return last of this week to Washington. I have not received any letter at all from Washington. H. J. Raymond[19] is home from Europe.

Give my best respects to Mrs. Burroughs—as I am coming back so soon, I will mention then what I have to say on the shirt question. I am living at 1194 Atlantic st. opposite Hamilton street. There is nothing specially new or important among my folks—they all wish me to give their best regards to you.

Walt Whitman.

249. *To Ellen M. O'Connor*

ENDORSED: "Sept. 21.—1867— | Ans'd." ADDRESS: Mrs. Ellen M. O'Connor, | Care of Benjamin Gardiner, | Jamestown, | Rhode Island. POSTMARK: Brooklyn | Sep | 23 | N. Y.

Brooklyn | September 21, 1867

My dear friend,

As you see by the date, &c. I am home, on a visit to my mother & the rest. Mother is about as well as usual—has occasionally some trouble with rheumatism, but is cheerful & keeps up amazingly. We speak of you

471–478. Interestingly, Mrs. Whitman wrote to her son on August 1: "you know i like . . . the good gray poet better than i doo borroughs book. Oconor shows the spirit its wrote in. i should form an idea of the man if i had never seen him by reading his writings" (Trent).

17. On October 3, Clapp sent WW a clipping from the New York *Times* about Garibaldi: "I wonder why it made me think of *you*!" (Feinberg; Traubel, I, 267). In the account (reprinted in Traubel, I, 268–269), Garibaldi is characterized as "a rowdy," an opponent stylistically of "the small flute of the Academies," "the expression of the land and the age that gave him birth," and "a mixture of the prophet and the child." When Traubel in 1888 asked how WW reacted to the newspaper article, he replied: "I can see some of the features—yes. . . . As to being any way associated with Garibaldi —that is the crowning tribute. Garibaldi belongs to the divine eleven!" (I, 270). On the envelope of Clapp's letter, WW jotted : "Quite good—read again."

18. See 246.

19. Editor of the New York *Times;* see 209.

every day, & I have to give minute particulars of you, William, little Jenny, & all. My brother George is very well, looks hearty & brown as ever—much like he used to, only more serious—Jeff is at St. Louis, on the Water Works. Martha & the little girls are well—they are here in Brooklyn, occupying temporary apartments.

I am well as usual, & go daily around New York & Brooklyn yet with interest, of course—but I find the places & crowds & excitements—Broadway, &c—have not the zest of former times—they have done their work, & now they are to me as a tale that is told—Only the majestic & moving river & rapid sea-water scenery & life about the islands, N. Y. and Brooklyn, tower into larger proportions than ever. I doubt if the world elsewhere has their equal, or could have, to me—The waters about New York & west end of Long-Island are real sea-waters, & are ever-rolling & rushing in or out—never placid, never calm—surely they please this uneasy spirit, Me, that ebbs & flows too all the while, yet gets nowhere, & amounts to nothing—

I am trying to write a piece, to be called *Democracy*, for the leading article in the December or January number of the *Galaxy*—in some sort a counterblast or rejoinder to Carlyle's late piece, *Shooting Niagara*, which you must have read, or at least heard about. Mr. Church strongly wishes it written. Mother & Martha send love, & I also, most truly—I shall probably return to Washington last of the week.

Walt.

250. *To William D. O'Connor*

ADDRESS: William D. O'Connor, | Light House Board, | Treasury Department, | Washington, | D. C. POSTMARKS: New York | Sep | 27; Carrier | Sep | 28 | 1 Del.

Brooklyn, | Friday, Sept 27, 1867.

My dear friend,

Your letter, & the two accompanying, came safe. I saw F. P. Church again yesterday—the arrangement is, that *Democracy* is to make an article of fifteen or sixteen pages, & is [to] be the leading article of the December number—it must be in his hands by the 25th of October. The *Ethiopia Commenting*[20] has been formally accepted, but is held back

20. See 246.

21. One of the objects of WW's Brooklyn visit was to arrange for the construction of a house for the family.

22. Timothy Titcomb was the pseudonym of Josiah Gilbert Holland (1819–1881), who was an editor of the Springfield *Republican* from 1850 to 1862, and author of *Titcomb's Letters to Young People, Simple and Married* (1858). While he was editor of

until the long article appears. I have felt that the *Galaxy* folks have received & treated me with welcome warmth & respect. F. P. Church is a sample of a New Yorker, a club man, (he pressingly invited me to a dinner at Atheneum Club—I declined,) young, cordial, refined, &c. He made no very decided impression on me, however—we will see how the acquaintance works & holds out in the future. The indirect & inferential of his tone & words in speaking to me would have satisfied your highest requirements—they evidently meant that in his opinion I was, or was soon to be, "one of the great powers."

Nothing new among my folks, or domestic matters. I have been purchasing property, or rather becoming responsible for the same[21]—

William, you needn't send any more of my letters to me here, after you receive this—keep them for me. I shall return within three or four days—I shall write out & finish *Democracy* there, as my leave extends two weeks yet. I suppose you rec'd the *Gazette*, containing T. Titcomb,[22] his opinion on such books as *Leaves of Grass*, etc.

I think it very likely I shall return on Monday 30th. I have seen Fred. Gray, Nathaniel Bloom[23]—the dear, good, affectionate young men—more kind, more affectionate than ever.

William, I do hope, it will come to you to buckle-to, & write something for Putnam—*et al.* You are talked about, & cause expectancies, curiosities, &c.—F. P. Church sent a florid & evidently genuine message to you by me—the meat of it is, a fervid appreciation of your literary genius, & a special request that you write for the *Galaxy*.[24] John Burroughs, I send you my love, & will soon be with you all again—

Walt.

251. *To F. P. and W. C. Church*

Washington, | October 13, 1867.

Messrs. Church. | Gentlemen:

I write merely to say that I have finished the article on *Democracy*; (that will be its name.) I feel persuaded that it will please you thoroughly. It will make thirteen pages in *Galaxy*—the arrangement that it appear as leader in December number, being of course carried out.

It will reach your hands by or before Monday next, 21st.

Walt Whitman.

Scribner's Monthly (1870–1881), WW submitted poems to him; see December 12, 1876.

23. See 40.

24. According to O'Connor's letter of October 28, the Churches rejected the works he submitted (NYPL). *The Galaxy*, however, published O'Connor's "The Ballad of Sir Ball" in March, 1868; see 292.

252. *To Dionysius Thomas* *10.13.* [*1867*]

ENDORSED (by WW): "Dion Thomas | Nassau st. bet Beekman & Spru[ce]."[25] DRAFT LETTER.

Washington Oct. 13

Dear Sir:

I write to ask your kind offices in the following described matter:

I sent to Doolady[26] six weeks ago an order

Mr. James Gray, Bookbinder 16 Spruce st. 14th floor, is the custodian of the sheets of my Leaves of Grass, & has been the binder for me. The sheets are now at his place.

I hear that he has become involved—in fact has failed. If so, I regret it much.[27]

I have been waiting now over six weeks for the fulfilment of orders I have sent him for bound books—& now, under that state of things, I suppose it will not be possible for him to do the work.

253. *To F. P. Church*

Washington, | October 19, 1867.

F. P. Church. | My dear Sir:

I send the article on Democracy. If satisfactory I should like $100 for it. You are to issue it in *Galaxy* with exclusive possession of the field, say for three months—after which I reserve to myself the right of any further use of it—as, for instance, issuing it with added Notes, Appendices, &c. in a pamphlet or small book—published by you, of course, if you are willing—I to receive copyright fee on sales, &c. &c.

But we can see better how the cat jumps after the article is before the public—& will leave that question open until then.

Please have it set up forthwith, read carefully by copy, & then, after correction, send me *two good proofs*. I want it to go forth in a perfect verbal &c. condition.

Walt Whitman.

Please acknowledge this, immediately on reception.

If any thing could be made by disposing of advance sheets in London,

25. In the Barrett Collection at the University of Virginia, there is an envelope, postmarked October 16, addressed to : "Dion Thomas, | Bookseller, &c | Nassau street, bet. Beekman & Spruce, | New York City."

26. See 256.1.

27. In 1888 WW spoke of "a history and a grief" in connection with the 1867 edition: "It was got up by a friend of mine, a young fellow, printed from type, in New York. One day I received the intelligence . . . that the place had been seized for debt.

to any magazine or publisher, I would suggest that it be done—the price procured to be divided equally between you & me.

W.

253.1 *To Alfred Pratt*

ATTORNEY GENERAL'S OFFICE,

Washington. Oct. 28, *1867.*

Alfred Pratt,[28] | Dear boy & Comrade,

I have been home to Brooklyn, N. Y., on a visit to my mother, but I am now back here again, and am well as usual, and working in the same place. Your letter of August 15, and the letter of Oct. 2, have both reached me, & I was very glad to hear from you & your folks, & to get such friendly letters. Dear boy, I should like much to pay you a visit, & to be with you for a while, & to become acquainted with your father & mother —it would be a real comfort to me, & I am determined to come one of these days—I often think about it, & about you too, dear friend, & one of these days we will see each other again.

There is nothing very new in my affairs. I have had quite a pleasant summer, & now the fall is here—the past three weeks has been splendid weather here, both days & nights—but to-day there is a heavy rain—looks as if it had set in for a long storm—

I am living at a boarding house, the same place where you come to see me, but new landlord & landlady[29]—472 M st.—it is quite pleasant —mostly young people, full of life & gayety—then I go to my work at 9, & leave at 3—so you see it is easy enough—In about three weeks more it will be lively times here in Washington, as Congress is to meet then, & there will be some important questions brought up—but I take all these things very coolly—&, since the war is over, dont allow myself to get excited—

You must write to me often as you can. I shall probably remain here this winter. I wish you to give my love to your father & mother. They do not seem at all like strangers to me.

I received a portion of the books remaining—the most of them were lost" (Traubel, II, 257).

28. See 164.1. In Pratt's letter on October 2, actually written on September 29, he was worried because he had not heard from WW: "As I have not heard anything from you in a great while I would rite you a few lines but as I rot last I think its your turn but I dont no [if you?] are ofended about some thing. if I have ofended you in any way I am vary sory for it and hope you will forgive me as I have ment no hurt" (Feinberg).

29. Mr. and Mrs. Newton Benedict; see 218.

And now, Alfred, I must bid you farewell for the present, my loving boy & comrade. When you write, write to me about the farm, & the farm-life, crops, horses, &c. for I like to hear about such things too.

Walt Whitman.

254. *To F. P. (?) Church*

ATTORNEY GENERAL'S OFFICE,

Washington. Nov. 1, 1867.

My dear Mr. Church:

I send herewith the proof of *Democracy*. Ask the proof-reader to revise it carefully, upon correction.

Please acknowledge the receipt of this.

Walt Whitman

255. *To Moncure D. Conway*

Washington | November 1, 1867.

Dear friend,

My feeling and attitude about a volume of selections from my Leaves by Mr. Rosetti, for London publication, are simply passive ones —yet with decided satisfaction that if the job is to be done, it is to be by such hands.[30] Perhaps, too, "good-natured," as you advise—certainly not ill-natured. I wish Mr. Rosetti to know that I appreciate *his* appreciation, realize his delicacy & honor, & warmly thank him for his literary friendliness.

30. On October 12 (Feinberg; Traubel, III, 296–298), Conway reported to WW that John Camden Hotten had "contracted with W. M. Rossetti to prepare and edit a volume of selections from your Poems." Rossetti received £25 and twelve copies of the book; see *Rossetti Papers*, 240. Conway noted as advantages of this new plan that a volume of selections would prepare the public for the complete work, and that it was better to have a well-known English critic introduce an American poet to the British public than an unknown American author like O'Connor (see 239). The irony, of course, was that WW had written the Introduction.

Hotten (1832–1873) printed Swinburne's *Poems and Ballads* when another publisher withdrew after the book caused a furor. Perhaps because he had lived in the United States from 1848 to 1856, Hotten introduced to an English audience such writers as Lowell, Artemus Ward, Oliver Wendell Holmes, and Bret Harte. After his death, his business was purchased by Chatto & Windus. In his letter to Conway on December 5, 1866, O'Connor had suggested Hotten as the English publisher of WW: "Seems to me the courage that prints *Laus Veneris* might dare this" (Yale).

31. In addition, Rossetti requested permission to delete "venereal sores or discolorations" and "any depravity of young men" (Feinberg; Traubel, III, 298). Rossetti noted in his diary, on November 28, O'Connor's "distaste" for the "concession to the outcry against W's indecencies" and his intimation that "Whitman, though resigned, is not really pleased at the publication of a mere selection from his poems" (*Rossetti Papers*, 244).

I have no objection to his substituting other words—leaving it all to his own tact, &c.—for "onanist," "father-stuff" &c.[31] Briefly, I hereby empower him, (since that seems to be the pivotal affair, & since he has the kindness to shape his action so much by my wishes—& since, indeed, the sovereignty of the responsibility is not at all mine in the case,)—to make verbal changes of that sort, wherever, for reasons sufficient to him, he decides that they are indispensable. I would add that it is a question with me whether the introductory essay or prose preface to the first edition is worth printing.

"Calamus" is a common word here. It is the very large & aromatic grass, or rush, growing about water-ponds in the valleys—[spears about three feet high—often called "sweet flag"—grows all over the Northern and Middle States—(see Webster's Large Dictionary—Calamus—definition 2).][32] The recherché or ethereal sense of the term, as used in my book, arises probably from the actual Calamus presenting the biggest & hardiest kind of spears of grass—and their fresh, aquatic, pungent bouquet.

I write this to catch to-morrow's steamer from New York. It is almost certain I shall think of other things—moving me to write you further in a week or so.

256. *To William D. O'Connor (For Moncure D. Conway)*[33] [*11.10. 1867?*]

ADDRESS: M. D. Conway, | 14 Milborne Grove, | Brompton W. | London, | England. DRAFT LETTER.

My dear Conway:

Mr. Whitman has shown me your letter of October 12, with news

32. The material in brackets has been supplied from the draft version. Someone cut out WW's signature in the original. Rossetti quoted this definition in a note; see *Poems by Walt Whitman*, 390*n*.

33. This letter was prepared by WW for O'Connor to copy and send to Conway, who was WW's agent for the forthcoming English edition (see 239 and 255). In 1888 WW did not remember whether O'Connor "had used it or not." "I must," he said to Traubel, "have been intending to assist him in something he was to say to Conway. If he used it at all he probably recast it in his own manner" (I, 381–382). The probabilities are that O'Connor sent it without substantial alteration. Rossetti noted in his diary, on November 28, that O'Connor "has written another letter (not yet in Conway's hands) setting forth the points he would wish insisted on in any prefatory work of mine. I replied to him in cordial terms, but to the effect that the Preface and part of the Selection are now in print, and cannot well be remodelled" (*Rossetti Papers*, 244).

The Feinberg draft contains two notations, written at different times: "Part of Wm O'Connor's | letter to Conway. | Nov. 10, 1867. . . . Good for | use in | review of Leaves | of Grass."

That WW took pains in composing the letter is evidenced by the many changes he made in the draft which he retained and which Traubel printed. He observed to Traubel: "It gives my idea of my own book: a man's idea of his own book—his serious idea—is not to be despised. I do not lack in egotism, as you know—the sort of egotism that is willing to know itself as honestly as it is willing to know third or fourth parties" (I, 383).

of Mr. Hotten's proposed London print of Leaves of Grass or selection therfrom, edited by Mr. Rosetti, with an Introductory Essay or preface, by Mr. R.

Now, in view of the latter, if I may take the liberty, I wish to speak of two or three points, or rather, enforce them—for no doubt they will, to a certain extent, have occurred to Mr. Rosetti. But as I have made Leaves of Grass & their author my study for the last seven years, & have had some fortuitous advantages, perhaps Mr. Rosetti would not consider it intrusive in me, that I send this letter, which I wish you to hand him.

Considering the attitude of the public, and their average calibre, and also considering the general bearing of most of the criticisms on Mr. Whitman's poetry, I would suggest the expediency, in any forthcoming, friendly examination of his genius & writings, of dwelling pretty strongly on the following points, & making them unmistakably appear:

1st—That personally the author of Leaves of Grass is in no sense or sort whatever the "rough," the "eccentric," "vagabond" or queer person, that the commentators, (always bound for the intensest possible sensational statement,) persist in making him. He has moved, & moves still, along the path of his life's happenings & fortunes, as they befall or have befallen him, with entire serenity & decorum, never defiant even to the conventions, always bodily sweet & fresh, dressed plainly & cleanly, a gait & demeanor of antique simplicity, cheerful & smiling, performing carefully all his domestic, social, & municipal obligations, his demonstrative nature toned very low, but eloquent enough of eye, posture, & expression, though using only moderate words; and offering to the world, in himself, an American Personality, & real Democratic Presence, that not only the best old Hindu, Greek, and Roman worthies would at once have responded to, but which the most cultured European, from court or academy, would likewise, on meeting to-day, see & own without demur. All really refined persons, and the women more than the men, take to Walt Whitman. The most delicate & even conventional lady only needs to know him to love him.[34]

2.[35] Critically, a significant, if not the most significant, fact about Leaves of Grass, is, that the genesis & fashioning of them have evidently not been for literary purposes, merely or mainly. Neither in mass nor detail have their pages been tried by the *sine qua non* of current literary or

34. This paragraph does not appear in WW's first draft. However, toward the end of that version appears this simple statement—"Personally the author is a man of normal characteristics, & of moderate, healthy, following a regular employment, averse to any display" (Feinberg; Traubel, I, 384).

35. The earlier draft begins at this point.

36. In criticizing Conway's article in the *Fortnightly Review* (see 197), O'Connor wrote on December 5, 1866: "The great, paramount, unmistakable thing about 'Leaves

esthetic standards. Instead of that, the Book is the product of the largest universal law & play of things, & of that sense of kosmical beauty, of which even literature is but a fraction. This is probably the clue to the explanation of the puzzle of the widely-vexatious formal & esthetic argument involved in Leaves of Grass.

3. The idea, however, which is this man's highest contribution, and which, compared even with the vastness of Biblical & Homeric poetry, still looms & towers—as, athwart his fellow-giants of the Himalayas, the dim head of Kunchainjunga rises over the rest—is the idea of Totality, of the All-successful, final certainties of each individual man, as well as of the world he inhabits. Joyousness, out of such sure ultimate happiness & triumph, rings throughout his verse. He holds the solution of each & every problem—the spell, giving full satisfaction; and his talisman is *Ensemble*. This is the word that epitomises the philosophy of Walt Whitman. Add the word *modernness*,[36] & you begin to unlock Leaves of Grass.

These are the points, my dear Conway, that I wish, through you, to submit to Mr. Rosetti. I have mentioned to Mr. Whitman my intention of writing him, & he, W., has made no objection. I would add, for myself, for Mr. Rosetti, that I hope he will not be deterred from giving fullest swing to what I am sure I have discovered in him, namely, an intuitional admiration & appreciation of our Poet, by the ostensibly timid attitude held at present by the critical & reading world toward Leaves of Grass—but hope he will strike at that loftier, honestly enthusiastic range of minds & readers, which, perhaps by the time Mr. Hotten's volume gets well in the hands of the public, will prove the genuine audience Mr. Whitman is certain of.

Again asking pardon of Mr. Rosetti for perhaps intruding these suggestions—yet placing them in any & every respect at his service should they be so fortunate as to strike him favorably—I remain &c &c

256.1 *To Michael Doolady*

ENDORSED (by WW): "sent M. Doolady[37] | 448 Broome st. | N. Y. DRAFT LETTER.

Nov. 13, 1867.

In reply to your note of some days since, in reference to acting as my agent, for sale of "Leaves of Grass," I would say as follows:

of Grass' is its *modernness*" (Yale). In *Notes on Walt Whitman, As Poet and Person* (1867), Burroughs wrote: ". . . as we gaze and gaze, and wish the unlocking word, gradually the dimness and the many-tinted, many-twining lines become illumined, definite, showing clearly the word—MODERNNESS" (36).

37. Bookseller and publisher. See the reference to him in 252. He was the publisher of Ada Clare's *Only a Woman's Heart* (1866).

I presume that Anderson & Archer, binders, No. 6 Reade street, N. Y., have now ready 100 copies, just bound. These you can have, if desired, as follows:

14 copies, as I understand from French & Richardson, are due you, having already been paid for by you. The remaining 76 copies you can have at $1(?)8cts [each], this is [*incomplete*][38]

257. *To William M. Rossetti*

Washington, U. S. | November 22, 1867.

My dear Mr. Rosetti:[39]

I suppose Mr. Conway has received, & you have read, the letter I sent over about three weeks since, assenting to the substitution of other words, &c. as proposed by you, in your reprint of my book, or selections therefrom.[40]

I suppose the reprint intends to avoid any expressed or implied character of being an expurgated edition. I hope it will simply assume the form & name of a selection from the various editions of my pieces printed here. I suggest, in the interest of that view, whether the adjoining might not be a good form of Title page:[41]

I wish particularly not only that the little figures numbering the stanzas, but also that the larger figures dividing the pieces into separate passages or sections be carefully followed & preserved, as in copy.

When I have my next edition brought out here, I shall change the title of the piece "When lilacs last in the dooryard bloom'd," to *President Lincoln's Funeral Hymn.*[42] You are at liberty to take the latter name, or the old one, at your option, (that is, if you include the piece.)

It is quite certain that I shall add to my next edition (carrying out my plan from the first,) a brief cluster of pieces, born of thoughts on the deep themes of Death & Immortality.

Allow me to send you an article I have written on "Democracy"—a

38. The publishing history of the 1867 edition of *Leaves of Grass* is confused. The first issue was printed by Chapin, and WW considered asking Huntington & Son to distribute it; see 188. One of the later issues, to which *Drum-Taps* was added, was bound by James Gray, who became bankrupt; see 252 and its notes. Apparently Anderson & Archer received and bound the sheets in Gray's possession. Dionysius Thomas (see 252) and Doolady, rather than Huntington & Son, evidently distributed the book. According to 272, WW paid Anderson & Archer $.35 each for binding *Leaves of Grass*.

39. This is WW's first letter to Rossetti, whose name he consistently misspelled.

40. See 255.

hasty charcoal-sketch of a piece, but indicative, to any one interested in Leaves of Grass, as of the audience the book supposes, & in whose interest it is made. I shall probably send it next mail.

Allow me also to send you (as the ocean-postage law is now so easy,) a copy of Mr. Burroughs's *Notes*,[43] & some papers. They go same mail with this.

And now, my dear sir, you must just make what use—or no use at all—of any thing I suggest or send—as your occasions call for. Very likely some of my suggestions have been anticipated.

I remain, believe me, with friendliest feelings & wishes,

Walt Whitman.

WALT WHITMAN'S

POEMS

Selected from the American Editions

By Wm. M. Rosetti.

— — —

— — — — —

— — — — — — — —

258. *To William D. O'Connor* *11.27. [1867]*

ADDRESS: William O'Connor.

Wednesday forenoon, | Nov. 27.

Dear William,

I wish you to come & take Thanksgiving Dinner with us to-morrow. Mrs. Benedict[44] specially joins in the request. No refusal permitted.

Walt.

No outside guests—our own boarders only—all decent fellows.

41. On December 8, Rossetti wrote to WW: "The form of title-page which you propose would of course be adopted by me with thanks & without a moment's debate, were it not that my own title-page was previously in print" (Feinberg; Traubel, III, 305).

42. Rossetti agreed to this change on December 8: "I had previously given it a title of my own, 'Nocturn for the Death of Lincoln' " (Feinberg; Traubel, III, 305–306). See "Postscript" to *Poems by Walt Whitman* (1868), 402.

43. Rossetti had seen the proofs of Burroughs' pamphlet in April; see 241.

44. WW boarded with Mrs. Newton Benedict in 1867; see 218.

259. *To William M. Rossetti*

Washington, | December 3, 1867.

My dear Mr. Rossetti:

I have just received, & have considered your letter of November 17. In order that there be the frankest understanding with respect to my position, I hasten to write you that the authorization in my letter of November 1st to Mr. Conway, for you, to make verbal alterations, substitute words, &c. was meant to be construed as an answer to the case presented in Mr. Conway's letter of October 12. Mr. Conway stated the case of a volume of selections in which it had been decided that the poems reprinted in London should appear verbatim, & asking my authority to change certain words in the Preface to first edition of poems, &c.[45]

I will be candid with you, & say I had not the slightest idea of applying my authorization to a reprint of the full volume of my poems. As such a volume was not proposed, & as your courteous & honorable course & attitude called & call for no niggardly or hesitating response from me, I penned that authorization, & did not feel to set limits to it. But abstractly & standing alone, & not read in connection with Mr. C's letter of October 12, I see now it is far too loose, & needs distinct guarding.

I cannot & will not consent of my own volition, to countenance an expurgated edition of my pieces. I have steadily refused to do so under seductive offers, here in my own country, & must not do so in another country.

I feel it due to myself to write you explicitly thus, my dear Mr. Rossetti, though it may seem harsh & perhaps ungenerous. Yet I rely on you to absolve me, sooner or later. Could you see Mr. Conway's letter of October 12, you would, I think, more fully comprehend the integrity of my explanation.

I have to add that the points made in that letter in relation to the pro-

45. WW was disturbed by the following passage in Rossetti's letter: "But now, after your letter [255] it seems to me that all or most of these poems, with some minimum of verbal modification or excision, may very properly be included: & indeed that there is nothing to prevent a reprint of the revised copy of your complete poems (which you sent to Mr Conway) coming out at once, *instead* of the mere selection—subject only to modification or excision here & there as above named" (Feinberg; Traubel, III, 300). However, in his next letter, on December 8, Rossetti informed WW that the publisher was unwilling to substitute a complete edition for the selections because printing was too far advanced. In the same letter, Rossetti stated the "two rules" which he had followed in making his selections: "1, to omit *entirely* every poem which contains passages or words which modern squeamishness can raise an objection to—& 2, to include, from among the remaining poems, those which I most entirely & intensely admire" (Feinberg; Trau-

posed reprint, as originally designed, exactly correspond with those, on the same subject, in your own late letter—& that the kind & appreciative tone of both letters is in the highest degree gratifying, & is most cordially & affectionately responded to by me—& that the fault of sending so loose an authorization has surely been, to a large degree, my own.

And now, my friend, having set myself right on that matter, I proceed to say, on the other hand, for you, & for Mr. Hotten, that if, before the arrival of this letter, you have practically invested in, & accomplished, or partially accomplished, any plan, even contrary to this letter, I do not expect you to abandon it, at loss of outlay, &c. but shall *bona fide* consider you blameless if you let it go on, & be carried out, as you may have arranged. It is the question of the authorization of an expurgated edition proceeding from me, that deepest engages me. The facts of the different ways, one way or another way, in which the book may appear in England, out of influences not under the shelter of my umbrage, are of much less importance to me. After making the foregoing explanation, I shall, I think, accept kindly whatever happens. For I feel, indeed know, that I am in the hands of a friend, & that my pieces will receive that truest, brightest of light & perception coming from love. In that, all other & lesser requisites become pale.

It would be better, in any Introduction, to make no allusion to me, as authorizing, or not prohibiting, &c.

The whole affair is somewhat mixed—& I write offhand[46] to catch to-morrow's New York steamer. But I guess you will pick out my meaning. Perhaps, indeed, Mr. Hotten has preferred to go on after the original plan—which, if so, saves all trouble.

I have to add that I only wish you could know how deeply the beautiful personal tone & passages of your letter of November 17, have penetrated and touched me.[47] It is such things that go to our hearts, and reward us, & make up for all else, for years. Permit me to offer you my friendship.

bel, III, 303–304). See also *Poems by Walt Whitman*, 20.

46. This was no offhand letter as a casual glance at the manuscript of the draft reveals: deletions and insertions appear in almost every line.

47. Rossetti had written on November 17: "I shall always hold it one of the truest & most prized distinctions of my writing career to be associated, in however modest a capacity, with the works of so great a poet & noble-hearted a man as you" (Feinberg; Traubel, III, 300). And on December 16, he replied to WW's offer of "friendship": "To be honoured by your friendship is as great a satisfaction & distinction as my life has presented or ever can present. I respond to it with all warmth & reverence, & the Atlantic seemed a very small space between us while I read and re-read your letter" (Feinberg; Traubel, III, 307).

I sent you hence Nov. 23d[48] a letter, through Mr. Conway. Also a copy of Mr. Burroughs's *Notes*, Mr. O'Connor's pamphlet, & some papers containing criticisms on *Leaves of Grass*. Also, later, a prose article of mine named *Democracy*, in a magazine.

Let me know how the work goes on, what shape it takes, &c. Finally I charge you to construe all I have written, through my declared & fervid realization of your goodness toward me, nobleness of intention, &, I am fain to hope, personal, as, surely, literary & moral sympathy & attachment. And so, for the present, Farewell.

Walt Whitman.

260. *To Gilbert A. Tracy*

Washington, | December 19, 1867

G. A. Tracy,[49] | My dear Sir:

Your note has been received. I published last edition of *Leaves of Grass* myself—& sell it. The price is $3. I send it from here by mail. Mr. Burroughs's *Notes* can be easily obtained by writing to the publishers, American News Company, 121 Nassau st., New York City. The price is $1.

Thanks for your kind wishes.

Walt Whitman

261. *To F. P. and W. C. Church*

Washington | December 30, 1867.

Messrs. Church. | My dear sirs:

I shall be in New York, & will call upon you, 2d of January. By the way, would you please have the little piece, the verses "Ethiopia Commenting,"[50] put in type, & a proof taken & ready for me?

Walt Whitman

48. The letter was written on November 22; see 257.

49. Gilbert A. Tracy (1835–1918) was at this time a clerk in the War Department. Before the war he had been a teacher in Connecticut. Later he became a noted collector of Lincolniana, and published *Uncollected Letters of Abraham Lincoln* (1917). For this information I am indebted to Mrs. Arthur Tracy.

50. See 246.

51. The publishers of *The Broadway Annual* (London) printed two sympathetic accounts of WW in 1867. W. Clark Russell termed him one of America's eminent poets,

262. *To Routledge & Sons*

ENDORSED: "letter to Messrs. Routledge | Dec. 30, 1867. . . . I sent 'Whispers | of Heavenly Death' | which they printed & paid handsomely for | in gold."
DRAFT LETTER.

Dec 30 | 1867.

Geo. Routledge & sons[51] | 416 Broome st | N. Y.

I have received the letter asking me to write for the "Broadway". I do not write much, but your invitation is cordially appreciated, and may serve as the spur toward something. I can at present only briefly say that should I be able to prepare an article, or poem, appropriate for the purposes of the magazine, I will send it on—& that I shall surely try to do so.

My address is at the Attorney General's office here. (New York house, please forward this to Mr. Edmund Routledge, London.)

263. *To William D. O'Connor* [*1867?*][52]

I have a half-hour's lull. If handy, send me down the proofs—or, if you prefer, (& can,) come down a moment.

Walt.

264. *To William D. O'Connor* [*1867?*]

ATTORNEY GENERAL'S OFFICE

Washington, 18

Dear William—

Come down a moment & have lunch with me—a biscuit & a glass of wine & water—& tell me about Nelly's getting off—I fully intended to be round this morning, & accompany her & you to the cars—but overslept myself—I was quite vexed at it.

Come immediately—

Walt

and Robert Buchanan devoted an entire article to WW; see I (1867), 45, 188–195. On December 28, the New York office of the firm requested "one or two papers or poems" (Feinberg; Traubel, I, 263). WW sent "Whispers of Heavenly Death," which appeared in October 1868, and for which he received $50; see 271.

52. I have included these three notes to O'Connor in this volume because they appear to belong to this period. The contents are too brief and indefinite to make dating certain. The first note, for example, can refer to any one of a number of publishing ventures in the period between 1865 and 1867, either O'Connor's or WW's.

265. *To William D. O'Connor* [*1867?*]

ATTORNEY GENERAL'S OFFICE,

Washington, 186

William:

The "*Citizen*" has the *Carol*[53] complete, & exactly reprinted. Get a copy or two, before they are gone—& tell Burroughs also.

Walt.[54]

265.1 *To John Jay Knox* [*1867?*][55]

ATTORNEY GENERAL'S OFFICE, OFFICIAL BUSINESS.

Mr. Knox, Office Comptroler of Currency

Please send me down John Burroughs's letter—which the same I will soon return—

Walt Whitman

53. "A Carol of Harvest for 1867," printed in *The Galaxy;* see 242. William Livingston Alden, associate editor of the New York *Citizen*, had asked WW for a poem on August 19, 1867, though he did not know "how much the *Citizen* would be able to pay for it" (Feinberg). When WW did not reply, Alden repeated his request on November 18 (Feinberg; Traubel, II, 211). On *August* 9, 1867, Alden had informed WW that he was printing Rossetti's article on the following day (Feinberg; Traubel, III, 259). See also 298. No copies of the *Citizen* are extant before July 10, 1869.

54. There are extant no letters from WW to his family for the latter part of the year, though, as "A Check list of Whitman's Letters" makes clear, he wrote frequently. There were no startling developments. While Jeff was in St. Louis, Martha lived with Mrs. Whitman, and her children ("the young fry department," as WW's mother termed them on December 15 [Trent]) continued to annoy their grandmother. George spent some time in Philadelphia in November on a job that Lane (see 31) evidently had obtained for him. Jeff returned to Brooklyn in December, and, on December 26 (Trent), Mrs. Whitman reported that he was taking his family to St. Louis.

55. It is impossible to date this note with any certainty. For Knox, see 215.

Appendix A

A LIST OF MANUSCRIPT SOURCES AND PRINTED APPEARANCES

The locations of the manuscripts transcribed in this volume appear in the following list, through an abbreviation explained in the list of abbreviations in the Introduction. If the version in this edition is based upon a printed source, or is derived from an auction record, the fact is indicated by the word TEXT. Unless otherwise indicated, the manuscripts have not previously appeared in print. I record all earlier printed appearances through the abbreviations CT (Complete Text) and PT (Partial Text). The location and printed appearances, if any, of draft letters are also noted. Occasionally the location of a letter is followed by a reference in parentheses to an envelope in another collection. In this way I have, artificially, restored the manuscript to its original state.

This list is followed by a list of the institutions and individuals whose manuscripts are represented in this volume, in order that scholars may readily tell which letters are to be found in a given collection.

Letters

1. WW's copy in Yale.
2. WW's copy in Yale. FACSIMILE: *UPP*, I, 84. CT: Nonesuch, 883.
3. Berg.
4. Berg.
5. Berg.
6. Berg.
7. Long Island Historical Society. CT: Nonesuch, 883.
8. Huntington (New York) Historical Society.
9. Long Island Historical Society.

9.1 New Hampshire Historical Society.

10. Feinberg. FACSIMILE: Traubel, IV, 152. CT: New York *Tribune*, October 10, 1855; Bucke, 138–139; Holloway, 118–119; Allen, *Handbook*, 127–128; Frederik Schyberg, *Walt Whitman* (1951), 126–127.
11. Papers of William Henry Seward, University of Rochester.
12. Huntington. CT: *AL*, VII (1935), 76–78; Nonesuch, 884–885. PT: Canby, 171; Allen, 217; Fredson Bowers, ed., *Whitman's Manuscripts—Leaves of Grass (1860)* (1955), xxxv–xxxvi.
13. TEXT: Henkels catalogue, June 14–15, 1901.
14. Colonel Richard Gimbel.
15. Feinberg.
16. Barrett. CT: Nonesuch, 886; *SB*, V (1952), 203–204.
17. Colonel Richard Gimbel.
18. Morgan. CT: *Putnam's Monthly*, V (November, 1908), 165; *NEQ*, I (1928), 358–359; Furness, 260–261; Nonesuch, 886–887. PT: Canby, 172.

19. Whitman House, Camden. CT: *American Mercury*, XVI (1929), 183–184. PT: *NEQ*, I (1928), 359–360; Furness, 261.
20. Feinberg.
21. Whitman House, Camden. CT: *American Mercury*, XVI (1929), 184–185. PT: *NEQ*, I (1928), 360–362; Furness, 261–262.
21.1 Draft letter in Feinberg.
21.2 Barrett.
22. Incomplete draft letter in Hanley.
23. Trent. CT: Gohdes and Silver, 68–69.
24. TEXT: Typescript in possession of Emory Holloway. CT: Nonesuch, 887.
25. Feinberg. CT: *Wound Dresser*, 47–50; *CW*, VII, 128–132; Holloway, 194–196; Nonesuch, 888–890.
26. Emerson Memorial Association, Harvard. CT: Rusk, ed. *The Letters of Ralph Waldo Emerson* (1939), V, 302.
27. Feinberg. CT: *Wound Dresser*, 51–55; *CW*, VII, 132–136; Nonesuch, 890–892. PT: Canby, 216–217.
28. National Archives.
29. Feinberg.
30. Feinberg.
31. Whitman House, Camden. CT: *American Mercury*, XVI (1929), 185–186.
32. Draft letter in Barrett.
33. Charles Roberts Autograph Collection, Haverford College. CT: *AL*, VII (1935), 79; Nonesuch, 893.
34. Feinberg. CT: *Wound Dresser*, 55–56; *CW*, VII, 136–137.
35. Feinberg. CT: *Wound Dresser*, 56–57; *CW*, VII, 137–138.
36. Feinberg. CT: *Wound Dresser*, 57–60; *CW*, VII, 138–141; Nonesuch, 893–895.
37. Rollo G. Silver. CT: *AL*, VII (1935), 79.
37.1 Whitman House, Camden.
38. Whitman House, Camden. CT: *AL*, VIII (1937), 417–418.
39. Whitman House, Camden. CT: *American Mercury*, XVI (1929), 186.
40. Barrett. CT: New York *Evening Post*, September 7, 1918; *UPP*, II, 21–26; Holloway, 200–205; Nonesuch, 895–900. PT: Canby, 146.
41. Feinberg. CT: *Wound Dresser*, 61–63; *CW*, VII, 142–144; Nonesuch, 900–901.
42. Feinberg. CT: *Wound Dresser*, 63–67; *CW*, VII, 144–148. PT: Canby, 220.
43. Draft letter in Berg. PT: Allen, 297–298.
44. Draft letter in Berg. PT: Allen, 298.
45. Feinberg. CT: *Wound Dresser*, 68–71; *CW*, VII, 149–152.
46. Feinberg. PT: *Wound Dresser*, 71–72; *CW*, VII, 152–153; Nonesuch, 902–903.
47. Draft letter in Feinberg.
48. Feinberg. CT: *Wound Dresser*, 72–75; *CW*, VII, 153–156.
49. Draft letter in Library of Congress.
50. Feinberg. PT: *Wound Dresser*, 75–78; *CW*, VII, 156–159; Nonesuch, 903–905. PT: Canby, 220.
51. Feinberg. CT: *Wound Dresser*, 78–80; *CW*, VII, 159–162.
52. Draft letter in Berg. PT: Allen, 299.
53. Feinberg. CT: *Wound Dresser*, 81–85; *CW*, VII, 162–166; Nonesuch, 905–907.
54. Feinberg. CT: *Wound Dresser*, 85–87; *CW*, VII, 166–168. PT: Canby, 220–221.
55. Berg. CT: *Wound Dresser*, 87–92; *CW*, VII, 168–173; Nonesuch, 908–911. PT: Canby, 221.
56. Feinberg. CT: *Wound Dresser*, 111–114; *CW*, VII, 193–195 (printed with 76). PT: Canby, 221–222.
57. Feinberg. CT: *Wound Dresser*, 92–93; *CW*, VII, 174–175.
58. Feinberg. CT: *Wound Dresser*, 93–96; *CW*, VII, 175–178; Nonesuch, 911–913.
59. New-York Historical Society.
60. Library of Congress. CT: Glicksberg, 94–95; Nonesuch, 913–915.
61. Draft letter in Feinberg. CT: Traubel, II, 127–129; Nonesuch, 919–921.
62. Draft letter in Feinberg. CT: Traubel, III, 386–388.
63. Draft letter in Feinberg. CT: Traubel, III, 367–370; Nonesuch, 915–917. PT: Canby, 146–147.
64. New-York Historical Society. DRAFT LETTER (in Feinberg): Traubel, I, 115–118.
65. Feinberg. CT: *Wound Dresser*, 96–99; *CW*, VII, 178–181.

66. Library of Congress. CT: Glicksberg, 96–97.
67. Library of Congress. CT: Glicksberg, 97–98.
68. Incomplete draft letter in Feinberg.
69. Feinberg. PT: *Wound Dresser*, 100–103; *CW*, VII, 181–184.
70. Feinberg. PT: *Wound Dresser*, 103–105; *CW*, VII, 184–187.
71. Draft letter in Berg.
72. Feinberg. CT: *Wound Dresser*, 106–108; *CW*, VII, 187–190.
73. Incomplete draft letter in Feinberg.
74. Charles A. Brown Collection, University of Rochester. PT: *Saturday Review of Literature*, XI (April 6, 1935), 598.
75. Draft letter in Feinberg. CT: Traubel, I, 233; Nonesuch, 917–918.
76. Feinberg. CT: *Wound Dresser*, 108–111; *CW*, VII, 190–193.
77. New-York Historical Society.
78. Feinberg. CT: *Wound Dresser*, 114–118; *CW*, VII, 196–200.
79. Draft letter in Feinberg.
80. Feinberg. CT: *Wound Dresser*, 118–121; *CW*, VII, 200–202.
81. Draft letter in Feinberg. CT: Traubel, I, 197–198; Nonesuch, 918–919.
82. Draft letter in Feinberg. CT: Traubel, II, 48–50; Nonesuch, 921–923.
83. Feinberg. CT: *Wound Dresser*, 121–124; *CW*, VII, 203–206. PT: Canby, 222.
84. Draft letter in Feinberg. CT: Traubel, III, 578–580; Nonesuch, 923–925. PT: Canby, 147.
85. Draft letter in Feinberg. CT: Traubel, I, 26–27.
86. Morgan. CT: Bucke, 38–40; *Wound Dresser*, 125–129; *CW*, VII, 206–211; Nonesuch, 926–928. PT: Canby, 145. DRAFT LETTER (in Feinberg).
87. Draft letter in Feinberg.
88. Feinberg. CT: *Wound Dresser*, 129–131; *CW*, VII, 211–213.
89. Feinberg. PT: *Wound Dresser*, 131–135; *CW*, VII, 213–217.
90. Trent. DRAFT LETTER (in Feinberg): Traubel, I, 434–435; Nonesuch, 928–929.
91. Draft letter in Yale. CT: Traubel, IV, 416–417.
92. Feinberg. CT: *Wound Dresser*, 135–139; *CW*, VII, 218–221. PT: Canby, 222–223.
93. Draft letter in Feinberg. CT: Traubel, I, 339–340; Nonesuch, 929–930.
94. Feinberg. CT: Traubel, III, 101–108. PT: Nonesuch, 930–934. DRAFT LETTER (in Feinberg).
95. Berg.
96. Lion. CT: Perry, 142–143; Allen, 305. PT: Barrus, 12–13; Barton, *Abraham Lincoln and Walt Whitman*, 71.
97. Draft letter in Berg.
98. Draft letter in Feinberg. CT: Traubel, II, 380–382; Holloway, 216–218; Nonesuch, 934–936. PT: Canby, 198.
99. TEXT: *Autograph Prices Current* (London), III (1917–1918), 243.
100. Feinberg.
101. Feinberg. CT: *Wound Dresser*, 139–141; *CW*, VII, 221–223.
102. TEXT: Copy in Stanford University Library, probably prepared by Trowbridge's daughter. PT: Glicksberg, 98–99.
103. Feinberg. CT: *Wound Dresser*, 143–146; *CW*, VII, 224–227. PT: Canby, 223.
104. Feinberg. CT: *Wound Dresser*, 146–147; *CW*, VII, 227–228.
105. Feinberg. CT: *Wound Dresser*, 147–148; *CW*, VII, 229–230. PT: Canby, 223.
106. TEXT: Perry, 144–146, and copy in Stanford University, probably prepared by Trowbridge's daughter.
107. Feinberg. CT: *Wound Dresser*, 149–152; *CW*, VII, 230–233; Nonesuch, 936–938.
108. Draft letter in Trent. CT: Gohdes and Silver, 70–72.
109. Feinberg. CT: *Wound Dresser*, 152–153; *CW*, VII, 233–235.
110. Draft letter in Berg.
111. Feinberg. CT: *Wound Dresser*, 154–155; *CW*, VII, 235–236.
112. Feinberg. CT: *Wound Dresser*, 155–157; *CW*, VII, 236–238.
113. Feinberg. PT: *Wound Dresser*, 157–159; *CW*, VII, 238–240; Nonesuch, 938–939; Canby, 223–224.
114. Feinberg. CT: *Wound Dresser*, 159–160; *CW*, VII, 240–242.

115. Feinberg. CT: *Wound Dresser*, 160–162; *CW*, VII, 242–244.
115.1 Missouri Historical Society. CT: *Missouri Historical Society Bulletin*, XVI (1960), 100–101.
116. Feinberg. CT: *Wound Dresser*, 162–164; *CW*, VII, 244–246; Nonesuch, 940–941.
117. Feinberg. CT: *Wound Dresser*, 165–166; *CW*, VII, 246–248.
118. Feinberg. CT: *Wound Dresser*, 166–170; *CW*, VII, 248–251; Nonesuch, 941–943.
119. Draft letter in Feinberg. CT: Carl Sandburg, *Lincoln Collector* (1949), 322–323.
120. Feinberg. CT: *Wound Dresser*, 170–172; *CW*, VII, 251–253.
121. Feinberg. CT: *Wound Dresser*, 172–174; *CW*, VII, 253–256.
122. Feinberg and Doheny. PT: *Wound Dresser*, 175–176; *CW*, VII, 256–258.
123. Feinberg. CT: *Wound Dresser*, 176–177; *CW*, VII, 258.
124. Feinberg. CT: *Wound Dresser*, 177–178; *CW*, VII, 259–260.
125. Feinberg. CT: *Wound Dresser*, 179; *CW*, VII, 260–261.
126. Feinberg. CT: *Wound Dresser*, 180–182; *CW*, VII, 261–263.
127. Feinberg. CT: *Wound Dresser*, 182–183; *CW*, VII, 263–264.
128. TEXT: Perry, 147–148, and copy in Stanford University, probably prepared by Trowbridge's daughter.
129. Feinberg. CT: *Wound Dresser*, 183–186; *CW*, VII, 264–267. PT: Canby, 224–225.
130. Feinberg. CT: *Wound Dresser*, 186–188; *CW*, VII, 267–269.
131. Feinberg. CT: *Wound Dresser*, 188–190; *CW*, VII, 269–271.
132. Feinberg. CT: *Wound Dresser*, 190–192; *CW*, VII, 271–273; Nonesuch, 943–945.
133. Feinberg. CT: *Wound Dresser*, 192–195; *CW*, VII, 273–276; Nonesuch, 945–947.
134. Feinberg. CT: *Wound Dresser*, 195–197; *CW*, VII, 277–278.
135. Feinberg. CT: *Wound Dresser*, 197–198; *CW*, VII, 278–279; Nonesuch, 947.
136. Feinberg. CT: *Wound Dresser*, 198; *CW*, VII, 279–280; Nonesuch, 948.
137. Berg.
138. Barrett. CT: *SB*, V (1952), 204–205.
139. Berg.
140. Yale.
141. Berg.
142. Berg.
143. Berg.
144. Berg. PT: Allen, 315–316.
145. Yale (Envelope: Feinberg). PT: Barrus, 19–20; Nonesuch, 948–949; Allen, 316.
146. Berg.
147. Draft letter in Trent. CT: Gohdes and Silver, 72.
148. Feinberg.
149. Berg. CT: Nonesuch, 949–951. PT: Perry, 150–152; William E. Barton, *Abraham Lincoln and Walt Whitman* (1928), 73–74; Canby, 234.
150. Berg.
151. Feinberg. CT: Traubel, III, 539–540; Nonesuch, 951–952. PT: Allen, 323.
152. Feinberg. CT: Traubel, III, 292–293.
153. FACSIMILE: George M. Williamson, *Catalogue of A Collector of Books, Letters, and Manuscripts Written by Walt Whitman* (1903).
154. Morgan. CT: Glicksberg, 106–107.
155. TEXT: Glicksberg, 99–100; Nonesuch, 953–954. PT: Perry, 152–153.
156. Feinberg. CT: Traubel, III, 201–202; Nonesuch, 951.
157. TEXT: Copy in Stanford University, probably prepared by Trowbridge's daughter. PT: Glicksberg, 100–101; Perry, 153.
158. Berg.
159. Berg. CT: Nonesuch, 954–955.
160. TEXT: *Overland Monthly*, XLIII (1904), 61, 63.
161. TEXT: *CW*, IV, 122–125; Nonesuch, 955–956.
162. Rutgers University. PT: *Drum-Taps*, ed. F. DeWolfe Miller (1959), xxxvi.

163. Whitman House, Camden, CT: *American Mercury*, XVI (1929), 187–188; Nonesuch, 958–960. PT: Canby, 255–256.
164. FACSIMILE: George M. Williamson, *Catalogue of A Collector of Books, Letters, and Manuscripts Written by Walt Whitman* (1903).
164.1 Feinberg.
164.2 Feinberg.
165. Doheny.
166. Berg.
167. TEXT: *The Collector*, XXVI (November, 1912), 3–4.
168. Berg.
169. Barrett.
170. TEXT: *Overland Monthly*, XLIII (1904), 61–62.
171. TEXT: *Overland Monthly*, XLIII (1904), 62.
172. Berg.
173. Berg. CT: *CW*, VIII, 173.
174. Berg. CT: *CW*, VIII, 173–174.
175. Hanley. CT: *CW*, VIII, 174.
176. Berg. CT: *CW*, VIII, 174–175.
177. Berg. CT: *CW*, VIII, 175–176; Nonesuch, 957–958.
178. Berg. CT: *CW*, VIII, 176–177.
179. TEXT: *Overland Monthly*, XLIII (1904), 62.
180. Berg. CT: *CW*, VIII, 177–178.
181. Trent. CT: *CW*, VIII, 178–180.
182. Trent. CT: *CW*, VIII, 180–181.
183. Berg. CT: *CW*, VIII, 181–182.
184. TEXT: Clara Barrus, *The Life and Letters of John Burroughs* (1925), I, 132, and Barrus, 42.
185. Morgan. CT: Glicksberg, 107.
186. Morgan. CT: *Putnam's Monthly*, V (1908), 166–167; Glicksberg, 107–108.
187. Yale. PT: Allen, 372.
188. Berg.
189. TEXT: Barrus, 43.
190. Lion. PT: Allen, 372.
191. TEXT: Anderson Galleries, February 11–13, 1924.
191.1 Feinberg.
192. TEXT: O'Connor's transcription, Yale. PT: *The Fortnightly Review*, VI (1866), 546–547; *Poems by Walt Whitman* (1868), 17–18.
192.1 Berg. CT: *CW*, VIII, 217–218 (dated 1867).
193. National Archives.
194. Morgan. CT: Glicksberg, 108–109. PT: New York *Evening Post*, May 31, 1919.
195. Berg (Envelope: Hanley). CT: *CW*, VIII, 182–183.
196. Fragment in Trent. CT: Gohdes and Silver, 78 (dated [Before May 23, 1873]).
197. Hanley. CT: *CW*, VIII, 183–184.
198. Clifford Odets. CT: *CW*, VIII, 184; Nonesuch, 960–961.
199. Barrett.
200. Hanley. CT: *CW*, VIII, 184–185.
201. Berg. CT: *CW*, VIII, 185–186; Nonesuch, 961–962.
202. Hanley. PT: *CW*, VIII, 186–187.
203. TEXT: *Overland Monthly*, XLIII (1904), 62.
204. Hanley. CT: *CW*, VIII, 187–188.
205. Hanley. CT: *CW*, VIII, 188–190.
206. Hanley. CT: *CW*, VIII, 190.
207. Morgan. CT: Glicksberg, 109–110.
208. Berg. CT: *CW*, VIII, 191.
209. Barrett. CT: *CW*, VIII, 191–193; Nonesuch, 962–963.
210. Feinberg.
211. Hanley. CT: *CW*, VIII, 193–194.
212. Hanley. CT: *CW*, VIII, 194–195.
213. Hanley. CT: *CW*, VIII, 195–197.
214. Berg. CT: *CW*, VIII, 197–200.
215. Hanley.
216. Hanley. CT: *CW*, VIII, 200–201.
217. Berg. CT: *CW*, VIII, 202–203.
218. Berg. CT: *CW*, VIII, 203–204.
219. Berg. CT: *CW*, VIII, 204–205.
220. New Jersey Historical Society. CT: *Proceedings of the New Jersey Historical Society*, LXXV (1957), 219.
221. Berg. CT: *CW*, VIII, 205–206.
222. Berg.
223. Berg. CT: *CW*, VIII, 207–208.
224. Berg. CT: *CW*, VIII, 208–210.
225. Morgan. CT: Glicksberg, 110–111.
226. Trent. CT: *CW*, VIII, 210–211.
227. Trent. CT: *CW*, VIII, 211–213.
228. Morgan. CT: Glicksberg, 111.
229. Berg. CT: *CW*, VIII, 213–214.
230. Draft letter in Feinberg.
231. Trent. PT: *CW*, VIII, 214–216.
232. Ohio Wesleyan and Berg. PT: *CW*, VIII, 216.
233. Trent. CT: *CW*, VIII, 216.
234. Trent. CT: *CW*, VIII, 217.
235. Berg.

236. Berg.
237. Draft letter in Feinberg.
238. Draft letter in Feinberg.
239. Barrett. CT: *Wake*, VII (1948), 13–14. DRAFT LETTER (in Feinberg): Traubel, II, 419; Nonesuch, 963.
240. Feinberg. DRAFT LETTER (in Feinberg).
241. Morgan. CT: Glicksberg, 111–112.
242. Mrs. Joseph Perkins. CT: *AL*, XXIII (1951), 335–336. DRAFT LETTER (in Feinberg).
243. Mrs. Francis Frederic Phillips. DRAFT LETTER (in Feinberg).
244. Morgan. PT: *Leaves of Grass*, ed. C. J. Furness (1939), vii.
245. Rollo G. Silver. CT: Traubel, III, 475.
246. NYPL. CT: *AL*, XXIII (1951), 336–337. DRAFT LETTER (in Feinberg).
247. Berg.
248. Yale. CT: *AL*, VIII (1937), 418–419.
249. Berg.
250. Berg. CT: *AL*, XXIII (1951), 338–339.
251. NYPL. CT: *AL*, XXIII (1951), 339.
252. Draft letter in Trent. CT: Gohdes and Silver, 72–73.
253. Mrs. Joseph Perkins. CT: *AL*, XXIII (1951), 340. DRAFT LETTER (in Feinberg).
253.1 Feinberg.
254. Mrs. Joseph Perkins. CT: *AL*, XXIII (1951), 340.
255. Robert H. Taylor. CT: *Rossetti Papers, 1862–1870* (1903), 275. DRAFT LETTER (in Feinberg): Traubel, III, 298–299; Nonesuch, 964.
256. Draft letter in Berg: Asselineau, 186–187 *n.* ANOTHER DRAFT (in Feinberg): Traubel, I, 383–384.
256.1 Draft letter in Feinberg.
257. Robert H. Taylor. CT: *Rossetti Papers, 1862–1870* (1903), 283–284. DRAFT LETTER (in Feinberg): Traubel, II, 358–359; Nonesuch, 964–965.
258. Berg.
259. Robert H. Taylor. CT: *Rossetti Papers, 1862–1870* (1903), 285–287. DRAFT LETTER (in Yale): Traubel, III, 301–303; Nonesuch, 965–967; Traubel, IV, 27–29. PT: Gilchrist, 179–182.
260. New Jersey Historical Society. CT: *Proceedings of the New Jersey Historical Society*, LXXV (1957), 219.
261. Mrs. Joseph Perkins. CT: *AL*, XXIII (1951), 343.
262. Draft letter in Feinberg. CT: Traubel, I, 263–264.
263. Berg.
264. Berg.
265. Berg.
265.1 Barrett.

Collections

Barrett, 16, 21.2, 32 (*draft*), 40, 138, 169, 199, 209, 239, 265.1.

Berg, 3, 4, 5, 6, 43 (*draft*), 44 (*draft*), 52 (*draft*), 55, 71 (*draft*), 95, 97 (*draft*), 110 (*draft*), 137, 139, 141, 142, 143, 144, 146, 149, 150, 158, 159, 166, 168, 172, 173, 174, 176, 177, 178, 180, 183, 188, 192.1, 195, 201, 208, 214, 217, 218, 219, 221, 222, 223, 224, 229, 232 (and Ohio Wesleyan), 235, 236, 247, 249, 250, 256 (*draft*), 258, 263, 264, 265.

Charles A. Brown Collection, University of Rochester, 74.

Doheny, 122 (and Feinberg), 165.

Emerson Memorial Association, Harvard, 26.

Feinberg, 10, 15, 20, 21.1 (*draft*), 25, 27, 29, 30, 34, 35, 36, 41, 42, 45, 46, 47 (*draft*), 48, 50, 51, 53, 54, 56, 57, 58, 61 (*draft*), 62 (*draft*), 63 (*draft*), 64 (*draft*), 65, 68 (*incomplete draft*), 69, 70, 72, 73 (*incomplete draft*), 75 (*draft*), 76, 78, 79 (*draft*), 80, 81 (*draft*), 82 (*draft*), 83, 84 (*draft*), 85 (*draft*), 86 (*draft*), 87 (*draft*), 88, 89, 90 (*draft*), 92, 93 (*draft*), 94 and draft, 98 (*draft*), 100, 101, 103, 104, 105, 107, 109, 111, 112, 113, 114, 115,

Feinberg (*cont.*)
116, 117, 118, 119 (*draft*), 120, 121, 122 (and Doheny), 123, 124, 125, 126, 127, 129, 130, 131, 132, 133, 134, 135, 136, env. 145, 148, 151, 152, 156, 164.1, 164.2, 191.1, 210, 230 (*draft*), 237 (*draft*), 238 (*draft*), 239 (*draft*), 240 and draft, 242 (*draft*), 243 (*draft*), 246 (*draft*), 253 (*draft*), 253.1, 255 (*draft*), 256 (*draft*), 256.1 (*draft*), 257 (*draft*), 262 (*draft*).
Colonel Richard Gimbel, 14, 17.
Hanley, 22 (*incomplete draft*), 175, env. 195, 197, 200, 202, 204, 205, 206, 211, 212, 213, 215, 216.
Huntington, 12.
Huntington (New York) Historical Society, 8.
Library of Congress, 49 (*draft*), 60, 66, 67.
Lion, 96, 190.
Long Island Historical Society, 7, 9.
Missouri Historical Society, 115.1.
Morgan, 18, 86, 154, 185, 186, 194, 207, 225, 228, 241, 244.
National Archives, 28, 193.
New Hampshire Historical Society, 9.1.
New Jersey Historical Society, 220, 260.
New-York Historical Society, 59, 64, 77.
NYPL, 246, 251.
Clifford Odets, 198.
Ohio Wesleyan, 232 (and Berg).
Mrs. Joseph Perkins, 242, 253, 254, 261.
Mrs. Francis Frederic Phillips, 243.
Charles Roberts Autograph Collection, Haverford College, 33.
Rutgers University, 162.
Papers of William Henry Seward, University of Rochester, 11.
Rollo G. Silver, 37, 245.
Stanford University, 102 (*copy*), 106 (*copy*), 128 (*copy*), 157 (*copy*).
Robert H. Taylor, 255, 257, 259.
Trent, 23, 90, 108 (*draft*), 147 (*draft*), 181, 182, 196 (*fragment*), 226, 227, 231, 233, 234, 252 (*draft*).
Whitman House, Camden, 19, 21, 31, 37.1, 38, 39, 163.
Yale, 1, 2, 91 (*draft*), 140, 145, 187, 192 (*transcript*), 248, 259 (*draft*).

Appendix B

A CHECK LIST OF WHITMAN'S LOST LETTERS

It is sometimes of importance to biographers and critics to know about letters WW wrote, even though the letters themselves are not extant. The entries in this check list include (1) the date, (2) the name of the recipient of WW's letter, and (3) the source of information which makes possible the reconstruction. Many of the dates are approximate because the information is based upon a letter addressed to WW, which simply informs us that the poet had written before the correspondent had replied. I have indicated the date and present location of correspondence addressed to WW. Allusions to lost letters in WW's own correspondence are designated WW and followed by the appropriate letter number. Auction records which contained no text are incorporated into this list, since the letters as of the moment are "lost." The abbreviations are explained in the table of abbreviations in the Introduction.

1848

March 27. To Mary Van Nostrand. WW 5.

1855

About December 19. To Hannah Heyde. Letter from Mrs. Heyde to Louisa Van Velsor Whitman, December 20 (Trent).

1856

June 11. To George I. Storms. Letter from Storms, June 29 (Feinberg).

1857

June 29. To Mrs. Sarah Tyndale. Letter from Mrs. Tyndale, July 1 (Feinberg).

1860

February 25. To Thayer & Eldridge. Letter from Thayer & Eldridge, February 27 (Feinberg).

About March 1. To Thayer & Eldridge. Letter from Thayer & Eldridge, March 2 (Feinberg).

March 8. To Thayer & Eldridge. Letter from Thayer & Eldridge, March 9 (Feinberg).

About March 20. To Fred Vaughan. Letter from Vaughan, March 21 (Feinberg).

About March 26. To Fred Vaughan. Letter from Vaughan, March 27 (Feinberg).

About March 26. To Henry Clapp. Letter from Clapp, March 27 (Feinberg; Traubel, I, 236).

About March 29. To Louisa Van Velsor Whitman. Letter from Mrs. Whitman, March 30 (Trent).

About March 29. To Louisa Van Velsor Whitman. Letter from Mrs. Whitman, March 30 (Trent): "I have received both of your letters."

About April 3. To Louisa Van Velsor Whitman. Letter from Mrs. Whitman, April 4 (Trent).

About April 29. To Fred Vaughan. Letter from Vaughan, April 30 (Feinberg).

About May 2. To Louisa Van Velsor Whitman. Letter from Mrs. Whitman, May 3 (Trent).

About May 17. To Hannah Heyde. Letter from Charles Heyde, May 18 (Trent; Gohdes and Silver, 215–216).

About May 20. To Fred Vaughan. Letter from Vaughan, May 21 (Feinberg).

About May 31. To Hannah Heyde. Letter from Mrs. Heyde to Louisa Van Velsor Whitman, June 1 (LC).

About June 13. To Thayer & Eldridge. Letter from Thayer & Eldridge, June 14 (Feinberg).

About July 26. To Thayer & Eldridge. Letter from Thayer & Eldridge, July 27 (Feinberg).

About August 16. To Thayer & Eldridge. Letter from Thayer & Eldridge, August 17 (Feinberg).

About October 10. To Thayer & Eldridge. Letter from Thayer & Eldridge, October 11 (Feinberg).

About October 14. To Thayer & Eldridge. Letter from Thayer & Eldridge, October 15 (Feinberg).

About November 12. To Charles L. Heyde. Letter from Mrs. Heyde, November 13 (LC).

1861

April 12. To W. W. Thayer. Letter from Thayer, April 19 (Feinberg).

About June 27. To George Washington Whitman. Letter from George to Louisa Van Velsor Whitman, June 28 (Trent).

1862

About March 11. To Silas S. Soule. Letter from Soule, March 12 (Feinberg).

June 10. To George Washington Whitman. Letter from George to Louisa Van Velsor Whitman, June 29 (Trent).

About November 5. To Hannah Heyde. Letter from Mrs. Heyde to Louisa Van Velsor Whitman, November 6–12 (LC).

About December 18. To Thomas Jefferson Whitman. WW 25.

December 19. To Louisa Van Velsor Whitman. WW 25.

December 19. To Hannah Heyde. WW 25.

About December 22. To Thomas Jefferson Whitman. WW 25.

December 30. To George Washington Whitman. WW 27.

1863

About January 1. To Thomas Jefferson Whitman. WW 27.

About January 12. To George Washington Whitman. Letter from George, January 13 (Trent).

About January 12. To Moses Lane. Letter from Jeff, January 13 (Feinberg).

About January 12. To Mr. Charles Botsfor(?). Letter from Jeff, January 13 (Feinberg).

About January 15. To Louisa Van Velsor Whitman. WW 31.

January 16. To Samuel Probasco. WW 31.

About January 21. To George Washington Whitman. Letter from George to Louisa Van Velsor Whitman, January 22 (Trent).

January 27. To George Washington Whitman. Letter from George, February 1 (Trent).

About January 31. To Tom (an orderly in George's Regiment). Letter from George, February 1 (Trent).

February 5. To George Washington Whitman. WW 34.

February 6. To George Washington Whitman. WW 34.

February 7. To Moses Lane. WW 34.

February 9. To Thomas Jefferson Whitman. Letter from Jeff, February 10 (Feinberg).

February 22. To George Washington Whitman. Letter from George, February 25 (Trent).

February. To James Redpath. Donaldson, 142.
March 1. To Thomas Jefferson Whitman. Letter from Jeff, March 3 (Feinberg).
March 14. To Louisa Van Velsor Whitman. WW 39.
March 16. To Louisa Van Velsor Whitman. WW 39.
About March 20. To Charles S. Kingsley. Letter from Kingsley, March 21 (Berg).
March 28. To Hannah Heyde. WW 41.
April 10. To George Washington Whitman. WW 42.
April 16. To George Washington Whitman. *Diary*, ed. Glicksberg, 132.
April 22. To Louisa Van Velsor Whitman. WW 45.
April 22. To George Washington Whitman. *Diary*, ed. Glicksberg, 132.
April 23. To "Futch" (Hugo Fritsch?). *Diary*, ed. Glicksberg, 132.
April 24. To George Washington Whitman. *Diary*, ed. Glicksberg, 133.
April 26. To Hannah Heyde. *Diary*, ed. Glicksberg, 133.
April 29. To Moses Lane. *Diary*, ed. Glicksberg, 133.
May 1. To George Washington Whitman. *Diary*, ed. Glicksberg, 133.
May 2. To Will W. Wallace. *Diary*, ed. Glicksberg, 133.
May 2. To Amos Vliet. *Diary*, ed. Glicksberg, 133.
May 5. To Moses Lane. *Diary*, ed. Glicksberg, 134.
May 8 or 9. To George Washington Whitman. *Diary*, ed. Glicksberg, 135.
About May 13. To Samuel Elliott. WW 48.
May 13. To Mrs. Eveline Ballou. *Diary*, ed. Glicksberg, 135.
May 13. To Moses Lane. *Diary*, ed. Glicksberg, 135.
May 16. To Mrs. Sarah A. Hudson. *Diary*, ed. Glicksberg, 135.
May 17. To Thomas Jefferson Whitman. *Diary*, ed. Glicksberg, 135.
May 18. To Hannah Heyde. *Diary*, ed. Glicksberg, 135.
May 18. To George Washington Whitman. *Diary*, ed. Glicksberg, 135.
June 1(?). To Hannah Heyde. WW 53.
June 8. To George Washington Whitman. WW 53.
About June 11. To Thomas Jefferson Whitman. Letter from Jeff, June 13 (Feinberg).
About June 18. To John J. Barker. Letter from Barker, June 19 (Texas).
About June 29. To Mrs. Redgate (mother of Stephen, a soldier). WW 55.
July 5. To George Washington Whitman. WW 57.
July 10(?). To George Washington Whitman. WW 57.
July 12. To Thomas Jefferson Whitman. WW 58.
July 15(?). To Hannah Heyde. WW 58.
July 17. To George Washington Whitman. Letter from George to Louisa Van Velsor Whitman, August 16 (Trent).
August 9. To Thomas Jefferson Whitman. WW 65.
About August 10. To George Washington Whitman. WW 65.
About August 10. To George Washington Whitman. WW 65: "I have sent George two letters within a week past."
August 13(?). To Hannah Heyde. WW 69.
August 13(?). To George Washington Whitman. WW 69.
About August 15. To William E. Vandermark. Letter from Vandermark, August 17 (Texas).
September 4. To Martha Whitman. WW 76.
About September 5. To Caleb H. Babbitt. Letter from Mary A. Babbitt, September 6 (Berg).
September 6. To Thomas Jefferson Whitman. WW 76.
About September 14. To George Washington Whitman. WW 78.
About September 14. To Hannah Heyde. WW 78.
About September 14. To Abby H. Price. WW 78.
September 15. To Thomas P. Sawyer. *Diary*, ed. Glicksberg, 136.
September 17. To Moses Lane. *Diary*, ed. Glicksberg, 136.

September 17. To Samuel Probasco. *Diary*, ed. Glicksberg, 136.
September 27. To Caleb H. Babbitt. Letter from Babbitt, October 1 (Berg).
September 28. To George Washington Whitman. WW 80.
About October 3. To Dr. Le Baron Russell. Letter from Russell, October 4 (Texas; Donaldson, 147).
October 5(?). To Bethuel Smith. *Diary*, ed. Glicksberg, 137.
October 10. To Caleb H. Babbitt. *Diary*, ed. Glicksberg, 137.
About October 12. To Julia Elizabeth Stilwell. Letter from Miss Stilwell, October 13 (Berg).
About October 12. To Hannah Heyde. WW 88.
About October 13. To Thomas Jefferson Whitman. Letter from Jeff, October 15 (Feinberg).
October 14. To George Washington Whitman. *Diary*, ed. Glicksberg, 137.
October 16. To Louisa Van Velsor Whitman. *Diary*, ed. Glicksberg, 137.
October 19. To George Washington Whitman. WW 89.
October 20. To John Stilwell. *Diary*, ed. Glicksberg, 138.
October 22(?). To Hannah Heyde. WW 92.
October 28. To George Washington Whitman. WW 92.
About November 9. To Elijah Douglass Fox. Letter from Fox, November 10 (Lion).
November 16. To Ellen M. O'Connor. *Diary*, ed. Glicksberg, 139.
November 17. To Hannah Heyde. *Diary*, ed. Glicksberg, 139.
November 17. To Elijah Douglass Fox. *Diary*, ed. Glicksberg, 139.
November 24. To Elijah Douglass Fox. Letter from Fox, December 9 (LC).
December 1. To George Washington Whitman. *Diary*, ed. Glicksberg, 139.
December 3. To Hannah Heyde. *Diary*, ed. Glicksberg, 140.
December 3. To George Washington Whitman. *Diary*, ed. Glicksberg, 140.
December 3. To Thomas Jefferson Whitman. *Diary*, ed. Glicksberg, 140.
December 3. To John Stilwell. *Diary*, ed. Glicksberg, 140.
December 11. To (?). Parke-Bernet, April 16–17, 1945.
December 12(?). To William E. Vandermark. Letter from Vandermark, December 16 (Berg).
December 17. To Thomas Jefferson Whitman. *Diary*, ed. Glicksberg, 140
December 17. To Caleb H. Babbitt. *Diary*, ed. Glicksberg, 140.
December 17. To Alonzo S. Bush. *Diary*, ed. Glicksberg, 140.
December 17. To Elijah Douglass Fox. Letter from Fox, December 24 (Lion).
December 19. To Livingstone J. Brooks. *Diary*, ed. Glicksberg, 140.
December 19. To John Stilwell. *Diary*, ed. Glicksberg, 140.
December 20(?). To Hannah Heyde. Letter from Mrs. Heyde to Louisa Van Velsor Whitman, January 5(?), [1864] (LC).
About December 28. To William E. Vandermark. Letter from Vandermark, December 29 (Berg).

1864

January 1(?). To Hannah Heyde. Letter from Mrs. Heyde to Louisa Van Velsor Whitman, January 5(?) (LC).
About January 8. To William H. Millis. Letter from Millis, January 9 (Berg).
January 30. To Hannah Heyde. WW 103.
February 8. To Louisa Van Velsor Whitman. WW 107.
February 22. To Alonzo S. Bush. Letter from Bush, March 7 (Texas).
March 19. To George Washington Whitman. Letter from George to Louisa Van Velsor Whitman, April 3 (Trent).
About March 21. To George Washington Whitman. WW 112.
About March 21. To Hannah Heyde. WW 112.
About March 28. To George Washington Whitman. WW 113.
April 6. To George Washington Whitman. WW 115.1.

April 27. To Hannah Heyde. WW 120.
May 5. To H. S. Cunningham. Letter from Cunningham, May 9 (Texas).
May 5. To George Washington Whitman. Letter from George to Louisa Van Velsor Whitman, May 20 (Trent).
About May 8. To Reuben Farwell. Letter from Farwell, May 10 (Trent).
May 12. To Louisa Van Velsor Whitman. WW 125.
May 16. To George Washington Whitman. WW 127.
About May 22. To George Washington Whitman. WW 129.
About May 22. To Hannah Heyde. WW 129.
May 24(?). To William E. Worthen. WW 130.
June 2. To H. S. Cunningham. Letter from Cunningham, June 11 (Berg).
June 9. To George Washington Whitman. WW 134.
June 11. To George Washington Whitman. Letter from George to Louisa Van Velsor Whitman, June 18 (Trent).
About June 13. To Hannah Heyde. WW 135.
June 25. To George Washington Whitman. Letter from George to Louisa Van Velsor Whitman, July 2 (Trent).
About July 13. To Elijah Douglass Fox. Letter from Fox, July 14 (Berg).
July 14. To George Washington Whitman. Letter from George to Louisa Van Velsor Whitman, July 26 (Trent).
August 2. To John Burroughs. Envelope in Feinberg.
August 4. To George Washington Whitman. Letter from George to Louisa Van Velsor Whitman, August 9–10 (Trent).
About August 29. To George Washington Whitman. Letter from George to Louisa Van Velsor Whitman, August 30 (Trent).
About August 29. To Bethuel Smith. Letter from Smith, August 30 (Feinberg).
About September 1. To James S. Stilwell. Letter from Stilwell, September 2(?) (Berg).
September 5(?). To Bethuel Smith. WW's notation on letter from Smith, August 30 (Feinberg).
September 8. To George Washington Whitman. Letter from George to Louisa Van Velsor Whitman, September 17 (Trent).
About September 26. To James S. Stilwell. Letter from Stilwell, September 27 (Berg).
About October 1. To Reuben Farwell. Letter from Farwell, October 2 (Trent).
October 7. To Reuben Farwell. WW's notation on letter from Farwell, October 2 (Trent).
About October 17. To William E. Babcock. Letter from Babcock, October 18 (Berg).
About October 20. To Jesse Mullery. Letter from Mullery, October 21 (Berg).
About November 20. To Reuben Farwell. Letter from Farwell, November 21 (Trent).
About December 24. To William E. Babcock. Letter from Babcock, December 25 (Berg).

1865

About January 5. To William T. Otto. WW 149.
About January 5. To J. Hubley Ashton. WW 149.
About January 10. To Herman Storms. Letter from Storms, January 11 (Berg).
About January 18. To J. Hubley Ashton. Letter from Ellen M. O'Connor, January 19 (Feinberg).
About January 19. To William T. Otto. WW 150.
About January 22. To Jesse Mullery. Letter from Mullery, January 23 (Berg).
About January 25. To Bethuel Smith. Letter from Mrs. Maria Smith, January 26 (Feinberg).
January 26. To Elliott F. Shepard. Letter from Shepard, February 16 (Feinberg).
About January 31. To Captain Julius Mason. WW 152.

February 6. To George Washington Whitman. *Diary*, ed. Glicksberg, 181.
About February 6. To Thomas Jefferson Whitman. Letter from Jeff, February 7 (Feinberg).
February 13. To Captain Julius Mason. *Diary*, ed. Glicksberg, 181.
February 24. To Louisa Van Velsor Whitman. *Diary*, ed. Glicksberg, 181.
February 27. To Lieutenant Colonel John Elmer Mulford. *Diary*, ed. Glicksberg, 181.
April 13. To Jesse Mullery. Letter from Mullery, May 3 (Berg).
April 24. To Jesse Mullery. Letter from Mullery, May 3 (Berg).
About May 3. To Louisa Van Velsor Whitman. Letter from Jeff, May 4 (Feinberg).
About May 13. To Thomas Jefferson Whitman. Letter from Jeff, May 14 (Feinberg).
June 3. To Louisa Van Velsor Whitman. Letter from Jeff, June 4 (Feinberg).
July 5. To George Washington Whitman. Letter from George, July 14 (Trent; Gohdes & Silver, 182).
About July 15. To Thomas Jefferson Whitman. Letter from Jeff, July 16 (Feinberg).
August 4. To Louisa Van Velsor Whitman. Letter from Mrs. Whitman, August 8 (Trent).
August 16. To Anson Ryder, Jr. Letter from Ryder, August 9 (Feinberg).
About August 22. To Thomas F. Bainbridge. Letter from Bainbridge, August 23 (Yale).
About September 10. To Louisa Van Velsor Whitman. Letter from Mrs. Whitman, September 11 (Trent).
About September 10. To Thomas Jefferson Whitman. Letter from Jeff, September 11 (Feinberg).
About September 20. To Louisa Van Velsor Whitman. Letter from Mrs. Whitman, September 21 (Trent).
September 26. To Louisa Van Velsor Whitman. Letter from Mrs. Whitman, September 27 (Trent).
November 20. To Benton H. Wilson. Letter from Wilson, November 11 (Feinberg).
December 1. To Louisa Van Velsor Whitman. Letter from Mrs. Whitman, December 3 (Trent).
December 8. To Louisa Van Velsor Whitman. Letter from Mrs. Whitman, December 10 (Trent).

1866

February 7. To Jesse Mullery. Letter from Mullery, February 20 (LC).
About March 22. To Louisa Van Velsor Whitman. WW 174.
About March 22. To Louisa Van Velsor Whitman. WW 174. "I wrote you three letters last week."
About March 23. To Hannah Heyde. Letter from Mrs. Heyde to Louisa Van Velsor Whitman, March 24 (LC).
June 1(?). To Louisa Van Velsor Whitman. WW 180.
June 30(?). To Hannah Heyde. WW 183.
October 9. To Louisa Van Velsor Whitman. WW 192.1.
About October 15. To Hannah Heyde. WW 192.1.
October 27. To Mrs. Aurelia Parker. WW 194.
November 6(?). To Louisa Van Velsor Whitman. WW 197.
November 10. To James Curphey, *Notebook* (*LC* #108).
November 23. To Hannah Heyde. WW 201.
November 30. To Hannah Heyde. WW 204.
About December 9. To Hannah Heyde. WW 206.
December 10. To Hugh B. Thomson. WW's notation on letter from Thomson, December 5 (Feinberg).
December 13. To Benton H. Wilson. WW's notation on letter from Wilson, December 9 (Feinberg).
About December 20. To William E. Worthen. Letter from Jeff, December 21 (Feinberg).

1867

About January 1. To Hannah Heyde. WW 211.
January 10. To Benton H. Wilson. WW's notation on letter from Wilson, December 16, 1866 (Feinberg).

January 26. To Hannah Heyde. WW 216.

January 31. To Benton H. Wilson. WW's notation on letter from Wilson, January 27 (Feinberg).

About February 23. To Anson Ryder, Jr. Letter from Ryder, February 24 (Feinberg).

February 23. To Hannah Heyde. WW 221.

About March 12. To Erastus Otis Parker. WW 225.

March 15. To Anson Ryder, Jr. WW's notation on letter from Ryder, February 24 (Feinberg).

March 15. To Benton H. Wilson. WW's notation on letter from Wilson, February 3 (Feinberg).

About March 18. To Hannah Heyde. WW 226.

March 30. To James Curphey. *Notebook* (LC #108).

April 9. To Louisa Van Velsor Whitman. WW 231.

About April 15. To Hannah Heyde. WW 231.

About May 21. To Thomas Jefferson Whitman. Letter from Jeff, May 23 (Feinberg).

June 13(?). To Louisa Van Velsor Whitman. Letter from Mrs. Whitman, June 20 (Trent).

June 17. To Abraham Simpson. WW's notation on letter from Simpson, May 31 (Feinberg).

June 18. To Louisa Van Velsor Whitman. Letter from Mrs. Whitman, June 20 (Trent).

About July 18. To H. J. Ramsdell. WW's notation on letter from Ramsdell, July 17 (Feinberg).

About August 1. To Thomas Jefferson Whitman. Letter from Jeff, August 2 (Feinberg).

August 3. To (?). "In reference to a photograph of himself." Henkels, June 7–8, 1907.

About August 18. To William Livingston Alden. Letter from Alden, August 19 (Feinberg).

September 23. To Benton H. Wilson. WW's notation on letter from Wilson, September 15 (Feinberg).

October 8(?). To Louisa Van Velsor Whitman. Letter from Mrs. Whitman, October 20 (Trent).

October 20. To Louisa Van Velsor Whitman. Letter from Mrs. Whitman, October 22 (Trent).

About October 25. To Benjamin Russell, Jr. Letter from Russell, October 26 (Feinberg).

October 29(?). To Louisa Van Velsor Whitman. Letter from Mrs. Whitman, October 30 (Trent).

October 29. To Benton H. Wilson. WW's notation on letter from Wilson, September 15 (Feinberg).

November 18(?). To Louisa Van Velsor Whitman. Letter from Mrs. Whitman, November 19 (Trent).

December 6(?). To Louisa Van Velsor Whitman. Letter from Mrs. Whitman, December [1–15] (Trent).

December 13(?). To Louisa Van Velsor Whitman. Letter from Mrs. Whitman, December 15 (Trent).

December 20(?). To Louisa Van Velsor Whitman. Letter from Mrs. Whitman, December 26 (Trent).

Appendix C

A CALENDAR OF LETTERS WRITTEN TO WHITMAN

This calendar includes extant letters written to WW. The following information appears in the entries: (1) the date; (2) the name of the correspondent, sometimes with a brief identification in order to indicate the nature of the correspondence; (3) the location of the letter, if known; and (4) appearance in print, if any. The letters to WW which are reproduced in this volume are marked WW, with the appropriate letter number. Excerpts from many of these letters appear in the notes. Abbreviations are explained in the table of abbreviations in the Introduction.

1852(?)

March 31. From Aaron Smith. Feinberg.

1855

July 21. From Ralph Waldo Emerson. Feinberg. WW 10.

1856

June 29. From George I. Storms, a friend. Feinberg.

September 16. From Charles S. Keyser. Feinberg.

June 7. From S. R. Wells. Feinberg.

1857

June 24. From Sarah Tyndale. Feinberg.

July 1. From Sarah Tyndale. Feinberg.

1860

February 10. From Thayer & Eldridge. Feinberg. CT: Allen, 236–237.

February 27. From Thayer & Eldridge. Feinberg.

March 2. From Thayer & Eldridge. Feinberg.

March 6. From Ticknor & Fields (for the *Atlantic Monthly*). Location unknown; CT: Traubel, IV, 77.

March 7. From Thayer & Eldridge. Feinberg.

March 9. From Thayer & Eldridge. Feinberg.

March 19. From Fred Vaughan, a friend. Feinberg.

March 21. From Charles Hine. Feinberg.

March 21. From Fred Vaughan. Feinberg.

March 27. From Henry Clapp, Jr. Feinberg. Location unknown. CT: *Traubel*, I, 236–237.

March 27. From Fred Vaughan. Feinberg.

March 30. From Louisa Van Velsor Whitman. Trent.

April 3. From Thomas Jefferson Whitman. Feinberg.

April 4. From Louisa Van Velsor Whitman. Trent.

April 6. From O. K. Sammis, a friend. Feinberg.

April 9. From Fred Vaughan. Feinberg.

April 16. From Thomas Jefferson Whitman. Feinberg.

April 23. From Frederick Baker. Feinberg.
April 30. From Fred Vaughan. Feinberg.
May 3. From Louisa Van Velsor Whitman. Trent.
May 14. From Henry Clapp, Jr. Feinberg. CT: Traubel, II, 375–376.
May 17. From Fred Vaughan. Feinberg.
May 18. From Charles L. Heyde. Trent. CT: Gohdes and Silver, 215–216.
May 21. From Fred Vaughan. Feinberg.
May 24. From Thayer & Eldridge. Feinberg.
June 5. From Thayer & Eldridge. Feinberg.
June 14. From Thayer & Eldridge. Feinberg.
June 25. From James Redpath. Feinberg. CT: Traubel, III, 460.
July 11. From Susan Garnet Smith, an admirer. CT: Traubel, IV, 312–313.
July 27. From Thayer & Eldridge. Feinberg.
August 16. From Wilhelmina Walton, an admirer. Feinberg.
August 17. From Thayer & Eldridge. Feinberg.
October 11. From Thayer & Eldridge. Feinberg.
October 15. From Thayer & Eldridge. Feinberg.
December 1. From Thayer & Eldridge. Feinberg.
December 5. From Thayer & Eldridge. Feinberg.

1861

February 6. From Harvey Jewell and C. S. Kendall, lawyers. Feinberg.
April 19. From W. W. Thayer. Feinberg.
October 10. From the Editors, the *Atlantic Monthly*. Feinberg. CT: Traubel, II, 213.

1862

January 8. From Lieutenant Silas S. Soule. Feinberg.
March 12. From Lieutenant Silas S. Soule. Feinberg.
March 25. From Ellen Eyre. Feinberg. CT: Allen, 279.
May 2. From Fred Vaughan. Feinberg.
August 31–September 6. From Thayer & Eldridge. Feinberg.
September 25. From Theodore Rich. LC.
December 19. From Thomas Jefferson Whitman. Feinberg.
December. From Hannah Heyde. Trent.
[1862?]. From Lieutenant Silas S. Soule. Feinberg.

1863

January 1–2. From Thomas Jefferson Whitman. Feinberg.
January 12. From Ralph Waldo Emerson. Feinberg. WW 30.
January 13. From George Washington Whitman. Trent.
January 13. From Thomas Jefferson Whitman. Feinberg.
January 15(?). From George Wood. Feinberg.
January 26. From Moses Lane. Feinberg.
February 1. From George Washington Whitman. Trent.
February 6. From George Washington Whitman. Trent.
February 6. From Thomas Jefferson Whitman. Feinberg.
February 10. From Thomas Jefferson Whitman. Feinberg.
February 12. From George Washington Whitman. Trent.
February 12. From Thomas Jefferson Whitman. Feinberg.
February 25. From George Washington Whitman. Trent.
February 25(?). From John Swinton. Feinberg. CT: Traubel, I, 416.
February 26. From *Harper's Weekly*. Feinberg.
March 3. From Thomas Jefferson Whitman. Feinberg.
March 7. From Louisa Van Velsor Whitman. Trent.
March 9. From Thomas Jefferson Whitman. Feinberg.
March 10. From Justus F. Boyd, soldier. Hanley.
March 10. From James Redpath. Location unknown. CT: Donaldson, 143.

March 12. From Thomas Jefferson Whitman. Feinberg.
March 19(?). From Louisa Van Velsor Whitman. Trent.
March 21. From Thomas Jefferson Whitman. Feinberg.
March 21. From Charles S. Kingsley, a New York friend. Berg.
March. From Louisa Van Velsor Whitman. Trent.
April 2. From Thomas Jefferson Whitman. Feinberg.
April 3. From Thomas Jefferson Whitman. Feinberg.
April 5. From Will W. Wallace, soldier. Feinberg, CT: *MLQ*, x (1949), 92–93.
April 6(?). From Thomas Jefferson Whitman. Feinberg.
April 11. From Thomas Jefferson Whitman. Feinberg.
April 15. From Thomas Jefferson Whitman. Feinberg.
April 20. From Thomas Jefferson Whitman. Feinberg.
April 25. From Thomas Jefferson Whitman. Feinberg.
April 26. From a friend of Thomas P. Sawyer, soldier. Berg.
April 27. From Justus F. Boyd. Hanley.
April 29. From Fred B. McReady, soldier. Berg.
April 30. From Moses Lane. LC.
May 1. From John F. S. ("Fred") Gray. Hanley.
May 2. From Thomas Jefferson Whitman. Feinberg.
May 2. From Moses Lane. LC.
May 5. From James Redpath. Historical Society of Pennsylvania. PT: Donaldson, 144.
May 7. From Will W. Wallace. Feinberg. CT: *MLQ*, x (1949), 93–94.
May 9. From Thomas Jefferson Whitman. Feinberg.
May 12. From Thomas Jefferson Whitman. Feinberg.
May 14. From Justus F. Boyd. Berg.
May 26. From Milford C. Reed, soldier. Yale.
May 27. From Thomas Jefferson Whitman. Feinberg.
May 27. From Moses Lane. Feinberg.
June 5. From John J. Barker, soldier. Hanley.
June 13. From Thomas Jefferson Whitman. Feinberg.
June 19. From John J. Barker. Hanley.
July 1. From Will W. Wallace. Berg. CT: *MLQ*, x (1949), 94–95.
July 7. From Thomas Jefferson Whitman. Feinberg.
July 8. From Thomas Jefferson Whitman. Feinberg.
July 10. From Lewis K. Brown, soldier. Hanley.
July 19. From Thomas Jefferson Whitman. Feinberg.
After July 23(?). From Louisa Van Velsor Whitman. Trent.
July 24. From Alvah H. Small, soldier. Berg.
July 27. From Lewis K. Brown. Hanley.
August 4. From Thomas Jefferson Whitman. Feinberg.
August 10. From Lewis K. Brown. Berg.
August 16–25(?). From Louisa Van Velsor Whitman. Trent.
August 17. From William E. Vandermark, soldier. Hanley.
August 18. From Mary A. Babbitt (for Caleb H. Babbitt, soldier). Berg.
August 22. From Lewis K. Brown. Hanley.
August 27. From S. B. & R. O. Haskell, parents of soldier. Hanley.
August 31. From C. L. Scott, soldier. Berg.
September 3(?). From Louisa Van Velsor Whitman. Trent.
September 3. From Thomas Jefferson Whitman. Feinberg.
September 3, evening. From Thomas Jefferson Whitman. Feinberg.
About September 3. From Louisa Van Velsor Whitman. Trent.
September 6. From Mary A. Babbitt, sister of soldier. Berg.
September 7. From William E. Vandermark. Hanley.
September 17. From Bethuel Smith, soldier. Feinberg.
September 17 (later). From Bethuel Smith. Feinberg.
September 18. From Caleb H. Babbitt. Berg.

September 21. From Dr. Le Baron Russell. Hanley. CT: Donaldson, 145–146.
September 22. From Thomas Jefferson Whitman. Feinberg.
September 24. From Thomas Jefferson Whitman. Feinberg.
September 25. From Fanny Van Nostrand. LC.
September 28. From Bethuel Smith. Feinberg.
October 1. From Caleb H. Babbitt. Berg.
October 1. From Margaret S. Curtis. Hanley. CT: Donaldson, 147.
October 4. From Dr. Le Baron Russell. Hanley. CT: Donaldson, 147–148.
October 6. From Dr. Le Baron Russell. Hanley.
October 6. From Hannah E. Stevenson. Hanley. CT: Donaldson, 150.
October 7. From Thomas Jefferson Whitman. Feinberg.
October 8. From Thomas Jefferson Whitman. Feinberg.
October 8. From James Redpath. Historical Society of Pennsylvania.
October 13. From Bethuel Smith. Feinberg.
October 13. From Julia Stilwell, sister of soldier. Berg.
October 14. From James Redpath. Location unknown. PT: Donaldson, 151.
October 15. From Thomas Jefferson Whitman. Feinberg.
October 20. From John and Margaret Stilwell, parents of soldier. Berg.
October 21(?). From Louisa Van Velsor Whitman. Trent.
October 22. From Thomas Jefferson Whitman. Feinberg.
October 24. From Dr. Le Baron Russell. Hanley.
October 25. From Margaret Stilwell, sister of soldier. Feinberg.
October 26. From Louisa Van Velsor Whitman. Trent.
October 26. From S. H. Childs (for Caleb H. Babbitt). Berg.
October 28. From James Redpath. Location unknown. CT: Traubel, IV, 418.
October (?). From Louisa Van Velsor Whitman. Trent. CT: Gohdes and Silver, 184–187.
November 2. From William E. Vandermark. Hanley.
November 5. From Lewis K. Brown. Hanley.
November 7. From Elijah Douglass Fox, soldier. Hanley.
November 8. From Dr. Le Baron Russell. Hanley. CT: Donaldson, 151.
November 10. From Elijah Douglass Fox. Lion.
November 10. From Ellen M. O'Connor. Feinberg.
November 11. From William H. McFarland, soldier. Hanley.
November 13–14. From Lewis K. Brown. Hanley.
November 21. From Livingston J. Brooks, soldier. Berg.
November 21. From Ellen M. O'Connor. Feinberg. CT: Traubel, III, 524–525.
November 24. From Ellen M. O'Connor. Feinberg.
December 3. From Thomas Jefferson Whitman. Feinberg. CT: Allen, 306.
December 4. From Louisa Van Velsor Whitman. Trent. CT: Gohdes and Silver, 187–190.
December 9. From Elijah Douglass Fox. LC.
December 14. From Benjamin Penhallow Shillaber. Feinberg. CT: Traubel, II, 96–97 (erroneously dated December 10).
December 15(?). From Louisa Van Velsor Whitman. Trent.
December 15. From Thomas Jefferson Whitman. Feinberg.
December 16. From Bethuel Smith. Feinberg.
December 16. From William E. Vandermark. Berg.
December 21. From John T. Trowbridge. Feinberg. CT: Traubel, II, 109.
December 22. From Livingston J. Brooks. Hanley.
December 22. From Alonzo S. Bush, soldier. Yale.
December 24. From Elijah Douglass Fox. Hanley.
December 25. From William E. Vandermark. Berg.
December 28. From Thomas Jefferson Whitman. Feinberg.
December 28. From Margaret Stilwell, sister of soldier. Feinberg.

December 29. From William E. Vandermark. Berg.
December 30. From John T. Trowbridge. Location unknown. CT: Traubel, IV, 290–291.

1864

January 8. From Thomas Jefferson Whitman. Feinberg.
January 9. From William H. Millis, Sr., father of soldier. Berg.
January 21. From Thomas P. Sawyer. Berg.
February 2. From Thomas B. Neat, soldier. Berg.
February 11. From Alonzo S. Bush. Hanley.
February 12. From John T. Trowbridge. Feinberg. CT: Traubel, II, 524.
February 20. From Andrew J. Liebenan, soldier. Hanley.
February 28. From Bethuel Smith. Feinberg.
March 5. From Alf. L. Lane, soldier. Hanley.
March 7. From Alonzo S. Bush. Hanley.
March 9. From W. A. Jellison, soldier. Hanley.
March 11. From Thomas Jefferson Whitman. Feinberg.
March 19. From Thomas Jefferson Whitman. Trent.
March 28. From Rodney R. Worster, soldier. Berg.
April 7. From William E. Vandermark. LC. CT: Glicksberg, 156*n*.
April 16. From George Washington Whitman. Trent.
April 21. From Mrs. George W. Briggs. Hanley.
April 29. From George Washington Whitman. Trent.
April 30. From Reuben Farwell, soldier. Trent.
May 5. From Reuben Farwell. Trent.
May 7. From John F. S. ("Fred") Gray. Berg.
May 7. From Isaac Linensparger, soldier. Berg.
May 9. From Helen S. Cunningham, sister of soldier. Hanley.
May 10. From Reuben Farwell, soldicr. Trent.
May 14. From Aaron Smith, soldier. Berg.
May 23. From W. E. Worthen. Feinberg.
May 30. From Charles H. Harris, soldier. Berg.
June 1. From Justus F. Boyd. Hanley.
June 8. From Reuben Farwell. Trent.
June 11. From Helen S. Cunningham. Berg.
June 16. From Reuben Farwell. Trent.
June 28. From John Burroughs. Feinberg.
July 2. From William D. O'Connor. Location unknown. CT: Traubel, IV, 366–368.
July 5. From Ellen M. O'Connor. Feinberg.
July 5. From James S. Stilwell, soldier. Berg.
July 6. From Lewis K. Brown. Berg.
July 13. From Aaron Smith. Berg.
July 14. From Elijah Douglass Fox. Berg.
July 18. From Lewis K. Brown. Berg.
July 18. From Ellen M. O'Connor. Feinberg.
July 24. From Ellen M. O'Connor. Feinberg.
August 2. From John Burroughs. Feinberg. CT: Traubel, II, 548–549. PT: Barrus, 19.
August 13. From William D. O'Connor. Feinberg; CT: Traubel, III, 337–340.
August 18. From Ellen M. O'Connor. Feinberg.
August 29. From Christopher and Marian Smith, parents of soldier. Feinberg.
August 30. From Bethuel Smith. Feinberg.
September 2(?). From James S. Stilwell. Berg.
September 5. From Lewis K. Brown. Berg.
September 5. From Joseph Harris, soldier. Berg.
September 17. From Lizzie H. Smith, cousin of Milton S. Roberts, soldier. Berg.
September 18. From Justus F. Boyd. Berg.
September 27. From James S. Stilwell. Berg.
October 2. From Reuben Farwell. Trent.

October 17. From Hannah Heyde. LC.
October 18. From Lieutenant William E. Babcock. Berg.
October 21. From William Mullery, father of soldier. Berg.
October 22. From Bethuel Smith. Feinberg.
November 7. From Reuben Farwell. Trent.
November 21. From Reuben Farwell. Trent.
November 30. From Ellen M. O'Connor. Feinberg.
December 12. From Lieutenant William E. Babcock. Berg.
December 26. From Jesse Mullery, soldier. Berg.
December 30. From William D. O'Connor. Feinberg. CT: Traubel, II, 400–403.

1865

January 4. From Dana F. Wright. Berg.
January 6. From John T. Trowbridge. Feinberg. CT: Traubel, II, 292–293.
January 11. From Herman Storms, soldier. Berg.
January 12. From William T. Otto. Lion. CT: Traubel, III, 470–471.
January(?) 12. From William H. Millis, soldier. Berg.
January 19. From Ellen M. O'Connor. Feinberg.
January 21. From Lieutenant William E. Babcock. Feinberg.
January 21. From Aaron Smith. Feinberg.
January 23. From Jesse Mullery. Berg.
January 24. From William T. Otto. Lion. CT: Traubel, III, 471.
January 26. From Thomas Jefferson Whitman. Feinberg.
January 26. From Christopher and Marian Smith, parents of soldier. Feinberg.
January 31. From Thomas Jefferson Whitman. Feinberg.
February 3. From Thomas Jefferson Whitman. Feinberg.
February 5. From John Swinton. Feinberg. CT: Traubel, II, 426.
February 7. From Thomas Jefferson Whitman. Feinberg.
February 16. From Colonel Julius W. Mason. Yale.
February 16. From Colonel Elliott F. Shepard. Feinberg.
February 24(?). From Louisa Van Velsor Whitman. Trent. PT: Allen, 328.
February 28. From Captain William Cook. Feinberg. CT: Traubel, III, 202–203.
March 5. From Louisa Van Velsor Whitman. Trent. CT: Gohdes and Silver, 190–192.
March 7. From Celie M. Burr, an admirer. Feinberg.
April 22. From Peter Eckler. Feinberg.
April 26. From Peter Eckler. Feinberg.
May 1. From Peter Eckler. Feinberg.
May 3. From Jesse Mullery. Berg.
May 4. From Thomas Jefferson Whitman. Feinberg.
May 4. From Peter Eckler. Feinberg.
May 11. From William T. Otto. Lion. CT: Traubel, III, 471.
May 14. From Thomas Jefferson Whitman. Feinberg.
June 3(?). From Louisa Van Velsor Whitman. Trent.
June 4. From Thomas Jefferson Whitman. Feinberg. PT: Allen, 343.
June 11. From Jesse Mullery. Berg.
June 18. From Kate Richardson, an admirer. Feinberg.
June 24. From Nicholas D. Palmer, soldier. Feinberg.
June 30. From James Harlan. Lion. CT: Traubel, III, 471; William E. Barton, *Abraham Lincoln and Walt Whitman* (1928), 117–118.
July 14. From George Washington Whitman. Trent. CT: Gohdes and Silver, 182.
July 16. From Thomas Jefferson Whitman. Feinberg. PT: Allen, 346–347.
July 17. From William Stewart, soldier. Yale.
July 30. From A. Van Rensellaer. Lion. FACSIMILE: William E. Barton, *Abraham Lincoln and Walt Whitman* (1928), 98. CT: Traubel, III, 178–179.
August 7. From Alfred Pratt, soldier. Feinberg.
August 8. From Louisa Van Velsor Whitman. Trent.

August 9. From Anson Ryder, Jr., soldier. Feinberg.
August 23. From William F. Bainbridge, soldier. Yale.
August 25. From Anson Ryder, Jr., soldier. Feinberg.
August 29. From Louisa Van Velsor Whitman. Trent.
September 5. From Louisa Van Velsor Whitman. Trent.
September 5. From Byron Sutherland, soldier. Feinberg.
September 11. From Louisa Van Velsor Whitman. Trent.
September 11. From Thomas Jefferson Whitman. Feinberg.
September 20. From Abraham Simpson. Feinberg. PT: F. DeWolfe Miller, ed., *Drum-Taps* (1959), xlviii.
September 21. From Louisa Van Velsor Whitman. Trent.
September 27. From Louisa Van Velsor Whitman. Trent.
September 29. From Thomas Jefferson Whitman. Feinberg.
October 17. From Ellen M. O'Connor. Feinberg.
October 19. From William D. O'Connor. Feinberg. CT: Traubel, I, 83–85.
October 22. From Anson Ryder, Jr. Feinberg.
October 25. From Margaret Stilwell. Berg.
November 1. From Ellen M. O'Connor. Feinberg.
November 11. From Benton H. Wilson, soldier. Feinberg.
November 14. From Louisa Van Velsor Whitman. Trent. CT: Gohdes and Silver, 192.
November 25. From Louisa Van Velsor Whitman. Trent.
December 3. From Louisa Van Velsor Whitman. Trent.
December 10. From Louisa Van Velsor Whitman. Trent.
December 25. From Louisa Van Velsor Whitman. Trent.
December 28. From Margaret Stilwell. Berg.

1866

February 20. From Jesse Mullery. LC.
February 21. From Charles J. Woodbury. Location unknown. CT: Barrus, 36–38.
March 27(?). From Louisa Van Velsor Whitman. Trent.
April 6. From Charlotte St. Clair, mother of soldier. Feinberg.
April. From Charles L. Heyde. Trent. CT: Gohdes and Silver, 222–223.
May 31. From Louisa Van Velsor Whitman. Trent.
June 7. From Louisa Van Velsor Whitman. Trent.
October 10. From Louisa Van Velsor Whitman. Trent.
November 12. From Bayard Taylor. Feinberg. CT: Traubel, II, 148–149.
November 16. From Horace Wentworth. Yale.
November 26. From Alexander Gardner. Feinberg. CT: Traubel, III, 346.
November 27. From Horace Wentworth. Feinberg.
December 1(?). From Charles L. Heyde. Trent. CT: Gohdes and Silver, 223–224.
December 2. From Bayard Taylor. Feinberg. CT: Traubel, II, 153.
December 5. From Hugh B. Thomson, soldier. Feinberg.
December 9. From Benton H. Wilson, soldier. Feinberg.
December 13. From Hugh B. Thomson. Feinberg.
December 16. From Benton H. Wilson. Feinberg.
December 17. From Horace Wentworth. Yale.
December 21. From Thomas Jefferson Whitman. Feinberg.

1867

January 1. From John T. Trowbridge. Feinberg.
January 4. From Senator George F. Edmunds. Feinberg.
January 17. From Louisa Van Velsor Whitman. Trent.
January 17. From Henry Wilson, father of soldier. Feinberg.
January 26. From Louisa Van Velsor Whitman. Trent.
January 27. From Benton H. Wilson. Feinberg.
February 3. From Benton H. Wilson. Feinberg.
February 8. From Charles Warren Stoddard. Feinberg.

February 19. From Louisa Van Velsor Whitman. Trent.
February 21. From Louisa Van Velsor Whitman. Trent.
February 24. From Anson Ryder, Jr. Feinberg.
February 27. From Louisa Van Velsor Whitman. Trent.
March 15. From Louisa Van Velsor Whitman. Trent.
March 21. From Louisa Van Velsor Whitman. Trent.
March 28. From Louisa Van Velsor Whitman. Trent.
March. From Charles L. Heyde. Trent.
[March]. From Abby H. Price. Yale.
April 7. From Benton H. Wilson. Feinberg.
April 8. From James Curphey(?). LC.
April 13. From Louisa Van Velsor Whitman. Trent.
April 21. From Benton H. Wilson. Feinberg.
April 27. From Louisa Van Velsor Whitman. Trent.
May 2. From Louisa Van Velsor Whitman. Trent.
May 8. From H. J. Ramsdell, Washington clerk. Feinberg.
May 9. From William D. O'Connor. Feinberg. CT: Traubel, III, 521–522.
May 10. From Abraham Simpson. Feinberg.
May 19. From Charles F. Wingate, an admirer. Feinberg.
May 23. From Thomas Jefferson Whitman. Feinberg.
May 24. From Hiram Sholes, soldier. Feinberg.
May 31. From Abraham Simpson. Feinberg.
June 8. From Hiram Sholes. Feinberg.
June 20. From Louisa Van Velsor Whitman. Trent.
June 21. From Judge Milton Kelly. National Archives.
June. From Charles L. Heyde. Trent.
July 3. From Abraham Simpson. Feinberg.
July 17. From H. J. Ramsdell. Feinberg.
July 20. From John T. Trowbridge. Feinberg. CT: Traubel, III, 506–507.
July 22. From H. J. Ramsdell. Feinberg.
August 1. From Louisa Van Velsor Whitman. Trent.
August 2. From Thomas Jefferson Whitman. Feinberg.
August 8. From W. C. Church. Feinberg.
August 9. From William Livingston Alden. Feinberg. CT: Traubel, III, 259.
August 9. From Judge Milton Kelly. Yale.
August 13. From F. P. Church. Feinberg.
August 14. From Scott & Williams, printers. Feinberg.
August 19. From William Livingston Alden. Feinberg.
August 26. From George W. Perrigo, a book order. Feinberg.
September 4. From F. P. Church. Feinberg.
September 10. From Moncure D. Conway. Feinberg. CT: Traubel, III, 267–268.
September 15. From Benton H. Wilson. Feinberg.
September(?) 29. From Alfred Pratt. Feinberg.
October 3. From Henry Clapp, Jr. Feinberg. CT: Traubel, I, 267.
October 7. From Louisa Van Velsor Whitman. Trent.
October 12. From Moncure D. Conway. Feinberg. CT: Traubel, III, 296–298.
October 15. From F. P. Church. Feinberg.
October 20. From Louisa Van Velsor Whitman. Trent.
October 21. From F. P. Church. Feinberg.
October 22. From Louisa Van Velsor Whitman. Trent.
October 26. From Benjamin Russell, Jr. Feinberg.
October 30. From Louisa Van Velsor Whitman. Trent.
November 7. From Moncure D. Conway. Feinberg. CT: Traubel, III, 322.
November 13(?). From Louisa Van Velsor Whitman. Trent.
November 17. From William Michael Rossetti. Feinberg. CT: Traubel, III, 299–301.
November 18. From William Livingston Alden. Feinberg. CT: Traubel, II, 211.
November 19. From Louisa Van Velsor Whitman. Trent.

December 1–15(?). From Louisa Van Velsor Whitman. Trent.

December 6. From George S. McWatters. Feinberg.

December 8. From William Michael Rossetti. Feinberg. CT: Traubel, III, 303–306.

December 15. From Louisa Van Velsor Whitman. Trent.

December 16. From William Michael Rossetti. Feinberg. CT: Traubel, III, 306–308.

December 23. From Dr. F. B. Gillette, an admirer. Feinberg. CT: Traubel, III, 465–466.

December 26. From Louisa Van Velsor Whitman. Trent.

December 28. From George Routledge & Sons. Feinberg. CT: Traubel, I, 263.

Appendix D

CHRONOLOGY OF WALT WHITMAN'S LIFE AND WORK

1819	Born May 31 at West Hills, near Huntington, Long Island.
1823	May 27, Whitman family moves to Brooklyn.
1825 - 30	Attends public school in Brooklyn.
1830	Office boy for doctor, lawyer.
1830 - 34	Learns printing trade.
1835	Printer in New York City until great fire August 12.
1836 - 38	Summer of 1836, begins teaching at East Norwich, Long Island; by winter 1837 - 38 has taught at Hempstead, Babylon, Long Swamp, and Smithtown.
1838 - 39	Edits weekly newspaper, the *Long Islander*, at Huntington.
1840 - 41	Autumn 1840, campaigns for Van Buren; then teaches school at Trimming Square, Woodbury, Dix Hills, and Whitestone.
1841	May, goes to New York City to work as printer in *New World* office; begins writing for the *Democratic Review.*
1842	Spring, edits a daily newspaper in New York City, the *Aurora;* edits *Evening Tattler* for short time.
1845 - 46	August, returns to Brooklyn, writes for *Long Island Star* from September until March.
1846 - 48	From March, 1846, until January, 1848, edits Brooklyn *Daily Eagle;* February, 1848, goes to New Orleans to work on the *Crescent;* leaves May 27 and returns *via* Mississippi and Great Lakes.
1848 - 49	September 9, 1848, to September 11, 1849, edits a "free soil" newspaper, the Brooklyn *Freeman.*
1850 - 54	Operates printing office and stationery store; does free-lance journalism; builds and speculates in houses.
1855	Early July, *Leaves of Grass* is printed by Rome Brothers in Brooklyn; father dies July 11.
1856	Writes for *Life Illustrated;* publishes second edition of *Leaves of Grass* in summer and writes "The Eighteenth Presidency!"
1857 - 59	From spring of 1857 until about summer of 1859 edits the Brooklyn *Times;* unemployed winter of 1859 - 60, frequents Pfaff's bohemian restaurant.
1860	March, goes to Boston to see third edition of *Leaves of Grass* through the press.
1861	April 12, Civil War begins; George Whitman enlists.

1862	December, goes to Fredericksburg, Virginia, scene of recent battle in which George was wounded, stays in camp two weeks.
1863	Remains in Washington, D. C., working part-time in Army Paymaster's office, visits soldiers in hospitals.
1864	Mid-June, returns to Brooklyn because of illness.
1865	January 24, appointed clerk in Department of Interior, returns to Washington; meets Peter Doyle; witnesses Lincoln's second inauguration; Lincoln assassinated, April 14; May, *Drum-Taps* is printed; June 30, is discharged from position by Secretary James Harlan but re-employed next day in Attorney General's office; autumn, prints *Drum-Taps and Sequel*, containing "When Lilacs Last in the Dooryard Bloom'd."
1866	William D. O'Connor publishes *The Good Gray Poet.*
1867	John Burroughs publishes *Notes on Walt Whitman as Poet and Person;* July 6, William Rossetti publishes article on Whitman's poetry in London *Chronicle;* "Democracy" (part of *Democratic Vistas*) published in December *Galaxy.*
1868	William Rossetti's *Poems of Walt Whitman* (selected and expurgated) published in England; "Personalism" (second part of *Democratic Vistas*) in May *Galaxy;* second issue of fourth edition of *Leaves of Grass*, with *Drum-Taps and Sequel* added.
1869	Mrs. Anne Gilchrist reads Rossetti edition and falls in love with the poet.
1870	July, is very depressed for unknown reasons; prints fifth edition of *Leaves of Grass*, and *Democratic Vistas* and *Passage to India*, all dated 1871.
1871	September 3, Mrs. Gilchrist's first love letter; September 7, reads "After All Not to Create Only" at opening of American Institute Exhibition in New York.
1872	June 26, reads "As a Strong Bird on Pinions Free" at Dartmouth College commencement.
1873	January 23, suffers paralytic stroke; mother dies May 23; unable to work, stays with brother George in Camden, New Jersey.
1874	"Song of the Redwood-Tree" and "Prayer of Columbus."
1875	Prepares Centennial Edition of *Leaves of Grass* and *Two Rivulets* (dated 1876).
1876	Controversy in British and American press over America's neglect of Whitman; spring, begins recuperation at Stafford Farm, at Timber Creek; September, Mrs. Gilchrist arrives and rents house in Philadelphia.
1877	January 28, gives lecture on Tom Paine in Philadelphia; during summer gains strength by sun-bathing at Timber Creek.
1878	Spring, too weak to give projected Lincoln lecture, but in June visits J. H. Johnson and John Burroughs in New York.
1879	April 14, first lecture on Lincoln in Philadelphia; September, makes trip to Colorado, long visit with brother Jeff in St. Louis.
1880	January, returns to Camden; summer, visits Dr. R. M. Bucke in London, Ontario.

1881	April 15, gives Lincoln lecture in Boston; returns to Boston in late summer to read proof of *Leaves of Grass*, being published by James R. Osgood; poems receive final arrangement in this edition.
1882	Osgood ceases to distribute *Leaves of Grass* because District Attorney threatens prosecution unless the book is expurgated; publication is resumed by Rees Welsh in Philadelphia, who also publishes *Specimen Days and Collect;* both books transferred to David McKay, Philadelphia.
1883	Dr. Bucke publishes *Walt Whitman*, biography written with poet's co-operation.
1884	Buys house on Mickle Street, Camden, New Jersey.
1885	In poor health; friends buy a horse and phaeton so that the poet will not be "house-tied"; November 29, Mrs. Gilchrist dies.
1886	Gives Lincoln lecture in Philadelphia.
1887	Gives Lincoln lecture in New York; is sculptured by Sidney Morse, painted by Herbert Gilchrist, J. W. Alexander, Thomas Eakins.
1888	Horace Traubel raises funds for doctors and nurses; *November Boughs* printed; money sent from England.
1889	Last birthday dinner, proceedings published in *Camden's Compliments.*
1890	Writes angry letter to J. A. Symonds, dated August 19, denouncing Symonds's interpretation of "Calamus" poems, claims six illegitimate children.
1891	*Good-Bye My Fancy* is printed, and the "death-bed edition" of *Leaves of Grass* (dated 1892).
1892	Dies March 26, buried in Harleigh Cemetery, Camden, New Jersey.

Index

Index

THIS BOOK is set in Monticello, a Linotype face designed after what was perhaps the first native American type face of real quality, cut by Archibald Binney probably in 1797. Printed on S. D. Warren Paper Company's University Text, the book was manufactured in its entirety by Kingsport Press, Inc.

The design and typography are by Andor Braun.